Lecture Notes in Computer

Commenced Publication in 1973
Founding and Former Series Editors:
Gerhard Goos, Juris Hartmanis, and Jan van Leeuwen

T0238556

Rafael E. Banchs   Fabrizio Silvestri
Tie-Yan Liu   Min Zhang   Sheng Gao
Jun Lang (Eds.)

Information Retrieval Technology

9th Asia Information Retrieval Societies Conference
AIRS 2013
Singapore, December 9-11, 2013
Proceedings

 Springer

Volume Editors

Rafael E. Banchs
Min Zhang
Sheng Gao
Jun Lang
Institute for Infocomm Research
Human Language Technology
1 Fusionopolis Way #21-01, Connexis South, Singapore 138632
E-mail: {rembanchs, mzhang, gaosheng, jlang}@i2r.a-star.edu.sg

Fabrizio Silvestri
Yahoo Labs
Avinguda Diagonal 177, 08018 Barcelona, Spain
E-mail: silvestr@yahoo-inc.com

Tie-Yan Liu
Microsoft Research Asia
No. 5, Danling Street, Haidian District, 100080 Beijing, China
E-mail: tyliu@microsoft.com

ISSN 0302-9743   e-ISSN 1611-3349
ISBN 978-3-642-45067-9   e-ISBN 978-3-642-45068-6
DOI 10.1007/978-3-642-45068-6
Springer Heidelberg New York Dordrecht London

Library of Congress Control Number: 2013953063

CR Subject Classification (1998): H.3, H.2, I.2.7, H.4, I.5

LNCS Sublibrary: SL 3 – Information Systems and Application,
incl. Internet/Web and HCI

Typesetting: Camera-ready by author, data conversion by Scientific Publishing Services, Chennai, India

Printed on acid-free paper

Springer is part of Springer Science+Business Media (www.springer.com)

Message from the Chairs

The Chinese and Oriental Languages Information Processing Society (COLIPS) was very proud to host the 9th Asia Information Retrieval Societies Conference (AIRS 2013) in Singapore, a well-communicated and uniquely vibrant conference city in Asia, during December 9–11, 2013.

This year's edition of AIRS aimed at bringing together researchers, engineers, and practitioners in the area of information retrieval (IR) to exchange new ideas and latest achievements in this field. The scope of the conference covers applications, systems, technologies and theory aspects of IR in text, audio, image, video and multimedia data.

The AIRS 2013 welcomed submissions of original papers in the broad field of IR. The technical areas covered include, but are not limited to, the following: IR models and theories; user study, evaluation and interactive IR; Web IR, scalability and IR in social media; multimedia IR; natural language processing for IR; machine learning and data mining for IR; and IR applications.

Following the tradition of previous editions, the AIRS 2013 proceedings are published as a Springer LNCS volume, demonstrating once more the high level of scientific achievement and technical research presented and discussed in this increasingly important venue.

We also want to thank all the persons who, with their hard work and effort, have contributed to ensuring the quality and success of AIRS 2013. Our special thanks and appreciation go to all members of the Program Committee, area chairs, authors and co-authors, as well as to all members of the local Organizing Committee, the publication and publicity chairs, our conference advisor, and the AIRS Steering Committee.

October 2013

Rafael E. Banchs
Min Zhang

Preface

During the last 20 years, information retrieval has come out from the libraries and resource centres into the daily life of thousands of millions of people across the globe. As a means to facilitating the access to an exponentially increasing amount of information in the digital era, information retrieval technologies have become one of the most valuable commodities of the modern information society.

Nevertheless, from the scientific point of view, information retrieval continues to be an exciting and active area of research, which is constantly challenged by the new possibilities of the information era and the complexities such possibilities imply. Cross-language, multilingualism, multimodality, multimedia, social media, user-generated content, personalization and recommendation are just a few examples of the new requirements information access presently faces, along with the necessity of faster, cheaper, and scalable algorithms and computational resources able to support the increasing demand for information retrieval in both traditional and mobile platforms.

It is within this context that AIRS (the Asia Information Retrieval Societies Conference) has become a prominent venue for the scientific discussion of information retrieval technologies and their applications. Originally targeting scientific production in the Asia and Asia-pacific region, AIRS has currently expanded its reach to the global scenario. For instance, this year's AIRS program included an international Program Committee of over 155 specialists within seven technical areas and from different research and commercial institutions, and it received a total of 109 technical submissions.

As a result of a comprehensive review process, 45 contributions were selected to appear in this final proceedings volume, 27 of which were selected for oral presentations and 18 for poster presentations in the AIRS conference program in Singapore during December 9–11, 2013.

Finally, we would like to express our gratitude to all the authors, area chairs, PC members and local Organizing Committee members. Without their active participation and contribution, we would not have had such an interesting technical program and a successful conference.

Rafael E. Banchs
Fabrizio Silvestri
Tie-Yian Liu

AIRS 2013 Organization

Conference Chairs

Rafael E. Banchs   Institute for Infocomm Research, Singapore
Min Zhang   Chinese and Oriental Language Information
     Processing Society

Publication Chairs

Sheng Gao   Institute for Infocomm Research, Singapore
Jun Lang   Chinese and Oriental Language Information
     Processing Society

Local Organizing Committee

Minghui Dong   Chinese and Oriental Language Information
     Processing Society
Seokhwan Kim   Institute for Infocomm Research, Singapore
Marta Ruiz Costa-jussà   Universitat Politecnica de Catalunya, Spain
Kheng Hui Yeo   Institute for Infocomm Research, Singapore
Tze Yuang Chong   Nanyang Technological University, Singapore
Parth Gupta   Universidad Politecnica de Valencia, Spain

Publicity Chairs

Min Yen Kan   National University of Singapore
Jens Grivolla   Barcelona Media Innovation Centre, Spain

Conference Advisor

Haizhou Li   Institute for Infocomm Research, Singapore

AIRS Steering Committee

Hsin-Hsi Chen   Taiwan
Gary Geunbae Lee   Korea
Wai Lam   Hong Kong
Alistair Moffat   Australia

Hwee Tou Ng   Singapore
Tetsuya Sakai   Mainland China
Dawei Song   UK
Masaharu Yoshioka   Japan

Program Committee Chairs

Fabrizio Silvestri   Istituto de Scienza e Tecnologia
                          ell'Informazione, Italy
Tie-Yan Liu   Microsoft Research Asia, China
Rafael E. Banchs   Institute for Infocomm Research, Singapore

Area Chairs

1.- IR Models and Theories
Bin Wang   Chinese Academy of Sciences, China
Craig Macdonald   University of Glasgow, UK

2.- User Study, IR Evaluation, and Interactive IR
Tetsuya Sakai   Microsoft Research Asia, China
Ben Carterette   University of Delaware, USA

3.- Web IR, Scalability, and IR in Social Media
Alistair Moffat   University of Melbourne, Australia
Min Zhang   Tsinghua University, China

4.- Multimedia IR
Kazunari Sugiyama   National University of Singapore, Singapore
Joemon Jose   University of Glasgow, UK

5.- Natural Language Processing for IR
Qi Haoliang   Heilongjiang Institute of Technology, China
Donald Metzler   Google Research, USA

6.- Machine Learning and Data Mining for IR
Sadao Kurohashi   Kyoto University, Japan
Roi Blanco   University of A Coruña, Spain

7.- IR Applications
Jimmy Huang   York University, Canada
Gabriella Pasi   Università di Milano Bicocca, Italy

Program Committee Members by Area

1.- IR Models and Theories

Pu-Jen Cheng	National Taiwan University, Taiwan, China
Ingo Frommholz	University of Bedfordshire, UK
Cathal Gurrin	Dublin City University, Ireland
Claudia Hauff	Delft University of Technology, The Netherlands
Ben He	University of Chinese Academy of Sciences, China
Katja Hofmann	University of Amsterdam, The Netherlands
Xuanjing Huang	Fudan University, China
Peng Li	Institute of Information Engineering, Chinese Academy of Sciences, China
Jun Miao	York University, Canada
Mandar Mitra	Indian Statistical Institute, India
Jian-Yun Nie	University of Montreal, Canada
Iadh Ounis	University of Glasgow, UK
Tao Qin	Microsoft Research Asia, China
Li Rui	Institute of Information Engineering, Chinese Academy of Sciences, China
Le Sun	Institute of Software, Chinese Academy of Sciences, China
Ming-Feng Tsai	National Chengchi University, Taiwan, China
Bo Wang	Tianjin University, China
Jun Xu	Huawei Tech., China

2.- User Study, IR Evaluation, and Interactive IR

Omar Alonso	Microsoft, USA
Javed Aslam	Northeastern University, USA
Peter Bailey	Microsoft, USA
Praveen Chandar	University of Delaware, USA
Charles Clarke	University of Waterloo, Canada
Maarten de Rijke	University of Amsterdam, The Netherlands
Atsushi Fujii	Tokyo Institute of Technology, Japan
Hideo Joho	University of Tsukuba, Japan
Diane Kelly	University of North Carolina, USA
Mounia Lalmas	Yahoo!, Spain
Stefano Mizzaro	University of Udine, Italy
Virgil Pavlu	Northeastern University, USA
Stephen Robertson	Microsoft, UK
Mark Sanderson	RMIT University, Australia
Falk Scholer	RMIT University, Australia
Mark Smucker	University of Waterloo, Canada
Ian Soboroff	NIST, USA
Ruihua Song	Microsoft, UK

Paul Thomas	CSIRO, Australia
Andrew Trotman	University of Otago, New Zealand
Andrew Turpin	University of Melbourne, Australia
Ellen Voorhees	NIST, USA
William Webber	University of Maryland, USA
Ke Zhou	University of Glasgow, UK

3.- Web IR, Scalability, and IR in Social Media

Ching-Man Au Yeung	Huawei Noah's Ark Lab, China
Rui Cai	Microsoft Research Asia, China
Mark Carman	Monash University, Australia
Nick Craswell	Microsoft Research, USA
Shane Culpepper	RMIT University, Australia
Kevin Duh	Nara Institute of Science and Technology, Japan
Wei Gao	Qatar Computing Research Institute, Qatar
Shlomo Geva	Queensland University of Technology, Australia
Xianpei Han	Chinese Academy of Sciences, China
Dave Hawking	Funnelback, Australia
Ben He	Chinese Academy of Sciences, China
Xiaodong He	Microsoft Research, USA
Adam Jatowt	Kyoto University, Japan
Jing Jiang	Singapore Management University, Singapore
Shasha Liao	New York University, USA
Yiqun Liu	Tsinghua University, China
Zhiyuan Liu	Tsinghua University, China
Jingjing Liu	MIT, USA
Kang Liu	Chinese Academy of Sciences, China
Zhengyu Niu	Baidu, China
Kristen Parton	Columbia University, USA
Laurianne Sitbon	Queensland University of Technology, Australia
Yang Song	Microsoft Research, USA
James Thom	RMIT University, Australia
Paul Thomas	CSIRO, Australia
Andrew Trotman	Otago University, New Zealand
Andrew Turpin	The University of Melbourne, Australia
Alexandra Uitdenbogerd	RMIT University, Australia
Tak-Lam Wong	The Hong Kong Institute of Education, SAR China
Xiaobing Xue	University of Massachusetts at Amherst, USA
Qi Zhang	Fudan University, China

4.- Multimedia IR

Liangcai Gao	Peking University, China
Kenji Hatano	Doshisha University, Japan
Ichiro Ide	Nagoya University, Japan

Hanmin Jung	Korea Institute of Science and Technology Information, Korea
In-Su Kang	Kyungsung University, Korea
Fuminori Kimura	Ritsumeikan University, Japan
Yiqun Liu	Tsinghua University, China
Zhiyuan Liu	Tsinghua University, China
Qiang Ma	Kyoto University, Japan
Akira Maeda	Ritsumeikan University, Japan
Mas Rina Mustaffa	Universiti Putra Malaysia, Malaysia
Toshiyuki Shimizu	Kyoto University, Japan
Aixin Sun	Nanyang Technological University, Singapore
Yu Suzuki	Nagoya University, Japan
Ichiro Yamada	NHK, Japan
Yi Yu	National University of Singapore, Singapore
Yin Zhang	Zhejiang University, China

5.- Natural Language Processing for IR

Niranjan Balasubramanian	University of Washington, USA
Timothy Baldwin	University of Melbourne, Australia
Xuanjing Huang	Fudan University, China
Hongfei Lin	Dalian University of Technology, China
Fuchun Peng	Google, USA
Satoshi Sekine	New York University, USA
Xiaojun Wan	Peking University, China
Lidan Wang	University of Illinois, USA
Yunqing Xia	Tsinghua University, China
Deyi Xiong	Institute for Infocomm Research, Singapore
Ruifeng Xu	Harbin Institute of Technology, China
Endong Xun	Beijing Language and Culture University, China
Jianmin Yao	Soochow University, Taiwan, China

6.- Machine Learning and Data Mining for IR

Lidong Bing	The Chinese University of Hong Kong, Hong Kong, SAR China
Pablo Castells	Universidad Autónoma de Madrid, Spain
Michael Chau	The University of Hong Kong, Hong Kong, SAR China
Pu-Jen Cheng	National Taiwan University, Taiwan, China
Georges Dupret	Yahoo! Labs, USA
Koji Eguchi	Kobe University, Japan
Atsushi Fujii	Tokyo Institute of Technology, Japan
Wei Gao	Qatar Research Institute, Qatar

Jiafeng Guo	Chinese Academy of Sciences, China
Yulan He	Aston University, UK
Xuanjing Huang	Fudan University, China
Minlie Huang	Tsinghua University, China
Jaap Kamps	University of Amsterdam, The Netherlands
Irwin King	The Chinese University of Hong Kong, Hong Kong, SAR China
Yanyan Lan	Chinese Academy of Sciences, China
Raymond Lau	Ramp Holdings, USA
Hang Li	Huawei, China
Claudio Lucchese	ISTI-CNR, Italy
Yugo Murawaki	Kyoto University, Japan
Issei Sato	University of Tokyo, Japan
Quan Wang	Peking University, China
Yunqing Xia	Tsinghua University, China
Xiaobing Xue	University of Massachusetts, USA
Qi Zhang	Fudan University, China

7.- IR Applications

Pavel Braslavski	Yandex, Russia
Pablo Castells	Universidad Autónoma de Madrid, Spain
Gerard de Melo	University of California, USA
Arjen de Vries	Delft University of Technology, The Netherlands
Gregory Grefenstette	Exalead, France
Qinmin Vivian Hu	York University, Canada
Gareth Jones	Dublin City University, Ireland
Yang Liu	Shangdong University, China
Mihai Lupu	Vienna University of Technology, Austria
Andrew MacFarlane	City University, UK
Raffaele Perego	Istituto di Scienza e Tecnologie dell'Informazione, Italy
Andrew Trotman	Otago University, New Zealand
Shusaku Tsumoto	Shimane University, Japan

Table of Contents

Part II: Clustering, Classification, and Detection

Clustering

Classification and Detection

Part III: Natural Language Processing for IR

Resources and Applications

Semantics and Relation Extraction

Part IV: Social Networks, User-Centered Studies, and Personalization

User-Centered Studies

Personalization and Recommendation

Part V: Applications

Seven Numeric Properties of Effectiveness Metrics

Alistair Moffat

Department of Computing and Information Systems,
The University of Melbourne, Australia

Abstract. Search effectiveness metrics quantify the relevance of the ranked document lists returned by retrieval systems. In this paper we characterize metrics according to seven numeric properties – boundedness, monotonicity, convergence, top-weightedness, localization, completeness, and realizability. We demonstrate that these properties partition the commonly-used evaluation metrics, and hence provide a framework in which the relationships between effectiveness metrics can be better understood, including their relative merits for different applications.

Keywords: Effectiveness metric, precision, NDCG, discounted cumulative gain, rank-biased precision, mean average precision, reciprocal rank.

1 Introduction

Search effectiveness metrics are used to quantify the relevance of the ranked document lists returned by retrieval systems, typically by *scoring* a ranking of length k, where k is a parameter of the experiment and might be 5, or 100, or 1,000, but is unlikely to be the number of documents in the underlying experimental collection. A very large number of metrics have been described in the literature, and used in retrieval experimentation [8]. More are developed each year, including for specialized applications.

An obvious question arises: is the diversity of metrics a consequence of them having different properties and behaviors? Or are they all connected in some fundamental manner? One way of comparing metrics is to look for correlations (and non-correlations) in their numeric scores, arguing that metrics that are non-strongly correlated supply evidence about different system behaviors, while metrics that are correlated are measuring similar aspects, whatever they may be. It is also possible to compare metrics according to their ability to attain similar system orderings on shared retrieval tasks; or based on their likelihood of generating statistically significant pairwise system comparisons; or based on their fit to observed user behavior.

In this paper we take a more fundamental approach, and describe seven simple numeric properties that a metric might or might not have: boundedness, monotonicity, convergence, top-weightedness, localization, completeness, and realizability. Each of the properties is a straightforward attribute; what is surprising is that the commonly-used metrics such as precision, reciprocal rank, average precision, and normalized discounted cumulative gain have different combinations of the seven attributes, and hence have distinctive numerical properties.

R.E. Banchs et al. (Eds.): AIRS 2013, LNCS 8281, pp. 1–12, 2013.

2 Effectiveness Metrics

Preliminaries: We suppose that a document ranking of length k is being scored and has been mapped, perhaps via human judgments, to a real-valued vector $\mathcal{R} = \langle r_i \rangle$. The interpretation is that $0 \leq r_i \leq 1$ is the utility to the user, in terms of the underlying information need, of the document at depth i in the ranking. It is also assumed that $\mathcal{R}$ can be thresholded in some way to make a vector $\mathcal{B} = \langle b_i \rangle$ of binary relevance values: $b_i = 1$ if $r_i \geq \theta$, and $b_i = 0$ otherwise. Graded relevance assessments provide the judges with multiple options – typically a set of ordered categories – that can be thresholded at different points if binary judgments are required. For example, a graded relevance scale with labels of *None*, *Low*, *Moderate*, *High*, and *Very High* might be translated to the set of utility contributions $\{0.0, 0.1, 0.3, 0.7, 1.0\}$ if numeric relevance scores are required; and might also be thresholded using $r_i \geq Moderate \Rightarrow b_i = 1$ in situations in which binary relevance values are desired. Naturally, different mappings (such as the use of $\{0.0, 0.125, 0.25, 0.5, 1.0\}$, or the use of $r_i \geq High$) affect the score that is generated by any particular metric.

In the development that follows, metrics that can only be applied to binary relevance judgments are shown with $\mathcal{B}$ as their argument; metrics that apply to real-valued relevance assessments (including binary-valued ones) are shown with an argument $\mathcal{R}$. Note also that some metrics rely more on k than do others; nevertheless, for consistency all metrics are shown as being evaluated down to a cutoff depth of k. The way in which metrics respond as k is altered is one of the numeric properties discussed in Section 4.

Standard Metrics: *Precision at depth k* is the fraction of the documents in the top k that are relevant (see Büttcher et al. [4] for descriptions of these standard mechanisms):

$$\text{Prec}@k(\mathcal{B}) = \frac{1}{k} \sum_{i=1}^{k} b_i .$$

The traditional counterpoint of precision is *recall at depth k*, the fraction of the relevant documents that appear in the first k positions of the ranking, $\text{Recall}@k(\mathcal{B}) = (k/R) \times \text{Prec}@k(\mathcal{B})$, where $R = \sum_{i=1}^{d} b_i$ is the total number of relevant documents in the d-document collection. Using the same definitions, *reciprocal rank at depth k* is

$$\text{RR}@k(\mathcal{B}) = \frac{1}{\min\{i \mid 1 \leq i \leq k \text{ and } b_i = 1\}} ;$$

and *average precision at depth k* is given by [2]:

$$\text{AP}@k(\mathcal{B}) = \frac{1}{R} \sum_{i=1}^{k} b_i \times \text{Prec}@i(\mathcal{B}) . \tag{1}$$

Note that it is important that the metric evaluation depth k be specified in all cases. Just as Prec@5 is a different metric to Prec@10, so too is AP@5 different to AP@10, and RR@5 different from RR@10. In the computation of AP@k in particular, there are zero contributions assumed from relevant documents outside the top k.

The four metrics introduced so far already display different properties. For example, Recall and AP are not defined if there are no relevant documents, that is, when $b_i = 0$ for all $1 \leq i \leq d$; and a special case of $RR@k = 0.0$ needs to be defined to cover the same situation. In contrast, provided $k \geq 1$, $Prec@k$ is well-defined even if there are no relevant documents in the top k, or if there are no relevant documents in the whole collection. That is, against just one criterion – whether the metric can be calculated if there are no relevant documents in the collection, the property denoted in Section 4 as *completeness* – there are differences to be found.

User Models: Before proceeding with further metrics, it is useful to note that a *user model* can be associated with each metric [15]. For example, $Prec@k$ corresponds to a user who examines exactly k documents in the ranking, and computes their "expected return" in units of "relevance per document inspected" (abbreviated RPDI for convenience). Similarly, $RR@k$ corresponds to a user who examines at most k documents, and stops either at depth k or as soon as they locate a useful one; the numeric RR score is again an expected return in units of RPDI. Robertson [17] describes a user model in which AP can also be interpreted as an RPDI value, but the user is presumed to have more complex behavior. If that model is adapted to the case of a ranking of depth k, then $AP@k$ corresponds to a user who knows how many relevant documents there are in the collection (the quantity R); chooses at random a number s between 1 and R inclusive; scans the ranking until they have encountered s relevant documents, even if that takes them beyond depth k; and then only actually takes benefit from the relevant documents that occur within the top k. Dupret and Piwowarski extend that model to graded relevance assessments [10].

Discounted Cumulative Gain: The *discounted cumulative gain at depth k* (or $DCG@k$) metric of Järvelin and Kekäläinen [11] is a variant of precision in which the ranks are top-weighted according to a weighting vector $\mathcal{W}$, so that a relevant document in the top position contributes more to the score than does a relevant document later in the ranking. The corresponding user model assumes that the user views all k documents in the ranking, but places more emphasis on items near the top. The weighting vector $\mathcal{W} = \langle w_i \rangle$ given by Järvelin and Kekäläinen is constant through until depth b, and then decays using logarithms base b; a variant, and the one used in the remainder of this paper, discounts the relevance ranking from the first position, taking $w_i = 1/\log(i + 1)$. In this "Microsoft DCG" version, the choice of b is no longer relevant, since logarithms to different bases are related by a multiplicative constant. In all of the numeric examples below, we take $b = 2$. Given a weighting vector $\mathcal{W}$, and a relevance vector $\mathcal{R}$, effectiveness is computed as:

$$DCG@k(\mathcal{R}) = \mathcal{W} \cdot \mathcal{R},$$

where the $\cdot$ operator represents vector inner product. Note that DCG is the first of the standard metrics that is expressly intended to be used with multi-value relevance assessments rather than binary assessments, and is defined using $\mathcal{R}$ rather than $\mathcal{B}$.

Scaled DCG: A drawback of DCG is that it is unbounded – a DCG effectiveness score might be 3.0, or 23.0, or 123.0. The latter value is attained only when then are 1,000 relevant documents at the head of the ranking, or some even more extensive combination of relevant documents further down the ranking; nevertheless, it is possible. Indeed, the unbounded nature of the sum $\sum_i 1/\log(i+1)$ means that *any* DCG@k_1 value computed for *any* prefix of length k_1 for one ranking can be exceeded by the DCG@k_2 score for a second ranking that commences with k_1 irrelevant documents, and then contains sufficiently many relevant documents. For example, the DCG@5 score of 1.63 assigned to the ranking $\mathcal{B} = $ "11000" is exceeded by the DCG@11 score assigned to the ranking $\mathcal{B} = $ "00000111111".

One way of introducing a bound is to scale $\mathcal{W}$ according to the sum to k terms of $1/\log(i+1)$, giving rise to a *scaled DCG at depth k* metric:

$$\text{SDCG@}k(\mathcal{R}) = \frac{\text{DCG@}k(\mathcal{R})}{\sum_{i=1}^{k} w_i} = \frac{\text{DCG@}k(\mathcal{R})}{\sum_{i=1}^{k} 1/\log(i+1)}.$$

In practical terms SDCG@k has much in common with Prec@k, and can be thought of as being a fixed-depth weighted-precision metric. As an example, $\mathcal{B} = $ "11000" has an SDCG@5 score of $(1.00 + 0.63)/(1.00 + 0.63 + 0.50 + 0.43 + 0.39) \approx 0.55$.

More Metrics: If the user will derive full satisfaction if any of the top k documents are relevant, a further metric can be defined: HIT@$k(\mathcal{R}) = \max\{r_i \mid 1 \leq i \leq k\}$. This metric is appropriate when a single answer is required, such as to a factoid question, or to a named-page finding task.

Following the lead of Järvelin and Kekäläinen [11], Moffat and Zobel [15] introduced *rank-biased precision*. Like SDCG, it is a weighted-precision metric; unlike SDCG, it makes use of an infinite sequence that is convergent, so that there is no requirement for subsequent scaling by a k-dependent denominator:

$$\text{RBP@}k(\mathcal{R}) = \mathcal{W} \cdot \mathcal{R} = (1-p)\left(\sum_{i=1}^{k} r_i p^{i-1}\right).$$

Moffat and Zobel also present a model of user behavior, in which p is the probability that the user will proceed from one document to the next in the ranking, with the RBP score representing the expected return per document inspected, the RPDI units introduced earlier. On any (finite) ranking, the RBP score is a bounded range, which narrows as documents are appended to the ranking. The lower bound of the range is reported as the RBP score, and the difference between it and the upper bound is specified as a *residual* [15]; that is, if we temporarily regard RBP@k as being a real-valued interval, then RBP@$k \supseteq$ RBP@$(k+1)$, and the intervals cannot diverge.

The key distinction between DCG/SDCG and RBP is that the latter uses a weighting vector $\mathcal{W}$ that sums to 1 in the limit, whereas DCG uses a weighting vector that has an unbounded sum, and must be truncated at k terms (hence the definition of SDCG) in order to achieve a bounded sum. There is thus a range of RBP-like metrics, each defined by a convergent infinite sequence of weights. For example, weights of $w_i = 1/(i(i+1))$ define a weighted-precision metric that has similar properties to RBP, since prefix sums of that sequence converge to one. Moffat et al. [14] describe such an inverse-squares weighting function; in the discussion below, we use RBP as a generic label for all metrics derived from infinite decreasing probability distributions.

3   Normalization

AP as a Normalized Metric: Aslam et al. [1] (see also Webber et al. [23]) introduced a *sum of precisions* metric, $\text{SP@}k(\mathcal{B}) = \sum_{i=1}^{k} b_i \times \text{Prec@}i(\mathcal{B})$. This computation results in an unbounded metric that shares properties with DCG. It is also related to AP, which is a *normalized* version of SP mapped to the range $[0, 1]$ as a consequence of the division by R. The transformation is useful in one respect, in that 1.0 always represents a "perfect" score; but the division by R means that there is a problem when $R = 0$.

NDCG as a Normalized Metric: Scaled DCG is always in the range $[0, 1]$, and a perfect ranking containing k relevant documents generates an SDCG@k score of 1.0. But if R is smaller than k, SDCG@k cannot be 1.0. An alternative normalization is to divide the actual DCG score by the highest DCG score that could be attained for this particular query, an approach denoted as *normalized discounted cumulative gain at depth k*, or NDCG@k [11]:

$$\text{NDCG@}k(\mathcal{R}) = \frac{\text{DCG@}k(\mathcal{R})}{\text{DCG@}k(Sort\_Decreasing(\mathcal{R}))} \, ,$$

where the denominator represents the DCG@k score that would be attained by an ideal reordering of the ranking, covering all d documents in the collection. Note that NDCG is another metric that is undefined when there are no relevant documents. The "percent perfect" measure of Losee [12] is also a normalized mechanism in this framework.

R-Precision as a Normalized Metric: The same issue also restricts Prec@k: if $R < k$, a score of 1.0 cannot be achieved. Imposing a cap on the score leads to a metric called *R-precision*, the value of Prec@R. For consistency, we also regard RPrec as being evaluated to some depth k, and define RPrec@k to be Prec@k if $k \leq R$; to be Prec@R if $k \geq R$; and to be undefined if $R = 0$.

Self Normalization: Computation of AP, NDCG, and RPrec requires that R be known – or, in the case of NDCG and RPrec, that $R \geq k$ be confirmed. In an experimental environment in which a collection of systems are being simultaneously scored, and relevance judgments can be shared across pooled runs, it may indeed be possible to make a reasonable estimate of R [26].

On the other hand, when a small number of systems are being scored, for example, in a simple "before" and "after" experiment, determination of even an approximate value of R might be difficult unless considerably more than k documents are judged for each topic. In such a resource-limited experiment an approach we call *self normalization* is tempting: each topic's relevance ranking is judged to depth k, and then an effectiveness metric is applied over the same k values, using R_k, the number of relevant items present in the top k, instead of R. Then *self normalized DCG at depth k*, or SN-DCG@k, is computed as SDCG@$k(\mathcal{R})$ divided by $\sum_{i=1}^{R_k}(1/\log(i+1))$. For example, SN-DCG@5 for the ranking $\mathcal{B} = $ "10100" is $(1.0 + 0.50)/(1.0 + 0.63) \approx 0.92$.

Table 1 summarizes the relationship between the three normalized versions of DCG. The sequence of increasingly precise normalizations is intended to adjust the effectiveness score to the bounds imposed by the query and the ranking generated for it. A

Table 1. Variants of DCG. In the case of SN-DCG@k, the scaling denominator is computed based solely on what is returned within the top k documents, and the scaling denominator is oblivious to any relevant documents outside the top k retrieved by the system being evaluated.

Method	Scaling denominator used to adjust DCG@k
DCG@k	No scaling performed
SDCG@k	Max score obtainable by *any* system on *any* query at depth k
NDCG@k	Max score obtainable by *any* system on *this* query at depth k
SN-DCG@k	Max score obtainable by *this* system on *this* query, permuting the top k

similar approach can be used to define *self normalized average precision at depth k*, or SN-AP, where the divisor in Equation 1 is R_k rather than R.

While the SN-DCG approach may appear to be a plausible solution to the question of determining R, it also gives rise to anomalous behavior. Consider the ranking $\mathcal{B} = $ "10101". It has one more relevant document than $\mathcal{B} = $ "10100". But now when SN-DCG is calculated, $R_k = 3$, and so SN-DCG@5 is computed as $1.89/2.13 = 0.88$. That is, the effectiveness score has *decreased*, even though an additional relevant document has *appeared* in the ranking. *Convergence* is one of the seven properties defined in the next section; and is a property that SN-DCG and SN-AP do not have.

4   Numeric Properties of Effectiveness Metrics

Having described a range of metrics, we now enumerate seven properties that might (or might not) be considered desirable in an effectiveness metric. As it turns out, there is tension between these properties, and it is not possible for any metric to attain all of them. Perhaps even more surprising is that the thirteen metrics described in Sections 2 and 3 span a total of ten different combinations of properties (summarized in Table 2).

(1) *Boundedness*: *The set of scores attainable by the metric is bounded, usually in the range* $[0, 1]$. When scores from experiments are being compared, it is desirable for them to be on the same scale. The maximum values of DCG@k and SP@k are functions of R, the number of relevant documents for this query, rather than constant, and so neither of DCG@k and SP@k are bounded. Metrics that are on different numeric scales – and perhaps even those that are not, see Mizzaro [13] – should not have mean scores computed across sets of topics, since they cannot be assumed to have the same units. Other aggregation techniques should be used [16], or standardized versions computed [23].

(2) *Monotonicity*: *If a ranking of length k is extended so that $k + 1$ elements are included, the score never decreases.* To see why P@k, SDCG@k, and NDCG@k are not monotonic, consider the ranking $\mathcal{B} = $ "11111", which has P@5, SDCG@5, and NDCG@5 scores all of 1.0. But if an additional relevance value is added and the ranking becomes $\mathcal{B} = $ "111110", then the P@6, SDCG@6, and NDCG@6 scores are 0.83, 0.89, and 0.89 (assuming that $R > 5$) respectively, less than the corresponding $k = 5$ scores. On the other hand, RR@6 can never be less than RR@5.

Table 2. Effectiveness metrics, ordered according to their combinations of properties in regard to one possible ordering of properties. All metrics are assumed to be evaluated over a ranking prefix of depth $k \geq 1$, where k is independent of R, the number of relevant documents for the query.

Metric	Bounded	Monoton.	Converg.	Top-wgt.	Localiz.	Complete	Realizb.
DCG@k	No	Yes	Yes	Yes	Yes	Yes	No
SP@k	No	Yes	Yes	Yes	Yes	Yes	No
RPrec@k	Yes	No	No	No	No	No	Yes
SN-DCG@k	Yes	No	No	Yes	Yes	No[d]	Yes
SN-AP@k	Yes	No	No	Yes	Yes	No[d]	Yes
Prec@k	Yes	No	Yes	No	Yes	Yes	No[e]
NDCG@k	Yes	No	Yes	Yes	No	No	Yes
SDCG@k	Yes	No	Yes	Yes	Yes	Yes	No[e]
HIT@k	Yes	Yes	No[b]	No[b]	Yes	Yes	Yes
RR@k	Yes	Yes	No[b]	No[b]	Yes[c]	Yes[c]	Yes
Recall@k	Yes	Yes	Yes	No	No	No	No[f]
AP@k	Yes	Yes	Yes	Yes	No	No	No[f]
RBP@k	Yes	Yes[a]	Yes[a]	Yes	Yes[a]	Yes	No

a. RBP@k yields a constrained range containing the score. The lower end of the range is taken to be the RBP score when a single value is required.
b. RR@k and HIT@k are not convergent or top-weighted because swaps of relevant documents to positions higher up the ranking are not guaranteed to increase the score.
c. RR@k is defined to be zero when there are no relevant documents in the prefix examined.
d. SN-DCG@k and SN-AP@k cannot be calculated when no relevant documents appear in the k-element prefix, even if $R > 0$.
e. SDCG@k and P@k can realize a value of 1.0 only if $k \leq R$.
f. Recall@k and AP@k can realize a value of 1.0 only if $k \geq R$.

Monotonicity is a desirable property when the reported results of an experiment are intended to be a conservative (that is, lower) bound on performance. Use of a monotonic effectiveness metric gives a reader the assurance that, should further relevance judgments be undertaken, the reported scores will increase rather than decrease. Resulted reported using non-monotonic metrics at shallow retrieval depths – for example, NDCG@5 or NDCG@10 – provide little indication as to how the same systems might be assessed in a comprehensive experiment using, say, NDCG@100.

(3) *Convergence: If a document outside the top k is swapped with a less relevant one (that is, has a lower r_i value) that is inside the top k, the score strictly increases.* This property complements monotonicity; if a metric is convergent and bounded, scores must strictly converge towards (typically) 1.0 as the density of relevant documents in the top k increases. As is noted in Table 2, there are several non-convergent metrics, most notably the self-normalized variants of NDCG and AP. Both of these can exhibit surprising behavior as relevant documents are inserted into the top k. For example, the ranking

$\mathcal{B}$ = "10000" has a SN-AP@5 score of 1.0, whereas $\mathcal{B}$ = "10001" has a SN-AP@5 score of 0.7. Reciprocal rank is also non-convergent according to this definition: the rankings $\mathcal{B}$ = "01000" and $\mathcal{B}$ = "01100" have the same RR@5 score.

(4) *Top-weightedness*: *If a document within the top k is swapped with a less relevant one (that is, has a lower r_i value) higher in the ranking, the score strictly increases.* A metric is top-weighted if, within the top k, the best score is attained when the relevant documents are in the first positions. The definitions of SDCG@k and RBP@k expressly introduce top-weighting to precision-like metrics, seeking to improve on Prec@k. The "strictly increases" requirement in the definition also implies that RR@k and HIT@k are not top-weighted, since RR@5 on $\mathcal{B}$ = "10001" and $\mathcal{B}$ = "11000" are the same.

Note that all four combinations of convergence and top-weightedness are in evidence in Table 2, and that they are independent concepts. Top-weightedness is similarly independent of monotonicity (as is convergence).

(5) *Localization*: *A score at depth k can be computed based solely on knowledge of the documents that appear in the top k.* The non-localized metrics – RPrec, NDCG, Recall, and AP – typically require specific knowledge of R, the number of relevant documents for the query, or, as a minimum, knowledge that $R \geq k$. As was noted in Section 3, requiring knowledge of R before being able to compute the score means that experimental evaluations are either expensive, with judgments required to depths rather greater than depth k; or must be carried out using approximate values of R derived from pooling; or must be done using self-normalization.

Two of the measures – RBP@k and RR@k – are localized in a slightly specialized sense, in that constrained ranges for the score can be determined after k documents have been judged, even if a single-value score cannot be. In the case of RR@k, either a relevant document is found in the top k, in which case the value of the metric is determined; or if no relevant document is identified, the score is taken to be 0.0. The RBP metric explicitly calculates a range in which the score lies, and as each document is added to the ranking, narrows that range. Regardless of k, the range is always non-zero. When a score value is required, the minimum value in the range is used.

(6) *Completeness*: *A score can be calculated even if the query has no relevant documents.* Metrics that compute normalized scores relative to the best that could be attained for that query – covering Recall, RPrec@k, NDCG@k, AP@k, and the two self-normalized metrics – must of necessity fail to produce a score when $R = 0$. And asserting that when $R = 0$ the score must "of course" be zero is inappropriate, since any ranking at all is "the best that could be attained" if there are no relevant documents, meaning that a score of 1.0 is no less appropriate.[1] The $R = 0$ situation arises in practice in retrieval experimentation, and can be vexing. In the TREC environment, query topics for which no relevant documents are identified in the corresponding collection are removed from the topic set, in order to bypass the awkwardness caused by effectiveness metrics that are not complete. Researchers who work with data subsets must

---

[1] One might also argue that the empty ranking, containing no documents at all, is more informative than any non-empty ranking of irrelevant documents, and hence should be the only ranking awarded a score of 1.0. As a further option, some researchers might feel that a "divide by zero" error when $R = 0$ is a less uninformative outcome than is a score of zero.

similarly prune topic sets so that they only include queries for which answers are available; one way of rationalizing this need is to argue that a query with no answers cannot differentiate between systems, regardless of what effectiveness score is assigned.

(7) *Realizability*: *Provided that the collection has at least one relevant document, it is possible for the score at depth k to be maximal.* To be realizable, a metric must be capable of generating its maximum value (typically 1.0), even when the number of relevant documents R is larger or smaller than the evaluation depth k. The precision-based metrics Prec@k, SDCG@k, and RBP@k, are unable to always generate a score of 1.0, regardless of how highly the relevant documents are ranked. Nor are Recall and AP realizable, since an evaluation at depth $k < R$ cannot attain a score of 1.0. On the other hand, NDCG generates a score relative to the best that could obtained for this topic, and can yield a score of 1.0 even when there is as few as one relevant document for the topic. Reciprocal rank also falls into this latter category.

All four combinations of completeness and realizability are demonstrated in Table 2, showing that they are independent.

Conflict Between the Properties: Is it possible for a metric to possess all seven of the properties? The answer is no, because monotonicity and convergence between them require that on any ranking that currently contains $k < R$ documents, the score assigned cannot yet be 1.0, making realizability impossible. Hence, of these seven properties, the best that can be achieved is six. Rank-biased precision attains six of the seven, sacrificing realizability. An interesting question is whether there is a metric that retains the other aspects of RBP, but swaps realizability for either monotonicity or convergence; and if such a metric exists, what behavior is implied by the corresponding user model.

5   Subjective Metric Evaluation Criteria

The categorization we have presented is based on objective numeric criteria, and each of the properties is an attribute that a metric either does, or does not, possess. But there are also other subjective criteria that are used when selecting a mechanism (or set of mechanisms) with which to report the results of retrieval experiments. Note that none of the objective criteria summarized in Table 2 implies any of these subjective desiderata.

Meaningfulness: Perhaps the most important attribute of a metric is its plausibility as a measurement tool, that is, whether the scores it generates correlate with the underlying behavior it is intended to represent. If the purpose of the metric is to quantify the overall usefulness of that ranking to the user, then a metric with a user model that doesn't ring true is unlikely to be of interest, regardless of its numeric properties. Normalized metrics, including Recall, have been criticized in this regard – it is difficult to see how the user's perception of the usefulness of a ranking of k documents can depend on the contents of the $d - k$ documents that they are not provided with [25]. More to the point, a range of user studies (see, for example, Turpin and Scholer [22]) have suggested that the link between the effectiveness score of a ranking and its usefulness to users may be tenuous. Even so, the aptness of the metric to the task at hand is an important subjective factor. Web search services are more likely to be measured using HIT@3 or SDCG@5 than via AP@1,000. A related aspect of this criteria is *scrutability*, whether the score generated by the metric can be readily explained.

Handling Partial Rankings: Another important subjective criterion is the behavior of the metric in the face of incomplete relevance judgments, including the case when a metric is being evaluated to depth k, but the ranking supplied by a system is only of length $j < k$. Buckley and Voorhees [3] introduced the AP-derived BPref metric in order to deal with this problem, with further contributions added by Yilmaz and Aslam [24], and by Sakai [19]. One approach is the use of *condensed rankings*, in which the non-judged documents are removed, and the remaining documents are scored as if that was the list returned by the search system.

A key motivation for RBP was to make explicit, via the provision of a score range, the degree of uncertainty attributable to unjudged documents [15]. Other precision-based metrics such as Prec and SDCG share this ability; whereas computation of score ranges is both more challenging and less informative for metrics such as AP.

Experimental Cost: Researchers designing experiments must construct a judgments budget – an estimate of the cost of carrying out the experiment – as part of their planning. Localized metrics allow such estimates to be made with a degree of confidence not possible with non-localized metrics. Other factors also come in to play when estimating costs, including the fidelity with which results will be presented. Being able to quantify the measurement uncertainty is a useful attribute of weighted-precision metrics; and in the other direction, if a score is required to be known to a given level of uncertainty, that constraint can be used to determine the depth k used in the experimentation [15].

Statistical Properties and Predictivity: Another important facet of metric behavior is the likelihood of statistically significant system differentiations being obtained. All other things being equal, metrics that are predictive of system performance (or system pair relativities) on unseen queries or unseen documents should be preferred to metrics that are not. Several studies have shown AP and NDCG to be useful in this regard [2,18,20,23], assuming that the evaluation depth k (and hence also the pooling depth used to determine R) is sufficiently deepNote that the range of statistical tests that can be used is affected by the metric's numeric properties – not all tests can be applied to bounded values, for example.

Recent Work: Measurement of retrieval effectiveness has been the focus of a range of recent work. For example, the *expected reciprocal rank* metric, ERR [7], is a blend of RR and RBP in which the user is modeled as scanning through to the first relevant document, and then with probability p deciding to scan for the next one, and so on. Other work has sought to compute effectiveness scores based on distributions over parameters (such as the persistence parameter p that governs RBP) so as to better model populations of users [6].

Carterette [5] examines a range of weighted precision metrics, including DCG and RBP, and evaluates them against a set of probability distributions. Carterette concludes that DCG has a number of subjective properties that make it attractive for retrieval experimentation, including that it can be fitted to click log data. Several earlier studies have also made use of click data in order to estimate parameters for user models (and vice versa); see, for example, Dupret and Piwowarski [9].

Most recently, Smucker and Clarke [21] have refined the assumption that user effort can be measured in terms of "documents inspected", and instead suggest that cost should be based on measured or estimated time. They propose a *time-biased gain* metric which differentiates between long documents and short documents, and between novel documents and repeat occurrences of those documents; Smucker and Clarke estimate parameters for their model through a user study, and via click log analysis.

Moffat et al. [14] consider the relationship between user behavior and effectiveness metrics, arguing that the behaviors modeled by a metric should correspond to the behaviors observed as users carry out search tasks.

6 Discussion

The seven properties that retrieval effectiveness metrics do or do not possess are not completely independent. Nevertheless, the groupings that are apparent in Table 2 show that there are multiple viable combinations. Researchers designing retrieval experiments should thus be alert to the implications associated with the metrics they use, and, conversely, should feel empowered to select metrics that will correctly recognize the behavior that they believe their experiment will reveal. The readers of research papers should be similarly aware of the implications arising from certain choices.

Our primary intention in this work has been to categorize, rather than to criticize. Nevertheless, a caution is in order: the two self-normalized metrics SN-DCG@k and SN-AP@k are counter-intuitive in their behavior, and need to be interpreted with care. Work that reports results using, for example, NDCG@5, should make it clear whether extensive judgments have been performed, or whether SN-DCG@5 is being used. The latter may be less costly to compute, but it is also less well behaved.

As a final remark, note that while the seven numeric criteria are all objective, the determination of them – deciding which properties were important enough to include – has been a subjective exercise. Moreover, the ordering of the columns in Table 2 generates the row ordering shown; with other column orderings yielding different row orderings. Researchers who prefer a different prioritization of the properties (or who feel that some of the listed properties fail to capture meaningful differences between metrics) can reorder the columns (and remove the ones they eschew) in order to focus on the metrics that meet their particular needs. Conversely, there may be additional numeric properties not recognized here – perhaps ones pertinent to metrics not yet considered – that can be added, in order to further refine the categorization.

Acknowledgments. James Allan, Falk Scholer, Paul Thomas, William Webber, and Justin Zobel provided helpful input, as did the anonymous referees via their extensive and thoughtful feedback. This work was supported by the Australian Research Council.

References

1. Aslam, J.A., Pavlu, V., Yilmaz, E.: A statistical method for system evaluation using incomplete judgments. In: Proc. SIGIR, Seattle, Washington, pp. 541–548 (2006)
2. Buckley, C., Voorhees, E.M.: Evaluating evaluation measure stability. In: Proc. SIGIR, Athens, Greece, pp. 33–40 (2000)
3. Buckley, C., Voorhees, E.M.: Retrieval evaluation with incomplete information. In: Proc. SIGIR, Sheffield, England, pp. 25–32 (2004)

4. Büttcher, S., Clarke, C.L.A., Cormack, G.V.: Information Retrieval: Implementing and Evaluating Search Engines. The MIT Press (2010)

5. Carterette, B.: System effectiveness, user models, and user utility: A conceptual framework for investigation. In: Proc. SIGIR, Beijing, China, pp. 903–912 (2011)

6. Carterette, B., Kanoulas, E., Yilmaz, E.: Simulating simple user behavior for system effectiveness evaluation. In: Proc. CIKM, Glasgow, Scotland, pp. 611–620 (2011)

7. Chapelle, O., Metzler, D., Zhang, Y., Grinspan, P.: Expected reciprocal rank for graded relevance. In: Proc. CIKM, Hong Kong, China, pp. 621–630 (2009)

8. Demartini, G., Mizzaro, S.: A classification of IR effectiveness metrics. In: Lalmas, M., MacFarlane, A., Rüger, S.M., Tombros, A., Tsikrika, T., Yavlinsky, A. (eds.) ECIR 2006. LNCS, vol. 3936, pp. 488–491. Springer, Heidelberg (2006)

9. Dupret, G., Piwowarski, B.: A user browsing model to predict search engine click data from past observations. In: Proc. SIGIR, Singapore, pp. 331–338 (2008)

10. Dupret, G., Piwowarski, B.: A user behavior model for average precision and its generalization to graded judgments. In: Proc. SIGIR, Geneva, Switzerland, pp. 531–538 (2010)

11. Järvelin, K., Kekäläinen, J.: Cumulated gain-based evaluation of IR techniques. ACM Trans. Inf. Sys. 20(4), 422–446 (2002)

12. Losee, R.M.: Percent perfect performance (PPP). Inf. Proc. Man. 43(4), 1020–1029 (2007)

13. Mizzaro, S.: The good, the bad, the difficult, and the easy: Something wrong with information retrieval evaluation? In: Macdonald, C., Ounis, I., Plachouras, V., Ruthven, I., White, R.W. (eds.) ECIR 2008. LNCS, vol. 4956, pp. 642–646. Springer, Heidelberg (2008)

14. Moffat, A., Thomas, P., Scholer, F.: Users versus models: What observation tells us about effectiveness metrics. In: Proc. CIKM, San Francisco, California (to appear, 2013)

15. Moffat, A., Zobel, J.: Rank-biased precision for measurement of retrieval effectiveness. ACM Trans. Inf. Sys. 27(1:2), 1–27 (2008)

16. Robertson, S.: On GMAP: and other transformations. In: Proc. CIKM, Arlington, Virginia, pp. 78–83 (2006)

17. Robertson, S.: A new interpretation of average precision. In: Proc. SIGIR, Singapore, pp. 689–690 (2008)

18. Sakai, T., Kando, N.: On information retrieval metrics designed for evaluation with incomplete relevance assessments. Inf. Ret. 11(5), 447–470 (2008)

19. Sakai, T.: Alternatives to BPref. In: Proc. SIGIR, Amsterdam, Netherlands, pp. 71–78 (2007)

20. Sanderson, M., Zobel, J.: Information retrieval system evaluation: Effort, sensitivity, and reliability. In: Proc. SIGIR, Salvador, Brazil, pp. 162–169 (2005)

21. Smucker, M.D., Clarke, C.L.A.: Time-based calibration of effectiveness measures. In: Proc. SIGIR, Portland, Oregon, pp. 95–104 (2012)

22. Turpin, A., Scholer, F.: User performance versus precision measures for simple search tasks. In: Proc. SIGIR, Seattle, Washington, pp. 11–18 (2006)

23. Webber, W., Moffat, A., Zobel, J.: Score standardization for inter-collection comparison of retrieval systems. In: Proc. SIGIR, Singapore, pp. 51–58 (2008)

24. Yilmaz, E., Aslam, J.A.: Estimating average precision with incomplete and imperfect judgments. In: Proc. CIKM, Arlington, Virginia, pp. 102–111 (2006)

25. Zobel, J., Moffat, A., Park, L.A.F.: Against recall: Is it persistence, cardinality, density, coverage, or totality? SIGIR Forum 43(1), 3–15 (2009)

26. Zobel, J.: How reliable are the results of large-scale information retrieval experiments? In: Proc. SIGIR, Melbourne, Australia, pp. 307–314 (1998)

How Intuitive Are Diversified Search Metrics? Concordance Test Results for the Diversity U-Measures

Tetsuya Sakai

Waseda University, Japan
tetsuyasakai@acm.org

Abstract. Most of the existing Information Retrieval (IR) metrics discount the value of each retrieved relevant document based on its rank. This statement also applies to the evaluation of diversified search: the widely-used diversity metrics, namely, α-nDCG, Intent-Aware Expected Reciprocal Rank (ERR-IA) and D$\sharp$-nDCG, are all rank-based. These evaluation metrics regard the system output as a list of document IDs, and ignore all other features such as snippets and document full texts of various lengths. In contrast, the U-measure framework of Sakai and Dou uses the *amount of text read by the user* as the foundation for discounting the value of relevant information, and can take into account the user's snippet reading and full text reading behaviours. The present study compares the diversity versions of U-measure (D-U and U-IA) with the state-of-the-art diversity metrics using the concordance test: given a pair of ranked lists, we quantify the ability of each metric to favour the *more diversified and more relevant* list. Our results show that while D$\sharp$-nDCG is the overall winner in terms of simultaneous concordance with diversity and relevance, D-U and U-IA statistically significantly outperform other state-of-the-art metrics. Moreover, in terms of concordance with relevance alone, D-U and U-IA significantly outperform all rank-based diversity metrics. Thus, D-U and U-IA are not only more realistic but also more relevance-oriented than other diversity metrics.

1 Introduction

For the past few decades, ranked retrieval (e.g. web search) has been evaluated using *rank-based* evaluation metrics such as Average Precision and *normalised Discounted Cumulative Gain* (nDCG) [7]. These metrics discount the value of each retrieved relevant document based on its rank. The situation is similar with *diversified search* which has gained popularity recently: diversity metrics such as α-nDCG [3], *Intent-Aware Expected Reciprocal Rank* (ERR-IA) [2] and D$\sharp$-nDCG [14] are also rank-based. These widely-used evaluation metrics regard the system output as a list of document IDs, and ignore all other features such as snippets and document full texts of various lengths.

The *U-measure* framework of Sakai and Dou [11] uses the *amount of text read by the user* as the foundation for discounting the value of relevant information,

R.E. Banchs et al. (Eds.): AIRS 2013, LNCS 8281, pp. 13–24, 2013.

and can take into account the user's snippet reading and full text reading behaviours. The present study compares the diversity versions of U-measure (*D-U* and *U-IA*) with state-of-the-art diversity metrics using the *concordance test*[10]: given a pair of ranked lists, we quantify the ability of each metric to favour the *more diversified and more relevant* list, by counting preference agreements with a pure diversity metric (namely, *intent recall* [14]) and a pure relevance metric (namely, precision). Our results show that while D♯-nDCG is the overall winner in terms of simultaneous concordance with diversity and relevance, D-U and U-IA statistically significantly outperform other state-of-the-art metrics. Moreover, in terms of concordance with relevance alone, D-U and U-IA significantly outperform all rank-based diversity metrics. Thus, D-U and U-IA are not only more realistic but also more relevance-oriented than other diversity metrics.

2   Prior Art

This section discusses existing studies on evaluation metrics for diversified search, which, given an ambiguous and/or underspecified query, aims to satisfy different user intents with a single search engine result page[1]. While traditional ranked retrieval only considers relevance, diversified search systems are expected to find the right balance between diversity and relevance. In diversified search evaluation, it is assumed that the following are available [14]:

- A set of ambiguous and/or underspecified topics (i.e., queries) $\{q\}$;
- A set of *intents* $\{i\}$ for each topic;
- The *intent probability* $Pr(i|q)$ for each intent;
- Per-intent (possibly graded) relevance assessments for each topic.

Because diversity metrics need to consider the above different factors to evaluate systems, they tend to be more complex than traditional ranked retrieval metrics. However, since the ultimate goal of IR researchers is to satisfy the user's information need, we want to make sure that the metrics are measuring what we want to measure. This is the focus of the present study.

The TREC[2] Web Track ran the Diversity Task from 2009 to 2012 [6]. In the present study, we use the TREC 2011 diversity data [4]: only the 2011 and 2012 data have *graded* relevance assessments, and the number of participating teams was higher in 2011 (9 vs. 8). At the TREC 2009 Diversity Task, the primary metric used for ranking the runs was α-nDCG; ERR-IA was used primarily in the subsequent years.

NTCIR[3] ran the INTENT task [12][4] at NTCIR-9 and -10, which also evaluated diversified search. The primary evaluation metric used there was D♯-nDCG,

---

[1] An example of an ambiguous query would be "office": does the user mean "workplace" or "Microsoft software"? An example of an underspecified query would be "harry potter": *Harry Potter books*? *Harry Potter films*? Or perhaps *Harry Potter the main character*?

[2] Text Retrieval Conference: http://trec.nist.gov/

[3] NII Testbeds and Community for Information access Research:
http://research.nii.ac.jp/ntcir/

[4] http://research.microsoft.com/INTENT/

which is a simple linear combination of *intent recall* (I-rec) and *D-nDCG* [14]. The NTCIR-10 INTENT-2 task also used additional metrics called *DIN-nDCG* and *P+Q* to evaluate the systems' ability to handle *informational* and *navigational* intents in diversified search. However, this *intent-type-sensitive* evaluation is beyond the scope of this paper, as very few teams have tackled this particular problem so far.

In this study, we compare D-U and U-IA with these official diversity metrics from TREC and NTCIR, namely, α-nDCG, ERR-IA and D($\sharp$)-nDCG, from the viewpoint of how "intuitive" they are. We use the *official* α-nDCG and ERR-IA performance values that were computed with the ndeval software[5], as well as D($\sharp$)-nDCG values computed with NTCIREVAL[6]. Below, we formally define these rank-based diversity metrics from TREC and NTCIR.

First, let us define the original nDCG for traditional IR, given graded relevance assessments per topic, where the relevance level x varies from 0 to H. In the present study, $H = 3$ (See Table 1 in Section 5), and $x = 0$ means "nonrelevant." Following previous work (e.g. [1,2]), we let the *gain value* of each x-relevant document be $gv_x = (2^x - 1)/2^H$: hence $gv_1 = 1/8$, $gv_2 = 3/8$ and $gv_3 = 7/8$. For a given ranked list, the gain at rank r is defined as $g(r) = gv_x$ if the document at r is x-relevant. Moreover, let $g^*(r)$ denote the gain at rank r in an *ideal* ranked list, obtained by sorting all relevant documents by the relevance level [7,9]. A popular version of nDCG [1] is defined as:

$$nDCG = \frac{\sum_{r=1}^{l} g(r)/\log(r+1)}{\sum_{r=1}^{l} g^*(r)/\log(r+1)} \tag{1}$$

where l is the *measurement depth* or *document cutoff*.

In diversified IR evaluation where each topic q has a set of possible intents $\{i\}$, (graded) relevance assessments are obtained for each i rather than for each q. Let $I_i(r)$ be one if the document at rank r is relevant to intent i and zero otherwise; let $C_i = \sum_{k=1}^{r} I_i(k)$. α-nDCG is defined by replacing the gains in Eq. 1 with the following *novelty-biased gain* [3]:

$$ng(r) = \sum_i I_i(r)(1 - \alpha)^{C_i(r-1)} \tag{2}$$

where α is a parameter, set to $\alpha = 0.5$ at TREC. Thus it discounts the value of each relevant document based on redundancy within each intent (Eq. 2) and then further discounts it based on the rank (Eq. 1). Although this definition requires the novelty-biased gains for the ideal list ($ng^*(r)$), the problem of obtaining the ideal list for α-nDCG is NP-complete, and therefore a greedy approximation is used in practice [3]. Note that α-nDCG cannot handle per-intent graded relevance: it defines the graded relevance of a document based solely on the number of intents it covers.

In contrast, ERR-IA utilises per-intent graded relevance assessments: let $g_i(r)$ denote the gain at rank r *with respect to intent i*, using the aforementioned gain

---

[5] http://trec.nist.gov/data/web/11/ndeval.c
[6] http://research.nii.ac.jp/ntcir/tools/ntcireval-en.html

value setting (i.e., $1/7, 3/8, 7/8$). This may be interpreted as the probability that the user with intent i is satisfied with this particular document at r. Then the ERR for this particular intent, ERR_i, is computed as:

$$ERR_i = \sum_r \prod_{k=1}^{r-1} (1 - g_i(k))g_i(r)\frac{1}{r} \; . \tag{3}$$

This is an intuitive metric: the user with intent i is dissatisfied with documents between ranks 1 and $r-1$, and is finally satisfied at r; the utility at this satisfaction point is measured by the reciprocal rank $1/r$. Finally, ERR-IA is computed as the expectation over the intents:

$$ERR\text{-}IA = \sum_i Pr(i|q)ERR_i \; . \tag{4}$$

The D♯ framework [14] used at the NTCIR INTENT task also utilises per-intent graded relevance assessments. First, for each document at rank r, the *global gain* is defined as:

$$GG(r) = \sum_i Pr(i|q)g_i(r) \; . \tag{5}$$

Then, by sorting all relevant documents by the global gain, a "globally ideal list" is defined for a given topic, so that the *ideal global gain* $GG^*(r)$ can be obtained. Note that unlike α-nDCG, there is no NP-complete problem involved here, and that, unlike ERR-IA, there is exactly one ideal list for a given topic. By replacing the gains in Eq. 1 with these global gain values, a *D-measure* version of nDCG, namely, *D-nDCG* is obtained. This is further combined with *intent recall*, defined as $I\text{-}rec = |\{i'\}|/|\{i\}|$ where $\{i'\}$ is the set of intents covered by the system output:

$$D\sharp\text{-}nDCG = \gamma I\text{-}rec + (1 - \gamma)D\text{-}nDCG \; . \tag{6}$$

Here, γ is a parameter ($0 \leq \gamma \leq 1$), simply set to 0.5 at NTCIR. D♯-nDCG is a single-value summary of the *I-rec/D-nDCG graph* used at the NTCIR INTENT task [12], which visualises the trade-off between diversity and overall relevance.

As we shall demonstrate later, α-nDCG and ERR-IA behave very similarly, as they both possess the per-intent *diminishing return* property [2]: whenever a relevant document is found, the value of the next relevant document is discounted for each intent. Because redundancy within each intent is penalised, diversity across intents is rewarded. Whereas, D-nDCG does not have this property, so it is combined with I-rec, a pure diversity metric, to compensate for this. However, none of these metrics used at TREC or NTCIR reflects the real user behaviours such as reading snippets and visiting the full text of a relevant document. The new diversity metrics that we advocate in this study, called D-U and U-IA, do just that.

The recently-proposed *Time-Biased Gain* (TBG) evaluation framework [17] is similar to the U-measure framework in that it can also take into account the

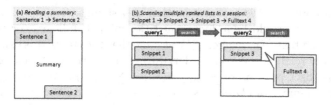

Fig. 1. Constructing trailtexts for summarisation and search session evaluation

user's snippet and full text reading behaviours: while U discounts the value of relevant information based on the *amount of text read so far*[7], TBG does this based on the *time spent so far*. The idea is basically equivalent if the user's reading speed is constant. However, TBG-based diversity evaluation has not been explored in the literature.

3   U-Measure, D-U and U-IA

This section defines U-measure and its diversity versions D-U and U-IA as described by Sakai and Dou [11].

First, we present the general U-measure framework. Figure 1 introduces *trailtexts*, the foundation of the U-measure framework. Part (a) shows a single textual query-biased summary being shown to the user. Suppose that we have observed (by means of, say, eyetracking or mousetracking) that the user read only the first and the last sentences of this summary. In this case, we define the trailtext as a simple concatenation of these two sentences: "**Sentence1 Sentence2.**"

Summarisation represents an information access task where the user-system interaction is minimal; at the other end of the spectrum, we may have search *sessions* with several query reformulations. Figure 1 Part (b) shows a session that involves one query reformulation: the user reads two snippets in the original ranked list, reformulates the query, reads one snippet in the new ranked list, and finally visits the actual document. The trailtext is then "**Snippet1 Snippet2 Snippet3 Fulltext4.**" Thus, the trailtext is a concatenation of all texts read by the user during her information seeking activity. If evidence from eyetracking/mousetracking etc. is unavailable, the trailtext can alternatively be constructed systematically under a certain user model, using document relevance assessments and or click data [11].

The general U-measure framework comprises two steps:

Step 1. Generate a trailtext, or multiple possible trailtexts, by either observing the actual user or assuming a user model;
Step 2. Evaluate the trailtext(s), based on relevant *information units* (e.g. documents, passages, nuggets) found within it, while discounting the value of each information unit based on its *position* within the trailtext.

---

[7] The U-measure framework is an extension of the *S-measure* framework [13] and hence text-oriented.

Formally, a trailtext tt is a concatenation of n strings: $tt = s_1 s_2 \ldots s_n$. Each string $s_k (1 \leq k \leq n)$ could be a document title, snippet, full text, or even some arbitrary part of a text (e.g. nugget). We assume that the trailtext is exactly what the user actually read, in the exact order, during an information seeking process. We define the offset position of s_k as $pos(s_k) = \sum_{j=1}^{k} |s_j|$. We measure lengths in terms of the number of *characters* [13]. Each s_k in a trailtext tt is considered either x-relevant or nonrelevant. In the present study, we assume that s_k is either a web search engine snippet of 200 characters or a part of a relevant web page; we also assume that the user examines the snippets starting from the top of the list, and that she reads exactly $F = 20\%$ of every relevant web page that she sees[8]. We define the *position-based gain* as $g(pos(s_k)) = 0$ if s_k is considered nonrelevant, and $g(pos(s_k)) = gv_x$ if it is considered x-relevant, where the gain value setting is the same as those for the rank-based metrics. In the present study where s_k is either a snippet or a part of a full text, $g(pos(s_k)) = gv_x$ if and only if s_k is a part of a full text of an x-relevant document; an example will be discussed later.

The general form of U-measure is given by:

$$U = \frac{1}{\mathcal{N}} \sum_{pos=1}^{|tt|} g(pos)D(pos) \tag{7}$$

where $\mathcal{N}$ is a normalisation factor, which we simply set to $\mathcal{N} = 1$ in this study, pos is an offset position within tt, and $D(pos)$ is a *position-based* decay function. Following the S-measure framework [13], here we assume that the value of a relevant information unit decays linearly with the amount of text the user has read:

$$D(pos) = \max(0, 1 - \frac{pos}{L})) . \tag{8}$$

Here, L is the amount of text at which all relevant information units become worthless, which we set to $L = 132000$ based on statistics from 21,802,136 sessions from Bing [11].

The U-measure framework can be extended to handle diversified IR evaluation in two ways. The first is to take the D-measure approach: as shown in Figure 2(a) and (b), given a ranked list, a single trailtext can be built by adding a 200-character snippet for each rank and 20% of each document full text which is relevant to at least one intent; then, the *global gain* at the end position of each relevant document is computed as:

$$g(pos(s_k)) = \sum_{i} P(i|q)g_i(pos(s_k)) \tag{9}$$

where $g_i(pos(s_k)) = gv_x$ if s_k is x-relevant to the i-th intent. This is then plugged in to Eq. 7, to obtain *D-U*. The second approach is to follow the Intent-Aware approach: as shown in Figure 2(a) and (c), a trailtext is built *for each intent*, and

---

[8] The snippet length for Microsoft's Bing is approximately 200 characters on average; Sakai and Dou [11] have shown that $F = 20\%$ is a reasonable choice.

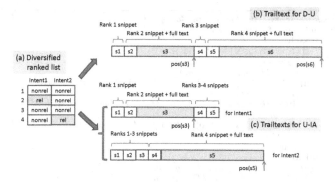

Fig. 2. Constructing trailtexts for D-U and U-IA [11]

a U value (U_i) is computed independently for each i. Finally, the Intent-Aware U is given as:

$$U\text{-}IA = \sum_i Pr(i|q)U_i \ . \tag{10}$$

D-U and U-IA are in fact very similar. Let $\{i'\}(\subseteq \{i\})$ be the set of intents covered by the system output; a document in this output is *strictly locally relevant* if it is relevant to at least one intent from $\{i'\}$ *and* nonrelevant to at least one intent from $\{i'\}$. It is easy to show that *if there is no strictly locally relevant document in the system output, then D-U = U-IA holds*. A corollary is that *if the system output covers only one intent, then D-U = U-IA holds* [11].

4   Concordance Test

Sakai and Dou [11] compared D-U and U-IA with D($\sharp$)-nDCG and a version of ERR-IA in terms of *discriminative power*: the ability of a metric to find statistically significant differences with high confidence for many system pairs. They reported that D-U, U-IA and ERR-IA underperform D($\sharp$)-nDCG in terms of discriminative power, probably because D($\sharp$)-nDCG does not possess the diminishing return property: it does not penalise "redundant" relevant documents, so it relies on more data points and is statistically more stable. However, discriminative power is only a measure of stability: it does not tell us whether the metrics are measuring what they are supposed to measure. To evaluate diversity metrics from the latter point of view, we adopt Sakai's concordance test [10].

Because diversity IR metrics are complex, the concordance test tries to examine how "intuitive" they are by using some very simple "gold-standard" metrics. Since we want both high diversity and high relevance in diversified search, it is possible to regard *intent recall* and/or *precision* (where a document relevant to at least one intent is counted as relevant) as the gold standard. Note that these gold-standard metrics themselves are not good enough for diversity evaluation: these merely represent the basic properties of the more complex diversity metrics that should be satisfied.

```
Disagreements = 0; Conc₁ = 0; Conc₂ = 0;
foreach pair of runs (X, Y)
    foreach topic q
        ΔM₁ = M₁(q, X) − M₁(q, Y);
        ΔM₂ = M₂(q, X) − M₂(q, Y);
        ΔM* = M*(q, X) − M*(q, Y);
        if( ΔM₁ × ΔM₂ < 0 ) then // M₁ and M₂ strictly disagree
            Disagreements + +;
            if( ΔM₁ × ΔM* ≥ 0) ) then// M₁ is concordant with M*
                Conc₁ + +;
            if( ΔM₂ × ΔM* ≥ 0) ) then // M₂ is concordant with M*
                Conc₂ + +;
        end if
    end foreach
    Conc(M₁|M₂, M*) = Conc₁/Disagreements;
    Conc(M₂|M₁, M*) = Conc₂/Disagreements;
```

Fig. 3. Concordance test algorithm for a pair of metrics M_1 and M_2, given the gold-standard metric M^* [10]

Figure 3 shows a simple algorithm for comparing two candidate metrics M_1 and M_2 given a gold standard metric M^*: concordance with multiple gold standards can be computed in a similar way. Here, for example, $M_1(q, X)$ denotes the value of metric M_1 computed for the output of system X obtained in response to topic q. Note that this algorithm focusses on the cases where M_1 and M_2 disagree with each other, and then turn to M^* which serves as the judge. While the condordance test relies on the assumption that the gold-standard metrics represent the real users' preferences[9], it is useful to be able to quantify exactly how often the metrics satisfy the basic properties that we expect them to satisfy, given many pairs of ranked lists. In our case, the specific questions we address are: (a) How often does a diversity metric agree with intent recall (i.e., prefer the more diversified list)?; (b) How often does it agree with precision (i.e., prefer the more relevant list)?; and (c) How often does it agree with intent recall and precision at the same time?

5   Experiments

Table 1 shows some statistics of the TREC 2011 Diversity Task data which we used for conducting the concordance tests. Note that as we have $17 * 16/2 = 136$ run pairs, we have $50 * 136 = 6,800$ pairs of ranked lists for the tests. The diversity evaluation metrics, D-U, U-IA, D(♯)-nDCG, α-nDCG and ERR-IA use the measurement depth of $l = 10$ as diversified search mainly concerns the *first* search engine result page. Computation of D-U and U-IA requires the document length statistics for all the relevant documents retrieved above top $l = 10$: the estimated lengths are available at http://research.microsoft.com/u/.

---

[9] Sanderson *et al.* [16] reported on experiments similar to the concordance test where Amazon Mechanical Turkers were used instead of the gold-standard metrics. However, they had to treat each intent of a topic as an independent topic. Hence their method does not evaluate the ability of a diversity metric to actually reward diversity.

Table 1. TREC 2011 Web Track Diversity Task data

Documents	ClueWeb09 (one billion web pages)
Intent probabilities	Not available
#intents/topic	3.3
#Topics	50
Pool depth	25
#runs	17 Category A runs
Per-intent relevance	graded (0, 1, 2, 3)
#Unique relevant/topic	100.6

As the TREC diversity data lack intent probabilities $Pr(i|q)$, we follow TREC and simply assume that the probability distribution across intents is uniform[10].

Table 2 summarises our concordance test results. Part (a) shows condordance with intent recall (i.e., the ability to prefer the more diversified result); (b) shows concordance with precision (i.e., the ability to prefer the more relevant result); and (c) shows simultaneous concordance with intent recall and precision. For example, Part (a) contains the following information for the comparison between U-IA and ERR-IA in terms of concordance with intent recall:

- U-IA and ERR-IA disagree with each other for 1,463 out of the 6,800 ranked list pairs;
- Of the above disagreements, U-IA is concordant 84% of the time, while ERR-IA is concordant 80% of the time;
- U-IA is significantly better than ERR-IA according to the sign test ($\alpha = 0.05$)[11].

Let "$M_1 \gg M_2$" denote the relationship: "M_1 statistically significantly outperforms M_2 in terms of concordance with a given gold-standard metric." Then our results can be summarised as follows[12]:

(a) Concordance with I-rec (pure diversity): D♯-nDCG $\gg \alpha$-nDCG $\gg$ U-IA $\gg$ D-U, D-nDCG, ERR-IA;
(b) Concordance with Prec (pure relevance): U-IA, D-U $\gg$ D-nDCG $\gg$ D♯-nDCG $\gg \alpha$-nDCG $\gg$ ERR-IA;
(c) Simultaneous concordance with I-rec and Prec : D♯-nDCG $\gg$ U-IA $\gg$ D-U $\gg$ D-nDCG $\gg \alpha$-nDCG $\gg$ ERR-IA.

Recall that D-U and U-IA are more realistic than the other metrics (including the gold-standard metrics), in that they consider the snippet and full text reading activities. Thus, we can conclude that D-U and U-IA are not only more realistic than other diversity metrics but also more relevance-oriented.

Finally, it can be observed that D-U and U-IA disagree with each other for only 54 out of the 6,800 ranked list pairs: thus, in practice, it is not necessary to

---

[10] Sakai and Song [15] have discussed the effect of utilising intent probabilities in diversity evaluation.

[11] Though not shown in the table, U-IA "wins" 273 times while ERR-IA "wins" 250 times.

[12] In general, note that pairwise statistical significance is not transitive. However, it turns out that our results do not violate transitivity.

Table 2. Concordance test results with the TREC 2011 Web Track Diversity Task data (50 topics; 17 runs). Statistically significant differences with the sign test are indicated by ‡'s ($\alpha = 0.01$) and †'s ($\alpha = 0.05$).

(a) gold standard: intent recall

	D-nDCG	D-U	U-IA	ERR-IA	α-nDCG
D♯-nDCG	100%/0%‡ (415)	100%/48%‡ (771)	100%/49%‡ (745)	99%/61%‡ (1106)	99%/71%‡ (913)
D-nDCG	-	81%/84% (562)	79%/86%‡ (568)	82%/82% (1044)	75%/91%‡ (974)
D-U	-	-	54%/94%‡ (54)	83%/81% (1472)	78%/89%‡ (1323)
U-IA	-	-	-	84%/80%† (1463)	79%/89%‡ (1299)
ERR-IA	-	-	-	-	42%/100%‡ (292)

(b) gold standard: precision

	D-nDCG	D-U	U-IA	ERR-IA	α-nDCG
D♯-nDCG	48%/71%‡ (415)	47%/76%‡ (771)	46%/77%‡ (745)	71%/53%‡ (1106)	69%/55%‡ (913)
D-nDCG	-	51%/74%‡ (562)	51%/75%‡ (568)	77%/49%‡ (1044)	75%/52%‡ (974)
D-U	-	-	74%/85% (54)	77%/48%‡ (1472)	76%/50%‡ (1323)
U-IA	-	-	-	77%/48%‡ (1463)	76%/49%‡ (1299)
ERR-IA	-	-	-	-	48%/76%‡ (292)

(c) gold standard: intent recall AND precision

	D-nDCG	D-U	U-IA	ERR-IA	α-nDCG
D♯-nDCG	48%/0%‡ (415)	47%/38%‡ (771)	45%/39%‡ (745)	70%/29%‡ (1106)	68%/35%‡ (913)
D-nDCG	-	42%/65%‡ (562)	40%/67%‡ (568)	66%/40%‡ (1044)	58%/48%‡ (974)
D-U	-	-	33%/80%‡ (54)	66%/40%‡ (1472)	62%/45%‡ (1323)
U-IA	-	-	-	67%/38%‡ (1463)	63%/43%‡ (1299)
ERR-IA	-	-	-	-	19%/76%‡ (292)

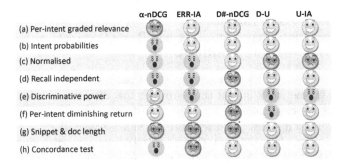

Fig. 4. Comparison of Diversified IR Metrics

use both of these metrics at the same time. Based on the above concordance test results, we recommend the use of U-IA. It can also be observed that α-nDCG and ERR-IA also behave similarly: they disagree with eath other for only 292 out of the 6800 ranked list pairs.

6 Conclusions and Future Work

Our results show that while D♯-nDCG is the overall winner in terms of simultaneous concordance with diversity and relevance, D-U and U-IA statistically significantly outperform other state-of-the-art metrics. Moreover, in terms of concordance with relevance alone, D-U and U-IA significantly outperform all rank-based diversity metrics. Hence D-U and U-IA are not only more realistic but also more relevance-oriented than the rank-based metrics. Moreover, as D-U and U-IA in fact behave extremely similarly, we recommend the use of of U-IA, which outperformed D-U according to the concordance tests.

Figure 4 summarises various properties of existing diversity evaluation metrics. Below, we provide additional comments for each row in this figure:

(a) As was mentioned in Section 2, α-nDCG lacks a mechanism for directly handling per-intent graded relevance.

(b) The original α-nDCG [5] did not consider $Pr(i|q)$, but it was incorporated later [3].

(c),(d) These are two sides of the same coin. α-nDCG requires an approximation of an ideal ranked list; there is a version of ERR-IA used at TREC that is normalised in a way similar to α-nDCG [3]. Normalisation generally implies the knowledge of all relevant documents: in this sense, the normalised metrics are recall-dependent. D(♯)-nDCG requires a globally ideal list which also implies the knowledge of all relevant documents. While normalised metrics assume that every topic is of equal importance, unnormalised merics such as D-U and U-IA assume that every *user effort* is of equal importance: the user needs to spend more effort for topics that have more relevant information.

(e) In terms of discriminative power, D(♯)-nDCG and α-nDCG outperform ERR-IA [14]; D(♯)-nDCG outperform D-U, U-IA and ERR-IA [11][13].

(f) α-nDCG, ERR-IA and U-IA possess the per-intent diminishing return property; as we have seen, D-U behaves similarly to U-IA, as the original U-measure has the *per-topic* diminishing return property.

(g) To date, D-U and U-IA are the only diversity metrics that take the user's snippet and full text reading behaviour into account.

(h) This row summarises the findings from the present study.

Our future work for diversity evaluation includes the following:

- Exploring different (possibly nonlinear) decay functions $D(pos)$ with U-IA for different types of search intents (e.g. navigational and informational);
- Comparing different information access styles (e.g. direct answers vs. diversified list of URLs) given ambiguous and/or underspecified queries on the U-measure framework;
- Exploring diversity evaluation methods without using explicit set of intents $\{i\}$, for example, based on relevant *information units* [8,13] rather than relevant documents.

---

[13] These two studies [14,11] used a version of ERR-IA, which is an "IA version of normalised ERR," not the official ERR-IA from TREC.

References

1. Burges, C., Shaked, T., Renshaw, E., Lazier, A., Deeds, M., Hamilton, N., Hullender, G.: Learning to rank using gradient descent. In: Proceedings of ICML 2005, pp. 89–96 (2005)
2. Chapelle, O., Ji, S., Liao, C., Velipasaoglu, E., Lai, L., Wu, S.L.: Intent-based diversification of web search results: Metrics and algorithms. Information Retrieval 14(6), 572–592 (2011)
3. Clarke, C.L., Craswell, N., Soboroff, I., Ashkan, A.: A comparative analysis of cascade measures for novelty and diversity. In: Proceedings of ACM WSDM 2011, pp. 75–84 (2011)
4. Clarke, C.L., Craswell, N., Soboroff, I., Voorhees, E.: Overview of the TREC 2011 web track. In: Proceedings of TREC 2011 (2012)
5. Clarke, C.L., Kolla, M., Cormack, G.V., Vechtomova, O., Ashkan, A., Büttcher, S., MacKinnon, I.: Novelty and diversity in information retrieval evaluation. In: Proceedings of ACM SIGIR 2008, pp. 659–666 (2009)
6. Clarke, C.L., Craswell, N., Voorhees, E.: Overview of the TREC 2012 web track. In: Proceedings of TREC 2012 (2013)
7. Järvelin, K., Kekäläinen, J.: Cumulated gain-based evaluation of IR techniques. ACM Transactions on Information Systems 20(4), 422–446 (2002)
8. Kato, M.P., Sakai, T., Yamamoto, T., Iwata, M.: Report from the NTCIR-10 1CLICK-2 Japanese subtask: Baselines, upperbounds and evaluation robustness. In: Proceedings of ACM SIGIR 2013 (2013)
9. Pollock, S.M.: Measures for the comparison of information retrieval systems. American Documentation 19(4), 387–397 (1968)
10. Sakai, T.: Evaluation with informational and navigational intents. In: Proceedings of WWW 2012, pp. 499–508 (2012)
11. Sakai, T., Dou, Z.: Summaries, ranked retrieval and sessions: A unified framework for information access evaluation. In: Proceedings of ACM SIGIR 2013, pp. 473–482 (2013)
12. Sakai, T., Dou, Z., Yamamoto, T., Liu, Y., Zhang, M., Kato, M.P., Song, R., Iwata, M.: Summary of the NTCIR-10 INTENT-2 task: Subtopic mining and search result diversification. In: Proceedings of ACM SIGIR 2013, pp. 761–764 (2013)
13. Sakai, T., Kato, M.P., Song, Y.I.: Click the search button and be happy: Evaluating direct and immediate information access. In: Proceedings of ACM CIKM 2011, pp. 621–630 (2011)
14. Sakai, T., Song, R.: Evaluating diversified search results using per-intent graded relevance. In: Proceedings of ACM SIGIR 2011, pp. 1043–1052 (2011)
15. Sakai, T., Song, R.: Diversified search evaluation: Lessons from the NTCIR-9 INTENT task. Information Retrieval 16(4), 504–529 (2013)
16. Sanderson, M., Paramita, M.L., Clough, P., Kanoulas, E.: Do user preferences and evaluation measures line up? In: Proceedings of ACM SIGIR 2010, pp. 555–562 (2010)
17. Smucker, M.D., Clarke, C.L.A.: Time-based calibration of effectiveness measures. In: Proceedings of ACM SIGIR 2012, pp. 95–104 (2012)

Estimating Intent Types
for Search Result Diversification

Kosetsu Tsukuda[1,*], Tetsuya Sakai[2], Zhicheng Dou[3], and Katsumi Tanaka[1]

[1] Kyoto University, Japan
{tsukuda,tanaka}@dl.kuis.kyoto-u.ac.jp
[2] Waseda University, Japan
tetsuyasakai@acm.org
[3] Microsoft Research Asia, China
zhichdou@microsoft.com

Abstract. Given an ambiguous or underspecified query, search result diversification aims at accommodating different user intents within a single Search Engine Result Page (SERP). While automatic identification of different intents for a given query is a crucial step for result diversification, also important is the estimation of intent types (informational vs. navigational). If it is possible to distinguish between informational and navigational intents, search engines can aim to return one best URL for each navigational intent, while allocating more space to the informational intents within the SERP. In light of the observations, we propose a new framework for search result diversification that is intent importance-aware and type-aware. Our experiments using the NTCIR-9 INTENT Japanese Subtopic Mining and Document Ranking test collections show that: (a) our intent type estimation method for Japanese achieves 64.4% accuracy; and (b) our proposed diversification method achieves 0.6373 in D♯-nDCG and 0.5898 in DIN♯-nDCG over 56 topics, which are statistically significant gains over the top performers of the NTCIR-9 INTENT Japanese Document Ranking runs. Moreover, our relevance oriented model significantly outperforms our diversity oriented model and the original model by Dou *et al.*.

Keywords: Search Result Diversity, Subtopic, Intent Type.

1 Introduction

Given an ambiguous or underspecified query, search result diversification aims at accommodating different user intents within a single Search Engine Result Page (SERP). For example, a query "red cliff" may represent several different search intents, such as "I want to go to the Red Cliff movie website" and "I want to read various reviews of the movie Red Cliff." Given a query, typical diversification algorithms first try to identify these different intents, and then rank documents so that "novel" documents (i.e. those that are dissimilar to the ones ranked above them) are included in the SERP [1,4,5,16,17].

---

* This research was conducted while the first author was an intern at Microsoft Research Asia.

R.E. Banchs et al. (Eds.): AIRS 2013, LNCS 8281, pp. 25–37, 2013.

While automatic identification of different intents for a given query is a crucial step for result diversification, we argue that also important is the estimation of *intent types* (informational vs. navigational [3]). If it is possible to distinguish between informational and navigational intents, search engines can aim to return one best URL for each navigational intent, while allocating more space to the informational intents within the SERP [13]. For example, consider the aforementioned navigational intent "I want to go to the Red Cliff movie website": the user probably wants one particular URL for this intent, so the search engine probably should try to allocate more space to the other more informational intents, for which more relevant documents basically means more informativeness.

In light of the above observations, we propose a new framework for search result diversification that is *intent type-aware*. The framework comprises the following steps:

Subtopic mining and clustering. We first obtain *subtopics* from query suggestions, query logs and search results. Here, a subtopic is an instance of a representation of a particular search intent given a query, which either disambiguates or specifies the original query[1]. As a single intent may be represented by several different subtopic strings, we automatically cluster the mined subtopics to identify intents. For example, subtopics "red cliff review" and "red cliff critique" may form the "red cliff review" cluster.

Intent importance estimation. Next, we estimate the importance of each intent by utilizing search engine results for the original query as well as those for the subtopics.

Intent type estimation. We also classify each intent to either navigational or informational using Support Vector Machine (SVM), so that we can allocate more space to the informational intents compared to the navigational intents in the SERP. Here, our interpretation of "navigational" is slightly broader than the original definition by Broder [3], as we shall discuss in Section 5.

Document reranking. Finally, we generate a diversified search result by leveraging the intents, estimated intent probabilities and types.

Except for the character type feature used in intent type estimation, our framework is basically language-independent.

Our experiments using the NTCIR-9 INTENT Japanese Subtopic Mining and Document Ranking test collections [18] show that: (a) our intent type estimation method for Japanese achieves 64.4% accuracy; and (b) our proposed diversification method achieves 0.6373 in D♯-nDCG [14] and 0.5898 in DIN♯-nDCG [12] over 56 topics, which are statistically significant gains over the top performers of the NTCIR-9 INTENT Japanese Document Ranking runs[2]. Moreover, our relevance oriented model significantly outperforms our diversity oriented model and the original model by Dou *et al.* [5].

---

[1] http://research.microsoft.com/INTENT/

[2] It should be noted, however, that the official top performers at NTCIR-9 worked under time pressure and that a postmortem comparison of this kind is only indicative.

2 Related Work

2.1 Intent Type Estimation

Lee, Liu and Cho [9] proposed a method for identifying the user goals (informational or navigational) based on user-click behavior and anchor-link distribution. Dou, Song and Wen [6] utilized the click entropy to estimate intent types of queries. These studies concern only head queries, for which reliable statistics can be obtained from clickthrough data. In contrast, we aim to estimate the intent type of *any* given subtopic, and therefore their methods are not directly applicable. Li, Wang and Acero [10] constructed click graphs based on clickthrough data and developed query intent classifiers. In order to compensate for the sparsity of a click graph, they also used the contents of documents. Our approach also utilises both clickthrough data and search engine results, as we shall describe in Section 5.

2.2 Search Result Diversification

Several search result diversification algorithms have been proposed in the literature [1,4,5,16,17]. The common approach is to first identify multiple possible subtopics (or intents) for the given query, and to try to cover as many subtopics as possible with the SERP, by minimizing retrieved redundant documents for each subtopic. State-of-the-art diversification algorithms include *IA-select* by Agrawal *et al.* [1], *xQuAD* by Santos, Macdonald and Ounis [16] and the algorithm by Dou *et al.* [5]. Santos, Macdonald and Ounis [17] also proposed a diversification approach which takes intent types (navigational and informational) into account. However, their approach does not aim to return one best URL for a navigational intent.

Our proposed algorithm uses the algorithm by Dou *et al.* as the starting point.

3 Subtopic Mining and Clustering

3.1 Subtopic Mining Resources

Our subtopic mining component mines subtopics of a given query from three different resources, as described below.

Query Suggestions. Query suggestions, which are "suggested queries" (a.k.a. query autocompletions) and "related queries," obtained from WSEs are an easy and effective choice for obtaining subtopics. As Santos, Macdonald and Ounis [16] suggest that suggested queries are more effective for search result diversification, we also decided to use suggested queries rather than related queries. In our experiments, we use the "official" Japanese suggested queries as we shall describe in Section 7.1.

Clickthrough Data. Another popular resource for obtaining subtopics is clickthrough data. In our experiments, we first obtained data that consists of approximately 14.8 million Japanese queries from Bing over a one month period (April 2012). Then, for each original query q, we used the following simple filters for obtaining candidate subtopics: extract all queries that (1) were issued by at least five unique users; and (2) are of the form "q plus an additional keyword." The first condition is designed to avoid subtopics that are too obscure; the second condition was devised based on the observation that most of the subtopics submitted by the NTCIR-9 INTENT Japanese Subtopic Mining participants conformed to this style[3].

Search Result Clusters. While either query suggestions or clickthrough data may work for simple phrase queries, these resources may not help when the original query is more complex. We therefore follow Zeng *et al.* [20] and use search result clusters for mining subtopic candidates. In their method, top N search results for the original query are grouped into K clusters based on key phrases (n-grams) extracted from snippets. As for the parameters, we used $N = 200$ and $K = 10$, following Zeng *et al.* [20].

The above method obtains words such as "reviews" and "dvd": we thus add the original query to the mined words to form subtopics such as "red cliff reviews." Also, the above method requires a search engine for obtaining a ranked list of URLs with snippets for a given query. For this purpose, we used Microsoft's internal web search platform WebStudio[4]. Unless otherwise noted, this is the search platform we use for creating document rankings throughout this paper.

3.2 Subtopic Clustering

Having obtained candidate subtopics for a given query, the next step is to cluster subtopics in order to identify the *intents*.

As Dou *et al.* [5] reported that combining subtopics from multiple sources is useful for discovering user intents, we first pool all subtopics extracted from query suggestions, clickthrough data and search result clusters. Recall that not all of our subtopics are head queries: thus click-based clustering methods [2,7] would not work for this purpose. Instead, we use a simple clustering approach based on search result contents.

First, we extract all terms from the titles and snippets in the top l web pages returned for each subtopic, using Bing API[5]. Then, we create a feature vector for each subtopic, where each element represents the tf-idf value for an extracted term. Here, "tf" is the total frequency of the term within the top l result (titles and snippets only) for the subtopic; "df" is the number of subtopics whose search results contain the term. By assuming that subtopics that share the same intent have similar search results, we can apply a clustering algorithm to the subtopics represented as vectors.

We apply the well-known Ward's method [19] for clustering subtopics. As Ward's method is a hierarchical agglomerative clustering (HAC) method, we stop clustering the subtopics when the minimum distance between two clusters is less than $d_{avg}(q) * h$, where $d_{avg}(q)$ represents the average distance between every pair of subtopics.

In this paper, we empirically set l and h to 200 and 0.3, respectively.

4   Intent Importance Estimation

Having obtained clusters of subtopics, we first estimate the importance of each subtopic. Then, the most important subtopic from each cluster is taken as a

---

[3] In the NTCIR-10 INTENT-2 task, participants were explicitly encouraged to submit subtopics of this form. See http://research.microsoft.com/INTENT/

[4] http://research.microsoft.com/en-us/projects/webstudio/

[5] http://msdn.microsoft.com/en-us/library/dd251056.aspx

representative subtopic, which we regard as a representation of a particular intent. Only the representative subtopics are used for diversifying the search result.

Our method for intent importance estimation is based on the overlap between a SERP for the original query and a SERP for each subtopic, and the rank information for each subtopic. The assumption is that the overlap between the sets of URLs near top ranks is more important than that between those at low ranks. Let $D_k(q)$ and $D_k(c_i)$ denote the set of top k retrieved URLs for a query q and a subtopic c_i, respectively. This method calculates the importance of c_i given q as:

$$P(c_i|q) = \sum_{d \in D_k(c_i) \cap D_k(q)} \frac{1}{rank(q, d)}, \tag{1}$$

where $rank(q, d)$ is the rank of the document d in the ranked list for q. In this paper, we empirically set k to 200.

5 Intent Type Estimation

Since Broder [3] proposed his taxnomy of search intents (informational, navigational and transactional), some researchers have addressed the problem of classifying queries into intent types, especially for the first two intent types [6,8,9]. In contrast to their faithful interpretation of "navigational" (*"The immediate intent is to reach a particular site"* [3]), we adopt a broader interpretation for the purpose of search result diversification, following Sakai and Song [15]. To be more specific, in addition to *homepage finding* intents, we also consider *single answer finding* intents as navigational. For example, if the user submits a query "president obama full name," probably exactly one good web page that answers this question suffices for this intent, and any additional web pages that contain the same information would be redundant. From the viewpoint of optimizing the SERP, these two types of intents can both be regarded as navigational.

We use SVM with RBF (Radial Basis Function) kernel to classify representative subtopics into navigational and informational intent types. Effective classification features were used in previous studies [6,8,9], but these are not suitable for our purpose for the following two reasons. First, as not all of the representative subtopics are head queries, statistics such as click entropy are not so reliable. Second, while these methods may be suitable for separating homepage finding intents from informational intents, they are probably not for separating single answer finding intents from informational intents. For example, different users may click different URLs to find the answer to the aforementioned question: "president obama full name," just like with informational intents.

In order to solve the above two problems, we propose two categories of features for SVM below: click features and character type features. Only the latter category of features was designed for Japanese queries and is language-dependent.

5.1 Click Features

Our first category of features for intent type estimation is based on clickthrough data. Recall that not all of our subtopics are head queries, and that therefore looking for occurrences of the subtopics in the clickthrough data would not work. Instead, we assume that the rightmost term (or *tail term*) of a query is often useful for estimating query intent types. For example, suppose that the user wants to read reviews of the movie Red Cliff: we assume that the user is likely to enter "red cliff review" rather than "review red cliff." Here, the tail term "review" suggests that the intent is informational: the user wants many relevant documents. Similarly, if the user wants to visit the Red Cliff official homepage, we assume that the user will enter "red cliff homepage": again, the tail term suggests that the intent is navigational. (Note that the actual queries and subtopics we currently handle are in Japanese.) Note that while the occurrrences of "red cliff review" may not be frequent in the clickthrough data, those of "review" probably are. Thus we try to avoid the sparsity problem.

More specifically, given a subtopic c, we first extract its tail term t. (If c consists of one term, then t is equal to c.) Then, we extract all queries that contain t as a tail term from the clickthrough data. As each record in our clickthrough data contain a user id, a query, a clicked URL and its position, we can compute the following features for t: (1) Average number of clicked pages per query per user; (2) Average number of unique clicked URLs per query; (3) Average rank of the first clicked web page for each query for each user; (4) Average rank of the last clicked web page for each query for each user; and (5) Average rank of any clicked web pages for each query for each user. The first feature represents how many pages are clicked after a user issues a query; if this is small, the query whose tail term is t may be navigational. The second feature approximates the number of relevant URLs for a query containing t; this should be small at least for homepage finding intents, if not for single answer finding intents. The other three features are to do with clicked ranks: for example, we can hypothesize that many homepage finding intents are easy to satisfy, as search engines often manage to return the home pages near the top ranks. In addition to these five features for t, we also compute the corresponding statistics for the most frequent query that has t as its tail term. Hence we use ten click features in total.

5.2 Character Type Features

Our second category of features for intent type estimation is designed specifically for Japanese, and is based on character types. Unlike English, Chinese and many other languages, the Japanese language uses three distinct character types that are outside the ascii codes: kanji, katakana and hiragana. Kanji, also known as Chinese characters, is an ideogram; Katakana and hiragana are phonograms. Just like our click features, we examine the tail term of a given subtopic as described below.

We observed that when the intent is informational, the tail term tends to be made up from a single character set, e.g. "*joho* (an all-kanji word meaning "information")" and "*osusume* (an all-hiragana word meaning "recommendation")." On the other hand, when the intent is navigational, the tail term tends to be more specific, e.g. "*shin-ruru-kaisetsu* (a kanji-katakana-combined word meaning "explanation of a new rule")." Moreover, we observed that the similar tendency is also seen about a query.

In light of this observation, we count how many times the character types change in the tail term and the original query, and use them as features. Orii, Song and Sakai [11] also used these features for a Japanese question classification task and found it effective.

6   Search Result Diversification

As we mentioned earlier, our proposed diversification framework builds on the one proposed by Dou et al. [5], which has been shown to outperform IA-Select [1] and MMR [4]. The framework was also used at the NTCIR-9 INTENT Japanese Document Ranking subtask, where it outperformed other participating teams. We first describe the algorithm by Dou et al., and then propose a few modifications below.

6.1   Dou et al.

Let C denote the set of representative subtopics obtained as described in Section 4 and let c be a member of C. We first generate a nondiversified ranked list for the original query q and for each representative subtopic c: following Dou et al. [5], we obtain 1,000 URLs for q and 10 URLs for each c. Let $rank(q, d)$ denote the rank of document d in the nondiversified ranked list of q. According to Dou et al., the relevance score of document d with respect to the original query q is given by $rel(q, d) = 1/\sqrt{rank(q, d)}$. Similarly, $rel(c, d)$, the relevance score of d with respect to a representative subtopic c is also computed.

Let R be the pool of candidate documents retrieved by the original query q and its subtopics, and let S_n denote the top n documents selected so far. Dou et al. [5] employs a greedy algorithm which iteratively selects documents and generates a diversified ranking list. The $n + 1$-th document is given by:

$$d_{n+1} = \arg \max_{d \in R \setminus S_n} [\rho \cdot rel(q, d) + (1 - \rho) \cdot \Phi(d, S_n, C)], \qquad (2)$$

where ρ is the parameter that controls the tradeoff between relevance and diversity and we use $\rho = 0.3$, following Dou et al. [5]; $\Phi(d, S_n, C)$ represents a topic richness score of d given the set S_n:

$$\Phi(d, S_n, C) = \sum_{c \in C} w_c \cdot \phi(c, S_n) \cdot rel(c, d), \qquad (3)$$

where w_c is the importance of subtopic c. In this paper, w_c is calculated by the method described in Section 4. $\phi(c, S_n)$ is the discounted importance of subtopic c given S_n:

$$\phi(c, S_n) = \begin{cases} 1 & \text{if } n = 0; \\ \prod_{d_s \in S_n} [1 - rel(c, d_s)] & \text{otherwise.} \end{cases} \qquad (4)$$

More details of this framework can be found in Dou et al. [5].

6.2   Proposed Framework

As the algorithm by Dou et al. does not consider intent types, we modify it in order to make it intent type-aware. We propose two modified methods, but first describe their common features.

In our intent type-aware models, the relevance score with respect to c is given by:

$$rel(c, d) = p_{inf}(c) \cdot rel_{inf}(c, d) + p_{nav}(c) \cdot rel_{nav}(c, d), \qquad (5)$$

where $p_{inf}(c)$ ($p_{nav}(c)$) is the probability that c is informational (navigational), as estimated by our SVM-based intent type estimation component. The key here is that the relevance score with respect to c is defined separately depending on intent types. In particular, we define the relevance score for the case where c is navigational as

$$rel_{nav}(c, d) = \begin{cases} 1 \text{ if } rank(c, d) = 1; \\ 0 \text{ otherwise,} \end{cases} \qquad (6)$$

to reflect the fact that we want exactly one relevant document for such an intent. Whereas, $rel_{inf}(c, d)$, the corresponding score for the informational case, differs according to our two models.

Relevance Oriented Model. In our first model, we let $rel_{inf}(c, d) = 1/\sqrt{rank(c, d)}$ just as in the original model. However, we modify $\phi(c, S_n)$: we still use Equation 4 if c is navigational, but let $\phi(c, S_n) = 1$ regardless of n if c is informational. This is because Equation 4 penalizes "redundant" documents for each c regardless of the intent type. In intent type-aware diversification, multiple relevant documents for an informational intent are not necessarily "redundant."

Diversity Oriented Model. In our second model, we first rerank each ranked list for each informational intent c to obtain a new rank for document d (denoted by $rerank(c, d)$), and let $rel_{inf}(c, d) = 1/\sqrt{rerank(c, d)}$. The reranking is intended to prioritize documents that cover many intents compared to those that are highly relevant to one particular intent. Thus, for each document d in the original ranked list for c, we first count the number of intents that also retrieved d. Using the number of covered intents as the first key (larger the better) and the original rank as the second key (smaller the better), we sort the original ranked list.

7 Experiments

This section reports on a component-by-component evaluation of our proposed framework using the NTCIR-9 Document Ranking test collections.

7.1 Data

Our experiments utilize the NTCIR-9 INTENT Japanese Subtopic Mining and Document Ranking test collections [18]. These test collections were constructed as follows:

1. In the Subtpic Mining subtask, 100 topics were released to participating teams, who returned a ranked list of subtopics for each topic;
2. The INTENT task organisers pooled the submitted subtopics and let assessors manually cluster them to form intents, and to provide a name for each intent;
3. The organisers then estimated intent probabilities based on assessor voting;
4. In the Document Ranking subtask, the same 100 topics were released to participating teams, who returned a diversified list of search results for each topic;
5. The organisers pooled the submitted documents and let assessors conduct per-intent graded relevance assessments, using the set of intents identified through the Subtopic Mining subtask.

Table 1. Intent type classification accuracy for the 481 intents

	true navigational	true informational	total
estimated as navigational	83	117	200
estimated as informational	54	227	281
total	137	344	481

As for the Document Ranking subtask, the document collection used in the Document Ranking task is the ClueWeb09-JA collection, which is the Japanese portion of ClueWeb09[6]. Per-topic graded relevance assessments are provided on a five-point scale: from $L0$ (judged nonrelevant) to $L4$ (highly relevant), based on assessments by two assessors for every topic.

The organisers released *query suggestion data*, which were scraped from Google, Bing and Yahoo, for the NTCIR-9 INTENT topics to its participants, in order to enhance the repeatability of the participants' experiments and to enable fair comparison. In our subtopic mining method, we also utilise this data set.

In addition to the above official data from the INTENT tasks, we obtained the *intent type labels* for the INTENT-1 Japanese topics from Sakai and Song [15], so that we can conduct intent type-aware evaluation. According to the intent type labels, only 56 topics of the 100 Japanese INTENT-1 topics contains at least one navigational and informational intents. For this reason, hereafter we use these 56 topics only. On average, each topic has 2.32 navigational intents (21%) and 8.89 informational intents (79%).

Evaluating search result diversification using an existing diversity test collection, however, is problematic. This is because existing diversity test collections are highly unlikely to be reusable, as their relevance assessments are obtained through shallow pooling [13]. For example, TREC 2010 and NTCIR-9 diversity test collections all used the pool depth of 20. Therefore, if a new system is evaluated using the official relevance assessments, the system is underestimated, as it returns many unjudged documents, some of which might be relevant. In light of this, we conducted some additional relevance assessments of our own to obtain more reliable results, following the relevance assessment procedure used at the INTENT task. We shall discuss this in Section 7.3.

7.2   Results of Intent Types Estimation

In this section, we discuss the accuracy of our intent type estimation component. As was described in Section 5, we use an SVM classifier to determine whether each given intent is likely to be navigational or informational. As SVM requires training data, we conducted the evaluation as follows. The 56 Japanese topics from the INTENT task had 1,902 (539 navigational and 1,363 informational) intents in total, but our subtopic mining and intent importance estimation components managed to identify only 481 of them (137 navigational and 344 informational). Since the remaining 1,421 (402 navigational and 1,019 informational) intents are never used in any part of our evaluation, these unused intents were utilized for training the SVM classifier. Furthermore, in order to avoid including extremely rare intents in the training data, only those that have at least 50 hits in our clickthrough data were used. This gave us 819 intents (231 navigational and 588

---

[6] http://lemurproject.org/clueweb09/

informational). Finally, to balance the amount of training data, we randomly sampled 231 informational intents.

Table 1 shows the classification results for the aforementioned 481 intents. The overall classification accuracy was $(83 + 227)/481 = 0.644$. It can be observed that navigational intents are more difficult to classify than the informational ones. From our classification results, we found that our approach that relies on tail terms has some clear limitations. In particular, it is often difficult to determine whether an intent is navigational or informational from its tail term alone. For example, "beijing image" (user wants pictures of Beijing) may be labelled as informational, as the information need is vague and it is not clear if any one particular image will completely satisfy the user. On the other hand, "dutch flag image" (user wants an image of the Dutch national flag) may be labelled as navigational, as returning one item may suffice. The gold standard data set itself contains some gray area: Sakai and Song [15] report that the kappa agreement of intent type labels between two assessors was .713 for TREC diversity topics. In short, our intent type classification task itself is a difficult one.

7.3 Results of Search Result Diversification

Evaluation Metrics. To finally evaluate the diversified search results, we use five evaluation metrics, namely, I-rec, *D-nDCG*, *D♯-nDCG* [14], *DIN-nDCG* and *DIN♯-nDCG* [13][7]. The first three measures are the official metrics used at the NTCIR-9 INTENT task: D♯-nDCG is a linear combination of I-rec (a pure diversity measure) and D-nDCG (an overall relevance measure). We evaluate the top 10 documents as our objective is to diversify the first search engine result page.

In contrast, the recently proposed DIN-nDCG and DIN♯-nDCG are more suitable for the purpose of intent type-aware diversity evaluation. DIN(♯)-nDCG is a simple modification of D(♯)-nDCG: the only difference is that, whenever multiple relevant documents are retrieved for a navigational intent, DIN(♯)-nDCG treats only the highest ranked relevant document as relevant to that intent. These intent type-aware metrics were used at the NTCIR-10 INTENT-2 Document Ranking subtasks.

More details on the evaluation metrics can be found elsewhere [13].

Evaluation with the Intent Data. We evaluate the overall performance of our diversified search system using the intent sets from the INTENT task. In this experiment, we compared three methods: the framework by Dou *et al.* [5] (**Dou**), the relevance oriented model proposed in Section 6.2 (**REL**), and the diversity oriented model proposed in Section 6.2 (**DIV**). In addition, we obtained top performing runs from the NTCIR-9 INTENT Japanese Document Ranking tasks: MSINT-D-J-3 and MSINT-D-J-2, which were the top two performers in terms of both I-rec@10 and D♯-nDCG@10; and uogTr-D-J-1 and uogTr-D-J-2, which were the top two performers in term of D-nDCG@10. (These official results suggest that the MSINT runs are diversity oriented while the uog runs are relevance oriented [18].)

As we briefly mentioned in Section 7.1, we conducted some additional relevance assessments for this experiment as some of the documents returned by our systems

---

[7] nDCG stands for normalized Discounted Cumulative Gain; D- stands for Diversification; DIN- stands for Diversification with Informational and Navigational intents.

Table 2. Diversification performances with the intents, importance and types obtained by the system (56 topics, each with all intents). The highest score is shown in bold. A two-sided t-test was used for significance testing. Significant differences with MSINT-D-J-2 is indicated by a $*$ ($\alpha = 0.05$) or a $**$ ($\alpha = 0.01$). Similarly, a $\star$, a $\dagger$ and a $\ddagger$ indicate significant differences with MSINT-D-J-3, uogTr-D-J-1 and uogTr-D-J-2, respectively.

	I-rec@10	D-nDCG@10	D♯-nDCG@10	DIN-nDCG@10	DIN♯-nDCG@10
uogTr-D-J-2	0.6843	0.4500	0.5671	0.3481	0.5162
uogTr-D-J-1	0.6832	0.4540	0.5686	0.3505	0.5169
MSINT-D-J-2	0.7626	0.4326	0.5976	0.3574	0.5600
MSINT-D-J-3	0.7649	0.4328	0.5988	0.3574	0.5611
Dou	0.7733 †† ‡‡	0.4557	0.6145 † ‡	0.3762	0.5748 †† ‡‡
DIV	0.7798 †† ‡‡	0.4551	0.6174 † ‡	0.3755	0.5777 †† ‡‡
REL	**0.7935** †† ‡‡	**0.4810** $**$ $\star\star$	**0.6373** $**$ $\star\star$ †† ‡‡	**0.3861** $*$ $\star$	**0.5898** $*$ $\star$ †† ‡‡

Table 3. Comparison of different diversification methods in terms of significant difference. A two-sided t-test was used for significance testing. Significant differences between two methods are indicated by a $*$ ($\alpha = 0.05$) or a $**$ ($\alpha = 0.01$). A method name written with a $*$ or a $**$ is a winner. A symbol "-" represents there is no significant difference between two methods.

	I-rec@10	D-nDCG@10	D♯-nDCG@10	DIN-nDCG@10	DIN♯-nDCG@10
Dou vs. REL	-	REL$*$	REL$*$	-	-
DIV vs. REL	-	REL$**$	REL$*$	-	-

are not covered by the official relevance assessments. The first two authors of this paper used the official relevance assessment tool from the INTENT task [18] to independently conduct relevance assessments for 97 unjudged documents, and the relevance assessments were merged with the official ones. The inter-assessor kappa agreement for this additional document set was 0.581, which is statistically significant at $\alpha = 0.01$.

Table 2 shows the performances of our seven runs (three proposed systems plus four official runs from NTCIR-9). The runs have been sorted by DIN♯-nDCG. It can be observed that **REL** significantly outperforms all top performing runs from the NTCIR-9 INTENT Japanese Document Ranking task in terms of D♯-nDCG and DIN♯-nDCG. Table 3 summarize the significant test results when different diversification methods are compared. Table 3 shows that **REL** is the best diversification method.

8 Conclusion

We proposed a new intent type-aware search result diversification framework, and conducted evaluation using the NTCIR-9 INTENT Japanese Subtopic Mining and Document Ranking test collections. Except for the character set-based feature used for intent type estimation, our proposed framework is basically language-independent.

Our main findings are as follows: (a) Our intent type estimation method for Japanese achieved 64.4% accuracy. Moreover, navigational intents were more difficult to classify than informational ones; and (b) For search result diversification, methods using the relevance oriented model significantly outperformed our diversity oriented model and the original model by Dou *et al.* [5]. Our best method achieved 0.6373 in D♯-nDCG and 0.5898 in DIN♯-nDCG over 56 topics, which are statistically significant gains over the top performers of the NTCIR-9 INTENT Japanese Document Ranking runs.

Our future work includes evaluation with English diversity test collections (i.e. TREC diversity data), and exploration of more sophisticated diversification methods. For example, our current models do not consider the contents of the documents already selected: some document features may be useful for estimating whether a document is likely to be relevant to a navigational intent or to an informational intent, or even both.

Acknowledgements. This work was supported in part by the following projects: Grants-in-Aid for Scientific Research (Nos. 24240013) from MEXT of Japan and JSPS KAKENHI Grant Number 243993.

References

1. Agrawal, R., Gollapudi, S., Halverson, A., Ieong, S.: Diversifying search results. In: Proc. of ACM WSDM 2009, pp. 5–14 (2009)
2. Beeferman, D., Berger, A.: Agglomerative clustering of a search engine query log. In: Proc. of ACM SIGKDD 2000, pp. 407–416 (2000)
3. Broder, A.: A taxonomy of web search. SIGIR Forum 36(2), 3–10 (2002)
4. Carbonell, J., Goldstein, J.: The use of MMR, diversity-based reranking for reordering documents and producing summaries. In: Proc. of ACM SIGIR 1998, pp. 335–336 (1998)
5. Dou, Z., Hu, S., Chen, K., Song, R., Wen, J.-R.: Multi-dimensional search result diversification. In: Proc. of ACM WSDM 2011, pp. 475–484 (2011)
6. Dou, Z., Song, R., Wen, J.-R.: A large-scale evaluation and analysis of personalized search strategies. In: Proc. of WWW 2007, pp. 581–590 (2007)
7. Hosseini, M., Abolhassani, H., Harikandeh, M.S.: Content free clustering for search engine query log. In: Proc. of SMO 2007, pp. 201–206 (2007)
8. Kang, I.-H., Kim, G.: Query type classification for web document retrieval. In: Proc. of ACM SIGIR 2003, pp. 64–71 (2003)
9. Lee, U., Liu, Z., Cho, J.: Automatic identification of user goals in web search. In: Proc. of WWW 2005, pp. 391–400 (2005)
10. Li, X., Wang, Y.-Y., Acero, A.: Learning query intent from regularized click graphs. In: Proc. of ACM SIGIR 2008, pp. 339–346 (2008)
11. Orii, N., Song, Y.-I., Sakai, T.: Microsoft Research Asia at the NTCIR-9 1CLICK Task. In: Proc. of NTCIR-9, pp. 216–222 (2011)
12. Sakai, T.: Evaluation with informational and navigational intents. In: Proc. of WWW 2012, pp. 499–508 (2012)
13. Sakai, T.: Web search evaluation with informational and navigational intents. Journal of Information Processing 21(1), 145–155 (2013)
14. Sakai, T., Song, R.: Evaluating diversified search results using per-intent graded relevance. In: Proc. of ACM SIGIR 2011, pp. 1043–1052 (2011)
15. Sakai, T., Song, Y.-I.: On labelling intent types for evaluating search result diversification. In: Banchs, R.E., Silvestri, F., Liu, T.-Y. (eds.) AIRS 2013. LNCS, vol. 8281, pp. 38–49. Springer, Heidelberg (2013)
16. Santos, R.L., Macdonald, C., Ounis, I.: Exploiting query reformulations for web search result diversification. In: Proc. of WWW 2010, pp. 881–890 (2010)

17. Santos, R.L., Macdonald, C., Ounis, I.: Intent-aware search result diversification. In: Proc. of ACM SIGIR 2011, pp. 595–604 (2011)
18. Song, R., Zhang, M., Sakai, T., Kato, M.P., Liu, Y., Sugimoto, M.: Overview of the NTCIR-9 INTENT Task. In: Proc. of NTCIR-9, pp. 82–105 (2011)
19. Ward, J.H.: Hierarchical grouping to optimize an objective function. Journal of the American Statistical Association 58(301), 236–244 (1963)
20. Zeng, H.-J., He, Q.-C., Chen, Z., Ma, W.-Y., Ma, J.: Learning to cluster web search results. In: Proc. of ACM SIGIR 2004, pp. 210–217 (2004)

On Labelling Intent Types for Evaluating Search Result Diversification

Tetsuya Sakai[1] and Young-In Song[2]

[1] Waseda University, Japan
tetsuyasakai@acm.org
[2] NHN Corporation, Korea
youngin.song@nhn.com

Abstract. Search result diversification is important for accommodating different user needs by means of covering popular and diverse query intents within a single result page. To evaluate diversity, we believe that it is important to consider the distinction between informational and navigational intents, as users would not want redundant information especially for navigational intents. In this study, we conduct intent type-sensitive diversity evaluation based on both *top-down labelling*, which labels each intent as either navigational or informational a priori, and *bottom-up labelling*, which labels each intent based on whether a "navigational relevant" document has actually been identified in the document collection. Our results suggest that reliable type-sensitive diversity evaluation can be conducted using the top-down approach with a clear intent labelling guideline, while ensuring that the desired URLs for navigational intents make their way into relevance assessments.

1 Introduction

Web search engine companies such as Google and Microsoft are addressing the problem of *search result diversification* for *ambiguous* and *underspecified* queries [1,10]. For example, by "office," the user could mean a workplace or a Microsoft product (ambiguity); by "harry potter," the user could mean the Harry Potter books, the films, or Harry Potter the main character, and so on (lack of specificity). Given such a query, search result diversification aims to satisfy different user *intents* with a single, short ranked list of web pages.

Unlike traditional information retrieval where *relevance* is all that matters, the evaluation of search result diversification, where relevance and *diversity* need to be balanced, is still an open problem. To evaluate a diversified search result, test collections are constructed in which each topic (i.e. query) has several possible intents, and each intent has its own set of (graded) relevant documents [5,7,8,17]. When utilising such data, we believe that it is important to take into account whether each intent can be regarded as *navigational* or *informational* [2]: while a navigational intent requires (say) one particular website, an informational intent requires as much relevant information as possible, and therefore the distinction should be useful for search engines to determine how much space within the search

R.E. Banchs et al. (Eds.): AIRS 2013, LNCS 8281, pp. 38–49, 2013.
© Springer-Verlag Berlin Heidelberg 2013

result page should be allocated to each intent. We call this approach (intent-)*type-sensitive* evaluation. For example, if one of the possible intents for "harry potter" is "I want to visit `pottermore.com`," a search engine that allocates five URLs for this navigational intent within its top ten results should be considered far from optimal, since exactly one URL is required to satisfy the intent. The search engine should allocate more space to other intents, especially informational ones.

The TREC Web track diversity test collections [5,7,8] appear to be useful for conducting type-sensitive diversity evaluation, as their intents (or "subtopics") already have informational and navigational labels. However, having carefully examined the 628 intents for topics 1-150 from the three TREC rounds, we found that the labels provided there are not always consistent. Table 1 shows some examples of possible inconsistencies within each round of TREC. For example, in the TREC 2009 topic file, while 28-4 (Topic 28 Intent 4) "I'm looking for InuYasha fan forums and websites" is labelled as navigational, 38-2 "Take me to the homepage of the Humane Society." is labelled as informational. Thus, for conducting reliable type-sensitive evaluation, we probably need a set of clear criteria for labelling the intent types appropriately and consistently.

In this study, we address the following main Research Questions:

RQ1 How can we systematically label informational and navigational intents for type-sensitive diversity evaluation?

RQ2 How do different methods for labelling the intent types affect the evaluation outcome?

More specifically, we explore both *top-down labelling*, which labels each intent as either navigational or informational by just looking at the intents, and *bottom-up labelling*, which labels each intent based on whether a "nav"-relevant document [8] has actually been found in the document collection during relevance assessment[1]. Here, a document is nav-relevant if the TREC assessor judged that the search intent is to obtain this exact document (and probably nothing else). Thus, top-down labelling is designed to reflect the user's expectations, while bottom-up labelling is designed to investigate what the search engines can do *given* a web corpus. Our results suggest that reliable type-sensitive diversity evaluation can be conducted using the top-down approach with a clear intent labelling guideline, while ensuring that the desired URLs for navigational intents make their way into relevance assessments.

2   Related Work

There are two main venues that evaluate search result diversification systems: the TREC web track diversity task [5,7,8] and the NTCIR INTENT Document Ranking subtask [14,17]. The properties of the data used in this study are summarised

---

[1] TREC has never utilised their intent type labels for evaluating systems; the NTCIR-10 INTENT-2 task has recently adopted the intent type labelling guidelines proposed in this paper to conduct type-sensitive diversity evaluation [14].

Table 1. Examples of possible inconsistencies in the TREC diversity intent types

TREC round	Topic-Intent	Type of info sought	intent (subtopic)	TREC intent type
2009	38-2	webpage	Take me to the homepage of the Humane Society.	inf
2009	28-4	webpage	I'm looking for InuYasha fan forums and websites.	nav
2010	58-4	image	Find penguin photos.	inf
2010	58-5	image	Find pictures of the penguins from the animated movie, "Madagascar".	nav
2010	54-6	factoid	What is the mailing address for the President of the United States?	inf
2010	59-4	factoid	Where can I buy materials for building a fence?	nav
2010	55-1	general	Find information about iron as an essential nutrient.	inf
2010	58-3	general	Find information about penguins.	nav
2011	135-3	map	map of the Nile River basin	inf
2011	126-2	map	Find a map of the area around the US Capitol, including nearby sites to visit.	nav
2011	115-5	factoid	Who operates (manages) PNL?	inf
2011	107-2	factoid	What was the 2008 budget for Cass County, MO?	nav

Table 2. TREC/NTCIR Test collections and runs used in this study

	TR2009Dg	TR2010D	TR2011Dg	INTENT1J
Language	English			Japanese
Documents	ClueWeb09 (one billion)			ClueWeb09-JA (67.3 million)
Intent probabilities	Not Available			Available, estimated from 10 assessors' votes
#Intents/topic	4.0	4.2	3.3	10.2
#Topics	50	48	50	100
Pool depth	20	20	25	20
#runs	25 (Category A)	22 (Category A)	17 (Category A)	15
Per-intent relevance	graded ($L0$-$L2$)	binary ($L0, L1$)	graded ($L0$-$L3$) where $L3$ means navigational	graded ($L0$-$L4$), sum of two assessors' grades
#Unique rel. /topic	98.8	136.5	100.6	88.96

in Table 2: *TR2009Dg* is the data from TREC 2009, with graded relevance assessments later added by Sakai and Song [15]; *TR2010D* is the data from TREC 2010 with binary relevance assessments; *TR2011Dg* is the data from TREC 2011 with official graded relevance assessments, which contained nav-relevant documents [8]. *INTENT1J* is the NTCIR-9 INTENT Japanese Document Ranking data (discussed in Appendix A). Note that we denote per-intent relevance levels as $L0, \ldots, L4$, where $L0$ means "judged nonrelevant." More details on the data sets can be found in the aforementioned TREC and NTCIR overview papers.

Most of the existing diversity evaluation metrics (e.g. α-$nDCG$ [6], *ERR-IA* [3] and $D\sharp$-$nDCG$ [15]) are *type-agnostic*: they do not consider the intent type labels. In light of this, Sakai [13] proposed diversity metrics called *DIN-nDCG* and *P+Q*, both of which are *type-sensitive* in that they utilise the intent type labels. DIN-nDCG is a simple generalisation of *D-nDCG* [15]: the difference is that the former ignores redundant relevant documents for each navigational intent; P+Q is a generalisation of the *intent-aware* approach to diversity evaluation [1]: it uses a graded-relevance metric called Q for each informational intent and another called P^+ for each navigational intent [13]. Moreover, $DIN\sharp$-$nDCG$ and $P+Q\sharp$ can be obtained by simply averaging the raw metrics with *intent recall* (I-rec), i.e. the proportion of known intents covered by the system's ranked list. We use these type-sensitive metrics (along with the type-unaware D($\sharp$)-nDCG) to address the aforementioned two research questions[2]. Recently, Chen *et al.* [4] have proposed a family of type-sensitive metrics that generalises DIN-nDCG, but their metrics require a greedy approximation of the ideal list just like α-nDCG [6]. Throughout our experiments, we use the document cutoff of 10 as we are interested in diversifying the first search engine result page.

The original web search query taxonomy of Broder [2] had a third category, namely *transactional*, where the "intent is to perform some web-mediated activity." Rose and Levinson [11] and Jansen, Booth and Spink [9] have independently refined the taxonomy. However, the focus of the present study is to evaluate search result diversification by considering whether each intent ideally requires one URL slot or more, rather than to provide a comprehensive taxonomy to cover all web search queries.

3   Top-Down Labelling

We first explore the top-down labelling approach for type-sensitive diversity evaluation, i.e., labelling each intent as either navigational or informational by just looking at it and referring to a guideline. Recall that this approach is designed to reflect the user's expectations for each intent.

As the official intent type labels from TREC (which we call **Official**) are not altogether reliable (See Table 1), we decided to set up a guideline for labelling each intent, and then re-labelled the intent types from scratch for all 150 TREC 2009-2011 topics, as described below. Since what matters is whether each intent ideally requires exactly one URL slot or more, we adopted a broader definition of a navigational intent compared to Broder's [2]: a navigational intent is a *one item search intent for a particular website, entity or object, or for a unique answer that satisfies a specific question.* An example of entity would be a particular person name; an example of object would be a particular pdf file. Based on this definition, the first author of this paper devised the following guideline to examine its effect on diversity evaluation:

Test 1: Expected Answer Uniqueness. Is the intent specific enough so that the expected relevant item (i.e. website, entity, object or answer) can be considered unique? Even if multiple relevant items exist, is it likely that there exists at least one searchable item that will completely satisfy the user and call for no additional information? If the answer is yes to one of these questions, the intent is navigational. Otherwise go to Test 2.

Test 2: Expected Answer Cohesiveness. If the desired item is not unique, are these items expected to lie within a single website (which could typically be a group of mutually linked web pages under the same domain name), so that this single website will completely satisfy the user and call for no additional information? If the answer is yes, the intent is navigational. Otherwise the intent is informational.

---

[2] Sakai and Song [15,16] have discussed some advantages of the D♯ framework over other type-agnostic divesity metrics, using *discriminative power* [12] and the *concordance test* [13] along with other analyses. The appendix of the present study reports on similar experiments with DIN(♯)-nDCG, P+Q(♯) and D(♯)-nDCG.

Table 3. Cohen's kappa for the TREC intent type labels. Two-sided z-test results are indicated by $*$ ($\alpha = .05$) and $**$ ($\alpha = .01$): significance means that the two label sets agree with each other.

		(a) Official vs. TD1			(b) Official vs. TD2			(c) Official vs. TD1+2			(d) TD1 vs. TD2		
		inf	nav	kappa	inf	nav	kappa	inf	nav	kappa	inf	nav	kappa
TR2009Dg	inf	131	46	.577**	130	47	.570**	144	33	.672**	120	14	.776**
	nav	3	63		3	63		3	63		13	96	
TR2010D	inf	103	39	.268**	123	19	.408**	125	17	.413**	134	3	.706**
	nav	34	41		36	39		37	38		25	55	
TR2011Dg	inf	65	65	.157*	88	42	.282**	92	38	.316**	71	4	.615**
	nav	10	28		12	26		12	26		29	64	
ALL	inf	299	150	.344**	341	108	.433**	361	88	.484**	325	21	.713**
	nav	47	132		51	128		52	127		67	215	

Following the above guideline, the first author labelled all ($243 + 217 + 168 =$) 628 intents of the 150 topics: we refer to this set of labels as **TD1** (where "TD" stands for "top-down"). Then, the second author of this paper read the same guideline and independently labelled the intents: we refer to this set of labels as **TD2**. Furthermore, to merge the two sets of labels and thereby reduce subjectivity, we took the conservative approach of taking the *intersection* of their "navigational" labels: we refer to this as **TD1+2**. We preferred this conservative approach because, once an intent has been labelled as navigational, the type-sensitive metrics will completely ignore "redundant" relevant documents for this intent. Note that we do not claim that our intent type labelling guideline is the best possible there could be: we merely want to examine the effect of using a guideline on the outcome of diversity evaluation.

We compared **TD1**, **TD2** and **TD1+2** with **Official**. For example, while 97-2 "Find maps of South Africa" was labelled as navigational in **Offcial** and informational in **TD1+2**, 35-6 "Find a street-level map of Hoboken, NJ" was labelled as informational in **Offcial** and navigational in **TD1+2**. The two labellers judged that the former intent is too vague, and that a single map of South Africa may not satisfy the intent entirely; in contrast, they judged that the latter intent is quite specific and therefore that a single street-level map will serve the purpose. While there will always be grey areas, the guideline helps boost the inter-labeller agreement, as discussed below.

Table 3 shows Cohen's kappa values for comparing **Official**, **TD1**, **TD2** and **TD1+2**. For example, Row "ALL" Column (c) shows that while **Offcial** has $52 + 127 = 179$ navigational labels out of 628 (29%), **TD1+2** has $88 + 127 = 215$ (34%), and the kappa between the two label sets is .484. A two-sided z-test suggests that these two sets actually agree with each other, even though **Official** does not rely on our guidelines. Thus, even though **Official** lacks consistency, the general understanding of what a navigational intent is appears to be similar to ours. However, the kappa values in Column (c) suggest that while the **Official** labels were quite consistent with our guidelines in 2009, they gradually deviated from them. According to z-tests for the *differences* between the kappa values in Column (c), the difference between TREC 2009 and 2010 is significant at $\alpha = 0.05$; that between 2009 and 2011 is significant at $\alpha = 0.01$; that between

Table 4. Informational/navigational intents lost

	TR2009Dg	TR2010D	TR2011Dg
Official	9/35	10/7	3/1
TD1+2	7/37	10/7	2/2

Table 5. τ and symmetric τ_{ap} for the TREC run rankings: **Official** vs. **TD1+2** using the same type-sensitive metric. Only topics that contain at least one navigational intent in either **Official** or **TD1+2** are used. Values higher than .9 are shown in bold.

	TR2009Dg	TR2010D	TR2011Dg
DIN-nDCG	**.947**/**.917**	.861/.648	**.926**/**.918**
P+Q	.833/.789	.835/.795	.868/.778
DIN♯-nDCG	**.967**/**.948**	**.974**/**.974**	**.956**/.842
P+Q♯	**.987**/**.980**	**.965**/**.976**	**.956**/**.907**

2010 and 2011 is not significant. More importantly, by comparing across the columns in Table 3, it is clear that the agreement between **TD1** and **TD2** is higher than the agreements with **Official**. In Row "ALL," the *difference* in kappa between Columns (a) and (d), that between (b) and (d), and that between (c) and (d) are all statistically significant at $\alpha = 0.01$.

Among the 628 intents we labelled, 44, 17 and 4 intents from each TREC round lacked relevant documents. We therefore use only $(199 + 200 + 164 =)$ 563 intents henceforth for evaluating the runs. Table 4 breaks down the lost intents by intent type: for example, according to **Official**, as many as 35 of the 44 lost intents are navigational. In fact, all of the 35 intents are *named page finding* intents such as 34-5 "Go to Nokia's home page." Unfortunatley, these named pages were not captured through *pooling* [5]. This analysis suggests that, when constructing a type-sensitive diversity test collection using a top-down approach, it is important to ensure that the named pages for the navigational intents are actually included in the relevance data.

Table 5 compares the TREC diversity run rankings based on **Official** and that based on **TD1+2** for each type-sensitive metric, in terms of Kendall's τ and *symmetric* τ_{ap}, which is more sensitive to the changes near the top than τ [18]. Here, only topics that contain at least one navigational intent according to either **Official** or **TD1+2** are used for ranking the runs: 30, 40 and 42 topics are used, respectively. It can be observed that, while the effect of revising the intent type labels is small for DIN♯-nDCG and P+Q♯ (as they reflect the property of the type-agnostic I-rec), it is not negligible for the raw DIN-nDCG and P+Q. For example, comparing the actual ranked run lists for TR2010D with DIN-nDCG (where it is shown in the table that $\tau = .861$) reveals that runs ranked at 1 and 4 according to **Official** trade places according to **TD1+2**, amongst other rank changes. The results demonstrate that how the intents are labelled in a top-down manner affects type-sensitive diversity evaluation considerably, and suggests that a labelling guideline may be useful.

Table 6. Cohen's kappa for the TR2011Dg intent type labels: **BU** vs. **TD/Official**. According to the z-test, we cannot conclude that any of the label set pairs agree with each other.

	inf	nav	kappa	inf	nav	kappa	inf	nav	kappa	inf	nav	kappa
	(a) **BU vs. TD1**			(b) **BU vs. TD2**			(c) **BU vs. TD1+2**			(d) **BU vs. Official**		
inf	62	70	.069	79	53	.011	80	52	−.043	103	29	.030
nav	13	23		21	15		24	12		27	9	

Table 7. τ and symmetric τ_{ap} for the TREC2011Dg runs: type-sensitive metrics using **TD1+2** vs. those using **BU**. Only topics that have at least one navigational intent in either **TD1+2** or **BU** are used.

DIN-nDCG	.941/.940	DIN♯-nDCG	.882/.749
P+Q	.853/.660	P+Q♯	.897/.858

4   Bottom-Up Labelling

Next, we explore the bottom-up labelling approach, i.e., labelling each intent as navigational only if at least one nav-relevant document exists for that intent. Here, we use the TR2011Dg data set only, as the other data sets lack nav-relevant judgments. Recall that this approach is designed to investigate what the search engines can do *given* a web corpus. We refer to the set of labels derived using the bottom-up approach as **BU**.

Table 6 compares **BU** with the aforementioned **TD** and **Official** labels in terms of Cohen's kappa. It is clear that **BU** is *completely* different from the **TD** labels. Note that, of the 168 intents (including the four lost ones), only 12 of them were unanimously labelled as navigational in **TD1+2** and **BU**. Also, **BU** has only 36 navigational labels, while **TD1+2** has 64 (and **Official** has 38). Thus, even though we have tried to identify navigational intents from the user's viewpoint to construct **TD1+2**, the test collection lacks the nav-relevant document for many of them. For example, while 150-3 "home page of the Tennesee highway Patrol" is navigational according to both **Official** and **TD1+2**, it is labelled as informational in **BU** due to lack of a nav-relevant document. Note that TR2011Dg was created via depth-25 pooling [8] (See Table 2): for both TD and BU approaches, a better mechanism for capturing nav-relevant documents is probably necessary. A simple solution would be to include manual runs in the pools that aim for high recall for the navigational intents.

On the other hand, we had ten cases labelled as navigational in **BU** even though they were labelled as informational in both **Official** and **TD1+2**. An example is 130-1 "Find information about the planet Uranus." Thus, a TREC assessor found a nav-relevant document for this intent, but it is unlikely that a user looking for general information on Uranus will be satisfied by reading just one document, unless it covers all possible relevant pieces of information. This analysis suggests that, for BU-based diversity evaluation, we need a better guideline that clearly defines what a nav-relevant document is.

Table 7 compares the run ranking based on **TD1+2** and that based on **BU** for each type-sensitive metric, in terms of τ and τ_{ap}. Only 40 topics that have at least one navigational intent according to either **TD1+2** or **BU** are used for ranking the runs. **TD1+2** and **BU** produce somewhat different rankings: for example, we found that the top two runs according to P+Q with **BU** are ranked at 2 and 4 by the same metric with **TD1+2** ($\tau = .853$).

5 Conclusions

Reliable evaluation environments are an absolute necessity for advancing the state of the art. Through experiments with existing diversity test collections, we addressed two research questions on type-sensitive diversification.

RQ1: How can we systematically label informational and navigational intents for type-sensitive diversity evaluation? RQ2: How do different methods for labelling the intent types affect the evaluation outcome?

We first explored top-down intent type labelling by devising a guideline. The inter-labeller agreement with our new labels was statistically significantly higher than that between the official TREC labels and our new labels, and our new labels produced type-sensitive evaluation results that are somewhat different from those based on the official labels. These results suggest that our guideline is useful. On the other hand, our analysis with the top-down labels showed that some of the desired URLs for the navigational intents are missing in the existing diversity test collections.

We have also explored the possibility of bottom-up labelling which relies on nav-relevant document labels. This approach looks at evaluation from the system's side, to show the best search engines can do given a set of (incomplete) relevance assessments. However, our analysis showed that the bottom-up labels are completely different from the top-down ones. This is due to two reasons. First, as was mentioned above, the TREC 2011 diversity test collection lacks nav-relevant documents for many intents that are clearly navigational from the user's point of view, due to the incompleteness of relevance assessments. Second, we found that some of the nav-relevant document labels in the test collection are not appropriate. The bottom-up approach may benefit from a clear guideline for *document relevance assessments*.

We observed some differences in the evaluation outcomes based on top-down and bottom-up labels. A practical recommendation for type-sensitive diversity evaluation would be to take the top-down approach with a clear intent labelling guideline *and* to ensure that the desired URLs for navigational intents make their way into relevance assessments. While we do not deny the possibility of bottom-up labelling with a clear document labelling guideline and a recall-enhancing mechanism to capture nav-relevant documents, this may still result in intent labels that are counterintuitive from the user's viewpoint, and therefore counterintuitive space allocation for different intents in the search result page. If the *user* feels that one intent is navigational while another is informational, perhaps this view deserves to be respected in the evaluation. For example, given the query "harry potter," a diversified search engine probably should not use up many URL slots for the "`pottermore.com`" intent.

References

1. Agrawal, R., Sreenivas, G., Halverson, A., Leong, S.: Diversifying search results. In: Proceedings of ACM WSDM 2009, pp. 5–14 (2009)
2. Broder, A.: A taxonomy of web search. SIGIR Forum 36(2) (2002)
3. Chapelle, O., Ji, S., Liao, C., Velipasaoglu, E., Lai, L., Wu, S.-L.: Intent-based diversification of web search results: Metrics and algorithms. Information Retrieval 14(6), 572–592 (2011)
4. Chen, F., Liu, Y., Zhang, M., Ma, S., Chen, L.: A subtopic taxonomy-aware framework for diversity evaluation. In: Proceedings of EVIA 2013, pp. 9–16 (2013)
5. Clarke, C.L., Craswell, N., Soboroff, I.: Overview of the TREC 2009 web track. In: Proceedings of TREC 2009 (2010)
6. Clarke, C.L., Craswell, N., Soboroff, I., Ashkan, A.: A comparative analysis of cascade measures for novelty and diversity. In: Proceedings of ACM WSDM 2011, pp. 75–84 (2011)
7. Clarke, C.L., Craswell, N., Soboroff, I., Cormack, G.V.: Overview of the TREC 2010 web track. In: Proceedings of TREC 2010 (2011)
8. Clarke, C.L., Craswell, N., Soboroff, I., Voorhees, E.: Overview of the TREC 2011 web track. In: Proceedings of TREC 2011 (2012)
9. Jansen, B.J., Booth, D.L., Spink, A.: Determining the informational, navigational, and transactional intent of web queries. Information Processing and Management 44, 1251–1266 (2008)
10. Rafiei, D., Bharat, K., Shukla, A.: Diversifying web search results. In: Proceedings of WWW 2010, pp. 781–790 (2010)
11. Rose, D.E., Levinson, D.: Understanding user goals in web search. In: Proceedings of WWW 2004, pp. 13–19 (2004)
12. Sakai, T.: Evaluating evaluation metrics based on the bootstrap. In: Proceedings of ACM SIGIR 2006, pp. 525–532 (2006)
13. Sakai, T.: Evaluation with informational and navigational intents. In: Proceedings of WWW 2012, pp. 499–508 (2012)
14. Sakai, T., Dou, Z., Yamamoto, T., Liu, Y., Zhang, M., Song, R., Kato, M.P., Iwata, M.: Overview of the NTCIR-10 INTENT-2 task. In: Proceedings of NTCIR-10, pp. 94–123. Springer (2013)
15. Sakai, T., Song, R.: Evaluating diversified search results using per-intent graded relevance. In: Proceedings of ACM SIGIR 2011, pp. 1043–1052 (2011)
16. Sakai, T., Song, R.: Diversified search evaluation: Lessons from the NTCIR-9 INTENT task. Information Retrieval 16(4), 504–529 (2013)
17. Song, R., Zhang, M., Sakai, T., Kato, M.P., Liu, Y., Sugimoto, M., Wang, Q., Orii, N.: Overview of the NTCIR-9 INTENT task. In: Proceedings of NTCIR-9, pp. 82–105 (2011)
18. Yilmaz, E., Aslam, J., Robertson, S.: A new rank correlation coefficient for information retrieval. In: Proceedings of ACM SIGIR 2008, pp. 587–594 (2008)

Appendix A: The Third Top-down Labelling Criterion

To investigate the feasibility of type-sensitive evaluation with the NTCIR INTENT test collections, we also applied the guideline described in Section 3 to the 100 Japanese topics of INTENT1J from NTCIR, which originally do not have the intent type labels. The first author of this paper labelled the 1,091 intents. We could not hire a second Japanese-speaking assessor for this data set, but our aim was to see if trends that are similar to TREC can be observed rather than to construct a highly reliable data set. Unlike the TREC case, the intents from the INTENT1J data are generally not natural languages sentences. Rather, they are *subtopic strings* [17,14] such as "Harry Potter and the Deathly Hallows author" (in English translation). Hence we used an additional test for selecting navigational intents:

Test 3: Navigational Need Reconstructability. From the intent string, is it possible to uniquely reconstruct a navigational intent that passes either Test 1 or Test 2? If the answer is yes, the intent is navigational. Otherwise, it is informational.

For example, the aforementioned subtopic string was reconstructed into "Who wrote Harry Potter and the Deathly Hallows?" (in English translation) and was labelled as navigational. A total of 130 intents (12%) were labelled as navigational in this way; there are 75 intents that lack known relevant documents, so only 1,016 intents are used in our evaluation experiments. Only eight of the 75 lost intents were navigational according to the first author's labels.

Appendix B compares several diversity evaluation metrics using the top-down labelled version of INTENT1J as well as the TREC data.

Appendix B: Choice of Evaluation Metrics

This appendix compares the diversity metrics discussed in this paper in terms of *discriminative power* (ability to detect statistically significant differences given a topic set size and a confidence level) [12] and the *concordance test* (how often the metric in question agrees with simple and intuitive "gold-standard" metrics) [13]. The algorithms for these experiments follow those of Sakai [13]; the gold-standard metrics used for the concordance tests are I-rec, *EfP* (effective precision, i.e. precision computed by ignoring redundant relevant documents for navigational intents) and the combination of both.

The discriminative power results with top-down labelling for the TREC and NTCIR data (Figures 1 and 2) generalise Sakai's finding with TR2009Dg [13]: DIN♯-nDCG and P+Q♯ are as discriminative as D♯-nDCG, but the raw P+Q, a generalised intent-aware metric, is substantially less discriminative[3].

Tables 8-10 summarise the concordance test results for the TREC data (top-down labelling), the NTCIR data (top-down labelling), and the TR2011Dg data (bottom-up labelling). For example, Table 8(c) Column "TR2009Dg" presents the following information: (1) There are 173 pairs of ranked lists for which D-nDCG and DIN-nDCG disagree with each other; DIN-nDCG is consistent with both I-rec and EfP for 73% of these disagreements, while D-nDCG is consistent with both I-rec and EfP for only 61% of them. (These percentages include cases where the ranked list pair is tied according to either the metric in question or

---

[3] The TREC2011 results are anomalous in that the discriminative power of I-rec is very low, and therefore that the combination of I-rec with other metrics is not successful. This is probably because it was relatively easy for many systems to achieve a high I-rec value, since the average number of intents for this data set is only 3.3 (Table 2).

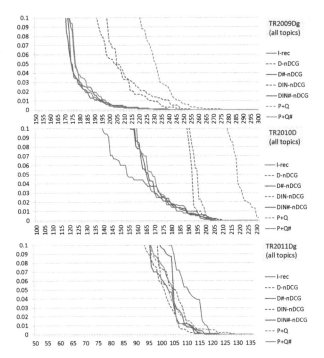

Fig. 1. ASL curves for the TREC data sets. Type-sensitive metrics use the **TD1+2** labels. The y axis represents the ASL (p-value) and the x axis represents run pairs sorted by the ASL.

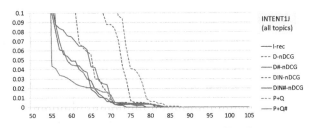

Fig. 2. ASL curves for INTENT1J

the gold standard [13].) This difference is statistically significant according to the sign test ($\alpha = 0.05$), and in this sense, DIN-nDCG is more "intuitive" than D-nDCG. (2) Similary, D-nDCG outperforms P+Q ($\alpha = 0.01$). (3) Similarly, DIN-nDCG outperforms P+Q ($\alpha = 0.01$). The overall result is that DIN-nDCG outperforms D-nDCG, which in turn outperforms P+Q.

Based on the results of our extensive discriminative power and concordance test experiments, we recommend the use of DIN($\sharp$)-nDCG for type-sensitive diversity evaluation. Note that DIN($\sharp$)-nDCG reduces to D($\sharp$)-nDCG when intent type labels are not available (i.e. when all intents are treated as informational).

Table 8. Concordance test results for the TREC data. Type-sensitive metrics use the **TD1+2** labels. Only topics that have at least one navigational intent in **TD1+2** are used. Significant differences according to a two-sided sign test is indicated by † ($\alpha = 0.05$) and ‡ ($\alpha = 0.01$).

	TR2009Dg		TR2010D		TR2011Dg	
	DIN-nDCG	P+Q	DIN-nDCG	P+Q	DIN-nDCG	P+Q
(a) gold standard: I-rec ("diversity")						
D-nDCG	80%/**85%** (173)	78%/78% (542)	55%/**83%**‡ (436)	53%/**76%**‡ (794)	74%/**88%**‡ (302)	75%/**78%** (557)
DIN-nDCG	-	**77%**/75% (511)	-	60%/**70%**‡ (660)	-	**78%**/72% (449)
(b) gold standard: Effective Precision ("relevance")						
D-nDCG	65%/**83%**‡ (173)	**79%**/63%‡ (542)	34%/**90%**‡ (436)	**73%**/50%‡ (794)	64%/64% (302)	**73%**/47% ‡ (557)
DIN-nDCG	-	**79%**/56%‡ (511)	-	**90%**/26%‡ (660)	-	**77%**/44% ‡ (449)
(c) gold standard: I-rec AND Effective Precision						
D-nDCG	61%/**73%**† (173)	**65%**/52%‡ (542)	29%/**77%**‡ (436)	**46%**/41% (794)	53%/**55%** (302)	**58%**/37%‡ (557)
DIN-nDCG	-	**63%**/45%‡ (511)	-	**54%**/17%‡ (660)	-	**60%**/32%‡ (449)

Table 9. Concordance test results for INTENT1J. Only topics that have at least one navigational intent are used.

	DIN-nDCG	P+Q
(a) gold standard: I-rec ("diversity")		
D-nDCG	59%/**79%**‡ (605)	65%/**68%** (1416)
DIN-nDCG	-	**69%**/64%† (1481)
(b) gold standard: Effective Precision ("relevance")		
D-nDCG	50%/**84%**‡ (605)	**80%**/78% (1416)
DIN-nDCG	-	**87%**/70%‡ (1481)
(c) gold standard: I-rec AND Effective Precision		
D-nDCG	32%/**69%**‡ (605)	**54%**/53% (1416)
DIN-nDCG	-	**61%**/45%‡ (1481)

Table 10. Concordance test results for TREC2011Dg, using the **BU** labels for the type-sensitive metrics. Only topics that have at least one navigational intent in **BU** are used.

	DIN-nDCG	P+Q
(a) gold standard: I-rec ("diversity")		
D-nDCG	78%/**88%**‡ (241)	**83%**/76% (262)
DIN-nDCG	-	**94%**/69%‡ (173)
(b) gold standard: Effective Precision ("relevance")		
D-nDCG	**73%**/67% (241)	**80%**/57%‡ (262)
DIN-nDCG	-	**81%**/54%‡ (173)
(c) gold standard: I-rec AND Effective Precision		
D-nDCG	62%/**64%** (241)	**72%**/50%‡ (262)
DIN-nDCG	-	**76%**/40%‡ (173)

Snippet Generation by Identifying Attribute Associated Information

Yoko Tanaka, Yoshihiko Suhara, Nobuaki Hiroshima, Hiroyuki Toda,
and Seiji Susaki

NTT Service Evolution Laboratories,
Yokosuka, Japan
{tanaka.yoko,suhara.yoshihiko,hiroshima.nobuaki,
toda.hiroyuki,suzaki.seiji}@lab.ntt.co.jp

Abstract. In this paper, we focus on the task of using a web search engine to find the entity that best fits the user's demand by comparing multiple entities of the same type. We call this task attribute-oriented entity search. As the primary task, we tackle the snippet generation problem. When users access a web search engine to locate entities, they input two kinds of queries; namely, type query and attribute query. Type query represents entity type. Attribute query represents specific entity attributes. We propose a method that generates snippets containing information associated with both type and attribute queries. Specifically, our model is an extension of the conventional query-biased summarization method, which consists of two probabilistic models. Our method introduces a novel probabilistic model, the ambiguous relevance model, to reflect the information about input attribute queries, which are written in a variety of words, in the generated snippet. The results of experiments show that our method can generate better snippets in terms of information about attribute queries than conventional methods while matching the performance of conventional methods with respect to information about type queries.

1 Introduction

It has become common for people to access search engines to gather information about entities such as restaurants to find the entity that fits the user's need. For example, the user chooses his/her destination from entities whose types are "restaurant near travel destination" by comparing the information of price from documents recovered by the search engine. In another example, before buying a cleaner, the user selects the entity, whose types are cleaner, that offers the best performance. In this way, it has become popular to use web search results to select an entity from multiple entities of the same type according one or more attributes of the entities. We call this search task *attribute-oriented entity search*.

When a user searches for a specific entity type, the user inputs a *type query* and an *attribute query* into a web search engine [13]. Type query represents the type of entities (e.g., "restaurants" or "hotels") or geographic-oriented information (e.g., "Kyoto"). Attribute query represents the demand for specific attribute(s) of each entity to allow selection, for example "price" or "atmosphere".

R.E. Banchs et al. (Eds.): AIRS 2013, LNCS 8281, pp. 50–61, 2013.

When users conduct a search, they first indicate the target by type query, then find the best entity by comparing with the information returned against the attribute query. For example, if the user wants a restaurant with nice atmosphere in Kyoto, he/she inputs "Kyoto restaurant" as the type query and "atmosphere" as the attribute query.

Entity search engines are not effective for this task because they target only structured information. Unfortunately, most documents that contain the information about a wide range of entity types and attributes are unstructured. Document authors use various words to express the information about the attributes of entities. For example, "romantic", "quiet and calm" or "noisy" are terms used to express the atmosphere of restaurants. This makes it difficult to extract and organize attribute information from the web.

The results of an attribute query should be shown in free format. This is because information that is written in free format such as "atmosphere", "characters of staff" may be lost by structuring. For example, though one restaurant is described as having "Beautiful night view" and the other as "We can see a famous spot from the windows" in web documents, both restaurants are stuck with the same tag of "Scenic View" after being structured. Users have to check the information by clicking each document, because the tag of "Scenic View" has very poor discrimination power. Moreover, the degree of attractiveness of the view is stripped from structured documents. Thus, our goal is to use unstructured documents on the web to satisfy the user's needs.

In this paper, we use the method of query-biased summarization to generate effective snippets of search results [1]. These snippets allow users to compare entities by looking at the information associated with the attribute query. They also allow users to select the best document. In their work, they used the objective function that consists of two factors; *Fidelity model* and *Relevance model*. Fidelity model summarizes documents so that users can imagine the contents of the original document. Relevance model confirms that the document contains the type query.

In the framework of our method, the conventional relevance model can be applied to type queries without any modification. Users are likely to compare entities of the same type as the input type query. Therefore, type query should be contained directly in the snippets. This requirement of a snippet corresponds to the function of the relevance model in the conventional method. However, this previous framework is ineffective for attribute queries because of the following issue. The words used in the attribute query may not be written in all documents. For example, "sight" can be expressed by words such as "view", "scenic location" or sentences such as "The scenery is beautiful.", "The interior design is good.". In a such case, the probability of the relevance model is set to be zero since the attribute query does not directly appear in the document. This makes the total probability be zero and thus the conventional method generates messy snippets as a result.

We resolve this problem by introducing a novel probabilistic model for attribute queries; it allows appropriate snippets to be generated in terms of both type and attribute queries. We refer to the probabilistic model as the *ambiguous relevance model* in this paper. The ambiguous relevance model uses a lot of words that are similar or related to the input attribute query to calculate the probability. Because of this, our method can generate snippets that contain information about an attribute query but written in a wide variety of words.

In this study, we assume that the type of input queries can be distinguished automatically. That is, the system can treat a type query and an attribute query separately. We consider that it is possible to identify the type of the input query automatically by modifying conventional methods since several studies [8,9,15] achieve stable accuracy in extracting entities and contexts (i.e., attribute queries in this paper) from a given query.

Our method makes it possible to generate snippets that contain not only type query responses but also the information that best satisfies the attribute query. Experiments that compare the proposed method with a conventional method show that our method can generate such snippets.

The major contributions of our research are:

- We introduce a novel probabilistic model, *ambiguous relevance model*, into the conventional method to develop a new snippet generation method, which treats type query and attribute query separately.
- We propose an implementation of the ambiguous relevance model. It expands the attribute queries to calculate the similarities among the expanded words in the document.
- We verify that our method can generate better snippets in terms of information about attribute queries than conventional methods while matching the performance of conventional methods with respect to information about type queries.

2   Related Work

There are many kinds of queries that user input to entity search engines. Pound [12,13] said that there are four kinds of queries: entity query, type query, attribute query, and relation query. In attribute-oriented entity search, a user inputs type query(ies) and attribute query(ies) to find the best-fit entity. Thus, we target type query and attribute query in this paper. Here, the definitions of type query and attribute query are identical to those of Pound's [12,13].

The conventional ranking method for entity search can be useful for ranking in attribute-oriented entity search. Dalton [4] proposed a ranking method for entity search based on the four kinds of queries proposed by Pound. We consider that the method would have a similar effect when it targets only two queries for ranking in attribute-oriented entity search. We suppose that the system for attribute-oriented entity search use the conventional method for ranking. Therefore, we preferentially address the problem of generating snippets of attribute-oriented entity search results in this paper.

This work is related to previous studies that treat search users' intents. Broder [3] outlined three main user intents: informational, navigational, and transactional. Rose [14] provided more subcategories in 11 finer-grained intents, and

Yin [18] proposed a method to organize taxonomies of phrases created to express these intents. Lin [6] addressed the problem of finding actions that can be performed on entities. Jain [5] proposed a method for open-domain entity extraction and clustering over query logs. Pantel [10,11] estimated what the user was searching for by classifying the user's intent into 70 types like Songs, Newspaper or Place based on the entity included in queries and the words input before and after the entity. All these studies focused on entity query to estimate user's intent by using query log data. Our method treats the attribute query as indicative of the user's intents. This is differ from previous research.

Snippet generation can be considered as the task of query-biased summarization [16]. Tombros [16] proposed a rule-based query-biased summarization method that gives a different score to each term in a document to generate a summary that contains relevant terms. Several studies have used the machine learning approach to realize query-biased summarization. Wang [17] formulated query-biased summarization as the task of classifying sentences in a document. Metzler [7] uses supervised machine learning to resolve the query-biased summarization task as a sentence ranking problem. Recently, it has become common to find the best combination of sentences/words that maximizes a pre-defined objective function. There are two tasks in the approach. The first task is how to model a suitable objective function. The second task is to develop a search algorithm that maximizes the objective function. In this paper, we tackle the first task by defining an objective function that reflects both type query and attribute query to generate an appropriate snippet in terms of the input queries. In the experiment conducted to verify the effectiveness of the objective function, we use greedy search as the search algorithm, but other search algorithms could be used.

3   Snippet Generation as Query-Biased Summarization

We propose a method to generate snippets that reflect type and attribute queries separately. Our method is based on a conventional method for query-biased summarization. In 3.1, we show the conventional method. Then, in 3.2, we describe a new model as an extension of the conventional model to treat attribute queries.

3.1   Probabilistic Models of Query-Biased Summarization

Berger [1] proposed a probabilistic method to generate a query-biased summary from a document and a given query consisting of one or more terms. The query-biased summary is a subset of sentences in the document. The method chooses the best subset that maximizes the objective function. The objective function in Berger's method is modeled as a product of two probabilistic models; the fidelity model and the relevance model.

Candidates are sentences in the document. Given document d and query q, query-biased summary s^* is created by

$$s^* = \operatorname*{argmax}_{s} P(s \mid d, q) \approx \operatorname{argmax} P(s \mid d) P(q \mid s). \tag{1}$$

Each summary is scored by these two probabilistic models: fidelity model $P(s \mid d)$ and relevance model $P(q \mid s)$.

The fidelity model: The fidelity model represents snippet accuracy. A summary should have content that accurately outlines the document because it is used as a substitute for the document. The model adopts $P(s \mid d)$ as the fidelity measure, that is, how well the words in the candidate summary express the content of the document. The method models fidelity by the multinomial distribution of word frequency in the candidate summaries generated from document d. $p_i = k_i/n$, where n is the total number of words in d. Candidate summary s contains words which appear each $c_1, ..., c_{|c|}$ times in s. Probability p_i is calculated by maximum likelihood estimation, i.e., $p_i = k_i/n$, where k_i is the occurrence number of the i-th word in document d. Fidelity score follows a multinomial distribution where each word is chosen c_i times in p_i, and $C \equiv \sum_{i=1}^{|c|} c_i$.

$$P(s \mid d) = \frac{C!}{\prod_i^{|c|} c_i!} \prod_i^{|c|} p_i^{c_i}. \tag{2}$$

The relevance model: The relevance model represents the relatedness between query and snippets. If a part of the document is related to the query while the others are not, the part is expected to contain more query terms than the other parts in the document. Thus, it is proper that the summary contains as many query terms as possible. $P(q \mid s)$ indicates how well the summary is related to the query. The method models $P(q \mid s)$ by a multinomial distribution of frequency of query terms q in summary s. If the words of type query appear each $t_1, ..., t_{|t|}$ times in q and the total number of query words is $T \equiv \sum_{i=1}^{|t|} t_i$, the relevance model follows a multinominal distribution when each query word appears t_i times with probability $p_i = k_i/n$ in the string of words of the candidate summary consisting of n words.

$$P(q \mid s) = \frac{T!}{\prod_i^{|t|} t_i!} \prod_i^{|t|} p_i^{t_i}. \tag{3}$$

As mentioned in Section 1, it is not effective to treat type and attribute queries the same way in this method.

3.2   Extended Probabilistic Model for Attribute Queries

We extend the conventional model to treat attribute queries independent of type queries to generate more informative snippets. Our model uses the conventional relevance model to calculate the score of type query responses. We note that the fidelity model is independent of the users' input.

First, we show how to add a new probabilistic model for attribute queries. The snippet that best reflects type and attribute queries is s^* given type query q, attribute query a, and a document d. We derive the conditional probability in a similar way to Berger's method.

$$s^* = \underset{s}{\operatorname{argmax}} P(s \mid d, q, a). \tag{4}$$

Applying Bayes' theorem,

$$P(s \mid d, q, a) = \frac{P(s \mid d)P(a \mid s, d)P(q \mid s, d, a)}{P(a \mid d)P(q \mid d, a)}. \tag{5}$$

$P(a \mid s, d)$ has the same value as $P(a \mid s)$ because s is a subset of d. $P(q \mid s, d, a)$ is also the same value as $P(q \mid s)$, because q is independent of a and d. Since the denominator is independent of s, Equation (5) is approximated as

$$s^* = \underset{w}{\operatorname{argmax}} P(s \mid d)P(a \mid s)P(q \mid s). \tag{6}$$

This model assumes that the snippet with the highest product of these three probabilities is the most suitable. The difference between our method and Berger's method is the use of $P(a \mid s)$ in Equation (6).

$P(a \mid s)$ expresses how much information snippet s contains that is relevant to attribute query a. In this paper, we call this model the *ambiguous relevance model*. The model calculates the score of all sentences in each candidate snippet. Given attribute query a that contains attributes $a_1, ..., a_{|a|}$ and candidate snippet s that contains the sentences $l_1, ..., l_{|l|}$, the ambiguous relevance model is given by

$$P(a \mid s) = \frac{|a|!}{Z} \prod_{x=1}^{|a|} \prod_{y=1}^{|l|} S(a_x, l_y). \tag{7}$$

where $S(a_x, l_y)$ is the similarity between sentence l_y in s and the attribute query a_x in a, Z is the normalizing constant. If there are multiple attribute queries in a query, it is virtually impossible to find one sentence that contains information about all attribute queries. To resolve this problem, the model considers only one attribute, the one that has the highest score among all attributes for the sentence, in calculating S. That is, we use

$$P(a \mid s) \approx \prod_{y=1}^{|l|} \max_x S(a_x, l_y). \tag{8}$$

as the probability of the ambiguous relevance model.

Here, we consider the fact that that words in the attribute query are frequently not written in the documents. For example, if the attribute query includes the word "sight", the document sentence "Night view was beautiful." is meaningful with regard to the attribute query. Because this sentence doesn't contain the word "sight", the system cannot understand that this sentence has information relevant to the attribute query. Because of this, we use not only direct word matches but also word similarity. However, while similarity is more effective than direct word matching, it still fails to extract the greatest possible amount of relevant information. For example, the sentence "We can see the blue sea" contains information relevant to sight. Though the most meaningful word "sea" is clearly associated with sight, "sea" is not a synonym of "sight" and so this sentence would not normally be part of the snippet. To counter this problem, we expand the semantic space of attribute words.

We introduce a method to create sets of associated attribute words. We use past queries held in the query logs to make these sets. The assumption is that the logs reflect the interests of a diverse range of users and thus coverage, in terms of associate attribute words, is sufficient. First, for each category, we select the most common type queries. For example, when users search in the category of "eating", type queries such as "lunch", "restaurants", "cafes" appear frequently in the query logs. The system extracts the queries that contain any one of these type queries and at least one other word, which is assumed to be the attribute word. The system drops type words, and clusters the remaining words, such as "atmosphere", "price" by using the K-means method. As a result of clustering, highly related words are put into the same cluster, for example "baby, child, baby food", "night view, sight, sea". These clusters are the sets of associated attribute words. When the attribute query contains "sight", all words in the set containing "sight" are selected as attribute words. This allows the meaning of "sight" to be used in extracting relevant information such as "night view" and "sea".

Our ambiguous relevance model is based on a measure of similarity between each word of the snippet sentence and the attribute word set. When attribute query a_x in a is a set of words, $n_{x1}, ..., n_{x|a_x|}$, and sentence l_y, one of the sentences of candidate summary s, is associated with words $w_{y1},...,w_{y|l_y|}$, we define the similarity, S, between a_x and l_y as

$$S(a_x, l_y) = \frac{1}{|a_x l_y|} \sum_{i=1}^{|a_x|} \sum_{j=1}^{|l_y|} sim(n_{xi}, w_{yj}), \tag{9}$$

where sim expresses the average similarity between a word of l_y and a word in the set of a_x. The method used to calculate word similarity can be chosen freely, for example thesaurus-based methods or word co-occurrence methods.

3.3   Algorithm

We detail here the algorithm of the method. The method used to make snippet candidates is set in Step 4-6. In this experiment, we select the greedy method to add sentences, one by one, from the document so as to maximize the score of the snippet. Given document d, type query q, attribute query a, and the total character count limit of the snippet, d is separated into sentences $l_1, ..., l_m$. The system calculates the probability score of each candidate of snippet $SUMM$. The candidate sentence that has the highest score is chosen as the temporary snippet $summMax$. Next, each sentence not included in the temporary snippet is added, one by one, to the snippet to create the next snippet candidate. If the candidate exceeds the total character count limit, the last addition is eliminated from the candidate. If no further updating is possible, the candidate is output as the snippet $bestSumm$ of the document. Finally the sentences of $bestSumm$ is sorted in the order they occur in the document (Step 18).

4   Experimental Evaluation

We conducted an experiment to verify that our method can generate better snippets than the conventional method in terms of attribute-oriented entity search.

In the experiments we use the following settings.

Algorithm 1. makeSummary($d,q,a,maxLength$)

1: $summMax \leftarrow \emptyset$
2: $scoreMax \leftarrow 0$
3: **while** $length(summ_{max}) < maxLength$ **do**
4:     **for all** $l \mid l \in d, l \notin summMax$ **do**
5:        $SUMM \leftarrow summMax \cup l$
6:     **end for**
7:     **for all** s *in* $SUMM$ **do**
8:        $F \leftarrow fidelity(s,d)$
9:        $R \leftarrow relevance(s,q)$
10:      $P \leftarrow ambiguous\_relevance(s,a)$
11:      $score \leftarrow F \times R \times P$
12:      **if** $score > scoreMax$ **then**
13:         $scoreMax \leftarrow score$
14:         $summMax \leftarrow s$
15:      **end if**
16:    **end for**
17: **end while**
18: $bestSumm \leftarrow sort(summMax)$
19: *return bestSumm*

Type Query: The queries used are listed in Table 1. We examined two situations "sightseeing" and "eating". We prepared four type queries for each situation. Each type query consisted of two words.

Attribute Query: We prepared six attribute queries for each situation. Six attribute queries were created, three consisted of one word and three consisted of two words (all pairs yielded by three words). We used the query log of a practical web search engine, gathered from January to June 2011, to produce the associated attribute word sets. We selected three words used frequently when searching for information related to each category from the query logs; "travel", "sightseeing", "drive" for sightseeing, and "restaurants", "cafes", "lunch" for eating. Next, we clustered the words that appeared with these words in the query log by the K-means algorithm, which yielded the associated attribute word sets used in the experiment.

Documents: The documents were the blog articles that the authors crawled. We collected 20 documents using each combination of type and attribute queries. We used two retrieval styles as follows.

1. AND retrieval of two query words. e.g) Disneyland AND lodgings
2. AND retrieval of type and attribute queries.
   e.g) Disneyland AND lodgings AND (price OR coupon OR cheap OR ...)

Given that some documents may contain no information relevant to the attribute query, we asked annotators to judge whether each document contained such information or not. We found that 57% of the documents collected by the two retrieval styles contained information relevant to the attribute queries.

Table 1. Type query and Attribute query

Situation	Type query	Attribute query
Sightseeing	Disneyland lodgings	price, family, eating,
	Hiroshima sightseeing	price AND family,
	Kyoto Hotel	price AND eating,
	Atami hotspring	family AND eating.
Eating	Izu lunch	price, scenery, atmosphere,
	Hayama restaurant	price AND scenery,
	Osaka Sta. cafe	price AND atmosphere,
	Minatomirai lunch	scenery AND atmosphere.

Snippets: The three types of snippets created in the experiment are as follows.

- Proposed method: Snippets reflect fidelity, relevance, and ambiguous relevance.
- Baseline A: Snippets reflect only fidelity and relevance, attribute query is not considered.
- Baseline B: Snippets reflect only fidelity and relevance, the relevance model treats type and attribute queries in the same way.

Total number of characters per snippet is limited to 120. To calculate word similarity we used the method based on the concept vectors statistically generated from the semantic expressions of words [2].

Evaluation method: The annotators were three people. They scored snippets on three levels based on two aspects: information about type query and information about attribute query. The evaluation guidelines are shown in Table 2.

4.1 Results

We show the average score for each method in Table 3. It shows that the proposed method matches baseline A in terms of type query evaluation. This shows that the proposed method can include information about the type query in the snippets, the same as the baseline. This indicates that our extension of the model does not degrade the merit of the conventional model.

With regard to the attribute query evaluation, the results show that the proposed method has higher score than either of the baselines. Therefore, the proposed method can generate snippets that contain more information, not only type query but also attribute query, than the baseline methods. The scores of method B are the smallest of the three methods so it is ineffective for generating useful snippets given type query and attribute query.

We show the average scores of documents for each combination of type and attribute query in Fig.3. More than 90% of the snippets output by the proposed method lie in the top right area (scores of both type query and attribute query exceed 2), so our snippets contain information satisfying both type and attribute queries. The result also says that most snippets yielded by baseline A lie in the right side of the graph. It means that most snippets by method A satisfy only

Table 2. Evaluation guideline

(a) Evaluation guideline for type query

score	information about query
3	contains information about both words of type query. e.g) Hayama AND restaurant
2	contains information about one word of type query. e.g) Hayama OR restaurant
1	contains information about neither word of type query.

(b) Evaluation guideline for attribute query

score	information about attribute query
3	contains information about one or more attribute queries.
2	contains information about attribute query but unrelated to the entity.
1	contains no information about attribute query.

Table 3. Average score for type query and attribute query evaluation. We show the standard deviations of the scores in parentheses.

	Proposed method	Baseline A	Baseline B
Score of Type query	2.76 ($\pm$ 0.25)	2.73 ($\pm$ 0.26)	1.26 ($\pm$ 0.38)
Score of Attribute query	**2.38***** ($\pm$ 0.48)	1.96 ($\pm$ 0.54)	1.60 ($\pm$ 0.43)

type queries, and only a few snippets satisfy attribute queries. This result is consistent with the feature of the baselines. Snippets generated by baseline B lie in the center and the bottom of the graph. This means that they don't satisfy attribute queries. Moreover, some method B snippets fail to satisfy either type or attribute queries. It means that it is not always possible to contain the attribute information in snippets if attribute queries are treated in the same way as type queries. This shows that type and attribute queries must be treated separately to make snippets that satisfy both queries.

Subjecting these results to the t-test shows that the difference in attribute query scores of information is significant (p value < 0.01). There is no significant difference in the type query scores between the proposed method and baseline A. It means that our method could contain the information about type query almost as much as conventional methods.

Next, we analyzed baseline B, the worst of the three methods. Its poor performance is caused by the snippet character limit, 120 in the experiment and the equal level of importance placed by baseline B on both type and attribute queries. In several instances, information satisfying the type query was added to the snippet which prevented the type query information from being added (assuming that this would exceed the character limit). These snippets are unsuitable for search results pages because our requirements for snippets, defined in Section 1, state that the snippets must contain words relevant to the type query. Without such words, users cannot find informative documents about the desired entities in the search results. Therefore methods that treat the two kinds of queries in the same manner cannot generate useful snippets. By contrast, our snippets give priority to type query words in a different manner than attribute query words. As a result, our proposed method is able to generate snippets that contain query information and information related to attribute query simultaneously, and so produces the most informative snippets.

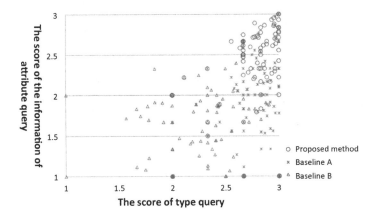

Fig. 1. Score of snippets from documents that contain information about at least one attribute query

5   Conclusion

In this paper, we tackled the problem of maximizing the effectiveness of attribute-oriented entity searches. We proposed a method that generates snippets that contain information about attribute queries as well as type queries. The model treats type queries and attribute queries differently to capture the key feature of the latter, the unstructured documents found on the web use many expressions to represent the same attribute. In addition to the fidelity model for documents and the relevance model for queries (baseline method), we proposed the ambiguous relevance model; it represents the similarity between words in the attribute queries and the words in the documents. We also proposed the method of calculating ambiguous relevance model scores. An experiment showed that the proposed method can generate better snippets that contain information clearly associated with both type query and attribute query than the conventional methods that employ only fidelity and relevance models. We plan to apply our method to other contents that contain information about entities, for example user's reviews in travel sites, shopping sites and so on.

Acknowledgments. We sincerely would like to thank Hitoshi Nishikawa of NTT Media Intelligence Laboratories, for his helpful comments and discussions which have enhanced this work.

References

1. Berger, A., Mittal, O.: Query-relevant summarization using FAQs. In: Proc. ACL 2000, pp. 294–301 (2000)
2. Bessho, K., Furuse, O., Kataoka, R., Oku, M.: Kanshinji Antenna: A japanese-language concept search system. International Journal of Human-Computer Interaction 23(1&2), 25–49 (2007)
3. Broder, A.: A taxonomy of web search. SIGIR Forum 36(2), 3–10 (2002)
4. Dalton, J., Blanco, R., Mika, P.: Coreference aware web object retrieval. In: Proc. CIKM 2011, pp. 211–220 (2011)
5. Jain, A., Pennacchiotti, M.: Open entity extraction from web search query logs. In: Proc. COLING 2010, pp. 510–518 (2010)
6. Lin, T., Pantel, P., Gamon, M., Kannan, A., Fuxman, A.: Active objects: Actions for entity-centric search. In: Proc. WWW 2012, pp. 589–598 (2012)
7. Metzler, D., Kanungo, T.: Machine learned sentence selection strategies for query-biased summarization. In: Proc. SIGIR 2008 Workshop Learning to Rank for Information Retrieval (2008)
8. Paşca, M.: Organizing and searching the world wide web of facts – step two: harnessing the wisdom of the crowds. In: Proc. WWW 2007, pp. 101–110 (2007)
9. Paşca, M.: Weakly-supervised discovery of named entities using web search queries. In: Proc. CIKM 2007, New York, NY, USA, pp. 683–690 (2007)
10. Pantel, P., Lin, D.: Discovering word senses from text. In: Proc. KDD 2002, pp. 613–619 (2002)
11. Pantel, P., Lin, T., Gamon, M.: Mining entity types from query logs via user intent modeling. In: Proc. ACL 2012, pp. 563–571 (2012)
12. Pound, J., Hudek, K., Ilyas, F., Weddell, G.: Interpreting keyword queries over web knowledge bases. In: Proc. CIKM 2012, pp. 305–314 (2012)
13. Pound, J., Mika, P., Zaragoza, H.: Ad-hoc object retrieval in the web of data. In: Proc. WWW 2010, pp. 771–780 (2010)
14. Rose, E., Levinson, D.: Understanding user goals in web search. In: Proc. WWW 2004, pp. 13–19 (2004)
15. Sekine, S., Suzuki, H.: Acquiring ontological knowledge from query logs. In: Proc. WWW 2007, pp. 1223–1224 (2007)
16. Tombros, A., Sanderson, M.: Advantages of query biased summaries in information retrieval. In: Proc. SIGIR 1998, pp. 2–10 (1998)
17. Wang, C., Jing, F., Zhang, L., Zhang, H.: Learning query-biased web page summarization. In: Proc. CIKM 2007, pp. 555–562 (2007)
18. Yin, X., Shah, S.: Building taxonomy of web search intents for name entity queries. In: Proc. WWW 2010, pp. 1001–1010 (2010)

Hyper-geometric Model
for Information Retrieval Revisited

Sha Lu, Ben He, and Jungang Xu

School of Computer and Control Engineering
University of Chinese Academy of Sciences
Beijing 100190, China
lusha12@mails.ucas.ac.cn, {benhe,xujg}@ucas.ac.cn

Abstract. DLH is a parameter-free divergence from randomness (DFR) model that is normally deployed as a standalone weighting model for retrieval applications. It assumes a hyper-geometric term frequency (*tf*) distribution which is reduced to a binomial distribution based on non-uniform *term* prior distribution. In this paper, we revisit the hyper-geometric model by showing that DLH is equivalent to deriving a Poisson-based DFR model based on a binomial distribution with non-uniform *document* priors. Moreover, instead of treating DLH as a standalone model, we suggest that the effectiveness of DLH can be improved by adding an *idf* component, since DLH considers only the *tf* information for the relevance weighting. Experimental results on standard TREC collections with various search tasks show that the newly proposed model with an additional *idf* component, called *PF1*, has comparable retrieval performance with the state-of-the-art probabilistic models, and outperforms them when query expansion is applied.

Keywords: Theory, Experimentation, Performance.

1 Introduction

A crucial issue underlying an IR system is to rank the returned documents by decreasing order of relevance. Generally, ranking is based on a weighting model. Most current probabilistic IR models assume a Poisson distribution of a query term's occurrences, namely the within-document frequency, in the document collection. Take BM25 for instance, its ranking function [11] is usually considered as a variant of the tf-idf weighting scheme, where the inverse document frequency (*idf*) is given by the Robertson Sparck-Jones weight [9] and the term frequency (*tf*) component is an approximation of the 2-Poisson distribution using a saturation function [10,11]. The PL2 model from the DFR family also follows the same Poisson assumption of the *tf* distribution.

An underlying assumption of the Poisson distribution is that the document prior $P(d)$, the probability of observing a query term in a given document, is uniform across all documents in the collection. Imagine a document corpora is a collection of balls (tokens) in different colors, where a set of balls in color

R.E. Banchs et al. (Eds.): AIRS 2013, LNCS 8281, pp. 62–73, 2013.
© Springer-Verlag Berlin Heidelberg 2013

t represents a unique term and a basket d is a document[1]. The occurrence of query term t can be seen as the event of randomly throwing a ball in color t, and $P(d)$ is the probability of the ball is found to be thrown into basket d. Poisson distribution assumes that the document prior $P(d)$ follows a uniform distribution, usually $\frac{1}{N}$, where N is the number of documents in the collection. In practice, since the lengths of different documents are highly diverse, it is natural that this assumption of the uniform prior distribution does not hold, hence the need for the so-called length normalization to penalize for the over-estimated term frequency in long documents.

Most current length normalization methods such as the saturation function of BM25 [11] and the Normalization 2 of PL2 [2] involve the use of a tunable parameter to control the trade-off between a "generous" and "harsh" normalization. Although the length normalization methods exhibit certain effectiveness, they also suffer from the robustness problem caused by the parameter tuning. More specifically, the optimal parameter setting varies with different types of queries and search tasks. Given that it is difficult to obtain the prior knowledge of query types in practice, the retrieval effectiveness can be hurt if an inappropriate parameter setting were used. Therefore, it is appealing to eliminate the normalization parameters while still having an adequate retrieval performance.

To this end, Amati proposed the DLH model based on the assumed hyper-geometric distribution of term frequency [1]. For the convenience of deriving a workable weighting function, the hyper-geometric distribution function is reduced to a binomial distribution with non-uniform *term* priors. Despite the encouraging performance shown by DLH, its retrieval effectiveness may still not be comparable with other state-of-the-art IR models such as BM25 and PL2, as shown in our experiments in Section 5 on four standard TREC collections.

In this paper, we first revisit the hyper-geometric model by deriving an equivalent parameter free model based on binomial distribution with non-uniform *document* priors. Thus, a query term t with *tf* occurrences in document d is seen as *TF* binomial trials with *tf* successes, where *TF* is the frequency of t in the whole collection. Next, since DLH takes only the *tf* information into account in the relevance weighting, we suggest the possibility of further improvement in the retrieval performance by extending DLH with an *idf* component. Finally, experimental results on multiple search tasks on various standard TREC test collections demonstrate the benefit brought by the additional *idf* component.

The major contributions of this paper are two-fold. First, we provide a link between the hyper-geometric model and the classical PL2 DFR model by deriving a parameter-free model based on the non-uniform *document* prior distribution. Second, we demonstrate the benefit of adding an *idf* component to DLH, which has been used as a standalone weighting model. To the best of our knowledge, this work is the first to combine the standalone DLH model with an explicit *idf* component.

---

[1] Although the urns and balls are used as examples, it does not necessarily imply that IR models are solely based on probabilistic models without replacement. For instance, the classical PL2 DFR model is derived from the binomial assumption.

The remainder of this paper is organized as follows. In Section 2, we review the above mentioned DLH model, which is then revisited in Section 3. In Section 4 and 5, we present our experimental settings and evaluation results. Finally, Section 6 concludes the work and suggests future research directions.

2   Related Work

In 2006, Amati proposes to eliminate the length normalization by assuming of the hyper-geometric distribution of term frequency [1]:

$$P(tf|d) = \frac{\binom{TF}{tf} \cdot \binom{TFC-TF}{l(d)-tf}}{\binom{TFC}{l(d)}} \tag{1}$$

where tf is the frequency of term t in document d, $l(d)$ is the document length, TF is the number of occurrences of t in the whole collection, and TFC is the number of tokens in the whole collection. There are $\binom{TF}{tf}$ different ways of combinations to choose tf occurrences of a term, and there are also $\binom{TFC-TF}{l(d)-tf}$ ways to choose $(l(d) - tf)$ occurrences of a different term.

For the convenience of deriving a workable model, the above hyper-geometric distribution is reduced to a binomial distribution as follows:

$$P(tf|d,p) \sim \binom{l(d)}{tf} p^{tf} \cdot (1-p)^{l(d)-tf} \tag{2}$$

where p is the probability of occurrence of term t, i.e. a success of the binomial trial.

The above binomial distribution assumes that a document d with length $l(d)$ is a sample of $l(d)$ trials from the collection, where a query term t is seen as tf successes of the $l(d)$ trials. Thus, a document can be considered as $l(d)$ binomial trials whose outcome can be either a success, namely an occurrence of the query term t, or a failure, namely an occurrence of a term other than t.

The prior probability of occurrence of the term t is given by the relative term-frequency in the collection, namely $P(t) = \frac{TF}{TFC}$, where TF and TFC are the frequency of t in the whole collection, and the number of tokens in the whole collection, respectively. Thus, the information content is used for measuring the importance of the query term in the document, which is a decreasing function of the probability as follows:

$$Inf(tf \parallel d) = -\log_2 P(tf|d, p = P(t)) \tag{3}$$

The final weighting function of DLH is given by a combination of the Laplace succession with an approximation of the above information content:

$$w(t,d) = \sum_{t \in Q} qtw(t) \cdot \frac{tf \cdot \log_2(\frac{tf}{l(d)} \cdot \frac{TFC}{TF}) + 0.5 \cdot \log_2(2\pi \cdot tf \cdot (1 - \frac{tf}{l(d)}))}{tf + 1} \tag{4}$$

where $qtw(t)$ is the query term weight of t. It is given by $\frac{qtf}{qtf_{max}}$, where qtf is the number of occurrences of t in the query, and qtf_{max} is the maximum qtf of all terms in the query.

3   Hyper-geometric Model Revisited

As aforementioned, most current probabilistic models such as BM25 and PL2 based on the uniform document prior assumption introduce length normalization components to deal with the over-estimated term frequency in long documents. Amati proposes the parameter free DLH model based on the hyper-geometric term frequency distribution, which is reduced to a binomial distribution with non-uniform term priors [1].

In this section, we revisit the hyper-geometric model by providing an alternative explanation on the reduction. We derive a *tf* weight based on the non-uniform document priors, which is shown to be highly similar to the DLH model. We then suggest not to use DLH as a standalone model as it is right now. Instead, we propose to extend DLH with an *idf* component so that the model takes both *tf* and *idf* into consideration for the relevance weighting.

To derive a *tf* weight based on non-uniform document priors, we start with assuming that a term t is a sample of TF binomial trials from the collection, where TF is the number of occurrences of t in the collection. Therefore, the term occurrence probability $P(tf|d, P(d))$ with a document prior $P(d)$ can be described by the binomial distribution as:

$$P(tf|d, P(d)) = \binom{TF}{tf} P(d)^{tf} \cdot (1 - P(d))^{TF-tf} \qquad (5)$$

where *tf* is the number of successes of the binomial trials.

If the document prior $P(d)$ is assumed to be uniform for all documents in the collection, the above formula is equivalent to the Poisson randomness model as in PL2 [2]. As our aim is to derive a parameter free model, here the document prior $P(d)$ is assumed to be non-uniform and depends on the document length:

$$P(d) = \frac{l(d)}{TFC} \qquad (6)$$

In this way, the length normalization 2 [2] of PL2 is no longer required. Then the information content of the term occurrence probability becomes:

$$-log_2 P(tf|d, P(d)) = -\log_2 \left[\binom{TF}{tf} P(d)^{tf} (1 - P(d))^{TF-tf} \right] \qquad (7)$$

Following a similar method with [1] to simplify the above formula, we use the approximation by Renyi [8]:

$$\mathcal{B}(TF, tf, P(d)) \sim \frac{2^{-TF \cdot \mathcal{D}(\hat{p}, P(d))}}{(2\pi \cdot tf (1 - \hat{p}))^{\frac{1}{2}}} \qquad (8)$$

where $\hat{p}$ is $\frac{tf}{TF}$ which is the maximum likelihood estimate (MLE) of the term in the document. The divergence $\mathcal{D}\left(\hat{p}, P\left(d\right)\right)$ can be given by the asymmetric Kullback-Leibler divergence:

$$KL(\hat{p} \parallel P(d)) = \hat{p} \cdot \log_2 \left(\frac{\hat{p}}{P(d)} \right) \tag{9}$$

Using the above approximation, we can further derive a simplified information content normalized by Laplace succession [2] as follows:

$$\frac{-log_2 P(tf|d, P(d))}{tf+1} \sim \frac{TF \cdot KL\left(\hat{p} \parallel P\left(d\right)\right) + 0.5 \cdot \log_2\left(2\pi \cdot tf \cdot (1 - \hat{p})\right)}{tf+1}$$

$$\sim \frac{tf \cdot \log_2\left(\frac{\hat{p}}{P(d)}\right) + 0.5 \cdot \log_2\left(2\pi \cdot tf \cdot (1 - \hat{p})\right)}{tf+1} \tag{10}$$

$$\sim \frac{tf \cdot \log_2\left(\frac{tf}{TF} \cdot \frac{TFC}{l(d)}\right) + 0.5 \cdot \log_2\left(2\pi \cdot tf \cdot \left(1 - \frac{tf}{TF}\right)\right)}{tf+1}$$

Despite the fact that the above formula and DLH in Equation (4) are derived based on different assumptions of the prior distribution, they share a similar form - the only difference is the last addendum of the numerator ($\frac{tf}{TF}$ against $\frac{tf}{l(d)}$). Indeed, the tf weight in Equation (10) is practically equivalent to DLH as they have almost identical results in our preliminary experiments.

Our above derivation provides an alternative explanation of the reduction from the hyper-geometric distribution to the binomial trials with non-uniform term priors. That is, the hyper-geometric model in its reduced form, namely the DLH model, can be seen as the classical PL2 model with non-uniform document priors without length normalization. Furthermore, as it turns out that DLH, having been used as a standalone model, takes only tf into account for the relevance weighting, it can be beneficial to expand DLH with an idf component. The inverse document frequency, namely the idf factor, considers the presence and absence of a given query term in the documents collection-wide. It implies that the more documents in which a term occurs, the less information is carried by the term. We then define a parameter free model called **PF1** after adding BM25's idf component [9]:

$$Score(d, Q) = \sum_{t \in Q} qtw\left(t\right) \cdot \left(w_{idf} + w_{tf}\right)$$

$$= \sum_{t \in Q} qtw\left(t\right) \cdot \left[- \log_2 \frac{df + 0.5}{N - df + 0.5} \right. \tag{11}$$

$$\left. + \frac{1}{tf+1} \cdot \left(tf \cdot \log_2(\frac{tf}{TF} \cdot \frac{TFC}{l(d)}) + 0.5 \cdot \log_2\left(2\pi \cdot tf \cdot (1 - \frac{tf}{TF})\right)\right)\right]$$

We define the relevance weight as the sum instead of the product of the idf and tf weights, as both are negative logarithms of probabilities.

Since the *tf* weight based on the non-uniform document priors in Equation (10) is practically equivalent to DLH, the above PF1 model can be seen as an extension of DLH by adding an *idf* component. PF1 can also be seen as a parameter free version of BM25 by replacing its *tf* weight with Equation (10), a DFR-based *tf* weight normalized by Laplace succession. In the following sections, we conduct extensive experiments to evaluate PF1.

4 Experimental Settings

4.1 Datasets and Indexing

All our experiments are conducted using an in-house extension of the open source Terrier 3.0 [7]. Moreover, the implementation of language model and its associated relevance feedback mechanism is migrated from the Lemur toolkit[2]. We use three standard TREC test collections in our study. Basic statistics about the test collections and topics are given in Table 1. The disk4&5 collection contains mainly the newswire articles from newspapers and journals. The WT10G collection is a medium size crawl of Web documents, which was used in the TREC 9 and 10 Web tracks. It contains 10 Gigabytes of uncompressed data. The DOT-GOV2 collection, which has 426 Gigabytes of uncompressed data, is a crawl from the .gov domain.

Each topic contains three fields, namely title, description and narrative. We only use the query terms in the title field for retrieval. The title-only queries are very short which are usually regarded as a realistic snapshot of real user queries.

Table 1. Information about the test collections used

Coll.	TREC Task	Query Topics	# Docs
disk4&5	Robust 2004	301-450, 601-700	528,155
WT10G	9, 10 Web	451-550	1,692,096
DOTGOV2	2004-2006 Terabyte Ad-hoc	701-850	25,178,548

4.2 Evaluation Methodology

We conduct two levels of comparisons to evaluate the effectiveness of our proposed parameter free model as follows.

The first level of evaluation compares the retrieval effectiveness of our proposed PF1 model with two popular statistical IR models, namely BM25 and KLLM (Kullback-Leibler divergence language model)[15,16], and also the parameter free DFR model, DLH. As both BM25 and KLLM have parameters that require tuning to provide a reliable retrieval performance, they are evaluated by cross-validation on the test collections used. In particular, they are evaluated by 2-fold cross-validation on disk4&5 and WT10G, and by 3-fold cross-validation on DOTGOV2. The query topics are partitioned into equal-size subsets by the year

---

[2] http://www.lemurproject.org/

of release on DOTGOV2, and by parity on WT10G and disk4&5. We use the TREC official evaluation measure in our experiments, namely the Mean Average Precision (MAP) [13]. All statistical tests are based on Wilcoxon matched-pairs signed-rank test. In all the tables presenting the experimental results, a * and †️ indicate a statistically significant difference at 0.05 and 0.01 level, respectively. Moreover, since DLH and PF1 are parameter-free, they are evaluated over all queries without any training.

In the second level of evaluation, the PF1 model is also evaluated when query expansion (QE), or pseudo relevance feedback, is applied. In particular, KLLM uses the RM3 method that is widely considered a state-of-the-art algorithm for relevance feedback [5,6]. The other retrieval models use an improved version of Rocchio's relevance feedback algorithm based on the KL-divergence term weighting, which shows comparable effectiveness to RM3 on the TREC collections used [4,14]. As the query expansion methods have multiple parameters that require tuning, all the models are evaluated by cross-validation. The query topics partitioning are the same as that for the first level of evaluation.

4.3 Parameter Tuning

The baseline retrieval models such as BM25 and KLLM, and the query expansion methods used, involve the use of several tunable parameters which need to be optimized on the training subsets. In all our experiments, the parameters with continuous values, such as BM25's k_1 and b, are optimized using Simulated Annealing by directly maximizing MAP. The parameters with discrete values, such as the feedback document set size $|ED|$ and the number of expansion terms $|ET|$ for query expansion, are optimized by grid search by maximizing MAP.

For BM25, we first tune parameters k_1 and k_3 by a 2-dimensional optimization. Next, we optimize the length normalization parameter b. For KLLM, only a one-dimensional optimization of its smoothing parameter μ is required. For the query expansion methods used, we first optimize the parameters $|ED|$ and $|ET|$ by grid search of every integer value within $[3, 20]$ for $|ED|$, and of every 5 integer value within $[10, 60]$ for $|ET|$.

5 Experimental Results

5.1 Evaluation Results without Query Expansion

Table 2 compares the retrieval performance measured by MAP of the baselines with our proposed parameter free model on the three collections used. In this table, the numbers after the MAP values of PF1 stand for the difference between their MAP values and the baseline model's MAP in percentage. From Table 2, we have the following observations. First, comparing to BM25, on all the three collections used, PF1 model performs equally well. No statistically significant difference between them are observed. Second, comparing to KLLM, there exists a statistically significant difference between the retrieval performance of KLLM

Table 2. Experimental results without using query expansion. The baselines are evaluated by cross-validation.

	BM25	PF1	KLLM	PF1	DLH	PF1
disk4&5	0.2563	0.2553,-0.410%	0.2531	0.2553,+0.869%	0.2487	0.2553,+2.65%†
WT10G	0.2043	0.2066,+1.13%	0.2152	0.2066,-4.01%*	0.1845	0.2066,+12.0%†
GOV2	0.3005	0.2980,-0.831%	0.2977	0.2980,+0.101%	0.2612	0.2980,+14.1%†

and PF1 on WT10G. However on the other two collections, disk4&5 and DOT-GOV2, PF1 has comparable retrieval performance with KLLM. Finally, comparing to DLH, PF1 consistently outperforms this parameter free baseline. The difference between their retrieval effectiveness measured by MAP is statistically significant on all three collections used. This shows that the introduction of an *idf* weight to the DLH model has a positive effect on the retrieval performance.

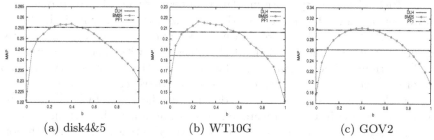

(a) disk4&5   (b) WT10G   (c) GOV2

Fig. 1. The parameter b of BM25 against the MAP obtained on the 3 collections used, compared with the MAP values obtained by the parameter free DLH and PF1 models

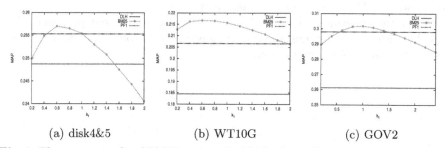

(a) disk4&5   (b) WT10G   (c) GOV2

Fig. 2. The parameter k_1 of BM25 against the MAP obtained on the 3 collections used, compared with the MAP values obtained by the parameter free DLH and PF1 models

We then take a close look at how the tunable parameters of BM25 and KLLM affect their retrieval performance, compared to the parameter free model. Figure 1 and 2 plot the MAP obtained by BM25 against its parameters b and k_1, respectively. For each of these two parameters, we scan a wide range of its possible values, while fixing the other parameter to its optimal setting. We do not plot

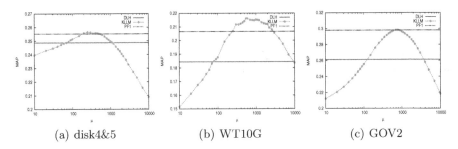

Fig. 3. The parameter μ of KLLM against the MAP obtained on the 3 collections used, compared with the MAP values obtained by the parameter free DLH and PF1 models

for parameter k_3 since this parameter has only negligible effect on the retrieval performance for title-only queries. Also, Figure 3 plots the MAP obtained by KLLM against its smoothing parameter μ. From Figures 1, 2 and 3, we can see that PF1, clearly outperforming DLH, appears to be able to provide the retrieval performance that is close to the optimized BM25 and KLLM. On the other hand, BM25 and KLLM are shown to need parameter tuning to guarantee their retrieval performance, as their MAP values vary with their parameter settings. Even though, the parameter of BM25 or KLLM appears to have a small range of safe settings across different collections. However, the optimal setting of the length normalization parameters depends on the search task, as shown by the experimentation in the literature, e.g. [13]. Experiments in Section 5.3 with non ad-hoc search tasks also show that the optimal settings of the length normalization parameters largely vary for different search tasks. Given the difficulty in guessing the information needs of different users in the dynamic real-world applications, it is therefore difficult to guarantee the retrieval effectiveness of BM25 and KLLM by using a fixed parameter setting.

Overall, the experimental results in this section show that our proposed PF1 model by adding an *idf* weight to DLH is indeed effective on ad-hoc search tasks without the use of query expansion.

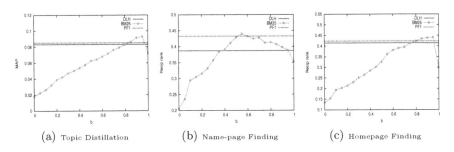

Fig. 4. The parameter b of BM25 Model (X-axis) against the retrieval performance obtained (Y-axis) on non-adhoc tasks by BM25, DLH and PF1

5.2   Evaluation Results with Query Expansion

Table 3 contains the results obtained using query expansion. Notations in this table are similar to those in Table 2 in the previous section.

Table 3. Experimental results with query expansion

	BM25	PF1	KLLM	PF1	DLH	PF1
disk4&5	0.2935	0.3016,+2.76%	0.2991	0.3016,+0.836%	0.3036	0.3016,-0.675%
WT10G	0.2280	0.2327,+2.04%*	0.2270	0.2327,+2.49%	0.2163	0.2327,+7.56%†
GOV2	0.3246	0.3416,+5.24%*	0.3350	0.3416,+1.97%	0.3074	0.3416,+11.1%†

From Table 3, we can see that our proposed PF1 model has at least comparable retrieval performance with the baselines. In particular, PF1 significantly outperforms BM25 and DLH on WT10G and DOTGOV2. We suggest that the marked effectiveness of PF1 over BM25 is due to the fact that the queries with the added expansion terms are much longer than the original title-only queries, which may affect the parameter sensitivity of BM25.

5.3   Evaluation Results for Non-adhoc Tasks

In this section, we further evaluate PF1 for non-adhoc search tasks. The experiments are conducted on the DOTGOV collection which is a medium crawl of the .gov domain with 1,247,753 indexed documents. The 225 topics of the TREC 2004 Web track [3] are used in our experiments. In particular, these 225 topics can be partitioned into three search tasks, namely topic-distillation (TD), named-page finding (NP), and homepage finding (HP). Each task has 75 associated query topics. These non-adhoc search tasks in general demand high-quality resources, for which query expansion usually hurts the retrieval performance because of the very small numbers of relevant documents for each query [3]. We therefore only conduct experiments without the use of query expansion.

For each search task, the 75 query topics are partitioned into three equal-size subsets by their topic numbers. We conduct a 3-fold cross-validation for the BM25 and KLLM baseline models. Table 4 contains the retrieval performance of the baseline models and our proposed parameter free model on three collections. According to the official TREC setting [3], the retrieval performance for the topic distillation task is measured by MAP, and that for the name-page finding and homepage finding tasks are measured by the mean reciprocal rank (MRR). Notations in this table are similar to those in Table 2 in the previous sections.

As shown by Table 4, PF1 provides again at least comparable retrieval performance with the baselines, and can achieve statistically significant improvement over KLLM and DLH for the topic distillation and named-page finding tasks, respectively. The encouraging retrieval effectiveness of PF1 may be due to the fact that these non-adhoc search tasks demand high-quality key resources, for which the models with tunable parameters may have high parameter sensitivity.

Table 4. Experimental results on DOTGOV

	BM25	PF1	KLLM	PF1	DLH	PF1
TD	0.0888	0.0852,-4.12%	0.0607	0.0852,+40.4%†	0.0833	0.0852,+2.28%
NP	0.4158	0.4329,+4.11%	0.3961	0.4329,+9.29%	0.3872	0.4329,+11.8%†
HP	0.4091	0.4231,+3.43%	0.4022	0.4231,+5.21%	0.4146	0.4231,+2.05%

To support this hypothesis, we again plot the retrieval performance of BM25 against its parameter b. We do not plot for k_1 and KLLM's parameter μ for space reason, as these two parameters have similar observations. From Figure 4, we can see that BM25 indeed suffers from the parameter sensitivity issue, as its parameter b has only a small range of "safe" values. Also, its optimal setting varies for different search tasks, from approximately 0.95 for topic distillation and homepage finding, 0.70 for named-page finding, and 0.35 for ad-hoc search. This supports our argument that it is not reliable to use a fixed parameter setting in practice. On the other hand, PF1 can provide near optimal retrieval performance in most cases without the need for parameter tuning.

In summary, we have evaluated the PF1 model by extensive experiments on four standard TREC test collections for a variety of search tasks that are different in nature. The experimental results can be summarized as follows. For the adhoc tasks without query expansion (see Section 5.1), it is encouraging to find out that the retrieval performance of PF1 is comparable with the state-of-the-art BM25 and KL-divergence language model (KLLM), and provide statistically significant improvement over DLH. For the adhoc tasks with query expansion (see Section 5.2), PF1 performs equally well to KLLM, and outperform BM25 and DLH. For the three non-adhoc tasks on DOTGOV (see Section 5.3), PF1 has overall comparable retrieval performance with BM25, and outperforms KLLM and DLH for the topic distillation and named-page finding tasks, respectively.

6   Conclusions and Future Work

We have revisited the parameter free hyper-geometric model in order to provide an alternative explanation on how the model is reduced to the binomial distribution. We follow a different approach for the *tf* weight estimation by assuming the non-uniform document priors, which depend on the actual lengths of the documents. Based on this assumption, we show that DLH can be seen as the classical PL2 model with non-uniform document priors without length normalization. Thus, we suggest that since DLH consists of only the normalized *tf* weight, it can be extended by adding an *idf* component which is also parameter free. Extensive experiments on the standard TREC test collections demonstrate the effectiveness of the new model, called PF1, which combines the *tf* weight based on the non-uniform document priors and BM25's *idf*.

In the future, we plan to further evaluate PF1 on other test collections for other search tasks, such as the real-time Twitter search in the TREC microblog track and the Web search tasks on the large-scale ClueWeb 09 collection, where the relevance judgments are relatively shallow compared to the test collections used in this paper. We also plan to extend PF1 model by proposing a term proximity component that take the adjacency between query terms into consideration. We also plan to extend this work to the language modelling based on the hyper-geometric distribution such as [12].

Acknowledgements. This work is supported in part by the National Natural Science Foundation of China (61103131/F020511), the President Fund of GUCAS (Y15101FY00 /Y25102HN00), and the National Key Technology R&D Program of China (2012BAH23B03).

References

1. Amati, G.: Frequentist and bayesian approach to information retrieval. In: Lalmas, M., MacFarlane, A., Rüger, S.M., Tombros, A., Tsikrika, T., Yavlinsky, A. (eds.) ECIR 2006. LNCS, vol. 3936, pp. 13–24. Springer, Heidelberg (2006)
2. Amati, G., van Rijsbergen, C.J.: Probabilistic models of information retrieval based on measuring the divergence from randomness. ACM Trans. Inf. Syst. 20(4), 357–389 (2002)
3. Craswell, N., Hawking, D.: Overview of the TREC-2003 Web track. In: Proceedings of the Thirteenth Text REtrieval Conference (TREC 2004), Gaithersburg, MD (2004)
4. Hui, K., He, B., Luo, T., Wang, B.: A comparative study of pseudo relevance feedback for ad-hoc retrieval. In: Amati, G., Crestani, F. (eds.) ICTIR 2011. LNCS, vol. 6931, pp. 318–322. Springer, Heidelberg (2011)
5. Lavrenko, V., Croft, W.B.: Relevance-based language models. In: SIGIR, pp. 120–127 (2001)
6. Lv, Y., Zhai, C.: A comparative study of methods for estimating query language models with pseudo feedback. In: CIKM, pp. 1895–1898 (2009)
7. Ounis, I., Amati, G., Plachouras, V., He, B., Macdonald, C., Johnson, D.: Terrier information retrieval platform. In: Losada, D.E., Fernández-Luna, J.M. (eds.) ECIR 2005. LNCS, vol. 3408, pp. 517–519. Springer, Heidelberg (2005)
8. Renyi, A.: Foundations of probability. Holden-Day San Francisco (1970)
9. Robertson, S.E., Sparck-Jones, K.: Relevance weighting of search terms. Journal of the American Society for Information Science 27, 129–146 (1976)
10. Robertson, S.E., Walker, S.: Some simple effective approximations to the 2-Poisson model for probabilistic weighted retrieval. In: SIGIR, pp. 232–241 (1994)
11. Robertson, S.E., Walker, S., Hancock-Beaulieu, M., Gatford, M., Payne, A.: Okapi at TREC-4. In: TREC (1995)
12. Tsagkias, M., de Rijke, M., Weerkamp, W.: Hypergeometric language models for republished article finding. In: SIGIR, pp. 485–494 (2011)
13. Voorhees, E.: TREC: Experiment and Evaluation in Information Retrieval. The MIT Press (2005)
14. Ye, Z., Huang, X., He, B., Lin, H.: York University at TREC 2009: Relevance feedback track. In: TREC, Gaithersburg, MD (2009)
15. Zhai, C.: Statistical language models for information retrieval: A critical review, 137–213 (2008)
16. Zhai, C., Lafferty, J.D., Lafferty, J.D.: A study of smoothing methods for language models applied to ad hoc information retrieval. In: SIGIR, pp. 334–342 (2001)

A Nonparametric N-Gram Topic Model with Interpretable Latent Topics*

Shoaib Jameel and Wai Lam

Department of Systems Engineering and Engineering Management,
The Chinese University of Hong Kong
{msjameel,wlam}@se.cuhk.edu.hk

Abstract. Most nonparametric topic models such as Hierarchical Dirichlet Processes, when viewed as an infinite-dimensional extension to the Latent Dirichlet Allocation, rely on the bag-of-words assumption. They thus lose the semantic ordering of the words inherent in the text which can give an extra leverage to the computational model. We present a new nonparametric topic model that not only maintains the word order in the topic discovery process, but also generates topical n-gram words leading to more interpretable latent topics in the family of the nonparametric topic models. Our experimental results show an improved performance over the current state-of-the-art topic models in document modeling and generating n-gram words in topics.

Keywords: Bayesian Nonparametrics, N-gram words, Perplexity, N-gram topic model, Collocations.

1 Introduction

Nonparametric topic models such as Hierarchical Dirichlet Processes (HDP) [28], when viewed as an infinite-dimensional extension to the fixed-dimension Latent Dirichlet Allocation (LDA) model [4] and [3], have gained immense popularity in recent years because in that one does not need to explicitly provide the number of topics apriori. However, a limitation of the HDP model is that it loses important structural information present in the text leading to undesirable effects such as producing ambiguous terms in topics. For example, due to its bag-of-words assumption, HDP discovers unigrams such as "networks" in a topic which does not seem to be that insightful. Instead finding n-gram words can convey more interpretable meaning to readers [31] and [23], for example, "neural networks". Also, word order is important to many aspects of linguistic processing [26] and [21]. Related works in parametric topic modeling, such as the bigram topic model (BTM) [30], the LDA Collocation model [18] (LDACOL), the topical n-gram model [31] (TNG), which maintain the order of the words in the document have shown to perform better than the bag-of-words counterpart models.

---

* The work described in this paper is substantially supported by grants from the Research Grant Council of the Hong Kong Special Administrative Region, China (Project Code: CUHK413510) and the Direct Grant of the Faculty of Engineering, CUHK (Project Code: 2050522). This work is also affiliated with the CUHK MoE-Microsoft Key Laboratory of Human-centric Computing and Interface Technologies.

R.E. Banchs et al. (Eds.): AIRS 2013, LNCS 8281, pp. 74–85, 2013.

Processing documents by keeping the word ordering intact, such as the existing parametric topic models mentioned earlier, does incorporate additional computational burden, nonetheless it gives an upper-hand over traditional bag-of-words topic models [19]. One useful advantage is to discover more interpretable latent topics. However, one common limitation of these existing parametric n-gram topic models which consider word order is that they require the number of topics to be supplied by the user in advance. In reality a user is completely ignorant about the number of topics that may uncover the true latent structure of the corpus. It is therefore more reasonable to develop a nonparametric model which can automatically infer a desirable number of latent topics via the data characteristics inherent in a collection of text documents.

We develop a new nonparametric topic model, which we name as NHDP, by extending the HDP model so that word order is taken into consideration during the topic discovery process. Our proposed NHDP model not only maintains the document's word order information, but also discovers topical n-gram words based on context. By generating n-gram in topics helps in better topic interpretation because n-gram words are more insightful to the reader than unigram words [23].

2   Related Work

Considering the importance of the word order in nonparametric setting is becoming to attract attention. For example, Goldwater et al. [15] presented two nonparametric word segmentation models where one of the models, called the bigram HDP model, maintains the ordering in text. Related extensions are described in [5] and [14]. They are well catered to the word segmentation task. In their model, contextual dependencies are distributed according to a Dirichlet Process (DP) specific to the words in a document and it closely resembles the hierarchical Pitman-Yor processes model [27] and [16]. In [11], the author introduced a nonparametric model that can extract phrasal terms based on the mutual rank relation. This model first extracts phrases and subsequently ranks them. It employs a heuristic measure for the identification of phrasal terms. In [25], the authors introduced the notion of extension pattern, which is a formalization of the idea of extending lexical association measures defined for bigrams. In [33], the authors presented a Bayesian nonparametric model for symbolic chord sequences. Their model is designed to handle n-grams in chord sequences for music information retrieval. Our proposed model is significantly different than the ones mentioned above. First, our model is an n-gram nonparametric topic discovery model capturing word dependencies in text. Consequently, it can generate more interpretable topics.

Some nonparametric language models have been proposed recently which maintain the word order, for example, [27], [32], etc. But there are differences between language models and topic models [29]. For example, language models do not discover topics, which typically is a probability distribution over words. Also, language models focus on representing local linguistic structure, as expressed by word order [8] whereas topic models focus on finding topics.

Parametric and nonparametric syntax based models also capture word dependencies using an extra layer of Hidden Markov Model (HMM). But they are different from our model in that we do not incorporate a HMM model in our NHDP model to capture word dependencies. For example, in [17] the authors introduced a parametric Bayesian topic model which can not only capture the semantic information inherent in the text, but also capture the syntax in the document by introducing an extra layer of HMM in the model. This model was later extended to a nonparametric setting [10] and [6] where the author introduced HDP model instead of its parametric counterpart, Latent Dirichlet Allocation (LDA) [4]. In [13], the authors presented the sticky HDP-HMM model for speaker diarization. Their model segments a piece of audio discourse using an augmented HDP-HMM that provides effective control over the switching rate in the audio data. The existing HMM based topic models are designed to capture the syntactic classes such as part-of-speech. In contrast, our model does not assume that syntax information is available.

Some existing parametric topic models discover n-gram words. But these models assume that the number of topics is known in advance. We believe that this is a major shortcoming because the desirable number of topics that describes the collection is typically not known in advance. One approach to solving this problem is to train several models with different numbers of topics and choose the one that performs reasonably well according to a performance measure [9]. But this is cumbersome and time consuming [10]. Note that selecting less number of topics than what the data can actually accommodate will result in under-fitting whereas selecting more number of topics will result in over-fitting. The LDA model [4], which is a basic parametric topic model, assumes "exchangeability" [1] among the words in the document. In [18], the authors proposed an extension to the LDA model, called the LDA Collocation (LDACOL) model. This model introduces a set of random variables which capture whether words in order form collocations. Each word has a topic assignment and a collocation assignment. The collocation variable can take on two values, namely, 0 and 1. If the collocation variable is 1, then the word is generated from the distribution based on just the previous word. Otherwise, the word is generated from a distribution associated with its topic. In this way, the model can generate both unigram and bigram words. Wang et al. [31] extended the LDA Collocation model and proposed the topical n-gram (TNG) model which makes it possible to decide whether to form a bigram for the same two consecutive words depending on their nearby context. However, this model suffers from some drawbacks such as words within a topical n-gram do not share the same topic. Moreover, the topic-specific bigram distributions share no probability mass between each other or with the unigram distributions. These shortcomings were addressed recently in another parametric topic model [23] based on the Hierarchical Pitman-Yor Processes [27]. However, their model becomes overly complex and it is inefficient for handling large datasets. Wallach in [30] proposed the bigram topic model which is an extension to the LDA and it maintains the word order in the document, but the model only generates bigrams in topics. In [20] Johnson described a connection between probabilistic context-free grammars PCFG and the LDA model. This paper shows how the LDA model can be expressed as a PCFG. The LDA model is employed to generate collocations of words apart from applying the model in other natural language processing task. The difference between Johnson's work in [20] and our paper is that we generate word collocations in a nonparametric setting whereas Johnson used the LDA model to generate word collocations. Recently, in [22] the authors presented a study where they considered bigrams as a single token and used bigrams as features to be given to a topic model. The authors presented extensive experiments how collocations can help improve a topic model in empirical evaluations. Their method has a limitation in that one has to manually supply bigrams to the model rather than the bigrams automatically discovered by the model itself. In [2] the authors presented an application of topic models to recommender systems. The authors presented topic models where the models maintain the ordering of the words in sequence and in turn obtain better empirical results in their experimental analysis. However, their model does not generate n-gram words based on the co-occurrences in the data.

3   Background

In order to circumvent the limitation prevalent in parametric topic models, Teh et al. [28] proposed the Hierarchical Dirichlet Processes (HDP) model. This model can be regarded as a nonparametric version of the LDA model [10]. We will mainly describe the HDP model in the context of topic modeling.

HDP is a nonparametric Bayesian model which is a Bayesian model on an ∞-dimensional parameter space. For nonparametric models, the number of parameters grows with the sample size. Here we give a succinct description of the HDP model whose one of the applications is also topic modeling. Inquisitive readers are requested to consult [28] for more details.

Given a collection of text documents, HDP is characterized by a set of random probability measures G_d for each document d in the collection. In addition, a global random probability measure G_0 which itself is drawn from a Dirichlet Process (DP) with the base probability measure H. The global measure G_0 selects all the possible topics from the base measure H, and then each G_d draws the topics necessary for the document d from G_0. The model is defined as:

$$G_0|\gamma, H \sim \mathbf{DP}(\gamma, H)$$
$$G_d|\alpha, G_0 \sim \mathbf{DP}(\alpha, G_0)$$
$$z_{di}|G_d \sim G_d$$
$$w_{di}|z_{di} \sim \mathbf{Multinomial}(z_{di})$$

where γ and α are the concentration parameters that govern the variability around G_0 and G_d respectively. The base probability measure H provides the prior distribution for the factors or topics z_{di}. Each z_{di} is a factor corresponding to a single observation w_{di} which is the word at the position i in the document d.

One perspective associated with the HDP mechanism can be expressed by the Chinese Restaurant Franchise (CRF) [28] which is an extension of the Chinese Restaurant Process (CRP). In order to describe sharing among the groups, the notion of "franchise" has been introduced that serves the same set of dishes globally. When applied to text data, each restaurant corresponds to a document. Each customer corresponds to a word. Each dish corresponds to a topic. A customer sits at a table, one dish is ordered for that table and all subsequent customers who sit at that table share that dish. The dishes are sampled from the base distribution H which corresponds to discrete topic distributions.

Multiple tables in multiple restaurants can serve the same dish. The factor values are shared both between and amongst documents. For a complete mathematical derivation of the CRF metaphor, we direct the reader to review [28].

4   Our N-Gram HDP Model (NHDP)

4.1   Model Description

We describe our n-gram nonparametric topic model, called NHDP, which is an extension to the basic HDP model described in Section 3. Unlike the basic HDP model, our proposed NHDP model is no longer invariant to the reshuffling of words in a document.

We introduce a set of binary random variables $\mathbf{x}$ which we term as the concatenation indicator variable that assume either of the two values which are 0 or 1. This variable indicates whether two words in consecutive order can be concatenated or not. Note that NHDP uses the first order Markov assumption on the words. There are two assignments per word w_{di} at position i in the document d, and $1 \leq i \leq N_d$ where N_d is the number of words (unigrams) in the document d. One assignment is the topic and the other assignment is the concatenation indicator variable x_{di} which relates to whether the word w_{di} can be concatenated with the previous word $w_{d,i-1}$. If $x_{di} = 1$, then w_{di} is part of a concatenation and the word is generated from a distribution that is dependent only on $w_{d,i-1}$. x_{di} is drawn from $P(x_{di}|w_{d,i-1})$. On the other hand, if $x_{di} = 0$, then w_{di} is generated from the distribution associated with its topic. We assume that the first indicator variable x_{d1} in a document is observed and set to 1, and only a unigram is allowed at the beginning of the document. In fact, we can also enforce other constraints in the model. Some examples are: no concatenation is allowed for sentence or paragraph boundary, only a unigram is allowed after a stopword is removed from that position, etc.

Note that NHDP can capture word dependencies in the document. The conditional probability $P(w_{di}|w_{d,i-1})$ can be written as:

$$P(w_{di}|w_{d,i-1}) = P(w_{di}|w_{d,i-1}, x_{di} = 1)P(x_{di} = 1|w_{d,i-1}) + P(w_{di}|w_{d,i-1}, x_{di} = 0)$$
$$P(x_{di} = 0|w_{d,i-1})$$
$$(1)$$

We can observe that $P(w_{di}|w_{d,i-1}, x_{di} = 0)$ can be computed using the basic HDP model. The full definition of our NHDP model is given as follows:

1   $G_0|\gamma, H \sim \mathbf{DP}(\gamma, H)$;
2   $G_d|\alpha, G_0 \sim \mathbf{DP}(\alpha, G_0)$;
3   $z_{di}|G_d \sim G_d$;
4   $x_{di}|w_{d,i-1} \sim \mathbf{Bernoulli}(\psi_{w_{d,i-1}})$;
5   **if** $x_{di} = 1$ **then**
6   $\quad | \quad w_{di}|w_{d,i-1} \sim \mathbf{Multinomial}(\sigma_{w_{d,i-1}})$
7   **end**
8   **else**
9   $\quad | \quad w_{di}|z_{di} \sim F(z_{di})$
10 **end**

Note that in the definition of our model the hyperprior of σ is δ. The hyperprior value of ψ is ϵ. Just as in the HDP model described earlier, the distribution $F(z_{di})$, is the Multinomial distribution in line 9 in the above generative process. We can obtain higher order n-grams by concatenating the current concatenated words with the next n-gram based on the value obtained by the next concatenation indicator variable. Although our model does not directly generate topic-wise n-grams, an n-gram can be associated with a topic via a simple post-processing strategy. One strategy is to take the topic of the first term in the n-gram as the topic for the whole n-gram. This technique has been used in [24] for the LDACOL model. Another strategy is to assume the topic of the n-gram as the most common topic occurring in the words involving in that n-gram [24].

4.2 Posterior Inference

Our inference scheme is based on the Chinese Restaurant Franchise scheme [28] with some modifications. In our scheme, we have to handle two different conditions. The first condition is concerned with $x_{di} = 0$ whereas the second condition is concerned with $x_{di} = 1$. Note that for some observed x_{di}, only z_{di} needs to be drawn.

In the document modeling setting, each document is referred to as a restaurant and words in the document are referred to as customers. The set of documents share a global menu of topics. The words in the document are divided into groups, each of which shares a table. Each table is associated with a topic and words around each table are associated with the table's topic.

The First Condition: The first condition refers to $x_{di} = 0$. In this setting, most of the modeling will resemble the HDP model as presented in [28], but in our case we need to derive updates for the HDP model for text data.

We will sample t_{di} which is the table index for each word w_{di} at the position i in the document d. We will then sample k_{dt} which is the topic index variable for each table t in d. $k_{d\hat{t}}$ is the new topic index variable created for a new table. Note that we will only sample the index variables here rather than the distributions themselves [10]. We define $\mathbf{w}$ as $(w_{di} : \forall d, i)$ and $\mathbf{w}_{dt}$ as $(w_{di} : \forall i$ with $t_{di} = t)$, $\mathbf{t}$ as $(t_{di} : \forall d, i)$ and $\mathbf{k}$ as $(k_{dt} : \forall d, t)$. In addition, we also define $\mathbf{x}$ as $(x_{di} : \forall d, i)$. When a superscript is attached to a set of variables or count, for example, $(\mathbf{k}^{-dt}, \mathbf{t}^{-di})$, it means that the variables corresponding to the superscripted index are removed from the set or from the calculation of the count. Each word whose $x_{di} = 0$ is assumed to be drawn from $F(z)$ whose density is written as $f(.|\phi)$ (f is just one part obtained from F). This density is the multinomial distribution with the parameter ϕ. The likelihood of w_{di} for $t_{di} = t$ where t is an existing table, denoted as $f_k^{-w_{di}}(w_{di})$, is the conditional density of w_{di} given all words in topic k except w_{di}:

$$f_k^{-w_{di}}(w_{di}) = \frac{\int f(w_{di}|\phi_k) \prod_{d'i' \neq di, z_{d'i'} = k} f(w_{d'i'}|\phi_k) h(\phi_k) d\phi_k}{\int \prod_{d'i' \neq di, z_{d'i'} = k} f(w_{d'i'}|\phi_k) h(\phi_k) d\phi_k} \quad (2)$$

where h is a probability density function of H and H is a Dirichlet distribution over a fixed vocabulary of size V. $h(.)$ is the Dirichlet distribution with the parameter η. ϕ_k is one of the global topics with which each table is associated which is indicated with a table-specific topic index k_{dt}. Furthermore, Equation 2 can be simplified as:

$$f_k^{\neg w_{di}}(w_{di} = \vartheta) = \frac{n_{..k}^{\neg w_{di},\vartheta} + \eta}{n_{..k}^{\neg w_{di}} + V\eta} \tag{3}$$

where $n_{..k}^{\neg w_{di}}$ is the number of words belonging to the topic k in the corpus whose $x_{di} = 0$ excluding w_{di}. $n_{..k}^{\neg w_{di},\vartheta}$ is the number of times the word ϑ is assigned with the topic k excluding w_{di} and whose x_{di} is 0. Furthermore, V is the number of words in the vocabulary which is typically fixed and is known. The likelihood of w_{di} for $t_{di} = \hat{t}$, where $\hat{t}$ is the new table being sampled, is written as:

$$P(w_{di}|t_{di} = \hat{t}, \mathbf{t}^{\neg di}, \mathbf{k}) = \sum_{k=1}^{K} \frac{m_{.k}}{m_{..} + \gamma} f_k^{\neg w_{di}}(w_{di}) + \frac{\gamma}{m_{..} + \gamma} f_{\hat{k}}^{\neg w_{di}}(w_{di}) \tag{4}$$

where $\hat{k}$ is the new topic being sampled. $m_{.k}$ is the number of tables belonging to the topic k in the corpus. $m_{..}$ is the total number of tables in the corpus. $f_{\hat{k}}^{\neg w_{di}}(w_{di}) = \int f(w_{di}|\phi)h(\phi)d\phi$ is the prior density of w_{di}. γ is the concentration parameter as described in Section 3. Since we follow the standard Chinese Restaurant Franchise sampling procedure, the conditional density for t_{di} for Gibbs sampling, the conditional densities for $k_{d\hat{t}}$ and k_{dt} can be found in [10].

The Second Condition: The second condition refers to $x_{di} = 1$. We only need to sample the probability of a topic in a document as the current word w_{di} is generated by the previous word $w_{d,i-1}$. In order to do this, we proceed as follows:

$$P(k_{dt} = k|\mathbf{t}, \mathbf{k}^{\neg dt}) \propto \begin{cases} m_{.k}^{\neg dt} f_k^{\neg \mathbf{w}_{dt}}(\mathbf{w}_{dt}) & \text{if } k \text{ is already used} \\ \gamma f_{\hat{k}}^{\neg \mathbf{w}_{dt}}(\mathbf{w}_{dt}) & \text{if } k = \hat{k} \end{cases} \tag{5}$$

where $f_k^{\neg \mathbf{w}_{dt}}(\mathbf{w}_{dt})$, which is the conditional density of $\mathbf{w}_{dt}$ given all words associated with the topic k leaving out $\mathbf{w}_{dt}$ is defined as:

$$f_k^{\neg \mathbf{w}_{dt}}(\mathbf{w}_{dt}) = \frac{\Gamma(n_{..k}^{\neg \mathbf{w}_{dt}} + V\eta)}{\Gamma(n_{..k}^{\neg \mathbf{w}_{dt}} + n^{\mathbf{w}_{dt}} + V\eta)} \times \frac{\prod_{\vartheta} \Gamma(n_{..k}^{\neg \mathbf{w}_{dt},\vartheta} + n^{\mathbf{w}_{dt},\vartheta} + \eta)}{\prod_{\vartheta} \Gamma(n_{..k}^{\neg \mathbf{w}_{dt},\vartheta} + \eta)} \tag{6}$$

where $n^{\mathbf{w}_{dt}}$ is the total number of words at the table t whose $x_{di} = 0$. $n^{\mathbf{w}_{dt},\vartheta}$ is the number of times the word ϑ appears at the table t with the assignment $x_{di} = 0$. $n_{..k}^{\neg \mathbf{w}_{dt}}$ is the number of words belonging to topic k in the corpus except $\mathbf{w}_{dt}$.

Sampling the Concatenation Indicator Variables: We present how to sample the values of the indicator variables. The idea is to compute the probabilities of how often two words consecutively occur in sequence. Then based on the probability value, the indicator variable is set to either 0 or 1. Let $n_0^{w_{d,i-1}}$ and $n_1^{w_{d,i-1}}$ be the number of times word $w_{d,i-1}$ has been drawn from a topic or formed a part of a concatenation respectively and all counts exclude the current case. ϵ_0 and ϵ_1 are the priors of the binomial distribution. $n_{w_{di}}^{w_{d,i-1}}$ is the number of times the word w_{di} comes after the word $w_{d,i-1}$. $n_{..k}^{\neg w_{di},\vartheta}$ and $n_{..k}^{\neg w_{di}}$ have been defined in Equation 3.

$$P(x_{di} = 0 | \mathbf{x}_{\neg di}, \mathbf{w}, \mathbf{k}) \propto \frac{n_0^{w_{d,i-1}} + \epsilon_0}{\sum_{c=0}^{1} n_c^{w_{d,i-1}} + \epsilon_0 + \epsilon_1} \times \frac{n_{..k}^{\neg w_{di},\vartheta} + \eta}{n_{..k}^{\neg w_{di}} + V\eta} \qquad (7)$$

$$P(x_{di} = 1 | \mathbf{x}_{\neg di}, \mathbf{w}, \mathbf{k}) \propto \frac{n_1^{w_{d,i-1}} + \epsilon_1}{\sum_{c=0}^{1} n_c^{w_{d,i-1}} + \epsilon_0 + \epsilon_1} \times \frac{n_{w_{di}}^{w_{d,i-1}} + \delta}{\sum_{v=1}^{V} n_v^{w_{d,i-1}} + V\delta} \qquad (8)$$

where δ is same as described in Section 4.1.

5 Empirical Evaluation

5.1 Test Collections

We used several corpora in our experiments. One corpus is the NIPS[1] collection often used in the topic modeling literature. Note that the original raw NIPS corpus consists of 17 years of conference papers. But we supplemented this corpus by including some new raw NIPS documents[2] and it has 19 years of papers in total. Our NIPS collection consists of 2,741 documents comprising of 4,536,069 non-unique words and 94,961 words in the vocabulary. The second corpus is the Associated Press (AP) corpus. We have obtained this corpus from the LDA-C[3] package. This corpus consists of 2,243 documents with 38,631 words in the vocabulary. We also use one of the datasets from the 20 Newsgroups corpus for showing qualitative results. We have chosen the computer (indexed as "comp" available in the corpus) dataset from the 20 Newsgroups corpus. We removed stopwords[4] from the collections, but did not perform word stemming.

5.2 Comparative Methods

One of the comparative methods is the basic HDP model proposed in [28]. We also chose the LDACOL model proposed in [18] for our comparative study. This model can be regarded as a parametric version close to our model. In addition to our proposed full NHDP, we also investigated a variant of our model, where we set all $x_{di} = 1$. We call this model as Bi-NHDP in the experiments. Note that we do not expect the Bi-NHDP model to generate interpretable latent topics because it always generates bigrams just like the BTM [30] model. We do not compare with the TNG model [31] because the TNG model performs topic sampling for every word in a bigram. Neither our model nor LDACOL employ this sampling. Also we only chose strong closely related comparative methods here. It has already been demonstrated through quantitative analysis in [31] that the LDACOL model is more powerful than the BTM model. Also, in [30] it has been has shown that the BTM outperforms the LDA model in several quantitative experiments. Hence we do not compare our model with the BTM and the LDA models.

---

[1] http://www.cs.nyu.edu/~roweis/data.html
[2] http://ai.stanford.edu/~gal/Data/NIPS/
[3] http://www.cs.princeton.edu/~blei/topicmodeling.html
[4] http://jmlr.csail.mit.edu/papers/volume5/lewis04a/
  all-smart-stop-list/english.stop

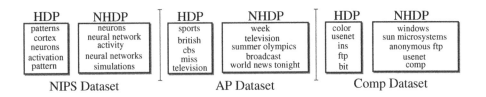

Fig. 1. Qualitative comparison of our model NHDP with the HDP model

5.3   Experimental Setup

The number of iterations for the Gibbs sampler for all models is 1,000. We have set $\delta = 0.1$, $\epsilon_0 = 0.1$, and $\epsilon_1 = 0.1$ which are the new parameters introduced in our model NHDP. We used a symmetric Dirichlet distribution with parameter of 0.5 for the prior H over topic distributions and the concentration parameters were set as $\gamma \sim$ Gamma$(1, 0.1)$ and $\alpha \sim$ Gamma$(1, 1)$ for our and the HDP models. η was set to 0.01. For the LDACOL model, following the notations described in [31], we set $\beta = 0.01$, $\alpha = 50/T$, $\gamma_0 = 0.1$, $\gamma_1 = 0.1$ and $\delta = 0.1$. Note that T is the number of topics which is pre-defined for the LDACOL model. The same hyperparameter values are also used in the LDACOL implementation available publicly[5]. Since the LDACOL model requires the number of topics to be supplied by the user, we conducted several runs by varying the number of topics and measured the performance at different number of topics. The best result value was chosen based on all values obtained.

5.4   Qualitative Results

We first show how our model generates more interpretable topics with topical n-grams. Here we employed a strategy that using the topic of the first word as the topic of the entire n-gram (refer Section 4.1 for more details). Our main comparative method for qualitative analysis is the HDP model which belongs to a family of nonparametric topic models. We manually chose top five words occurring with high probability in some topics. From Figure 1, we can see that compared to the HDP model, our NHDP model has generated words which are more coherent and has provided an extremely salient summary about "neural networks" in the NIPS collection, media related information obtained from the Associated Press (AP), and computer technology related words from the 20 Newsgroups computer dataset (denoted as "Comp Dataset" in Figure 1). The results show that our model has produced interpretable topics.

Both LDACOL and NHDP can generate bigrams such as "neural networks", etc. But the merit of NHDP lies in the fact that it does not require the number of topics to be specified explicitly by the user and it is automatically inferred from the data characteristics. Moreover, NHDP can produce topical n-grams, not only restricted to bigrams. We thus investigate how well they perform in some typical text analysis tasks, such as document modeling, as described next.

---

[5] http://psiexp.ss.uci.edu/research/programs_data/toolbox.htm

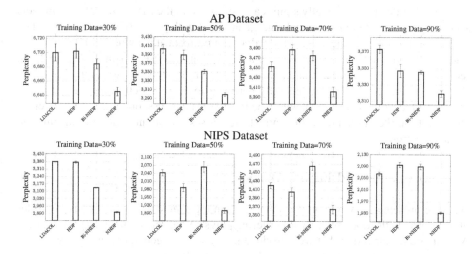

Fig. 2. Perplexity results for the AP and NIPS datasets

5.5 Document Modeling

Several works in the topic modeling literature have used perplexity analysis to compare the generalization ability of the model on unseen data as exemplified in [12]. Evaluation using perplexity is important for our model because it is well suited for models where word order in the document is maintained [7]. Generally the documents in the collection are treated as unlabeled. Thus, our goal is density estimation. We wish to achieve a high likelihood on the held-out test set. We first train the parameters of the model using a training set and subsequently the unseen data is fed to the learnt model in order to measure its generalization ability. A commonly used metric is the perplexity score. A lower perplexity score indicates better generalization performance. More formally, for a test set $\mathbf{D}$ consisting of D documents, the perplexity score is written as:

$$\text{Perplexity}(\mathbf{D}) = \exp\left\{ -\frac{\sum_{d=1}^{D} \log \text{P}(\mathbf{w}_d)}{\sum_{d=1}^{D} N_d} \right\} \tag{9}$$

where $\mathbf{w}_d$ are the words in the document d and N_d is the number of words in the document d.

We conducted perplexity analysis by experimenting on two datasets described earlier (AP and NIPS datasets). Perplexity analysis was conducted by running the Gibbs sampler 3 times each with 1,000 iterations and the average of the three perplexity values was taken. For all the datasets, we split the datasets randomly into two subsets each. One subset is the training set and the other subset is the testing set. We conducted several runs by varying the split proportion obtaining different amounts of the training set from 30% to 90% in steps of 20%. The purpose is to study how the models perform on different sizes of the training set.

From the results depicted in Figure 2, our model outperforms all comparative models in terms of generalizing on the unseen data. The computed average perplexity values for our NHDP model are statistically significant compared to the HDP and LDACOL models according to a two-tailed statistical significance test with $p < 0.05$ in all corpora. The variant of our model, namely, Bi-NHDP does not perform at par with our NHDP model. The LDACOL model also does not generalize well on the unseen data. In Figure 2, we see the effect of varying the training size on different models. For example, in the AP and NIPS datasets, our model generally performs extremely well in different training portions. One can note that even when the training data is less, our NHDP model generalizes well on the unseen data. In contrast, HDP loses important structural information in the document.

6   Conclusions and Future Work

We have presented a new nonparametric n-gram topic model that maintains the order of the words in the document. Word ordering plays a vital role in many linguistic tasks. An important innovation that we introduce in our work is generating n-gram words in topics where the number of topics need not be specified by the user. We have shown better quantitative performance in generalizing on an unseen data in two document collections. Our model generates more interpretable latent topics with n-gram words, whereas the existing nonparametric topic model HDP fails to generate such n-grams which are more insightful to a reader.

In the future, we intend to extend our model in generating n-gram words in topics over time as test collections in general are dynamic and topics change over time. Another direction which we wish to investigate is to incorporate text segmentation in a nonparametric setting and capturing n-gram words in each segment.

References

1. Aldous, D.: Exchangeability and related topics. Ecole d'Ete de Probabilites de Saint-Flour XIII-1983, pp. 1–198 (1985)
2. Barbieri, N., Manco, G., Ritacco, E., Carnuccio, M., Bevacqua, A.: Probabilistic topic models for sequence data. Machine Learning 93(1), 5–29 (2013)
3. Blei, D.M.: Probabilistic topic models. Commun. ACM 55(4), 77–84 (2012)
4. Blei, D., Ng, A., Jordan, M.: Latent Dirichlet allocation. JMLR 3, 993–1022 (2003)
5. Blunsom, P., Cohn, T., Goldwater, S., Johnson, M.: A note on the implementation of hierarchical Dirichlet processes. In: Proc. of ACL-IJCNLP, pp. 337–340 (2009)
6. Boyd-Graber, J., Blei, D.M.: Syntactic topic models. In: Proc. of NIPS (2008)
7. Caballero, K.L., Barajas, J., Akella, R.: The generalized Dirichlet distribution in enhanced topic detection. In: Proc. of CIKM, pp. 773–782 (2012)
8. Chen, S.F., Goodman, J.: An empirical study of smoothing techniques for language modeling. In: Proc. of ACL, pp. 310–318 (1996)
9. Claeskens, G., Hjort, N.: Model selection and model averaging. Cambridge Books (1993)
10. Darling, W.: Generalized Probabilistic Topic and Syntax Models for Natural Language Processing. Ph.D. thesis (2012)
11. Deane, P.: A nonparametric method for extraction of candidate phrasal terms. In: Proc. of ACL, pp. 605–613 (2005)
12. Fang, Y., Si, L., Somasundaram, N., Yu, Z.: Mining contrastive opinions on political texts using cross-perspective topic model. In: Proc. of WSDM, pp. 63–72 (2012)

13. Fox, E., Sudderth, E., Jordan, M., Willsky, A.: A sticky HDP-HMM with application to speaker diarization. The Annals of Applied Statistics 5(2A), 1020–1056 (2011)
14. Goldwater, S., Griffiths, T., Johnson, M.: A Bayesian framework for word segmentation: Exploring the effects of context. Cognition 112(1), 21–54 (2009)
15. Goldwater, S., Griffiths, T.L., Johnson, M.: Contextual dependencies in unsupervised word segmentation. In: Proc. of ACL, pp. 673–680 (2006)
16. Goldwater, S., Griffiths, T., Johnson, M.: Interpolating between types and tokens by estimating power-law generators. In: Proc. of NIPS, vol. 18, p. 459 (2006)
17. Griffiths, T.L., Steyvers, M., Blei, D., Tenenbaum, J.: Integrating topics and syntax. In: Proc. of NIPS, vol. 17, pp. 537–544 (2005)
18. Griffiths, T., Steyvers, M., Tenenbaum, J.: Topics in semantic representation. Psychological Review 114(2), 211–244 (2007)
19. Gruber, A., Rosen-Zvi, M., Weiss, Y.: Hidden topic Markov models. In: Proc. of AISTATS (2007)
20. Johnson, M.: PCFGs, topic models, adaptor grammars and learning topical collocations and the structure of proper names. In: Proc. of ACL, pp. 1148–1157 (2010)
21. Kim, H.D., Park, D.H., Lu, Y., Zhai, C.: Enriching text representation with frequent pattern mining for probabilistic topic modeling. JASIST 49(1), 1–10 (2012)
22. Lau, J.H., Baldwin, T., Newman, D.: On collocations and topic models. ACM Trans. Speech Lang. Process. 10(3), 10:1–10:14 (2013)
23. Lindsey, R.V., Headden, W.P., Stipicevic, M.J.: A phrase-discovering topic model using hierarchical Pitman-Yor processes. In: Proc. of EMNLP, pp. 214–222 (2012)
24. McCallum, A., Wang, X.: A note on topical N-grams. Department of Computer Science, University of Massachusetts, Amherst (2005)
25. Petrović, S., Šnajder, J., Bašić, B.: Extending lexical association measures for collocation extraction. Computer Speech & Language 24(2), 383–394 (2010)
26. Steyvers, M., Griffiths, T.: Probabilistic topic models. Handbook of Latent Semantic Analysis 427(7), 424–440 (2007)
27. Teh, Y.: A hierarchical Bayesian language model based on Pitman-Yor processes. In: Proc. of ACL, pp. 985–992 (2006)
28. Teh, Y., Jordan, M., Beal, M., Blei, D.: Hierarchical Dirichlet processes. JASA 101(476), 1566–1581 (2006)
29. Wallach, H.M.: Structured topic models for language. Ph.D. thesis (2008)
30. Wallach, H.: Topic modeling: beyond bag-of-words. In: Proc. of ICML, pp. 977–984 (2006)
31. Wang, X., McCallum, A., Wei, X.: Topical N-grams: Phrase and topic discovery, with an application to information retrieval. In: Proc. of ICDM, pp. 697–702 (2007)
32. Wood, F., Teh, Y.W.: A hierarchical nonparametric Bayesian approach to statistical language model domain adaptation. Journal of Machine Learning 5, 607–614 (2009)
33. Yoshii, K., Goto, M.: A vocabulary-free infinity-gram model for nonparametric Bayesian chord progression analysis. In: Proc. of ISMIR (2011)

Extracting Categorical Topics from Tweets
Using Topic Model

Lei Zheng[1] and Kai Han[2]

[1] Shenzhen Institutes of Advanced Technology, Chinese Academy of Sciences, Shenzhen 518055, China
zhenglei@siat.ac.cn
[2] Shenzhen Graduate School, Harbin Institute of Technology, Shenzhen 518055, China
hankai@cs.hitsz.edu.cn

Abstract. Over the past few years, microblogging websites, such as Twitter, are growing increasingly popular. Different with traditional medias, tweets are structured data and with a lot of noisy words. Topic modeling algorithms for traditional medias have been studied well, but our understanding of Twitter still remains limited and few algorithms are specially designed to mine Twitter data according to its own characteristics. Previous studies usually employ only one type of topic to analyze hot topics of the Twitter community and are greatly affected by the large amount of noisy words in tweets. We have observed that, in the Twitter community, users tend to discuss two types of topics actually. One mainly focuses on their personal lives and the other on hot issues of the society. These two types of topics usually yield different distributions. In this paper, we introduce the Categorical Topic Model. This model incorporates the features of Twitter data to divide topics into two types in semantic and introduce a word distribution for background words to filter out noisy words. Our model is able to discover different types of topics efficiently, indicate which topics are interested by an user and find hot issues of the Twitter community. Employing the Gibbs sampling, we compare our model with Latent Dirichlet Allocation and Author Topic Model on the TREC2011 data set and examples of discovered public topics and personal topics are also discussed in our paper.

Keywords: Twitter, Topic Model, Gibbs Sampling.

1 Introduction

Twitter, as a microblogging website, is becoming more and more popular. The number of Twitter users has exceeded 500 million since July, 2012. The number of active users is over 200 million per month. The structure of Twitter contents is strictly constrained and it differs from the traditional medias in many aspects.

One tweet is much shorter than a traditional document and its length is strictly constrained to 140 words. So, only a little information is conveyed in a tweet and much of the content in a tweet is noisy. Because of these characteristics of Twitter data, traditional topic models, such as LDA, can not yield interpretable experiment results. From our observations of real tweets, users tend to discuss some public issues of the whole

R.E. Banchs et al. (Eds.): AIRS 2013, LNCS 8281, pp. 86–96, 2013.
© Springer-Verlag Berlin Heidelberg 2013

society or share their personal lives with their friends. Previous studies are unable to discover interests of each user and hot issues of the whole community since they usually treat all tweets as a whole to discover interests of all users.

To filter out noisy words, we introduce a background word distribution into our model. Moreover, we divide topics into two main types in semantics: personal topics and public topics. Personal topics are usually interested by several users and could strongly depict one user's personal interests, such as *autos* and *weight loss*, while public topics, such as *Boston marathon bombing*, are usually interested by the whole community and could strongly depict hot issues of the society.

Hashtag which is a word or phrase prefixed with the symbol # indicates the tweet is discussing a public topic. In the Twitter community, users are inclined to use a hashtag as a public topic label. So, in order to analyze these two categories of topics, the presence of hashtags is taken into account while selecting topic of one tweet in our model.

A novel topic model is proposed in this paper. Using a background word distribution, the proposed model can clearly extract public topics and personal topics separately. The potential useage of these two kinds of topic distributions is very great. For example, we can extract the hottest public topic using the public topic distribution. And we can also recommend the users of same interests to each other.

2   Related Works

Many algorithms for topic mining in text exist. An early solution for this problem is to transfer the text data into vectors and cluster with some traditional methods like K-means[1]. In the popular td-idf scheme[2], each document in the corpus is reduced to a fixed-length list of numbers, roughly corresponding to the frequency of appearance for a basic set of words within that document.

Later, the LSI model[3] uses the singular value decomposition (SVD) of the word-by-document matrix from td-idf to identify a subset of the feature space that captures the most variance. Probabilistic latent semantic indexing (pLSI)[4], which allows each document to contain multiple topics, has been introduce naturally.

Blei & Jordan proposed Latent Dirichlet Allocation (LDA) topic model in 2003 [5]. This is an unsupervised, statistical approach proposed for modeling text corpora by discovering latent semantic topics in large collections of text documents. LDA has become a standard tool in topic modeling. A number of extensions of LDA has been proposed. Because tweets are much shorter than the traditional text and with a lot of noisy words, traditional topic models do not work well with the Twitter data.

Few works has presented a systematic analysis of content on Twitter. [6] characterizes content on Twitter and other "Social Awareness Streams" via a manual coding of tweets into categories of varying specificity, from "Information Sharing" to "Self Promotion". Some have focused on modeling conversations on Twitter[7]. [8] has studied features of Twitter social network, such as topological and geographical properties, patterns of growth, and user behaviors. Ramage et al. applied Labeled Latent Dirichlet Allocation (Labeled LDA) model to Twitter context [9,10]. But, this method relies on hashtags and may lose topics without hashtags. In order to overcome the difficulty of short text in Twitter context, unlike traditional LDA model, [11] associated one tweet, rather than one word, with only one topic. Nevertheless, previous works equally analyze all topics as one type and can not discover personal interests of each user and public issues from the given corpus, the problem we approach here.

3   The Proposed Model

3.1   Preliminaries

A *vocabulary* consists of a set of V unique words in a set of tweets.

A *userlist* consists of a set of U unique users.

A *word* is the basic unit of data, which is an item from a vocabulary indexed by $\{1, ..., V\}$. The v_{th} word can be represented by a V-vector such that the v_{th} element is one and other elements are zero.

A *corpus* C is a collection of M tweets $C = \{w_1, w_2, ..., w_M\}$.

A tweet is divided into three parts:

- Text $w_m = \{w_{m1}, w_{m2}, ..., w_{mN}\}$ is a sequence of N words, where w_{mn} is the n_{th} word of the tweet text w_m in the sequence and N is the number of words in text w_m.
- Hashtag flag h is a Boolean variable denoting whether the tweet contains hashtags. If it contains, h denoted as one, otherwise zero.
- User u is a user number indexed by the userlist of the tweet. This variable indicates the author of the tweet.

A *topic* is a random variable z_n on $\{1, ..., K\}$ where n indicates the n_{th} word in the tweet and K is the number of topics.

Personal topic: topics focusing on personal life strongly depicts one user's interests.

Public topic: topics focusing on hot issues depicts the public's interests.

3.2   Categorical Topic Model

In our model, denoted as Θ and π, two latent variables representing personal topic distribution and public topic distribution are introduced. Besides, a background word distribution, denoted as ρ, is introduced to filter background words for all topics. Bayesian network of the proposed Categorical Topic Model is shown in Figure 1. Here, we introduce the following model parameters:

κ is a symmetric Dirichlet hyperparameter for personal topic mixtures and public topic mixtures.

η is a symmetric Dirichlet hyperparameter for words distribution.

α are symmetric Dirichlet hyperparameter for word distribution selection.

ψ is a Muiltnomial parameter to govern the process of selecting users.

And, seven latent variables of our model are introduced:

β_k is the Multinomial words distribution over topic k. It remains the same meaning with original LDA.

ρ is the Multinomial background words distribution.

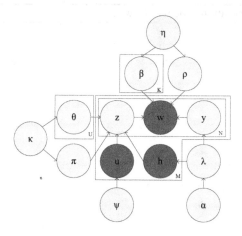

Fig. 1. Bayesian Network of Categorical Topic Model

π stands for public topic distribution of all users. $\pi = \{\pi_1, \pi_2, ..., \pi_K\}$.

z is the topic indicator of a word in the tweets of one user.

Θ is $U * K$ multinomial parameters matrix in which each column represents topic multinomial distribution of one user.

y is a binary parameter governing the selection of word distributions.

λ is a Bernoulli parameter which represents the probability of generating a word from the background word distribution.

We also introduce:

n_u^k is the number of words of user u under topic k in tweets without hashtags.

n_M^k is the number of words under topic k in tweets with hashtags.

n_k^v is the times that word v appears under topic k in all tweets.

n_M^v is the times that word v appears as a background word.

n_M^c is the number of background words(c=1) or the number of non-background words(c=0).

In the generating process, the topics of tweets are selected according to its presence of hashtags. When a tweet with hashtags is generated, its topic is selected from the public topic distribution. Otherwise, if one tweet without hashtags is generated, its topic is selected from the user's personal topic distribution. Variable y_{mn} is acted as a background word indicator. When it equals one, word w_{mn} is selected from β_k, otherwise ρ. Formal generating process of our model is in Algorithm 1.

3.3 Deriving a Gibbs Sampler for Our Model

According to Figure 1, when the corpus is given, **h** and **u** can be observed, prior λ and prior ψ are d-separated from the rest of the model. Given **h,u** and hyperparameters: α, κ, η, the joint probability of w,z,y can be computed with Equation 1.With the joint distribution of w,z,y, full conditional distribution for the current word can be

Algorithm 1. The Generation Process of Tweets

---

for $k = 1$ to K **do**
    draw $\beta_k \sim Dir(\eta)$
end for
draw $\rho \sim Dir(\eta)$
draw $\pi \sim Dir(\kappa)$
for $u = 1$ to U **do**
    draw $\theta_u \sim Dir(\kappa)$
end for
draw $\lambda \sim Dir(\alpha)$
for $w_m = w_1$ to w_M **do**
    draw $h_m \sim Multi(\lambda)$
    draw $u_m \sim Multi(\psi)$
    for $w_{mn} = w_{m1}$ to w_{mN} **do**
        if $h_m = 1$ **then**
            draw $z_{mn} \sim Multi(\pi)$
        else
            draw $z_{mn} \sim Multi(\theta_{u_m})$
        end if
        draw $y_{mn} \sim Multi(\lambda)$
        if $y_{mn} = 1$ **then**
            draw $w_{mn} \sim Multi(\beta_{z_{mn}})$
        else
            draw $w_{mn} \sim Multi(\rho)$
        end if
    end for
end for

---

derived as Equation 2 by using Euler integration and one property of Gamma function $\Gamma(x+1) = x\Gamma(x)$.

$$
\begin{aligned}
&p(\boldsymbol{w}, \boldsymbol{z}, \boldsymbol{y} | \boldsymbol{h}, \boldsymbol{u}, \boldsymbol{\kappa}, \boldsymbol{\eta}, \boldsymbol{\alpha}) \\
&= p(\boldsymbol{z} | \boldsymbol{\kappa}, \boldsymbol{h}, \boldsymbol{u}) p(\boldsymbol{w} | \boldsymbol{\eta}, \boldsymbol{y}) p(\boldsymbol{y} | \boldsymbol{\alpha}) \\
&= \int \prod_{u=1}^{U} \frac{\Gamma(\sum_{k=1}^{K}\kappa_k)}{\prod_{k=1}^{K}\Gamma(\kappa_k)} \prod_{k=1}^{K} \theta_{u,k}^{n_u^k+\kappa_k-1} d\theta \int \frac{\Gamma(\sum_{k=1}^{K}\kappa_k)}{\prod_{k=1}^{K}\Gamma(\kappa_k)} \prod_{k=1}^{K} \pi_k^{n_M^k+\kappa_k-1} d\pi \\
&\quad \int \prod_{k=1}^{K} \frac{\Gamma(\sum_{v=1}^{V}\eta_v)}{\prod_{v=1}^{V}\Gamma(\eta_v)} \prod_{v=1}^{V} \beta_{k,v}^{n_k^v+\eta_v-1} d\beta \int \frac{\Gamma(\sum_{v=1}^{V}\eta_v)}{\prod_{v=1}^{V}\Gamma(\eta_v)} \prod_{v=1}^{V} \rho_v^{n_v^v+\eta_v-1} d\rho \\
&\quad \int \frac{\Gamma(\sum_{c=1}^{2}\alpha_c)}{\prod_{c=1}^{2}\Gamma(\alpha_c)} \prod_{c=1}^{2} \lambda_c^{n_M^c+\alpha_c-1} d\lambda
\end{aligned}
\tag{1}
$$

$$
\begin{aligned}
&p(z_{m,n}, y_{m,n} | \boldsymbol{z}_{\neg(m,n)}, \boldsymbol{y}_{\neg(m,n)}, \boldsymbol{w}, \boldsymbol{h}, \boldsymbol{u}, \boldsymbol{\alpha}, \boldsymbol{\kappa}, \boldsymbol{\eta}) = \frac{p(\boldsymbol{z}, \boldsymbol{w}, \boldsymbol{y} | \boldsymbol{h}, \boldsymbol{u}, \boldsymbol{\alpha}, \boldsymbol{\kappa}, \boldsymbol{\eta})}{p(\boldsymbol{z}_{\neg(m,n)}, \boldsymbol{w}, \boldsymbol{y}_{\neg(m,n)} | \boldsymbol{h}, \boldsymbol{u}, \boldsymbol{\alpha}, \boldsymbol{\kappa}, \boldsymbol{\eta})} \\
&\propto \frac{p(\boldsymbol{z}, \boldsymbol{w}, \boldsymbol{y} | \boldsymbol{h}, \boldsymbol{u}, \boldsymbol{\alpha}, \boldsymbol{\kappa}, \boldsymbol{\eta})}{p(\boldsymbol{z}_{\neg(m,n)}, \boldsymbol{w}_{\neg(m,n)}, \boldsymbol{y}_{\neg(m,n)} | \boldsymbol{h}, \boldsymbol{u}, \boldsymbol{\alpha}, \boldsymbol{\kappa}, \boldsymbol{\eta})} = \frac{n_{u_m,\neg(m,n)}^{z_{m,n}}+\kappa_{z_{m,n}}-1}{\sum_{k=1}^{K} n_{u_m,\neg(m,n)}^{k}+\kappa_k-1} \frac{n_{M,\neg(m,n)}^{z_{m,n}}+\kappa_{z_{m,n}}-1}{\sum_{k=1}^{K} n_{M,\neg(m,n)}^{k}+\kappa_k-1} \\
&\quad \frac{n_{z_{m,n},\neg(m,n)}^{w_{m,n}}+\eta_{w_{m,n}}-1}{\sum_{v=1}^{V} n_{z_{m,n},\neg(m,n)}^{v}+\eta_v-1} \frac{n_{M,\neg(m,n)}^{w_{m,n}}+\eta_{w_{m,n}}-1}{\sum_{v=1}^{V} n_{M,\neg(m,n)}^{v}+\eta_v-1} \\
&\quad \frac{n_{M,\neg(m,n)}^{y_{m,n}}+\alpha_{y_{m,n}}-1}{\sum_{c=1}^{2} n_{M,\neg(m,n)}^{c}+\alpha_c-1}
\end{aligned}
\tag{2}
$$

If one further manipulates the above formula , one can turn them into separated update equations for the topic and the background word indicator of each token. With the Gibbs updating rule, topic distribution and word distribution can be derived as Equation 3, Equation 4 , Equation 5 and Equation 6.

$$\theta_{uk} = \frac{n_u^k + \kappa_k - 1}{\sum_{k=1}^{K} n_{u_d}^k + \alpha_k - 1} \tag{3}$$

$$\pi_k = \frac{n_M^k + \kappa_k - 1}{\sum_{k=1}^{K} n_M^k + \kappa_k - 1} \tag{4}$$

$$\beta_{kv} = \frac{n_k^v + \eta_v - 1}{\sum_{t=1}^{V} n_k^t + \eta_v - 1} \tag{5}$$

$$\rho_v = \frac{n_M^v + \eta_v - 1}{\sum_{t=1}^{V} n_M^t + \eta_v - 1} \tag{6}$$

Algorithm 2. Sampling Algorithm

Require:
  Corpus $C = \{w_1, ..., w_M\}$
  α, κ, η
Ensure:
  Public topic distribution π
  Personal topic distribution θ
  Topic word distribution β Background word distribution ρ
  repeat
    initialize each word w_{mn} in corpus C with a random topic and a background word indicator.
    for $w_m = w_1$ to w_M **do**
      for $w_{mn} = w_{11}$ to w_{mN} **do**
        Sample its topic and background word indicator
        update $n_u^k, n_M^k, n_k^v, n_M^c$
      end for
    end for
  until converged
  compute π, θ, β, ρ by Eq. 3, Eq. 4, Eq. 5 and Eq. 6

Because the exact inference of LDA is intractable, Heinrich introduced Gibbs sampling for approximate inference [12]. Gibbs sampling is a special case of Markov-chain Monte Carlo (MCMC) simulation. It often yields relatively simple algorithms for approximate inference in high-dimensional models such as LDA. Therefore it is also utilized for the proposed model.

The procedure of Gibbs sampling for our model is shown in Figure 2. All words in the corpus are set with an initial topic and a background word indicator randomly. Then, variables n_u^k, n_M^k, n_k^v, n_M^v and n_M^c can be computed. The probability of current word for each topic and its background word indicator are calculated. $z_{(m,n)}$ and $z_{\neg(m,n)}$

indicate topic assignments for the current word and the rest of words in the corpus respectively. When the probabilities of each topic and its background word indicator are calculated, a topic and its background word indicator for the current word is sampled based on the probability distribution. The same procedure is done to the other words in the corpus. The procedure runs iteratively until all distributions have been converged. The algorithm is shown in Algorithm 2.

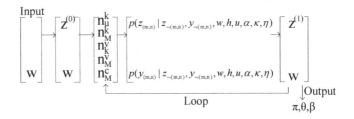

Fig. 2. Gibbs sampling procedure of our model

4   Experiments and Discussion

4.1   Data Set and Preprocessing

In order to test and illustrate our model, we use the data set provided officially by the Micro-blog Track at Text Retrieval Conference (TREC) 2011. The data set contains approximately 16 million tweets, posted over a period of 2 weeks from January 23, 2011 to February 8, 2011. In this corpus, each tweet record has five attributes: tweet remark, user remark, status codes, posted time and tweet content. Five types of status code are included in the corpus: 200, 302, 403, 404 and null, which means ok, found, forbidden, not found and nothing respectively. The statistic result of the dataset is showed in Table 1.

Table 1. Data set information

Tweet Type	Total	200	302	403	404	null	hashtag
Tweet Number	15679761	13274705	1067138	326987	1010931	1397311	1812243

Because only records with status code 200 and 302 are useful, tweets with status code 403 and 404 are cleared. We also have conducted Stemming operation for all the left tweets. And, URLs, stop words, punctuation, RT labels, words not in the dictionary (Alan Beales Core Vocabulary is used here) are also filtered. Eventually, the users who posted less than 50 tweets and their corresponding tweets are removed. After preprocession, tweet number, user number and vocabulary size are 87292, 1210 and 4840 respectively.

4.2 Parameter Settings

Referring to [13], our hyper-parameters are set as $\alpha = 1.0$, $k = 1.0$, $\eta = 0.1$. The topic number is set as 50 (Numbered from 0 to 49) at the beginning of the experiment.

4.3 Evaluation Metrics

In order to evaluate the results, perplexity is employed here. It is a criterion of clustering quality that does not require priori categorisations and it is a measure of the ability of a model to generalize the unseen data. Perplexity is defined as reciprocal geometric mean of per-word likelihood of a test corpus. A lower perplexity indicates a better generalization performance. The perplexity is shown in Equation 7, where C is the corpus, w_d is the observed words in d_{th} tweet.

$$Perplexity(C) = \exp\left\{\frac{-\sum_{d=1}^{M}\log p(w_d)}{\sum_{d=1}^{M}N_d}\right\} \tag{7}$$

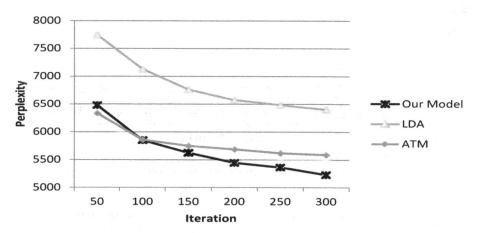

Fig. 3. Comparing perplexity for LDA, ATM and the proposed model

4.4 Performance Comparison

The comparison bewteen LDA, ATM and our model on perplexity are illustrated in Figure 3. When the iteration number is set less than 150, the perplexity of the proposed method is better than LDA. When the iteration number is over 150, our model can yield the best performance of the three. Figure 4 shows an example of top 10 words for 4 topics and background words. Clearly, Topic4, Topic8, Topic20, Topic39 can be interpreted as "*weight loss*", "*Pornography*", "*Terrorist attack*" and "*Politics*" respectively. In the background words column, common words have been listed and filtered out from topic words. As we can see, background words usually do not convey definite meanings and are not helpful to illustrate a topic.

Topic4		Topic8		Topic20		Topic39		Background words	
WORD	PROB.	WORD	PROB.	WORD	PROB.	WORD	PROB.	WORD	PROB.
weight	0.0519	porn	0.0463	terrorist	0.0683	protest	0.0778	great	0.0476
food	0.0504	sex	0.0417	death	0.0519	parade	0.0712	long	0.0463
loss	0.0421	cock	0.0311	kill	0.0508	resign	0.0637	hour	0.0451
eat	0.0401	video	0.0305	injure	0.0484	egypt	0.0549	kick	0.0432
health	0.0312	hot	0.0236	crash	0.0412	corruption	0.0489	view	0.0415
fat	0.0303	girl	0.0229	bomb	0.0329	election	0.0478	kind	0.0401
train	0.0248	fuck	0.0211	cop	0.0416	president	0.0329	time	0.0396
diet	0.0221	love	0.0135	president	0.0361	conflict	0.0314	set	0.0386
secret	0.0206	suck	0.0124	instigate	0.0349	price	0.0303	big	0.0378
cure	0.0182	tit	0.0115	explosive	0.0314	loss	0.0285	person	0.0325

Fig. 4. Top 10 words for 4 topics and background words

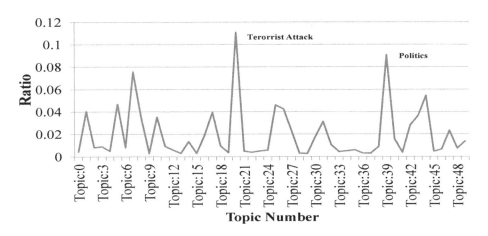

Fig. 5. Example of public topic distribution

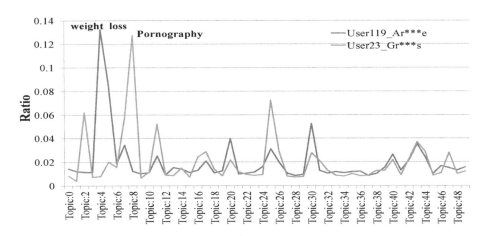

Fig. 6. Example of personal topic distribution

Public topic distribution and personal topic distribution are illustrated in Figure 5 and Figure 6. From these two types of distributions, we could see that the two types of topics have different probability distribution. As shown in Figure 5, Topic 20 and Topic 39, related to *"Terrorist attack"* and *"Politics"*, have relatively high ratio of all the topics. Both of the two topics are hot issues of the society at that time. Figure 6 illustrates an example of personal topic distribution for two users. Clearly, these two users have different interests. User23 and User119 are strongly interested in *"weight loss"* and *"Pornography"* separately. Obviously, both topics mainly focus on personal lives.

5 Conclusion

In this paper, the Categorical Topic Model is presented for extracting topics from tweets. By introducing a background word distribution, common words have been effectively filtered and topics extracted by our model are more interpretable. According to the presence of hashtags, we divide topics into two types in semantics: personal topics and public topics. Thus, personal interests and hot issues can be clearly analyzed in the same model. The derivation of approximated inference via Gibbs sampling is illustrated for the model. Compared with the previous research, our model could discover personal interests and hot issues and achieve comprehensive and interpretable experimental results.

References

1. Xu, R., Donald, Wunsch, o.: Survey of clustering algorithms. IEEE Transactions on Neural Networks 16(3), 645–678 (2005)
2. Chowdhury, G.: Introduction to modern information retrieval. Facet publishing (2010)
3. Deerwester, S., Dumais, S.T., Furnas, G.W., Landauer, T.K., Harshman, R.: Indexing by latent semantic analysis. Journal of the American Society for Information Science 41(6), 391–407 (1990)
4. Hofmann, T.: Probabilistic latent semantic indexing. In: Proceedings of the 22nd Annual International ACM SIGIR Conference on Research and Development in Information Retrieval, pp. 50–57. ACM (1999)
5. Blei, D.M., Ng, A.Y., Jordan, M.I.: Latent dirichlet allocation. The Journal of Machine Learning Research 3, 993–1022 (2003)
6. Naaman, M., Boase, J., Lai, C.H.: Is it really about me?: message content in social awareness streams. In: Proceedings of the 2010 ACM Conference on Computer Supported Cooperative Work, pp. 189–192. ACM (2010)
7. Ritter, A., Cherry, C., Dolan, B.: Unsupervised modeling of twitter conversations (2010)
8. Krishnamurthy, B., Gill, P., Arlitt, M.: A few chirps about twitter. In: Proceedings of the First Workshop on Online Social Networks, pp. 19–24. ACM (2008)
9. Ramage, D., Hall, D., Nallapati, R., Manning, C.D.: Labeled lda: A supervised topic model for credit attribution in multi-labeled corpora. In: Proceedings of the 2009 Conference on Empirical Methods in Natural Language Processing, vol. 1, pp. 248–256. Association for Computational Linguistics (2009)
10. Ramage, D., Dumais, S., Liebling, D.: Characterizing microblogs with topic models. In: International AAAI Conference on Weblogs and Social Media, vol. 5, pp. 130–137 (2010)

11. Zhao, W.X., Jiang, J., Weng, J., He, J., Lim, E.-P., Yan, H., Li, X.: Comparing twitter and traditional media using topic models. In: Clough, P., Foley, C., Gurrin, C., Jones, G.J.F., Kraaij, W., Lee, H., Mudoch, V. (eds.) ECIR 2011. LNCS, vol. 6611, pp. 338–349. Springer, Heidelberg (2011)
12. Heinrich, G.: Parameter estimation for text analysis (2005),
    http://www.arbylon.net/publications/text-est.pdf
13. Griffiths, T., Steyvers, M.: Probabilistic topic models. In: Latent Semantic Analysis: A Road to Meaning (2006)

Topic Assisted Fusion to Re-rank Texts for Multi-faceted Information Retrieval

Rajendra Prasath[1], Aidan Duane[2], and Philip O'Reilly[1]

[1] University College Cork (UCC), Cork, Ireland
[2] Waterford Institute of Technology, Waterford, Ireland
{R.Prasath,Philip.OReilly}@ucc.ie, aduane@wit.ie

Abstract. We propose to develop a framework for an intelligent business information system with multi-faceted data analysis capabilities that supports complex decision making processes. Reasoning and Learning of contextual factors from texts of financial services data are core aspects of the proposed framework. As part of the proposed framework, we present an approach for the ordering of contextual information from textual data with the help of latent topics identified from the web corpus. The web corpus is prepared by specifically using a number of financial services sources on the web that describe various aspects of mobile payments and services. The proposed approach first performs weighting of query terms and retrieves the initial set of texts from the web corpus. We use Latent Dirichlet Allocation (LDA) on this web corpus to identify the topics that relate to the contextual features of various financial services/products. The retrieved texts are scored based on the identified topics that could cover a variety of contextual factors. We performed subjective evaluation to identify the relevance of the contextual information retrieved, and found that the proposed approach captures a variety of key contexts pertaining to user information needs in a better way with the support of topic assisted contextual factors.

1 Introduction

The commercial importance for companies in generating effective business models is emphasised by Teece [1], who states that adopting the correct business model when offering new products and services is critical for organisational performance management and enterprise success. In order to adopt and implement an appropriate business model, it is necessary for organisations to have an in-depth knowledge of the existing market and to learn from successful product/service implementations which the organisation already has in the market[1]. Following a review of the patent library, it is evident that there is no commercially available decision support system that enables organisations to research the specifics of the market in which they operate, in order to enable them, to review the marketplace and to develop, test and validate suitable business models for their products/services.

With the advent of the semantic web and the great amount of business data available online, this research focuses on transforming the highly interlinked

R.E. Banchs et al. (Eds.): AIRS 2013, LNCS 8281, pp. 97–108, 2013.

documents of the world wide web into a rich knowledge base[2]. The primary focus is on developing an intelligent business information system with multi-faceted data analysis for better decision making in relation to business models. In this paper, we present an approach based on topic assisted information fusion to perform a re-ranking of texts retrieved for a given information need. The preliminary analysis shows that the proposed algorithm records a much greater depth and quality of results vis a vis the baseline.

2   Motivation

In the business model domain, the state of the art is very descriptive. Osterwalder's paper, based on the business model canvas[3], is typically used as an application by which practitioners can analyse and construct business models for their business ecosystem. While this framework is acknowledged within industry as being the "state of the art", an analysis of same reveals a number of key limitations like poor predictive capacity, no correlated evaluation of factors associated with business ecosystem, inability to combine internal and external knowledge base on a specific product or service. Many organisations struggle to get external information pertaining to current market trends, innovations and competitors in an efficient way. Many managers within organisations utilise commercial search engines like Google, Bing, etc to retrieve information and manually navigate through them. This is an inefficient, time consuming approach and is typically not fused with an organisations' internal knowledge base.

There are interesting fusion based reasoning approaches in the literature. Chang *et al.* [4] proposed an interactive reasoner abbreviated as *Pequliar* that applies progressive query language and interactive reasoning (cum learning) for information fusion support. However, this research is limited in that the reasoner is guided by humans to elaborate the query by means of some rule and then a query processor uses this to produce a more informative answer. Park and Kim [5] proposed an interactive grey-zone case based reasoning model that makes decisions focusing additional attention on cases near cut-off point. This work emphasizes organisations' need to learn from previous cases and experiences, especially in relation to designing and commercialising new products and services. Especially each organization is supposed to have internal knowledge about their products, services, partners and customers. External sources would have information illustrating the impacts of their products, voices of their customers and business critics in the market. By fusing an organisations' internal knowledge with that from external sources, organisations would have a greater insight on the market and be in a position to learn and apply similar contexts to solve current similar problems which they face. In order to assist organisations to capture external knowledge efficiently, we have derived a framework that uses topic assisted information fusion to capture similar contexts, and then apply these contexts to learn to solve similar instances from a knowledge base in an non-interactive way. Subsequently we would fuse this external knowledge with the internal knowledge of the interested companies involved in mobile payments sector. In this paper, the term "context" means the semantic association between the specific user query and the retrieved set of texts. The terms, *aspect* or *facet*, are used interchangably to represent the type of contextual relations between the query and the retrieved set of texts.

3 Latent Dirichlet Allocation

Latent Dirichlet Allocation (LDA) is a generative probabilistic topic model [6,7]. To analyse a discrete collection of data, especially text corpora, LDA applies three-level hierarchical Bayesian model, in which each item of a collection is modelled as a finite mixture over an underlying set of topics. Each topic is, in turn, modelled as an infinite mixture over an underlying set of topic probabilities. In the context of text modelling, the topic probabilities provide an explicit representation of a document. LDA defines the marginal distribution of a document as a continuous mixture distribution, as follows,

$$p_i(x) = p(d|\alpha_i, \beta_i) = \int p(\theta|\alpha) \left(\prod_{j=1}^{n} p(w_j|\theta, \beta) \right) d\theta \tag{1}$$

where d is a document with n words. $p(\theta|\alpha)$ and $p(w_j|\theta, \beta)$ are actually multinomial distributions with Dirichlet prior. $p(w_j|\theta, \beta)$ describes $K-$dimensional topic-word distributions. The parameters α, β are estimated by means of Gibbs sampling [8]. Here α is the symmetric Dirichlet prior for all documents and β is the symmetric Dirichlet prior for all topics.

4 Topic Assisted Information Fusion

Reasoning about data with lots of dynamics is vital for many applications where the basic data sources come from different types, and the generated data is heterogeneous. Data obtained from such sources are often ambiguous and associated with certain levels of uncertainty. Topic models could narrow down the search to specific areas by reducing the level of uncertainty to a greater extent. The use of topic models in information retrieval is well studied in the literature [9]. In this work, we use data from multiple web sources and perform information fusion assisted by the information on latent topics to improve the quality of text retrieval. The retrieved texts provide market and organisational knowledge to the user, enabling better decision making. The original query is expanded based on these aspects that a set of more informative answers to the specific users information needs is retrieved. We plan to capture the aspects of the query in terms of distinct topics covered by it. Then using these topics associated information, we score the retrieved texts and re-rank them to bring the informative content to the top. Then the reasoner accepts the top ranked texts and identifies the matching of similar texts/cases that could potentially represent similar contexts. The learner is enforced to work on these text segments to perform context sensitive assessments so as to update both the learning experience and the knowledge base.

4.1   The System Design

The proposed framework, as shown in Figure. 1, consists of three major components: *Query Processing, Topic Assisted Information Fusion,* and *Knowledge Management Process.*

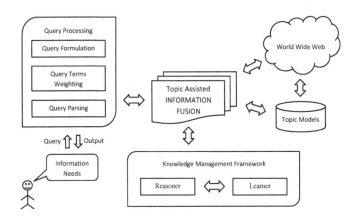

Fig. 1. The proposed retrieval framework with reasoner and learner

Query Processing: The user enters their information needs in terms of a set of keywords or key phrases or short sentences typically consisting of 3-5 keywords. Bai and Nie [10] used query expansion using term relations based on language models that integrates several contextual factors to adapt specific query contexts. The proposed system obtains the query terms and processes them to find the associated aspects and then the query term weighting is applied to identify their individual weights depending on the corpus statistics. The weighting of a query term q_i is computed as follows:

$$qtw(q_i) = averageTF(q_i) * IDF(q_i), \forall i \in [1, n] \tag{2}$$

where $averageTF(q_i)$ is computed as the ratio between the total number of occurrences of the given query term across the texts in the collection and the total number of texts (in terms, the total number of texts in which the term occurs) and $IDF(q_i) = \log(\frac{N}{df(q_i)})$ where N = total number of texts and $df(q_i)$ = frequency of texts given the query term q_i.

The proposed query term weighting technique focuses on important query terms that may represent an entity (the primary focus), rather than other associated query terms of this entity. For example, consider the query: *countries adopting mobile payments.* In this query, "countries" is the main focus and it might represent the number of countries adopting mobile payments, or the name of the countries adopting mobile payments or the type of payment services in countries adopting mobile payments or the status of the countries offering mobile payments. We obtain the following weight for each of these query terms [weights in brackets] as follows: countries[6.3057], adapting[4.2886], mobile[1.0530], payments[2.0595].

Consider another query: *How will mobile payments integrate coupons?* In this query, customer loyalty services such as special offers, coupons, bonus points for either using their service or buying their products are the main focus. This reflects in the weight estimated for the individual term: mobile[1.4307], payments[1.7373], integrate[2.8587], coupons[2.9401]. These weights are used as the boost factors in the formulation of the expanded query. In this paper, we considered the system employing this weighting approach as the *baseline* system for the retrieval of texts. Here "text" means a meaningful sentence or passage having qualitative and quantitative information pertaining to the user query.

Topic Assisted Information Fusion: This component first seeks the interpretation of the query with latent topic models and infers the user information need in terms of the coverage of a variety of topics learned from the given corpus. It then uses the expanded query to retrieve information from the index and applies fusion on each text retrieved with the topic associated information to compute the contextual similarity score. The contextual similarity score of each retrieved text is computed as follows:

$$tscore(td_i) = s * \sum_{j=1}^{m} qtw(w_j) + (1 - s) * \frac{1}{|td_i|} \sum_{j=1}^{m} \frac{1}{nt} * \sum_{l=1}^{p} prob(w_j|T_l) \quad (3)$$

where $td_i = \{w_1, w_2, \cdots, w_m\}$, $s = cosine(query, retrieved\ text)$, nt denotes the number of topics in which the term is associated with and $|td_i|$ denotes the number of unique words in the retrieved text. Here the topic model probability contributes the likelihood score of a term given an aspect and cosine similarity score contributes the degree of relevance of the retrieved text given a query. So the combined *tscore* is used to represent a variety of aspects that are relevant to the user needs. Then the retrieved texts are ranked in decreasing order of their contextual similarity. This produces a set of top ranked texts containing key information pertaining to the user's query. This task is different from cluster based approaches, as described in [11], in which is the query is matched against the cluster of documents instead of individual documents and clusters are ranked based on their similarity to the query.

Knowledge Management (KM) Process: This consists of two tasks: *Reasoning* and *Learning*. The proposed KM framework is supposed to process the top ranked list of documents and identify similar text segments from the index. This task is yet to mature for reporting. Actually we plan to find the patterns of similar text fragments, with high matching scores, that are sent to the learner with the actual user query to perform context sensitive assessments. The knowledge gained by the learner could be reused to solve similar scenarios as guided by Case Based Reasoning(CBR) [12,13].

4.2   Proposed Approach

The proposed system works as follows: A user enters their information needs in the form of a query - a sequence of keywords. The system receives this query and applies the proposed query terms weighting approach using corpus statistics to understand the level of importance attached to these query terms, in order to capture the actual context of the user's query. Using the weight computed for each query term, the system re-formulates the given query into the weighted query. This weighted query is used to retrieve texts from the search system. The initial set of results retrieved by the search system is assumed to be relevant, as similar to the Pseudo-Relevance Feedback (PRF) approach. We use the standard cosine similarity as the scoring function during the texts retrieval. The retrieved results are fused with topic assisted information and re-ranked based on their contextual similarity. Then the re-ranked results are evaluated subjectively to compute the retrieval efficiency of the top 20 results. This research is evolving towards the goal of developing a more sophisticated fusion approach that combines the results obtained with multiple sources.

The pseudo code of the proposed approach is illustrated in Algorithm 1.

Algorithm 1. Topic Assisted Information Fusion to Re-rank Texts

---

Require: A Searcher - gets user query and retrieves top k texts $D = \{td_1, td_2, \cdots, td_k\}$
where $td_i = \{w_1, w_2, \cdots, w_m\}$
Input: Query Q having a sequence of keywords: $\{q_1, q_2, \cdots, q_n\}$
Description:
  Input: Enter the user query into the system
  Query Terms Weighting: Extract the query terms and use corpus statistics to determine their individual weights using Equation. 2.
  Text Retrieval: Compute $s = cosine(Q, D)$ and retrieve top k texts
  Topic Assisted Information Fusion:
  Create the topic model with p topics (fixed) by applying LDA on the entire corpus
  for all $td_i \in D$ **do**
    Compute weights of each term in td_i, $qtw(w_j)$ and take their summation.
    Compute $tscore(td_i)$ using Equation. 3
    Update Texts with the computed $tscore(td_i)$
  end for
  Re-Rank: Choose top k texts based on high $tscore(td_i)$ scores
  return top k texts $(k \leq n)$
Output: The ranked list of top $k \leq n$ texts pertaining to the query context

---

5   Experimental Results

5.1   Corpus

We have created a collection of web documents / reports crawled from the websites of various financial companies using open source web crawlers. We collected 14,764 web documents containing a total of 296,983 words. Actually we do not have the idea about the coverage of documents pertaining to mobile payments sector in the TREC web collections. So we have chosen to crawl much more focused information pertaining to mobile payments. To achieve this, we have selected 20 contextually different types of user information needs pertaining to mobile payments and created the web corpus. These queries are chosen as the representative sample of the statistical population that comes from the documents in the underlying web corpus. However, the test of significance has to be done to justify this choice. We used the open source implementation of JGibbLDA[1] for building the topic models. For this, we are limited to 200 latent topics with 1,000 iterations to build the topic model (assumed other LDA parameters: $\alpha = 0.5$ and $\beta = 0.1$).

The selected queries that pertain to the specific information needs in the mobile payment sector are listed in Table. 1. Most of the queries contain the phrase, "mobile payments" due to the fact that the underlying information needs are very much specific to the issues in mobile payments. Even though

Table 1. List of Queries

QID	Actual Information Needs (Queries)
Q1	What are mobile payments?
Q2	How will mobile payments benefit consumers?
Q3	How will mobile payments benefit retailers?
Q4	What is the cost to consumers of using mobile payments?
Q5	What is the cost to retailers of mobile payments?
Q6	How is the mobile payments security addressed?
Q7	How is the mobile payments privacy addressed?
Q8	What technology do retailers need to accept mobile payments?
Q9	How will mobile payments integrate coupons?
Q10	What challenges arise with mobile payments?
Q11	How are mobile payments protected by legislation?
Q12	What types of mobile payments are available?
Q13	How big is the global mobile payments market?
Q14	How mature is the global mobile payments market?
Q15	What is the most common type of mobile payment?
Q16	What is the most common value of mobile payments?
Q17	What companies are the biggest players in the global mobile payments market?
Q18	Can mobile payments be hacked?
Q19	Will mobile payments replace cash?
Q20	Which retailers accept mobile payments?

the above listed queries represent questions and look like seeking answers, as in the Q & A systems, the primary focus is on retrieving texts whose context matches the actual context of the given query. By representing the "context" of the query, we mean different aspects pertaining to the focused information need of the given query. For example, consider query - Q4 (Table. 1) which searches for mobile payment models. The retrieved texts should contain the details about the

---

[1] http://jgibblda.sourceforge.net

payment models currently available in the market. Business models of payment services would also be considered as the relevant context.

5.1.1   Evaluation Methodology

We have used the following steps for the subjective evaluation to test the quality of the content retrieved:

- The focus is on evaluating the quality or goodness of the document content in terms of the coverage of informative subtopics pertaining to the query.
- We have used 2 evaluators to judge the quality of the content in the top 20 results retrieved two systems: the standard *vector space model*(VSM) [14] with the proposed query weighting approach as the baseline system and the system with the proposed re-ranking approach.
- The evaluator reviewed one query at a time and the top 20 ranked documents retrieved for that query.
- For each query, each evaluator picked up top 20 ranked texts and evaluated them by analysing their context. The number of facets covered by each text pertaining to the query is identified. Then, depending on the variety of facets and their importance pertaining to the query, the quality of the content is scored in the 3 point scale as outlined in Table. 2.
- Final scores are used to compute precision at top d texts ($p@d$) for both lists

It is not a fair idea to consider VSM as the baseline method rather than other standard PRF methods like Rocchio or probabilisitc methods because the primary focus is on incorporating information pertaining to latent topics in payments sector. The following scale is used for subjective evaluation:

Table 2. Guidelies for the subjective evaluation

Score	Description
1.0	various aspects of the query context
0.5	partial information of the query context
0	NOISY / irrelevant information

While evaluating the pieces of information retrieved by the base line and the proposed systems, the evaluators are instructed to focus on the relevance of the texts retrieved with respect to the query context. We do not apply deep NLP parsing on the textual content (except sentence level parsing with '.', '?', '!' as sentence markers). But in this work, we try to get PROBABLE Text fragments that could represent the expected context of the user information needs(especially financial service payment oriented queries).

We applied the following evaluation measure: $p@d$ to evaluate the ranked list of top d ($= 5, 10, 20$) results retrieved for each query. We used the three different tiny datasets for this experiment with the same set of queries listed in Table. 1. The top 5, 10 and 20 results were manually evaluated and the observations relating to the retrieved texts are discussed in the subsequent section.

6   Discussion

In this section, we present our key observations on the nature of the texts retrieved for the specific information needs. During the analysis, we have considered the top 5, 10 and 20 texts retrieved for each query and analysed the context represented by the texts. The context of the texts retrieved is analysed to find its matching with the context of the query. Figure. 2 shows the text retrieval performance of the baseline and the proposed approach with "Precision @ top 5" (p@5) scores. We present some of our key observations

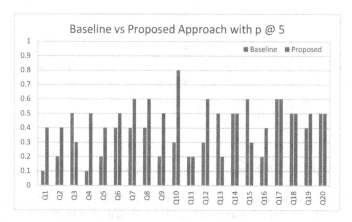

Fig. 2. $p@5$ comparison: Baseline vs Proposed retrieval approach

in analysing the top 5 texts retrieved. For query Q1, the primary focus of the user is to find information pertaining to the cost to be paid by the customers to use mobile payment services. The baseline results have only one partially relevant result whereas the proposed system fetched texts having the information on the cost imposed by the payment service providers to access their mobile payment services. Similar observations were observed for query Q4, in finding the cost involved in using mobile payment services and for Q5, in identifying the cost-benefit trends of retailers of mobile payments sector. The best performance is achieved for query Q10, which identifies the distinct types of mobile payments activity observed in the market. For this query, we retrieved texts having the details of various messaging services like text messaging, simple message services (SMS), etc. Also we have identified qualitative information having the details of various electronic accessaries involved in mobile payments sector. We also observed a better performance in query Q9, in which the security related aspects of mobile payments are well addressed in the retrieved texts and the query Q12, in which benefits of the retailers are well addressed with the information on their low and high margins.

Query drifting takes place for specific queries Q3, Q13 and Q15 with the topic assisted approach. We analyse these queries individually. The query Q3 focuses on the information about the coupons offered by mobile payments service providers to attract their customers. The retrieved texts constitute more context-insensitive collections of information than are associated with the statistics of loyalty programs in mobile payments sector. For query Q13, the

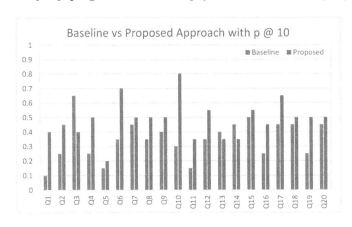

Fig. 3. $p@10$ comparison: Baseline vs Proposed retrieval approach

query is intended to find the possible pitfalls in hacking of mobile payments. But the retrieved texts contain descriptions on hacked histories pertaining to various companies and phones involved in mobile sector. "7500 mobile phones had been hacked live in China" and "hacking of SquareUp mobile payment system" are some observations in the retrieved texts. For query Q15, the actual intent is to find the size of the global mobile payments market. For this query, noisy texts, that are not filtered during content extraction, result in the decrease of performance. However the retrieval performance improved with the subsequent 15 texts retrieved.

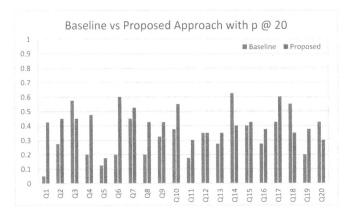

Fig. 4. $p@20$ comparison: Baseline vs Proposed retrieval approach

Figure. 3 shows the text retrieval performance of the baseline and the proposed approaches with p@10 scores. We analyse the top 10 texts retrieved for each query in this section. The retrieval performance has increased for queries Q6, Q11, Q15, Q17 and Q19 significantly. The effects of query drift has been observed for two queries Q13 and Q14. The decrease in the retrieval performance for query 13 is the same as the one described in the above paragraph. For query 14, texts with noisy data degraded the performance with p@10. The overall retrieval task is much improved for the rest of the queries.

Figure. 4 shows the text retrieval performance of the baseline and the proposed approaches with p@20 scores. The top 20 text retrieval performance is effective for queries Q1, Q4, Q6, Q8, Q10, Q17 and slightly degraded performance has been observed for a few queries, namely Q3, Q18 and Q20. For query Q14, the texts retrieved at the later part of the top 20 consists of partial matching contexts of the query. So the overall $p@20$ score reached 0.4 which is better than the retrieval performance of top 10 texts. For query Q17, we observed equal

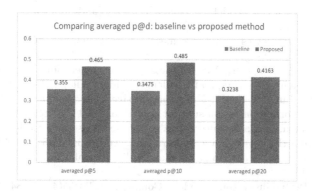

Fig. 5. Averaged $p@d$ comparison: Baseline vs Proposed retrieval approach

performance with baseline and the proposed method. The proposed method for this query fetched texts having, "54% consumers found mobile payments as quick and easy way" and "majority of customers realized convenience and gained benefits via loyalty programs". In the mean time, the baseline approach fetched texts having similar observations like "customers benefit through the ability to control/monitor their finance" and "36% customers reported mobile payments as the easiest way". However, the retrieval performance is consistent with Q17 whose $p@d$ scores remained on an average of 0.61. Finally we have presented the overall performance of the proposed approach vs the baseline approach with the averaged $p@d$ scores across all 20 queries in Figure 5. Subsequently, we plan to incorporate the reasoning and learning processes to identify relation axioms, as in [15], from the web corpus.

7 Conclusion

We proposed a framework towards developing an intelligent business information system with multi-faceted data analysis and decision support. As part of the proposed framework, we present an approach for re-ranking of texts with the help of latent topics identified from the web corpus. The proposed approach first performs weighting of query terms and retrieves the initial set of texts from web corpus. We used Latent Dirichlet Allocation method on the same web corpus to find out the topics distribution that cover the contextual features of various financial services/products. The retrieved texts are fused with topic distribution information and re-ranked based on the contextual features. Our experimental results show that the proposed approach captures a variety of key contexts of user information needs in a better way with the support of topics distribution.

Acknowledgments. A part of this work is supported by B-MIDEA project funded by Enterprise Ireland.

References

1. Teece, D.J.: Business models, business strategy and innovation. Long Range Planning 43(2-3), 172–194 (2010)
2. Horrocks, I.: Ontologies and the semantic web. Commun. ACM 51(12), 58–67 (2008)
3. Osterwalder, A., Pigneur, Y.: Business Model Generation: A Handbook for Visionaries, Game Changers, and Challengers. John Wiley & Sons, USA (2010)
4. Chang, S.K., Jungert, E., Li, X.: A progressive query language and interactive reasoner for information fusion support. Inf. Fusion 8(1), 70–83 (2007)
5. Park, Y.J., Kim, B.C.: An interactive case-based reasoning method considering proximity from the cut-off point. Expert Syst. Appl. 33(4), 903–915 (2007)
6. Blei, D.M., Ng, A.Y., Jordan, M.I.: Latent dirichlet allocation. J. Mach. Learn. Res. 3, 993–1022 (2003)
7. Blei, D.M.: Probabilistic topic models. Commun. ACM 55(4), 77–84 (2012)
8. Griffiths, T.: Gibbs sampling in the generative model of latent dirichlet allocation. Technical report, Stanford University (2002)
9. Yi, X., Allan, J.: A comparative study of utilizing topic models for information retrieval. In: Boughanem, M., Berrut, C., Mothe, J., Soule-Dupuy, C. (eds.) ECIR 2009. LNCS, vol. 5478, pp. 29–41. Springer, Heidelberg (2009)
10. Bai, J., Nie, J.Y.: Adapting information retrieval to query contexts. Inf. Process. Manage. 44(6), 1901–1922 (2008)
11. Liu, X., Croft, W.B.: Cluster-based retrieval using language models. In: Proc. of the 27th ACM SIGIR Conf. on Information Retrieval, SIGIR 2004, pp. 186–193. ACM, New York (2004)
12. Aamodt, A., Plaza, E.: Case-based reasoning: Foundational issues, methodological variations, and system approaches. AI Commun. 7(1), 39–59 (1994)
13. Öztürk, P., Aamodt, A.: A context model for knowledge-intensive case-based reasoning. Int. J. Hum.-Comput. Stud. 48(3), 331–355 (1998)
14. Salton, G., Wong, A., Yang, A.C.S.: A vector space model for automatic indexing. Communications of the ACM 18, 229–237 (1975)
15. Sánchez, D., Moreno, A., Del Vasto-Terrientes, L.: Learning relation axioms from text: An automatic web-based approach. Expert Syst. Appl. 39(5), 5792–5805 (2012)

A Collaborative Document Ranking Model for a Multi-faceted Search

Laure Soulier, Lynda Tamine, and Wahiba Bahsoun

IRIT Laboratory - 118 Route de Narbonne, 31062 Toulouse Cedex 9
{soulier,tamine,wbahsoun}@irit.fr

Abstract. This paper presents a novel collaborative document ranking model which aims at solving a complex information retrieval task involving a multi-faceted information need. For this purpose, we consider a group of users, viewed as experts, who collaborate by addressing the different query facets. We propose a two-step algorithm based on a relevance feedback process which first performs a document scoring towards each expert and then allocates documents to the most suitable experts using the Expectation-Maximisation learning-method. The performance improvement is demonstrated through experiments using TREC interactive benchmark.

Keywords: collaborative information retrieval, multi-faceted search.

1 Introduction

It is well-known in information retrieval (IR) domain that one critical issue is the understanding of users' search goals hidden behind their queries, in attempt to get a better insight of how to explore the information space towards relevant documents [2]. Most retrieval approaches consider that a query addresses mainly a single topic whereas multi-faceted search-based approaches [1,13] have highlighted the need of considering the topical coverage of the retrieved documents towards different aspects of the query topic, named facets. One multi-faceted query example, extracted from the TREC Interactive dataset [17], is "Hubble Telescope Achievements". For this query, users have manually identified, for instance, several aspects: "focus of camera", "age of the universe space telescope" and "cube pictures". The key emerging challenges from multi-faceted search are how to infer the different query facets and how to exploit them jointly to select relevant results. To tackle the underlying issues, a first category of work attempts to enhance the query representation in order to identify the query facets [5,22], whereas a second line of work in the same category [4,12] considers result diversification towards query facets.

Another category of work [15,19] arisen from the Collaborative IR (CIR) domain underlines that collaboration could benefit complex tasks and more particularly exploratory queries. Indeed, complex problems can be difficultly solved within ad-hoc IR due to the single searcher's knowledge or skills inadequacy [19]. A collaborative framework enables overcoming this lack considering that a group of users may analyze more in-depth the different query facets in contrast

R.E. Banchs et al. (Eds.): AIRS 2013, LNCS 8281, pp. 109–120, 2013.
© Springer-Verlag Berlin Heidelberg 2013

to a single user who performs individually the first level of the information need. Shah [19] introduces the notion of the synergic effect of collaborative search in so far as *"the whole (is) greater than the sum of all"*. Therefore, CIR is another response to tackle multi-faceted search issues in which multiple users search documents together in response to a shared information need considering their different knowledge expertise and points of view with respect to the same query.

In this paper, we present a collaborative document ranking model suited to solve a multi-faceted query. Our approach allows to leverage the users' different knowledge expertise and assigns them implicit knowledge-based roles towards at least one query facet. These facets are modeled through document and user topical-based representations using the LDA generative model. Documents are allocated to experts using the Expectation-Maximization algorithm.

In section 2, we discuss related work. Section 3 describes our collaborative ranking approach involving an expert group. Section 4 presents our experimental evaluation. Finally, section 5 concludes the paper and introduces future work.

2   Related Work

The multi-faceted search issue can arise within two search settings, namely the individual-based search and the collaborative based-one.

Individual-based search is a classic IR setting in which one user aims at satisfying an information need. We address particularly in this paper a complex information need expressed by means of a multi-faceted query. There are two lines of work in this area. The first one remains on identifying explicit query facets prior to performing a facet-based retrieval model [5,6,9]. Authors use different tools or methods addressed at the query level such as terminological resources for building a hierarchy among the detected facets [5]. Other methods [9] remain on the analysis of the user navigation for classifying query facets using document features. In contrast, generative probabilistic-based models [3,6] aim at modeling documents as topical-based vectors in which each component expresses a query facet. Another line of work [4,24] dealing with multi-faceted search focuses on the diversification of the search results without highlighting the query facets. The key idea is to select a diversified document subset either using a term-frequency distribution [4] or a graph modeling approach [24].

Unlike individual-based search, the collaborative-based one is a retrieval setting in which several users collaborate for satisfying a shared information need. Considering a multi-faceted information need, the integration of collaboration within a search task enables to benefit from the *synergic effect* of collaboration [19] in so far as people with different backgrounds and points of view search relevant documents together with respect to a multi-faceted shared information need. Collaboration principles [10], namely *awareness, sharing of knowledge* and *division of labor*, enable to leverage from users their different skills and search abilities by warming collaborators of actions of their pairs, transmitting the information flow among users and avoiding redundancy. Previous work in the CIR domain [10,16,18,21] rely on different retrieval strategies, such as designing user roles and relevance feedback techniques, in order to explore the different query facets. We distinguish two main categories of work depending on if they integrate user roles or not. The first category remains on a relevance feedback process without integrating user roles [10,16], providing iteratively a ranked list of documents either at the user level [10,16] or at the group level [16]. The second category of work, more close to ours, consists in integrating a supplementary layer based on user roles [18,21] by assigning to each collaborator a specific task for avoiding redundancy. Pickens et al. [18] model the *prospector* and *miner* roles which respectively aim at ensuring the quality of the selected documents and favoring the diversity of the search results in response to the multi-faceted information need by means of query suggestion. This model is guided by the division of labor and sharing of knowledge principles throughout a relevance feedback process.Shah et al. [21] introduce another couple of roles, namely the *gatherer* and the *surveyor* relying on different predefined tasks: respectively, performing a quick overview of documents for detecting relevant ones or a better understanding of the topic to explore other subtopic areas in accordance to the multi-faceted query.

In this paper, we focus on a collaborative context in which a multi-faceted information need is solved by a group of users. Unlike previous work based on explicit user roles [18,21], our model assigns to users implicit roles considering their domain knowledge mined through a relevance feedback process. Therefore, our model enables to leverage users' skills in which they are the most effective, in opposition to other models [18,21] based on explicit roles which assign predefined users roles or domain expertise. For this purpose, we model topical-based profiles for estimating the knowledge expertise of users and propose an iterative document ranking model using a learning-based algorithm in order to assign documents to the most likely suited users according to their domain knowledge.

3   The Model

Several underlying concerns of multi-faceted search within a CIR context may arise, such as identifying the most suitable users for solving a multi-topical information need or performing a collaborative retrieval task according to the different query facets. We focus here on the second concern. More specifically, we address two main research questions: 1) How to mine the query facets? 2) How to build collaborative document rankings?

3.1   Mining Query Facets

First, given an initial document dataset $\mathcal{D}$ and a multi-faceted query Q, we extract a subset $\mathcal{D}^*$ of n documents which satisfies the condition of being relevant with respect to the query topic and ensuring a broad topical coverage. For this purpose, we use the *Maximal Marginal Relevance* (MMR) [4] that selects document $D^* \in \mathcal{D}$ with the highest relevance and marginal diversity score considering subset $\mathcal{D}^*$:

$$D^* = \arg \max_{D_i \in \mathcal{D}} [\gamma sim_1(D_i, Q) - (1 - \gamma) \max_{D_{i'} \in \mathcal{D}^*} sim_2(D_i, D_{i'})] \qquad (1)$$

where $sim_1(D_i, Q)$ and $sim_2(D_i, D_{i'})$ express the similarity between document D_i and query Q, respectively document $D_{i'}$. $\gamma \in [0,1]$ is a weighting factor.

Second, we use the generative probabilistic algorithm named LDA [3] applied on the diversified document dataset $\mathcal{D}^*$ in order to identify latent topics. Each topic is assimilated to a facet of query Q. The algorithm computes a word-topic distribution $\phi_{w|t}$ and document-topic distribution $\theta_{D_i|t}$ for respectively estimating the probability of word w and document D_i given topic t. The optimal number of topics T for the document dataset $\mathcal{D}^*$ is generally tuned using a likelihood measure:

$$l(T^*|w, t) = \arg \max_T \sum_{w \in W} log(\sum_{t \in T} p(w|t)) \tag{2}$$

where W is the set of words extracted from document dataset $\mathcal{D}^*$. The probability $p(w|t)$ corresponds to the word-topic distribution $\phi_{w|t}$.

Each document $D_i \in \mathcal{D}^*$ is represented using a topical distribution $D_i = (w_{1i}, \ldots, w_{ti}, \ldots, w_{Ti})$ where w_{ti} represents the weight of mined topic t by the LDA algorithm for document D_i expressed by the probability $\theta_{D_i|t}$. Each expert $E_j \in E$ is characterized by a knowledge profile built using the previously selected documents and inferred on the document representation using the LDA inference method. The profile of expert E_j is noted $\pi(E_j)^{(k)} = (w_{1j}^{(k)}, \ldots, w_{tj}^{(k)}, \ldots, w_{Tj}^{(k)})$, where $w_{tj}^{(k)}$ represents the expertise of expert E_j towards topic t at iteration k.

3.2 Collaborative Document Ranking

Expert-Based Document Scoring. The expert-based document scoring aims at reranking documents with respect to each expert's domain expertise towards the query facets. It provides a first attempt for document ranking given experts which is, then, used within the collaborative learning method. We estimate, at iteration k, the probability $p^{(k)}(d_i|e_j, q)$ of document D_i given expert E_j and query Q as follows:

$$p^{(k)}(d_i|e_j, q) = \frac{p^{(k)}(e_j|d_i, q)p(d_i|q)}{p(e_j|q)} \tag{3}$$

where d_i, e_j and q are random variables associated respectively with document D_i, expert E_j and query Q. Considering the probability $p(e_j|q)$ is not discriminant and assuming that expert e_j and query q are independent, we obtain:

$$p^{(k)}(d_i|e_j, q) \propto p^{(k)}(e_j|d_i, q)p(d_i|q) \tag{4}$$
$$\propto p^{(k)}(e_j|d_i)p(d_i|q)$$

We first estimate the probability $p(d_i|q)$ of document D_i given query Q as:

$$P(d_i|q) = \frac{\frac{p(d_i).p(q|d_i)}{p(q)}}{\sum_{D_{i'} \in \mathcal{D}^*} \frac{p(d_{i'}).p(q|d_{i'})}{p(q)}} \propto \frac{p(d_i).p(q|d_i)}{\sum_{D_{i'} \in \mathcal{D}^*} p(d_{i'}).p(q|d_{i'})} \tag{5}$$

with $\mathcal{D}^*$ is the reference dataset. The probability $p(d_i)$ of document D_i is independent of the query and can be estimated as a uniform weight: $p(d_i) = \frac{1}{|\mathcal{D}|}$.

Considering the facet-based distribution of document D_i, we estimate $p(q|d_i)$ by combining two similarity scores $RSV_{LDA}(Q|D_i)$ and $RSV_{BM25}(Q, D_i)$ respectively based on the LDA-based document ranking model detailed in [11] and a BM25-based document scoring:

$$p(q|d_i) = \lambda RSV_{LDA}(Q|D_i) + (1 - \lambda)RSV_{BM25}(Q, D_i) \qquad (6)$$

$$with\ RSV_{LDA}(Q|D_i) = \prod_{w\in Q} \sum_{t=1}^{T} p(w|t).p(t|d_i)$$

where $p(w|t)$ represents the probability of term w given topic t estimated by $\phi_{w|t}$ and $p(t|d_i)$ is the probability of topic t given document D_i, previously noted w_{ti} in the document representation. We estimate the probability $p^{(k)}(e_j|d_i)$ as a cosine similarity sim_{cos} comparing the two topical distributions of document D_i and knowledge profile $\pi(E_j)^{(k)}$ associated to expert E_j at iteration k as:

$$p^{(k)}(e_j|d_i) = \frac{sim_{cos}(D_i, \pi(E_j)^{(k)})}{\sum_{D_{i'} \in \mathcal{D}^*} sim_{cos}(D_{i'}, \pi(E_j)^{(k)})} \qquad (7)$$

Expert-Based Document Allocation. Here, we aim at allocating documents to the most suitable experts considering document scores computed in Equation 3. For this aim, we use the learning *Expectation Maximization* algorithm [7]. The EM-based collaborative document allocation method runs into two stages, as detailed in Algorithm 1. Notations are detailed in Table 1.

1. Learning the document-expert mapping. The aim is to learn through an EM-based algorithm how experts are likely to assess the relevance of a document. This method is divided into two steps:
- The *E-step* estimates the probability $p(c_j = 1|X_i^{(k)})$ of relevance of document D_i towards expert E_j considering all experts at iteration k considering document score vector $X_i^{(k)}$. The probability $p(c_j|X_i^{(k)})$ is estimated using a mixture model that considers Gaussian probability laws ϕ_j to model the relevance c_j of documents for expert E_j at iteration k:

$$p(c_j = 1|X_i^{(k)}) = \frac{\alpha_j p_{ij}^{(k)}}{\alpha_j p_{ij}^{(k)} + (1 - \alpha_j)\bar{p}_{ij}^{(k)}} = \frac{\alpha_j p_{ij}^{(k)}}{\sum_{l=1}^{m} \alpha_l p_{il}^{(k)}} \qquad (8)$$

$$with\ \begin{cases} p_{ij}^{(k)} = p(c_j = 1)p(x_{ij}^{(k)}|c_j = 1) \\ \bar{p}_{ij}^{(k)} = p(c_j = 0)p(x_{ij}^{(k)}|c_j = 0) \end{cases}$$

If we consider the fact that document irrelevance towards expert E_j, noted $c_j = 0$, can be formulated by the probability of being relevant for another expert, noted $c_l = 1\ \forall l = \{1, \dots, m\}$ with $l \neq j$, the denominator corresponds to the sum of the probabilities expressing the document relevance, noted $c_l = 1$, towards

Table 1. Notations used in Algorithm 1

$X_i^{(k)} = \{x_{i1}^{(k)}, ..., x_{im}^{(k)}\}$	The scoring vector where each element $x_{ij}^{(k)}$ is estimated by equation 4.
$X^{(k)} \in \mathcal{R}^{n \times m}$	The matrix including the n vectors $X_i^{(k)}$.
$c_j = \{0, 1\}$	The hidden variable referring to the irrelevance, respectively relevance, of a document of belonging to category c_j of expert E_j.
ϕ_j	The Gaussian probability density function of relevant documents respectively according to expert E_j.
θ_j	The parameters for the Gaussian score distribution ϕ_j related to expert E_j, namely μ_j and σ_j.
α_j	The coefficient of the mixture model assuming that $\sum_{j=1}^{m} \alpha_j = 1$.

Algorithm 1. EM-based collaborative document ranking

Data: $\mathcal{D}$, $X^{(k)}$, E
Result: $M^{EM,k} \in \mathcal{R}^{n \times m}$
begin

    /* Stage 1: Learning the document-expert mapping   */
    while *nonconvergence* **do**

        /* E-step   */
        forall the *documents* $D_i \in \mathcal{D}$ **do**
            forall the *experts* $E_j \in E$ **do**

$$p(c_j = 1|X_i^{(k)}) = \frac{\alpha_j \phi_j(x_{ij}^{(k)})}{\sum_{l=1}^{m} \alpha_l \phi_l(x_{il}^{(k)})}$$
$$M_{ij}^{EM,k} = p(c_j = 1|X_i^{(k)})$$

        /* M-step   */
        forall the *experts* $E_j \in E$ **do**

$$\alpha_j = \frac{1}{n}\sum_{h=1}^{n} p(c_j = 1|X_h^{(k)})$$
$$\mu_j = \frac{1}{S_j}\sum_{h=1}^{n} p(c_j = 1|X_h^{(k)}).x_{hj}^{(k)}$$
$$\sigma_j = \frac{1}{S_j}\sum_{h=1}^{n} p(c_j = 1|X_h^{(k)}).(x_{hj^{(k)}} - \mu_j)^2$$

    /* Stage 2: Allocating documents to experts   */
    $M^{EM,k} = odds(M^{EM,k})$
    Return $M^{EM,k}$

---

expert E_l. Thus, we replace the probabilities $pij^{(k)}$ and $p_{il}^{(k)}$ by the Gaussian density values $\phi_j(x_{ij}^{(k)})$ and $\phi_l(x_{il}^{(k)})$ for obtaining the final estimated probability.
- The *M-step* updates the parameters θ_j and allows estimating the "Expected Complete Data Log Likelihood":

$$\mathcal{L}(c_j = 1|X_j^{(k)}, \theta_j) = \sum_{h=1}^{n}\sum_{l=1}^{m} log(p(c_l = 1|X_h^{(k)}))p(c_l = 1|X_h^{(k)}) \quad (9)$$

The algorithm convergence is reached when the log-likelihood is maximized.

2. Allocating documents to experts. The key issue is to detect which expert is more likely to assess the relevance of a document. Similarly to the probabilistic model assumption, we assign to each matrix element $M_{ij}^{EM,k}$ the odds value $odds(M_{ij}^{EM,k})$, computed as the ratio between the probability of relevance $M_{ij}^{EM,k}$ and the probability of irrelevance, estimated by $\sum_{\substack{l=1 \\ l \neq j}}^{m} M_{il}^{EM,k}$. The classification is done using this output matrix $M^{EM,k}$ where document D_i is allocated to expert E_j by maximizing the probability $p(c_j|X_i^{(k)})$ that document D_i is relevant for expert E_j considering its scores $X_i^{(k)}$:

$$\forall D_i, \ \exists \ E_j^*; \ E_j^* = \arg\max_{E_j \in E} M_{ij}^{EM,k} \tag{10}$$

Moreover, we propose an additional layer which ensures division of labor by removing from document allocation towards user u_j, documents already displayed within collaborators' lists.

4   Experimental Evaluation

Considering that it does not exist online collaborative search log, except proprietary ones [15,19], the retrieval effectiveness of our model was evaluated through a simulation-based framework which is an extension of the experimental framework proposed in Foley et al [10]. We used the same dataset, namely the TREC 6-7-8 Interactive one[1] which models users' interactions within an interactive-based IR task. One of the goals of users who perform this task is to identify several instances, namely aspects, related to the information need [17].

4.1   Experimental Setup

Dataset. We use the TREC Financial Times of London 1991-1994 Collection (Disk 4 of the TREC ad-hoc Collection) which includes 210 158 articles. We performed our effectiveness evaluation on 277 collaborative query search sessions extracted from dataset runs and built upon 20 TREC initial topics. The latter are analyzed for checking whether they are multi-faceted by estimating the diversity coverage of the top 1000 documents. We use the Jaccard distance between documents in pairs which avoids document length bias. We retained the whole set of 20 TREC topics, characterized by diversity coverage values very close to 1. Considering our collaborative model, we retain the 10 participants who have provided "rich format data" including the list of documents selected by the user and their respective selection time-stamp label. For each TREC topic, we retained as relevance judgments the respective feedback provided by TREC participants. For improving their reliability, we ensured the agreement between users by considering only documents which have been assessed twice as relevant. The agreement level is tuned in section 4.2 for testing the stability of our model.

---

[1] http://trec.nist.gov/data/interactive.html

Collaboration Simulation. Here, we extend the experimental protocol proposed in [10] by building groups of experts. Considering that experts use generally a more specific vocabulary [21,23], we analysed the expertise level $Expertise(U_j, Q)$ of each user U_j with respect to query Q using relevance feedback expressed through their respective TREC runs. For this purpose, we estimate the average specificity of the selected document set $\mathcal{D}^{S_Q(U_j)}$ using the specificity indicator $Pspec$ [14] for search session S_Q related to query Q:

$$Expertise(U_j, Q) = \frac{\sum_{D_i \in \mathcal{D}^{S_Q(U_j)}} \mathcal{L}_s(D_i)}{|\mathcal{D}^{S_Q}(U_j)|} \tag{11}$$

with $\mathcal{L}_s(D_i) = \underset{t \in D_i}{avg} Pspec(t) = \underset{t \in D_i}{avg} (-log(\frac{df_t}{N}))$. The document frequency of term t is noted df_t and N is the number of documents in the collection.

For each query Q, we performed a 2-means classification of users from all the participant groups who have achieved an interactive task considering their respective expertise level as criteria. We identified as experts users who belong to the class with the highest average expertise level value. Within each participant group and for each query, we perform all the combinations of size m, with $m \geq 2$, for building the set of 277 groups of experts. We notice that 19 TREC topics enable to form at least one group of experts of size $m \geq 2$. For each group of experts, we identified the time-line of relevance feedback which represents the whole set of selected documents by all the experts of the group synchronized chronologically by their respective time-stamp feature. We carefully consider the time-line of the collaborative search session by ensuring that every document assessed as relevant is displayed in the user's document list. Moreover, assuming that a user focuses his attention on the 30 top documents within a ranked list [10], only those are displayed to the user.

Metrics. We highlight here that CIR implies a different effectiveness evaluation approach compared to ad-hoc IR. Indeed, even if the goal of a collaborative document ranking model is to select relevant documents, the main objective remains on supporting the collaboration within the group [20]. For estimating the retrieval effectiveness of our model at the session level, we used metrics proposed in [20]. We consider measures at rank 30 considering the length of the displayed document lists. The evaluation metrics are the following:

- $Cov@R$: the coverage ratio at rank R for analysing the diversity of the search results displayed during the whole search session:

$$Cov@R = \frac{1}{|\theta|} \sum_{Q \in \theta} \frac{1}{|E_Q|} \sum_{e \in E_Q} \frac{Coverage(L_{e,Q})}{\sum_{l \in L_{e,Q}} |l|} \tag{12}$$

where θ is the set of TREC topics, E_Q represents the set of groups e of experts who have collaborated for solving query Q and $L_{e,Q}$ is the set of displayed lists related to query Q for group e. $Coverage(L_{e,Q})$ corresponds to the number of distinct documents displayed to expert group e for query Q. The total number of documents displayed throughout the same session is noted $|l|$.

- *RelCov@R*, the relevant coverage ratio at rank R which adds the supplementary layer to the coverage measure by including the condition that distinct displayed documents should be relevant:

$$RelCov@R = \frac{1}{|\theta|} \sum_{Q \in \theta} \frac{1}{|E_Q|} \sum_{e \in E_Q} \frac{RelevantCoverage(L_{e,Q})}{\sum_{l \in L_{e,Q}} |l|} \qquad (13)$$

where $RelevantCoverage(L_{e,Q})$ corresponds to the number of distinct relevant documents displayed to expert group e for query Q.

- *P@R*: the average precision at rank R:

$$P@R = \frac{1}{|\theta|} \sum_{Q \in \theta} \frac{1}{|E_Q|} \sum_{e \in E_Q} \frac{1}{|L_{E,Q}|} \sum_{l \in L_{e,Q}} \frac{D_{SelRel}(Q,l)}{\sum_{l \in L_{e,Q}} |l|} \qquad (14)$$

where $D_{SelRel}(Q,l)$ represents the number of relevant documents retrieved within document list l related to query Q.

Baselines. We performed four scenarios considering either an individual-based search or a collaborative-based one:

- *W/oEMDoL* is the individual version of our model which integrates only the expert-based document scoring presented in section 3.2.
- *W/oDoL* is our collaborative-based model detailed in section 3 by excluding the division of labor principle.
- *W/oEM* is our collaborative-based model by excluding the expert-based document allocation, detailed in section 3.2.
- *OurModel* is our collaborative-based model detailed in section 3.

4.2   Results

Here, we present the results obtained throughout our experimental evaluation. We adopt a learning-testing method through a two-cross validation strategy in order to tune the retrieval model parameters and then test its effectiveness. For this purpose, we randomly split the 277 search sessions into two equivalent sets, noted Q_A and Q_B. In what follows, we detail the parameter tuning, for both baselines and our model, and the retrieval effectiveness results.

Parameter Tuning. First, we tune the weighting parameter γ in Equation 1, used for the diversification of the search results using the MMR score [4]. The diversity criteria considered for building the subset of documents $\mathcal{D}^*$ of size $n = 1000$ is inversely proportional to the value of γ. For both subsets of queries Q_A and Q_B, the retrieval effectiveness is optimal for a γ value equal to 1.

Second, we estimate the optimal number of topics used for the topical distribution of documents. For each multi-faceted query, we perform the LDA algorithm with a number of topics T from 20 to 200 with a step of 20. The number of topics is tuned using the likelihood, presented in Equation 2. We retain $T = 200$ as the optimal value for both query sets Q_A and Q_B. Considering that previous work [8] found that the number of query subtopics is lower than 10 for most of the queries, we add a supplementary layer for modeling query facets by considering the top f facets among the 200 ones of the topical distribution of the query valued by the probability $\theta_{Q|t}$. Documents and experts are therefore represented by extracting these f facets from their topical vector.

Third, we jointly tune the number f of the top facets and the parameter λ which combines a similarity score based on the topical modeling and the BM25 algorithm within the document scoring step in equation 6. In order to tune $\lambda \in [0; 1]$ and $f \in [1; 10]$, we rank, for each TREC topic $Q \in \theta$, the top 1000 diversified documents $D_i \in \mathcal{D}^*$ according to their topical distribution. We retain the value $\lambda = 0.6$ and $f = 5$ which maximizes the retrieval effectiveness for both sets of queries Q_A and Q_B.

Model Effectiveness Evaluation. Table 2 compares the obtained results using our collaborative model with those obtained by the three scenarios, detailed in section 4.1. The reported precisions show that our model generally overpasses the baseline models without the EM step, namely *W/oEM* and *W/oEMDoL*. More particularly, the improvement is significant compared to the scenario *W/oEM* for the query testing set Q_B with a value of +20.61%. This highlights the importance of allocating documents to experts, as detailed in section 3.2, considering the whole set of experts in contrast to a ranking algorithm only based on a personalized document scoring towards a particular expert, as detailed in equation 4. We notice that the scenario performed without division of labor, namely *W/oDoL*, provides better results than our model considering the precision measures. On a first point of view, we could conclude that division of labor is inappropriate for solving collaboratively a multi-faceted information need. However, this statement is counterbalanced by the analysis of coverage-based measures, detailed in section 4.1. In fact, we notice that our model provides in most of the cases higher values of the coverage-based measures with several significant improvements around +17.69% for the *Cov*@30 metric and up to +55.40% for the *RelCov*@30 one. These results show that our model ensures both diversity of the displayed documents throughout the coverage measure *Cov*@30 and relevance of these diversified documents within the displayed lists by means of the *RelCov*@30 measure. This contrast between precision measures and coverage-based ones is explained by the fact that the latter takes into account the residual relevance feedback within the displayed document lists whereas the second one does not consider document redundancy between successive displayed lists. In summary, the results show that our collaborative ranking model is more appropriate for satisfying a multi-faceted information need compared to an individual one, namely through scenario *W/oEMDoL*; moreover, as reported by coverage-based measures we confirm that our model favors the topical diversity of the search results thanks to the division of labor principle.

Complementary Analysis. We perform further analysis to show the impact of two parameters, namely the relevance agreement level and the group size, on the model effectiveness. Figure 1 plots the retrieval effectiveness variation within these two parameters. We can see that our model curve overpasses baseline curves for both parameters. The decreasing trend of curves in Figure 1(a) can be explained

Table 2. Comparative analysis of the retrieval effectiveness of our model - %Ch: our model improvement. Student test significance *: $0.01 < t \leq 0.05$; **: $0.001 < t < 0.01$; ***: $t < 0.001$.

Learning set → Testing set	Scenario	Cov@30	%Ch	RelCov@30	%Ch	P@30	%Ch
$Q_B \rightarrow Q_A$	W/oDoL	0.486	+12.01	0.131	+19.58*	0.388	-0.30
	W/oEM	0.571	-4.60	0.124	+26.73*	0.309	+20.60*
	W/oEMDoL	0.454	+17.56***	0.101	+55.40**	0.369	+1.13
	OurModel	0.545		**0.157**		0.372	
$Q_A \rightarrow Q_B$	W/oDoL	0.481	+10.78***	0.147	+4.29	0.414	-2.12***
	W/oEM	0.526	+1.38	0.134	+14.77	0.379	+7.01
	W/oEMDoL	0.453	+17.69***	0.131	+17.16	0.394	+ 2.73
	OurModel	**0.533**		**0.156**		0.406	

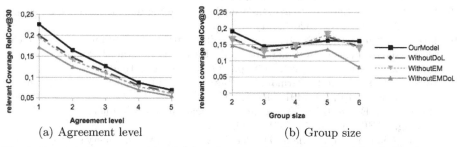

(a) Agreement level   (b) Group size

Fig. 1. Impact of agreement level (a) and group size (b) on the retrieval effectiveness

by the fact that higher is the agreement level, fewer documents are assessed as relevant within the search session and this favors the search failure regardless of the retrieval model. From Figure 1(b), we notice that the curve of our model is generally stable even with the increasing size of the collaborator group. These statements confirm that the retrieval model improvements are stable within different configurations of collaborative search settings.

5   Conclusion and Future Work

In this paper, we propose a collaborative ranking model for satisfying a multi-faceted information need considering a group of experts. We propose an iterative relevance-feedback process for automatically updating expert's document list by means of the Expectation-Maximization learning method for collaboratively ranking documents. Our model was evaluated using a collaboration simulation-based framework and has shown effective results. Future work will focus on the design of other formal methods to emphasize division of labor and the modeling of user profile through his behavior in addition to his relevance feedback.

References

1. Allan, J., Raghavan, H.: Using part-of-speech patterns to reduce query ambiguity. In: SIGIR 2007, pp. 307–314 (2002)

2. Ashkan, A., Clarke, C.L., Agichtein, E., Guo, Q.: Classifying and characterizing query intent. In: Boughanem, M., Berrut, C., Mothe, J., Soule-Dupuy, C. (eds.) ECIR 2009. LNCS, vol. 5478, pp. 578–586. Springer, Heidelberg (2009)
3. Blei, D.M., Ng, A.Y., Jordan, M.I.: Latent dirichlet allocation. J. Mach. Learn. Res. 3, 993–1022 (2003)
4. Carbonell, J., Goldstein, J.: The use of mmr, diversity-based reranking for reordering documents and producing summaries. In: SIGIR 1998, pp. 335–336 (1998)
5. Dakka, W., Dayal, R., Ipeirotis, P.G.: Automatic discovery of useful facet terms. In: SIGIR 2006, pp. 18–22 (2006)
6. Deerwester, S., Dumais, S.T., Furnas, G.W., Landauer, T.K., Harshman, R.: Indexing by latent semantic analysis. JASIST 41, 391–407 (1990)
7. Dempster, A.P., Laird, N.M., Rubin, D.B.: Maximum likelihood from incomplete data via the em algorithm. Journal of the Royal Statistical Society, Series B 39(1), 1–38 (1977)
8. Deveaud, R., SanJuan, E., Bellot, P.: Unsupervised latent concept modeling to identify query facets. In: RIAO 2013 (2013)
9. Dou, Z., Hu, S., Luo, Y., Song, R., Wen, J.-R.: Finding dimensions for queries. In: CIKM 2011, pp. 1311–1320 (2011)
10. Foley, C., Smeaton, A.F.: Synchronous collaborative information retrieval: Techniques and evaluation. In: Boughanem, M., Berrut, C., Mothe, J., Soule-Dupuy, C. (eds.) ECIR 2009. LNCS, vol. 5478, pp. 42–53. Springer, Heidelberg (2009)
11. Harvey, M., Ruthven, I., Carman, M.: Ranking social bookmarks using topic models. In: CIKM 2010, pp. 1401–1404 (2010)
12. He, J., Meij, E., de Rijke, M.: Result diversification based on query-specific cluster ranking. JASIST 62(3), 550–571 (2011)
13. Hu, Y., Qian, Y., Li, H., Jiang, D., Pei, J., Zheng, Q.: Mining query subtopics from search log data. In: SIGIR 2012, pp. 305–314 (2012)
14. Kim, G.: Relationship between index term specificity and relevance judgment. Inf. Process. Manage. 42(5), 1218–1229 (2006)
15. Morris, M.R., Horvitz, E.: Searchtogether: an interface for collaborative web search. In: UIST 2007, pp. 3–12 (2007)
16. Morris, M.R., Teevan, J., Bush, S.: Enhancing collaborative web search with personalization: groupization, smart splitting, and group hit-highlighting. In: CSCW 2008, pp. 481–484 (2008)
17. Over, P.: The trec interactive track: an annotated bibliography. Inf. Process. Manage. 37(3), 369–381 (2001)
18. Pickens, J., Golovchinsky, G., Shah, C., Qvarfordt, P., Back, M.: Algorithmic mediation for collaborative exploratory search. In: SIGIR 2008, pp. 315–322 (2008)
19. Shah, C.: Collaborative Information Seeking: The Art and Science of Making The Whole Greater Than The Sum of All. Springer (2012)
20. Shah, C., González-Ibáñez, R.: Evaluating the synergic effect of collaboration in information seeking. In: SIGIR 2011, pp. 913–922 (July 2011)
21. Shah, C., Pickens, J., Golovchinsky, G.: Role-based results redistribution for collaborative information retrieval. Inf. Process. Manage. 46(6), 773–781 (2010)
22. Wang, Q., Cao, Z., Xu, J., Li, H.: Group matrix factorization for scalable topic modeling. In: SIGIR 2012, pp. 375–384 (2012)
23. White, R.W., Dumais, S.T., Teevan, J.: Characterizing the influence of domain expertise on web search behavior. In: WSDM 2009, pp. 132–141 (2009)
24. Zhu, X., Goldberg, A.B., Van, J., Andrzejewski, G.D.: Improving diversity in ranking using absorbing random walks. In: SIGIR 2009 (2009)

Using Dempster-Shafer's Evidence Theory for Query Expansion Based on Freebase Knowledge

Dazhao Pan[1], Peng Zhang[1], Jingfei Li[1], Dawei Song[1,2], Ji-Rong Wen[3],
Yuexian Hou[1], Bin Hu[4], Yuan Jia[5], and Anne De Roeck[2]

[1] Tianjin University, Tianjin, China
[2] The Open University, Milton Keynes, UK
[3] Microsoft Research Asia
[4] Lanzhou University, Lanzhou, China
[5] Institute of Linguistics, Chinese Academy of Social Sciences, China
{dazhaopan,darcyzzj,dawei.song2010,krete1941}@gmail.com
tjucsljf@foxmail.com,jrwen@microsoft.com
bh@lzu.edu.cn,summeryuan_2003@126.com,anne.deroeck@open.ac.uk

Abstract. Query expansion is generally a useful technique in improving search performance. However, some expanded query terms obtained by traditional statistical methods (e.g., pseudo-relevance feedback) may not be relevant to the user's information need, while some relevant terms may not be contained in the feedback documents at all. Recent studies utilize external resources to detect terms that are related to the query, and then adopt these terms in query expansion. In this paper, we present a study in the use of Freebase [6], which is an open source general-purpose ontology, as a source for deriving expansion terms. FreeBase provides a graph-based model of human knowledge, from which a rich and multi-step structure of instances related to the query concept can be extracted, as a complement to the traditional statistical approaches to query expansion. We propose a novel method, based on the well-principled Dempster-Shafer's (D-S) evidence theory, to measure the certainty of expansion terms from the Freebase structure. The expanded query model is then combined with a state of the art statistical query expansion model – the Relevance Model (RM3). Experiments show that the proposed method achieves significant improvements over RM3.

Keywords: Query Expansion, Freebase, Dempster-Shafer theory.

1 Introduction

The information needs of the searchers are often formulated as keyword queries. However, searchers tend to use short and incomplete queries. Consequently the original query input by the user may miss some important information, resulting in a negative impact on the retrieval effectiveness. To address this problem, query expansion (QE) has been widely used [5] [7] [15].

Pseudo-relevance feedback (PRF) is a typical query expansion method [8] [7] [19] [33]. It selects expansion terms from top-ranked documents in the first-round retrieval as feedback documents, by assuming that feedback documents

R.E. Banchs et al. (Eds.): AIRS 2013, LNCS 8281, pp. 121–132, 2013.
© Springer-Verlag Berlin Heidelberg 2013

are relevant and contain the key concepts related to the query. However, in practice the top ranked documents may not all be truly relevant, so that many expansion terms derived may be irrelevant. The uncertainty of the relevance of expansion terms may cause the query drifting problem [8].

To tackle this problem, recent research attempts to make use of external knowledge, such as click data, user log, Wikipedia or simple ontology data Word-Net. The analysis of the user search history (e.g., click data) may avoid the query drifting problem, but the coverage of such knowledge is limited[10]. The emergence of the Web and large-scale human edited knowledge (e.g., Wikipedia and Freebase) provides access to new sources of high quality term associations for query expansion [34].

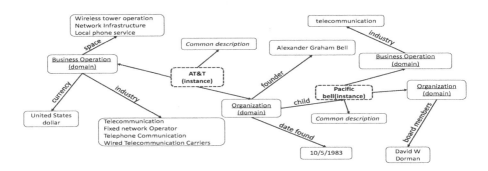

Fig. 1. Fragment of the entity-relationship graph of Freebase

In this paper, we focus on studying the use of an ontology-structured knowledge source - Freebase, as the source of obtaining expansion terms. Freebase employs the entity-relation model to describe the data in the knowledge base. It has over 37 million topics about real-world entities like people, places and events. We choose Freebase for three reasons. First, it contains a large amount of knowledge, covering different aspects of the world, such as location, people, event, military, music, film, literature and business. As an illustration, we searched the TREC queries in the Freebase, and found that 90% of the queries (we used in our experiments) have matches of some relevant knowledge. Second, unlike Wikipedia that describes human knowledge with a long detailed article, Freebase describes the human knowledge using an ontological structure, and describes each property with keywords. Therefore, the relevant concepts underneath a query can be quickly located. Third, different from the WordNet which mainly contains synonymy relations, Freebase not only describes entities, but also contains different properties and entity-relationships. Thus one can walk through the entity-relation graph to find deeper relationships.

A fragment of the entity-relation graph in Freebase is shown in Figure 1. We can see that all the information about an instance (e.g., AT&T) is contained in its properties (e.g., space, industry, currency). We can also find other instances that are related to the current one. For example, starting from AT&T and walking through the Organization Domain, we can find AT&T's successor node

- "Pacific bell", which is also an instance. For a query, we can find the matched instances as well as their parent and child instances up to a certain step, and treat them as different aspects that describe the query. Then it is key to fuse the relevant information from different aspects. In this paper, we propose to solve the fusion problem by using the Dempster-Shafer's (D-S) evidence theory [23]. D-S theory allows one to combine evidence from different sources and arrive at a degree of belief that takes into account all the available evidences. Treating different instances as different evidences for determining query expansion terms from Freebase, we redefine the Basic Probability Assignment (BPA) and Belief functions in the D-S theory, and define a new measure, called *Certainty*, to represent a term's importance in the knowledge structure. Under the framework of D-S theory, we also define the transitivity of the nodes in the knowledge structure. Finally, we integrate the above parameters in a single model (see Section 4.3).

The knowledge terms are then combined with the terms given by the relevance model (RM3) [17] [18]. In the combination process, we balance the knowledge term's Certainty values by D-S theory and the original weights by RM3, in order to compute the final term weights in the query expansion model. Our experiments show that the selected knowledge terms are complementary to the initial query (Table 2). Combining the knowledge terms and the RM3 terms can significantly improve the retrieval effectiveness.

2 Related Work

Pseudo relevance feedback (PRF) is an effective query expansion method by reformulating the original query using terms derived from the pseudo-relevance documents [8] [7] [19] [33]. Based on the assumption that top-ranked documents are relevant to the query, several PRF algorithms are proposed, e.g., Okapi [22], relevance model [15] and mixture model [35].

Despite the large number of studies in this area, a crucial question is that the expansion terms extracted from the pseudo-relevant documents are not all useful [8]. It was found that one of reasons for the failure of query expansion is the lack of relevant documents in local relevance feedback collection. Recently, some researches attempt to capture and utilize lexico-semantic relationships, based on the association hypothesis formulated by van Rijsbergen [25]. Early global expansion techniques [11] [12] [33] aim to determine the strength of semantic relatedness between terms based on the term co-occurrence statistics. The emergency of hand-crafted general purpose or domain-specific ontologies also provide access to high quality term associations for query expansion. Several approaches have been proposed to utilize external resources, such as query logs [10], WordNet [9], Wikipedia [34], ConceptNet [13], etc. Yin et al. proposed an expansion method based on random walking through URL graph [12]. Voorhees [32] experimentally determined an upper bound of the WordNet based on query expansion.

Furthermore, there has been an emerging line of research on ontology-based query expansion. Vallet et al. [3] used an ontology query language to search for relevant documents. Nagypal et al. [20] combined the use of ontology with the vector space model. Braga et al. [2] used ontologies for information extraction and filtering across multiple domains. Ozcan et al. [4] adopted ontologies to represent concepts which are expanded by using WordNet. Meij et al. [16] showed that discriminative semantic annotations of documents using domain-specific ontologies, such as MeSH, can effectively improve retrieval effectiveness.

Several methods which combine multiple resources have also been proposed. Mandala et al. [31] proposed a method to combine three different thesaurus types for query expansion. Bodner et al. [27] combined WordNet and co-occurrence based thesauri for query expansion. In the work of Collins-Thompson and Callan [30], a Markov chain based framework were proposed for query expansion by combining multiple sources of knowledge on term associations. In Cao et al. [28], term relationships from co-occurrence statistics and WordNet were used to smooth the document language model.

Dempster-Shafer (D-S) theory has been applied to IR in several previous studies. In [21], D-S theory has been used to combine content and link information in Web IR, and in [24], it is used to combine textual and visual evidences for image retrieval. Theophylactou and Lalmas [14] also used D-S theory to model a compound term as a set of single terms. In our work, we employ the D-S theory to measure the scores of the terms in Freebase that are matched against a query, and to determine the weights of the expanded terms based on such scores.

3   Query Matching in Freebase

Given a query, in order to find matched instances in Freebase, we first split a query into sequences of words. For example, the query "commercial satellite launches" can be split into three phrases: "commercial satellite launches", "commercial satellite" and "satellite launches". We search these three phrases in Freebase and get relevant instances. Note that we do not split the query to single terms, because we think that single terms will more likely match non-relevant instances, due to lack of context. For example, the query "Black Monday" describes the largest one-day percentage decline in recorded stock market history. If we split it to "Black" and "Monday", the two separate terms, individually, are irrelevant to the query. In our experiment, the minimum splitting unit is two sequential terms.

After getting the phrases from the query, we then adopt a two-round matching process to find candidate instances. In the first round, we will find whether a phrase extracted from query is recorded in the Freebase using exact match. If the phrase is recorded, we will get the corresponding instance and extract the notable domain from the instance. in the second round, we employ the Freebase's API to search for (partially) matched instances within the notable domain. For example, for the phrase "Black Monday", in the first round matching, we get the exactly matched instance "black Monday" and extract its notable domain "event". In the second round, we only search the instances belonging to the "event" domain. Through the two-round matching, we get the matched instances. The Match

Score provided by the Freebase's API, is used to measure the relevance degree between a query phrase and an instance.

As shown in Fig.1, one instance's property may be another instance. Therefore, in addition to the two round matching strategy described above, we go deeper in the Freebase graph by walking through the path as follows:

$$instance_j \dashrightarrow property_{jk} \dashrightarrow instance_k \dashrightarrow property_{kw}$$

where $property_{jk}$ is the $k-th$ property of $instance_j$. We use the $property_{jk}$ to find the child $instance_k$ and finally we can get the property of $instance_k$. In our paper, we call the instances directly from the two round matching process as the **first level instances** and their successor instances as **second level instances**.

4   Ranking Knowledge Terms Based on Dempster-Shafer Theory

Table 1. Notations

Parameters	Definition
Q	Query
q_i	term in Query
I_i	first level Instance
$FS(I_i)$	instance I_i's Freebase score provided by Freebase
Ip_i	second level Instance
$tf_k(t_i)$	term t_i's term frequency in instance I_k
$m_k(t_i)$	basic probability assignment (BPA) in instance I_k
$Bel_k(t_i)$	belief of term in instance I_k
$Bel_k(Ip_i)$	belief of second level instance in instance I_k
$Pl_k(t_i)$	plausibility of term in instance I_k
$Pl_k(Ip_j)$	plausibility of second level instance in instance I_k
$Certainty(I_k)$	initial I_k's relevance degree with query
$Certainty(Ip_i)$	the measure of certainty of the second level instance
$Certainty(t_i)$	the measure of certainty of the single term

4.1   An Introduction to Dempster-Shafer Theory

The Dempster-Shafer (D-S) theory is a mathematical theory of evidence [23]. It allows one to combine evidence from different sources and arrive at a degree of belief that takes into account all the available evidence. It is developed to account for the uncertainty. Specifically, let θ represent all possible states (or elements) under consideration. Function m: $2^\theta \to [0,1]$ is called a basic probability assignment (BPA), which assigns a probability mass to each element. It has two properties:

First, the empty set is assigned the value 0:

$$m(\emptyset) = 0$$

Second, the sum of the probabilities assigned to all elements of θ is 1:

$$\sum_{X \in 2^\theta} m(X) = 1$$

Based on the mass assignments, the upper and lower bounds of a probability interval can be defined. This interval contains the precise probabilities of a set of elements (denoted as A), and is bounded by two non-additive continuous measures called belief (or support) and plausibility:

$$Bel(A) \leq P(A) \leq Pl(A)$$

The belief $Bel(A)$ for a set A is defined as the sum of all the masses of subsets of A:

$$Bel(A) = \sum_{B:B \subseteq A} m(B)$$

That is, $Bel(A)$ gathers all the evidence directly in support of A. The plausibility $Pl(A)$ is the sum of all the masses of the sets B that intersect A:

$$Pl(A) = \sum_{B:B \cap A \neq \emptyset} m(B) = 1 - Bel(\overline{A})$$

It defines the upper bounds of A.

Dempster-Shafer theory corresponds to the traditional probability theory when m assigns non-zero probabilities only to individual elements. The Dempster's rule of combination provides a method to fuse the evidences for an element from multiple independent sources and calculate an overall belief for the element. In our paper, we use the Dempster's rule to measure the Certainty of a term from different matched instances, detailed in the next subsection.

4.2   Using D-S Theory to Rank the Candidate Terms

We treat different instances as different sources of evidence. Our objective is to measure the certainty of a term that is contained in multiple instances. We assume the hypothesis space is composed of all the candidate terms extracted from Freebase, e.g., $instance \longrightarrow \{a, b, c, d, e, \{d, e\}\}$, where d, e are second level instances. We use P to represent the hypothesis space.

We measure the basic probability assignment(BPA) of a single term t_i in P as follows:

$$m_k(t_i) \propto tf_k(t_i)Certainty(I_k) \tag{1}$$

where $tf_k(t_i)$ represents t_i's term frequency in the Instance I_k, and we define the initial $Certainty(I_k)$ as the Match score of the Instance I_k with respect to the query. We adopt different strategies to measure the Certainty for instances got from the two round matching process. Intuitively, if an instance contains more terms from query, the instance is more relevant to the query. Therefore we use the length of the first round matched instance to measure I_1's Certainty.

$$Certainty(I_1) = \frac{length(I_1)}{length(Q)} \tag{2}$$

Table 2. Top ranked terms extracted from Freebase combined (by D-S theory) with expanded terms from Feedback documents (by RM3) on AP collection

Query	Top Knowledge Terms(AP)
Black Monday	finance stock market crash industrial
Diversify of Pacific Telesis	pactel bell commun telecom wireless
Conflict in Horn of Africa	east somalia eritrea ethiopia djibouti
Nuclear Prolifer	weapon india treati north korea
McDonnell Douglas Contracts Military Aircraft	germani navi radar bomber jet

For the instances got from the second round retrieval, we initialize their Certainty according to the comparison with I_1:

$$Certainty(I_i) = \frac{FS(I_i)}{FS(I_1)} Certainty(I_1) \tag{3}$$

where $FS(I_i)$ represents the *Match Score* provided by Freebase and $i \neq 1$. We use the $FS(I_1)$ as a standard value, and use $\frac{FS(I_i)}{FS(I_1)}$ to represent the ratio between $FS(I_i)$ and $FS(I_1)$, where $FS(I_i) < FS(I_1)$.

For the single term, we calculate the $Bel(t_i)$ as follows:

$$Bel_k(t_i) \propto tf_k(t_i)Certainty(I_k) \tag{4}$$

For the second level instance Ip_i, we calculate the $Bel(Ip_i)$ as follows:

$$Bel_k(Ip_i) \propto \sum_{t_i:t_i \in Ip_i} tf_k(t_i)Certainty(I_i) \tag{5}$$

According to the Dempster-Shafer evidence theory, the plausibility of the second level instance calculated as follows:

$$Pl_k(Ip_i) \propto Certainty(I_k) - Bel_k(\overline{Ip_i}) \tag{6}$$

As mentioned in Section **4.2**, the plausibility of the single term is the same as Bel. So, $Pl(t_i) = Bel(t_i)$.

Fusion. Recall that, we treat different instances as different sources of evidence, and Dempster's rule of combination that aggregates two or more bodies of evidence (defined within the same frame of discernment) into one body of evidence. Let m_j and m_k be two different BPA calculated from I_j and I_k. A as the common terms. we calculate the combined BPA as follows :

$$m(A) \propto (m_j \oplus m_k)(A)$$

$$= \frac{\sum_{B \cap C = A \neq \emptyset} (tf_j(B)Certainty(I_j)) \times (tf_k(C)Certainty(I_k))}{(1-K)} \tag{7}$$

$$K \propto \sum_{B \cap C = \emptyset} (tf_j(B)Certainty(I_j)) \times (tf_k(C)Certainty(I_k)) \tag{8}$$

Where B and C are two hypothesis space from two different Instances. According to the Dempster's rule of combination, we fuse the term's BPA from different instances. We calculate the Bel using the uniformed BPA.

Transitivity. In order to measure the second level instance's properties, we need to measure the *Certainty* of the second level instance, and according to the *Bel* and *Pl*, we measure the second level instance as follows:

$$Certainty(Ip_i) \propto Bel_{Ip_i} + \frac{|Ip_i|}{|P|}(Pl_k(Ip_i) - Bel_k(Ip_i)) \qquad (9)$$

where $|Ip_i|$ indicates the length of the instance property, and $|P|$ indicates the number of the elements in P. Therefore we get the Certainty of the second level instance which is passed through its precursor's instance. After that, we can use such method to calculate Certainty of second level instance's property. We use Certainty to represent term's final score in the Freebase (Considering $Bel = Pl$ for single term. So, $Certainty(t_i) = Bel(t_i)$).

4.3   Extended Relevance Model

In the framework of Relevance Model(RM), we estimate the probability distribution $P(w|R)$, where w is an arbitrary word and R is the unknown underlying relevance model, which is usually extracted by RM based on the top-ranked documents of the initial retrieval.

Although the candidate expansion words extracted from knowledge are relevant to the query in Freebase, we do not know whether such knowledge words are suitable to the local corpus. In order to measure the relevance of the knowledge words in the local corpus, we measure two features of knowledge candidate words. First, we will count the co-occurrence of the candidate expanded knowledge term and query term in a Window (we segment the documents to small passages). It is formulated as follows:

$$co - occurrence_{(q_i,t_i)} = \#win_n(t_i, q_i) \qquad (10)$$

We filter the knowledge terms using the co-occurrence feature, by removing the terms that don't co-occur with the query terms. Second, based on the assumption, if a knowledge candidate term is relevant to the query, it will occur in the top-ranked feedback documents. We calculate two term distributions: 1) the term frequency in the top-ranked feedback documents, 2) the term frequency in the whole corpus. Using the method mentioned in the work of Parapar and Barreiro [29]. We assume that the term with a big divergence is important. Combing with the Certainty from knowledge, we measure the term score as follows:

$$Socre(t_i) = Certainty(t_i)log(\frac{tf(t_i|D)}{tf(t_i|C)})IDF(t_i|D) \qquad (11)$$

$$IDF(t_i) = log(\frac{|C|}{|j : t_i \in d_j|}) \qquad (12)$$

where D is the top-ranked documents, C is the whole corpus and $Certainty(t_i)$ is the measure of term's Certainty in the Freebase. We use the *log* operation to smooth the distribution gap. *IDF* is used to represent the importance of term in the corpus. $|C|$ represents the total amount of documents in the corpus. $|j : t_i \in d_j|$ represents the amount of documents that contain the term t_i. We think that the Freebase term with a higher IDF and a bigger divergence of term distribution is more relevant to the query. We use the score computed by Eq. 11 to measure the importance of the terms. Table 2 shows the top ranked knowledge terms.

We will combine our knowledge terms with the Relevance Model (RM3). Specifically, we formulate the new query Q_{new} as follows:

$$Q_{new} \propto \lambda Q_{ori} + (1 - \lambda)(Q_{exp} + Q_{kb}) \tag{13}$$

where Q_{ori} is the original query, Q_{exp} is the expanded query by RM, and Q_{kb} represents the terms extracted from Freebase. We do not involve extra parameters in Eq. 13, where λ is the parameter of RM3 (i.e., $\lambda Q_{ori} + (1 - \lambda)Q_{exp}$).

5 Experiment

5.1 Experimental Settings

We use three standard TREC collections: AP8889 with topics.101-150; WSJ with topics.101-150; ROBUST04 with topics.301-450. Table 3 shows the detail of the collections. We use mean average precision(MAP) to evaluate the retrieval effectiveness. Lemur4.12 is used for indexing and retrieval. Documents and queries are stemmered with the Porter stemmer and the stopwords are removed through the Stopwords list.

Table 3. Overview of TREC collections and topics

Corpus	Size	# of Doc	Topics
AP8889	0.6G	164,597	101-150
WSJ	0.5G	173,252	101-150
ROBUST04	1.8G	528,155	301-450

5.2 Baseline Models

In our experiments, we select two baselines. One is the query-likelihood language model (QL), and the other is the relevance Model (RM3). RM3 is a strong baseline which is widely used, and we choose the parameters of RM3 to get its optimal result on each collection. RM3 + FB1 and RM3 + FB are the results that we didn't apply D-S. RM3 + FB1 is the result that we just use the first level of the Freebase, RM3 + FB is the result that we use both level of the Freebase.

5.3 Parameter Settings

In our experiment, we adopt the Dirichlet smoothing method and set the Dirichlet prior as the default 1000. RM3 + KB is our model that combines the RM3 terms

Table 4. Performance comparisons on all the topics

Method	Topics.101-150(AP8889)	Topics.101-150(WSJ)	Topics.301-450(ROBUST04)
QL	0.2423	0.2629	0.2480
RM3	0.3077	0.2941	0.2550
RM3 + FB1	0.3105(0.90%)	0.2970(0.986%)	0.2554(0.157%)
RM3 + FB	0.3142(2.10%)	0.2921(-0.680%)	0.2558(0.317%)
RM3 + KB	*0.3197(3.90%)	*0.3008(2.28%)	0.2598(1.18%)

* indicates statistically significant improvements (at level 0.05) over RM3.

and Freebase terms using D-S theory. Both RM3 and RM3 + KB methods have parameters N, k, λ. For number of feedback documents, we tested N from 10, 20, 30, 40, 50. We evaluated the λ for different values: 0.1, 0.2, 0.3, 0.4, 0.5. And for the feedback terms number k , we tested :10, 20, 30, 40, 50. When N = 10, k = 50 and λ = 0.1, RM3 gets the optimal result. In Eq. 13, we combine knowledge candidate terms and RM3 terms, so we denote the new query model in Eq. 13 as RM3+KB. RM3+KB adopts the same parameter (i.e., λ) as RM3 model.

5.4 Experiment Results

As can be seen from the Table 4, RM3 largely outperforms QL, which demonstrates RM3 is an effective query expansion method on all collections. For RM3+KB, On AP8889 and WSJ, it has a significant performance improvement over the RM3 model. For ROBUST04, RM3+KB also improves the performance over RM3. RM3+KB also outperforms RM3 + FB1 and RM3 + FB in which the D-S theory is not involoved. We can see that RM3+KB performs the best on all collections.

Table 5. Performance comparisons on the topics for which related knowledge instances can be found in Freebase

Method	Topics.101-150(AP8889)	Topics.101-150(WSJ)	Topics.301-450(ROBUST04)
QL	0.2446	0.2532	0.2351
RM3	0.3045	0.2858	0.2406
RM3 + KB	*0.3207(5.32%)	*0.2945(3.04%)	0.2459(2.20%)

* indicates statistically significant improvements (at level 0.05) over RM3.

As we have mentioned, not all of queries have the relevant knowledge in Freebase, e.g., for Topics.101-150, about 90% queries can find relevant instance in Freebase. We then report the results of the topics for which the related instances can be found in Freebase. From the result showed by Table 5, we can see that on AP8889 collection, the performance is improved by RM3 + KB about 5% over RM3, and on WSJ collection, performance is improved about 3% over RM3. For ROBUST04, the performance is also improved about 2% over RM3. These results indicate that the terms extracted from the Freebase are relevant to the query and RM3 with knowledge terms works better than using RM3 terms only.

6 Conclusions

In this paper, we have explored the use of Freebase as a resource for query expansion. In our work, we adopt a two round query match in Freebase to find knowledge instances related to query. We propose to apply the Dempster-Shafer evidence theory to rank relevant terms for the query. We then combine the extracted terms (from Freebase) with the expanded terms (from feedback documents) by RM3. The experiment result shows that terms extracted from Freebase have a significant improvement performance over RM3, which is a state-of-the-art query expansion method.

Acknowledgments. This work is funded in part by the Chinese National Program on Key Basic Research Project (973 Program, grant no. 2013CB329304 and 2014CB744604), the Natural Science Foundation of China (grant no. 61272265), and the European Union Framework 7 Marie-Curie International Research Staff Exchange Programme (grant no. 247590).

References

1. Ciorascu, C., Ciorascu, I., Stoffel, K.: Knowler-ontological support for information retrieval systems. In: SIGIR 2003, vol. 2 (2003)
2. Braga, R.M.M., Werner, C.M.L., Mattoso, M.: Using ontologies for domain information retrieval. In: Database and Expert Systems Applications, pp. 836–840 (2000)
3. Vallet, D., Fernández, M., Castells, P.: An ontology-based information retrieval model. In: The Semantic Web: Research and Applications, pp. 455–470 (2005)
4. Ozcan, R., Aslangdogan, Y.A.: Concept based information access using ontologies and latent semantic analysis. Dept. of Computer Science and Engineering 8 (2004)
5. Bendersky, M., Croft, W.B.: Discovering key concepts in verbose queries. In: SIGIR 2008, pp. 491–498 (2008)
6. Bollacker, K., Evans, C., Paritosh, P., Sturge, T., Taylor, J.: Freebase: a collaboratively created graph database for structuring human knowledge. In: SIGMOD 2008, pp. 1247–1250 (2008)
7. Buckley, C., Salton, G., Allan, J., Singhal, A.: Automatic query expansion using smart: Trec 3. NIST Special Publication SP, pp. 69-69 (1995)
8. Cao, G., Nie, J.Y., Gao, J., Robertson, S.: Selecting good expansion terms for pseudo-relevance feedback. In: SIGIR 2008, pp. 243–250 (2008)
9. Collins-Thompson, K., Callan, J.: Query expansion using random walk models. In: ACM International Conference on Information and Knowledge Management, pp. 704–711 (2005)
10. Cui, H., Wen, J.R., Nie, J.Y., Ma, W.Y.: Query expansion by mining user logs. IEEE Transactions on Knowledge and Data Engineering, 829–839 (2003)
11. Gauch, S., Wang, J.: A corpus analysis approach for automatic query expansion. In: Proceedings of the Sixth International Conference on Information and Knowledge Management, pp. 278–284 (1997)
12. Jing, Y., Croft, W.B.: An association thesaurus for information retrieval. In: Proceedings of RIAO 1994, vol. 94, pp. 146–160 (1994)
13. Kotov, A., Zhai, C.: Tapping into knowledge base for concept feedback: leveraging conceptnet to improve search results for difficult queries. In: ACM International Conference on Web Search and Data Mining, pp. 403–412 (2012)
14. Lalmas, M., Ruthven, I.: Representing and retrieving structured documents using the dempster-shafer theory of evidence: Modelling and evaluation. Journal of Documentation, 529–565 (1998)

15. Lavrenko, V., Croft, W.B.: Relevance based language models. In: SIGIR 2001, pp. 120–127 (2001)
16. Meij, E., Trieschnigg, D., De Rijke, M., Kraaij, W.: Conceptual language models for domain-specific retrieval. In: Information Processing & Management, pp. 448–469 (2010)
17. Lavrenko, V., Croft, W.B.: Relevance based language models. In: ACM SIGIR, pp. 120–127 (2001)
18. Lv, Y., Zhai, C.: A comparative study of methods for estimating query language models with pseudo feedback. In: ACM Conference on Information and Knowledge Management, pp. 1895–1898 (2009)
19. Metzler, D., Croft, W.B.: Latent concept expansion using markov random fields. In: SIGIR 2007, pp. 311–318 (2007)
20. Nagypál, G.: Improving information retrieval effectiveness by using domain knowledge stored in ontologies. In: Meersman, R., Tari, Z. (eds.) OTM-WS 2005. LNCS, vol. 3762, pp. 780–789. Springer, Heidelberg (2005)
21. Plachouras, V., Ounis, I.: Dempster-shafer theory for a query-biased combination of evidence on the web. In: Information Retrieval, pp. 197–218 (2005)
22. Robertson, S.E., Walker, S., Beaulieu, M.M., Gatford, M., Payne, A.: Okapi at trec-4. In: Text Retrieval Conference, pp. 73–97 (1996)
23. Shafer, G.: A mathematical theory of evidence, vol. 1. Princeton University Press, Princeton (1976)
24. Urban, J., Jose, J.M., Van Rijsbergen, C.J.: An adaptive technique for content-based image retrieval. In: Multimedia Tools and Applications, pp. 1–28 (2006)
25. Van Rijsbergen, C.J.: A non-classical logic for information retrieval. The Computer Journal, 481–485 (1986)
26. Bai, J., Song, D., Bruza, P., Nie, J.Y., Cao, G.: Query expansion using term relationships in language models for information retrieval. In: ACM International Conference on Information and Knowledge Management, pp. 688–695 (2005)
27. Bodner, R.C., Song, F.: Knowledge-based approaches to query expansion in information retrieval. In: McCalla, G.I. (ed.) Canadian AI 1996. LNCS, vol. 1081, pp. 146–158. Springer, Heidelberg (1996)
28. Cao, G., Nie, J.Y., Bai, J.: Integrating word relationships into language models. In: SIGIR 2005, pp. 298–305 (2005)
29. Parapar, J., Barreiro, Á.: Promoting divergent terms in the estimation of relevance models. In: Amati, G., Crestani, F. (eds.) ICTIR 2011. LNCS, vol. 6931, pp. 77–88. Springer, Heidelberg (2011)
30. Collins-Thompson, K., Callan, J.: Query expansion using random walk models. In: ACM International Conference on Information and Knowledge Management, pp. 704–711 (2005)
31. Mandala, R., Tokunaga, T., Tanaka, H.: Combining multiple evidence from different types of thesaurus for query expansion. In: SIGIR 1999, pp. 191–197 (1999)
32. Voorhees, E.M.: Query expansion using lexical-semantic relations. In: SIGIR 1994, pp. 61–69 (1994)
33. Xu, J., Croft, W.B.: Query expansion using local and global document analysis. In: SIGIR 1996, pp. 4–11 (1996)
34. Xu, Y., Jones, G.J., Wang, B.: Query dependent pseudo-relevance feedback based on wikipedia. In: SIGIR 2009, pp. 59–66 (2009)
35. Zhai, C., Lafferty, J.: Model-based feedback in the language modeling approach to information retrieval. In: The Tenth International Conference on Information and Knowledge Management, pp. 403–410 (2001)

Optimization of an Integrated Model for Automatic Reduction and Expansion of Long Queries

Dawei Song[1,2], Yanjie Shi[1], Peng Zhang[1], Yuexian Hou[1], Bin Hu[3], Yuan Jia[4], Qiang Huang[5], Udo Kruschwitz[6], Anne De Roeck[2], and Peter Bruza[7]

[1] Tianjin University, Tianjin, China
[2] The Open University, Milton Keynes, UK
[3] Lanzhou University, Lanzhou, China
[4] Chinese Academy of Social Sciences, Beijing, China
[5] University of East Anglia, Norwich, UK
[6] University of Essex, Colchester, UK
[7] Queensland University of Technology, Brisbane, Australia
{dawei.song2010,sandy.y.shi,darcyzzj,krete1941}@gmail.com
bh@lzu.edu.cn,summeryuan_2003@126.com,h.qiang@uea.ac.uk
udo@essex.ac.uk,anne.deroeck@open.ac.uk,p.bruza@qut.edu.au

Abstract. A long query provides more useful hints for searching relevant documents, but it is likely to introduce noise which affects retrieval performance. In order to smooth such adverse effect, it is important to reduce noisy terms, introduce and boost additional relevant terms. This paper presents a comprehensive framework, called Aspect Hidden Markov Model (AHMM), which integrates query reduction and expansion, for retrieval with long queries. It optimizes the probability distribution of query terms by utilizing intra-query term dependencies as well as the relationships between query terms and words observed in relevance feedback documents. Empirical evaluation on three large-scale TREC collections demonstrates that our approach, which is automatic, achieves salient improvements over various strong baselines, and also reaches a comparable performance to a state of the art method based on user's interactive query term reduction and expansion.

1 Introduction

Long queries can be viewed as a rich expression of a user's information need and have recently attracted much attention [1,12]. An example long query (the description field of TREC topic 382) is shown in Figure 1.

Long queries may only form a fraction of queries actually submitted by searchers on the Web but they do represent a significant part [6]. For more specialized search engines long queries are very common, e.g. the queries submitted to the legal search service *Westlaw* are on average about 10 words long [15]. Medical search engines have also been developed to handle long queries such as plain English text [14]. Furthermore, one could also see pseudo-relevance feedback as an attempt to make the query longer.

R.E. Banchs et al. (Eds.): AIRS 2013, LNCS 8281, pp. 133–144, 2013.
© Springer-Verlag Berlin Heidelberg 2013

> *Identify documents that discuss the use of hydrogen as a fuel for piston driven automobiles (safe storage a concern) or the use of hydrogen in fuel cells to generate electricity to drive the car*

Fig. 1. An example of a long query

Intuitively, the useful hints and rich information carried by a long query can be leveraged to improve search performance. However, the rich information is also likely to bring interference caused by possible irrelevant terms and the verbosity surrounding the key concepts in the long queries [1]. One type of "bad" terms are those completely irrelevant to user's information need, such as "identify" and "documents" in the above example, and can be viewed as noise. The other type are terms that are weakly relevant, such as "drive" and "storage" in the example. They may result in query shift although they do carry some useful information. Table 1 shows the retrieval performances of TREC Topics 251 $\sim$ 300 on ROBUST05 collection using the title and description fields of each topic, respectively. The title field's average length is about 3 terms per topic. The description field is much longer, on average about 17 terms per topic. We can find that using title field as query generates higher precision and recall than the use of description field, over two typical IR models (vector space model based on TF-IDF and language model using Kullback-Leibler (KL) divergence), and a widely used pseudo-relevance feedback model - the Relevance Model (RM) [13].

Table 1. The retrieval performances of queries 251-300 on ROBUST05 collection

	ROBUST05					
	Title+TFIDF	Des.+TFIDF	Title+KL	Des.+KL	Title+RM	Des.+RM
Precision	**0.1721**	0.1154	**0.1951**	0.1544	**0.2297**	0.1994
Recall	**0.3729**	0.3143	**0.3876**	0.3651	**0.3892**	0.3806

Therefore, to improve the retrieval effectiveness for long queries, it is crucial to identify and boost the important terms and meanwhile eliminate the negative effects of "bad" terms in the original or expanded queries.

1.1 Related Work

One way of alleviating the problem is to use interactive techniques and let users select some terms or combinations of various terms, as key concepts, from long queries, through interactive query reduction (IQR) and interactive query expansion (IQE) [11,10,4,18,9]. IQR in general aims to help users remove noisy information - the first type of interference we described earlier. However, it is not good at handling the second type of "bad" terms. This is because users often can only decide, approximately, whether a term is important or not, rather than accurately quantifying the importance of these terms. Moreover, it cannot introduce additional relevant terms to the original query. Thus interactive query expansion (IQE) is used to help users remove irrelevant terms suggested by automatic query expansion techniques. Further, [11] integrates IQR and IQE into a single framework for Selective Interactive Reduction and Expansion (SIRE). Although both IQR and IQE can result in salient improvements for document retrieval with long queries, such user-dependent approaches have their limitations. Too much user interference may increase the time and cognitive overhead, if users are required to read through each long query and the search results from a baseline system and decide which terms should be selected. On the other hand, users may not be able to easily give an accurate estimation of the weight for each selected term, which can be effectively computed from automatic methods. In any case, it is well recognized that users are reluctant to leave any explicit feedback when they search a document collection [3,8,16].

Therefore, it makes sense to process long queries automatically to estimate the importance of query terms. In [1], a method to identify key concepts in verbose queries using supervised learning is proposed. However, it relies on pre-labeled training data. In term of automatic query expansion, there has been many approaches in the literature. One of the state of the art automatic query expansion methods is the Relevance Model. Although it does not distinguish the combinations of multiple query terms as IQR or IQE does in [18], it estimates the probability distribution of expanded terms. Thus it can improve the positive effects of some key terms and reduce the negative effects caused by noisy and/or redundant information.

However, as shown in Table 1, existing automatic approaches such as TFIDF, as a basis for query reduction, and RM, as a basis for selecting expansion terms, are less effective for long queries. We think a possible reason is that these approaches treat the query terms as independent of each other. In reality, particularly for long queries, the cohesion of query terms, largely determined by the intra-query term dependencies, plays a key role in deciding which terms should be used to represent the information need.

The overall aim of this paper is to develop an effective automatic query reduction and expansion approach for long queries, which should take into account the intra-query term dependencies.

1.2 Our Approach

In this paper, we propose a method that effectively integrates query expansion and query reduction. First, an existing robust query expansion approach, called the Aspect Query Language Model (AM) [19], is used as a basis for an overall framework to derive an expanded query model (Query Expansion). In AM, the query terms are considered as latent variables over a number of observed top ranked documents after initial retrieval. Secondly, a Hidden Markov Model (HMM) is established over the AM structure, leading to an Aspect Hidden Markov Model (AHMM), to estimate the dependencies between the latent variables (as states of the HMM), and in turn to identify an optimal probabilistic distribution over the states (Query Reduction). The details of our approach will be introduced in the next section.

2   Model Construction

2.1   The Aspect Query Language Model (AM)

This section gives a brief description of the AM [19], where the subsets of query terms are viewed as latent variables (representing query aspects) over a number of top-ranked documents from the initial retrieval. The query aspects are treated as latent variables, as they (and their optimal weighting) can only be derived through the top ranked documents that we observe.

The AM structure is shown in Figure 2. S_j is a latent variable in the set $\mathbf{S}$ ($\mathbf{S} = \{S_1, \cdots, S_N\}$), and w is a word whose occurrence probability in the expanded query model (formally denoted as θ_Q) to be estimated. The latent variable S_j is generated from the original query $Q = \{q_1, \cdots, q_M\}$, where each S_j is in general defined as a query term or a combination of query terms. The size of $\mathbf{S}$ is $(2^M - 1)$ if we use all the combinations of query terms. For instance, given $Q = \{q_1, q_2\}$, the set of latent variables can be transformed into $\mathbf{S} = \{\{q_1\}, \{q_2\}, \{q_1, q_2\}\}$. In practice, we can only use the combinations of up to k query terms as latent variables in order to reduce the computational complexity. Indeed, our experimental results indicate little difference in effectiveness between the use of combinations of 2-3 terms and the combinations of more terms as states.

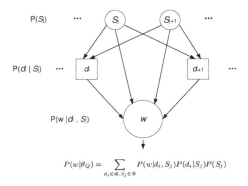

$$P(w|\theta_Q) = \sum_{d_i \in \mathbf{d}, S_j \in \mathbf{S}} P(w|d_i, S_j)P(d_i|S_j)P(S_j)$$

Fig. 2. Structure of Aspect Query Language Model

The relationship between the word w and the latent variable S_j is derived from the relevance feedback documents. In practice, such as in Web search, the number of top ranked documents actually observed by users is often small [7], which will lead to the data sparsity problem given the large number of latent variables for a long query. Furthermore, not all the top ranked documents are truly relevant to the query. Even for a relevant document, it is not necessarily true that every part within the document is relevant. Thus, smaller chunks of the documents (e.g., segmented through a sliding window) are used to connect S_j and w in order to expand the observation space to overcome the data sparsity problem and improve the quality of parameter optimization.

Based on the structure in Figure 2, the following formula can be derived:

$$P(w|\theta_Q) = \sum_{d_i \in \mathbf{d}, S_j \in \mathbf{S}} P(w|d_i, S_j)P(d_i|S_j)P(S_j) \tag{1}$$

$P(S_j)$ is the prior distribution of latent variables, $P(d_i|S_j)$ is the probability of an observed document chunk d_i given a latent variable S_j, and $P(w|d_i, S_j)$ is the probability of a word w in a chunk d_i given S_j.

An on-the-fly training data construction method is developed to automatically label the document chunks with query term(s). The Expectation Maximization (EM) algorithm is then used to fit the parameters of Equation 1. Despite the proven effectiveness of the AM, it does not take into account the intra-query term dependencies (i.e., dependencies between the latent variables).

2.2 Aspect Hidden Markov Model (AHMM)

We now present an AHMM approach that extends the original AM and allows a natural incorporation of the intra-query dependencies through the HMM mechanism. There has been evidence that the source of natural language text can be modelled as an "ergodic" Markov process, meaning the corresponding Markov chain is aperiodic (i.e., words can be separated by any number of intermediate words) and irreducible (i.e., we can always get from one word to another by continuing to produce text) [5]. As shown in Figure 3, based on the dependencies among S_j, d_j and w, we extend the AM by adding links between S_j and S_{j+1}.

The HMM is a finite set of states ($\mathbf{S} = \{S_1, \cdots, S_M\}$), each of which is associated with a probability distribution ($\pi = \{P(S_1), \cdots, P(S_M)\}$). Transitions among the states ($A = \{S_{j',j}\}$, $S_j, S_{j'} \in \mathbf{S}$) are governed by a set of probabilities called transition probabilities. For a particular state, an observation d_i can be generated according to the associated probability distribution denoted as $B = \{P(d_i|S_j)\}$. Figure 4 shows an example structure of a 3-state ergodic HMM.

We now need to design a parameter estimation framework based on effective optimization mechanisms in HMM. The application of the HMM can not only estimate the prior distribution of each S_j, but also integrate the dependence between any two latent variables (as states) and their underlying observables (document chunks) through a state transition matrix. Given the observation chunks $\mathbf{d} = \{d_1, \cdots, d_T\}$ and a model $\Lambda = (A, B, \pi)$, the HMM can choose a corresponding state sequence ($S_1, \cdots, S_T$) that is optimal (i.e., best "explains" the observations). For the purpose, the Viterbi algorithm is used. Due to space limit, the algorithm is not detailed here (See [17] for details).

In this paper, the query terms are used as HMM states (S_j), which are not really "hidden" in a strict sense. We adopt the HMM structure for the effective optimization mechanisms that HMM provides. In the process of learning the model, we utilize the Baum-Welch algorithm to optimize the state distribution and transition matrix and the Viterbi algorithm to search the optimal path [17]

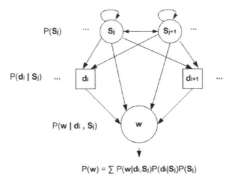

Fig. 3. Structure of Aspect Hidden Markov Model

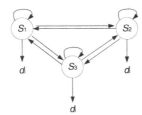

Fig. 4. An example of three-state Ergodic Hidden Markov Model

to update the probability distribution of each chunk in different states. The update of $P(d_t|S_j)$ is based on:

$$P(d_i|S_j) = \frac{\sum_{t=1, d_t=d_i}^{T} \gamma_t(j)}{\sum_{t=1}^{T} \gamma_t(j)} \tag{2}$$

where $\gamma_t(j) = P(S_j|d_t, \Lambda)$. The value of $\gamma_t(j)$ is estimated by using an iterative computation detailed in Fig. 5.

In summary, the HMM would seem to provide a mechanism to estimate the parameters listed in Eq. 1.

3   Model Optimization

For estimation of the probabilities in Eq. 1 within the AHMM structure, we adapt the original parameter estimation algorithms in AM [19] to AHMM, as shown in Figure 5.

3.1   Data Pre-processing (Step 1)

The same data pre-processing procedure used in AM is applied here. Step 1.1 takes the query term combinations as states, as discussed in Section 2.1. Step 1.2 selects relevance feedback documents. In Step 1.3, each feedback document is segmented with an overlapped sliding window, as discussed in Section 2.1.

1. **Pre-processing**
   1.1 View the single query terms in query Q as "hidden" states.
   1.2 Select N top-ranked relevant or pseudo-relevant documents according to the initial retrieval results.
   1.3 Segment the selected document into chunks with an overlapped sliding window.
   1.4 Retain the chunks containing any query terms and discard the rest.
   1.5 Assign those chunks containing query terms into various clusters, labelled by the "hidden" states that share one or more query terms with the chunks.
2. **Optimize Aspect Hidden Markov Model**
   2.1 Set the initial values of the model parameters.
   $$P(S_j) = 1/M, \quad (M = |\mathbf{S}|, \quad S_j \in \mathbf{S})$$
   $$P(S_{j'}|S_j) = 1/M, \quad (M = |\mathbf{S}|), \quad S_j, S_{j'} \in \mathbf{S})$$
   $$P(d_i|S_j) = \frac{\sum_{t=1, d_t = d_i}^{T} \gamma_t(j)}{\sum_{t=1}^{T} \gamma_t(j)}$$
   where $\gamma_t(j) = P(S_j|d_t, \Lambda)$, and $P(S_j|d_t, \Lambda)$ can be approximately derived by the pseudo code as follows:
   $$d_{i,k} = \{w_1, \cdots, w_k\}, \quad d_i = d_{i,K} \ (K = |d_i|)$$
   $$P(S_j|d_{i,0}) = P(S_j)$$
   for k = 1 : K,
   $$P(S_j|d_{i,k}) = \frac{1}{k+1} \frac{P(w_k|S_j) P(S_j|d_{i,k-1})}{\sum_{S_t} P(w_k|S_t) P(S_t|d_{i,k-1})} + \frac{k}{k+1} P(S_j|d_{i,k-1})$$
   end
   $$P(S_j|d_i) = P(S_j|d_{i,K})$$
   The computation of $P(w_k|S_j)$ is detailed in Section 3.2.
   2.2 Apply Viterbi algorithm to searching the optimal state sequences.
   2.3 Collect the labelled chunks of each "state" and update the occurrence probability of the observed term w_k, namely $P(w_k|S_j)$, then $P(d_i|S_j)$.
   2.4 Optimize the model iteratively by repeating Step 2.1 $\sim$ Step 2.3.
3. **Derive the language model**
   Compute the final probability of $P_{AHMM}(w|\theta_Q)$ using Eq. 1.

Fig. 5. Outline of framework

Step 1.4 can be seen as a coarse data refinement by keeping only the chunks containing at least one query term. Step 1.5 can be considered as an automatic on-the-fly training data construction process, which labels the selected chunks with different states. With these automatically labeled chunks, we can compute the initial word probability given a state S_j, denoted as $P(w|S_j)$. These initial computations are then used to optimize the AHMM in Step 2.

3.2   Model Estimation (Steps 2 & 3)

According to the description of AHMM in Section 2.2, we initialize the model parameters by setting the state distribution $P(S_j)$ and the state transition probability $P(S_{j'}|S_j)$ to be the chance probability $\frac{1}{M}$. Here M is the number of states in the HMM. A recursive method is used to compute $P(d_i|S_j)$. This method for $P(d_i|S_j)$ was also used in [2] for an online estimation. In this recursive equation, $d_{i,k}$ denotes the first k words in chunk d_i and $d_{i,K} = d_i$, where K is the window size. $P(S_j|d_{i,0})$ as an initial value is set to be $P(S_j)$. The conditional probability $P(w_k|S_j)$ is computed as:

$$P(w_k|S_j) = \frac{\sum_{d_i} \#w_{k,i} * P(d_i|S_j)}{\sum_{w_k} \sum_{d_i} \#w_{k,i} * P(d_i|S_j)} \tag{3}$$

where $\#w_{k,i}$ is the occurrence frequency of w_k in d_i. The probability $P(w_k|S_j)$ is then applied to the recursive equation to compute $P(S_j|d_i)$.

In Step 2.2, we apply the Viterbi algorithm to searching the optimal state sequence, then we update the HMM iteratively by re-computing the model parameters $\Lambda = \{\pi, A, B\}$. Finally, the two probability parameters $P(S_j)$ and $P(d_i|S_j)$ in Eq. 1 are updated according to the AHMM. Since the contribution of $P(d_i|S_j)$ has been considered in Eq. 3 to compute $P(w_k|S_j)$, Eq. 1 can be simplified as:

$$P(w|\theta_Q) = \sum_{S_j} P(w_k|S_j) * P(S_j) \tag{4}$$

4   Experimental Setup

We evaluate our method using TREC topics 251–300 on the TREC5 collection (TREC disk 2 and 4), topics 303–689 (50 selected queries) on the ROBUST05 collection (AQUAINT collection), and topics 301–450 and 601–700 on the RO-BUST04 collection (TREC disk 4 and 5 excluding the *Congressional Record*). The *description* field of the topics are used as queries (with an average query length of 15-17 words). They are selected because they have varied content and document properties. The Robust tracks are known to be difficult, and conventional IR techniques have failed on some of them [11]. In our experiments, a standard stopword list and the Porter stemmer are applied to all data collections. Note that the same experimental setting was also used in [11] for user interactive IQR and IQE. This allows a direct comparison of our method with this interactive approach.

Three baselines are used for comparison including a language model based on Kullback-Leibler (**KL**) divergence, the Relevance Model (**RM**) and the AM. We also compare our methods with the user based interactive system based on its results reported in [11]. For pseudo-relevance feedback, all the methods are tested with a certain number N of top-ranked documents from the initial retrieval results. Here, we only select $N = 30$ documents as feedback, as we think this is close to real web search scenarios. Note that we have tested a range of N (10, 20, ..., 100), and the performance of our approach is in general quite stable with respect to N. The documents are then segmented into chunks using a sliding window of 15 words with 1/3 overlapping between two consecutive windows. After applying each query expansion algorithm, we choose the top ranked 100 terms as expansion terms. All the experiments are carried out using the Lemur toolkit 4.0[1]. The initial retrieval is run by a widely used language model based on KL-divergence. The expanded queries derived from three different query language modeling methods (RM, AM and AHMM) are used to perform the second round of retrieval using KL divergence. Our primary evaluation metric is mean average precision (MAP). The Wilcoxon singed rank test is used to measure the statistical significance of the results.

---

[1] http://www.lemurproject.org

5   Result and Analysis

5.1   Illustration of AHMM Optimization

When the AHMM is applied, its probability parameters is iteratively optimized. Let us consider the example in Figure 1 again. Table 2 shows the changes of the probability of each query term and the query's retrieval performance (average precision) for each iteration. In the original query, some terms, such as *cell*, *safe*, *storage* and *gener*, seem only weakly relevant to the intention of the query. After a few iterations, their probability values are reduced. Simultaneously, the corresponding values of some key terms, such as *car* and *fuel*, are increased, This table also shows the positive trend of the performance when more iterations are run. The performance peaks at iteration 4 but then drops slightly at the 5th. This may be due to the overfitting caused by the data sparsity when optimizing the model. An in-depth investigation on this issue is left as future work.

Table 2. Illustration of AHMM optimization

Term	#Iter				
	1	2	3	4	5
automboil	0.0503	0.0489	0.0446	0.0435	0.0459
fule	0.0423	0.0543	0.0677	0.0834	0.0928
discuss	0.0377	0.0368	0.0410	0.0414	0.0439
safe	0.0823	0.0785	0.0798	0.0787	0.0778
electr	0.0646	0.0814	0.0922	0.0845	0.0893
car	0.0717	0.0926	0.1056	0.1061	0.1039
gener	0.1102	0.0999	0.0855	0.0853	0.0884
document	0.0545	0.0606	0.0635	0.0628	0.0624
concern	0.0333	0.0359	0.0388	0.0379	0.0397
storage	0.0653	0.0602	0.0543	0.0463	0.0382
hydrogen	0.0944	0.0816	0.073	0.0717	0.06
driv	0.0492	0.0556	0.0633	0.0633	0.0662
driven	0.0635	0.0704	0.0688	0.0695	0.0661
piston	0.0706	0.0597	0.0516	0.0522	0.0511
cell	0.1100	0.0836	0.0703	0.0734	0.0743
AP	**0.3982**	**0.4267**	**0.4447**	**0.4619**	**0.4483**

5.2   Comparisons in Query Expansion

The results of KL baseline, RM, AM and our approach are listed in Table 3. We can find that the AHMM shows good performance on all three data collections, and generates significant improvements over the KL baseline, RM and AM.

As a further comparison, we list the performances using user based interactive system (UIS) [11] in Table 4. In [11], the interactive query expansion (IQE) relies on users' help to select query expansion terms. In the comparison with IQE, our AHMM can also generate better performance on two data collections, TREC5

Table 3. Performance comparison (MAP) of KL, RM, AM and AHMM

Collection	KL	RM	AM	AHMM	Improv. (%) of AHMM over KL & RM & AM		
TREC5	0.1353	0.1484	-	**0.1715**	+26.7*	+15.6*	-
ROBUST05	0.1544	0.1994	-	**0.2435**	+57.7*	+22.1*	-
ROBUST04	0.2439	0.2375	0.2314	**0.2735**	+12.1*	+15.1*	+18.2*

* Statistically significant at $p = 0.05$ (Wilcoxon signed rank test).

Table 4. Performance comparison (MAP) with user based interactive query expansion

Collection	UIS-IQE	AHMM	Improv. (%)
TREC5	0.168	0.1715	+2.08
ROBUST05	0.237	0.2435	+2.74
ROBUST04	0.292	0.2735	-6.3

and ROBUST05, while the MAP value of our approach is lower than IQE on ROBUST04. Since the query set for ROBUST04 is a known difficult one, our model, as an automatic method, still gives a good performance.

5.3   Robustness of the Model

To further test the robustness of our model, we run another set of experiments, where we remove some "noisy" information in advance from the queries, through a process of *pre- query reduction*. This test is based on the assumption that the retrieval performance of the AHMM should keep a stable status, i.e., it is robust regardless of the selective removal of some noisy query terms.

Unlike the interactive query reduction, which is based on user manual selection, in our experiment, we use a simple automatic method for the pre- query reduction. We first collected all the queries we are using. Since there is an overlap between the query sets for ROBUST04 and ROBUST05, we obtain 300 queries altogether. We then counted the query frequency of each query term.

Our idea is to remove several query terms with high query frequencies, which can be viewed as "stop words" in the query set, such as "identifi", "document", etc. We set a threshold in term of the ratio of the query frequency to the total number of queries. In our experiments, it is set to be 0.1, a small number, because we want to be conservative and not to risk too much of mistakenly removing some useful terms.

Table 5 summarizes the performance of KL, RM, AM and the AHMM after applying the query term reduction. We observe a performance improvement on all models and collections, compared with the results without applying pre- query reduction (Table 3). The AHMM still outperforms the other three methods. The performance difference of AHMM with and without applying pre- query reduction is smaller than that of the other models. The observations reflect the robustness of the AHMM.

Table 5. Performance comparison (MAP) of KL, RM, AM and AHMM, after pre-query reduction

Collection	KL	RM	AM	AHMM	Improv. (%) of AHMM over KL & RM & AM		
TREC5	0.1482	0.1605	-	**0.1725**	+17.7*	+7.5*	-
ROBUST05	0.1611	0.2228	-	**0.2502**	+55.3*	+12.3*	-
ROBUST04	0.2500	0.2456	0.2364	**0.2758**	+10.3*	+12.3*	+16.7*

* Statistically significant at $p = 0.05$ (Wilcoxon signed rank test).

In both scenarios (i.e., with and without pre- query reduction), for RO-BUST04, a well-known difficult collection where RM and AM underperform the KL baseline, AHMM achieves significant improvements over all the other models. The AM itself performs less well for long queries (in contrast of the good performance for short queries as reported in [19]). By adding the HMM layer on top of the AM structure, the performance is largely improved. This indicates our method learns more reasonable weights for query terms than the AM through the HMM-based model optimization process.

6   Conclusions and Future Work

We have presented an AHMM method for effective query expansion and query reduction for long queries, by estimating the intra-query term dependencies and the relationships between query terms and other words through observed relevance feedback documents. Our experimental results show that our method achieves significant improvements in comparison with three baselines: KL, RM and AM, showing the effectiveness and robustness of the proposed approach. Even when compared with the user-based interactive system used in [11], our approach, which is automatic, still shows a comparable performance. In the future, it would be interesting to study how to effectively and efficiently combine the user interactions with our automatic algorithm. In addition, to tackle the data sparsity problem when selecting fewer number of documents, we will consider smoothing our model with the background collection model.

Acknowledgments. This work is funded in part by the Chinese National Program on Key Basic Research Project (973 Program, grant no. 2013CB329304 and 2014CB744604), the Natural Science Foundation of China (grant no. 61272265), and the European Union Framework 7 Marie-Curie International Research Staff Exchange Programme (grant no. 247590).

References

1. Bendersky, M., Croft, W.B.: Discovering key concepts in verbose queries. In: SIGIR 2008, pp. 491–498 (2008)
2. Blei, D.M., Moreno, P.J.: Topic segmentation with an aspect hidden Markov model. In: SIGIR 2001, pp. 343–348 (2001)

3. Dumais, S., Joachims, T., Bharat, K., Weigend, A.: SIGIR 2003 workshop report: implicit measures of user interests and preferences. In: SIGIR Forum, pp. 50–54 (2003)
4. Harman, D.: Towards interactive query expansion. In: SIGIR 1998, pp. 321–331 (1998)
5. Hoenkamp, E., Bruza, P., Song, D., Huang, Q.: An effective approach to verbose queries using a limited dependencies language model. In: Azzopardi, L., Kazai, G., Robertson, S., Rüger, S., Shokouhi, M., Song, D., Yilmaz, E. (eds.) ICTIR 2009. LNCS, vol. 5766, pp. 116–127. Springer, Heidelberg (2009)
6. Huston, S., Croft, W.B.: Evaluating verbose query processing techniques. In: SIGIR 2010, pp. 291–298 (2010)
7. Jansen, B.J., Spink, A., Bateman, J., Saracevic, T.: Real life information retrieval: A study of user queries on the web. In: SIGIR Forum, pp. 5–17 (1998)
8. Jansen, B.J., Spink, A., Saracevic, T.: Real life, real users, and real needs: a study and analysis of user queries on the web. In: Information Processing and Management, pp. 207–227 (2000)
9. Kelly, D., Dollu, V.D., Fu, X.: The loquacious user: a document-independent source of terms for query expansion. In: SIGIR 2005, pp. 457–464 (2005)
10. Kumaran, G., Allan, J.: A case for shorter queries, and helping users create them. In: HLT-NAACL 2007, pp. 220–227 (2007)
11. Kumaran, G., Allan, J.: Effective and efficient user interaction for long queries. In: SIGIR 2008, pp. 11–18 (2008)
12. Kumaran, G., Carvalho, V.R.: Reducing long queries using query quality predictors. In: SIGIR 2009, pp. 564–571 (2009)
13. Lavrenko, V., Croft, W.B.: Relevance-based language models. In: SIGIR 2001, pp. 120–127 (2001)
14. Luo, G., Tang, C., Yang, H., Wei, X.: Medsearch: A specialized search engine for medical information retrieval. In: CIKM 2008, pp. 143–152 (2008)
15. Manning, C.D., Raghavan, P., Schütze, H.: Introduction to Information Retrieval. Cambridge University Press (2008)
16. Markey, K.: Twenty-five years of end-user searching, Part 1: Research findings. Journal of the American Society for Information Science and Technology, 1071–1081 (2007)
17. Rabiner, L.R.: A tutorial on hidden markov models and selected applications in speech recognition. Proceedings of the IEEE 77, 257–286 (1989)
18. Ruthven, I.: Re-examining the potential effectiveness of interactive query expansion. In: SIGIR 2003, pp. 213–220 (2003)
19. Song, D., Huang, Q., Bruza, P., Lau, R.: An aspect query language model based on query decomposition and high-order contextual term associations. In: Computational Intelligence, pp. 1–23 (2012)

Clustering Short-Text Using Non-negative Matrix Factorization of Hadamard Product of Similarities

Krutika Verma[1], Mukesh K. Jadon[2], and Arun K. Pujari[3]

[1] Sambalpur University Institute of Information Technology, Sambalpur, Odisha, India
verma.kirtika6@gmail.com
[2] Department of CSE, The LNMIIT, Jaipur, Rajasthan, India
jadonmukesh30@gmail.com
[3] School of Computer and Information Sciences, University of Hyderabad, Hyderabad, Andhra Pradesh, India
arun.k.pujari@gmail.com

Abstract. Short-texts mining has become an important area of research in IR and data mining. *Ncut-term* weighting is recently proposed for clustering of short-texts using non-negative matrix factorization. Non-negative factorization can be employed for such term weighting when the similarity measure is the inner product of term-document matrix. We propose a new weighting scheme and devise a new clustering algorithm using Hadamard product of similarity matrices. We demonstrate that our technique yields much better clustering in comparison to *ncut weighting* scheme. We use three measures for evaluating clustering qualities, namely purity, normalized mutual information and adjusted Rand index. We use standard benchmark datasets and also compare the performance of our algorithm with well-known document clustering technique of Ng-Jordan-Weiss. Experimental results suggest that the weighting process by Hadamard product gives better clustering of document of short-texts.

Keywords: Short-text clustering, ncut-weighting, non-negative matrix factorization, Hadamard product, kernel distance.

1   Introduction

With the increasing popularity of micro-blogging and social networking, the documents collected from the web are becoming more and more condensed. Social media allows users to post short texts. Facebook status length is limited to 420 characters. Twitter limits the length of each Tweet to 140 characters. A personal status message on Windows Live Messenger is restricted to 128 characters. Most of the categories in Yahoo! Answers have an average post length of less than 500 characters. Thus uses of short-texts are increasing and it becomes necessary to relook at the existing text mining techniques to handle the large corpora of short texts. A basic representation of a document is bag of words in which a document is represented as a vector of words whose entries are non-zero if the corresponding terms appear in the document. When the number of terms in a text is very small, the vector is very sparse and hence do not

R.E. Banchs et al. (Eds.): AIRS 2013, LNCS 8281, pp. 145–155, 2013.
© Springer-Verlag Berlin Heidelberg 2013

have enough statistical information for distinguishing different documents. Thus, though there have been very large number of algorithms for document clustering and classification, these are not found to be suitable for short-text document set. Short-text documents require different approaches in data mining and study on special algorithms for short text documents has evolved as a major research area of data mining in recent years [2, 10, 14, 18-19].

Recently, an efficient algorithm for clustering of short-text document is proposed [18]. Since different terms have different importance in a given document, a term-weight is normally associated with every term. These weights are often derived from the frequency of terms within a document or a set of documents. Most widely used term weighting scheme is *tfidf* which is a simple and efficient representation. However, it eliminates some contextual information such as phrases, sequential patterns. Other widely used term weighting methods [3-4, 11, 13] include: mutual information [13], ATC, Okapi [4] and LTU[3]. In [18], weights are derived from well-known *normalized cut* method [17] and it is shown that efficiency of clustering can be substantially improved. Hypotheses advocated in this work are that the proposed *ncut*-weighting is better than *tfidf* weighting and assigning weights to terms is better than assigning weights to documents. A major shortcoming of this method is that spectral clustering with such term-weighting can be achieved by non-negative matrix factorization with similarity matrix S= XX^T, where X is term-document matrix. Thus there is an implicit assumption of pairwise similarity derived from XX^T. Choice of similarity measure plays a very important role in clustering and classification and there are several similarity measures proposed in literature to achieve more accurate clustering. A question that naturally arises is whether the proposed method can be extended with other similarity measures.

The objective of this paper is to study different weighting schemes (not limiting to term weighting) and different similarity measures (not limiting to Cosine similarity) in order to devise an efficient clustering of short-text collection of documents. A new clustering algorithm is proposed through rigorous experiments, it is demonstrated that the proposed method yields better clustering than the other existing methods. Major contributions of the present work are the followings.

- The *ncut-weighting* method is extended to other similarity measure. We call this as weighted similarity.
- The concept of term-weighting is extended to term-pair weighting and we devise a new method of weighting. We obtain weights by a Hadamard product of multiple similarity measures.
- Our experimental experiences on benchmark datasets show that the proposed method is better than earlier methods.

In Section 2, we discuss *ncut*-weighting scheme proposed in [18]. We also discuss the background of our extension. In Section 3, the technique of weighted similarity is introduced. Section 4 outlines our proposed clustering algorithm which makes use of non-negative matrix factorization of Hadamard product of similarities matrices. We consider two similarity measures in our study. Section 5 discusses the performance measures for cluster quality and Section 6 outlines our experimental results.

2   Ncut Weighting Method

A set of N documents with M distinct terms can be represented as a matrix $X = \{x_{ij}\} \in R^{M \times N}$. The element x_{ij} of matrix X can be determined by many ways such as term frequency (*tf*) or term frequency and inverse document frequency (*tfidf*). We assume x_{ij} as binary and defined as follows.

$$x_{ij} = \begin{cases} 1 \; if \; term \; i \; occurs \; in \; document \; j \\ 0 \; otherwise \end{cases}$$

Consider the similarity matrix $S = XX^T$ and the degree matrix $D \in R^{M \times M}$ is diagonal matrix with diagonal elements $D_{ii} = \sum_{j=1}^{M} S_{ij}$.

A *ncut-term-weighting* is introduced in [18] and each row of X (corresponding to each term) is assigned a weight to obtain a weighted matrix Y as $Y = D^{-1/2} X$. It is proved that when $S = XX^T$, spectral clustering of documents can be achieved through nonnegative factorization of Y. It is shown that *ncut-term-weighting* yields better clustering compared to other well-known term weighting such as *tf* and *tfidf*. Authors emphasize here that weighting of terms have advantage over document-weighting.

The similarity matrix S is a $n \times n$ pairwise symmetric matrix of documents, where S_{ij} represents some notion of similarity between X_i and X_j. Many clustering algorithms, particularly those of the spectral variety rely on a suitable similarity measure to cluster data points. The pairwise similarity matrix $S = XX^T$ is un-normalized form of cosine similarity and can also be viewed as standard inner-product linear Kernel matrix. It is worthwhile to examine the suitability of other kernel function for short-text clustering.

Cosine Similarity
Given two documents columns X_i and X_j, the cosine similarity as

$$S^1 = CosSim((X_i, X_j)) = \frac{X_i.X_j}{\|X_i\|.\|X_j\|} = \frac{\sum_{k=1}^{M} x_{ik}.x_{jk}}{\sqrt{\sum_{k=1}^{M} x_{ik}^2}.\sqrt{\sum_{k=1}^{M} x_{jk}^2}}$$

Gaussian Similarity (Kernel Similarity)
Given two documents columns X_i and X_j, the Gaussian Kernel is defined as follows.

$$S^2 = \exp\left(-\frac{\|X_i - X_j\|^2}{2\sigma^2}\right)$$

where σ is a scaling parameter to control the rapid reduction in S_{ij} with the distance in X_i and X_j. This kernel trick has been applied to several problems because of its applicability in feature space of higher dimension.

3   Hadamard Product of Similarities

One can view the concepts of term-weighting and document-weighting as assigning weights to rows or columns of X, respectively. A natural extension can be to weigh each individual element of S separately. A similarity measure has its own inherent characteristics of capturing a specific type of statistical property. To take advantage of multiple characteristics exhibited by different similarity measures, we propose a method to assign weights to similarity measure of a pair of documents by another similarity measure. We call this as *weighted similarity*. Given two similarity measures S^1 and S^2, *weighted similarity* is defined as $S^1 \oplus S^2$ where $\oplus$ is Hadamard Product or element-wise multiplication of two matrices. We think of non-negative factorization of $Y = S^1 \oplus S^2$.

NMF has been investigated by many researchers, but it has gained popularity through the works of Lee and Seung published in Nature and NIPS [7-8]. Based on the argument that the non negativity is important in human perception they proposed simple algorithms (often called the Lee-Seung algorithms) for finding nonnegative representations of nonnegative data and images. The basic NMF problem can be stated as follows: Given a nonnegative data matrix $Y \in R^{N \times M}$ (with $y_{ij} \geq 0$) and a reduced rank K ($K \leq min(M, N)$), find two nonnegative matrices $V \in R^{K \times N}$ and $U \in R^{M \times K}$ which factorize Y as correctly as possible. The factors U and V may have different physical meanings in different applications. In clustering problems, V is the basis matrix, while U denotes the weight matrix. The nonnegative factorization can be reformulated as trace maximization problem as follows.

$$||Y - UV||_f^2 = trace(YY^T) - 2trace(V^T U^T Y) + trace(V^T U^T UV)$$

With the above formulation, it becomes easy to see that when Y is a Hadamard product of two symmetric matrices, the NMF of Y boils down to an NMF of S^1 weighted by S^2. There are many interesting properties of factorization of Hadamard products which we intend to explore separately. Some authors have proposed weighted NMF [5] but conceptually our method of weighting the factors through Hadamard product is different from weighting the errors of Y as UV. Weighted NMF (WNMF) was first used to deal with missing values in the distance matrix for predicting distances in large scale networks [5].

4   Our Method-KCNMF

In this section we propose a new method of clustering of documents of short length. The method is generic in the sense that it makes use of Hadamard product of any two similarity matrix. But, in the present context, we consider only Gaussian Kernel and Inner product linear Kernel for short-text clustering. The motivation for selecting these two similarity measures is from earlier research in a different context where it was shown that the weighting of one of similarity with another yields better results [15-16]. We also experimented with several combinations of similarity measures but we observe the combination of Gaussian kernel with inner product yields very satisfactory results. We term this algorithm as Kernel-Cosine with NMF (KC-NMF).

Using term-document matrix X, we compute similarity matrices S^1 and S^2 corresponding to two different similarity measures. The Hadamard product of S^1 and S^2, $S^1 \oplus S^2$ is the weighted similarity matrix. We first normalize this similarity matrix by scaling each element by square-root of the row sum of the matrix as follows.

We use the alternating non-negative least-square (ANLS) algorithm [6] to find NMF of Y. The following iterative process is used as ANLS.

> Initialize U with k random columns of Y
> Repeat until maximum number iteration
> $V \leftarrow \max ((U^T U + \lambda I)^{-1} U^T Y), 0)$
> $U \leftarrow \max (YV^T (VV^T + \lambda I)^{-1}, 0)$

Above steps are repeated till a predetermined number of iterations or when U and V become stationary. Then we normalize U and scale V accordingly as follows.

$$\alpha_i \leftarrow \Sigma_i^N U_{ij} \ , \ U_{ij} \leftarrow \frac{U_{ij}}{\alpha_i} \ , \ V_{ij} \leftarrow \alpha_i V_{ij}$$

It may be noted that any scaling of U is essentially a post multiplication of a diagonal matrix and corresponding scaling of V is pre-multiplication of the inverse of the diagonal matrix. Hence, such normalization keeps the factorization invariant. Finally document clustering is achieved by assigning the document to a cluster which corresponds to maximum entry in each column of V.

5   Cluster Quality

In order to evaluate clustering quality in terms of high intra-cluster similarity and low inter-cluster similarity against all other algorithms, we use three external measures. Let the clusters obtained by any algorithm for N documents be $\{C'_1, C'_2, C'_3, ..., C'_K\}$ and the predefined classes are $C_1, C_2, ...$ and C_k . The measures *purity, NMI* and *ARI* are defined as follows.

Purity
For a given cluster C'_i, we determine the dominant class as the class C_j with the highest number of common elements. Purity denotes the ratio of sum of common elements in dominant class to the total number of elements. When element of same class mapped in one cluster the purity goes high. Purity with value 1 or value tends to 1 symbolizes good clustering while value near to 0 represents bad cluster.

$$purity(C',C) = \frac{1}{N} \sum_i \max_j |C'_i \cap C_i|$$

Normalized Mutual Information (NMI)
Normalized mutual information is defined as the measure that allows us to evaluate the quality of clustering against the number of clusters. It lies in between 0 to 1

$$NMI(C',C) = \frac{\sum_{i,j} \frac{|c'_i \cap c_j|}{n} log \frac{|c'_i||c_j|}{n|c'_i \cap c_j|}}{(\sum_i^k \frac{c'_i}{n} log \frac{c'_i}{n} + \sum_j^p \frac{c_j}{n} log \frac{c_j}{n})/2}$$

Adjusted Random Index

The Rand Index measures the accuracy of pair wise decision i.e., the ratio of pair of objects, both of which are located in the same cluster and same class or both in different cluster or different class. Adjusted Random Index is the corrected for chance version of Random index. Its value lies in [-1,1]. Higher value shows more resemblance between clustering result and label.

$$\text{ARI}(C', C) = \frac{\Sigma_{i,j}\binom{|C'_i \cap C_j|}{2} - \left[\Sigma_i\binom{|C'_i|}{2}\Sigma_j\binom{|C_j|}{2}\right]/\binom{n}{2}}{\frac{1}{2}\left[\Sigma_i\binom{|C'_i|}{2} + \Sigma_j\binom{|C_j|}{2}\right] - \left[\Sigma_i\binom{|C'_i|}{2}\Sigma_j\binom{|C_j|}{2}\right]/\binom{n}{2}}$$

6   Experimental Analyses

In order to evaluate the efficiency of the proposed method, we carried out experiments with several benchmark datasets. Some datasets are not text datasets but as our proposed method is on short text, we try to use the short text concept to those non-text datasets by assuming their characteristic vector as a term vector in the document. We try to show that the proposed method is independent of the content. It can not only deals with the sparse problem but also it is easier to implement. We have also used the combination of normal and short text for our experiments. We report here the experimental results for the following datasets.

Iris dataset

Fisher's Iris data base [22] is perhaps the best known database to be found in the pattern recognition literature. The dataset contains 3 classes of 50 instances each, where each class refers to a type of iris plant. One class is linearly separable from the other two; the latter are not linearly separable from each other.

Pendigit dataset

PENDIGIT dataset is one of UCI benchmark data repository [21]. We consider one easy instance, namely PENDIGIT 01 with 2286 instances and one hard instance, namely PENDIGIT 17 with 1557 instances.

AGBlog dataset

AGblog [1] is an undirected hyperlink network mined from 1222 political blogs. It contains 2 clusters pertaining to the liberal and conservative divisions.

20Ng dataset

The 20 Newsgroups collection is an archive of 1000 messages from each of 20 different Usenet newsgroups. We have selected different versions of this dataset such as 20NgA, 20NgB, 20NgC and 20NgD. Dataset A contains 100 documents of two groups-*misc for sale* and *soc.religion.christian*. Dataset B is an expanded dataset with 200 documents of each class. Dataset C has three classes obtained from dataset B by appending an additional class *talk.politics.guns* with 200 documents. Similarly dataset D has 4 classes obtained by appending yet another class *rec.sport.baseball* with 200 classes to dataset C.

Each of these datasets were preprocessed by removing the stopwords, stemming, and removing very highly frequent words. Here high frequent word signifies, words which are more common in the corpus have high frequencies than the word which are less common. Applying certain thresholds to this list of words, words which comes under the thresholds are considered to be important and they are used as an feature for the documents. We compare the performance of our method with two techniques namely, Normalized-Cuts (NC-NMF) [18] and the Ng-Jordan-Weiss algorithm (NJW) [12]. Since the present work is a sort of extension of NC-NMF, we feel it mandatory to compare the performance of our algorithm with NC-NMF. NJW clustering is one of the most cited [9] clustering techniques for documents and we consider this as our benchmark for performance evaluation. For each data set, experiments were carried out with different values of k in the range [2, 15] in steps of 2. We experimented 50 times for each combination of the parameters. We take the best value among all combinations. The experimental results comparing purity, NMI and ARI of three algorithms are summarized in Table 1. The last row of Table 1 gives the average value of these measures when average is taken over all datasets. It can be seen that except for Pendigit01 and for 20ngA, the proposed method yield better results.

Table 1. Three measures of quality of clustering –purity, NMI and ARI are compared for different datasets for three different algorithms

Datasets	k	KC-NMF			NC-NMF			NJW		
		purity	NMI	ARI	purity	NMI	ARI	purity	NMI	ARI
IRIS	3	**0.9067**	**0.7337**	0.6911	0.6733	0.7235	0.7779	0.7667	0.6083	**0.797**
PEN_DIGIT01	2	0.9987	0.9313	0.9619	**1.000**	**1.000**	**1.000**	**1.000**	**1.000**	**1.00**
PEN_DIGIT17	2	**0.9724**	**0.4376**	0.4113	0.7550	0.2066	**0.6301**	0.7550	0.2043	0.630
AGBLOG	2	**0.9484**	**0.7955**	**0.7003**	0.5205	0.0060	0.5006	0.5205	0.0006	0.500
20ngA	2	**0.9600**	0.7236	0.8081	**0.9600**	**0.7594**	**0.9232**	**0.9600**	**0.7594**	0.923
20ngB	2	**0.9400**	**0.6829**	**0.7735**	0.5050	0.0096	0.5001	0.5523	0.0842	0.505
20ngC	3	**0.8050**	**0.3668**	0.3384	0.6183	0.3295	0.6750	0.6317	0.3488	**0.686**
20ngD	4	**0.8800**	**0.6746**	**0.7031**	0.4750	0.2385	0.6312	0.5150	0.2959	0.682
Average		**0.9264**	**0.6682**	0.6734	0.6883	0.4091	0.7048	0.7126	0.4126	**0.715**

k defines the predefined labels present in the data set.

A detailed experimental comparison is carried out between KC-NMF and NC-NMF for each dataset and for each of the three measures, the performance of two algorithms are compared for different values of K.

Figures 1-3 depicts three cluster measures for KC-NMF and NC-NMF for 20ngA dataset for different values of k. It can be seen that there is a noticeable improvement of performance of KC-NMF in terms of purity. Figures 4-6 give the similar results for 20ngB dataset. It can be seen that KC-NMF performs better for all values but improvement over NC-NMF decreases for higher values of k. Figures 7-9 depict similar results for dataset 20ngC. It is interesting to note that for dataset 20ngD, Figures 10-12, there is a significant improvement in terms of all the three measures. Mixed performance is observed for AGBlog dataset (Figures 13-15).

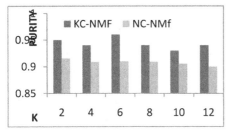

Fig. 1. Comparison of purity for 20ngA

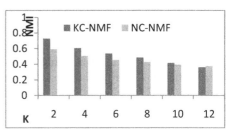

Fig. 2. Comparison of NMI for 20ngA

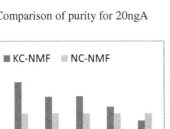

Fig. 3. Comparison of   ARI for 20ngA

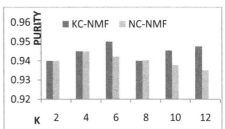

Fig. 4. Comparison of purity for 20ngB

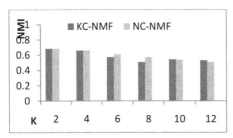

Fig. 5. Comparison of NMI for 20ngB

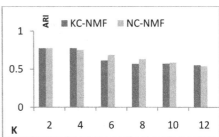

Fig. 6. Comparison of ARI for 20ngB

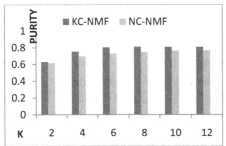

Fig. 7. Comparison of purity for 20ngC

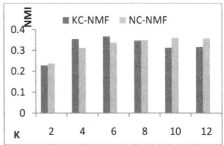

Fig. 8. Comparison of NMI for 20ngC

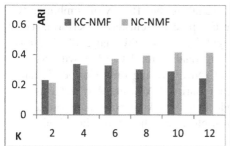

Fig. 9. Comparison of ARI for 20ngC

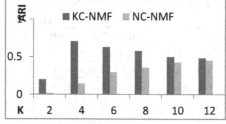

Fig. 10. Comparison of purity for 20ngD

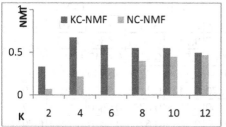

Fig. 11. Comparison of NMI for 20ngD

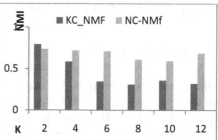

Fig. 12. Comparison of ARI for 20ngD

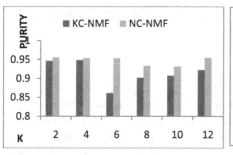

Fig. 13. Comparison of purity for AGBlog

Fig. 14. Comparison of   NMI for AGBlog

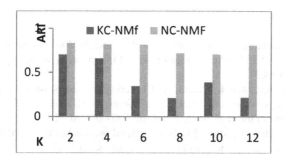

Fig. 15. Comparison of ARI for AGBlog

We carried out another set of experiment to analyze the efficacy of combining two similarity measures. In this experiment, we compare the clustering performance of $S^1 \oplus S^2$ with S^1 and S^2 individually. We use eight datasets for this and Table 2 summarizes the three external measures of clustering quality for KC-NMF with K-NMF (taking only kernel similarity measure) and C-NMF (taking only Cosine similarity measure). It is evident that $S^1 \oplus S^2$ gives better Purity, NMI, and ARI value for the benchmark datasets and hence, we conclude that by taking Hadamard product of two similarity measures we get better result of clustering than clustering obtained by taking individual similarity measure.

Table 2.

Datasets	k	KC-NMF			K-NMF			C-NMF		
		purity	NMI	ARI	purity	NMI	ARI	purity	NMI	ARI
IRIS	3	**0.9067**	**0.7337**	**0.6911**	0.7267	**0.7337**	0.5681	0.6800	0.2524	0.1276
PEN_DIGIT01	2	**0.9987**	**0.9313**	**0.9619**	0.9983	0.5313	0.4194	0.9517	0.5941	0.7359
PEN_DIGIT17	2	**0.9724**	**0.4376**	**0.4113**	0.9531	0.3904	0.3276	0.8750	0.4230	0.5173
AGBLOG	2	**0.9484**	**0.7955**	**0.7003**	0.7070	0.2423	0.1197	0.9422	0.3953	0.3975
20ngA	2	**0.9600**	**0.7236**	**0.8081**	0.9400	0.5748	0.6721	0.9600	0.6913	0.7720
20ngB	2	0.9400	0.6829	0.7735	0.9300	0.5626	0.6727	**0.9450**	**0.7214**	**0.7911**
20ngC	3	0.8050	**0.3668**	0.3384	0.6075	0.1803	0.1489	**0.8350**	0.3432	**0.2671**
20ngD	4	**0.8800**	**0.6746**	**0.7031**	0.4600	0.1693	0.0370	0.8700	0.6548	0.6782
Average		**0.9264**	**0.6682**	**0.6734**	0.7093	0.4230	0.3706	0.8823	0.5094	0.5358

7   Conclusions

In this paper a new algorithm for clustering of short-texts is proposed and it is shown that the new algorithm yields better clustering for benchmark dataset. The new technique makes use of Hadamard product of similarity matrices and it is viewed as weighted similarity. This improves the earlier technique of *ncut*-term-weighting proposed recently. In our future work, we propose to investigate theoretical advantages of non-negative factorization of Hadamard product of two symmetric matrices.

References

1. Adamic, L., Glance, N.: The political blogosphere and the 2004 u.s. election: Divided they blog. In: LinkKDD 2005: Proceedings of the 3rd International Workshop on Link Discovery, pp. 36–43 (2005)
2. Banerjee, S., Ramanathan, K., Gupta, A.: Clustering short texts using wikipedia. In: SIGIR 2007: Proceedings of the 30th Annual International ACM SIGIR Conference on Research and Development in Information Retrieval, pp. 787–788. ACM, New York (2007)
3. Buckley, C., Singhal, A., Mitra, M.: New retrieval approaches using SMART. In: Proc. of the 4th Text Retrieval conference (TREC-4), Gaithersburg (1996)

4. Jin, R., Falusos, C., Hauptmann, A.G.: Meta-scoring: automatically evaluating term weighting schemes in IR without precision-recall. In: Proc. of the 24th ACM International Conference on Research and Development in Information Retrieval (SIGIR 2001), pp. 83–89 (2001)
5. Kim, Y.-D., Choi, S.: Weighted non negative matrix factorization. In: ICASSP (2009)
6. Kim, H., Park, H.: Sparse non-negative matrix factorization via alternating non-negativity-constrained least squares for microarray data analysis. Bioinformatics 23, 1495–1502 (2007)
7. Lee, D.D., Seung, H.S.: Learning the parts of objects by non-negative factorization. Nature 401, 788–791 (1999)
8. Lee, D.D., Seung, H.S.: Algorithms for non-negative factorization. In: Advances in Neural Information Processing Systems, vol. 13, pp. 556–562 (2001)
9. Lin, F., Cohen, W.: Power iteration clustering. In: 27th International Conference on Machine Learning (ICML), Haifa, Israel (2010)
10. Makagonov, P., Alexandrov, M., Gelbukh, A.: Clustering abstracts instead of full texts. In: Sojka, P., Kopeček, I., Pala, K. (eds.) TSD 2004. LNCS (LNAI), vol. 3206, pp. 129–135. Springer, Heidelberg (2004)
11. Manning, C., Raghavan, P., Schutze, H.: Introduction to information retrieval, vol. 1. Cambridge University Press, Cambridge (2008)
12. Ng, A., Jordan, M., Weiss, Y.: On spectral clustering: analysis and an algorithm. In: Advances of Neural Information Processing Systems, vol. 14 (2001)
13. Pantel, P., Lin, D.: Document clustering with committees. In: Proc. of the 25th ACM International Conference on Research and Development in Information Retrieval (SIGIR 2002), pp. 199–206 (2002)
14. Pinto, A.: On Clustering and Evaluation of Narrow Domain Short-Text Corpora. PhD thesis, Universidad Politécnica de Valencia, Spain (2008)
15. Rawat, S., Gulati, V.P., Pujari, A.K.: Frequency and ordering based similarity measure for host-based intrusion detection. Info. Mngt. Computer Security 12(5), 411–421 (2004)
16. Sharma, A., Pujari, A.K., Paliwal, K.K.: Intrusion detection using text processing techniques with a kernel based similarity measure. Computer & Security 26(7-8), 488–495 (2007)
17. Shi, J., Malik, J.: Normalized cuts and image segmentation. IEEE Trans. PAMI 22(8), 888–905 (2000)
18. Yan, X., Guo, J.: Clustering Short Text Using Ncut-weighted Non-negative Matrix Factorization. In: CIKM 2012, Mami, HI, USA, pp. 2259–2262 (2012)
19. Yan, X., Guo, J.: Learning Topics in short text Using Ncut-weighted non-negative matrix Factorization on term correlation matrix,
http://xiaohuiyan.com/papers/TNMF-SDM-13.pdf
20. Yu, S., Shi, J.: Multiclass spectral clustering. In: Proceedings of Ninth IEEE International Conference on Computer Vision, pp. 313–319. IEEE (2003)
21. http://archive.ics.uci.edu/ml/datasets/
Pen-Based+Recognition+of+Handwritten+Digits
22. http://archive.ics.uci.edu/ml/datasets/Iris

Various Document Clustering Tasks
Using Word Lists

Yaakov HaCohen-Kerner and Orr Margaliot

Dept. of Computer Science, Jerusalem College of Technology, 9116001 Jerusalem, Israel
kerner@jct.ac.il, ormargol@gmail.com

Abstract. This research investigates whether it is appropriate to use word lists as features for clustering documents to their authors, to the documents' countries of origin or to the historical periods in which they were written. We have defined three kinds of word lists: most frequent words (FW) including function words (stopwords), most frequent filtered words (FFW) excluding function words, and words with the highest variance values (VFW). The application domain is articles referring to Jewish law written in Hebrew and Aramaic. The clustering experiments have been done using The EM algorithm. To the best of our knowledge, performing clustering tasks according to countries or periods are novel. The improvement rates in these tasks vary from 11.53% to 39.43%. The clustering tasks according to 2 or 3 authors achieved results above 95% and present superior improvement rates (between 15.61% and 56.51%); most of the improvements have been achieved with FW and VFW. These findings are surprising and contrast the initial assumption that FFW is the prime word list for clustering tasks.

Keywords: Authorship attribution, Composition country, Document clustering, Historical period, Word lists.

1 Introduction

In light of the proliferation in available data in general and text documents, which are usually unlabeled, in particular, there is a growing necessity for Unsupervised Learning. Unsupervised Learning in Machine Learning (ML) refers to the method used for seeking out similarities between pieces of data in order to determine whether they can be characterized as forming a group (cluster). Many methods employed in unsupervised ML are based on data mining methods used to preprocess data. Approaches to unsupervised ML include clustering methods, such as K-means, Expectation Maximization (EM), and hierarchical clustering. Surveys of various clustering methods can be seen at [13, 22].

Text clustering is an automatic unsupervised grouping of text documents into clusters. Clustering text documents is the process of detecting groups of documents with similar content. Clustering typically results in a set of clusters, where each cluster consists of documents. The quality of clustering is considered to be superior when more similarities appear within one cluster, in the contents of the documents,

R.E. Banchs et al. (Eds.): AIRS 2013, LNCS 8281, pp. 156–169, 2013.

and when more dissimilarities can be found between the various clusters. However, it is rare to achieve a perfect clustering result, since the result varies between applications and might even differ between users. Researchers can influence the results of a clustering algorithm by using subsets of features only or by using specific similarity measures.

There is a widespread variety of clustering applications. The most popular ones are: (1) document clustering related to classification and information retrieval, and (2) word clustering to produce groups of similar words or concept hierarchies. Examples of clustering applications are presented below.

He and Hui [10] propose a mining process to automate the author co-citation analysis (ACA) based on the Web Citation Database. Their mining process uses agglomerative hierarchical clustering as the mining technique for author clustering and multidimensional scaling for displaying author cluster maps. The clustering results and author cluster map have been incorporated into a citation-based retrieval system known as PubSearch to support author retrieval of Web publications.

A graph-clustering algorithm, called Chinese Whispers [1], is used for various natural language processing (NLP) tasks such as language separation, acquisition of syntactic word classes, and word sense disambiguation. Document clustering is used to produce an overview of the recent trends in data mining activities [20]. Production of domain clusters for domestic and international news in four languages: English, German, Chinese and Russian, was done by Sharoff [21]. Integration of clustering and ranking for heterogeneous information network analysis is presented by Sun et al. [23]. Chan at el. [2] developed a system that visualizes relationships and groupings of authors using keyword clustering and author clustering. They found that authors tend to be grouped together correctly because the co-citation and joint publications imply an extent of collaboration between the authors in the same clusters.

This study focuses on a special form of documents called responsa. The responsa are usually unlabeled answers written by foremost Jewish rabbis in response to various questions submitted to them. These documents are taken from a widespread variety of Jewish domains, e.g.: customs, holidays, kosher food, and laws. Each responsa is based on both ancient Jewish writings and answers given by previous rabbis over the years. The responsa are written in two Semitic languages: Hebrew and Aramaic.

In this research, we are interested in discovering various types of clusters of responsa from the viewpoints of their authors, the places (countries) in which the documents were written or the periods in which they were written. In particular, we want to explore whether the use of three kinds of word lists: (1) FFW (most frequent words excluding function words), (2) FW (most frequent words including function words), and (3) VFW (words with the highest variance values), as features is appropriate for these clustering tasks. The initial assumption is that FFW will be superior to FW and VFW for clustering tasks because function words have little lexical meaning and words with the highest variance values are not considered good features.

This paper is organized as follows: Section 2 presents several previous text clustering systems that use words. Section 3 presents our model. Section 4 describes the examined corpora. Section 5 details the experimental results and analyzes them. Section 6 summarizes and proposes future directions for research.

2   Text Clustering Using Words

Text clustering presents challenges due to the large number of training documents, the vast amount of features present in the documents set, and the dependencies between the features. Effective feature selection is essential to make the learning task efficient and higher in accuracy. In text clustering one typically uses a 'bag of words' model, where each position in the input feature vector corresponds to a given word or phrase. Feature selection is critical in order to make large problems computationally efficient—conserving computation, storage and network resources for the training phase and for every future use of the classifier. Moreover, appropriate features and an appropriate number of features can improve clustering capability substantially, or equivalently, reduce the amount of training data necessary in order to obtain a desired level of performance.

Supervised classification of Hebrew-Aramaic documents has been presented in a few previous works. Several works presented by HaCohen-Kerner et al. [7, 8] use stylistic feature sets. Other works presented by Koppel et al., [14, 15] use a few hundreds of single words. HaCohen-Kerner et al. [6] investigate as a supervised ML task the use of 'bag of words' for the classification of Hebrew-Aramaic documents according to their historical period and the ethnic origin of their authors.

Hotho et al. [11, 12] implement text documents clustering based on ontologies. Their method includes the following stages: (1) representation of the original text document as a 'bag of words', (2) removal of 571 stopwords taken from a standard list, (3) stemming, (4) pruning rare terms, (5) TF-IDF weighting, and (6) integrating sets of synonyms as background knowledge achieved through the Wordnet ontology. They found that the best background knowledge method always improves performance compared to the best baseline.

Miao et al. [18] implement three methods for document clustering: (1) using words (after removing stopwords, stemming, pruning rare terms and tfidf weighting), (2) using terms (based on their C Value , i.e., a frequency-based weight that accounts for nested terms), and (3) using frequent character n-grams. They found that the n-gram-based representation gives the best performance with the lowest dimensionality.

Li and Chung [16] and Li et al. [17] implement text clustering based on frequent word sequences and frequent word meaning sequences instead of 'bag of words'. A word meaning is the concept expressed by synonymous word forms. Using these two kinds of sequences they reduce the high dimensionality of the documents and measure the closeness between documents.

Yu [25] uses function words[1] to solve the Chinese authorship attribution problem (C-FWAA) in three different genres: the novel, essay, and blog. Her system is able to distinguish three authors in each genre with various levels of success. C-FWAA is the most effective in distinguishing authors of novels (averaged accuracy 90%), followed by essays (85%), and with blogs being the most difficult (68%).

---

[1] Function words express grammatical relationships. Function words include articles (e.g., the, a), pronouns (e.g., he, him, she, her), particles (e.g., if, then, well, however, thus), and conjunctions (e.g., for, and, or, nor, but, yet, so), auxiliary verbs (be, have, shall, will, may, and can). Function words were probably first proposed by Mosteller and Wallace [19].

With the exception of Yu [25], all studies mentioned above that use 'bags of words', inter alia process removal of stop words from their 'bags of words'. Moreover, they neither use the most frequent words nor words with the highest variance values.

Forman [4] presents an empirical study of twelve feature selection metrics, which were evaluated on a benchmark of 229 text classification problem instances that originated from Reuters. Forman claims that overly common words (stopwords), such as 'a' and 'of', may be removed on the grounds that they are ambiguous and occur so frequently as to not be discriminating for any particular cluster. In his research, a common word was identified if it occurred in over 50% all documents.

3   The Model

As mentioned above, Forman claims that stopwords should be removed when utilizing the feature selection methods. We chose to examine his claim by conducting two sets of experiments: one uses all the words including stopwords and the other without the stopwords. In both sets, we used a normalized frequency for each feature. In addition, we examined a third word-list: words with the highest variance values.

We have defined the following terms:
1. **Common Features (CF)** – a word is identified as a common feature if it occurs in over 50% of all documents (at least once in each document). 84 CF have been found in these corpora. Based on our findings, 82 (!) of them are stopwords.
2. **Frequent Words (FW)** – Most frequent words including CF.
3. **Filtered Frequent Words (FFW)** – Most frequent words excluding CF.
4. **Variance Features (VFW)** - Words with the highest variance values.

We have defined the following algorithm:
For each experiment E done for task T on corpus C
    For each word list: FW, FFW and VFW
        select: 100, 200, …, 1000 as the number of its features
        Measure the performance of the EM algorithm

The EM algorithm [3] is a general approach to iterative computation of maximum-likelihood estimates when the observations are viewed as incomplete data. Each algorithm's iteration consists of an expectation step followed by a maximization step. The EM method was chosen by us, due to its simplicity, generality and relatively quick run time, and due to the wide range of examples which fall under its definition.

In our work, the EM algorithm has been applied on a widespread variety of clustering tasks: clustering of documents to their authors or to countries where the documents were written or the historical period when they were written. For each task, various experiments (depending of the number of chosen words) have been performed. Each experiment has been applied for each one of the 3 word lists: FW, FFW, and VFW. The accuracy measured in all experiments is the fraction of the number of documents correctly clustered to the total number of possible documents to be clustered. We applied the EM implementation of Weka [24, 9] using the default values as done by Forman [4]. Model tuning is left for future research.

4   The Examined Corpora

The application domain contains responsa written in Hebrew and Aramaic. The responsa are answers written by foremost Jewish rabbis in response to various questions submitted to them. These documents are taken from a widespread variety of Jewish domains, e.g.: customs, holidays, kosher food, and laws. Each responsa is based on both ancient writings and answers given by previous rabbis.

The examined corpora were downloaded from The Global Jewish Database (The Responsa Project[2]) at Bar-Ilan University. These corpora include 1,370 documents (responsa), which contain 1,769,072 words composed by six authors who lived in two consecutive generations (the first starting around 1800 and the second starting around 1850) from 3 countries (Germany, Lithuania and Morocco). Tables 1-3 present full statistical information concerning these corpora.

Table 1. General statistical information about the examined corpora

#	Book's Hebrew title (pronounced in English)	Author's Hebrew name (pronounced in English)	Country	Lifetime	Era: Old/ New	Period	# of Docu- ments	# of words	Average # of words per document
1	Binyan Tzion	R. Jacob Ettlinger	Germany	1798-1871	Old	1800-1900	358	240871	672.82
2	Melamed Le-Ho'il	R. David Tzvi Hoffmann	Germany	1843-1929	New	1850-1950	373	201744	540.87
3	Meshiv Davar	R. Naftali Tzvi Judah Berlin	Lithuania	1817-1893	Old	1800-1900	260	347651	1337.12
4	Achiezer	R. Chaim Ozer Grodzinsky	Lithuania	1863-1940	New	1850-1950	170	560674	3298.08
5	Yoru Mishpatecha Le-Ya'akov	R. Yaakov Abu-Chatzeira	Morocco	1806-1880	Old	1800-1900	146	175620	1202.88
6	Asher Li-Shlomo	R. Solomon b. Moses Ibn Denan	Morocco	1848-1929	New	1850-1950	69	242512	3514.67

Table 2. Statistical information about the corpora from the location (country) viewpoint

#	Country	Documents	Words	Average # of words per document
1	Germany	731	442615	605.49
2	Lithuania	430	908325	2112.38
3	Morocco	215	418132	1944.8

Table 3. Statistical information about the corpora from the period viewpoint

#	Era	Documents	Words	Average # of words per document
1	Old (1798-1880)	764	764142	1000.19
2	New (1848-1940)	612	1004930	1642.04

[2] http://www.biu.ac.il/ICJI/Responsa/index.html

5   Experimental Results

In sub-section 5.1, we detail the results and the analyses of the clustering task according to countries or periods of composition. In sub-section 5.2, we detail the results and the analyses of the clustering task according to the documents' authors.

5.1   Clustering Experiments According to Countries or Periods

We have performed eight clustering experiments (combinations of 2 or 3 countries of composition and 2 periods of composition). Tables 4-6 present the clustering results for the 3 word lists: FW, FFW, and VFW, respectively.

Table 4. Clustering results for the FFW

#	Countries	Clustering type	# of features									
			100	200	300	400	500	600	700	800	900	1000
1	Germany –	Country	73.04%	69.16%	69.16%	69.16%	69.16%	69.16%	69.16%	69.16%	69.16%	69.16%
2	Lithuania	Era	55.30%	85.36%	85.36%	85.36%	85.36%	85.36%	85.36%	85.36%	85.36%	85.36%
3	Germany –	Country	77.59%	62.16%	62.16%	62.16%	62.16%	62.16%	62.16%	62.16%	62.16%	62.16%
4	Morocco	Era	63.53%	92.71%	92.71%	92.71%	92.71%	92.71%	92.71%	92.71%	92.71%	92.71%
5	Lithuania –	Country	92.40%	93.95%	92.71%	91.94%	90.39%	91.63%	90.70%	90.08%	90.08%	89.77%
6	Morocco	Era	54.26%	51.63%	53.49%	53.80%	54.11%	54.57%	55.50%	55.50%	70.23%	71%
7	Germany –	Country	64.54%	70.28%	70.42%	52.18%	60.97%	59.52%	59.23%	58.50%	58.14%	57.12%
8	Lithuania – Morocco	Era	55.81%	%82.70	82.63%	82.63%	82.63%	82.63%	82.63%	82.63%	82.63%	82.63%

Table 5. Clustering results for the FW

#	Countries	Clustering type	# of features									
			100	200	300	400	500	600	700	800	900	1000
1	Germany –	Country	73.82%	72.52%	69.16%	69.16%	69.16%	69.16%	69.16%	69.16%	69.16%	69.16%
2	Lithuania	Era	51.68%	57.02%	85.36%	85.36%	85.36%	85.36%	85.36%	85.36%	85.36%	85.36%
3	Germany –	Country	81.61%	62.16%	62.16%	62.16%	62.16%	62.16%	62.16%	62.16%	62.16%	62.16%
4	Morocco	Era	56.34%	92.71%	92.71%	56.34%	92.71%	56.34%	92.71%	56.34%	92.71%	92.71%
5	Lithuania –	Country	77.52%	93.49%	92.40%	91.63%	90.85%	90.54%	90.54%	90.54%	89.92%	90.70%
6	Morocco	Era	65.58%	53.02%	54.42%	54.88%	55.50%	55.50%	55.97%	85.89%	86.36%	53.80%
7	Germany –	Country	46.08%	69.40%	70.35%	69.84%	58.65%	58.43%	57.49%	58.58%	58.07%	57.56%
8	Lithuania – Morocco	Era	53.34%	66.50%	82.63%	82.63%	82.63%	82.63%	82.63%	82.63%	82.63%	82.63%

Table 6. Clustering results for the VFW

#	Countries	Clustering type	# of features									
			100	200	300	400	500	600	700	800	900	1000
1	Germany –	Country	71.23%	72.78%	71.75%	71.32%	72.61%	73.56%	72.18%	71.75%	74.50%	73.90%
2	Lithuania	Era	55.30%	57.19%	57.62%	77%	73.99%	62.02%	75.97%	81.40%	78.81%	79.41%
3	Germany –	Country	91.12%	93.13%	91.97%	92.49%	93.23%	92.18%	63.85%	68.82%	62.16%	62.16%
4	Morocco	Era	58.25%	55.39%	56.77%	56.87%	58.25%	58.46%	89.75%	84.99%	92.71%	92.71%
5	Lithuania –	Country	76.12%	84.19%	91.63%	90.85%	90.08%	90.85%	90.70%	90.85%	90.39%	89.77%
6	Morocco	Era	67.60%	61.40%	53.95%	55.66%	55.97%	55.50%	55.81%	55.66%	81.09%	56.43%
7	Germany –	Country	67.73%	62.14%	69.69%	73.33%	65.84%	52.40%	61.63%	65.41%	58.28%	72.24%
8	Lithuania – Morocco	Era	51.24%	50.36%	59.81%	54.51%	57.92%	57.78%	60.90%	62.72%	76.89%	73.26%

Table 7. Improvement rates for the clustering tasks according to countries or periods

#	Countries	Clustering type	Baseline - Majority	The best result	Achieved by	Improvement rate
1	Germany – Lithuania	Country	62.97%	74.50%	VFW(900)	11.53%
2		Period	53.23%	85.36%	FFW(200)	32.13%
3	Germany – Morocco	Country	77.27%	93.23%	VFW(500)	15.96%
4		Period	53.28%	92.71%	Both FFW(200) & FW(200)	39.43%
5	Lithuania – Morocco	Country	66.67%	93.95%	FFW(5)	27.28%
6		Period	62.95%	85.36%	FW(900)	22.41%
7	Germany – Lithuania	Country	53.36%	73.33%	VFW(400)	19.97%
8	– Morocco	Period	55.77%	82.70%	FFW(200)	26.93%

Almost all superior clustering results for the first two word lists: FW and FFW (Tables 4-5) have been achieved by 100 or 200 or 300 words, i.e., there is no need to use more words. However, most of the superior clustering results for VFW (Table 6) have been achieved by 800 or 900 words. Table 7 presents the best clustering results versus the baseline results for all 8 experiments. The baseline classifier is the "majority" method, which assumes that every document belongs to the larger of the two or three categories (depending on the experiment). This baseline is reasonable since almost all the experiments are for two categories and the categories do not include the same number of documents, i.e. most of the baseline values are relatively high especially for clustering tasks, which are usually not as successful as classification tasks.

The improvement rates for the clustering tasks according to countries or periods presented in Table 7 are significant. The improvement rates from the "majority" (the baseline result) to the best result vary from 11.53% to 39.43%.

When considering all 8 experiments (Tables 4-6), FFW has been found as the superior set with 4 best results (one of them tied with FW), VFW with 3 best results, and FW with 2 best results (one of them tied with FW). When considering the clustering experiments according to period, FFW has been found as the superior set with 3 best results. FFW contains the most frequent words excluding function words, i.e. the set of the most frequent content words is the best set for clustering according to periods. A possible explanation is that different content words are used in different periods.

However, a surprising finding has been discovered when considering the clustering experiments according to countries. VFW has been found as the best set with 3 best results (out of 4). VFW contains the words with the highest variance values. A possible explanation is that frequent words that their distribution is non-uniform over the documents are the best set for clustering according to countries.

The FFW set was better than the FW set in the clustering experiments performed in sub-section 5.1. This finding strengthens Forman's claim, which stopwords do not support the classification task. Nevertheless, FW achieved some surprising results. Moreover, VFW achieved even more surprising results. Another interesting finding is as follows: the greater the distance between the countries, the greater the success rate of clustering results according to countries in comparison to those according to periods (Germany-Lithuania 1300 km, Germany-Morocco 3300 km and Lithuania-Morocco 4600 km). The clustering result for Germany versus Lithuania, which are relatively close geographically, is quite poor (74.50%) with a rather small improvement rate (11.53%), while the clustering results for Germany or Lithuania versus Morocco are much higher (93.23% and 93.95% respectively) with higher improvement rates.

5.2   Clustering Experiments According to Authors

Document clustering according to authors is one of the most popular clustering tasks. A few relevant works have been presented in the first two sections. In our work, we have performed clustering experiments for all combinations of 2 or 3 authors. All six examined authors are the same authors mentioned in the previous sub-section with the same serial numbers.

Tables 8-10 present the clustering results for all 15 possible combinations of 2 authors (out of 6 authors) for the 3 word lists: FW, FFW, and VFW, respectively. When taking into account the number of optimal results (100%), FW is the superior set with 7 optimal results, VFW is second best with 6 optimal results, and FFW is least successful with only 3 optimal results. When taking into account the average of the best 10 results (one for each row), for each one of the word lists, we observe that VFW is the best set with an average of 98.58%, FW is the second with a very close result of 98.49%, and FFW is least successful with an average of only 95.41%.

FW includes function words, which are common to many authors and therefore are usually regarded as words that have little lexical meaning. Thus, these results are rather surprising and contrast Forman's opinion that common words should not be used for classification tasks. A more surprising result is the success of VFW, which represents words that are unusually distributed over the documents. Improvement rates of clustering to 2 authors are presented in Table 14. These findings reveal that function words and words with the highest variance values are relevant for such clustering tasks.

Table 8. Clustering results for 2 authors using the FFW

#	# of authors	# of features									
		100	200	300	400	500	600	700	800	900	1000
1	1,2	93.98%	93.16%	95.76%	97.67%	97.81%	93.98%	93.84%	95.35%	95.08%	95.49%
2	1,3	85.76%	90.61%	89.48%	92.23%	91.59%	91.91%	92.72%	92.07%	92.07%	91.91%
3	1,4	90.91%	96.78%	98.67%	98.67%	98.67%	99.24%	99.62%	99.62%	99.81%	99.81%
4	1,5	97.42%	98.02%	97.42%	99.01%	99.01%	98.81%	99.01%	98.81%	98.61%	98.81%
5	1,6	65.81%	98.59%	99.53%	99.53%	99.77%	99.53%	99.53%	99.53%	99.77%	99.77%
6	2,3	86.41%	85.31%	64.46%	64.46%	64.46%	64.46%	64.46%	57.35%	57.35%	57.35%
7	2,4	94.11%	96.69%	98.90%	100%	100%	100%	100%	50.28%	100%	100%
8	2,5	95.76%	98.46%	98.46%	99.61%	99.81%	52.02%	52.02%	100%	100%	100%
9	2,6	52.49%	50.91%	50.91%	50.91%	50.91%	50.91%	61.09%	61.09%	61.09%	61.09%
10	3,4	92.09%	98.14%	98.37%	96.74%	98.84%	53.26%	53.26%	53.26%	53.26%	53.26%
11	3,5	97.04%	99.01%	98.52%	98.03%	98.03%	99.26%	99.26%	99.01%	98.77%	98.77%
12	3,6	81.46%	96.66%	96.96%	98.18%	67.48%	57.45%	58.97%	58.36%	98.48%	55.93%
13	4,5	96.52%	95.25%	95.89%	96.20%	98.73%	98.73%	98.73%	99.37%	98.73%	99.05%
14	4,6	79.92%	96.65%	98.74%	98.33%	97.07%	98.74%	99.58%	99.58%	100%	100%
15	5,6	73.49%	91.63%	93.02%	98.60%	96.74%	96.74%	96.74%	96.74%	93.95%	91.63%

Table 9. Clustering results for 2 authors using the FW

#	# of authors	# of features									
		100	200	300	400	500	600	700	800	900	1000
1	1,2	100%	100%	100%	100%	100%	100%	100%	100%	100%	100%
2	1,3	76.05%	71.36%	73.14%	73.79%	89.81%	90.13%	90.61%	90.13%	90.61%	90.29%
3	1,4	96.02%	97.92%	89.77%	91.67%	92.23%	91.67%	92.05%	92.05%	92.23%	91.86%
4	1,5	97.82%	93.85%	95.63%	95.04%	94.25%	100%	100%	100%	100%	100%
5	1,6	77.05%	89.23%	90.63%	89.70%	89.46%	89.46%	89.23%	89.46%	89.46%	89.46%
6	2,3	100%	100%	100%	100%	100%	100%	100%	100%	100%	100%
7	2,4	93.37%	100%	100%	100%	100%	100%	100%	100%	100%	100%
8	2,5	100%	100%	100%	100%	100%	100%	100%	100%	100%	100%
9	2,6	100%	100%	100%	100%	100%	100%	100%	100%	100%	100%
10	3,4	90%	93.72%	98.37%	99.07%	99.30%	96.28%	97.67%	98.14%	97.67%	97.44%
11	3,5	97.54%	98.03%	98.52%	99.26%	99.51%	99.26%	99.51%	99.51%	99.75%	99.75%
12	3,6	77.51%	95.14%	97.57%	98.78%	98.48%	100%	99.70%	58.36%	99.70%	99.70%
13	4,5	99.37%	99.37%	99.68%	99.37%	99.37%	99.68%	99.68%	99.68%	100%	100%
14	4,6	99.16%	97.49%	89.96%	99.58%	99.16%	92.47%	88.70%	86.61%	93.72%	97.91%
15	5,6	90.23%	86.98%	89.30%	88.84%	92.09%	96.74%	96.74%	97.67%	99.53%	99.53%

Table 10. Clustering results for 2 authors using the VFW

#	# of authors	# of features									
		100	200	300	400	500	600	700	800	900	1000
1	1,2	74.69%	88.37%	91.24%	100%	100%	100%	100%	100%	100%	100%
2	1,3	72.17%	82.85%	86.89%	89.64%	91.26%	92.23%	93.69%	94.50%	93.69%	94.82%
3	1,4	84.47%	91.67%	94.13%	96.59%	97.92%	98.48%	98.11%	98.86%	98.86%	98.30%
4	1,5	98.02%	98.02%	98.81%	98.21%	98.41%	98.21%	98.02%	97.82%	99.01%	99.21%
5	1,6	95.78%	97.89%	98.59%	99.30%	99.30%	98.83%	98.83%	98.83%	98.59%	100%
6	2,3	77.88%	99.84%	99.21%	99.37%	99.68%	100%	100%	100%	100%	100%
7	2,4	91.16%	93.74%	94.66%	96.13%	100%	99.82%	99.45%	99.26%	100%	100%
8	2,5	98.07%	98.27%	98.27%	98.07%	98.46%	100%	100%	100%	100%	100%
9	2,6	94.57%	96.15%	97.06%	96.61%	97.51%	61.09%	99.77%	99.77%	100%	100%
10	3,4	79.77%	85.35%	88.14%	89.77%	91.40%	92.79%	94.42%	95.12%	96.74%	97.21%
11	3,5	97.04%	98.28%	97.78%	97.78%	98.03%	99.01%	99.01%	98.52%	98.77%	98.77%
12	3,6	74.16%	96.96%	98.48%	98.78%	98.78%	97.57%	98.18%	79.94%	79.94%	79.94%
13	4,5	97.47%	98.73%	99.05%	99.37%	99.37%	99.37%	99.37%	99.37%	99.37%	99.37%
14	4,6	85.36%	78.66%	75.73%	93.31%	79.50%	74.48%	72.80%	74.48%	72.38%	73.22%
15	5,6	88.84%	86.51%	87.44%	90.23%	89.30%	93.95%	93.95%	97.67%	98.14%	92.09%

Tables 11-13 present the clustering results for all 20 possible combinations of 3 authors (out of 6 authors) for the 3 word lists: FW, FFW, and VFW, respectively. When taking into account the number of optimal results (100%), FW is again the best set with 2 optimal results, VFW is in the second place with 1 optimal result, and FFW is in the last place with no optimal results. Additional results concerning clustering to 3 authors are given in Tables 13 and 15.

When taking into account the average of the best 10 results (one for each row), for each of the word lists (Tables 11-13), we observe again that VFW is the best set with an average of 96.38%, FFW is in the second place with 95.85%, and FW is in the last place with an average of 95.41%. Again, VFW appears to be better than the other word lists for clustering according to 3 authors.

The improvement rates for the clustering tasks according to 2 authors presented in Table 14 vary from 15.61% to 48.97%. The improvement rates for the clustering tasks according to 3 authors presented in Table 15 vary from 24.39% to 56.51%.

Table 11. Clustering results for 3 authors using the FFW

#	# of authors	100	200	300	400	500	600	700	800	900	1000
						# of features					
1	1,2,3	75.68%	82.24%	83.15%	83.45%	83.65%	83.96%	84.06%	84.26%	94.45%	93.95%
2	1,2,4	87.24%	98.89%	91.01%	91.68%	95.56%	95.23%	95.23%	95.56%	95.45%	95.56%
3	1,2,5	98.63%	98.18%	97.38%	96.69%	96.69%	96.58%	95.67%	95.78%	99.89%	95.67%
4	1,2,6	68.75%	85.25%	94.50%	94.25%	94.38%	94.38%	94.13%	94.13%	93.75%	78.50%
5	1,3,4	66.50%	58.12%	91.88%	71.70%	90.61%	92.13%	91.88%	92.77%	67.39%	70.69%
6	1,3,5	82.46%	89.14%	89.14%	89.66%	90.97%	92.67%	92.15%	92.02%	92.54%	92.54%
7	1,3,6	59.83%	64.92%	72.93%	90.83%	75.69%	78.02%	92.43%	92.58%	91.99%	91.85%
8	1,4,5	90.06%	94.51%	95.55%	96.88%	97.48%	97.63%	97.92%	98.22%	98.96%	99.11%
9	1,4,6	94.97%	95.31%	97.99%	79.06%	99.16%	99.33%	96.98%	87.27%	86.93%	87.77%
10	1,5,6	74.35%	68.06%	82.20%	95.64%	95.29%	94.76%	97.56%	75.57%	80.98%	74.52%
11	2,3,4	66.63%	89.04%	94.52%	99.13%	99.50%	60.40%	60.40%	74.97%	74.97%	60.40%
12	2,3,5	85.62%	98.46%	99.10%	98.84%	98.97%	62.26%	99.23%	98.84%	99.23%	99.10%
13	2,3,6	56.98%	84.90%	65.67%	66.67%	66.95%	57.98%	59.54%	69.09%	49.57%	48.86%
14	2,4,5	87.81%	94.05%	96.81%	97.39%	98.55%	98.69%	67.34%	67.34%	47.17%	66.47%
15	2,4,6	87.75%	89.38%	94.61%	78.10%	51.96%	56.21%	51.96%	51.96%	54.25%	52.45%
16	2,5,6	61.73%	62.93%	95.07%	59.35%	69.39%	70.75%	70.75%	70.75%	70.75%	70.75%
17	3,4,5	93.06%	95.49%	96.35%	97.05%	96.18%	95.66%	95.66%	94.10%	63.89%	64.06%
18	3,4,6	83.37%	75.95%	63.73%	76.95%	96.19%	87.37%	57.11%	54.31%	55.71%	56.91%
19	3,5,6	79.37%	70.32%	88.84%	73.05%	75.16%	76.63%	81.47%	97.26%	66.74%	66.53%
20	4,5,6	87.79%	92.73%	91.43%	92.21%	91.95%	77.14%	72.99%	82.34%	82.34%	78.70%

Table 12. Clustering results for 3 authors using the FW

#	# of authors	100	200	300	400	500	600	700	800	900	1000
						# of features					
1	1,2,3	75.88%	94.45%	82.34%	83.65%	83.96%	83.75%	83.65%	94.05%	94.05%	94.15%
2	1,2,4	77.36%	98.78%	99.22%	92.79%	95.34%	95.23%	95.34%	95.23%	95.12%	95.45%
3	1,2,5	88.37%	99.09%	96.01%	96.92%	96.58%	96.47%	96.81%	96.24%	100%	100%
4	1,2,6	75.13%	86.38%	94.50%	94%	94%	94.13%	94%	94%	94%	78.50%
5	1,3,4	51.14%	87.56%	77.28%	57.11%	76.52%	79.57%	68.27%	68.15%	68.15%	61.68%
6	1,3,5	79.84%	89.53%	75.52%	75.39%	75.79%	77.88%	77.36%	77.36%	90.45%	90.97%
7	1,3,6	59.97%	64.92%	63.17%	73.22%	74.53%	73.07%	72.05%	91.41%	72.63%	90.68%
8	1,4,5	89.61%	95.99%	96.59%	97.33%	97.63%	93.03%	93.03%	93.03%	93.03%	92.88%
9	1,4,6	87.44%	98.16%	82.41%	87.94%	75.88%	80.74%	80.90%	90.79%	80.74%	81.07%
10	1,5,6	68.76%	93.89%	87.78%	87.61%	87.78%	88.31%	88.31%	89.01%	90.40%	89.70%
11	2,3,4	78.70%	97.88%	98.75%	99.25%	99.50%	98.63%	60.40%	60.40%	60.40%	60.40%
12	2,3,5	87.93%	98.59%	98.97%	99.23%	98.84%	99.36%	99.36%	99.49%	99.74%	99.74%
13	2,3,6	71.08%	83.48%	70.09%	69.09%	69.09%	69.09%	69.09%	69.09%	69.09%	69.09%
14	2,4,5	85.92%	99.56%	99.71%	99.71%	99.71%	99.71%	99.71%	99.71%	99.85%	99.71%
15	2,4,6	65.85%	97.22%	100%	100%	100%	64.54%	64.54%	64.54%	64.54%	64.54%
16	2,5,6	85.54%	96.09%	95.41%	95.92%	70.75%	63.10%	63.10%	63.10%	70.75%	70.75%
17	3,4,5	85.59%	92.71%	97.22%	96.18%	96.53%	96.01%	96.18%	95.83%	96.70%	64.76%
18	3,4,6	66.93%	85.17%	97.39%	70.94%	68.54%	67.33%	95.79%	98%	64.53%	61.52%
19	3,5,6	81.89%	83.79%	92.21%	91.79%	93.47%	95.37%	84.42%	81.47%	73.68%	67.16%
20	4,5,6	95.06%	90.39%	92.99%	93.25%	80.26%	81.82%	93.77%	94.03%	94.29%	93.51%

Table 13. Clustering results for 3 authors using the VFW

#	# of authors	# of features									
		100	200	300	400	500	600	700	800	900	1000
1	1,2,3	63.87%	88.29%	89.10%	91.73%	94.05%	58.83%	58.83%	71.14%	58.83%	78.71%
2	1,2,4	62.04%	65.59%	71.25%	82.69%	92.23%	93.78%	96%	99.56%	99.78%	72.81%
3	1,2,5	63.85%	60.89%	75.14%	84.61%	89.28%	98.97%	99.20%	98.75%	99.20%	99.20%
4	1,2,6	75.50%	84.50%	87.88%	88.50%	92.50%	72.88%	78.50%	78.50%	78.50%	78.50%
5	1,3,4	58.50%	66.37%	72.08%	78.17%	81.47%	82.11%	88.96%	89.72%	89.34%	68.65%
6	1,3,5	75.79%	84.42%	79.97%	87.70%	89.92%	91.62%	92.41%	93.46%	93.72%	94.63%
7	1,3,6	71.03%	79.91%	60.84%	65.36%	74.96%	92.14%	93.60%	72.78%	95.05%	77.73%
8	1,4,5	80.71%	91.25%	95.99%	95.10%	94.96%	95.25%	97.92%	97.92%	73.15%	73%
9	1,4,6	77.05%	85.09%	91.96%	94.81%	94.97%	96.82%	97.65%	84.92%	72.70%	85.93%
10	1,5,6	92.67%	90.58%	93.54%	96.16%	87.96%	95.64%	81.33%	81.50%	81.68%	81.68%
11	2,3,4	65.38%	71.73%	82.57%	92.90%	91.41%	94.15%	95.52%	96.89%	98.88%	77.71%
12	2,3,5	81.26%	88.32%	94.48%	97.18%	97.56%	97.18%	98.33%	99.36%	99.10%	99.36%
13	2,3,6	81.20%	85.33%	98.43%	68.80%	65.81%	64.96%	64.25%	64.96%	99.86%	69.09%
14	2,4,5	85.78%	91.73%	95.07%	94.63%	96.08%	99.71%	99.71%	99.27%	98.98%	99.71%
15	2,4,6	80.23%	91.18%	93.30%	94.44%	94.12%	100%	100%	100%	99.84%	100%
16	2,5,6	91.33%	93.03%	91.84%	93.03%	94.39%	91.16%	95.92%	95.92%	96.26%	96.26%
17	3,4,5	72.22%	87.50%	88.89%	91.49%	94.44%	94.97%	96.01%	94.44%	96.53%	94.97%
18	3,4,6	68.94%	65.33%	76.55%	78.16%	93.99%	92.79%	91.98%	94.79%	94.19%	82.97%
19	3,5,6	74.95%	70.95%	92.21%	93.05%	94.53%	94.74%	94.32%	94.74%	95.16%	94.95%
20	4,5,6	80.26%	86.23%	83.90%	90.39%	88.57%	90.39%	80%	79.48%	86.49%	90.39%

When considering all 15 experiments according to 2 authors (rows 1-15 in Table 14), FW has been found to be the best set with 11 best results, VFW with 8 best results, and FFW with only 4 best results. When considering all 20 experiments according to authors (rows 1-20 in Table 15), FW has been found again as the best set with 9 best results, FFW with 8 best results, and VFW with only 6 best results.

Table 14. Improvement rates for the clustering tasks according to 2 authors

#	Authors	Baseline - Majority	The best result	Achieved by	Improvement rate
1	1,2	51.03%	100%	FW(100) & VFW(400)	48.97%
2	1,3	57.93%	94.82%	VFW(1000)	36.89%
3	1,4	67.80%	99.81%	FFW(900)	32.01%
4	1,5	71.03%	100%	VFW(1000)	28.97%
5	1,6	83.84%	100%	FW(100) & VFW(1000)	16.16%
6	2,3	58.93%	100%	FW(100) & VFW(600)	41.07%
7	2,4	68.69%	100%	FFW(400) & FW(200) & VFW(500)	31.31%
8	2,5	71.87%	100%	FFW(800) & FW(100) & VFW(600)	28.13%
9	2,6	84.39%	100%	FW(100) & VFW(900)	15.61%
10	3,4	60.47%	99.30%	FW(500)	38.83%
11	3,5	64.04%	99.75%	FW(900)	35.71%
12	3,6	79.03%	100%	FW(600)	20.97%
13	4,5	53.80%	100%	FW(900)	46.20%
14	4,6	71.13%	100%	FFW(900)	28.87%
15	5,6	67.91%	99.53%	FW(900)	31.62%

Table 15. Improvement rates for the clustering tasks according to 3 authors

#	Authors	Baseline-Majority	The best result	Achieved by	Improvement rate
1	1,2,3	37.64%	94.15%	FW(1000)	56.51%
2	1,2,4	51.03%	99.78%	VFW(900)	48.75%
3	1,2,5	51.03%	100%	FW(900)	48.97%
4	1,2,6	51.03%	94.50%	FFW(300) & FW(300)	43.47%
5	1,3,4	57.93%	92.77%	FFW(800)	34.84%
6	1,3,5	57.93%	94.63%	VFW(1000)	36.70%
7	1,3,6	57.93%	95.05%	VFW(900)	37.12%
8	1,4,5	67.80%	99.11%	FFW(1000)	31.31%
9	1,4,6	67.80%	99.33%	FFW(600)	31.53%
10	1,5,6	71.03%	97.56%	FFW(700)	26.53%
11	2,3,4	58.93%	99.50%	FFW(500(& FW(500)	40.57%
12	2,3,5	58.93%	99.74%	FW(900)	40.81%
13	2,3,6	58.93%	99.86%	VFW(900)	40.93%
14	2,4,5	68.69%	99.85%	FW(900)	31.16%
15	2,4,6	68.69%	100%	FW(300) & VFW(600)	31.31%
16	2,5,6	71.87%	96.26%	VFW(900)	24.39%
17	3,4,5	60.47%	97.22%	FW(300)	36.75%
18	3,4,6	60.47%	98.00%	FW(800)	37.53%
19	3,5,6	64.04%	97.26%	FFW(800)	33.22%
20	4,5,6	53.80%	94.29%	FW(900)	40.49%

6   Summary and Future Work

In this research, we investigate whether the use of words as features is appropriate for clustering of documents according to their authors, to the countries in which the documents were written or the historical period in which they were written. To the best of our knowledge, performing clustering tasks according to countries or periods are novel.

The clustering tasks for 2 countries are rather successful (74.50%, 93.23%, and 93.95%). An interesting finding is that as the countries are geographically farther apart, the clustering results achieved were more successful. For the more complex clustering tasks (3 countries), a lower result was achieved (73.33%). The clustering results for the period tasks were reasonable (between 82.70% and 92.71%).

The clustering tasks according to 2 or 3 authors have been highly successful (above 95%), especially when using FW and VFW. A possible explanation is that function words and words with the highest variance values are relevant for such clustering tasks.

Future directions for research are: (1) tuning of the model, (2) defining and applying additional types of features such as: special content word lists, n-grams, morphological features (e.g.: nouns, verbs and adjectives), syntactic features (frequencies and distribution of parts of speech tags, such as: noun, verb, adjective, adverb), key-phrases [5], collocations and references unique to each class, and (3) applying various kinds of models in other domains (especially those which are important for historians or other humanities researchers), applications and languages.

References

1. Biemann, C.: Chinese Whispers - An Efficient Graph Clustering Algorithm and its Application to Natural Language Processing Problems. In: Proceedings of the HLT-NAACL 2006 Workshop on Textgraphs 2006, New York, USA, pp. 73–80 (2006)

2. Chan, S., Pon, R., Cardenas, A.: Visualization and Clustering of Author Social Networks. In: Distributed Multimedia Systems Conference, pp. 174–180 (2006)
3. Dempster, A.P., Laird, N.M., Rubin, D.B.: Maximum Likelihood from Incomplete Data via the EM Algorithm. J. Royal Stat. Soc. B. 39(1), 1–38 (1977)
4. Forman, G.: An Extensive Empirical Study of Feature Selection Metrics for Text Classification. Journal of Machine Learning Research 3, 1289–1305 (2003)
5. HaCohen-Kerner, Y., Stern, I., Korkus, D., Fredj, E.: Automatic Machine Learning of Keyphrase Extraction from Short Html Documents Written in Hebrew. Cybernetics and Systems 38(1), 1–21 (2007)
6. HaCohen-Kerner, Y., Mughaz, D., Beck, H., Yehudai, E.: Words as Classifiers of Documents According to their Historical Period and the Ethnic Origin of their Authors. Cybernetics and Systems 39(3), 213–228 (2008)
7. HaCohen-Kerner, Y., Beck, H., Yehudai, E., Rosenstein, M., Mughaz, D.: Cuisine: Classification using Stylistic Feature Sets and/or Name-Based Feature Sets. JASIST 61(8), 1644–1657 (2010a)
8. HaCohen-Kerner, Y., Beck, H., Yehudai, E., Mughaz, D.: Stylistic Feature Sets as Classifiers of Documents According to their Historical Period and Ethnic Origin. Applied Artificial Intelligence 24(9), 847–862 (2010b)
9. Hall, M., Frank, E., Holmes, G., Pfahringer, B., Reutemann, P., Witten, I.H.: The WEKA Data Mining Software: an Update. ACM SIGKDD Explorations Newsletter 11(1), 10–18 (2009)
10. He, Y., Hui, S.C.: Mining a Web Citation Database for Author Co-Citation Analysis. Information Processing & Management 38(4), 491–508 (2002)
11. Hotho, A., Staab, S.: Stumme. G.: Ontologies Improve Text Document Clustering. In: Proceedings of the International Conference on Data Mining, pp. 541–544. IEEE Press (2003)
12. Hotho, A., Staab, S., Stumme. G.: Wordnet Improves Text Document Clustering. In: Proc. of the Semantic Web Workshop at SIGIR- 2003, 26th Annual Int. ACM SIGIR Conference (2003b)
13. Jain, K., Murty, M.N., Flynn, P.J.: Data Clustering: A Review. ACM Comput. Surveys 31, 264–323 (1991)
14. Koppel, M., Schler, J.: Mughaz. D.: Text Categorization for Authorship Verification. In: Proc. of the 8th Symposium on Artificial Intelligence and Mathematics, Fort Lauderdale, FL (2004)
15. Koppel, J., Mughaz, D., Akiva, N.: New Methods for Attribution of Rabbinic Literature, Hebrew Linguistics: A Journal for Hebrew Descriptive. In: Computational and Applied Linguistics, vol. 57, pp. v-xviii. Bar-Ilan University Press (2006)
16. Li, Y.J., Chung, S.M.: Document Clustering Based on Frequent Word Sequences. In: Proceedings of the 14th ACM International Conference on Information and Knowledge Management (CIKM), pp. 293–294 (2005)
17. Li, Y.J., Chung, S.M., Holt, J.: Text Document Clustering based on Frequent Word Meaning Sequences. Data & Knowledge Engineering 64, 381–404 (2008)
18. Miao, Y., Keselj, V., Milios, E.: Document Clustering using Character N-grams: A Comparative Evaluation with Term-based and Word-based Clustering. In: Proc. of the 14th ACM Int. Conference on Information and Knowledge Management, pp. 357–358 (2005)
19. Mosteller, F., Wallace, D.L.: Inference and Disputed Authorship: The Federalist. Addison-Wesley, Reading (1964)

20. Peng, Y., Kou, G., Shi, Y.: Recent Trends in Data Mining (DM): Document Clustering of DM Publications. In: Proceedings of the International Conference on Service Systems and Service Management, vol. 2, pp. 1653–1659 (2006)
21. Sharoff, S.: Classifying Web Corpora into Domain and Genre Using Automatic Feature Identification. In: Proc. of Web as Corpus Workshop, Louvain-la-Neuve (September 2007)
22. Steinbach, M., Ertoz, L., Kumar, V.: Challenges of Clustering High Dimensional Data. In: Wille, L.T. (ed.) New Vistas in Statistical Physics – Applications in Econophysics, Bioinformatics, and Pattern Recognition. Springer (2003)
23. Sun, Y., Han, J., Zhao, P., Yin, Z., Cheng, H., Wu, T.: Rankclus: Integrating Clustering with Ranking for Heterogeneous Information Network Analysis. In: Proc. of the 12th International Conference on Extending Database Technology, pp. 565–576. ACM, New York (2009)
24. Witten, I.H., Frank, E.: Data Mining: Practical Machine Learning Tools and Techniques, 2nd edn. Morgan Kaufmann (2005)
25. Yu, B.: Function Words for Chinese Authorship Attribution. In: Proceedings of the NAACL-HLT 2012 Workshop on Computational Linguistics for Literature, pp. 45–53. Association for Computational Linguistics (June 2012)

Clustering with Error-Estimation for Monitoring Reputation of Companies on Twitter

Muhammad Atif Qureshi[1,2], Colm O'Riordan[1], and Gabriella Pasi[2]

[1] Computational Intelligence Research Group, Information Technology,
National University of Ireland, Galway, Ireland
[2] Information Retrieval Lab, Informatics, Systems and Communication,
University of Milan Bicocca, Milan, Italy
{muhammad.qureshi,colm.oriordan}@nuigalway.ie,
pasi@disco.unimib.it

Abstract. The aim of this research is to easily monitor the reputation of a company in the Twittersphere. We propose a strategy that organizes a stream of tweets into different clusters based on the tweets' topics. Furthermore, the obtained clusters are assigned into different priority levels. A cluster with high priority represents a topic which may affect the reputation of a company, and that consequently deserves immediate attention. The evaluation results show that our method is competitive even though the method does not make use of any external knowledge resource.

Keywords: Monitoring social streams, Clustering, Priority-level assessment.

1   Introduction

Social media have given birth to a new form of marketing known as electronic word-of-mouth marketing (*eWOM*) [9]. There is also an increasing trend of users on social media to express their opinions about various companies and their products. This phenomenon is particularly evident on Twitter[1] due to its real-time nature, and hence tweets serve as a significant repository for a company to monitor its online reputation and thereby take the necessary steps to tackle threats to it. Furthermore, such real-time social streams (e.g. Twitter) have motivated a whole new area of research known as Online Reputation Management. A fundamental task within Online Reputation Management is continuous "monitoring" of social streams for early identification of topics that may have an impact (either positive or negative) on the reputation of an entity of interest. The RepLab Monitoring Task at CLEF 2012 [1] introduced a task to tackle the "monitoring" problem in tweets within the context of Online Reputation Management, the main characteristics of which are:

- clustering tweets based on their topics: for example, the company Apple would have separate topical clusters for iPhone, iPad and iPod etc.

---

[1] http://twitter.com

R.E. Banchs et al. (Eds.): AIRS 2013, LNCS 8281, pp. 170–180, 2013.
© Springer-Verlag Berlin Heidelberg 2013

– ordering tweets by priority to the company: the idea is that tweets critical to the company's reputation require an immediate action, and they have a higher priority than tweets that do not require immediate attention. For example, a tweet heavily criticizing a company's customer service may damage the company's reputation, and thus it should be processed with a high priority.

In this paper we focus on the task of "monitoring" tweets for a company's reputation, in the context of the RepLab2012, where we are given a set of companies and for each company a set of tweets, which contain different topics pertaining to the company with different levels of priority. Performing such a monitoring of tweets is a significantly challenging task as tweet messages are very short (140 characters) and noisy. We alleviate these problems through the idea of core term expansion in tweets. We perform the two phases of clustering and priority level assessment separately, where the clustering applies an unsupervised technique, while a supervised technique is used for priority level assessment.

The rest of the paper is organized as follows. Section 2 presents a description of the problem in more detail. Section 3 presents an overview of work related to ours along with a description of how we differ from past approaches. Section 4 presents our technique for clustering and assigning priority levels to the clusters. Section 5 describes the experiments and finally Section 6 concludes the paper.

2   Problem Description

In this section we briefly define the problem statement related to this contribution. It is important to outline that this contribution aims at presenting a formal method that was evaluated (but never formally presented in a previous publication) within a CLEF campaign. We have a stream of tweets for different companies collected by issuing a query corresponding to the company name. The stream of tweets for the companies were then divided into a training set and a test set. In the training set each stream of tweets for a company was clustered according to their topics. Furthermore, these clusters were prioritized into five different levels as follows:

Alert >average priority >low priority >'other' cluster >'irrelevant'

The 'Alert' category corresponds to the cluster of tweets that deserves immediate attention by the company. Likewise, the tweet clusters with average and low priority deserve attention as well but with relatively less urgency than those with alert priority level. The label 'other' refers to a cluster of tweets that are about the company but that do not qualify as interesting topics, and that are negligible to the monitoring purposes. Finally, 'irrelevant' labels the cluster of tweets that do not refer to the company.

Our task is to cluster the stream of unseen tweets (test set) of a given company with respect to topics. Furthermore, we have to assign these clusters a priority level chosen from the above-mentioned five levels.

3   Related Work

The analysis and organization of tweet messages is a rapidly evolving research area with a significant amount of interest from the academic community [6]. The relative freshness of the area leads to new problems being defined almost every day[2]. This section attempts to present an overview of the huge body of works on tweets' content mining while at the same time explaining how we differ from existing works. Within the area of mining tweets the proposed works are organized into the following categories: a) event detection via tweets, b) sentiment analysis of tweets, and c) summarization and detection of topics in tweets.

Table 1. Example of "alert-level" tweets from RepLab2012 dataset

Entity	Tweet
Marriott	I'm at Teaneck Marriott at Glenpointe (100 Frank W Burr Blvd, Teaneck) w/ 2 others http://4sq.com/zBlS9x
Lufthansa	Lufthansa to Launch 29 New Routes from Berlin Brandenburg http://www.whichbudget.com/blog/en/news/1235-lufthansa-to-launch-29-new-routes-from-berlin-brandenburg-from-june-2012 via @ WhichBudget
Apple	Steve Jobs used patents to pressure Bill Gates into 1997 investment in Apple: Apple co-founder Steve Jobs was not... http://adf.ly/5wB1d

Given the real-time nature of textual data in Twitter streams, a lot of work has been done to extract real-world events from these streams [3] [8] [12] [15]. Most of these techniques formulate event detection as a classification problem and use various features within tweets such as keywords occurring frequently in bursts, context surrounding events, and temporal signals such as tweet volume within a time interval. Some different event detection approaches however utilize word or topic clustering based [5] [17] approaches. Event detection approaches cannot be directly applied to the task of monitoring a company's reputation as it is often the case that something that is beneficial or detrimental to the reputation of a company is not a major event in most of the cases.

Sentiment analysis of Twitter messages has gained significant attention over the past few years [4] [10] [11] and consists in classifying tweets with respect to their polarities (positive, negative) or to their subjectivities. The sentiment analysis approaches for Twitter utilize a machine learning framework largely relying on use of emoticons and hashtags as indications of polarity and sentiment. Despite the overlaps between the company reputation monitoring task and tweets' sentiment analysis task there are some differences between the two which make traditional sentiment analysis techniques unsuitable for the task at hand. We explain with the help of example tweets in Table 1; it can be seen that the example tweets for the three companies Marriott, Lufthansa and Apple contain no

---

[2] Note that the tweets' monitoring task that we address in this paper is a newly defined problem in the context of Online Reputation Management defined by CLEF RepLab2012 organizers.

obvious expression of sentiment (subjectivity) and yet they fall into the "alert" priority level according to labels assigned by reputation management experts.

Topical analysis of tweet messages has also gained increasing attention over the past few years. The works in this direction involve use of latent dirichlet allocation ("LDA") to form topical representations of tweet content [7] [13] [18]. One limitation of such topical based representations is however their application to authors of tweets whereby a single author's tweets are aggregated to help build a topic profile for that particular Twitter user. We argue that such approaches are not well-suited to the task under consideration on account of the fact that tweets expressing opinions about companies' reputation is independent of the users expressing it and often come from a diverse number of sources.

4   Methodology

The proposed method solely involves processing the tweets' contents, i.e., it does not use any external knowledge resource such as Wikipedia or the content of any Web page. Before applying our method we expand the shortened URL mentioned inside a tweet into a full URL in order to avoid redundant link forwarders to the same URL. In the following subsections we present the strategy we used for the monitoring tweets' task.

4.1   Pre-processing

In this section we describe two necessary pre-processing steps. We first perform both of them so that the outputs from these steps can be used in the main algorithm that we explain later.

4.1.1 Tweet Core Terms Extraction

In the first step we extract core terms (i.e., important terms) from each tweet in the training and test set so as to be able to identify a topic. To achieve this goal, we filter out the trivial components from each tweet's content such as mentions, RT, MT and URL string. Then, we apply POS tagging to identify the terms having a label 'NN', 'NNS', 'NNP', 'NNPS', 'JJ' or 'CD' as a core term. For the purpose of POS tagging, we use the Stanford POS tagger [16] which achieves an accuracy of 80% on tweets [14] and such an accuracy serves well for the task at hand.

4.1.2 Training Priority Scores for Core Terms

In this step each core term extracted from the training set is associated with multiple weights, which represent the strength of association of the core term with each priority level. The applied algorithm is shown in Procedure 1. We employ the training data, where each cluster of tweets is labelled with a priority level. First we associate each tweet in a cluster with the label of that cluster i.e., we borrow the label from the tweet's cluster as shown in Step 1 of Procedure 1 (here, a label implies a priority level out of the five priority levels discussed in

Section 2). Then we count the number of occurrences of each core term in tweets belonging to a priority level (label) as Steps 2-7 show. The intuition is that if a core term is frequently appearing in tweets that belong mostly to one unique priority level, then that core term is very likely to belong to this level.

Procedure 1. Assigning priority scores to core terms

Require: Tweet clusters in training data ($\{TweetCluster_{Training}\}$)
1: $\{Tweet_{Text}\}$, $\{TweetLevel_{Label}\}$ ← Split $\{TweetCluster_{Training}\}$ into tweets and corresponding label borrowed from the cluster
2: **for all** $tweet$ in $\{Tweet_{Text}\}$, $\{TweetLevel_{Label}\}$ **do**
3:    **for all** $core_{term}$ in $tweet$ **do**
4:       $level$ ← $tweet.TweetLevel_{Label}$
5:       $core_{term}.trainedPriorityScore[level]$ ← $core_{term}.trainedPriorityScore[level] + 1$
6:    **end for**
7: **end for**

4.2 Main Algorithm

Once the preliminary steps have been completed, the algorithm described in this section is applied to cluster the stream of tweets (test set) with respect to their topics, and to assign them a priority level. The algorithm iteratively learns two threshold values i.e., the content threshold and the specificity threshold ($content_{threshold}$ and $specificity_{threshold}$ in Procedure 2 and 3 respectively) from a list of threshold values provided to it as explained in the following subsections.

Clustering. We cluster the tweets according to the similarity of their contents, to the specificity of core terms in tweets, and to common URL mentions in tweets. We explain these three clustering phases as follows:

1. An initialization phase of clusters is applied according to tweets' content similarity (see Procedure 2). Initially, the similarity between all pairs of tweets is measured. An initial set of clusters is created when this similarity is above a specified threshold, i.e., if two tweets are similar, they are placed in the same cluster. Having generated this initial set of clusters we merge two clusters together if they have a non-null intersection, i.e. if they have a tweet in common.

2. The second phase aims to cluster tweets according to the specificity of core terms in the tweets (see Procedure 3). We exploit core terms that are specific to a cluster in order to expand that particular cluster. For identification of core terms specific to a cluster we exploit the ratio between the two document[3] frequencies: a) document frequency of core term within the cluster and, b) document frequency of the same core term but in the rest of the corpus (Steps 12-15 of Procedure 3). The intuition behind calculation of these ratios is that the greater the value of the ratio, the greater the chance that

---

[3] Each tweet is treated as a document.

the core term is specific to a particular cluster. Once we have gathered these ratio scores for all core terms in each cluster, we check for the occurrence of these core terms in the tweets which are not present inside a given cluster and if a tweet contains some core terms whose aggregated score is greater than that of specificity threshold we make changes to clusters (Steps 16-19 of Procedure 3 and Procedure 4). The tweet that passes the specificity threshold constraint gets added into the new cluster (expansion) across which ratio scores were generated while the same tweet leaves the cluster to which it was previously assigned (contraction). The process repeats until every cluster has been processed.

3. In the final step of clustering according to URL similarity we exploit the URL mentioned inside the content of a tweet in order perform an expansion of clusters similar to the previous step (i.e, every expansion follows a contraction). In this step we iterate over each cluster, and during the iteration we collect the number of URLs mentioned in the tweets of each cluster. A cluster of tweets that mentions a specific URL most frequently compared to other clusters (of tweets) becomes the home cluster for that specific URL. The intuition is to assign that specific URL as a representative URL for the discovered home cluster so as to serve as a means for inclusion of other tweets mentioning the same URL. The tweets which are outside of the home cluster but mention the home cluster's specific URL now join the home cluster (expansion) and leave their previously discovered cluster (contraction).

Procedure 2. Cluster initialization

Require: Tweets in test data ($\{Tweets_{Test}\}$)
1: **for all** $pair_{tweets}$ in $\{Tweets_{Test}\}$ **do**
2:    $similarity \leftarrow$ cosinesimilarity($pair_{tweets}$)
3:    **if** $similarity < content_{threshold}$ **then**
4:       Cluster together $pair_{tweets}$
5:    **end if**
6: **end for**
7: Repeatedly merge any two clusters that have a common item.

Predicting Priority Levels. In this step, we assign a priority level to each cluster. To this aim, we first estimate a priority level for each tweet in the corpus, and then by using the assignment of priority level to the tweets we decide a priority for each cluster. The process is explained here below.

Estimation of Priority Level for Each Tweet: First, we generate five aggregations across each priority level for a tweet. Then, the highest aggregation corresponding to a priority level becomes the priority level for that tweet. Each aggregation is computed by aggregating each core term's priority score (as estimated in Section 4.1.2) corresponding to the priority level for that tweet.

Procedure 3. Cluster expansion via specificity of core terms in clusters

---

Require: Cardinality-ordered tweet clusters ($\{Ordered_{Cluster}\}$)

1: **for all** $current_{cluster}$ in $\{Ordered_{Cluster}\}$ **do**
2:     **if** $current_{cluster}$.cardinality< 2 **then**
3:        break
4:     **end if**
5:     $currentclusterexpand_{possible} \leftarrow True$
6:     **while** $currentclusterexpand_{possible}$ is $True$ **do**
7:        $currentclusterexpand_{possible} \leftarrow False$
8:        $current_{cluster}$.vocab $\leftarrow$ set of terms in tweets of $current_{cluster}$
9:        $current_{cluster}$.df $\leftarrow$ vector of normalized frequency for every term in $current_{cluster}$.vocab
10:       $dfcorpus \leftarrow$ vector of normalized frequency for every term in $corpus$ - $current_{cluster}$.vocab
11:       $dfratio_{sum} \leftarrow 0.0$
12:       **for all** $term$ in $current_{cluster}$.vocab **do**
13:          $dfratio_{term} \leftarrow current_{cluster}.df_{term}^{const}/dfcorpus_{term}$
14:          $dfratio_{sum} \leftarrow dfratio_{term}+dfratio_{sum}$
15:       **end for**
16:       **for all** $tweet$ not in $current_{cluster}$ **do**
17:          $expansionsimilarityscore_{tweetid} \leftarrow$ findExpandSimilartityScore($tweetid$, $dfcorpus$, $dfratio$, $dfratio_{sum}$, $current_{cluster}$.vocab)
18:       **end for**
19:       $\{Tweet_{OrderSimilarityScore}\} \leftarrow$ Order by score set of tweets in $expansionsimilarityscore_{tweetid}$ (from highest to lowest)
20:       **for all** $tweetid$, $score$ in $\{Tweet_{OrderSimilarityScore}\}$ **do**
21:          **if** $score < specificity_{threshold}$ **then**
22:             break
23:          **else**
24:             $current_{cluster} \leftarrow$ Push $tweet[tweetid]$
25:             Remove $tweet[tweetid]$ from previous cluster
26:             $currentclusterexpand_{possible} \leftarrow True$
27:          **end if**
28:       **end for**
29:    **end while**
30: **end for**

Procedure 4. $findExpandSimilarityScore()$

Require: $tweetid$, $dfcorpus$, $dfratio$, $dfratio_{sum}$, $current_{cluster}$.vocab

1: $terms_{intersection}. \leftarrow (tweet[tweetid] \cap current_{cluster}$.vocab$)$
2: $dfratio_{scores} \leftarrow 0.0$
3: **for all** $term$ in $terms_{intersection}$ **do**
4:     $dfratio_{scores} \leftarrow dfratio_{scores} + dfratio_{term}$
5: **end for**
6: **return** $dfratio_{scores}/dfratio_{sum}$

Estimation of Priority Level for Each Cluster: Since each cluster is composed of tweets, the assigned priority level for a tweet is counted as a vote for a cluster's priority level, and the priority level that gets the maximum number of votes (for a cluster) becomes the priority level for that cluster.

Global Error Estimates and Optimization. This step enables the algorithm to learn optimized threshold values. To this aim, we estimate the global error as follows. We first estimate the number of errors per cluster by counting the number of inconsistencies (i.e., non-uniformity) among the priority levels assigned to the tweets of a cluster. Here, inconsistencies refers to mismatch among priority levels for each tweet in the cluster; note that the priority levels assigned to each tweet come from the priority assigned to the individual core terms as explained previously. We finally aggregate these errors estimates across each cluster to define a global error estimate. The threshold values across which the global error estimation is minimum are declared to be optimized threshold values. Note that the threshold values are optimized again for each company in the test dataset. The output corresponding to the optimized threshold values is reported as the final output of the algorithm.

Table 2. Results of Monitoring task of RepLab2012

Team	R Clustering (BCubed precision)	S Clustering (BCubed recall)	F(R,S) Clustering	R Prior	S Priority	F Priority	R	S	F(R,S)
UNED_3	0.72	0.32	0.4	0.25	0.3	0.26	0.32	0.26	0.29
CIRG_IRDISCO	0.95	0.24	0.35	0.24	0.3	0.24	0.29	0.22	0.25
OPTAH_1	0.7	0.34	0.38	0.19	0.16	0.16	0.37	0.19	0.22
UNED_2	0.85	0.34	0.39	0	0	0	0.85	0.09	0.14
UNED_1	0.9	0.2	0.3	0	0	0	0.9	0.05	0.1

5   Experimental Results

5.1   Data Set

We performed our experiments by using the data set provided by the Monitoring task of RepLab2012 [1]. In this data set 37 companies were provided, out of which six were in the training set, while the remaining 31 were in the test set. For each company a few hundred tweets were provided with the language of the tweets being English and Spanish; furthermore, most of the tweets are in Spanish and we translate a tweet that is not written in English using the Bing Translation API[4].

5.2   Evaluation Measures

The measures used for the purposes of evaluation are Reliability and Sensitivity, which are described in detail in [2].

---

[4] http://www.microsofttranslator.com/

In essence, these measures consider two types of binary relationships between pairs of items: relatedness – two items belong to the same cluster – and priority – one item has more priority than the other. Reliability is defined as precision of binary relationships predicted by the system with respect to those that derive from the gold standard. Sensitivity is similarly defined as the recall of relationships. When only clustering relationships are considered, Reliability and Sensitivity are equivalent to BCubed Precision and Recall [2].

5.3   Results and Discussion

Table 2 presents a snapshot of the official results for the Monitoring task of RepLab, where CIRG_IRDISCO is the name of our team. It shows that our algorithm performed competitively, and is the second from the top. In addition, our algorithm shows the best BCubed precision for the clustering of tweets compared to other algorithms. Our algorithm did not perform well for the priority level assignment to clusters on account of extremely scarce training data[5]. Table 3 shows the details of individual companies for which our proposed technique beats the systems submitted by other teams. The top three companies in the table perform well because of the presence of similar companies in the training set: Telefonica and Yahoo! have tweets similar in nature to Apple, while Ferrari has tweets similar in nature to Armani [6]. Given these encouraging results, we believe the algorithm to be quite promising for the task of "real-time monitoring" in social streams with the availability of even a modest amount of training data.

Table 3. Details of Specific Companies within RepLab2012 Monitoring Task

CompanyID (Company Name)	R Clustering (BCubed precision)	S Clustering (BCubed recall)	F(R,S) Clustering	R Prior	S Priority	F Priority	R	S	F(R,S)
RL2012E07 (Telefonica)	0.94	0.34	0.5	0.55	0.34	0.42	0.56	0.31	0.4
RL2012E09 (Yahoo!)	0.99	0.07	0.14	0.19	0.4	0.26	0.2	0.19	0.2
RL2012E29 (Ferrari)	0.92	0.11	0.19	0.43	0.41	0.42	0.44	0.32	0.37
RL2012E11 (Bing)	0.96	0.21	0.34	0.41	0.42	0.42	0.42	0.31	0.36
RL2012E28 (Chevrolet)	0.93	0.51	0.66	0.3	0.36	0.32	0.36	0.4	0.38

Another interesting observation we made with respect to per entity (company) evaluation results is that our algorithm suffers due to translation issues[7]. This is particularly obvious for entities with high percentage of English tweets e.g., our algorithm performed best for the entity RL2012E11 (Bing) which had 98% of tweets in English and RL2012E28 (Chevrolet) which had 96.75% of tweets in English (shown as bottom two rows of Table 3).

---

[5] This was purposefully done by the RepLab organizers so that traditional machine learning methods may not be applied on the data.

[6] The six companies that were given as training set included Apple, Lufthansa, Alcatel-Lucent, Armani, Barclays and Marriott.

[7] The Bing Translate API does not correctly translate all Spanish tweets into English e.g., it translates name of company Telefonica into telephone.

6   Conclusion

We proposed an algorithm for clustering tweets and for assigning them a priority level for companies. Our algorithm did not make use of any external knowledge resource and did not require prior information about the company. Even under these constraints our algorithm showed competitive performance. Our approach for monitoring "real-time social streams" may open a promising new dimension as witnessed by the evaluation results.

References

1. Amigó, E., Corujo, A., Gonzalo, J., Meij, E., de Rijke, M.: Overview of replab 2012: Evaluating online reputation management systems. In: CLEF 2012 Labs and Workshop Notebook Papers (2012)
2. Amigo, E., Gonzalo, J., Verdejo, F.: Reliability and Sensitivity: Generic Evaluation Measures for Document Organization Tasks. UNED, Madrid, Spain, Technical Report (2012)
3. Becker, H., Naaman, M., Gravano, L.: Beyond trending topics: Real-world event identification on twitter. In: Proceedings of the Fifth International AAAI Conference on Weblogs and Social Media, ICWSM 2011 (2011)
4. Davidov, D., Tsur, O., Rappoport, A.: Enhanced sentiment learning using twitter hashtags and smileys. In: Proceedings of the 23rd International Conference on Computational Linguistics: Posters, pp. 241–249. Association for Computational Linguistics (2010)
5. Diao, Q., Jiang, J., Zhu, F., Lim, E.-P.: Finding bursty topics from microblogs. In: Proceedings of the 50th Annual Meeting of the Association for Computational Linguistics: Long Papers, vol. 1, pp. 536–544. Association for Computational Linguistics (2012)
6. Ellen, J.: All about microtext: A working definition and a survey of current microtext research within artificial intelligence and natural language processing. In: Proceedings of the Third International Conference on Agents and Artificial Intelligence (2011)
7. Hong, L., Davison, B.D.: Empirical study of topic modeling in twitter. In: Proceedings of the First Workshop on Social Media Analytics, pp. 80–88. ACM (2010)
8. Ilina, E., Hauff, C., Celik, I., Abel, F., Houben, G.-J.: Social event detection on twitter. In: Brambilla, M., Tokuda, T., Tolksdorf, R. (eds.) ICWE 2012. LNCS, vol. 7387, pp. 169–176. Springer, Heidelberg (2012)
9. Jansen, B.J., Zhang, M., Sobel, K., Chowdury, A.: Twitter power: Tweets as electronic word of mouth. J. Am. Soc. Inf. Sci. Technol. 60(11), 2169–2188 (2009)
10. O'Connor, B., Balasubramanyan, R., Routledge, B.R., Smith, N.A.: From tweets to polls: Linking text sentiment to public opinion time series. In: Proceedings of the International AAAI Conference on Weblogs and Social Media, pp. 122–129 (2010)
11. Pak, A., Paroubek, P.: Twitter as a corpus for sentiment analysis and opinion mining. In: LREC (2010)
12. Petrović, S., Osborne, M., Lavrenko, V.: Streaming first story detection with application to twitter. In: Human Language Technologies: The, Annual Conference of the North American Chapter of the Association for Computational Linguistics, HLT 2010, pp. 181–189. Association for Computational Linguistics, Stroudsburg (2010)

13. Ramage, D., Dumais, S., Liebling, D.: Characterizing microblogs with topic models. In: International AAAI Conference on Weblogs and Social Media, vol. 5, pp. 130–137 (2010)
14. Ritter, A., Clark, S., Mausam, Etzioni, O.: Named entity recognition in tweets: an experimental study. In: Proceedings of the Conference on Empirical Methods in Natural Language Processing, EMNLP 2011, pp. 1524–1534. Association for Computational Linguistics, Stroudsburg (2011)
15. Sakaki, T., Okazaki, M., Matsuo, Y.: Earthquake shakes twitter users: real-time event detection by social sensors. In: Proceedings of the 19th International Conference on World Wide Web, WWW 2010, pp. 851–860. ACM, New York (2010)
16. Toutanova, K., Manning, C.D.: Enriching the knowledge sources used in a maximum entropy part-of-speech tagger. In: Proceedings of the 2000 Joint SIGDAT Conference on Empirical Methods in Natural Language Processing and Very Large Corpora: Held in Conjunction with the 38th Annual Meeting of the Association for Computational Linguistics, EMNLP 2000, vol. 13, pp. 63–70. Association for Computational Linguistics, Stroudsburg (2000)
17. Weng, J., Lee, B.-S.: Event detection in twitter. In: Proceedings of the 5th International AAAI Conference on Weblogs and Social Media, vol. 3 (2011)
18. Weng, J., Lim, E.-P., Jiang, J., He, Q.: Twitterrank: finding topic-sensitive influential twitterers. In: Proceedings of the Third ACM International Conference on Web Search and Data Mining, pp. 261–270. ACM (2010)

Weighted Cumulative Voting-Based Aggregation Algorithm for Combining Multiple Clusterings of Chemical Structures

Faisal Saeed[1,2,*] and Naomie Salim[1]

[1] Faculty of Computing, Universiti Teknologi Malaysia, Malaysia
[2] Information Technology Department, Sanhan Community College, Sana'a, Yemen
alsamet.faisal@gmail.com

Abstract. Many consensus clustering methods have been applied for combining multiple clusterings of chemical structures such as co-association matrix-based, graph-based, hypergraph-based and voting-based methods. However, the voting-based consensus methods showed the best performance among these methods. In this paper, a Weighted Cumulative Voting-based Aggregation Algorithm (W-CVAA) was developed for enhancing the effectiveness of combining multiple clusterings of chemical structures. The effectiveness of clusterings was evaluated based on the ability of clustering to separate active from inactive molecules in each cluster and the results were compared to Ward's method, which is the standard clustering method for chemoinformatics applications. The chemical dataset MDL Drug Data Report (MDDR) was used. Experimental results suggest that the weighted cumulative voting-based consensus method can improve the effectiveness of combining multiple clustering of chemical structures.

Keywords: Compound selection, Cumulative voting, Ensemble clustering, Graph partitioning, Mutual Information, Shannon Entropy.

1 Introduction

Many clustering methods have been applied for chemical structures datasets [1-8], which are mainly used for the purpose of reducing the high costs and lengthy time needed to discover new drugs, especially in the process of High-Throughput Screening (HTS), in which hundreds of thousands of chemical compounds are screened for testing the biological activity. The clustering helps the pharmaceutical industries to find faster and more effective ways of discovering and producing chemical compounds that can effectively react to the examined disease [9].

There are different types of clustering methods that can be grouped based on the problem they intend to solve, the general strategy they use, or others. For example Jain *et al.* [10] organized the clustering methods into five opposing approaches which are agglomerative versus divisive, hard versus soft, monothetic versus polythetic, deterministic versus stochastic and incremental versus non incremental. Recently, individual clustering has been used versus consensus clustering.

---

[*] Corresponding author.

R.E. Banchs et al. (Eds.): AIRS 2013, LNCS 8281, pp. 181–190, 2013.

Consensus clustering involves two main steps: (i) partitions generation and (ii) combination using consensus function. In the first step, as many as possible individual partitions are generated. In the second step, there are two main approaches: objects co-occurrence based and median partition based approaches. In the first one, the idea is to determine which cluster label must be associated to each object in the consensus partition. To do that, it is analyzed how many times an object belongs to one cluster (for the voting-based methods) or how many times two objects belong together to the same cluster (for the co-association matrix-based and graph-based methods). Therefore, the consensus partition is obtained through a voting process among the objects, such that each object should vote for the cluster to which it will belong in the consensus partition. In the second combination approach, the consensus partition is obtained by the solution of an optimization problem, which is the problem of finding the median partition with respect to the cluster ensemble [11].

In the literature, there are many voting-based consensus clustering methods [12-18], in which the consensus partition is derived by seeking an optimal relabeling of the ensemble partitions. In general, the optimal relabeling of the ensemble partitions is addressed through a pairwise relabeling of each ensemble partition with respect to a representative partition [18]. Then, the voting process is used to assign object to the higher voted cluster in order to obtain the consensus partition [17-18].

For clustering of chemical structures datasets, it is most unlikely that any single method will yield the best classification under all circumstances, even if attention is restricted to a single type of application [19]. Chu, et al. [19] used similarity matrix consensus methods on sets of chemical structures and concluded that the consensus clustering methods can outperform Ward's method. However, based on the implemented methods, it was not the case if the clustering is restricted to a single consensus method. In addition, Saeed et al. [20] examined the use of the graph-based consensus clustering method, Cluster-based Similarity Partitioning Algorithm (CSPA) and Hypergraph Partitioning Algorithm (HGPA) [21], for clustering of the MDDR dataset and concluded that they can improve the effectiveness of individual clusterings and provide robust and stable clustering. Moreover, Saeed et al. [22] used a cumulative voting-based aggregation algorithm (CVAA) for combining multiple clusterings of chemical structures and found that it could significantly improve the quality of clustering. In addition, an enhanced voting-based consensus method (E-CVAA) was developed by Saeed et al. [23] to obtain the final consensus partition. In this paper, a weighted cumulative voting-based aggregation algorithm is developed as improvement for E-CVAA method by making each vote as a weighted contribution.

2   Materials and Methods

2.1   Dataset

The MDL Drug Data Report (MDDR) database [24] was used for experiments, which consists of 102,516 molecules. The MDDR subset dataset was chosen from the MDDR database which has been used in the previous consensus clusterings experiments [20, 22, 23]. The MDDR dataset contains eleven activity classes (8294 molecules), which involves homogeneous and heterogeneous active molecules. Details of this dataset are listed in Table 1. Each row in the table contains an activity class, the number of molecules belonging to the class, and the diversity of the class, which was computed as the mean pairwise Tanimoto similarity calculated across all pairs of molecules in the class. For the clustering experiments, two 2D fingerprint descriptors were used which were developed by Scitegic's Pipeline Pilot [25]. These were 120-bit ALOGP and 1024-bit ECFP_4 fingerprints (more details about these fingerprints in [26-28]).

Table 1. MDDR Activity Classes for DS1 Data Set

Activity Index	Activity class	Active molecules	Pairwise similarity
			Mean
31420	Renin Inhibitors	1130	0.290
71523	HIV Protease Inhibitors	750	0.198
37110	Thrombin Inhibitors	803	0.180
31432	Angiotensin II AT1 Antagonists	943	0.229
42731	Substance P Antagonists	1246	0.149
06233	Substance P Antagonists	752	0.140
06245	5HT Reuptake Inhibitors	359	0.122
07701	D2 Antagonists	395	0.138
06235	5HT1A Agonists	827	0.133
78374	Protein Kinase C Inhibitors	453	0.120
78331	Cyclooxygenase Inhibitors	636	0.108

2.2   Partitions Generation

The ensemble includes six partitions that were generated by using six individual clustering algorithms (for each fingerprint). These algorithms were: the single linkage, complete linkage, average linkage, weighted average distance, Ward and K-means clustering methods. The thresholds of 500, 600, 700, 800, 900 and 1000 were used to generate partitions with different sizes (number of clusters in each partition). Every individual clustering method was applied by using Jaccard coefficient.

2.3   Weighted Cumulative Voting-Based Aggregation Algorithm

The first step of cumulative voting-based algorithms is to obtain the optimal relabeling for all partitions, which is known as the voting problem. Then, the voting-based aggregation algorithm is used to obtain the aggregated partition. The cumulative voting-based aggregation algorithm (CVAA) was described by Ayed and Kamel [17-18], and enhanced by developing a weighted cumulative voting-based aggregation algorithm (W-CVAA) in this paper.

Let χ denote a set of n data objects, and let a partition of χ into k clusters be represented by an $n \times k$ matrix $\mathbf{U}$ such that $\sum_{q=1}^{k} u_{jq} = 1$, for $\forall$ j. Let $u = \{\mathbf{U}^i\}_{i=1}^{b}$ denote an ensemble of partitions, where b is the number of partitions. The voting-based aggregation problem is concerned with searching for an optimal relabeling for each partition $\mathbf{V}^i$ with respect to representative partition $\mathbf{U}^0$ (with k^0 clusters) and for a central aggregated partition denoted as $\bar{\mathbf{U}}$ that summarises the ensemble partitions. The matrix of coefficients $\mathbf{W}^i$, which is a $k^i \times k^0$ matrix of w_{lq}^i coefficients, is used to obtain the optimal relabeling for ensemble partitions such that $w_{lq}^i = \dfrac{n_{lq}^i}{n_l^i}$, where n_{lq}^i is the number of objects assigned to clusters c_l^i and c_q, and n_l^i is the number of objects assigned to cluster c_l^i.

Let $H(C)$ denote the Shannon entropy associated with cluster C, which measures the average amount of information associated with C and is defined as a function of its distribution $p(c)$ as follows [29]:

$$H(c) = -\sum_{c \in C} p(c) \log p(c) \tag{1}$$

And

$$P(c) = \frac{N}{n} \tag{2}$$

where N refers to the total number of molecules in a certain cluster, and n refers to the total number of molecules in the dataset.

In this algorithm, the fixed-reference approach is used, whereby an initial reference partition is used as a common representative partition for all the ensemble partitions. Unlike the CVAA [22], A-CVAA and E-CVAA [23], the W-CVAA gives different weights to the individual clustering methods that are used to generate the ensemble based on the mutual information associated with each method, which is measured by the Shannon entropy, as shown in Eq. 3. In each partition, each compound will be assigned to any cluster with a given weight that is associated with the individual clustering method. Thus, the weights of assigning compounds to clusters will not be the same using different individual clusterings.

$$T^i = \frac{H(C^i)}{\displaystyle\sum_{i=1}^{b} H(C^i)} \tag{3}$$

The weighted cumulative voting based aggregation algorithm can be viewed as improvements of the E-CVAA method [23] and described as follows:

Weighted Cumulative Voting-based Aggregation Algorithm

1: Re-order $\mathcal{U}$, s.t.

    U^i partitions are sorted as (the number of partitions $= b$):

    Weighted Average Distance partition> Ward partition>

    Average Linkage partition > Single-Linkage partition > Complete Linkage

    partition > K-means partition.

2: Assign U^1 to U^0

3: for $i = 2$ to b do

4:    $W^i = (U^{iT} U^i)^{-1} U^{iT} U^0$

5:    $V^i = U^i W^i$

6:    $U^0 = \dfrac{i-1}{i} U^0 + \dfrac{T^i}{i} V^i$

7: end for

8: $\bar{U} = U^0$.

2.4   Performance Evaluation

The results were evaluated based on the effectiveness of the methods to separate active from inactive molecules using two measures: the F-measure [30] and Quality Partition Index (QPI) measure [31]. If the cluster contains n compounds, that a of these are active and that there is a total of A compounds with the chosen Activity. The precision, P, and the recall, R, for that cluster are [19]:

$$P = \frac{a}{n} \tag{4}$$

$$R = \frac{a}{A} \tag{5}$$

$$F = \frac{2PR}{P+R} \tag{6}$$

This calculation is carried on each cluster and the F-measure is the maximum value across all clusters.

Also, an active cluster is defined as a non-singleton cluster for which the percentage of active molecules in the cluster is greater than the percentage of active molecules in the dataset as a whole. Let p be the number of actives in active clusters, q be the number of inactives in active clusters, r be the number of actives in inactive clusters (i.e., clusters that are not active clusters) and s be the number of singleton actives. The high value occurs when the actives are clustered tightly together and separated from the inactive molecules. The QPI is defined to be [7]:

$$QPI = \frac{p}{p+q+r+s} \tag{7}$$

Then, the results were compared with that of Ward's method and other consensus clustering methods such as the CSPA, HGPA, A-CVAA and E-CVAA.

3   Results and Discussion

The two ensembles were combined using the weighted cumulative voting-based consensus clustering (W-CVAA) method and other consensus clustering methods: CSPA, HGPA, A-CVAA and E-CVAA.

The mean of the F-measure and QPI values were averaged over the eleven activity classes of the dataset. Figures 1-4 show the effectiveness of the MDDR dataset clustering for the ALOGP and ECFP_4 fingerprints.

Visual inspection of the F-measure and QPI values in Figures 1-4 enables comparisons to be made between the effectiveness of the consensus clustering methods and Ward's method for clustering of chemical structures.

In Figures 1-2, the performance of the weighted cumulative voting-based aggregation algorithm (W-CVAA) outperformed Ward's method using the F-measure for the ALOGP and ECFP_4 fingerprints. In comparison to other consensus clustering methods, the W-CVAA outperformed all other consensus methods using the ALOGP and obtained similar results to that of E-CVAA using the ECFP_4 fingerprint. In addition, the performance of the CSPA was inferior to others methods.

Similarly, the experimental results show consistent superior performance of the W-CVAA method using the QPI measure comparing to other clustering methods, as shown in Figures 3-4. For instance, the W-CVAA outperformed Ward's method using the QPI measure for the ALOGP and ECFP_4. In addition, the W-CVAA outperformed all other consensus methods using the ALOGP and obtained similar performance of E-CVAA using the ECFP_4.

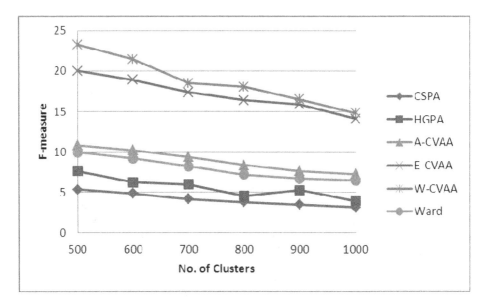

Fig. 1. Effectiveness of clustering the MDDR dataset using the F-Measure: ALOGP Fingerprint

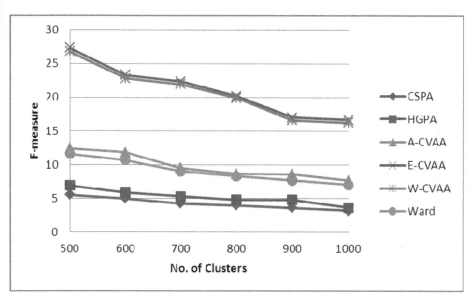

Fig. 2. Effectiveness of clustering the MDDR dataset using the F-Measure: ECFP_4 Fingerprint

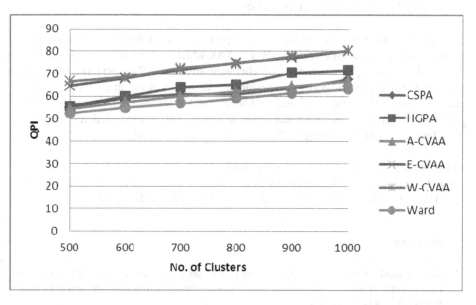

Fig. 3. Effectiveness of clustering the MDDR dataset using the QPI: ALOGP Fingerprint

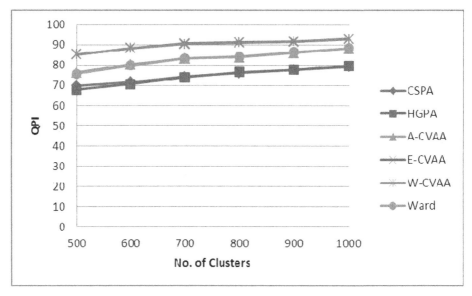

Fig. 4. Effectiveness of clustering the MDDR dataset using the QPI: ECFP_4 Fingerprint

4   Conclusion and Future Work

The experimental results show the superior performance of the weighted cumulative voting-based aggregation algorithm (W-CVAA), which can improve the effectiveness of combining multiple clusterings of chemical structures. The performance of the W-CVAA consensus clustering outperformed Ward's method and other consensus clustering methods using the F and QPI measures for the ALOGP and ECFP_4 fingerprints. In future work, other weighting schemes will be examined for improving the effectiveness of combining multiple clusterings of chemical structures.

Acknowledgment. This work is supported by the Ministry of Higher Education (MOHE) and Research Management Centre (RMC) at the Universiti Teknologi Malaysia (UTM) under Research University Grant Category (VOT 02H99).

References

1. Downs, G.M., Barnard, J.M.: Clustering of Chemical Structures on the Basis of Two-Dimensional Similarity Measures. Journal of Chemical Information and Computer Science 32, 644–649 (1992)
2. Willett, P.: Similarity and Clustering in Chemical Information Systems. Research Studies Press, Letchworth (1987)
3. Downs, G.M., Willett, P., Fisanick, W.: Similarity searching and clustering of chemical-structure databases using molecular property data. J. Chem. Inf. Comput. Sci. 34, 1094–1102 (1994)

4. Brown, R.D., Martin, Y.C.: The information content of 2D and 3D structural descriptors relevant to ligand–receptor binding. J. Chem. Inf. Comput. Sci. 37, 1–9 (1997)
5. Downs, G.M., Barnard, J.M.: Clustering methods and their uses in computational Chemistry. In: Lipkowitz, K.B., Boyd, D.B. (eds.) Reviews in Computational Chemistry, vol. 18. John Wiley (2002)
6. Holliday, J.D., Rodgers, S.L., Willet, P.: Clustering Files of chemical Structures Using the Fuzzy k-means Clustering Method. Journal of Chemical Information and Computer Science 44, 894–902 (2004)
7. Varin, T., Bureau, R., Mueller, C., Willett, P.: Clustering files of chemical structures using the Székely–Rizzo generalization of Ward's method. Journal of Molecular Graphics and Modeling 28(2), 187–195 (2009)
8. Brown, R.D., Martin, Y.C.: Use of structure-activity data to compare structure-based clustering methods and descriptors for use in compound selection. J. Chem. Inf. Compute. Sci. 36, 572–584 (1996)
9. Salim, N.: Analysis and Comparison of Molecular Similarity Measures. University of Sheffield. PhD Thesis (2003)
10. Jain, A.K., Murty, M.N., Flynn, P.J.: Data Clustering: a review. ACM Computing Surveys 31 (1999)
11. Vega-Pons, S., Ruiz-Schulcloper, J.: A survey of clustering ensemble algorithms. International Journal of Pattern Recognition and Artificial Intelligence 25(3), 337–372 (2011)
12. Fischer, B., Buhmann, J.M.: Bagging for path-based clustering. IEEE Transactions on Pattern Analysis and Machine Intelligence 25(11), 1411–1415 (2003)
13. Dudoit, S., Fridlyand, J.: Bagging to improve the accuracy of a clustering procedure. Bioinformatics 19(9), 1090–1099 (2003)
14. Evgenia, D., Andreas, W., Kurt, H.: A combination scheme for fuzzy clustering. International Journal of Pattern Recognition and Artificial Intelligence 16(7), 901–912 (2002)
15. Gordon, A.D., Vichi, M.: Fuzzy partition models for fitting a set of partitions. Psychometrika 66(2), 229–248 (2001)
16. Topchy, A., Law, M., Jain, A.K., Fred, A.: Analysis of consensus partition in clustering ensemble. In: Proceedings of IEEE Intl. Conf. on Data Mining 2004, Brighton, UK, pp. 225–232 (2004)
17. Ayad, H.G., Kamel, M.S.: Cumulative voting consensus method for partitions with a variable number of clusters. IEEE Transactions on Pattern Analysis and Machine Intelligence 30(1), 160–173 (2008)
18. Ayad, H.G., Kamel, M.S.: On voting-based consensus of cluster ensembles. Patt. Recogn. 43, 1943–1953 (2010)
19. Chu, C.-W., Holliday, J., Willett, P.: Combining multiple classifications of chemical structures using consensus clustering. Bioorgan. Med. Chem. 20(18), 5366–5371 (2012)
20. Saeed, F., Salim, N., Abdo, A., Hentabli, H.: Graph-Based Consensus Clustering for Combining Multiple Clusterings of Chemical Structures. Journal of Molecular Informatics 32(2), 165–178 (2013)
21. Strehl, A., Ghosh, J.: Cluster Ensembles - A Knowledge Reuse Framework for Combining Multiple Partitions. J. Machine Learning Research 3, 583–617 (2002)
22. Saeed, F., Salim, N., Abdo, A.: Voting-based consensus clustering for combining multiple clusterings of chemical structures. J. Cheminf, 4, Article 37 (2012), http://www.jcheminf.com/content/4/1/37 (accessed March 20, 2013)
23. Saeed, F., Salim, N., Abdo, A.: Consensus methods for combining multiple clusterings of chemical structures. Journal of Chemical Information and Modeling 53(5), 1026–1034 (2013)

24. Sci Tegic Accelrys Inc., the MDL Drug Data Report (MDDR) database is available from at `http://www.accelrys.com/` (accessed June 1, 2013)
25. Pipeline Pilot, Accelrys Software Inc., San Diego (2008)
26. Ghose, A.K., Crippen, G.M.: Atomic physicochemical parameters for three-dimensional structure-directed quantitative structure–activity relationships 1. Partition coefficients as a measure of hydrophobicity. J. Comput. Chem. 7, 565–577 (1986)
27. Ghose, A.K., Viswanadhan, V.N., Wendoloski, J.J.: Prediction of hydrophobic (lipophilic) properties of small organic molecules using fragmental methods: An analysis of ALOGP and CLOGP methods. J. Phys. Chem. A. 102, 3762–3772 (1998)
28. Rogers, D., Hahn, M.: Extended-connectivity fingerprints. J. Chem. Inf. Model. 50, 742–754 (2010)
29. Cover, T.M., Thomas, J.A.: Elements of Information Theory. Wiley, New York (1991)
30. Van Rijsbergen, C.J.: Information Retrieval. Butterworth, London (1979)
31. Varin, T., Saettel, N., Villain, J., Lesnard, A., Dauphin, F., Bureau, R., Rault, S.J.: 3D Pharmacophore, hierarchical methods, and 5-HT4 receptor binding data. Enzyme Inhib. Med. Chem. 23, 593–603 (2008)

Learning to Classify Subjective Sentences from Multiple Domains Using Extended Subjectivity Lexicon and Subjective Predicates

Sylvester Olubolu Orimaye

Faculty of Information Technology, MONASH University Sunway Campus, Malaysia
sylvester.orimaye@monash.edu

Abstract. We investigate the performance of subjective predicates and other extended predictive features on subjectivity classification in and across different domains. Our approach constructs a semi-supervised subjective classifier based on an extended subjectivity lexicon that includes *subjective annotations* resulting from a manually annotated subjectivity corpus, a list of manually constructed *subjectivity clues*, and a set of *subjective predicates* learned from a large collection of likely subjective sentences. Using the extended lexicon, we extracted high precision subjective sentences from multiple domains and constructed *in-domain* and *cross-domain* subjectivity classifiers. Experimental results on multiple datasets show that the proposed technique performed comparatively better than a high precision subjectivity classification baseline and has improved cross-domain accuracy. We report 97.7% precision, 73.4% recall and 83.8% F-Measure for *in-domain* subjectivity classification and a accuracy level of 84.6% for *cross-domain* subjectivity classification.

Keywords: subjectivity, sentence, predicates, clues, annotations.

1 Introduction

Sentence subjectivity is very crucial to Opinion Mining and Sentiment Classification. Therefore, it is very important to differentiate between subjective and objective sentences such that subjective sentences get higher weights compared to objective sentences. The process of identifying such subjective sentences is termed *subjectivity classification*. Subjective sentences contain certain level of subjectivity (e.g. presence of modifiers (adjectives), intensifiers and diminishers) or express a private state such as described in [1]. Given the many ways subjectivity can be expressed, it is often difficult to efficiently identify subjective sentences from opinionated documents. The problem has indeed been the focus of the research community over the past decade. Subjectivity may not only be determined by modifiers and intensifiers. Study has also shown nouns (e.g. garbage and prank) and verbs (e.g. admire, prefer and hate) to be very good indicators of subjectivity in sentences [1,2]. Interestingly, objective sentences (factual sentences) may also express subjectivity. For example, the sentence *"The phone worked for an hour and no more"* expresses certain level of "undesirable" fact

R.E. Banchs et al. (Eds.): AIRS 2013, LNCS 8281, pp. 191–202, 2013.

about the entity "phone". Such subjectivity is often difficult to identify in sentences. Idiomatic and Sarcastic expressions may also be subjective. For example, *"Ford is a giant in the auto industry"* and *"A cubicle is just a padded cell without a door"* are two idiomatic and sarcastic sentences, respectively. While the former expresses appraisal on the Ford brand of automobile (very commonly used in news), the latter *expresses discomfort* on an office cubicle. In our experience, such sentences are very challenging to classify as subjective or not.

In this study, we investigate a semi-supervised approach that uses a novel and extended set of predictive features to classify sentences from different domains. The idea is to understand how best we might capture subjective sentences across different domains, and with good precision. First we developed a pattern-based algorithm that extracts subjective predicates from a large collection of blog documents. The subjective predicates are then combined with an extended subjectivity lexicon that contains subjective clues and subjective annotations derived from the MPQA corpus [1]. The resulting lexicon including the subjective predicates is then used to identify subjective sentences for training a subjective classifier. On different datasets, we show that our approach outperform a state-of-the-art High-precision subjectivity classifier in terms of precision, recall and F-measure, respectively. Finally, we perform cross-domain subjective classification, training with a balanced mixture of subjective sentences from different domains (e.g. blogs, news, and movie reviews) and objective sentences from Wikipedia. The classifier achieved a better cross-domain accuracy of 84.6%.

The rest of this paper is organized as follows. We discuss related research work in Section 2. Section 3 describes the construction of the extended lexicon with multiple subjectivity clues. In Section 4, we extracted subjective predicates from a large collection of subjective sentences and add such predicates to our extended lexicon. Experiments and results are presented in Section 5. Finally, we give conclusions on our study in Section 6.

2   Related Work

In the literature, subjectivity classification is often treated as supervised learning problem. Early works such as [3,4] use machine learning techniques (e.g. Naïve Bayes(NB) and Support Vector Machines (SVM)) with different types of features. In [3], the presence of pronouns; adjectives; cardinals; modals (except *will*); and verbs (except *not*) were used as features to classify subjective sentences. In [4], a subjectivity detector was used to detect subjective sentences based on minimum cuts in sentence graph. The technique first built sentence graph using local labelling consistences that produce association score between two sentences. Sentences with similar association scores are more likely to belong to the same subjective or objective classes. More recently, [5] used nouns abstraction for in-domain and cross-domain subjectivity classification. While the above approaches have performed moderately, however, it is still difficult to determine effective features for subjectivity classification [1,2,6].

Unsupervised and semi-supervised techniques have also been applied to subjectivity classification. [7] used an unsupervised technique to detect the presence of subjective expressions using opinion seed words and similar words based on distributional similarity. [8,9,10] used the number of subjective adjectives that occur within a sentence window to retrieve subjective documents. Those techniques recorded certain level of success and show that subjective adjectives can indeed be beneficial to subjectivity classification. [11] proposed a semi-supervised technique that uses a bootstrapping process to learn extraction pattern for subjective sentences. The technique first used a High-precision subjective classifier to label subjective sentences using set of subjective clues. Linguistic patterns are then extracted from the subjective sentences using a learning algorithm similar to AutoSlog-TS [12]. Additional subjective sentences are further identified with the linguistic patterns for the purpose of training a subjective classifier.

Our technique differs from existing works by using a large number of *subjective predicates* (which are independent of any domain) combined with various subjectivity indicators. This allows the classifier to be used for both in-domain and cross-domain subjectivity classification with better performance.

3 Extended Subjectivity Lexicon

In this section, we describe the extended subjectivity lexicon creation technique. The technique is further improved in Section 4 using the subjective predicates approach. Our goal is to automatically identify likely subjective sentences with high precision using a set of 8221 *subjective clues* [13], and the *subjective annotation spans* which are manually annotated in the MPQA corpus [1].

The 8221 subjective clues presented in [13] was aggregated from different sources including the subjective adjectives presented in [8] and the subjectivity clues presented in [14]. The subjective annotations in MPQA corpus was achieved by using the annotation technique described in [1]. 535 news articles from 187 different sources were manually annotated using the GATE[1] implementation. Using the MPQA corpus, we extract subjective expressions which satisfy the following MPQA subjectivity annotation pattern:

INSIDE(text: "Alice love Chocolate";
source:writer/Ryan);
DIRECT-SUBJECTIVE(text: "love";
    intensity: high;
    expression-intensity: high;
    polarity: positive;
    insubstantial: false;
    source: writer/Alice;
    target: Chocolate);

---

[1] http://gate.ac.uk/

Using the subjectivity annotation pattern, a sentence is considered subjective if the output contains a "direct-subjective" annotation component. In addition, the "intensity" attribute must be "high"; the "expression-intensity" attribute must be "high"; and the "insubstantial" attribute must be "false". A sentence is also considered subjective if and only if the annotation output contains an "expressive-subjectivity" annotation component with all "intensity" attributes that must not be "low" [1].

It could be straightforward to directly train a subjective classifier using the subjective sentences extracted by the patterns above. However, the application of such classifier would give less performance on other domains without adequate domain adaptation technique [15]. It is important to state that the MPQA corpus consists of news articles. Thus, extracting only the necessary and independent subjective features from the subjective sentences could increase the performance of a subjective classifier. An evaluation results to that effect is presented in our experiment Section 5. Since our goal is to construct a high precision domain-independent subjective classifier, we did not use the entire MPQA subjective sentences for training. Instead, we extracted only the *annotated spans* from the subjective sentences in the corpus. We noticed that each annotated span consists of a "word" or a "phrase" or rarely, a clause, in the annotated discourse. In MPQA corpus, an annotated span is the *start* and *end* byte of an annotation [1]. For example, an annotation could span from byte 718 to byte 748 in a paragraph of a news article as shown in Figure 1. In this case, the subjective annotation is *"feeling of uncertainty"*.

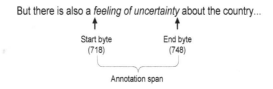

Fig. 1. Example of annotated span in MPQA news article

Thus, we combined the extracted subjective annotations with the 8221 *subjective clues* to form an extended subjectivity lexicon. Using an *empirical threshold* ε, the lexicon is used to automatically identify subjective sentences from each of our datasets. Where ε is the number of clues and/or annotations that must be present in a subjective sentence.

In order to select an optimal threshold, we conducted a pilot study on a labelled subjective and objective datasets by setting ε to 1, 2, 3 and 5, respectively. The subjective dataset[2] was introduced in [4]. It contains 5000 subjective sentences or snippets from *Rotten Tomatoes*[3]. However, we did not use its set of objective sentences which are from IMDb *plot summaries*. Our pilot study reveals that the *plot summaries* contains considerable number of subjective words. Rather, we used 5000 Wikipedia sentences that were extracted across the eight

---

[2] http://www.cs.cornell.edu/people/pabo/movie-review-data/

[3] http://www.rottentomatoes.com/

Wikipedia categories. We assume Wikipedia could be a good source of objectivity. Thus, using the subjectivity lexicon, we extracted subjective sentences from the *Rotten Tomatoes* dataset by setting ε one after the other. This process was also repeated on the Wikipedia sentences. The idea was to identify what ε retrieves a *larger percentage* of the labelled subjective sentences and at the same time minimises the number of objective (Wikipedia) sentences retrieved. We set $\varepsilon \geq 3$ to retrieve subjective sentences across all our multiple datasets. Given a sentence, the subjectivity is determined as follows:

$$S_{sbjv} = \begin{cases} subjective \ if \ C_s \geq \varepsilon \\ objective \ \ \ otherwise \end{cases} \tag{1}$$

where S_{sbjv} is the subjectivity determinant and C_s is the number of subjectivity clues in a given sentence S. A subjective sentence is identified when C_s is more than or equal to ε, otherwise the sentence is objective.

Table 1. Pilot thresholds and percentage of "subjective" sentences extracted

ε	Rotten/subjective	Wiki/objective	IMDb/objective
≥ 1	99.6%	55%	99.5%
≥ 2	99%	47.8%	98.8%
≥ 3	98.3%	44%	97.4%
≥ 5	95%	37%	93.7%

Table 1 shows the result of a comparative pilot study on different thresholds. Interestingly, we found $\varepsilon \geq 3$ to retrieve a larger percentage of subjective sentences (98.3%) and when the same threshold is used on the Wikipedia sentences, it found 44% subjective sentences leaving 56% as true objective sentences. $\varepsilon \geq 3$ also retrieved a combination of short, medium and long sentences compared to starting with a higher threshold such as 5. Note that higher thresholds may likely reduce the number of subjective sentences. Nevertheless, our result is comparatively better than using the IMDb plot summaries from which we retrieved 97.4% subjective sentences on an assumed "objective" dataset[4]. It also confirms our assumption about Wikipedia as a likely source of objectivity.

In order to verify the quality of the extracted subjective sentences, we trained a subjective classifier and evaluated its performance on a different test set containing 1000 manually identified subjective and objective sentences from blogs. With 5-fold cross-validation using NB [16], we achieved 89% precision and 71.5% recall, respectively (see Table 4). This result makes sense given the difficulty of the task on unseen sentences [2]. To improve on this performance, we therefore propose to extract *subjective predicates* from a large collection of subjective sentences. The subjective predicates will be added to the extended lexicon for improved accuracy.

---

[4] http://www.cs.cornell.edu/people/pabo/movie-review-data/
   subjdata.README.1.0.txt

4   Subjective Predicates

We define "subjective predicates" as predicates that exist within an already identified subjective sentence. A predicate contains a verb or verb phrase with optional compliments. Predicate "verbs" are *transitive verbs* because they require one or two compliments unlike "intransitive verbs". Below, we show an example sentence with a predicate:

*"The president **fascinates me** about the economy."*

In the example sentence, *fascinates me* is a predicate with a direct object "me" and indirect object "economy". Thus we could see that the verb "fascinates" has two compliments (the direct and indirect objects) which makes it a transitive verb. The sample sentence also illustrates a subjective predicate - "fascinates me". The idea of using subjective predicates to detect subjective sentences is that some sentences may not necessarily contain *explicit* subjective words such as adjectives (e.g. love, hate, good), yet they may express certain level of subjectivity or private state. The example sentence above meets this criteria as it expresses a "favourable" subjectivity about the subject (entity) "President". Further examples of *subjective predicates* are shown below:

The car **drives slowly**.
The product **works for me** and my family.

Therefore, extracted *subjective predicates* can be combined with the existing "subjective clues" and "subjective annotations" to form a more extended *subjectivity lexicon*. The lexicon can then be used to identify further subjective sentences which are used to improve the accuracy of subjective classifiers.

The proposed technique is similar to the bootstrapping technique proposed in [11]. However, rather than learning case frame-based extraction patterns, we directly extract *subjective predicates* to automatically detect additional or omitted subjective sentences. Adding the subjective predicates to the extended lexicon retrieves further subjective sentences from the *classified objective sentences* (sentences that do not contain subjective clues or subjective annotations by using the previous lexicon) and improves the precision and recall of the subjective classifier substantially. In total, we extracted 10618 subjective predicates from 20000 subjective sentences from blogs. Table 2 shows the composition of the extended subjectivity lexicon.

We identify subjective predicates from subjective sentences using the template patterns below:

1. <transitive-verb><Opt: ANY><punctuation>
2. <transitive-verb><Opt: ANY><Opt: ADJECTIVE><NOUN>

We determine Part-of-Speech using [18]. Below, we show different subjective predicates extracted from some example subjective sentences.

Table 2. Composition of the extended subjectivity lexicon

Subjectivity Type	Number of clues	Source
Clues	8221	Subjectivity clues[13]
Annotations	18,215	MPQA[1]
Predicates	10,618	TREC Blog Dataset [17]

Sentence I: The technology *amazes me.*

The template pattern 1 extracts the subjective predicate "amazes me" as follows:

<transitive-verb>= "amazes", <Opt: ANY>= "me" (optional), <punctuation> = ".".

Sentence II: The government *killed many citizens* during the civil war.

The template pattern 2 extracts the subjective predicate "killed many citizens" as follows:

<transitive-verb>= "killed", <Opt: ANY>= "many" (optional, any word after the transitive verb), <Opt: ADJECTIVE>= " " (optional), <NOUN>= "citizens".

Sentence III: He *deceived many American taxpayers* in the name of peace in the middle-east.

The template pattern 2 extracts the subjective predicate "deceived many American taxpayers" as follows:

<transitive-verb >= "deceived", <Opt: ANY>= "many" (optional), <Opt: ADJECTIVE>= "American" (optional), <NOUN>= "taxpayers".

Table 3 shows additional examples of subjective predicates and their equivalent probability of occurrence in a different sample data other than the data from which the subjective predicates were extracted. The probability was computed as the ratio of each predicate to the total number of sentences in the sample data. The idea is to show that the subjective predicates are likely to appear at least once in any randomly selected sample data. This shows the benefit of subjective predicates in training data.

5   Experiments and Results

5.1   Datasets

Blogs: Using the extended subjectivity lexicon and the threshold discoursed earlier, we randomly select sample 5000 subjective sentences and 5000 objective

Table 3. Sample subjective predicates and probability of occurrence in sample data

Predicate	Prob.
waiting for	0.0016
going to be a	0.0012
seems to be a	0.0006
come a long way	0.0002
tell you	0.0032
have changed	0.0002
feel welcome	0.0002
are thinking	0.0006
caught up	0.0004
falling apart	0.0004
know that	0.0054

sentences from the TREC Blog08 dataset which was crawled over different time frames[17]. The sentences are not specific to a particular topic or entity but a sample data that represents how sentences are generally written in blog documents. Also, the sample data contains different types of blog domains such as music, video, and technology, thus making the sample data quite representative of blogs written from different perspectives.

Rotten Tomatoes/IMDb: This subjectivity dataset was used in [4]. It contains 5000 subjective sentences or snippets which are extracted from *Rotten Tomatoes* movie reviews. The dataset also contains 5000 objective sentences from IMDb *plot summaries* following the assumption made in [4], that the IMDb plot summaries are mostly objective sentences.

MPQA/News: The MPQA opinion corpus contains 535 news articles from 187 different sources. The corpus was manually annotated for different kinds of subjectivity. The annotation scheme used for identifying subjective sentences in MPQA has been discussed earlier in this paper. Using such mechanism, we identified 5000 subjective sentences and 5000 objective sentences for our experiment.

Mixed-Subjective: Again, using the extended subjectivity lexicon and appropriate threshold, we selected a combination of 5000 subjective sentences from the TREC blog dataset, rotten tomatoes movie reviews, and the MPQA news corpus. Note that this set of sentences are completely different from the sentences used in the datasets described earlier. The idea is that, as long as the extended lexicon with the subjective predicates is used, it does not matter where one selects subjective sentences for training subjective classifiers, although, we suggest it should be a combination of more than one domain. We will use this dataset for the cross-domain subjective training set.

Wikipedia: We mentioned earlier that Wikipedia is a likely source of objectivity following the outcome of our pilot study (see Table 1). Thus, we selected 5000 random sentences from Wikipedia articles using the Wikipedia corpus described in [18]. Again, the dataset is a combination of sentences from the eight top Wikipedia categories[5] (i.e. Arts, Biography, Geography, History, Mathematics, Science, Society, and Technology). We believe that these categories could be sufficient to capture objectivity from different domains/datasets. We will use the Wikipedia sentences for the cross-domain objective training set.

5.2 Classification

We used two baselines in our experiments. One is our implementation of the High-Precision subjective classifier proposed in [11]. Again, the technique used case frame-based extraction patterns to identify subjective sentences. The other baseline is a *self baseline* using the performance of the *in-domain/domain-specific* classification on each of the three datasets (Blogs, Rotten Tomatoes, and MPQA). We used the first baseline to validate the significance of the extended lexicon with the subjective predicates over the baseline technique on the same data. The second baseline is used to further measure the performance of the extended lexicon with the subjective predicates in cross-domain classification.

We performed three different classification experiments to validate the proposed technique. First, using the different subjectivity criteria for building the extended lexicon, we experimented with a Naïve Bayes classifier and show the significance of the proposed extended lexicon with the subjective predicates on an out-of-sample blog data (see Table 4). Second, using 5-fold cross validation, we trained another NB classifier and a Language Model (LM) classifier[19], with 60% of each dataset and and tested with the remaining 40%. As per [4], we used *unigram* features for the NB classifier, denoting the independent count of each word learned from the training set. We used *n*-gram features for the LM classifier by setting *n*-gram=6. The study in [20] suggested *n*-gram> 5 leads to improved classification for LM. Finally, we evaluated the performance of our technique using *cross-domain* classification. Specifically, we trained the two classifiers on the *Mixed-Subjective* dataset and tested with the testing set of each domain-specific dataset (i.e. 40%-Blogs, 40%-Rotten Tomatoes, and 40%-MPQA). Both NB and LM classifiers were implemented using the LingPipe[6] NLP APIs.

Table 4. Performance of NB subjective classifier using different criteria to extract the training sentences

Training set criteria	Precision	Recall	F-Measure ($\beta = 1$)
Subjective clues, annotations, & predicates	97.7%	73.4%	83.8%
Subjective clues & annotations only	89%	70%	78.3%
Baseline	87.2%	63.9%	73.75%

---

[5] http://en.wikipedia.org
[6] http://alias-i.com/lingpipe/

We refer to Table 4 for the first experiment. We could see that the subjective classifier that combines *subjective clues* and *subjective annotations* to extract training sentences has a *precision* of 89% on the subjective test set (i.e. 89% of the subjective sentences are subjective) and a *recall* of 70% (i.e. 70% of the entire test set were found to be subjective). The *F-measure* 78.3% is also encouraging, while β is the *relative weight of precision*. The interesting thing is that both precision and recall are comparatively high. The performance is also better than the baseline technique. However, our aim is to further increase the performance of the subjectivity classifier while maintaining the same order of precision and recall. Which is why we proposed the *subjective predicates* as described in Section 4. We see that the precision of the subjective classifier improved upon introducing the subjective predicates. The precision is increased by 8.7% and the recall increased by 3.4%. This shows that subjective predicates is likely to improve subjectivity classification. Overall, the subjective classifier performs better as both precision and recall values are high.

Table 5. Accuracies of NB and LM subjective classifier for in-domain classification

	Rotten/IMDb	Blogs	MPQA
NB	85%	82.8%	67.4%
LM	92.2%	83.8%	84.4%

Table 6. Accuracies of NB and LM subjective classifier for cross-domain classification

	Rotten/IMDb	Blogs	MPQA
NB	80.2%	76.6%	71.6%
LM	84.6%	81.2%	84.4%

In Table 5, we could see that the LM classifier outperforms the NB classifier on all datasets. We believe this confirms the benefit of using higher order $n-$gram as suggested in [20]. Also, a better improvement is noticed on MPQA news corpus. We suggest this could be as a result of news articles often containing a lot of sarcastic and/or idiomatic expressions[2]. Thus, we think the n-gram based LM classifier was able to capture such expressions as a sequence of words rather than using the NB's independent assumption which avoids dependencies between words.

Table 6 shows the effect of the extended lexicon with subjective predicates on cross-domain classification. The result is rather encouraging given the nature of the cross-domain classification task[15]. Furthermore, the results are comparatively better than those reported in [5]. They reported 73.9% using Support Vector Machines (SVM) on the Chesley[7] dataset and 74.5% using Linear Discriminant Analysis (LDA) on blogs/wiki dataset. We could also see that the difference between the performance of the cross-domain and the in-domain classifications is less than 10% for both NB and LM. We suggest that this is an

---

[7] http://www.tc.umn.edu/~ches0045/data/

expected trade-off given the difficulty of the cross-domain classification problem. On the other hand, we improved the accuracy of the NB cross-domain classifier on the MPQA corpus, while the LM cross-domain classifier performed comparably with the in-domain LM classifier. Thus, we believe that the proposed extended subjectivity lexicon including the subjective predicates could be helpful to high precision subjectivity classification.

6   Conclusion

In this study, we have used an extended subjectivity lexicon including subjective predicates to improve in-domain and cross-domain subjectivity classifications. The proposed subjectivity classification technique is comparatively better than a in-domain baseline technique and has improved accuracy on cross-domain subjectivity classification. The significance of the technique is that it identifies subjective sentences with high precision regardless of the domain. This suggests the improved accuracy on the cross-domain subjectivity classification. In future, we will investigate additional linguistic features that could improve the accuracy of both in-domain and cross-domain classifiers.

References

1. Wiebe, J., Wilson, T., Cardie, C.: Annotating expressions of opinions and emotions in language. Language Resources and Evaluation 39(2/3), 165–210 (2005)
2. Liu, B.: Sentiment analysis and opinion mining. Synthesis Lectures on Human Language Technologies 5(1), 1–167 (2012)
3. Wiebe, J.M., Bruce, R.F., O'Hara, T.P.: Development and use of a gold-standard data set for subjectivity classifications. In: Proceedings of the 37th Annual Meeting of the Association for Computational Linguistics on Computational Linguistics, ACL 1999, pp. 246–253. Association for Computational Linguistics, Stroudsburg (1999)
4. Pang, B., Lee, L.: A sentimental education: sentiment analysis using subjectivity summarization based on minimum cuts. In: Proceedings of the 42nd Annual Meeting on Association for Computational Linguistics, Barcelona, Spain, p. 271. Association for Computational Linguistics (2004)
5. Lambov, D., Dias, G., Noncheva, V.: High-level features for learning subjective language across domains. In: Proceedings of International AAAI Conference on Weblogs and Social Media, ICWSM (2009)
6. Liu, B.: Sentiment analysis and subjectivity. In: Handbook of Natural Language Processing, 2nd edn. (2010)
7. Wiebe, J.M.: Learning subjective adjectives from corpora (2000)
8. Hatzivassiloglou, V., McKeown, K.R.: Predicting the semantic orientation of adjectives. In: Proceedings of the Eighth Conference on European Chapter of the Association for Computational Linguistics, Madrid, Spain, pp. 174–181. Association for Computational Linguistics (1997)
9. Turney, P., Littman, M.L.: Unsupervised learning of semantic orientation from a hundred-billion-word corpus. Technical report (2002)
10. Vechtomova, O.: Using subjective adjectives in opinion retrieval from blogs (2008)

11. Riloff, E., Wiebe, J.: Learning extraction patterns for subjective expressions. In: Proceedings of the 2003 Conference on Empirical Methods in Natural Language Processing, EMNLP 2003, pp. 105–112. Association for Computational Linguistics, Stroudsburg (2003)

12. Riloff, E.M.: Automatically generating extraction patterns from untagged text (1996)

13. Wilson, T., Wiebe, J., Hoffmann, P.: Recognizing contextual polarity in phrase-level sentiment analysis. In: Proceedings of the Conference on Human Language Technology and Empirical Methods in Natural Language Processing, Vancouver, British Columbia, Canada, pp. 347–354. Association for Computational Linguistics (2005)

14. Wiebe, J.M.: Recognizing subjective sentences: a computational investigation of narrative text. PhD thesis, Buffalo, NY, USA (1990)

15. Blitzer, J., Dredze, M., Pereira, F.: Biographies, bollywood, boom-boxes and blenders: Domain adaptation for sentiment classification. Association of Computational Linguistics (ACL) (2007)

16. Domingos, P., Pazzani, M.: On the optimality of the simple bayesian classifier under zero-one loss. Machine Learning 29, 103–130 (1997)

17. Macdonald, C., Santos, R.L., Ounis, I., Soboroff, I.: Blog track research at trec. SIGIR Forum 44(1), 58–75 (2010)

18. Torsten, Z., Christof, M., Iryna, G.: Extracting lexical semantic knowledge from wikipedia and wiktionary (2009)

19. Peng, F., Schuurmans, D., Wang, S.: Augmenting naive bayes classifiers with statistical language models. Information Retrieval 7(3), 317–345 (2004)

20. Cui, H., Mittal, V., Datar, M.: Comparative experiments on sentiment classification for online product reviews. American Association for Artificial Intelligence (AAAI) (2006)

Duplicate News Story Detection Revisited

Omar Alonso[1], Dennis Fetterly[2], and Mark Manasse[2]

[1] Microsoft Corporation
omalonso@microsoft.com
[2] Microsoft Research, Silicon Valley Lab
{fetterly,manasse}@microsoft.com

Abstract. In this paper, we investigate near-duplicate detection, particularly look-ing at the detection of evolving news stories. These stories often consist primarily of syndicated information, with local replacement of headlines, captions, and the addition of locally-relevant content. By detecting near-duplicates, we can offer users only those stories with content materially different from previously-viewed versions of the story. We expand on previous work and improve the performance of near-duplicate document detection by weighting the phrases in a sliding win-dow based on the term frequency within the document of terms in that window and inverse document frequency of those phrases. We experiment on a subset of a publicly available web collection that is comprised solely of documents from news web sites. News articles are particularly challenging due to the prevalence of syndicated articles, where very similar articles are run with different headlines and surrounded by different HTML markup and site templates. We evaluate these algorithmic weightings using human judgments to determine similarity. We find that our techniques outperform the state of the art with statistical significance and are more discriminating when faced with a diverse collection of documents.

Keywords: News story near-duplicate detection, web similarity, crowdsourcing.

1 Introduction

Near-duplicate document detection is a problem with a long history spanning many applications. Notable applications include duplicate result suppression for web search engines, better filesystem compression through careful dictionary seeding, reduced stor-age requirements for backups, improved bandwidth utilization using delta compression on similar packets, copyright infringement or plagiarism detection, and visual image clustering by recognizing rotation, scale, and lighting invariant features. Near-duplicate documents are those where the documents are not identical, so a hash-based compar-ison of the full content will fail, but are comprised of a plurality of identical features. Near-duplication is not necessarily transitive: $a \approx b$ and $b \approx c$ do not guarantee $a \approx c$.

In a web search service, algorithms for near-duplicate document detection face many real-world challenges, such as pages containing common navigational text, legal no-tices, user-generated content, contents of form fields (including lists of months and days), and content from services that suggest related pages or articles. These challenges are even greater in collections of news articles, due to syndication, markup from soft-ware used by the publisher to control layout, local event listings, neighborhood shoppers

R.E. Banchs et al. (Eds.): AIRS 2013, LNCS 8281, pp. 203–214, 2013.
© Springer-Verlag Berlin Heidelberg 2013

(free papers) with repeated content, and section summaries mostly containing a single article from the section's subject in addition to abstracts for a number of additional articles.

In 2008, Theobald *et al.* investigated a set of techniques, *SpotSigs*, for detecting near-duplicate news items. Inspired by this, and newly armed with a tool for approximating arbitrary non-negative weighted Jaccard values, we seek to find algorithmic weightings (based solely on the corpus' statistical properties) that yield comparable or better results, without the *ad-hoc* explicit choice of a preferred set of stop words, unlike SpotSigs.

To evaluate our techniques when facing these real-world challenges, we experiment on subsets of a publicly available web collection. We evaluate our algorithmic weightings using human judgments by the authors and from crowdsourcing to evaluate similarity and relevance when detecting duplicate news stories. All variants of our techniques which eliminate templates outperform (with statistical significance) previous efforts, with better discrimination in a more diverse collection of relevant documents.

The remainder of this paper is laid out as follows. In Section 2 we discuss related work, Section 3 describes our approach, and the experiments are described in Section 4.

2   Related Work

Near-duplicate detection algorithms have been utilized in a variety of ways. Some of the more significant ones, which we do not consider further in this paper, include: plagiarism detection [11,13,22], sub-document replication [6,2,7,18], Winnowing [21], finding near-duplicate files in a local or remote filesystem [15,25,17,23], and web crawling [16].

Our consideration of the Theobald, *et al.* SpotSigs paper [24] suggested that the primary aspect differentiating their technique from the sampling approaches they rejected (shingling [3] and SimHash [5]) is that the Theobald approach is highly selective in the choice of phrases from which to draw samples. While SimHash (a technique for approximating cosine similarity) is easily tuned to offer weighted sampling, the individual samples are words, not phrases. Preferentially weighting stop words would result in frequency matching of occurrences of those words (or their immediate successors), which cannot distinguish news stories from one another. Shingling, as described, used phrases, but allowed for integer phrase weighting.

Gollapudi and Panigrahy [9] found a weighted sampling technique running in time logarithmic to the weights, suitable for weights larger than some given positive constant; Manasse *et al.* [14] presented an expected constant-time sampling algorithm for arbitrary non-negative weights. Ioffe [12] subsequently improved this to a Monte Carlo randomized algorithm running in constant time.

Recently, Gibson *et al.* [8] considered the specific problem of news story deduplication, principally using a text extractor to reduce news pages to just the story, followed by the use of known sketching algorithms. We also tried a news story extractor in some of our algorithms to try to restrict our attention to just the news content of the story. Our techniques improve on Gibson by using aspects of the feature selection suggested by SpotSigs. We omit this comparison due to space limatations.

3   Algorithmic Approach

From Theobald [24], we take the idea that phrases beginning with common words are more likely to be body text of an article than to be captions or headlines. These phrases are likely to be preserved as a news story evolves, or as articles transit from a wire service to appearance in a newspaper. We therefore investigate phrase weightings giving higher weight to phrases beginning with oft-used terms as measured by term frequency.

From Broder [3], we take the efficiency of replacing exact Jaccard computation by sample-based approximation, allowing the identification of most highly-similar pairs drawn from billions of documents.

From Henzinger's comparison of shingling to SimHash [10], we take seriously that unweighted shingling is often inferior to the weighted term selection of SimHash.

Ioffe's work on consistent sampling [12] offers a Monte Carlo constant-time technique for approximating weighted Jaccard values, allowing us to use arbitrary non-negative weightings of phrases. We use information retrieval standards, such as term and document frequency, and modifications of such weightings using logarithms and powers.

We seek weighting schemes offering heightened probability of selection to those phrases SpotSigs prefers, but allowing some probability of selection to all phrases. We use weight-proportional sampling to create compact document sketches. Unlike Spot-Sigs, compact sketches and supershingles allow significantly larger corpora to be considered.

SpotSigs chooses a small set of *antecedent* words common in English. It then selects samples beginning after an element of the antecedent set skipping antecedents and a configurable number of terms. SpotSigs chose a test collection starting from a small number of known news stories, building 68 clusters of near-duplicate articles, and evaluating recall and precision for variants of SpotSigs within this collection.

We identify news stories within a large pool of documents selected from known news source web sites. We use a probabilistic approximation to weighted Jaccard to identify likely near-duplicates in this collection. The weights are based on term and phrase frequencies. We do not explicitly choose a preferred set of antecedents, and generally give all phrases which do not appear to be boilerplate some positive weight.

To elaborate and unify the computations involved, all of the algorithms assign a weight to every phrase of a chosen target length. SpotSigs confounds this simplification by picking phrases which omit the antecedent words; a behavior we did not attempt to replicate. SpotSigs assigns weight one to phrases beginning at the position of a word in the antecedent set, and weight zero to all other phrases.

Weighted Jaccard for non-negative weightings W_1 and W_2 over a universe of phrases U is defined to be

$$\frac{\sum_{u \in U} \min(W_1(u), W_2(u))}{\sum_{u \in U} \max(W_1(u), W_2(u))} = \frac{\|\min(W_1, W_2)\|_1}{\|\max(W_1, W_2)\|_1}.$$

For binary weightings, the numerator is the cardinality of the intersection of W_1 and W_2, while the denominator is the cardinality of the union of W_1 and W_2, viewing W_1 and W_2 as sets containing those elements with weight one, resulting in the conventional definition for the Jaccard value.

In choosing weightings, we considered term frequency (both within a document, and in the entire corpus), and approximations or exact computation of phrase frequency in the corpus, in order to reduce the impact of boilerplate text.

Due to working with a corpus of considerable size, we call the one percent of phrases found in more than forty-two distinct documents *common*. This set can be efficiently stored in a relatively small amount of memory on even a modest computer. Features that utilize both the presence and absence of a phrase in this set can be derived. We chose to work with unbiased estimates of the Jaccard value, rather than computing the exact value for all pairs. The SpotSigs paper computes exactly the set of document pairs whose Jaccard value exceeds a chosen threshold, but it does this in a corpus where the number of pairs is bounded by a few million; we aim for corpora in which the number of individual documents is best measured in billions, resulting in quintillions of document pairs, rendering even the enumeration of all pairs impractical. We also seek to understand whether our algorithms help separate news stories from non-news, at least when one of the articles is judged as news. As such, we evaluated pairs across the spectrum of Jaccard similarity, rating selected pairs as irrelevant (two non-news stories), and duplicate or not. In our first experiments, as follows, we viewed the identification of a non-news story as a near-duplicate of a valid news story to be a false positive, reducing our precision value.

We discovered a few encouraging things: many variants of weighting produced results comparable to one another and to SpotSigs, as measured by F1 value and Matthews coefficient. We further discovered that SpotSigs performed surprisingly (to us) poorly on our broader collection, marking many documents as duplicates which shared only a significant amount of boilerplate text – for instance, the text associated with the navigational controls on different pages from a single news site – leading to low precision numbers for SpotSigs and for our first proposed weightings when applied to our test set.

We then refined some of the algorithms by down-weighting common phrases, using both a variant of inverse document frequency (IDF) for phrases, and a simple threshold cut-off for phrases common to more than a few dozen documents. The resulting techniques significantly outperform SpotSigs on the judged portion of our collection.

Computations using the algorithms described above are highly parallelizable – samples for different documents can be drawn independently in time linear in the document length multiplied by the number of samples to be drawn, if the phrase frequencies to determine weightings are in memory.

4   Evaluation

4.1   Experimental Setup

This section describes the data and computational infrastructure that we used to carry out our experiments. We started with the 503 million page "Category A" English subset of the ClueWeb09 dataset[1]. Additionally, we retrieved the RDF version of the Open Directory Project site on September 23, 2010. In order to build a large test corpus comprised primarily of news documents, we filter the ClueWeb pages to contain only those

---

[1] `http://boston.lti.cs.cmu.edu/Data/clueweb09/`

from one of the 7,261 distinct hostnames in the ODP News category, resulting in a set of 11,826,611 web pages. We then removed all content from Wikipedia and exact duplicate pages by including only one representative from each group of exactly matching text pages. The resulting collection of 5,540,370 web pages forms our corpus.

To evaluate the effectiveness of near-duplicate detection algorithms, we first need to compute the similarity of the documents in the collection. It is computationally infeasible to compute the pairwise similarity of all 5.5 million documents. Past work [8,24] has built small collections of documents either via clustering or by querying a search engine with an existing news article's title and retrieving the results to obtain duplicate stories. We took a different approach, which we believe yields a collection that surfaces many of the thorny issues in near-duplicate document detection.

We begin by extracting the potential news article from each of the documents in our corpus using the Maximum Subsequence Segmentation approach described in [19]. We then parse the documents using an HTML parser producing a sample of document pairs where the articles share at least one seven word phrase whose IDF is in the interval $[0.2, 0.85]$. From each group of documents that share a phrase, samples are drawn uniformly for all pairs in that group. The number of samples drawn is proportional to the number of pairs in the group. Once we have obtained the distinct set of pairs from all groups, we compute the unweighted Jaccard coefficient of the pairs of extracted articles. A histogram of these Jaccard values was then calculated and used to obtain a sample of 456 document pairs distributed approximately evenly across the set of Jaccard values.

Two authors labeled all of these pairs of pages, assigning a label with potential values of Containment, Duplicate, Non-duplicate, Duplicate Irrelevant, and Non-duplicate Irrelevant. The two sets of labels were compared for agreement, and the pairs where the labels were not in agreement were rejudged in consultation in order to obtain a set of labels with complete agreement. We refer to this dataset as CW1 for the remainder of this paper. The distribution of labels is depicted in Table 1. The labels, along with the set of document identifiers that form our corpus, are available from the project page at http://research.microsoft.com/projects/newsdupedetect/.

Table 1. Distribution of labels for CW1

Label	Frequency
Duplicate	42
Containment	10
Non-duplicate	252
Duplicate, Irrelevant	10
Non-duplicate, Irrelevant	142

Table 2. Distribution of Phase 1 raw labels

Label	Frequency
Yes	4,235
No	7,877
I don't know	208
Other	412
Non English	45

4.2 Crowdsourced Labels

Like many others, when attempting to scale the labeled dataset, we turned to crowdsourcing, where tasks are outsourced to an unknown set of workers. Using the same methodology as for CW1, we initially sampled 4,107 pairs of documents from our corpus. While labeling CW1, the authors used a labeling tool (implemented specifically for this task) that presented both documents at the same time, and assigned a label to the pair. We streamlined this process for the labels we generated via crowdsourcing, which includes using a more generic tool for implementing the tasks. To validate the new experimental design, we took the CW1 data set and ran it through Phase 1 of the crowdsourcing pipeline. We compared the agreement between us and the workers using Cohen's Kappa and reported $\kappa = 0.766$, which indicates substantial agreement.

At a high level, we follow the same process described in [1] by using an iterative approach for the design and implementation of each experiment. We designed and tested both designs (Figure 3 depicts Phase 2) with small data sets before involving crowds. We batched the data sets and adjusted quality control using honey pots and manually checking for outliers. We now describe each step in more detail.

We designed a crowdsourced labeling pipeline that consisted of two separate experiments: news identification (Phase 1) and duplicate detection assessment (Phase 2). The labeling process works as follows: Once we had our initial sample, we generated a list of distinct documents from the sampled pairs, and then asked workers to determine if a document was or was not a news article, or if the worker was unable to determine. After computing agreement, we then filtered the list of document pairs to include only those where both documents had been labeled as news articles. We asked workers if the articles in the pair were about the same event and if one had more detail than the other. The Microsoft Universal Human Relevance System [20] gathered all crowd assessments.

Quality control is a key part in any crowdsourcing task and our workflow combines different crowds at each phase. Initially, we use a small data set to test the design of phase 1 experiments. Each URL was assessed by the authors and all disagreements resolved in person. The output was used as a honey-pot data set to check the quality of the same phase using a different crowd. In this step, an overlapping medium size data set is used and each URL is assessed by 2 workers. All URLs where both workers agree are then used to generate the URL pairs, which are the input for phase 2. In this second phase, each URL pair was assessed by 3 workers and for those few cases where at least 2 of the additional workers disagree with the initial judgment, we provided an extra label to compute the final list. Figure 2 describes the quality control mechanisms we used.

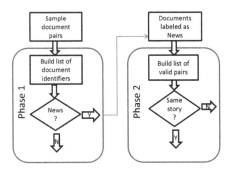
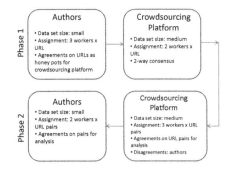
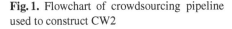

Fig. 1. Flowchart of crowdsourcing pipeline used to construct CW2

Fig. 2. Flowchart of work quality control for phases 1 and 2

We assessed 4,107 pairs in phase one, containing 3,992 distinct ids. Each document was assessed as a news article or not by two workers where the values were one of Yes, No, I don't know, or Other. The assessments we received resulted in a Cohen's Kappa $\kappa = 0.73$, indicating substantial agreement. Table 2 lists the distribution of labels.

Please only consider the article itself (not the surrounding template). Ignore ads, images and formatting. We are only considering the core text of the articles. Note that headlines can be different.

1. Are these 2 news articles about the same event/topic?

- **Yes**. These news articles are about the same.
- **No**. These news articles are not the same.
- **I don't know**. I can't tell if the news articles are the same or not.
- **Other**. Web page didn't load/error message/etc.
- **Non English**. This document is not in English.

2. Does one document cover more detail than the other?

- Document A covers more detail than document B.
- Document B covers more detail than document A.
- No

Fig. 3. Experiment design for Phase 2

Once we had a set of documents that was labeled as news articles or not news articles, we returned to the list of document pairs that we initially sampled and considered each pair where both documents had been labeled as news articles. For Phase 2, we report agreement using Fleiss' Kappa $\kappa = 0.74$, indicating again substantial agreement.

For the assessments from Phase 2, we directly take all URL pairs assessed as news. Table 3 shows the results of this task. When comparing these results against CW1, note that Table 1 identifies duplicates and containment separately, while Table 3 counts all incidents of containment also as a duplicate. Due to the two-phase nature of the crowdsourced pipeline, many sampled pairs were not carried forward from Phase 1 to Phase 2 because at least one article in the pair was not labeled as a news article. Despite the similar magnitude of the results in Tables 1 and 3, the scale of the crowdsourced experiment was much larger because of the labels obtained in Phase 1. We refer to this dataset as CW2 and these labels are also available from the project webpage.

4.3 Experimental Results

In order to compute sample values for our documents, we use Ioffe's [12] constant time weighted sampling technique, which extends shingling to select a weighted sketch [5] of each document. We consider a document to be equivalent to its set of *phrases*, consecutive terms from the document. A weighted document is a document together with a weighting function, mapping each phrase to a non-negative weight. Symbolically, the set of phrases in a document is $\{\rho_i\}$, and a weight function maps each i to a non-negative value $W(i)$. A weighted sample $<\rho, w>$ is a pair where, for some i, $\rho = \rho_i$

Table 3. Phase 2 label Distribution

Label	Frequency
Yes	323
No	386
I don't know	0
Other	1

Table 4. Functions used for final weight

uniform	$\log^2 DF$	DF^2
DF	$\log^3 DF$	DF^3
$\log DF$	$\log^4 DF$	DF^4
$\log(DocumentCount/DF)$	$\log^{10} DF$	

and $0 \le w < W(i)$. We want a family of sampling functions $\{\mathcal{F}_i\}$ where averaged over that family, the expected probability of agreement is equal to the Jaccard value. Thus, $Prob_i(\mathcal{F}_i(A) = \mathcal{F}_i(B)) = J(A,B)$. Such estimators are *unbiased*.

Ioffe produces such a family by picking a family of pseudo-random generators of values. For each phrase ρ, we seed the generator with ρ, and uniformly pick five numbers $u_1, u_2, v_1, v_2, \beta \in [0,1)$. Let $r = \frac{1}{u_1 u_2}$ and $t = \lfloor \beta + \log_r w \rfloor$. The weight y associated with phrase ρ is $r^{t-\beta}$, and the associated value is $a = \frac{-\ln v_1 v_2}{ry}$. From all phrases, choose as the sample the $<\rho, y>$ with the numerically least a value.

We experiment with several families of algorithms for setting weights. First, we generalize the SpotSigs approach of taking samples that occur immediately after one of a small number of antecedents. SpotSigs assigns equal weight to all antecedents. Variants of SpotSigs have antecedent sets that vary from the single term *is* to the 571 stopwords used in SMART [4]. We combine two values to compute the weight for a given sample. First, we consider the document frequency (DF) of the first term in the window. Second, we either scale this by the IDF of the complete phrase or multiply that by a binary value, which is 1 if the phrase is a "rare" phrase or 0 is the phrase is common, as detailed in Section 4.5. A function from Table 4 is then applied to the combined weight in order to determine a final weight for this phrase. Many of the values we utilize when calculating the weights are readily computed during the index construction phase for a search engine, or can be independently calculated with a pass over the corpus.

4.4   Results on ClueWeb Labeled Data

As described in Section 4.1, we drew plausible pairings by examining the Jaccard similarity of paired pages. We took samples of roughly equal size from small ranges of similarity, so that our samples would span the gamut of syntactic similarity. We chose the uniform distribution so that we could explore our techniques in a variety of settings.

We utilize the F1 measure to assess the quality of our techniques. The threshold values we use for cutoffs are largely unrelated. Accordingly, we set the threshold for each technique by choosing a sample of the document pairs, and finding the threshold value resulting in the maximum F1 score on this set. We then use this threshold on the full set of pairs and compute and report the F1 scores. Because of the differing scales for each technique, we then compare the F1 scores for thresholds in small neighborhoods of the predetermined threshold, to assess sensitivity of our techniques to the choice of threshold value. The F1 measure is easily described in terms of recall and precision, which measure the fraction of detected positives, $\frac{TP}{TP+FN}$, and the fraction of positives which are correct, $\frac{TP}{TP+FP}$. Using these, F1 is $2\frac{recall \times precision}{recall + precision} = \frac{2TP}{2TP+FN+FP}$.

In a particular example we considered weights equal to the fourth power of document frequency for the first word in a phrase, divided by the document frequency of the entire phrase. We computed recall, precision, and F1 curves at a range of thresholds from zero to one. In this case, the curve stayed reasonably flat from thresholds of $\frac{1}{4}$ to $\frac{3}{4}$, suggesting relative insensitivity to the precise setting of the threshold.

The experiments in this paper use a phrase length of 7. SpotSigs does not consider phrase windows of a fixed size, instead, "chains" of some chain length c are constructed where the the non-stopwords that are at least d terms apart are selected. The SpotSigs results are for a chain length of 3 plus a distance of 2, akin to our phrase length of 7 in the absence of stopwords within the phrase window: we include the first term in the phase window while SpotSigs omits it. Future work could consider other phrase lengths.

Table 5. Maximum F1 scores for SpotSigs similarity

Antecedent list	Max F1
Is	0.7394
The	0.8375
Is,The	0.8321
Is,The,Said	0.8373
Is,The,Said,Was	0.8382
Is,The,Said,Was,There	0.8385
Is,The,Said,Was,There,A	0.8392
Is,The,Said,Was,There,A,It	0.8446
The,A,Can,Be,Will,Have,Do	0.8263
Smart stopword list	0.8202

Table 6. Maximum F1 scores for rare phrase weighting functions

Weighting function	Max F1
uniform	0.8693
DF	0.8625
$\log DF$	0.8732
$\log IDF$	0.8692
DF^2	0.8825
DF^3	0.8815
DF^4	0.8824
$\log^2 DF$	0.8698
$\log^3 DF$	0.8710
$\log^4 DF$	0.8776
$\log^{10} DF$	0.8807

4.5 Rare Phrases

We also experimented with considering various fractions of rare (or not-so-rare) phrases. We calculated results for all of the functions in Table 4 where we set the weight for a phrase to 0 if it occurred in more than 1, 5, 25, 50, 75, 95, or 99% of documents. For the ClueWeb09 dataset, this table of rare phrases contains at most 847,281 elements, which can be easily stored with the counts in an in-memory hashtable. While all of the rare phrase variants of our technique perform well, we find that considering the bottom 50% performs best. Table 6 lists the F1 value we compute for each weighted sampling technique at 50%. The F1 values we computed for all rare phrase variants are superior to all other techniques, including SpotSigs, which are listed in Table 5, primarily due to the presence of significant amounts of boilerplate in newspaper formatting, which has little to do with the contents of an individual story.

We compared SpotSigs similarity against Rare Phrase similarity by looking at all of our pairs of documents. We scored each algorithm by whether it correctly predicted the judged assessment of similarity. Looking at just the judgments, all of our algorithms compared to the best SpotSigs algorithm produced a large number of points of agreement with the judges and with one another. Simple χ^2 testing revealed no significant differences: both disagreed about equally often with each often choosing positive.

However, as Table 6 shows, our F1 scores are typically 6% better than SpotSigs, and, when considering whether we agree with the judges at points of disagreement, the likelihood of that improved F1 score being due to chance is almost always below 2% as measured by χ^2, and often vanishingly small as measured using a two-sided T-Test.

4.6   Matthews Correlation

The Matthews Correlation Coefficient, or MCC, which is defined to be

$$\frac{TP \times TN - FP \times FN}{\sqrt{(TP+FP)(TP+FN)(TN+FP)(TN+FN)}}$$

is a correlation coefficient with a value in the range $[-1, 1]$ commonly used to evaluate machine learning algorithms. A correlation coefficient value of 1 indicates perfect classification. Figure 4 shows the MCC for a select few of the methods we experimented with compared to the ground truth data from CW1. We selected the best-performing methods within each class of technique; other methods performed similarly.

We observe that our rare phrase variants do quite well compared to the best variant of SpotSigs, except for a small range of thresholds. We consider this acceptable: the variants we chose concentrate around a threshold of roughly $\frac{1}{4}$ to $\frac{1}{2}$. There is no intrinsic correlation between the thresholds for different methods; it makes sense to select a value for each that typically performs well.

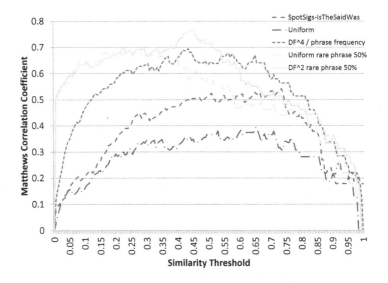

Fig. 4. Matthews Correlation Coefficient for a selection of techniques on CW1

Again, the worst-performing methods are a uniform weighting (which closely approximates shingling), and the best variant of SpotSigs. As noted by Henzinger, straight shingling is an inferior method, falling prey to a host of irrelevancies in the document. The inverse phrase-frequency weighting has intermediate performance: better than SpotSigs, roughly equal to uniform rare phrase (but with a flatter range for tuning), and inferior to an exponentially-weighted rare phrase variant. Although not depicted (to save space), these comparisons are consistent across the gamut of variants.

5 Conclusion

We have presented an algorithm for effectively detecting near duplicate news stories. This algorithm generalizes SpotSigs by using the term and phrase frequencies to weight sample choices. Non-binary weights give our approach more of a SimHash flavor, addressing issues raised by Henzinger. Our experimental results significantly improve performance using a battery of statistical tests on a test set presenting real-world challenges. We make both our algorithm and our test set available for use by the research community.

We plan to test the suitability of this technique across multiple languages. By using DF as a term weight, we hope this will work even in languages without stopwords.

In this work, we took note of only very-common phrases due to the difficulty of exact counting of frequency given the large number of uncommon phrases. In the future, approximate counting Bloom filters might be an economical way to find most of the heavy hitters. We had the opportunity to use exact counting, but given that we used frequency for rarity only as a binary decision, fuzzier counts would suffice.

While we may think that assessing duplicate documents is a simple task, in practice it is difficult and demanding. There are a number of presentation issues (e.g., formatting, broken images, different styles, etc.) that the assessor has to deal with to locate the "core" of the document. Different news agencies often produce different paragraph breaks making it difficult for workers to find visual anchors to compare similarity.

We also introduced a crowdsourcing pipeline that consists of two phases for gathering labels and improves the overall label quality. The two phase pipeline let us maximize the utility of our assessment effort, since many candidate pairs were dropped from consideration after Phase 1 after an element was assessed to be non-news. Initially sampling candidate documents and then for those judged to be news, pairing to documents with desired similarity as a three phase process might have increased the yield.

Assessing archival or historical reference collections where part of the visual material is not available is a challenge as workers have to make an effort to locate the important pieces of material first, before producing any labels.

Acknowledgments. We thank Jeff Pasternack for the use of his Maximum Subsequence Segmentation library (http://www.jeffreypasternack.com/software.aspx) for news article extraction.

References

1. Alonso, O.: Implementing crowdsourcing-based relevance experimentation: An industrial perspective. In: Information Retrieval, pp. 1–20 (2012)
2. Bendersky, M., Croft, W.B.: Finding text reuse on the web. In: WSDM, pp. 262–271 (2009)
3. Broder, A.Z., Glassman, S.C., Manasse, M.S., Zweig, G.: Syntactic clustering of the web. In: WWW, pp. 1157–1166 (1997)
4. Buckley, C., Salton, G., Allan, J.: Automatic retrieval with locality information using SMART. In: TREC-1, pp. 69–72 (1992)
5. Charikar, M.S.: Similarity estimation techniques from rounding algorithms. In: ACM STOC, pp. 380–388 (2002)
6. Chowdhury, A., Frieder, O., Grossman, D., McCabe, M.C.: Collection statistics for fast duplicate document detection. ACM TOIS 20(2) (2002)
7. Fetterly, D., Manasse, M., Najork, M.: Detecting phrase-level duplication on the world wide web. In: ACM SIGIR, pp. 170–177 (2005)
8. Gibson, J., Wellner, B., Lubar, S.: Identification of duplicate news stories in web pages. In: Proceedings of the 4th Web as CorpusWorkshop, WAC-4 (2008)
9. Gollapudi, S., Panigrahy, R.: Exploiting asymmetry in hierarchical topic extraction. In: ACM CIKM, pp. 475–482 (2006)
10. Henzinger, M.: Finding near-duplicate web pages: A large-scale evaluation of algorithms. In: ACM SIGIR, pp. 284–291 (2006)
11. Hoad, T.C., Zobel, J.: Methods for identifying versioned and plagiarized documents. J. Am. Soc. Inf. Sci. Technol. 54(3), 203–215 (2003)
12. Ioffe, S.: Improved consistent sampling, weighted minhash and ℓ_1 sketching. In: IEEE ICDM, pp. 246–255 (2010)
13. Kienreich, W., Granitzer, M., Sabol, V., Klieber, W.: Plagiarism detection in large sets of press agency news articles. In: Database and Expert Systems Applications, pp. 181–188 (2006)
14. Manasse, M., McSherry, F., Talwar, K.: Consistent weighted sampling. Technical Report MSR-TR-2010-73, Microsoft Research (2010)
15. Manber, U.: Finding similar files in a large file system. In: USENIX WTEC, Berkeley (1994)
16. Manku, G.S., Jain, A., Das Sarma, A.: Detecting near-duplicates for web crawling. In: WWW, pp. 141–150 (2007)
17. Muthitacharoen, A., Chen, B., Mazières, D.: A low-bandwidth network file system. In: ACM SOSP, pp. 174–187 (2001)
18. Najork, M.: Detecting quilted web pages at scale. In: ACM SIGIR (2012)
19. Pasternack, J., Roth, D.: Extracting article text from the web with maximum subsequence segmentation. In: WWW, pp. 971–980 (2009)
20. Patel, R.: UHRS overview, http://research.microsoft.com/en-us/um/redmond/events/fs2012/presentations/Rajesh_Patel.pdf
21. Schleimer, S., Wilkerson, D.S., Aiken, A.: Winnowing: Local algorithms for document fingerprinting. In: ACM SIGMOD, pp. 76–85 (2003)
22. Stein, B., zu Eissen, S.M., Potthast, M.: Strategies for retrieving plagiarized documents. In: ACM SIGIR, pp. 825–826 (2007)
23. Teodosiu, D., Bjørner, N., Gurevich, Y., Manasse, M., Porkka, J.: Optimizing file replication over limited-bandwidth networks using remote differential compression. Technical Report MSR-TR-2006-157, Microsoft Research (2006)
24. Theobald, M., Siddharth, J., Paepcke, A.: Spotsigs: robust and efficient near duplicate detection in large web collections. In: ACM SIGIR, pp. 563–570 (2008)
25. Tridgell, A., Mackerras, P.: The rsync algorithm. Technical Report TR-CS-96-05, Australian National University, Dept. of Computer Science (June 1996), http://rsync.samba.org

A Composite Kernel Approach for Detecting Interactive Segments in Chinese Topic Documents

Yung-Chun Chang[1,2], Chien Chin Chen[1], and Wen-Lian Hsu[2]

[1] Department of Information Management, National Taiwan University
No. 1, Sec. 4, Roosevelt Rd., Taipei City 10617, Taiwan (R.O.C)
[2] Institute of Information Science, Academia Simica
No. 128, Sec. 2, Academia Rd., Taipei City 11529, Taiwan (R.O.C)
{changyc,hsu}@iis.sinica.edu.tw, patonchen@ntu.edu.tw

Abstract. Discovering the interactions between persons mentioned in a set of topic documents can help readers construct the background of a topic and facilitate comprehension. In this paper, we propose a rich interactive tree structure to represent syntactic, content, and semantic information in text. We also present a composite kernel classification method that integrates the tree structure with a bigram kernel to identify text segments that mention person interactions in topic documents. Empirical evaluations demonstrate that the proposed tree structure and bigram kernel are effective and the composite kernel approach outperforms well-known relation extraction and PPI methods.

Keywords: Topic Mining, Interaction Detection, Rich Interactive Tree, Composite Kernel.

1   Introduction

The web has become a powerful medium for disseminating information about diverse topics, such as political issues and sports tournaments. While people can easily find documents that cover various perspectives of a topic, they often have difficulty assimilating the information in large documents. The problem has motivated the development of several topic mining methods to help readers digest enormous amounts of topic information. For instance, Nallapati et al. [13] and Feng and Allan [5] grouped topic documents into clusters, each of which represents a theme in a topic. The clusters are then connected chronologically to form a timeline of the topic. Chen and Chen [1] developed a method that summarizes the incidents of a topic's timeline to help readers quickly understand the whole topic. The extracted themes and summaries distill the topic contents clearly; however, readers still need to expend a great deal of time to comprehend the extracted information about unfamiliar topics.

Basically, a topic is associated with specific times, places, and persons [13]. Thus, discovering the interactions between persons mentioned in topic document can help readers construct the background of the topic and facilitate comprehension. For instance, if readers know the interactions of the key persons in a presidential campaign, they can understand documents about the campaign more easily. Interaction discovery is an active

R.E. Banchs et al. (Eds.): AIRS 2013, LNCS 8281, pp. 215–226, 2013.
© Springer-Verlag Berlin Heidelberg 2013

research area in the bioinformatics field. A number of studies [e.g., 15, 18] have investigated the problem of protein-protein interaction (PPI) which focuses on discovering the interactions between proteins mentioned in biomedical literature. Specifically, discovering PPIs involves two major tasks: *interaction detection* and *interaction extraction* [10]. The first task decomposes medical documents into text segments and identifies the segments that convey interactions between proteins. Then, the second task applies an information extraction algorithm to extract interaction tuples from the identified segments. In this paper, we focus on interaction detection in Chinese topic documents and identify text segments (called *interactive segments* hereafter) that convey interactions between persons. According to [17], such interactions exemplify types of human behavior that make people consider each other or influence each other. Examples of person interactions include compliments, criticism, collaboration, and competition. The detection of interactions between topic persons is more difficult than the task in PPI because the latter tries to discover permanent interactions between proteins, such as binding. By contrast, the interactions between persons are dynamic and topic-dependent. For instance, during the 2012 U.S. presidential election, the Democratic candidate, incumbent President Barack Obama often criticized Mitt Romney (the Republican candidate) for his political views. However, in the topic about Obama forming a new cabinet, President Obama broke bread with Mitt Romney at the White House, and even considered offering him a position in the new cabinet.

To detect interactive segments from topic documents effectively, we model interaction detection as a classification problem. We develop a rich interactive tree structure to represent syntactic, content, and semantic information in text segments. Furthermore, to identify interactive segments in topic documents, we develop a composite kernel classification method that integrates the tree structure with a bigram kernel to support vector machines (SVM) [7]. The results of experiments demonstrate that the composite kernel classification method is effective in detecting interactive segments. In addition, the proposed rich interactive tree structure and bigram kernel successfully exploits the syntactic structures, interaction semantics, and content of text segments. Consequently, the method outperforms the tree kernel-based PPI method [15]; the feature-based interaction detection method [2]; and the shortest path-enclosed tree (SPT) detection method [21], which is widely used to identify relations between named entities.

2   Related Work

Our research is closely related to relation extraction (RE), which was introduced as a part of the template element task in the sixth Message Understanding Conference (MUC-6). The goal of RE is to discover the semantic relations between the following five types of entities in text: persons, organizations, locations, facilities, and geo-political entities. Many RE methods [e.g., 4, 6, 8, 19] treat relation extraction as a supervised classification problem. Given a training corpus containing a set of manually-tagged examples of predefined relations, a supervised classification algorithm is employed to train an RE classifier to assign (i.e., classify) a relation type to a new text segment (e.g., a sentence). Feature-based approaches [6, 8] and kernel-based approaches [4, 19] are frequently used for RE. Feature-based methods exploit instances of positive and negative relations in a training corpus to identify effective text features for relation extraction. For instance, Hong [6] applied a set of features that included lexical tokens, syntactic structures, and semantic entity types, to SVM for relation extraction. In addition, Kambhatla [8] integrated lexical, syntactic, and semantic features of text into a maximum entropy model to extract relations between entities in the Automatic Context Extraction (ACE) datasets[1]. Feature-based methods often have difficulty finding effective features to extract entity relations. To resolve the problem, Collins and Duffy [3] developed a convolution tree kernel (CTK) that computes the similarity between two text segments in terms of the degree of overlap between their constituent parsing trees. A relation type is assigned to a text segment if the segment is similar to instances of the relation type in the training corpus. Moschitti [12] also utilized a CTK in the predicate argument classification task, which is a special case of relation extraction. Zhang et al. [21] further refined the convolution tree kernel by using the shortest path-enclosed tree (SPT) structure, which is the sub-tree enclosed by the shortest path linking two entities in a parsing tree. Their experiment results showed that the SPT successfully represents syntactic information in text and therefore achieves a superior relation extraction performance on the ACE dataset. In recent years, a technique that combines CTK with SPT has been applied by many RE methods [20].

Our research is also related to the protein-protein interaction (PPI) detection [14], which focuses on discovering protein interactions mentioned in biomedical literature. In medical research, determining protein interaction pairs is crucial to understanding both the functional role of individual proteins and the organization of the entire biological process. Originally, methods on PPI are feature-based. The methods extract text features from sentences to construct learning models, which are then used to detect sentences that mention protein interactions. For instance, Ono et al. [14] manually defined a set of syntactic rule-based features covering word and part-of-speech patterns to represent complex sentences. Xiao et al. [18] exploited maximum entropy models to combine diverse lexical, syntactic, and semantic features for PPI extraction. However, the above features hardly represent structured and dependency-based syntactic information in a constituent, which is essential for detecting interactions between proteins. To address the issue, several tree-based kernel approaches have been developed. For example, Qian et al. [16] defined a set of hand-crafted heuristics to identify the informative parts of a constituent parsing tree. The identified sub-trees are then examined by a classification model, which assigns a relation type to the proteins mentioned in a text segment. Miyao et al. [11] combined constituent parsing trees with a bag-of-words kernel to improve PPI performance. Recently, Qian and Zhou [15] developed a novel tree-based kernel. In their approach, the parsing tree of text generated by a constituent syntactic parser is revised by the shortest dependency path between two proteins derived from a dependency parser. Their experiment results show that the tree-based kernel is efficient in PPI detection. Our research differs from RE and PPI, which detect static and permanent relations. In contrast, our research detects interactions between persons, which are dynamic and topic-dependent.

---

[1] http://www.itl.nist.gov/iad/mig/tests/ace/

3   The Composite Kernel Approach for Interaction Detection

Figure 1 shows the proposed interaction detection method, which is comprised of three key components: *candidate segment generation*, *rich interactive tree construction*, and *composite kernel classification*. We regard interaction detection as a classification problem. The candidate segment generation component processes a set of Chinese topic documents to extract text segments (called *candidate segments* hereafter) that may mention interactions between topic persons. Then, each candidate segment is represented by a rich interactive tree that integrates the syntactic, content, and semantic information extracted from the segment. Finally, the composite kernel classification component combines the rich interactive tree with a bigram kernel for SVM to classify interactive segments. We discuss each component in detail in the following sub-sections.

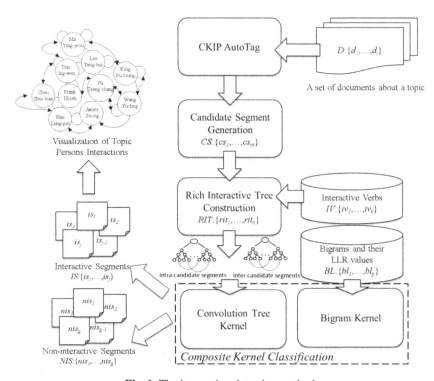

Fig. 1. The interaction detection method

3.1   Candidate Segment Generation Component

For a Chinese topic document d, we first apply the Chinese word segmentation system CKIP AutoTag[2] to decompose the document into a sequence of sentences $S = \{s_1,...,s_k\}$.

---

[2] http://ckipsvr.iis.sinica.edu.tw/

CKIP also labels the tokens in the sentences that represent a person's name. We observed that the rank-frequency distribution of the labeled person names followed Zipf's law [9], which means that many of them rarely occurred in the topic documents. Low frequency names usually refer to persons that are irrelevant to the topic (e.g., journalists), so they are excluded from the interaction detection process. Let $P = \{p_1,\ldots,p_e\}$ denote the set of important topic person names. For any topic person name pair (p_i, p_j) in P, the candidate segment generation component extracts text segments that are likely to mention the pair's interactions from the document. The component processes a set of document sentences S one by one and considers a sentence as the initial sentence of a candidate segment if it contains person name p_i (p_j). Because the interaction between p_i and p_j may be narrated by a sequence of sentences, we consider two types of candidate segments, namely, *intra-candidate segments* and *inter-candidate segments*. The component then examines the initial sentence and subsequent sentences until it reaches an end sentence that contains the person name p_j (p_i). If the initial sentence is identical to the end sentence, the process generates an intra-candidate segment; otherwise, it generates an inter-candidate segment. However, if there is a period in the inter-candidate segment, we drop the segment because, in Chinese, a period indicates the end of a discourse. In addition, if p_i (p_j) appears more than once in an inter-candidate segment, we truncate all the sentences before the last p_i (p_j) to make the candidate segment concise. By running all person name pairs of P over the topic documents, we obtain a candidate segment set $CS = \{cs_1,\ldots, cs_m\}$.

3.2   Rich Interactive Tree Construction Component

A candidate segment is represented by the rich interactive tree (RIT) structure, which is the shortest path-enclosed tree (SPT) of the segment enhanced by three operators: *branching*, *pruning*, and *ornamenting*. To facilitate comprehension of the operators, the inter-candidate segment shown in Fig. 2(a), which mentions the interaction between "歐巴馬(Barack Obama)" and "羅姆尼(Mitt Romney)", serves as an example.

(1) RIT branching
In [21], the authors show that the SPT is effective in identifying the relation between two entities mentioned in a segment of text. Given a candidate segment, the SPT is the smallest sub-tree of the segment's syntactic parsing tree that links person names p_i and p_j, but the information in the SPT is often insufficient for interaction detection. For instance, in Fig. 2(a), "延攬(recruit)" and the corresponding syntactic constituent are critical for recognizing the interaction between Obama and Romney. However, they are excluded from the SPT, as shown in Fig. 2(b). To include useful segment context information, the branching operator extends the SPT by examining the syntactic structure of the candidate segments. By default, we utilize the SPT as our RIT sapling. However, if the last person name and the verb following it form a verb phrase in the syntactic parsing tree, we treat the verb as a modifier of the last person name and extend the RIT to the end of the verb phrase. As shown in Fig. 2(c), the extended RIT includes richer context information than the SPT.

(2) RIT pruning
To make the RIT concise and clear, we prune redundant elements via the following procedures.

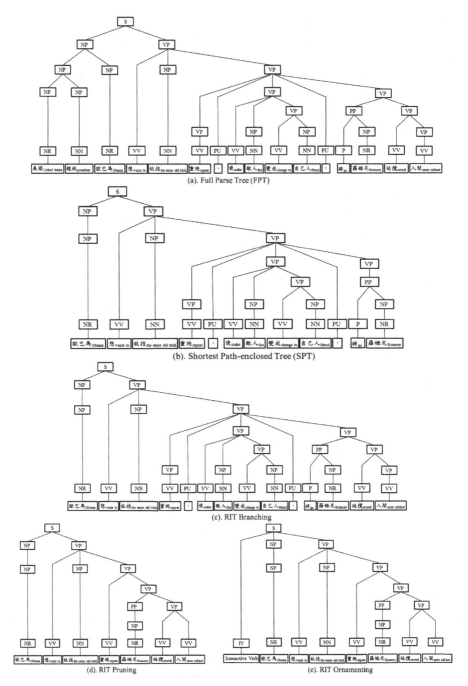

Fig. 2. The rich interactive tree construction procedure for an inter-candidate segment "美國總統歐巴馬想故技重施，使敵人變成自己人，將羅姆尼延攬入閣(United States President Obama wants to repeat the same old trick by changing from foe to friend and recruit Romney to join the cabinet)"

- Truncating inter-candidate segments: We observe that the middle sentences of inter-candidate segments do not normally contain information that can be used to detect interactions between persons. For instance, in Fig. 2(c), the middle sentence "使敵人變成自己人(changing from foe to friend)" is not useful for recognizing the interaction "延攬(recruit)" between Obama and Romney. In each inter-candidate segment, we remove all the middle sentences if the segment is composed of more than two sentences. The corresponding elements in the RIT and the punctuation are also deleted to concatenate the initial and end clauses.

- Removing indiscriminative RIT elements: Frequent words are not useful for expressing interactions between topic persons. For instance, the word "將(let)" in Fig. 2(c) is a common Chinese word and cannot discriminate interactive segments. To remove stop words and the corresponding syntactic elements from the RIT, we sort Chinese words according to their frequency in the text corpus. Then, the most frequent words are used to compile a stop word list. Moreover, to refine the list, person names and verbs are excluded from it because they are key constructs of person interactions.

- Merging duplicate RIT elements: We observe that nodes in an RIT are sometimes identical to their parents. For instance, the branch "重施$_{repeat}$→VV→VP→VP" in Fig. 2(c) contains two successive VP's. The tree-based kernel we use to classify a candidate segment computes the overlap between the RIT structure of the segment and that of the training segments. Because complex RIT structures degrade the computation of the overlap, we merge all duplicate elements to make the RIT concise.

(3) RIT ornamenting

Verbs are often good indicators of interactive segments, but not all verbs express person interactions. Highlighting verbs (called *interactive verbs* hereafter) closely associated with person interactions in an RIT would improve the interaction detection performance. We used the log likelihood ratio (LLR) [9], which is an effective feature selection method, to compile a list of interactive verbs. Given a training dataset comprised of interactive and non-interactive segments, the LLR calculates the likelihood that the occurrence of a verb in the interactive segments is not random. A verb with a large LLR value is closely associated with the interactive segments. We rank the verbs in the training dataset based on their LLR values and select the top 150 to compile the interactive verb list. For each RIT that contains an interactive verb, we add an IV tag as a child of the tree root to incorporate the interactive semantics into the RIT structure (as shown in Fig. 2(e)).

3.3   Composite Kernel

Kernel approaches are frequently used in SVM to compute a dot product (i.e., similarity) between instances modeled in a complex feature space. In this study, we employ a composite kernel approach that integrates the convolution tree kernel (CTK) [12] with a bigram kernel to determine the similarity between segments.

(1) Convolution Tree Kernel

We leverage the convolution tree kernel to capture the syntactic similarity between rich interactive trees. Specifically, the convolution tree kernel K_{CTK} counts the number of common sub-trees as the syntactic similarity between two rich interactive trees RIT_1 and RIT_2 as follows:

$$K_{CTK}(RIT_1, RIT_2) = \sum_{n_1 \in N_1, n_2 \in N_2} \Delta(n_1, n_2) \tag{1}$$

where $N1$ and $N2$ are the sets of nodes in $RIT1$ and $RIT2$ respectively. In addition $\Delta(n_1, n_2)$ evaluates the common sub-trees rooted at n_1 and n_2 and is computed recursively as follows:

(1) if the productions (i.e. the nodes with their direct children) at n_1 and n_2 are different, $\Delta(n_1, n_2) = 0$;
(2) else if both $n1$ and $n2$ are pre-terminals (POS tags), $\Delta(n_1, n_2) = 1 \times \lambda$;
(3) else calculate $\Delta(n_1, n_2)$ recursively as:

$$\Delta(n_1, n_2) = \lambda \prod_{k=1}^{\#ch(n_1)} (1 + \Delta(ch(n_1, k), ch(n_2, k))), \tag{2}$$

where $\#ch(n_1)$ is the number of children of node n_1; $ch(n, k)$ is the kth child of node n; and $\lambda (0<\lambda<1)$ is the decay factor used to make the kernel value less variable with respect to different sized sub-trees.

(2) Bigram Kernel

In addition to the syntactic similarity, we consider the content similarity. Since most Chinese keywords are comprised of two characters, we design the following bigram kernel $K_{BK}(.)$, which examines the bigrams in a candidate segment cs and a training segment ts to measure their content similarity as follows:

$$K_{BK}(cs, ts) = \sum_i \sum_j C(cs \cdot b_i, ts \cdot b_j), \tag{3}$$

where b_i and b_j represent the ith bigram of cs and j^{th} bigram of ts respectively. The function $C(.)$ returns the LLR value of $cs.b_i$ if $cs.b_i$ and $ts.b_j$ are identical; otherwise, it returns 0. As the LLR value of an interactive verb, a bigram's LLR value indicates the weight of bigram associated with interactive or non-interactive segments. Consequently, the value of K_{BK} will be high if the bigram overlap between cs and ts is large, and the overlapping bigrams are discriminative.

Finally, a composite kernel approach is used to interpolate the convolution tree kernel and the bigram kernel. We exploit polynomial interpolation [21], which integrates the two kernels as follows:

$$K_{COM}(cs, ts) = \alpha \cdot K_{BK}^P(cs, ts) + (1 - \alpha) \cdot K_{CTK}(RIT_{cs}, RIT_{ts}), \tag{4}$$

where cs denotes a candidate segment, ts is a training segment in the training corpus, and RIT_{cs} and RIT_{ts} are the corresponding rich interactive trees. $K^P(\bullet, \bullet) = (K(\bullet, \bullet) + 1)^d$ and it is the polynomial expansion of kernel $K(\bullet, \bullet)$. The parameters d and α are the polynomial degree and weight coefficient respectively.

4   Performance Evaluation

4.1   Experimental Setting

To the best of our knowledge, there is no official corpus for person interaction detection. The relations defined in the Automatic Context Extraction (ACE) datasets, such as *capital of,* are static and irrelevant to person interactions. Therefore, we compiled a data corpus for the performance evaluations, as shown in Table 1. It contains 10 topics related to political events from 2004 to 2012; and each topic consists of 50 Chinese news documents (all longer than 250 words) collected from Yahoo News. As mentioned in Section 3, many of the person names labeled by CKIP rarely occur in topic documents, and low frequency names usually refer to persons that are irrelevant to the evaluated topics. Hence, for each topic, we evaluated the person names whose frequency reached 70% of the total person name frequency in the topic documents. All the evaluated names represent important topic persons. We used the candidate segment generation algorithm to extract 1754 candidate segments from the topic documents, and two experts labeled 651 of the segments as interactive. The Kappa statistic of the labeling process is 0.834, which means that our data corpus is reliable.

Table 1. The statistics of data corpus

# of topics	10
# of topic documents	500
# of tagged person names	332
# of evaluated person names	67
# of person name pairs	276
# of interactive segments (intra)	338
# of interactive segments (inter)	313
# of non-interactive segments (intra)	380
# of non-interactive segments (inter)	723

We use the SVMLight package [7] to implement our composite kernel classification component; and set the polynomial kernel parameters d and α at 2 and 0.23 respectively, as suggested in [20, 21]. In addition, we use Moschitti's tree kernel toolkit [12] to develop the convolution kernel of an RIT. To derive credible evaluation results, we utilize the leave-one-out cross validation method [9]. The evaluation metrics are the precision rate, recall rate, and F1-score [9]. The F1 value is used to determine relative effectiveness of the compared methods.

4.2   Results and Discussion

The proposed RIT structure uses three operators, *branching, pruning,* and *ornamenting,* to enhance the SPT. In the following, we evaluate the performance of the operators to demonstrate the effectiveness of RIT. Table 2 shows the marginal performances of applying RIT branching, pruning, and ornamenting, denoted as +RIT$_{branching}$, +RIT$_{pruning}$, and +RIT$_{ornamenting}$ respectively. In addition, to demonstrate the efficacy of the proposed method, we detail the results of applying our composite kernel classification component (denoted as RIT+BK), which integrates the RIT with the bigram kernel. As shown in the table, only RIT branching (i.e., +RIT$_{branching}$) outperforms the SPT. This is because the branching operator correctly extends useful context information to remedy the context-limited problem of the SPT (see Sec. 3.2). The pruning operator further improves the system performance because it successfully eliminates indiscriminative and redundant RIT elements and thereby helps SVM learn representative syntactic structures of person interactions. The RIT ornamenting operator improves the F1 performance significantly. Moreover, the compiled interactive verbs are highly correlated with person interactions, so tagging them in the RIT structure helps our method discriminate interactive segments. Notably, our composite kernel classification component achieves the best performance. As the bigram kernel examines the content of segments to identify interactive segments, it does not conflict with the RIT, which analyzes syntactic and semantic information in the segments. Consequently, applying them together improves the system performance.

Table 2. Incremental contribution of the RIT branching, pruning, and ornamenting operators

RIT Structure	Intra-segment	Inter-segment	Micro-average	Macro-average
	Precision, Recall, F1-score (%)			
SPT	69.42 / 57.10 / 62.66	45.74 / 13.74 / 21.13	63.44 / 36.25 / 46.14	57.58 / 35.42 / 41.90
+RIT$_{branching}$	69.15 / 60.36 / 64.45	49.56 / 17.89 / 26.29	63.73 / 39.94 / 49.10	59.36 / 39.12 / 45.37
+RIT$_{pruning}$	76.76 / 64.50 / 70.10	43.66 / 18.81 / 27.25	62.70 / 43.59 / 51.43	60.21 / 42.16 / 48.68
+RIT$_{ornamenting}$	83.56 / 72.19 / 77.46	73.55 / 56.87 / 64.14	79.03 / 64.82 / 71.22	78.56 / 64.53 / 70.80
RIT + BK	**85.16 / 78.11 / 81.48**	**77.27 / 59.74 / 67.36**	**81.70 / 69.28 / 74.98**	**81.22 / 68.93 / 74.44**

In addition to the SPT and the proposed method, we evaluate FISER [2] and SDP-CPT [15]. To ensure the fairness of our evaluation, systems used for comparison are also developed using the SVMLight package [7] and Moschitti's tree kernel toolkit [12]. It has been shown that SPT is an effective relation extraction method [21]. FISER exploits nineteen features that cover parts-of-speech, context and semantic information in text to detect interactive segments in topic documents. SDP-CPT is an effective tree kernel-based PPI method that analyzes the syntactic dependency tree of a piece of text to identify protein interactions. In this paper, we use it to identify person interactions. As shown in Table 3, the proposed method significantly outperforms SPT and SDP-CPT. This is because SPT and SDP-CPT only examine the syntactic structures of candidate segments and cannot sense the semantics of person interactions in those segments. By contrast, our method analyzes the semantics (i.e., interactive verbs) and content (i.e., bigrams) of segments to identify person interactions. Hence, its performance is superior to that of SPT and SDP-CPT. It is noteworthy that SPT and SDP-CPT cannot deal with inter-candidate segments effectively. The reason is that the syntactic structure of inter-candidate segments is usually long and complex, and that affects the methods' detection performance. The proposed method prunes indiscriminative and redundant syntactic constructs in text, so it is effective in detecting inter-candidate segments. SDP-CPT is superior to SPT in terms of intra-candidate segments because the segments are usually short. The corresponding dependency structure is clear that the shortest dependency path of SDP-CPT represents person interactions well. Consequently, it performs better than SPT. FISER also outperforms SPT and SDP-CPT as it incorporates semantic features to distinguish interactive segments. However, FISER ignores the syntactic structures of text, which are effective in extracting the relations between named entities from text as demonstrated in [21]. It is therefore inferior to our method.

To summarize, the proposed rich interactive tree and bigram kernel approach successfully integrates the syntactic, semantic, and content information in text to identify interactive segments. Hence, it achieves the best precision, recall, and F1 scores among the compared methods, as shown in Table 3.

Table 3. The interaction detection results of the compared methods

System	Intra-segment	Inter-segment	Micro-average	Macro-average
	Precision, Recall, F1-score (%)			
SPT	69.42 / 57.10 / 62.66	45.74 / 13.74 / 21.13	63.44 / 36.25 / 46.14	57.58 / 35.42 / 41.90
SDP-CPT	74.34 / 66.86 / 70.40	44.79 / 13.74 / 21.03	67.25 / 41.32 / 51.19	59.57 / 40.30 / 45.72
FISER	80.70 / **81.66** / 81.18	**82.17** / 33.87 / 47.96	81.10 / 58.69 / 68.09	**81.44** / 57.76 / 64.57
Our method	**85.16** / 78.11 / **81.48**	77.27 / **59.74** / **67.36**	**81.70** / **69.28** / **74.98**	81.22 / **68.93** / **74.44**

5   Concluding Remarks

A topic is associated with specific times, places, and persons. Thus, discovering the interactions between the persons would help readers construct the background of the topic and facilitate document comprehension. To this end, we developed a method that combines the rich interactive tree structure and bigram kernel to analyze the syntactic, semantic, and content information in text. It then exploits the derived information to identify interactive segments in topic documents. Our experiment results demonstrate that the proposed method is effective and also outperforms well-known relation extraction and PPI methods.

In the future, we will investigate the syntactic dependency tree and sentimental information in candidate segments to incorporate further syntactic and semantic information into the rich interactive tree structure. We will also utilize information extraction algorithms to extract interaction tuples from interactive segments and construct an interaction network of topic persons.

Acknowledgements. This research was supported by the National Science Council of Taiwan under grant NSC 100-2628-E-002-037-MY3, NSC101-3113-P-001-004, and NSC102-3111-Y-001-012.

References

1. Chen, C.C., Chen, M.C.: TSCAN: A content anatomy approach to temporal topic summarization. IEEE Transactions on Knowledge and Data Engineering 24, 170–183 (2012)
2. Chang, Y.-C., Chuang, P.-H., Chen, C.C., Hsu, W.-L.: FISER: An effective method for detecting interactions between topic persons. In: Hou, Y., Nie, J.-Y., Sun, L., Wang, B., Zhang, P. (eds.) AIRS 2012. LNCS, vol. 7675, pp. 275–285. Springer, Heidelberg (2012)
3. Collins, M., Duffy, N.: Convolution kernels for natural language. In: Proceedings of Annual Conference on Neural Information Processing Systems, pp. 625–632 (2001)

4. Culotta, A., Sorensen, J.: Dependency tree kernels for relation extraction. In: Proceedings of the 42nd Annual Meeting on Association for Computational Linguistics, pp. 423–429 (2004)
5. Feng, A., Allan, J.: Finding and linking incidents in news. In: Proceedings of the 16th ACM International Conference on Information and Knowledge Management, pp. 821–830 (2007)
6. Hong, G.: Relation extraction using support vector machine. In: Proceedings of the 2nd International Joint Conference on Natural Language Processing, pp. 366–377 (2005)
7. Joachims, T.: Text categorization with support vector machine: learning withmany relevant features. In: Proceedings of 10th European Conference on Machine Learning, pp. 137–142 (1998)
8. Kambhatla, N.: Combining lexical, syntactic, and semantic features with maximum entropy models for extracting relations. In: Proceedings of the 42nd Annual Meeting of the Association for Computational Linguistics on Interactive Poster and Demonstration Sessions, pp. 178–181 (2004)
9. Manning, C.D., Schütze, H.: Foundations of statistical natural language processing, 1st edn. MIT Press, Cambridge (1999)
10. Miwa, M., Thompson, P., Ananiadou, S.: Boosting automatic event extraction from the literature using domain adaptation and coreference resolution. Bioinformatics 28(13), 1759–1766 (2012)
11. Miyao, Y., Sagae, K., Satre, R., Matsuzaki, T., Tsujii, J.: Evaluating contributions ofnatural language parsers to protein-protein interaction extraction. Bioinformatics 25(3), 394–400 (2009)
12. Moschitti, A.: A study on convolution kernels for shallow semantic parsing. In: Proceedings of the 42nd Annual Meeting of the Association for Computational Linguistics, pp. 21–26 (2004)
13. Nallapati, R., Feng, A., Peng, F., Allan, J.: Event threading within news topics. In: Proceedings of the 13th ACM International Conference on Information and Knowledge Management, pp. 446–453 (2004)
14. Ono, T., Hishigaki, H., Tanigam, A., Takagi, T.: Automated extraction of informationon protein-protein interactions from the biological literature. Bioinformatics 17(2), 155–161 (2001)
15. Qian, L.H., Zhou, G.D.: Tree kernel-based protein–protein interaction extraction from biomedical literature. Journal of Biomatical Informatics 45(3), 535–543 (2012)
16. Qian, L.H., Zhou, G.D., Zhu, Q.M., Qian, P.D.: Exploiting constituent dependencies fortree kernel-based semantic relation extraction. In: Proceedings of 22nd International Conference on Computational Linguistics, pp. 697–704 (2008)
17. Vernon, G.M.: Human interaction: An introduction to sociology, 1st edn. Ronald Press Co., New York (1965)
18. Xiao, J., Su, J., Zhou, G.D., Tan, C.L.: Protein-protein interaction extraction: a supervisedlearning approach. In: Proceedings of the 1st International Symposium on Semantic Mining in Biomedicine, pp. 51–59 (2005)
19. Zelenko, D., Aone, C., Richardella, A.: Kernel methods for relation extraction. The Journal of Machine Learning Research 3, 1083–1106 (2003)
20. Zhou, G.D., Qian, L.H., Fan, J.X.: Tree kernel-based semantic relation extraction with rich syntactic and semantic information. Journal of Information Science 180(8), 1313–1325 (2010)
21. Zhang, M., Zhang, J., Su, J., Zhou, G.D.: A composite kernel to extract relations between entities with both flat and structured features. In: Proceedings of the 21st International Conference on Computational Linguistics and the 44th Annual Meeting of the Association for Computational Linguistics, pp. 825–832 (2006)

Pornography Detection with the Wisdom of Crowds

Cheng Luo*, Yiqun Liu, Shaoping Ma, Min Zhang,
Liyun Ru, and Kuo Zhang

State Key Laboratory of Intelligent Technology and Systems
Tsinghua National Laboratory for Information Science and Technology
Department of Computer Science and Technology, Tsinghua University
Beijing 100084, China
c-luo12@mails.thu.edu.cn, {yiqunliu, z-m, msp}@mail.thu.edu.cn
lyru@vip.sohu.com, zhangkuo@sogou-inc.com
http://www.thuir.cn

Abstract. With rapid development of the Internet, much attention has been paid to the problem of children exposed to Internet pornography. Existing detection techniques, which mainly focus on pornography content analysis have obtained much success. However, they still meet challenges in practical Web environment due to the great computational costs and the difficulties in dealing with various pornography forms. We attempt to solve this problem from a new perspective with the wisdom of crowds in search engine click-through logs. Inspired by the idea that different pornography Web pages may be oriented by similar search keywords, a label propagation method on click-through bipartite graph is proposed which can locate pornography Web pages from a small set (a few hundreds) of manually labeled seed pages. Experiments performed on datasets collected from both English and Chinese search engines show that the proposed algorithm can identify different forms of Internet pornography both effectively and efficiently.

Keywords: Pornography Detection, Click-through Graph, Semi-supervised Learning.

1 Introduction

The Internet is increasingly prominent in young people's lives. A global Internet usage survey in the year of 2008 revealed that, among young people between 12 and 14 years old in the United States, 88% used the Internet; the percentage of Internet users in this age group was 100% in the United Kingdom, 98% in Israel, 95% in Canada, and over 70% in Singapore[1].

Coupled with the very large number of pornographic Web pages, concern has been raised that increasing accessibility could lead to a rise in pornography seeking among children and adolescents, with potentially serious ramifications for their sexual development. Ropelato's statistics shows that there are 420 million pornographic Web pages on the Internet, and 42.7% of Internet users saw pornographic content in 2006 [2].

---

* This work was supported by Natural Science Foundation (60903107, 61073071) and National High Technology Research and Development (863) Program (2011AA01A205) of China.

R.E. Banchs et al. (Eds.): AIRS 2013, LNCS 8281, pp. 227–238, 2013.

In many countries, sexual materials on the Internet are subject to censorship and legal restraints on their publication on the grounds of that they are obscene and that adolescents must be protected from inappropriate information[3][4]. However, the Internet has no boundaries, which means that pornography from a place where there are no effective restrictions imposed on Internet pornography can be easily accessed.

There have been several proposals to protect children from pornographic information on the Web. Traditional filtering techniques regard it as a classification problem which relies on features extracted from contents. Different types of page content are taken into account, such as texts, images and videos. Many approaches, including neural networks[5], statistical natural language processing[6] and pattern recognition[7], have been used to train a classifier to identify Web pages with pornographic content. Most of these content-based methods are usually dependent on the form of pornographic material and are limited by the efficiency of the algorithms. It is sometimes difficult to adopt these methods on practical Web environment due to the costs of a large amount of computational resources, especially for those with multimedia contents.

With explosive growth of Web resources, search engine become one of the most important portals for all kinds of Web pages including pornographic ones. The click behaviors on pornographic pages usually reflect the 'search for porn' intent of the users. Because of this similar search intent, different users often use similar queries to search for pornography on the Web. Therefore, the aggregation of a large number of user clicks is likely to provide valuable implicit evidence of whether one page being pornography or not. We can utilize the correlations between queries and URLs to detect pornographic Web pages. In other words, this approach can be regarded as a type of wisdom of crowds. Inspired by this idea, we try to utilize the correlations between queries and URLs to detect pornographic Web pages. We construct a bipartite graph from click-through data with queries/URLs as nodes and user clicks as edges. After that, a propagation based algorithm is performed on the graph to estimate the possibility of a Web page containing pornography.

The major contribution of this work is that we propose a highly efficient method to identify pornography based on a click-through bipartite graph. In this way, there is no need to crawl Web pages and perform time-consuming content analysis on them. To the best of our knowledge, we are among the first to address the problem of pornography detection using only click-through data.

The remainder of this paper is organized as follows: Section 2 provides a brief review of the related literature. Section 3 presents our motivations for detecting pornography, discusses our algorithm in detail and gives a proof of its convergence. In Section 4, an experimental validation is conducted, and the analysis of the results demonstrates that our method can detect pornography both effectively and efficiently. Our conclusions are given in Section 5.

2   Related Work

To fight against pornographic content on the Web, there are a number of major content-filtering approaches that are adopted, including the Platform for Internet Content Selection (PICS), URL blocking, keyword filtering, and intelligent content analysis.

PICS is a voluntary labeling system that allows Web publishers to associate labels or metadata with Web pages[8]. RSACi and SafeSurf are the two most popular PICS systems. Currently, Microsoft Internet Explorer and several other popular Web browsers offer PICS support with embedded PICS rating labels. However, PICS is not adopted by all major content providers and is not very reliable because of the mislabeling problem, either by negligence or by intent.

The second common approach focuses on URL blocking systems that restrict or allow access by comparing the requested Web page's URL with URLs in a stored list. Usually, two types of lists are maintained, namely a black-list and a white-list[9]. Lee et al. proposed an inverse chi-square based classification method and an incremental updating mechanism[10]. It's not necessary for URL blocking technology to consume a large amount of computational resources to perform content analysis. It also avoids the risk of virus infections. However, it is quite difficult to maintain a black-list for the practical Web environment because of the rapid growth of the Web pages.

Keyword filtering[11] blocks access to Web pages when the occurrence of harmful words or phrases exceeds a predefined threshold by comparing the text in the retrieved Web page to a dictionary of prohibited words and phrases. Gui-yang et al. proposed a keyword-matching method to filter harmful text[12]. One of the greatest challenges of keyword blocking is over-blocking. Nevertheless, it can be adopted to decide whether further content analysis is needed, which might require more time.

Intelligent content analysis attempts to gain a semantic understanding of the context on a Web page. Existing methods usually train a model using statistical computing of the discriminative features extracted from texts or images to make a decision. Lee et al. used the frequency that keywords appear in a text and the relevant Web page feature to train a neural network classifier[5]. Polpinij et al. proposed a filtering system that combines both text and images[7].

To summarize, while adopted to practical Web environment, PICS and URL blocking meet the problem of keeping prior information both credible and up-to-date. Keyword filtering can be regarded as a kind of content analysis method because they both rely on content features and suffer from the problem of obtaining and dealing with contents from Web pages that are usually noisy, ill-formed and unreliable. For those methods which adopt multimedia content features, they are further constrained by limited computational resources and high-efficiency requirement. Different from these detection methods, we utilize user behavior information stored in search engine click-through logs and therefore avoid the problem of (multimedia) content analysis of numerous Web pages. Because search engines have oriented a large part of user visits for most Web sites including pornography ones, we believe that this method can deal with most pornography problems on the Web although it doesn't require crawling these pages.

3 Pornography Detection with Click-Through Data

3.1 Motivation

Traditional pornography detection systems usually focus on various content analysis techniques. The major limitation of the approaches mentioned above might be the computational cost. The behavior of search engine users offers some information that is helpful for pornography detection. Pornographic Web pages usually select some attractive keywords that reflect the 'search for porn' intent to boost the ranking of their pages/sites in corresponding search results lists. In the other way, the users who want to access pornography by search engine most likely issue similar queries. Therefore, our basic assumption is that users share similar queries to search for pornography, which are most likely to be popular on Web pages that contain pornographic materials. The collection of queries that are related to a certain URL can be considered to be a profile of a Web page. If a large percentage of queries contain implicit pornographic intent, then the reason is most likely that there was pornographic content on the Web page.

By noticing the relationship between pornographic Web pages and porn-intent queries, we designed a label propagation algorithm on click-through data. First, a small number of seed pages are selected and each labeled with a pornographic score. Then, their labels are propagated on the click-through bipartite graph to identify other possible instances of pornography. The input comprises a set of labeled URLs, a set of unlabeled URLs and a set of constraints between URLs and the queries in the log. The goal is to find unlabeled pornographic pages from labeled pages.

3.2   Problem Formulation

Before formulating our problem, some definitions should be given.

I. Click-through data C and bipartite graph G.

The click log is a set of triples $\langle q, u, f_{qu} \rangle$, where q is a query, u is a URL, and f_{qu} is the times URL u is clicked when query q is issued. Define $Q = \{q | q \ appears \ in \ C\}$,and $U = \{u | u \ appears \ in \ C\}$. Click-through data C can be presented as another equivalent form – a click-through bipartite graph $G = (Q, U, E)$. There are two types of nodes in the graph, queries and URLs. For a certain edge(q, u), each q/u is assigned a score p_q/p_u, which denotes how likely this query/URL is to be a pornographic query/page. A sample portion of a bipartite graph constructed with search engine log, as shown in Figure 1.

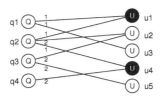

Fig. 1. An Example of Query-URL Bipartite Graph

The click-through graph can be constructed either at the page level or at the site level. In this study, we choose the URL itself to construct graph because the structure and content of a Web site might be very comprehensive.

II. Labeled Seed URL set L.

All of the URLs in L are selected from C(or G) and are manually labeled as porn. Formally, $L = \{u | u \ is \ labeled \ as \ a \ pornographic \ page\}$. We will discuss the construction details of L in Section 4.1.

III. URL result set RU and query result set QU.

Respectively, RU and QU contain all of the $\langle u, p_u \rangle$ and $\langle q, p_q \rangle$ pairs. After the algorithms ends, each URL u or query q in C(or G) will receive a score p_u/p_q, which denotes the possibility that this URL or query is a porn one.

Given $G = (Q,U,E)$ and $L \subset U$, the goal of this problem is to obtain the results set RU, which is by definition the set contains all of the possible pornographic pages in G.

3.3 Algorithm Design

First we will propose a label propagation algorithm for the the detection of pornography. Specifically, for every URL u, we could calculate the probability p_u of a certain URL u by incorporating all of the label information of its adjacent query nodes. Similarly we could calculate p_q for every query q. This procedure can be described formally as follows.

For $\forall q/u$, l_q/l_u denotes its label, which is **P** for pornography and **N** for non-pornography. Thus, every URL u in L would receive a label, such as **P** or **N**, which means that P(l_u=**P**)=1 or P(l_u=**P**)=0 initially while every URL u in the set $U - L$ has P(l_u=**P**)=0. Then, we have

$$P(l_u = \mathbf{P}) = \sum_{q:(q,u)\in E} (t_{qu}P(l_q = \mathbf{P})) \tag{1}$$

where

$$t_{qu} = \frac{\omega_{qu}}{\sum_{q':(q',u)\in E} \omega_{q'u}} \tag{2}$$

and

$$\omega_{qu} = f_{qu} \tag{3}$$

t_{qu} can be interpreted as the transition probability from query q to URL u and ω_{qu} is the weight of edge (q, u) in the bipartite graph. From equations (1) and (2) that q's label is determined by both its neighbors' labels and the relationship of the connection. The larger the value of ω_{qu} is, the more influence its corresponding node has on the label determining the label of q.

Similarly, for each query q in Q, the probability P(l_q=**P**) is computed as

$$P(l_q = \mathbf{P}) = \sum_{u:(q,u)\in E} (t_{uq}P(l_u = \mathbf{P})) \tag{4}$$

where

$$t_{uq} = \frac{\omega_{qu}}{\sum_{u':(q,u')\in E} \omega_{qu'}} \tag{5}$$

t_{uq} can be interpreted as the transition probability from URL u to query q.

Using the equations above, we can obtain P(l_q=**P**) and P(l_u=**P**) recursively for all of the queries and URLs in the click-through bipartite graph. A concise representation of this iterative process is stated as follows.

Suppose that there are $|Q|$ queries and $|U|$ URLs. Define possibility vectors as follows:

$$\mathbf{P_Q} = (P(l_{q1} = \mathbf{P}), P(l_{q2} = \mathbf{P})...P(l_{q|Q|} = \mathbf{P}))^T \qquad (6)$$

$$\mathbf{P_U} = (P(l_{u1} = \mathbf{P}), P(l_{u2} = \mathbf{P})...P(l_{u|U|} = \mathbf{P}))^T \qquad (7)$$

and the transition probability matrixes as:

$$\mathbf{T_{qu}} = (t_{qu})_{|Q| \times |U|} \quad and \quad \mathbf{T_{uq}} = (t_{uq})_{|U| \times |Q|} \qquad (8)$$

Then, in the ith iteration,

$$\mathbf{P_Q^i} = \mathbf{T_{qu}} \mathbf{P_U^{i-1}} \quad and \quad \mathbf{P_U^i} = \mathbf{T_{uq}} \mathbf{P_Q^{i-1}} \qquad (9)$$

It should be noted that the possibility of the labeled nodes should be clamped before each round of iteration, which means that all of the URLs in the seed set L should be re-assigned their initial label. In this way, the algorithm converges. The convergence will be proved in Section 3.5.

3.4   Bidirectional Edge Weight Definition

In the naive definition of the edge's weight shown in Equation(3), the weight is related only to the amount of clicks in click-through log. However, we find that in experiment the naive definition has to face the positive feedback problem and the reliability problem. More specifically, the problems that naive definition faces are stated as follows:

The Positive Feedback Problem. Label propagation algorithms or random walks on click-through bipartite graphs usually face positive feedback problems. For example, u_3 in Figure 1 is connected only to q_1. If we use the naive weight definition for iteration, after the first iteration, $P(l_{u3}=\mathbf{P})=0.5$. Before the second iteration begins, we will set $P(l_{u1}=\mathbf{P})$ to be 1 because u_1 is a seed URL. It is easy to see that $P(l_{u3}=\mathbf{P})$ is 0.75 after the second iteration and converges to 1 as the iteration process proceeds. The reason is that u_3 is a 1-degree node, which means that the score of u_3 will flow back to q_1; from this process, it obtains its original pornography score. We call this effect the positive feedback problem, which would magnify the noise and distort the final results.

Suppose that a non-typical user issues a query q to the search engine and then clicks a pornographic page while most of the other users use this query to navigate to ordinary sites. After applying this label propagation algorithm, all of the pornography scores of the URLs will converge to 1 after our algorithm is applied on the graph. Although the 1-degree nodes will be removed from results, it will most likely misinterpret the real explanation of other pages.

The Reliability Problem. Another important challenge that we must face is the reliability problem. In a naive label propagation algorithm, the score of one specific node comes from its adjacent nodes, and the weight of each score is related only to the weight of the edge, which is click times in the query log. However, the correlation between a

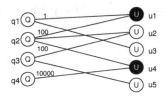

Fig. 2. A Case for the Reliability Problem

query node and an URL node should be determined by the click distribution of both of these nodes jointly. The naive definition fails to take this factor into account. Consider another sample portion of a bipartite graph, as shown in Figure 2.

Based on the naive weight definition, for query node q_2, the score of u_1 and u_4 are equally weighted. Let us focus on u_1 and u_4; u_1's clicks are almost all from q_2 while u_4 has the same clicks from q_2, but most of its clicks are from q_4. Obviously, the score from u_1 is more convincing for q_2 than for u_4.

Based on these two observations, we take the click distribution of both the query and the URL into account and propose a novel bidirectional edge weight definition. For edge $(q, u) \in E$, the weight is defined as:

$$\omega_{qu} = \frac{f_{qu}}{\left(\sum_{q':(q',u)\in E} f_{q'u}\right)\left(\sum_{u':(q,u')\in E} f_{qu'}\right)} \tag{10}$$

Essentially, our bidirectional edge weight definition will help the iterative process to magnify the influence from nodes with a close relationship and to minimize the effect of noisy nodes(e.g., a query seldom issued or URLs with few clicks). To summarize, the outline of our algorithm is as follows:

Algorithm 1. Pornography detection algorithm

Input: labeled seed set L, click-through data $C(G)$
Output: $P(l_u=\mathbf{P})$ for all URLs in G
 1: **repeat**
 2:    for $u \in L$, set $P(l_u=\mathbf{P}) = 1$ due to they are in seed set
 3:    for all $q \in Q$, calculate $P(l_q=\mathbf{P})$ as $\mathbf{P_Q} = \mathbf{T_{qu}P_U}$
 4:    for all $u \in Q$, calculate $P(l_u=\mathbf{P})$ as $\mathbf{P_U} = \mathbf{T_{uq}P_Q}$
 5: **until** Algorithm converges
 6: Output $P(l_u=\mathbf{P})$ for every URL u in U

3.5   Convergence of the Algorithm

Let us look into $\mathbf{M_{qu}}$ and $\mathbf{M_{uq}}$, each of whose rows is composed of nonnegative real numbers, with each row summing to 1. They are right stochastic matrixes. Consider $\mathbf{M_{uu}} = \mathbf{M_{uq}M_{qu}}$.

For each element t_{ij} in $\mathbf{T_{uu}}$, $\omega_{ij} = \sum_j \omega_{ik}\omega'_{kj}$, where $\omega_{ik} \in \mathbf{T_{uq}}$ and $\omega'_{kj} \in \mathbf{T_{qu}}$. Thus, we have

$$\sum_j t_{ij} = \sum_j \sum_k \omega_{ik}\omega'_{kj} = \sum_k \sum_j \omega_{ik}\omega'_{kj} = \sum_k \omega_{ik} \sum_j \omega'_{kj} = \sum_k \omega_{ik} = 1 \quad (11)$$

$\mathbf{T_{uu}}$ is also a right stochastic matrix. Next, look into $\mathbf{P_U}$; the iteration process can be represented as,

$$\mathbf{P_U^i} = \mathbf{T_{uu}}\mathbf{P_U^{i-1}} = \mathbf{T_{uq}}\mathbf{T_{qu}}\mathbf{P_U^{i-1}} \quad (12)$$

Let T_l be the top l rows of T(the labeled pages), and let T_u be the remaining u rows. Note that T_l never really changes because it is re-assigned in every iteration.Define the probability vector $\mathbf{P_U} = (\mathbf{P_L}\ \mathbf{P_R})$, where $\mathbf{P_L}$ are the top l rows of $\mathbf{P_U}$(the labeled pages) while $\mathbf{P_R}$ are the remaining rows. We can split $\mathbf{T_{uu}}$ into 4 sub-matrixes

$$T_{uu} = \begin{pmatrix} T_{ll} & T_{lr} \\ T_{rl} & T_{rr} \end{pmatrix} \quad (13)$$

It is noted that $\mathbf{P_L}$ never really changes. Zhu et al. proved that P_L converges to $(\mathbf{I} - \mathbf{T_{rr}})^{-1}\mathbf{T_{rl}}\mathbf{P_T}$ if $\mathbf{T_{uu}}$ is a right stochastic matrix[13]. Thus, the initial value of $\mathbf{P_L}$ is inconsequential. Using the same approach, we could prove that $\mathbf{P_Q}$ also converges.

4   Experiments and Discussion

4.1   Experiment Setups

The goal of our experiments is to evaluate whether our algorithm is effective in detecting pornographic Web pages. Given a labeled seed set L, our algorithm will return a list of pages that are ranked according to the possibility of being pornography. Seed pages are not included in this list, and the pages connected with only one query are also removed from this list because we think it is arbitrary to make a decision from only one query.

We use two datasets to build the bipartite graphs separately. From both datasets, we extract the information of the query, URL and timestamp. Private information is reduced as much as possible without introducing any ID or IP information.

The first query log dataset was collected from May 1, 2012 to May 14, 2012, with the help of a popular commercial search engine company in China. We pruned all of the query-URLs that appear only once in dataset because they could be noisy and potentially private. After that, the query log comprised 2,625,029 unique queries, 4,699,150 unique URLs and 72,106,874 query-URL pairs, which involve 717,916,107 individual clicks.

The second dataset is the America Online(AOL) query logs released in 2006 for research[1][14].This dataset contains 16,946,938 unique(normalized) queries, which were collected from March 1, 2006 to March 31, 2006.

---

[1] More information about the AOL dataset : http://www.gregsadetsky.com/aol-data/

4.2 Seed Set Selection and Labeling Criteria

The seed set contains labeled pages for our detection algorithm. On the Chinese dataset, we obtained a pornographic page list that contains 700 popular Web pages with the help of the same search engine that provides click-through data. This list was annotated by professional assessors, and each of the pages was double checked by us. A total of 691 pages appear in our click-through data, and we use them as the seed set for our algorithm.

For the English dataset, we picked out the URLs which contains 'sex' or 'porn' in the domain name to generate a candidate set. From the candidates, we randomly select a group of Web pages and have three human annotators with professional skills to label them as pornography or not. The labeling process stops when there are 500 pornographic pages in the seed set. The labeling criteria is stated as follows:

- NONPORN - The page contains no porn materials.
- BORDERLINE - The page contains some sexual material but no pornography.
- PORN - The page contains pornographic material.
- CAN NOT CLASSIFY - The page can not be accessed or the accessor could not classify it.

We also use these criteria to evaluate the results of our algorithm. It should be noted that we adopt a a relatively strict judgment rule on the pornographic pages in the seed selection step. All of the "BORDERLINE" pages are as "NONPORN", because the cost of mislabeling a normal page as pornography seed is much higher than the opposite situation. All of the "CAN NOT CLASSIFY" pages are removed in both the seed selection step and the result evaluation step.

When we labeled the seed set and results, some of the pages could not be accessed for different reasons. We attempted to label them according to the snapshots obtained from commercial search engines. If snapshots could not be obtained, we labeled them as "CAN NOT CLASSIFY".

4.3 Performance Comparison

We conducted our algorithm on both the Chinese dataset and the English dataset and compared their performances by the area under the receiver operating characteristic curve (AUC) and precision score.

We observed that the possibility of pornography changed little after 20 iterations. Specifically, we ran the iteration process 20 times in our experiment and then output the results. On a PC with a Intel CPU of 3.3 GHz and 32 GB RAM, the algorithm finished 20 iterations in 45 minutes on Chinese dataset and in 20 minutes on English dataset.

After the algorithm ends, we rank the URLs by the possibilities of pornography in descending order. Similar with the annotation approaches adopted by Gyöngyi et al in[15] , we separate the URLs into ten buckets sequentially and make sure that each bucket has an equal sum of possibilities that belong to the URLs in it. From each bucket, we randomly label 50 URLs with the criteria in Section 4.2, and we rank all of the URLs by their probabilities in descending order to generate the results list. We evaluate this list with both AUC and the precision, which are calculated based on the list. Content analysis based methods were not used for comparison in this step because their methods mainly focus on the classification of specific Web page sets while our method addresses the pornography detection within a large set of Web pages.

The experiment results are shown in Figure 3.

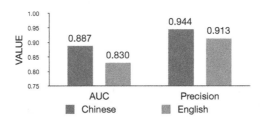

Fig. 3. Performance Comparison between the Chinese Dataset and the English Dataset

From this figure, we can see that the AUC values are greater than 0.83 and the precision values are greater than 0.91, which suggests that our algorithm is effective in detecting pornography. The performance on the Chinese dataset is slightly better than on the English dataset, probably because the size of the English dataset is smaller and the Chinese dataset is more up-to-date.

We also want to see our algorithm's performance on detecting various forms of pornography. We randomly selected 280 URLs from the Chinese results that represent pornography on the Web page and manually classified their main pornographic forms into 4 categories: Text, Image, Video and Others(e.g., pornographic audio, pornographic chatting service). Of all the Web pages, 42% represent pornography information with text, most likely because this venue is the cheapest way to attract traffic from a search engine. Other research regarding anti-spam[16] shows that pornographic terms are one of the most important categories that lead to spam pages on Chinese Web pages. In our experiment, we also find that many of the porn pages are spammy with the purpose of cheating.

4.4 Discussion: Pornography Score as Feature

In practical Web application, it is difficult to identify pornography Web pages only with the pornography scores given by our algorithm. However, we can use this method to generated candidates for further context analysis. This will help to reduce the number of pages to be analyzed. Also, we can use the pornography score as a feature to classify whether the Web pages contains inappropriate material. We implement a text-analysis method on the Chinese dataset and compare the performance by adding the pornography score(PS) as a feature. In our implementation, each Web page is represented as a vector of TF-IDF values. Classification results on 812 Web pages(4-fold cross-validation) is shown in Table 1.

Experiment result shows that we can get better classification performance by adding the feature of pornography scores. However, the improvement is limited because classifiers have already reach a quite good performance with only text features.

Table 1. Performance Comparision by Adding Pornography Score Feature

	Precision	Recall	F-measure
SVM	0.924	0.924	0.924
SVM+PS	**0.963**	**0.962**	**0.962**
Naive Bayes	0.919	0.909	0.907
Naive Bayes+PS	**0.952**	**0.952**	**0.952**

4.5 Discussion: Algorithm Robustness

Seed selection is very important in semi-supervised algorithms. Therefore, an experiment was conducted to see how robust our algorithm is. We only conducted this experiment on the Chinese dataset because it is newer and much larger than the English one. We randomly split the pornographic page seed set into 14 subsets(each one contains approximately 50 seed sites) and then gradually added the subsets into the seed set to observe the influences on the performance. The results are summarized in Figure 4.

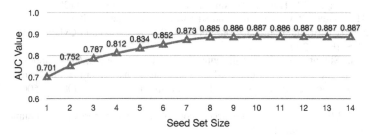

Fig. 4. Performance on Different Sizes of Seed Sets

It can be observed that our algorithm is very robust because it can achieve a relatively stable AUC value after only 400 pornographic pages are added. This experiment shows that our algorithm gained a stable performance in detecting pornography from a small number of seed set.

5   Conclusions

The very large number of pornographic Web pages has raised concerns about protecting children and adolescents. Traditional pornography detection methods focus on the extraction of textual or multimedia features from Web content, which consumes a large amount of computational resources. This paper attempts to solve the problem from a new perspective by proposing a novel method that is based on label propagation on a large scale bipartite click-through graph. First, a bidirectional edge weight definition is introduced to measure the correlation between the query and the URL reasonably. Then, we propagate the pornographic possibilities for all of the URLs iteratively on the click-through graph from a small set of seed URLs. The experiment that was conducted on both the Chinese and English datasets indicates that our method can detect pornography in different forms both effectively and efficiently. We hope that this method will be useful for protecting children and adolescents from pornography. For future work, we plan to combine our pornography detection method with traditional content-based methods to improve performance. More specifically, our algorithm could return a candidate set for further content analysis efficiently.

References

1. Guan, S.S.A., Subrahmanyam, K.: Youth internet use: risks and opportunities. Current opinion in Psychiatry 22(4), 351–356 (2009)
2. Ropelato, J.: Internet pornography statistics. TopTenReviews.com, internetfilter-review (2006), toptenreviews.com/internetpornographystatistics.html (accessed December 3, 2012)
3. Ybarra, M.L., Mitchell, K.J.: Exposure to internet pornography among children and adolescents: A national survey. CyberPsychology & Behavior 8(5), 473–486 (2005)
4. Goldstein, M.P.: Congress and the courts battle over the first amendment: Can the law really protect children from pornography on the internet. J. Marshall J. Computer & Info. L. 21, 141 (2002)
5. Lee, P.Y., Hui, S.C., Fong, A.C.M.: An intelligent categorization engine for bilingual web content filtering. IEEE Transactions on Multimedia 7(6), 1183–1190 (2005)
6. Ho, W.H., Watters, P.A.: Statistical and structural approaches to filtering internet pornography. In: 2004 IEEE International Conference on Systems, Man and Cybernetics, vol. 5, pp. 4792–4798. IEEE (2004)
7. Polpinij, J., Sibunruang, C., Paungpronpitag, S., Chamchong, R., Chotthanom, A.: A web pornography patrol system by content-based analysis: In particular text and image. In: IEEE International Conference on Systems, Man and Cybernetics, SMC 2008, pp. 500–505. IEEE (2008)
8. Resnick, P., Miller, J.: Pics: Internet access controls without censorship. Communications of the ACM 39(10), 87–93 (1996)
9. Lee, P.Y., Hui, S.C., Fong, A.C.M.: Neural networks for web content filtering. IEEE Intelligent Systems 17(5), 48–57 (2002)
10. Lee, L.H., Luh, C.J.: Generation of pornographic blacklist and its incremental update using an inverse chi-square based method. Information Processing & Management 44(5), 1698–1706 (2008)
11. Du, R., Safavi-Naini, R.: andW. Susilo. Web filtering using text classification. In: The 11th IEEE International Conference on Networks, ICON 2003, pp. 325–330. IEEE (2003)
12. Su, G., Li, J., Ma, Y., Li, S.: Improving the precision of the keyword-matching pornographic text filtering method using a hybrid model. Journal of Zhejiang University-Science A 5(9), 1106–1113 (2004)
13. Zhu, X., Ghahramani, Z.: Learning from labeled and unlabeled data with label propagation. Technical report, Technical Report CMU-CALD- 02-107, Carnegie Mellon University (2002)
14. Pass, G., Chowdhury, A., Torgeson, C.: A picture of search. In: Proceedings of the 1st International Conference on Scalable Information Systems, p. 1. Citeseer (2006)
15. Gyöngyi, Z., Garcia-Molina, H., Pedersen, J.: Combating web spam with trustrank. In: Proceedings of the Thirtieth International Conference on Very Large Data Bases, vol. 30, pp. 576–587. VLDB Endowment (2004)
16. Wei, C., Liu, Y., Zhang, M., Ma, S., Ru, L., Zhang, K.: Fighting against web spam: a novel propagation method based on click-through data. In: Proceedings of the 35th International ACM SIGIR Conference on Research and Development in Information Retrieval, SIGIR 2012, pp. 395–404. ACM, New York (2012)

Web Spam Detection: New Approach
with Hidden Markov Models

Ali Asghar Torabi[1], Kaveh Taghipour[2,*], and Shahram Khadivi[1]

[1] Human Language Technology Lab, Department of Computer Engineering and IT, Amirkabir
University of Technology
{a.torabi,khadivi}@aut.ac.ir
[2] Department of Computer Science, National University of Singapore, 13 Computing Drive,
Singapore 117417
kaveh@comp.nus.edu.sg

Abstract. Web Spam is the result of a number of methods to deceive search engine algorithms so as to obtain higher ranks in the search results. Advanced
spammers use keyword and link stuffing methods to create farms of spam pages. Most of the recent works in the web spam detection literature utilize graph
based methods to enhance the accuracy of this task. This paper is basically a
probabilistic approach that uses content and link based features to detect the
web spam pages. Since we observe there is a high connectivity between web
spam pages, we adopt a method based on Hidden Markov Model to exploit
conditional dependency of a sequence of hosts and their spam/normal class distribution of each host. Experimental results show that the proposed method can
significantly improve the performance of baseline classifier.

Keywords: web spam, link spam, hidden Markov models, ant colony optimization.

1 Introduction

Given the vast amount of information on the web, users have to use search engines to
locate the useful web pages that are relevant to their interests and inquiries. The goal
of search engines as the main information retrieval machines for web is to provide
higher ranks for pages that are most important and relevant to the users' query. Therefore, search engines need to distinguish the normal web pages from Spam pages so as
to prevent misleading of the users [1].

In order to find desired contents, Search engines use specific textual similarity
measures for determining the relevancy of a page and a query. To measure the importance of the pages there are several global query-independent indicators like Page
Rank [2] that often are calculated from web link structure [3]. While these two important criteria are used in search engines for evaluating web pages, a new industry of
Search Engine Optimizers has developed (SEO) recently. Malaga and Ross [4]

---

* This research was conducted at the time Taghipour was in AmirKabir University of Tehran.

R.E. Banchs et al. (Eds.): AIRS 2013, LNCS 8281, pp. 239–250, 2013.

grouped the SEO methods into two categories: White hat SEOs that stay within the guidelines by search engines and Web Spams (also known as Black hat SEOs) that violate the rules and transgress accepted norms. Web Spamming means boosting the rates of web pages undeservedly, without improving the true value of a page.

The web Spamming methods cause crucial problems for search engines, e.g., they tremendously waste the resources for indexing illegitimate web pages, unduly decrease the quality of retrieval process, damage search engines [5].

According to [3] Web Spam techniques can be categorized to the following types:

- Content Spam: If Spammers target textual similarity measures it is a content spam generation method. The content of pages is filled by popular words so that they are relevant to more popular users' queries. In [6] the term "keyword-stuffing" is used to refer to this method.
- Link Spam: There is a general belief that pages with more incoming links are more popular and important than others. As mentioned, Search engines use some link-based measures like Page Rank to assess importance of a web page. Spamming methods that intend to influence these algorithms are named Link Spam. Spammers create so many pages that link to the target page to increase its popularity.

Extensive researches have been presented to reduce the impact of Web Spam. Most of the proposed solutions such as [6, 7] considered Web Spam detection as a classification problem. This research considers hosts as train/test instances and features are extracted from content of pages within the host and links among them. Previous experiences show that in Web Spam Detection, instances are not independent and data labels are unbalanced [8]. In this paper we present a new approach to handle biasness of data and model the dependency between hosts. To our knowledge this is the first time that Hidden Markov Model (HMM) is used to do this. The proposed system starts by building a classifier based on Aggregating One Dependence Estimators (AODE) [9]. Hidden Markov Model helps us to consider the dependency of web hosts during the prediction process and boost the performance of AODE. A simple method to adopt HMM for this task is to find the most frequent sequences of visiting hosts. In the proposed system, Ant Colony Optimization algorithm is used to generate the required sequences of hosts.

The paper is organized as follows. In Section 2, we provide an overview of previous works. In Section 3, feature selection and classification method are described. In Section 4, we propose a method that extracts sequences of hosts that we need to apply HMM on these sequences. Finally, we conclude by summarizing key principals of our approach.

2   Related Work

Several automatic techniques for web spam detection have been presented in the literature. Fetterly et al. [10] justified the statistical difference between machine generated spam pages and normal web pages. They presented some features based on page content, linkage structure and page evolution. In their next following paper [6] they also proposed several content based features and a decision tree, classifying Spam and Normal pages. Piskorski et al [11] studied on some linguistic features and discovered several discriminative features that are available publicly for others. Moreover in [12] Araujo et al, They offered a new approach rooted in combination of link based features and language model based ones. They observed the semantic relation between linked pages and found them to be useful to improve the performance of the classification task.

In addition to traditional learning models many papers used graph based methods to boost the performance of Web Spam Detection by considering topological dependency between the hosts. Link propagation as one the most popular methods in graph based problems has been widely used in web spam detection. Becchetti et al. [13] performed a statistical analysis on link structure of web pages in a large collection. Their experiments show that link based metrics like TrustRank and Truncated Page-Rank can improve the performance of Web Spam classifiers. TrustRank separates an initial set of good pages. It starts with a seed of good pages and then follows the link structure to propagate the rank thorough the related pages. Implementation of this method is described in [14]. Truncated PageRank is a version of PageRank that ignores the direct contribution of near neighbors according to a damping function. Experiments by Becchetti and others in [13, 15] show that Truncated PageRank is a discriminative feature. Castillo et al [5] proposed stacked graphical learning for propagating labels across the web graph. In addition to content and link based features the average of probability of Spam for neighboring hosts is added to the feature vector of each host and thus is considered in decision process.

Link refinement, elimination and regularization methods are other methodologies that exploit link structure to improve performance of basic classifiers. Elimination of Nepotistic links is one of the proposed method to reduce the impact of the link stuffing by removing certain links of the web graph [16]. Jacob Abernethy et al in [17] presented a graph regularization based algorithm, WITCH, that learns simultaneously from graph structure, content and link based features.

There are also other works and experiences in this regard. For additional studies on the above mentioned topics, you can refer to the Survey on Web Spam Detection by Nikita Spirin and Jiawei Ha [8] , that is a good survey covering many papers and proposed systems to date.

3   Classification and Feature Selection

The following paper has tested and trained the proposed method by WebSpam-Uk2006 [18] which is a public Web Spam dataset. This collection contains 11402 hosts from the .uk domain. For each host 263 features have been extracted from links and content of pages. Additional information about feature types and list of them is available at [6, 13]. In this dataset, 7473 hosts are labeled by a group of volunteers into three categories of Spam, Normal and Borderline. Here, we use the first two categories to build a model that recognizes spam hosts from normal ones.

In this research several classifiers such as decision trees, neural networks and statistical classifiers were examined and compared against each other. We use F-measure value as a criterion to compare efficiency of different classification methods. The results showed that AODE was superior to other competitive methods. AODE is a statistical classifier that achieves higher accuracy by averaging over all naïve Bayes models. The core of above mentioned classifier is to consider weaker independency assumption for Naïve Bayes. Thus it has less error rate and still is as fast as possible in training and test phases. In comparison with other methods like Bayesian networks, AODE benefits from the advantage of not performing model selection while it's accuracy is comparable with none parametric models like decision trees and neural networks [9]. The proposal has taken advantage of AODE by using its implementation in Weka [19].

A subset of two sorts of link based and content based features have been used in this paper. The paper approach is to use Wrapper Feature Selection method with which evaluates features by using a learning model [20] and chooses the most discriminative and relevant features. After feature selection process, only 22 of 263 features have been selected. By using cross validation and a bidirectional search an optimal feature subset has been found that results the best accuracy for AODE classifier. Table 1 shows the performance for different feature selection models and AODE classifier. In this paper "true positive" and "false positive" rates are respectively about "the rate of correctly detected spam hosts" and "normal hosts that are detected as spam incorrectly". Tables 1 and 3-5 are result of cross validation with 10 folds.

Table 1. Comparision of feature selection methods

	Correlation Attribute Evaluation	Principal Component Analysis	Wrapper feature selection
True positive rate	74%	77.2%	81.2%
False positive rate	9%	10.4%	4.9%
F-Measure	0.72	0.724	**0.825**

Reported results show that Wrapper feature selection improves the result by increasing true positive and reducing false positive ratio which has resulted in the selection of AODE and the new feature space to setup the proposed system.

4   Smoothing

In this Section, the research proposes a method to detect Web spam by using topological dependency between hosts. It started by representing the web spam detection as a graph based problem. In this presentation each host is a node in graph $G = (V, E)$ of Web hosts V and links E. For each pair of nodes i and j we have $e(i, j)$ the number of links from host i to j.

Most of the traditional classifiers presuppose that instances are independent and identically distributed. But in web spam problem, samples are topologically dependent [21, 22]. Therefore lots of latent information in the link structure between hosts are missed if we confine ourselves to use only the base classifier in the previous Section. The proposed system is based on smoothness assumption of semi-supervised learning. According to this, nodes which are closer to each other are more likely to share a label [23]. In web graph for each pair of nodes the paper declared a closeness factor:

$$\log{(1 + e(i,j))} \tag{1}$$

On the other hand Castillo et al [5] showed in their experiments that normal nodes tend to be linked by very few Spam nodes and they mainly link to other normal nodes while Spam nodes are mainly linked to Spam nodes. In Table 2 the results of our study on WebSpam-Uk2006 dataset are shown. Probability of transition from a spam host to a normal host is 23% and that is much lower than transition to other spam host.

Table 2. Dependency of Spam and Normal classes

	Spam	*Normal*
Spam	77%	23%
Normal	13%	87%

Considering the conditional dependency of Spam and Normal hosts to each other and topological dependency of hosts in the web graph, and also hidden category of each host; it is intuitively obvious that Hidden Markov Model would be a useful learning schema to build a pattern of dependency between nodes and handle imbalance between spam and normal labels.

HMM is a probabilistic method to model sequence of data [24]. Indeed, to take HMM into use we need a sequence of connected hosts. This paper proposes Ant colony optimization algorithm to extract sequences of related hosts according to similarity measure (1). Fig. 1 presents the workflow of the proposed system.

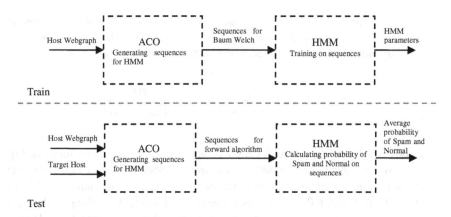

Fig. 1. Web spam detection workflow

4.1   Ant Colony Optimization

In computer science, Ant Colony Optimization refers to a general propose method of finding the best solution of an optimization problem. In ACO, artificial ants build solutions and exchange information by depositing pheromone on the ground in order to remark favorable path to the optimization problem [25]. To use ACO it is needed to represent the problem space as a graph and declare three fundamental components:

- Edge selection: Artificial ants move from vertex to vertex along the edges of the graph. A stochastic mechanism is hired to guide each ant to choose edge (i, j) in each step of walk. This mechanism uses a probability distribution based on heuristic function η_{ij} and pheromone values τ_{ij}. The probability function is defined as:

$$P_{ij}{}^k = \begin{cases} \dfrac{\tau_{ij} \times \eta_{ij}}{\sum_{l \in N(i)} \tau_{il} \times \eta_{il}} & if (i, j) \in N(i) \\ 0 & otherwise \end{cases} \tag{2}$$

In equation (2) τ_{ij} and η_{ij} are "the pheromone value on edge (i, j)" and "heuristic function", respectively. $N(i)$ represents a set of the neighboring hosts l pointing to host i that has not yet visited by ant k.

- Heuristic function: The heuristic function has been defined using the assumptions we mentioned at the beginning of this Section. Equation (3) illustrates heuristic function η_{ij} that is the same as similarity measure in equation (1). Therefore an ant that is in the web host i chooses an edge (j, i) that has more input links than others.

$$\eta_{ij} = log \left(1 + e(j, i)\right) \tag{3}$$

- Pheromone update: According to [25] each artificial ant should update pheromone on edge (i, j) after each step of walk to communicate with other ants. These pheromone's updates incrementally specify the best paths of connected hosts.

$$\tau_{ij}(t) = (1 - \alpha) \times \frac{\tau_{ij}(t - 1)}{t} + \alpha \times \frac{e(j, i)}{\sum_{l \in N(j)} e(j, l)} \tag{4}$$

This study combines offline and local pheromone updates [25] in one formula. Equation (4) explains the defined pheromone's update function. $\tau_{ij}(t)$ represents the value of pheromone on edge (i, j) in iteration t and $e(j, i)$ is the number of links from j to i. Real number $0 < \alpha < 1$ is a decay coefficient. According to the proposed equation, amount of pheromone on each edge decreases over time. Higher value of α gives a greater chance to other paths to be selected by edge selection method in the next following iterations and as a result we will have more paths of connected hosts.

4.2   Hidden Markov Model

HMM is a stochastic extension of Markov Model with hidden states. In this model, states are not visible but probability of states and transition between them are given by state dependent functions [24, 25]. This paper defined two states Spam and Normal. The visible output and emission probability functions are respectively the 22 dimensional feature vectors and AODE model that was presented in Section 3. Since AODE is a probabilistic model [9] that here predicts posterior class probabilities, this model is appropriate to be used as emission probability of HMM.

Fig. 2. Sequences of hosts to host t

In training phase, Baum Welch algorithm is run on generated sequences from ACO to estimate the transition matrix a_{ij} and the initial probabilities π_i. All HMM parameters are recalculated in maximization step of Baum Welch except emission probabilities $b_i(X)$ that have already been estimated using an AODE classifier.

In test phase, the label of host t will be predicted by the proposed system. It first extracts sequences of hosts that are linked to the t by ACO. Fig. 2 illustrates an example of host sequences with length three that are linked to the target web host. The forward algorithm, Equation (5) is used to calculate probability of normal and spam hosts according to each sequence.

$$P(Z_k|X_{1:k}) \; \forall Z_k \in \{spam, normal\}$$

$$= \sum_{Z_{k-1} \in \{spam, \; normal\}} P(Z_k, Z_{k-1}, X_{1:k}) \tag{5}$$

$$= \sum_{Z_{k-1} \in \{spam, \; normal\}} P(X_k|Z_k) \times P(Z_k|Z_{k-1}) \times P(Z_{k-1}, X_{1:k-1})$$

$P(X_k|Z_k = \text{spam})$ is the probability of observing feature vector X_k in the state spam. $P(Z_1, X_1)$ refers to the initial probabilities of spam and normal and $P(Z_k|Z_{k-1})$ is the transition probability distribution. Four possible transitions are as follows:

— $Spam \rightarrow Spam$
— $Spam \rightarrow Normal$
— $Normal \rightarrow Spam$
— $Normal \rightarrow Normal$

Finally to predict the label of target host, average probabilities of $P(Z_k = \text{spam}|X_{1:k})$ and $P(Z_k = \text{nomal}|X_{1:k})$ over all sequences are used. In Table 3, the performance of the new classification method is shown.

Table 3. Smoothing by one HMM

	AODE	HMM
True positive rate	81.2%	81.8%
False positive rate	4.9%	4.3%
F-Measure	0.825	**0.836**

4.3   Multiple HMMs

So far, we only use the output of ACO algorithm in the system, i.e., we only use the best sequences to train a single HMM. In this Section, we use the values of pheromones to better estimate the HMM parameters. We assume the pheromone values of each edge as a measure of conditional dependency between two hosts. Here, we introduce a technique for label smoothing by using multiple HMMs.

In Fig. 3, the results of our experiments on .uk 2006 dataset are shown. In these experiments, we first use ACO with 100 artificial ants and then we extract sequences with length 2. Then a discretization with 10 equal depth bins is performed on pheromone values. Afterwards, we train a Hidden Markov Model for each bin, so we have ten different HMMs. Prior probability of spam $P(Z_1 = \text{spam})$ and transition probability $P(Z_2 = \text{spam}|Z_1 = \text{spam})$ for each bin are presented in Fig. 3. According to the reported parameters, the label of destination point is conditionally more dependent on the source point when there is more pheromone on the edge between them. Furthermore, it illustrates that probability of spam has an inverse relation with amount of pheromone.

The result of the above experiment is convincing enough to make use of different HMM components to model relation between points with different dependency values (Pheromones). For sequences with length two implementation of such a system with non-parametric models is straightforward. But for sequences with length of three or higher we should present a technique that considers pheromones in edges in depth two or higher in addition to pheromones in first step of sequences. Please note that since we aim to use non-parametric models in HMM, we need to discretize the edge values so as to decrease the amount of sparsity.

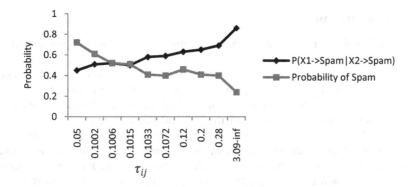

Fig. 3. Dependency between HMM parameters and pheromone value

In this paper two approaches were examined for sequences with length three. In the first one, a weight for each sequence of two edges was defined by multiplication of pheromones of the edges. Afterwards the binning was performed on these weights. In the second approach, the binning is applied two times. First on the edges connected to the target host, and second time on the edges connected to the neighbors of the target host.   The binning algorithm introduces ten bins in each run. Therefore, a 10×10 table of 100 HMM component was created. Each sequence was assigned to one of the HMM components according to the amount of pheromone on their edges. For example if the first edge of sequences belonged to bin 3 and second edge belonged to bin 6 the system assigned the sequence to the HMM number 18 in row 3 and column 6 of the pheromone table.

The train and test phases are the same as before; unless $P(Z_k = \text{spam}|X_{1:k})$ and $P(Z_k = \text{nomal}|X_{1:k})$ should be computed according to the appropriate HMM component. Table 4 shows the result of the experiments.

Table 4. Camparison of proposed approaches

	HMM	Multiple HMMs of order 2	Multiple HMMs of order 3 first approach	Multiple HMMs of order 3 second approach
True positive rate	81.8%	88.1%	87.6%	91.7%
False positive rate	4.3%	6.5%	6.7%	6.9%
F-Measure	0.836	0.843	0.838	**0.859**

As you can see in Table 4, the proposed system achieves an improvement by using several HMM components on sequences with length 2. The performance of system but then is reduced when first approach was used to model sequences with length 3. However it is raised again when the second approach is used.

According to our experiments the general trend of using this method is a considerable increase of 10 percent in detection rate of baseline classifier while F-measure has also improved from 0.825 to 0.859. Next Section is a comparison of the result of this study and other existing methods to show to what extent the application of HMMs is contributed to the improvement for Web spam detection.

5   Conclusion

For many applications like Web spam detection the i.i.d assumption would fail to exploit dependency patterns between data points. This study proposed a system to detect web spam according to the content and link based features and dependency between points in web host graph. To our knowledge this is the first attempt to boost the performance of web spam detection using Hidden Markov Models. Table 5 shows a comparison between the presented method and other systems according to the F-Measure value. Experimental results show that the proposed method is effective and yields better performance in comparison with other works on the same feature set. Geng et al in [26] boosted the performance of classification task using under sampling method and reached F-measure 0.759. Castillo et al [5] as one of the most significant studies on the web spam detection reports F-Measure 0.763 using stacked graphical learning. Benczúr et al [27] reported F-measure 0.738 following the same methodology as Castillo et al [5].

To compare the performance of the proposed system with the results of the participants in web spam challenge [28] The study also evaluated the proposed method on the test set provided by the organization.

Table 5. Comparing performance of systems

Web Spam Detection system	F-Measure	
	Test Set	Cross Validation
Our Proposed system	0.90	0.85
Castillo et al	NA	0.76
Geng et al	0.87	0.75
Benczúr et al	0.91	0.73
Filoche et al	0.88	NA
Abou et al	0.81	NA
Fetterly et al	0.79	NA
Cormack	0.67	NA

One disadvantage of the proposal system is the number of the needed HMMs in the second approach. For instance using the second approach needs to create 1000 HMM models for sequences of length 4; which is a proof that it is time consuming to estimate parameters of these HMMs. In near future, we plan to propose a HMM with parametric transition probabilities that can handle the weights of the edges. Moreover we intend to employ a new content based feature using language modeling techniques. Based on the ongoing researches and studies on the topic we strongly believe that it is possible to achieve better performance using these new features.

References

1. Henzinger, M.R., Motwani, R., Silverstein, C.: Challenges in web search engines. In: ACM SIGIR Forum, pp. 11–22. ACM (2002)
2. Bianchini, M., Gori, M., Scarselli, F.: Inside pagerank. ACM Transactions on Internet Technology (TOIT) 5, 92–128 (2005)

3. Gyongyi, Z., Garcia-Molina, H.: Web spam taxonomy. In: First International Workshop on Adversarial Information Retrieval on the Web, AIRWeb 2005 (2005)
4. Malaga, R.A.: Search Engine Optimization—Black and White Hat Approaches. Advances in Computers 78, 1–39 (2010)
5. Castillo, C., Donato, D., Gionis, A., Murdock, V., Silvestri, F.: Know your neighbors: Web spam detection using the web topology. In: Proceedings of the 30th Annual International ACM SIGIR Conference on Research and Development in Information Retrieval, pp. 423–430. ACM (2007)
6. Ntoulas, A., Najork, M., Manasse, M., Fetterly, D.: Detecting spam web pages through content analysis. In: Proceedings of the 15th International Conference on World Wide Web, pp. 83–92. ACM (2006)
7. Mahmoudi, M., Yari, A., Khadivi, S.: Web spam detection based on discriminative content and link features. In: 2010 5th International Symposium on Telecommunications (IST), pp. 542–546. IEEE (2010)
8. Spirin, N., Han, J.: Survey on web spam detection: principles and algorithms. ACM SIGKDD Explorations Newsletter 13, 50–64 (2012)
9. Webb, G.I., Boughton, J.R., Wang, Z.: Not so naive Bayes: aggregating one-dependence estimators. Machine Learning 58, 5–24 (2005)
10. Fetterly, D., Manasse, M., Najork, M.: Spam, damn spam, and statistics: Using statistical analysis to locate spam web pages. In: Proceedings of the 7th International Workshop on the Web and Databases: Colocated with ACM SIGMOD/PODS 2004, pp. 1–6. ACM (2004)
11. Piskorski, J., Sydow, M., Weiss, D.: Exploring linguistic features for Web spam detection: A preliminary study. In: Proceedings of the 4th International Workshop on Adversarial Information Retrieval on the Web, pp. 25–28. ACM (2008)
12. Araujo, L., Martinez-Romo, J.: Web spam detection: new classification features based on qualified link analysis and language models. IEEE Transactions on Information Forensics and Security 5, 581–590 (2010)
13. Becchetti, L., Castillo, C., Donato, D., Leonardi, S., Baeza-Yates, R.: Link-based characterization and detection of web spam. In: 2nd Intl. Workshop on Adversarial Information Retrieval on the Web (AIRWeb), pp. 1–8 (2006)
14. Gyöngyi, Z., Garcia-Molina, H., Pedersen, J.: Combating web spam with trustrank. In: Proceedings of the Thirtieth international conference on Very Large Data Bases, vol. 30, pp. 576–587. VLDB Endowment (2004)
15. Becchetti, L., Castillo, C., Donato, D., Leonardi, S., Baeza-Yates, R.: Using rank propagation and probabilistic counting for link-based spam detection. In: Proc. of WebKDD (2006)
16. Davison, B.D.: Recognizing nepotistic links on the web. Artificial Intelligence for Web Search, 23–28 (2000)
17. Abernethy, J., Chapelle, O., Castillo, C.: Web spam identification through content and hyperlinks. In: Proceedings of the 4th International Workshop on Adversarial Information Retrieval on the Web, pp. 41–44. ACM (2008)
18. Yahoo! Research: Web Spam Collections, http://barcelona.research.yahoo.net/webspam/datasets/ Crawled by the Laboratory of Web Algorithmics, University of Milan, http://law.dsi.unimi.it/ (retrieved August 8, 2012)
19. Hall, M., Frank, E., Holmes, G., Pfahringer, B., Reutemann, P., Witten, I.H.: The WEKA data mining software: an update. SIGKDD Explor. Newsl. 11, 10–18 (2009)

20. Kohavi, R., John, G.H.: Wrappers for feature subset selection. Artificial intelligence 97, 273–324 (1997)
21. Menczer, F.: Mapping the semantics of Web text and links. IEEE Internet Computing 9, 27–36 (2005)
22. Chakrabarti, S., Joshi, M.M., Punera, K., Pennock, D.M.: The structure of broad topics on the web. In: Proceedings of the 11th International Conference on World Wide Web, pp. 251–262. ACM (2002)
23. Chapelle, O., Schölkopf, B., Zien, A.: Semi-supervised learning. MIT Press (2006)
24. Rabiner, L., Juang, B.: An introduction to hidden Markov models. IEEE ASSP Magazine 3, 4–16 (1986)
25. Dorigo, M., Birattari, M., Stutzle, T.: Ant colony optimization. IEEE Computational Intelligence Magazine 1, 28–39 (2006)
26. Geng, G.-G., Wang, C.-H., Li, Q.-D., Xu, L., Jin, X.-B.: Boosting the performance of web spam detection with ensemble under-sampling classification. In: Fourth International Conference on Fuzzy Systems and Knowledge Discovery, FSKD 2007, pp. 583–587. IEEE (2007)
27. Benczúr, A., Bíró, I., Csalogány, K., Sarlós, T.: Web spam detection via commercial intent analysis. In: Proceedings of the 3rd International Workshop on Adversarial Information Retrieval on the Web, pp. 89–92. ACM (2007)
28. Web Spam Challenge (2007), http://webspam.lip6.fr/

Building a Microblog Corpus for Search Result Diversification

Ke Tao, Claudia Hauff, and Geert-Jan Houben

TU Delft, Web Information Systems, Delft, The Netherlands
{k.tao,c.hauff,g.j.p.m.houben}@tudelft.nl

Abstract. Queries that users pose to search engines are often ambiguous - either because different users express different query intents with the same query terms or because the query is underspecified and it is unclear which aspect of a particular query the user is interested in. In the Web search setting, search result diversification, whose goal is the creation of a search result ranking covering a range of query intents or aspects of a single topic respectively, has been shown in recent years to be an effective strategy to satisfy search engine users. We hypothesize that such a strategy will also be beneficial for search on microblogging platforms. Currently, progress in this direction is limited due to the lack of a microblog-based diversification corpus. In this paper we address this shortcoming and present our work on creating such a corpus. We are able to show that this corpus fulfils a number of diversification criteria as described in the literature. Initial search and retrieval experiments evaluating the benefits of de-duplication in the diversification setting are also reported.

1 Introduction

Queries that users pose to search engines are often ambiguous - either because different users express different query intents with the same query terms or because the query is underspecified and it is unclear which aspect of a particular query the user is interested in. Search result diversification, whose goal is the creation of a search result ranking covering a range of query intents or aspects of a single topic respectively, has been shown in recent years to be an effective strategy to satisfy search engine users in those circumstances. Instead of a single query intent or a limited number of aspects, search result rankings now cover a set of intents and wide variety of aspects. In 2009, with the introduction of the diversity search task at TREC [1], a large increase in research efforts could be observed, e.g. [2–5].

Recent research [6], comparing users' query behaviour on microblogging platforms such as Twitter and the Web has shown that Web search queries are on average longer than Twitter queries. This is not surprising, as each Twitter message (tweet) is limited to 140 characters and a longer query might remove too many potentially relevant tweets from the result set. Considering the success of diversity in Web search, we believe that it is an even more important technology on microblogging platforms due to the shortness of the queries.

R.E. Banchs et al. (Eds.): AIRS 2013, LNCS 8281, pp. 251–262, 2013.

However, to our knowledge, no publicly available microblogging data set (i.e. a corpus and a set of topics with subtopic-based relevance judgments) exists as of yet. In order to further the work on diversity in the microblog setting, we created such a corpus[1] and describe it here.

Specifically, in this paper we make the following contributions: (i) we present a methodology for microblog-based corpus creation, (ii) we create such a corpus, and, (iii) conduct an analysis on its validity for diversity experiments. In the second part of the paper we turn to the question of (iv) how to improve search and retrieval in the diversity setting by evaluating the recently introduced de-duplication approach to microblogging streams [7].

2   Related Work

Users of (Web) serach engines typically employ short keyword-based queries to express their information needs. These queries are often underspecified or ambiguous to some extent [8]. Different users who pose exactly the same query may have very different query intents. In order to satisfy a wide range of users, search results diversification was proposed [9].

On the Web, researchers have been studying the diversification problem mostly based on two considerations: novelty and facet coverage. To increase novelty, maximizing the marginal relevance while adding documents to the search results [10, 11] has been proposed. Later studies have focused on how to maximize the coverage of different facets [2] of a given query. Furthermore, there are works that consider a hybrid solution to combine benefits from both novelty-based and coverage-based approaches [12, 3].

In order to evaluate the effectiveness of search result diversification, different evaluation measures have been proposed. A number of them [13–16] have been employed at the Diversity Task [1] of the Text REtrieval Conference (TREC), which ran between 2009 and 2012.

Given the difference [6] in querying behavior on the Web and microblogging sites, we hypothesize that the diversification problem is more challenging in the latter case due to the reduced length of the queries. Tao et al. [7] recently proposed a framework to detect (near-)duplicate messages on Twitter and explored its performance as a search result diversification tool on microblogging sites [7]. The approach can be categorized as novelty-based since it exploits the dependency between documents in the initial result ranking. The evaluation though was limited due to the lack of an explicit diversity microblogging corpus (i.e. a corpus with topics and subtopics as well as relevance judgments on the subtopic level). In this paper, we now tackle this very issue. We describe our methodology for the creation of a Twitter-based diversity corpus and investigate its properties. Finally, we also employ Tao et al.'s framework [7] and explore its effectiveness on this newly developed data set.

---

[1] The corpus is publicly available at `http://wis.ewi.tudelft.nl/airs2013/`.

3   Methodology: Creating a Diversity Corpus

We collected tweets from the public Twitter stream between February 1, 2013 and March 31, 2013 - the dates were chosen to coincide with the time interval of the TREC Microblog 2013 track[2].

After the crawl, in order to create topics, one of this paper's authors (*Annotator 2*) consulted Wikipedia's *Current Events Portal*[3] for the months February and March 2013 and selected fifty news events. We hypothesized that only topics with enough importance and more than local interests are mentioned here and thus, it is likely that our Twitter stream does contain some tweets which are pertinent to these topics. Another advantage of this approach is that we were able to also investigate the importance of time - we picked topics which are evenly distributed across the two-month time span.

Having defined the documents and topics, two decisions need to be made: (i) how to derive the subtopics for each topic, and, (ii) how to create a pool of documents to judge for each topic (and corresponding set of subtopics). Previous benchmarks have developed different approaches for (i): e.g. to derive subtopics post-hoc, i.e. after the pool of documents to judge has been created or to rely on external sources such as query logs to determine the different interpretations and/or aspects of a topic. With respect to (ii), the setup followed by virtually all benchmarks is to create a pool of documents to judge based on the top retrieved documents by the benchmark participants, the idea being that a large set of diverse retrieval systems will retrieve a diverse set of documents for judging.

Since in our work we do not have access to a wide variety of retrieval systems to create the pool, we had to opt for a different approach: one of this paper's authors (*Annotator 1*) *manually* created complex Indri[4] queries for each topic topics. We consider this approach a valid alternative to the pool-based approach, as in this way we still retrieve a set of diverse documents. A number of examples are shown in Table 1. The Indri query language allows us to define, among others, synonymous terms within $< .. >$ as well as exact phrase matches with #1(...). The #*combine* operator joins the different concepts identified for retrieval purposes. Since we do not employ stemming or stopwording in our retrieval system, many of the synonyms are spelling variations of a particular concept. The queries were created with background knowledge, i.e. where necessary, *Annotator 1* looked up information about the event to determine a set of diverse terms. The created Indri queries are then deployed with the query likelihood retrieval model. Returned are the top $10,000$ documents (tweets) per query. In a post-processing step we filter out duplicates (tweets that are similar with cosine similarity > 0.9 to a tweet higher in the ranking) and then present the top 500 remaining tweets for judging to *Annotator 1* and *Annotator 2*. After

---

[2] TREC Microblog 2013 track: `https://github.com/lintool/twitter-tools/wiki/TREC-2013-Track-Guidelines`

[3] Wikipedia Current Events Portal, `http://en.wikipedia.org/wiki/Portal:Current_events`

[4] Indri is a query language supported by the Lemur Toolkit for Information Retrieval, `http://www.lemurproject.org/`.

the manual annotation process, the duplicates are injected into the relevance judgments again with the same relevance score and subtopic assignment as the original tweet.

Table 1. Examples of (i) news events selected, (ii) the corresponding Indri queries to generate a diverse result ranking for annotation purposes, (iii) the adhoc queries used in the retrieval experiments, and, (iv) examples of subtopics found during the annotation process (not all identified subtopics are shown)

News Event Topics	Manually created Indri queries	Adhoc queries	Identified Subtopics
Hillary Clinton steps down as United States Secretary of State	#combine(<#1(hillary clinton) #1(hilary clinton) #1(secretary clinton) #1(secretary of state)> <#1(steps down) #1(step down) leave leaves resignation resigns resign #1(stepping down) quit quits retire retires>)	hillary clinton resign	Clinton's successor what may be next for Clinton details of resignation Clinton's political positions
Syrian civil war	#combine(<syria syrian aleppo daraa damascus homs hama jasmin baniyas latakia talkalakh> <#1(civil war) war unrest uprising protest protests protestors demonstration demonstrators rebel rebels rebellion revolt revolts revolting resistance resisting resist clash clashes clashing escalation escalate escalated fight fights fighting battle battles offensive>)	syria civil war	casualties positions of foreign governments infighting among rebels
Boeing Dreamliner battery problems	#combine(<#1(Boeing Dreamliner) #1(boeing 787) #1(787 dreamliner)> <test tests testing tested check checks checked trial trials try> <battery batteries lithium-ion #1(lithium ion)>)	dreamliner battery	battery incidents cause of battery problems criticism Boeing tests

The annotators split the 50 topics among them and manually determined for each of the 500 tweets whether or not they belong to a particular subtopic (and which one). Thus, we did not attempt to identify subtopics beforehand, we created subtopics based on the top retrieved tweets. Tweets which were relevant to the overall topic, but did not discuss one or more subtopics were considered non-relevant. For example, for the topic *Hillary Clinton steps down as United States Secretary of State* we determined the first tweet to be relevant for subtopic *what may be next for Clinton*, while the second tweet is non-relevant as it only discusses the general topic, but no particular subtopic:

1. *Hillary Clinton transition leaves democrats waiting on 2016 decision. Hillary Clinton left the state department < URL >.*

2. *Clinton steps down as secretary of state. Outgoing us secretary of state Hillary Clinton says she is proud of < URL >.*

Thus, during the annotation process, we focused on the content of the tweet itself, we did not take externally linked Web pages in the relevance decision into account - we believe that this makes our corpus valuable over a longer period of time, as the content behind URLs may change frequently. This decision is in contrast to the TREC 2011 Microblog track, where URLs in tweets were one of the most important indicators for a tweet's relevance [17].

We note, that defining such subtopics is a subjective process - different annotators are likely to derive different subtopics for the same topic. However, this is a problem which is inherent to all diversity corpora which were derived by human annotators. In order to show the annotator influence, in the experimental section, we not only report the results across all topics, but also on a per-annotator basis.

At the end of the annotation process, we had to drop three topics, as we were not able to identify a sufficient number of subtopics for them. An example of a dropped topic is *2012-13 UEFA Champions League*, which mostly resulted in tweets mentioning game dates but little else. Thus, overall, we have 47 topics with assigned subtopics that we can use for our diversity retrieval experiments.

4   Topic Analysis

In this section, we perform a first analysis of the 47 topics and their respective subtopics. Where applicable, we show the overall statistics across all topics, as well as across the topic partitions according to the two annotators.

The Topics and Subtopics. In Table 2, we list the basic statistics over the number of subtopics identified, while Figure 1 shows concretely for each topic the number of subtopics. On average, we find 9 subtopics per topic. The large standard deviation indicates a strong variation between topics with respect to the number of subtopics (also evident in Figure 1). On a per annotator basis we also observe a difference in terms of created subtopics: *Annotator 1* has a considerably higher standard deviation than *Annotator 2*. This result confirms our earlier statement - subtopic annotation is a very subjective task.

The topics yielding the fewest and most subtopics, respectively, are as follows:

- *Kim Jong-Un orders preparation for strategic rocket strikes on the US mainland* (2 subtopics)
- *Syrian civil war* (21 subtopics)
- *2013 North Korean nuclear test* (21 subtopics).

Table 2. Subtopic statistics

	All topics	Topics annotated by	
		Annotator 1	*Annotator 2*
Av. num subtopics	9.27	8.59	9.88
Std. dev. subtopics	3.88	5.11	2.14
Min. num. subtopics	2	2	6
Max. num. subtopics	21	21	13

The annotators spent on average 6.6 seconds on each tweet in the annotation process and thus the total annotation effort amounted to 38 hours of annotations.

Apart from a very small number of tweets, each relevant tweet was assigned to exactly one subtopic - this is not surprising, considering the small size of the documents.

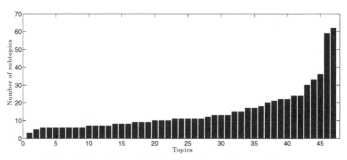

Fig. 1. Number of subtopics found for each topic

The Relevance Judgments. In Figure 2 we present the distribution of relevant and non-relevant documents among the 500 tweets the annotators judged per topic[5]. Twenty-five of the topics have less than 100 relevant documents, while six topics resulted in more than 350 relevant documents. When considering the documents on the annotator-level, we see a clear difference between the annotators: *Annotator 1* judged on average 96 documents as relevant to a topic (and thus 404 documents as non-relevant), while *Annotator 2* judged on average 181 documents as relevant.

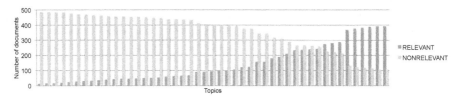

Fig. 2. Number of tweets per topic identified as (non-)relevant during the annotation process

We also investigated the temporal distribution of the relevant tweets. In Figure 3 we plot for each topic the number of days that have passed between the first and the last relevant tweet in our data set. Since our data set spans a two-month period, we note that a number of topics are active the entire time (e.g. the topics *Northern Mali conflict* and *Syrian civil war*) while others are active froughly 24 hours (e.g. the topics *BBC Twitter account hacked* and *Eiffel Tower, evacuated due to bomb threat*). We thus have a number of short-term topics and a number of long-term topics in our data set. Inn contrast to the TREC Microblog track 2011/12, we do not assign a particular querytime to each topic (therefore we implicitly assume that we query the data set one day after the last day of crawling). We do not consider this a limitation, as a considerable number of topics are covered across weeks.

---

[5] As described earlier, the near-identical tweets that were removed to ease the annotation load are later added to the qrels again; they are not taken into account in the analysis presented here.

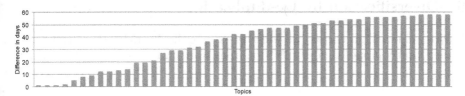

Fig. 3. Difference in days between the earliest and the latest *relevant* tweet for each topic

Diversity Difficulty. Lastly, we consider the extent to which the search results can actually be diversified. Diversification does not only depend on the ambiguity or the underspecification of the query, it is also limited by the amount of diverse content *available in the corpus.* Golbus et al. [18] recently investigated this issue and proposed the *diversity difficulty* measure (*dd*) which is a function of two factors: the amount of diversity that a retrieval system can achieve at best and the ease with which a retrieval system can return a diversified result list. Intuitively, a topic has little inherent diversity if the maximum amount of diversity a retrieval system can achieve is small. A topic is considered "somewhat more diverse" by Golbus et al. in the case where a diverse result list can be achieved but it is difficult for the system to create one. A topic has a large amount of diversity if a retrieval system not tuned for diversity is able to return a diverse result list. These intuitions are formalized in a diversity formula with $dd \in [0,1]$. A large score ($dd > 0.9$) indicates a diverse query, while a small score ($dd < 0.5$) either indicates a topic with few subtopics or a fair number of subtopics which are unlikely to be discovered by an untuned retrieval system. In Table 3 we present the diversity difficulty average and standard deviation our topics achieve - they are very similar for both annotators and also in line with the diversity difficulty scores of the TREC 2010 Web diversity track [18]. We thus conclude, that in terms of diversity our topic set presents a well constructed data source for diversity experiments.

Table 3. Diversity difficulty scores across all topics - a higher score is indicative of more diverse topics

	All topics	Topics assigned to Annotator 1	Annotator 2
Av. diversity difficulty	0.71	0.72	0.70
Std. dev. diversity difficulty	0.07	0.06	0.07

Finally, we observe that the diversity difficulty score of *long-term topics*, that is topics whose first and last relevant tweet cover at least a 50 day timespan, is higher ($dd_{long\text{-}term} = 0.73$), than the diversity difficulty score of *short-term* topics (the remaining topics) where $dd_{short\text{-}term} = 0.70$.

5   Diversification by De-duplication

Having analyzed our corpus, we will now explore the diversification effectiveness of the recently proposed de-duplication framework for microblogs [7] on this data set.

5.1   Duplicate Detection Strategies on Twitter

In [7] it was found that about 20% of search results returned by a standard adhoc search system contain duplicate information. This finding motivated the development of a de-duplication approach which detects duplicates by employing (i) *Sy*ntactical features, (ii) *Se*mantic features, and (iii) *Co*ntextual features in a machine learning framework[6]. By combining these feature sets in different ways, the framework supports mixed strategies named after the prefixes of the feature sets used: **Sy**, **SySe**, **SyCo** and **SySeCo**. Not surprisingly, the evaluation showed that the highest effectiveness was achieved when all features were combined.

Given an initial ranking of documents (tweets), each document starting at rank two is compared to all higher ranked documents. The duplicate detection framework is run for each document pair and if a duplicate is detected, the lower ranked document is filtered out from the result ranking.

5.2   Diversity Evaluation Measures

As researchers have been studying the diversification problem intensively on the Web, a number of measures have been proposed over the years to evaluate the success of IR systems in achieving diversity in search results. We evaluate our de-duplication experiments according to the following measures:

α-(n)DCG [14]. This measure was adopted as the official diversity evaluation measure at TREC 2009 [1]. It is based on Normalized Discounted Cumulative Gain (nDCG) [19] and extends it by making the gain of each document dependent on the documents ranked above it.

Precision-IA [13]. We evaluate the ratio of relevant documents for different subtopics within the top k items by the measure **Precision-IA**.

Subtopic-Recall [20]. We report the subtopic recall (in short **S-Recall**) to show the number of subtopics covered by the top k documents. The measures ranges from 0 to 1, where larger values indicate a better coverage of subtopics.

Redundancy The measure shows the ratio of repeated subtopics among all relevant documents within the top k ranked documents. For diversity experiments, a lower redundancy value indicates a better performance.

---

[6] The paper also consider the use of features derived from Web pages linked to in tweets. We ignore these features, as we did not consider URL content in the annotation process.

5.3   Analysis of De-duplication Strategies

We evaluate the different de-duplication strategies from two perspectives: (i) we compare their effectiveness on all 47 topics, and, (ii) we make side-by-side comparisons between two topic splits, according to the annotator and the temporal persistence. This enables us to investigate the annotator influence and the difference in diversity between long-term and short-term topics.

Apart from the de-duplication strategies we also employ three baselines: the **Automatic run** is a standard query likelihood based retrieval run (language modeling with Dirichlet smoothing, $\mu = 1000$) as implemented in the Lemur Toolkit for IR. The run **Filtered Auto** builds on the automatic run by greedily filtering out duplicates by comparing each document in the result list with all documents ranked above it - if it has a cosine similarity above 0.9 with any of the higher ranked documents, it is removed from the list. The de-duplication strategies also built on top of the Automatic Run by filtering out documents (though in a more advanced manner). All these runs take as input the adhoc queries (i.e. very short keyword queries) as defined in Table 1.

The only exception to this rule is the **Manual run** which is actually the run we derived from the manually created complex Indri queries that we used for annotation purposes with cosine-based filtering as defined above.

Overall comparison. In Table 4 the results for the different strategies averaged over all 47 topics are shown. Underlined is the best performing run for each evaluation measure; statistically significant improvements over the *Filtered Auto* baseline are marked with † (paired t-test, two-sided, $\alpha = 0.05$). The *Manual Run* - as expected - in general yields the best results which are statistically significant in all measures at level @20.

We find that the de-duplication strategies *Sy* and *SyCo* in general outperform the baselines *Automatic Run* and *Filtered Auto*, though the improvements are not statistically significant. Not surpisingly, as the de-duplication strategies take *Automatic Run* as input, Preicision-IA degrades, especially for Precision-IA@20. On the other hand, in terms of lack of redundancy, the de-duplication strategies perform best. De-duplication strategies that exploit semantic features (*SySe* and *SySeCo*) show a degraded effectiveness, which is in stark contrast to the results reported in [7]. We speculate that the main reason for this observation is the recency of our corpus. Semantic features are derived from named entities (NE) recognized in the top-ranked tweets and queries. Since in [7] a corpus (documents and topics) from 2011 was used, it is likely that many more NEs were recognized (i.e. those NEs have entered the Linked Open Data cloud) than for our very recent topics. As a concrete example, the topic *Syrian civil war* retrieves tweets which contain person names and locations important to the conflict, but they have not been added to standard semantics extraction services such as DBpedia Spolight[7].

---

[7] DBPedia Spotlight, `http://spotlight.dbpedia.org/demo/`

Table 4. Comparison of different de-duplication strategies on our 47 diversity topics. Statistically significant improvements over the *Filtered Auto* baseline are marked with † (paired t-test, two-sided, $\alpha = 0.05$) for α-nDCG, Precision-IA and S-Recall. The Redundancy measure performs best when it is lowest.

Measure	α-nDCG		Precision-IA		S-Recall		Redundancy	
	@10	@20	@10	@20	@10	@20	@10	@20
Automatic Run	0.312	0.338	0.079	0.075	0.315	0.413	0.471	0.580
Filtered Auto	0.339	0.358	0.079	0.072	0.370	0.454	0.380	0.514
Sy	0.347	0.362	0.080	0.066	0.382	0.457	0.358	0.497
SySe	0.340	0.357	0.075	0.063	0.363	0.452	<u>0.357</u>	0.481
SyCo	0.346	0.360	0.080	0.065	0.381	0.464	0.371	<u>0.478</u>
SySeCo	0.341	0.358	0.077	0.064	0.365	0.457	0.376	0.489
Manual Run	<u>0.386</u>	<u>0.443</u>†	<u>0.104</u>†	<u>0.099</u>†	<u>0.446</u>	<u>0.623</u>†	0.482	0.601

Influence of Annotator Subjectivity and Temporal Persistence. In Table 5, the results are shown when splitting the topic set according to the annotators. Here we find that although the absolute scores of the different evaluation measures for *Annotator 1* and *Annotator 2* are quite different, the general trend is the same for both. The absolute α-nDCG scores of the various de-duplication strategies are higher for *Annotator 2* than for *Annotator 1*, which can be explained by the fact that *Annotator 2*, on average, judged more documents to be relevant for a topic than *Annotator 1*. The opposite observation holds for the *Manual Run*, which can be explained by the inability of cosine filtering to reduce redundancy. Given that there are more relevant documents for *Annotator 2*'s topics, naturally the redundancy problem is more challenging than for *Annotator 1*'s topics.

Table 5. Comparison of different de-duplication strategies when splitting the 47 topics according to the two annotators (due to the small topic size, significance tests were not performed)

Measure	α-nDCG		Precision-IA		S-Recall		Redundancy	
	@10	@20	@10	@20	@10	@20	@10	@20
Annotator 1								
Automatic Run	0.298	0.325	0.085	0.078	0.317	0.405	0.512	0.563
Filtered Auto	0.317	0.337	0.083	0.073	0.366	0.425	0.361	0.497
Sy	0.321	0.344	0.085	0.069	0.366	0.448	0.365	0.518
SySe	0.315	0.337	0.079	0.060	0.366	0.447	0.375	0.477
SyCo	0.318	0.346	0.086	0.067	0.359	0.466	<u>0.339</u>	0.464
SySeCo	0.321	0.344	0.083	0.062	0.358	0.466	0.362	<u>0.460</u>
Manual Run	<u>0.442</u>	<u>0.489</u>	<u>0.127</u>	<u>0.111</u>	<u>0.537</u>	<u>0.667</u>	0.451	0.582
Annotator 2								
Automatic Run	0.325	0.350	0.074	0.073	0.314	0.420	0.444	0.593
Filtered Auto	0.359	0.377	0.075	0.071	0.374	0.479	0.393	0.526
Sy	<u>0.371</u>	0.377	0.075	0.064	0.395	0.466	<u>0.352</u>	<u>0.482</u>
SySe	0.362	0.374	0.072	0.065	0.360	0.456	0.372	0.493
SyCo	<u>0.371</u>	0.373	0.075	0.063	<u>0.400</u>	0.462	0.369	<u>0.482</u>
SySeCo	0.359	0.371	0.073	0.066	0.371	0.448	0.386	0.509
Manual Run	0.338	<u>0.403</u>	<u>0.087</u>	<u>0.090</u>	0.367	<u>0.583</u>	0.505	0.615

Finally, Table 6 shows the results when comparing short-term and long-term queries. For long-term topics, the de-duplication strategies consistently outperform the baselines, while the same cannot be said about the short-term topics. We hypothesize that short-term topics do not yield a large variation in vocabulary (often a published news report is repeated in only slightly different terms) so that features which go beyond simple term matching do not yield significant benefits. Long-term topics on the other hand develop a richer vocabulary during the discourse (or the course of the event) and thus more complex syntactic features can actually help.

Table 6. Comparison of different de-duplication strategies when splitting the 47 topics according to temporal persistence

Measure	α-nDCG		Precision-IA		S-Recall		Redundancy	
	@10	@20	@10	@20	@10	@20	@10	@20
			Long-term Topics					
Automatic Run	0.346	0.386	0.074	0.075	0.336	0.494	0.518	0.597
Filtered Auto	0.387	0.415	0.075	0.072	0.431	0.560	0.371	0.518
Sy	0.400	0.419	0.077	0.069	0.458	0.558	<u>0.336</u>	0.499
SySe	0.389	0.414	0.072	0.066	0.421	0.548	0.354	0.493
SyCo	<u>0.401</u>	0.416	0.078	0.068	<u>0.459</u>	0.554	0.358	<u>0.486</u>
SySeCo	0.386	0.412	0.074	0.069	0.417	0.545	0.376	0.501
Filtered Manual	0.373	<u>0.431</u>	<u>0.084</u>	<u>0.087</u>	0.416	<u>0.596</u>	0.457	0.619
			Short-term Topics					
Automatic Run	0.293	0.311	0.082	0.075	0.304	0.367	0.437	0.571
Filtered Auto	0.312	0.326	0.081	0.072	0.336	0.393	0.402	0.510
Sy	0.318	0.329	0.081	0.065	0.338	0.400	0.388	0.495
SySe	0.312	0.325	0.077	0.061	0.330	0.397	<u>0.375</u>	<u>0.464</u>
SyCo	0.315	0.329	0.081	0.063	0.337	0.413	0.396	0.471
SySeCo	0.316	0.328	0.080	0.061	0.335	0.407	0.391	0.472
Manual Run	<u>0.391</u>	<u>0.448</u>	<u>0.116</u>	<u>0.106</u>	<u>0.464</u>	<u>0.638</u>	0.492	0.590

6 Conclusions

In this paper, we presented our efforts to create a microblog-based corpus for search result diversification experiments. A comprehensive analysis of the corpus showed its suitability for this purpose. The analysis of the annototators' influence on subtopic creation and relevance judgments revealed considerable subjectivity in the annotation process. At the same time though, the de-duplication retrieval experiments showed that the observed trends with respect to the different evaluation measures were largely independent of the specific annotator.

The performance of the de-duplication strategies and their comparison to the results reported in [7] indicate the importance of the feature suitability for the topic type (long-term vs. short-term topics and topic recency).

In future work we plan to further analyze the impact of the different strategies and the annotator subjectivity. We will also implement and evaluate the de-duplication strategy with diversification approaches which have been shown to perform well in the Web search setting, e.g. [4, 5]. Furthermore, we will investigate the potential sources (influences and/or motivations) for the observed annotator differences.

References

1. Clarke, C.L.A., Craswell, N., Soboroff, I.: Overview of the trec 2009 web track. In: TREC 2009 (2009)
2. Carterette, B., Chandar, P.: Probabilistic models of ranking novel documents for faceted topic retrieval. In: CIKM 2009, pp. 1287–1296 (2009)
3. Slivkins, A., Radlinski, F., Gollapudi, S.: Learning optimally diverse rankings over large document collections. In: ICML 2010, pp. 983–990 (2010)
4. Santos, R.L.T., Macdonald, C., Ounis, I.: Intent-aware search result diversification. In: SIGIR 2011, pp. 595–604 (2011)
5. Santos, R.L.T., Macdonald, C., Ounis, I.: Aggregated search result diversification. In: Amati, G., Crestani, F. (eds.) ICTIR 2011. LNCS, vol. 6931, pp. 250–261. Springer, Heidelberg (2011)
6. Teevan, J., Ramage, D., Morris, M.R.: #TwitterSearch: a comparison of microblog search and web search. In: WSDM 2011, pp. 35–44 (2011)
7. Tao, K., Abel, F., Hauff, C., Houben, G.J., Gadiraju, U.: Groundhog day: Near-duplicate detection on twitter. In: WWW 2013, pp. 1273–1284 (2013)
8. Cronen-Townsend, S., Croft, W.B.: Quantifying query ambiguity. In: HLT 2002, pp. 104–109 (2002)
9. Bennett, P.N., Carterette, B., Chapelle, O., Joachims, T.: Beyond binary relevance: preferences, diversity, and set-level judgments. SIGIR Forum 42(2), 53–58 (2008)
10. Carbonell, J., Goldstein, J.: The use of mmr, diversity-based reranking for reordering documents and producing summaries. In: SIGIR 1998, pp. 335–336 (1998)
11. Zhai, C., Lafferty, J.: A risk minimization framework for information retrieval. Inf. Process. Manage. 42(1), 31–55 (2006)
12. Yue, Y., Joachims, T.: Predicting diverse subsets using structural svms. In: ICML 2008, pp. 1224–1231 (2008)
13. Agrawal, R., Gollapudi, S., Halverson, A., Ieong, S.: Diversifying search results. In: WSDM 2009, pp. 5–14 (2009)
14. Clarke, C.L., Kolla, M., Cormack, G.V., Vechtomova, O., Ashkan, A., Büttcher, S., MacKinnon, I.: Novelty and diversity in information retrieval evaluation. In: SIGIR 2008, pp. 659–666 (2008)
15. Chapelle, O., Metlzer, D., Zhang, Y., Grinspan, P.: Expected reciprocal rank for graded relevance. In: CIKM 2009, pp. 621–630 (2009)
16. Clarke, C.L.A., Kolla, M., Vechtomova, O.: An effectiveness measure for ambiguous and underspecified queries. In: Azzopardi, L., Kazai, G., Robertson, S., Rüger, S., Shokouhi, M., Song, D., Yilmaz, E. (eds.) ICTIR 2009. LNCS, vol. 5766, pp. 188–199. Springer, Heidelberg (2009)
17. Tao, K., Abel, F., Hauff, C., Houben, G.J.: What makes a tweet relevant for a topic? In: #MSM2012 Workshop, pp. 49–56 (2012)
18. Golbus, P., Aslam, J., Clarke, C.: Increasing evaluation sensitivity to diversity. Information Retrieval, 1–26 (2013)
19. Järvelin, K., Kekäläinen, J.: Cumulated gain-based evaluation of ir techniques. ACM Trans. Inf. Syst. 20(4), 422–446 (2002)
20. Zhai, C.X., Cohen, W.W., Lafferty, J.: Beyond independent relevance: methods and evaluation metrics for subtopic retrieval. In: SIGIR 2003, pp. 10–17 (2003)

Generating New LIWC Dictionaries by Triangulation

Guillem Massó, Patrik Lambert, Carlos Rodríguez Penagos, and Roser Saurí

Barcelona Media Innovation Center
Av. Diagonal 77, 08025 Barcelona, Spain
{guillem.masso,roser.sauri}@gmail.com, patrik.lambert@upf.edu,
carlos.rodriguez@barcelonamedia.org

Abstract. This work aims at exploring a triangulation-based methodology for generating a sentiment dictionary in a language from equivalent dictionaries in other languages. Direct machine translation of dictionaries generally leads to incomplete or wrong results, but multilingual translation can help disambiguate and improve these data. More precisely, we want to translate the LIWC dictionary (Linguistic Inquiry and Word Count) into Catalan from the original English dictionary, complemented with other versions in Romance languages close to Catalan, that is, Spanish, French and Italian. Comparing translations from these dictionaries allows us to identify the most reliable solutions, namely, those common to the different languages. Since LIWC classifies words by categories, assigning the correct ones to the chosen translations is also an important issue, specially when the source categories are different. We present the results of a semi-automatic approach and the challenges that had to be addressed in the translation process.

Keywords: sentiment analysis, translation, triangulation, LIWC, sentiment dictionary.

1 Introduction

With the development of the Web 2.0, a massive amount of text expressing personal sentiments is published daily on the internet. The automatic analysis of these texts is extremely valuable to many institutions and companies since it allows them to know the general sentiment about them or about their products or services. Sentiment analysis has become a very active research field, boosted both by its scientific interest and this commercial value. The main approaches to perform sentiment analysis use lists of sentiment words with their opinion polarity or their sentiment category, either to craft classification rules or as features of machine learning algorithms [1]. While the subjective texts available on the web is increasingly multilingual[1] because most people prefer to write and read information in their own language, sentiment and subjectivity dictionaries are still not available for most languages, especially for minority languages.

---

[1] Statistics of Internet world users by language on www.internetworldstats.com.

R.E. Banchs et al. (Eds.): AIRS 2013, LNCS 8281, pp. 263–271, 2013.
© Springer-Verlag Berlin Heidelberg 2013

In this paper we investigate the feasibility of the translation of the Linguistic Inquiry and Word Count (LIWC) [2] sentiment dictionary. To keep manual work minimal, we propose a semi-automatic approach based on triangulation from LIWC dictionaries existing in four languages. We test our investigations on the translation of LIWC into the Catalan minority language.

Table 1. LIWC 2001 categories, with id code and name (emotion-related ones bolded)

Cat.	Dimension	Cat.	Dimension
I. STANDARD LINGUISTIC DIMENSIONS		**III. RELATIVITY**	
1	Total pronouns	37	Time
2	1st person singular	38	Past tense verb
3	1st person plural	39	Present tense verb
4	Total first person	40	Future tense verb
5	Total second person	41	Space
6	Total third person	42	Up
7	Negations	43	Down
8	Assents	44	Inclusive
9	Articles	45	Exclusive
10	Prepositions	46	Motion
11	Numbers	**IV. PERSONAL CONCERNS**	
II. PSYCHOLOGICAL PROCESSES		47	Occupation
12	Affective or Emotional Processes	48	School
13	Positive Emotions	49	Job or work
14	Positive feelings	50	Achievement
15	Optimism and energy	51	Leisure activity
16	Negative Emotions	52	Home
17	Anxiety or fear	53	Sports
18	Anger	54	Television and movies
19	Sadness or depression	55	Music
20	Cognitive Processes	56	Money and financial issues
21	Causation	57	Metaphysical issues
22	Insight	58	Religion
23	Discrepancy	59	Death and dying
24	Inhibition	60	Physical states and functions
25	Tentative	61	Body states, symptoms
26	Certainty	62	Sex and sexuality
27	Sensory and Perceptual Processes	63	Eating, drinking, dieting
28	Seeing	64	Sleeping, dreaming
29	Hearing	65	Grooming
30	Feeling	**APPENDIX:**	
31	Social Processes	**EXPERIMENTAL DIMENSIONS**	
32	Communication	66	Swear words
33	Other references to people	67	Nonfluencies
34	Friends	68	Fillers
35	Family		
36	Humans		

LIWC is a text analysis software calculating the degree to which any text uses positive or negative emotions, self-references or causal words, among other language dimensions. Its aim is to provide an efficient and effective method for studying the various emotional, cognitive, structural, and process components present in individuals' verbal and written speech samples. LIWC contains a list of word categories (see Table 1) and a dictionary of words with a set of related categories. For example, the categories associated to the word "love" are Affect, Positive emotion, Positive feeling, Present, Physical and Sexual.

2 Related Work

We are not aware of any semi-automatic method reported to translate the LIWC dictionary. However, some research has already been conducted on translation of subjectivity or sentiment polarity dictionaries. Mihalcea et al. [3] translated a subjectivity dictionary directly with a bilingual dictionary. They reported that only a small fraction of the lexicon entries preserve their subjectivity in the translation, mainly because of the ambiguous entries in the source and target languages. To alleviate this problem, Steinberger et al. [4] proposed a triangulation method. They first produced high-level gold-standard sentiment dictionaries for two languages and then translated them automatically into third languages. The idea is that the overlapping target language word lists are likely to have senses similar to that of the two source languages. For example, "esperar" in Spanish has two translations into French: "attendre" (to wait), which has negative polarity, and "espérer" (to hope), which has positive polarity. In English, there is only the positive sense "to hope". Thus triangulation into English allows to disambiguate the polarity of the French translations.

Other approaches mentioned in the literature to build or translate sentiment lexicons include bootstrapping based on lexicon relations [5] or graph relations [6]. Lexicon bootstrapping consists of expanding a set of manually chosen seeds and their corresponding polarity with related words, and then filter the candidate words. Banea et al. [5] expand the seed words with words of the text of their definition, as well as with synonym and antonym words found in a dictionary. To translate an English sentiment lexicon, Scheible et al. [6] first build monolingual graphs based on 2 relation types: coordination between adjectives (e.g. healthy and tasty) and adjective-noun modification (e.g. healthy food). They then use a sentiment lexicon to determine the sentiment polarity in English graph nodes and a bilingual lexicon to draw seed relations between the English and foreign graphs. They finally expand the English-foreign relations with the SimRank algorithm, which determines the similarity between 2 nodes in different graphs.

These two bootstrapping approaches expand a set of seeds based on similarity or dissimilarity between words in a dictionary (such as synonyms or antonyms) or nodes in a graph. They thus only work because each word has only one binary polarity attribute (positive or negative). These methods cannot be applied to translate the LIWC dictionary, in which there are more than 60 possible categories and each word may be associated to several categories.

Another approach mentioned in the literature and which could be applied to the proposed task is Wordnet-based lexicon generation. Banea et al. [7] showed that for about 90% of Wordnet senses the subjective meaning does hold across languages (in this case Romanian and English). This property is exploited by Perez-Rosas et al. [8] and Hassan et al. [9] to build sentiment lexicons in a foreign language using multilingual Wordnet resources. However, in the present work, we wanted to develop a method applicable to languages in which Wordnet resources are not available.

3   Methodology

This section details how to generate a Catalan translation of the LIWC dictionary from LIWC dictionaries in other languages. Comparing translations from several dictionaries allows us to distinguish the more reliable ones, namely, these common to the different languages.

Since LIWC classifies words by categories, assigning the correct ones to translations is also an important issue, mainly when the source categories are different. Furthermore, there are two LIWC versions (2001 and 2007) and not all the dictionaries are available in both versions. We describe below the steps of the whole process, from mapping categories of LIWC versions to assigning the most appropriate categories to the obtained translations.

3.1   Multilingual Translation and Alignment

As source language dictionaries, we choose Romance languages (namely Spanish, French and Italian) because of their closeness to Catalan. We also used the English dictionary as it is the original one created in the LIWC project. We used LIWC 2001 categories because most selected dictionaries were available in this format. For the French dictionary, only available with 2007 categories, we manually mapped 2007 categories to 2001 ones. Note that 2007 categories cannot all been mapped unambiguously to 2001 categories. The dictionaries were translated using the bilingual dictionaries of Apertium [10]. Apertium is a free and open-source rule-based machine translation platform, focused on Romance languages and other language pairs such as English-Catalan.

The LIWC dictionaries are rather different in different languages. The English one has 2318 words, the Spanish one, 7475, the French one, 39164, and the Italian one, 5153. The large amount of words in the French dictionary is due to repeated words with different clitics (i.e. *abandonne, j'abandonne, l'abandonne, m'abandonne, n'abandonne, s'abandonne* and *t'abandonne*). After the translation process, we obtained 8526 Catalan words: 3359 have source words in the English dictionary, 5517 in the Spanish one, 3299 in the French one and 1807 in the Italian one. As the translation was direct and using bilingual dictionaries, not all the words were translated and the translated Catalan words are lemmas. As for roots, represented as *root**, we got the translations of all the words beginning with the root. For this reason, the number of translated words from the English dictionary is larger than the number of words of the dictionary.

The next step was to automatically align the different source words of each Catalan word. From this alignment, we observed the following figures. Only 76 words have source words in every language with the same categories. Other 499 words have source words in every language but with different categories. There are also 979 translations with source words in three languages, 205 of which have the same categories. There are 1773 Catalan words with source words in two languages, 631 of them with the same categories. Finally, 5199 translations have source words in only one language. We thus observed few reliable translations but a great amount of hardly reliable ones. In between, there is a range of increasingly unreliable translations. The degree of reliability for a Catalan word depends on the number of source languages it was translated from (the more, the better) as well as the number of shared and different categories of the corresponding source words (the more similar, the better). A further analysis is clearly needed, and we deal with it in the next section.

4   Analysis of Results

4.1   Analysis of LIWC Categories

Each word of the LIWC dictionaries is annotated with a code composed of one or more category identifiers. These categories are hierarchical and grouped by linguistic or semantic criteria: *Affective Processes* are divided into *Positive Emotions* and *Negative Emotions*, and these categories are divided into other subcategories. A code can contain categories of the same or different groups. We have used the 2001 version categories, listed in Table 1.

For each group, there is a main category (i.e. *1-Pronouns, 12-Affective Processes, 20-Cognitive Processes*, etc.). This category can be the only one of the group in a code or there can be other categories of the same group. On the other hand, the secondary categories hardly go without their main category. However, we observed that some secondary categories are rather independent, such as *25-Tentative, 26-Certainty, 38-Past, 39-Present, 40-Future, 44-Inclusive, 45-Exclusive, 50-Achievement, 52-Home, 58-Religion, 59-Death* and *65-Grooming*. These categories often appear in codes without their main category.

The category groups are classified as Standard Linguistic Dimensions, Psychological Processes, Relativity Personal Concerns and Experimental Dimensions. As for the Standard Linguistic Dimensions, the categories are grammatical, while the other categories are basically semantic. An exception could be the categories *38-Past, 39-Present* and *40-Future*: they have a morphological role when they are related to a tense verb, but they have a semantic role when they are related to adverbs or other temporal expressions. On the other hand, *7-Negations* and *8-Assents* are linguistic categories but with a strong polarity, so they will have an important role if the dictionary is focused on sentiment analysis.

The Italian dictionary has additional categories which are included in the Standard Linguistic Dimensions. As they are very specific, we have not taken them into account. This is not the only difference among languages. We can notice some different criteria, such as those for the Catalan translation *cèlebre*, whose source words have different categories: in Spanish, *célebre* has the categories 51 and 54, focused on the celebrities of movies or TV; in French, *célèbre* has the categories 31 and 50, as a social achievement, and in Italian, *celebre* is tagged as a positive emotion. All of them are acceptable and are different approaches to the semantics of the word. This happens with several words.

The roots are another source of problems. An extreme case is the Italian article root *l**, which is translated into all Catalan words beginning with l. There are also less dramatic mistakes: the Spanish root *sex** (categories 60 and 62) is shared by *sexo* ('sex') and *sexto* ('sixth'). If there are other source words, these mistakes can be solved by multi-lingual translation.

4.2   Analysis of Translations

We have aligned all the source category codes for each Catalan translation and we have automatically compared them. If we analyse the overall results, we can first see that the most frequent divergent categories are linguistic (1-6, 9 and 10) and verb tense (38-40) categories. This means that these categories are less consistent among languages or that they are more language-dependent. The second important issue is that many aligned codes share main categories but have different secondary categories. We can then consider that the source words belong to the same semantic group, although they can receive different nuances in different languages. It is also possible to find source words sharing secondary categories but not main categories. In this case, we can also think that they belong to the same semantic group but there are some annotation differences among languages.

When we analyse each Catalan translation with more than one source category code, we can rank their reliability by number of source languages and by qualitative differences among codes. The translations from four languages with a very similar code will be much more reliable than the translations from two languages with completely different codes. We classify the similarity among codes as:

- Case 5: all the categories within the different codes belong to the same group (i.e. *humor*: EN *mood* [12], *humour** and *humor** [12 13], SP *humor** [12 13 14], FR *humeur** [12], IT *umorismo* [12 13]).
- Case 4: all the codes share categories from the same group, but they have other categories as well (i.e. *problema*: EN *troubl** [12 16], SP *problema* [12 16 17 18], FR *problème** [12 16 20 23], IT *problem** [12 16 24]).
- Case 3: similar to case 5, but some language has a second (or third, fourth, etc.) word with a completely different code (i.e. *nou*: EN *new* [37], SP *nuevo** [37] and *nueve* [11], FR *nouveau* [37] and *neuf** [11], IT *nuov** [37]).
- Case 2: similar to case 4, but some language has a second (or third, fourth, etc.) word with a completely different code (i.e. *bonic*: EN *beaut** [12 13] and *pretty* [20 25], SP *bonito* [12 13] and *guapo** [12 13 14], FR *bel* and *beau* [12 13 27 28], IT *carin** [12 13]).
- Case 1: there is not any common group shared by every language, but most of the languages share some category group (i.e. *fortuna*: EN *fortune** [56], SP *fortuna* [56], FR *fortune** [56], IT *fortun** [25]).
- Case 0: every code is completely different (i.e. *asseure*: EN *settl** [20], SP *sentar* [52], FR *asseoir* [1 2 4], IT *sedere* [60 61]).

We consider that cases 2-5 are reliable and case 1 is slightly reliable when there are source words in 3 or 4 languages, cases 2-5 are slightly reliable if there are 2 source languages, and case 0 is always unreliable. Table 2 shows the number of translations per case.

Table 2. Translations with several source languages and category codes

	Case 0	Case 1	Case 2	Case 3	Case 4	Case 5	Total
2 languages	418	-	22	33	475	194	1142
3 languages	40	201	33	32	340	128	774
4 languages	4	113	54	22	248	58	499
Total	462	314	109	87	1063	380	2415

Even if all the categories within the different codes belong to the same group (case 5), we can choose to assign only the common categories to the translation, or to assign it all the categories. The other cases are more challenging and there are more options to assign a category code to the Catalan word. If we choose the most conservative option, the new codes will be very simple and we can lose some semantic nuances. On the other hand, if we accept all the categories, the codes could be too complex. In fact, the linguistic categories *1-Pronouns*, *9-Articles*, *10-Prepositions* and *11-Numbers*, and the categories *38-Past*, *39-Present* and *40-Future* are problematic when they are not shared by (almost) all the codes. After analysing several options, we decided to accept the categories of the common groups and also the categories that complement the common ones in some code except for the problematic ones. For example, if the source codes of *garantia* ('guarantee') are '26', '12 13 15 26', '12 13 15 26 39' and '20 26 38 47', the suggested code is '12 13 15 20 26 47'. As for case 1, the criteria are similar but we ignore the divergent code. In case 0, it is not possible to suggest any code.

With these results, we can create a restrictive dictionary formed by 1203 Catalan translations with source words from 3 or 4 languages: 281 translations with only one source code and 922 from cases 2-5. We can also create a less restrictive dictionary with 1669 additional translations: 631 with only one code from 2 languages, 724 from cases 2-5 and 2 source languages and 314 from case 1. Nevertheless, there are still 5661 unreliable translations which should be manually revised.

Since our ultimate objective was to create a sentiment dictionary for languages not covered by LIWC, we evaluated those entries that (a) belonged to the Positive and Negative Emotions (codes 12 to 19, inclusive), and where a translation was found in 3 or 4 of the triangulation languages with those codes (regardless if other codes were included). From the resulting supposedly (high-precision) 509 entries we selected 171 for manual evaluation by 3 linguists that assigned (without knowing the original, pre-translation entries) an 'S' where the entry in Catalan can be assigned the emotional concepts in the codes attributed to it (e.g., "positive emotion", "anger", etc.), or 'N' if in Catalan that was not the case. 'I' was reserved for 'undecidable', as in cases like "sensibly" where no apriori polarity could be assigned to it. We tested our Kappa inter annotator agreement in 11 of those entries, and obtained perfect agreement in them. Overall, 146 (85%) were acceptable transpositions of emotional meaning, and 11 (6%) were not. 14 (8%) were undecidable, according to our evaluators.

5   Conclusions and Further Work

The proposed semi-automatic approach based on triangulation from four LIWC dictionaries in different languages is not trivial. Less than a half of the translations are slightly to highly reliable. However, these translations are lemmas, which can be expanded into more word forms, and we can obtain a reasonable dictionary size. We have to deal with several problems, such as the translation of roots into inaccurate words and the differences of criteria among languages. The triangulation process resolves partially these problems, but we still need a human check if we want an optimal result.

As for the translation of roots, a dictionary with derivatives would be useful, but we would need one for each source language. Furthermore, it would be useful to increase the coverage of the bilingual dictionaries to increase the number of source languages per target entry and thus improve the reliability of translations. On the other hand, we found that such triangulation can effectively provide us with a core, high-quality dictionary of emotional words, since these codes are transported effectively when these entries are found in more than 50% of the translation dictionaries. For these purposes, the approach seems to be feasible, although evaluating it as a method for creating full LWIC dictionary for novel languages (to aid in Information Retrieval ranking and aggregation for results from less-developed languages) needs further study.

Acknowledgments. The authors would like to thank Barcelona Media Innovation Center for their support and permission to publish this work.

The research leading to these results has received funding from the Seventh Framework Program of the European Commission through the Intra-European Fellowship (CrossLingMind-2011-300828) Marie Curie Actions.

References

1. Liu, B.: Sentiment Analysis and Opinion Mining. Synthesis Lectures on Human Language Technologies. Morgan & Claypool Publishers (2012)
2. Pennebaker, J.W., Francis, M.E., Booth, R.J.: Linguistic inquiry and word count: LIWC 2001. Lawrence Erlbaum Associates, Mahway (2001)
3. Mihalcea, R., Banea, C., Wiebe, J.: Learning multilingual subjective language via cross-lingual projections. In: Proceedings of the 45th Annual Meeting of the Association of Computational Linguistics, pp. 976–983. Association for Computational Linguistics, Prague (2007)
4. Steinberger, J., Ebrahim, M., Ehrmann, M., Hurriyetoglu, A., Kabadjov, M., Lenkova, P., Steinberger, R., Tanev, H., Vázquez, S., Zavarella, V.: Creating sentiment dictionaries via triangulation. Decision Support Systems 53(4), 689–694 (2012)
5. Banea, C., Mihalcea, R., Wiebe, J.: A bootstrapping method for building subjectivity lexicons for languages with scarce resources. In: Proceedings of the International Conference on Language Resources and Evaluations (LREC), Marrakech, Morocco, pp. 2764–2767 (May 2008)

6. Scheible, C., Laws, F., Michelbacher, L., Schüze, H.: Sentiment translation through multi-edge graphs. In: Coling 2010: Posters, Beijing, China, pp. 1104–1112 (August 2010)
7. Banea, C., Mihalcea, R., Wiebe, J.: Sense-level subjectivity in a multilingual setting. Computer Speech & Language 28(1), 7–19 (2014)
8. Perez-Rosas, V., Banea, C., Mihalcea, R.: Learning sentiment lexicons in spanish. In: Proceedings of the Eight International Conference on Language Resources and Evaluation (LREC 2012), Istanbul, Turkey, pp. 3077–3081 (May 2012)
9. Hassan, A., AbuJbara, A., Jha, R., Radev, D.: Identifying the semantic orientation of foreign words. In: Proceedings of the 49th Annual Meeting of the Association for Computational Linguistics: Human Language Technologies, Portland, Oregon, USA, pp. 592–597 (June 2011)
10. Forcada, M.L., Ginestí-Rosell, M., Nordfalk, J., O'Regan, J., Ortiz-Rojas, S., Pérez-Ortiz, J.A., Sánchez-Martínez, F., Ramírez-Sánchez, G., Tyers, F.M.: Apertium: a free/open-source platform for rule-based machine translation. Machine Translation 25(2), 127–144 (2011)

Stemming for Kurdish Information Retrieval

Shahin Salavati[1], Kyumars Sheykh Esmaili[2], and Fardin Akhlaghian[3]

[1] University of Kurdistan
Sanandaj, Iran
shahin.salavati@ieee.org
[2] Nanyang Technological University
Singapore
kyumarss@ntu.edu.sg
[3] University of Kurdistan
Sanandaj, Iran
f.akhlaghian@uok.ac.ir

Abstract. Resource scarcity along with diversity –in both dialect and script– are the two primary challenges in Kurdish language processing. In this paper we aim at addressing these two problems by building stemmers for the two main dialects of the Kurdish language (i.e. Sorani and Kurmanji) and investigate their effectiveness on Kurdish Information Retrieval.

More specifically, we build *Jedar*, the first rule-based stemmer for both Sorani and Kurmanji. We also implement *GRAS* –as a state-of-the-art statistical stemming technique– and apply it to both of the Kurdish dialects. We then conduct a comprehensive experimental study to compare the effectiveness of these stemmers.

Our experimental results show that stemming can significantly –up to %35– improve the retrieval performance on Kurdish documents. Furthermore, they indicate that the gains from the rule-based and the statistical approaches are comparable.

1 Introduction

Stemming is a common form of language processing in most information retrieval (IR) systems. Stemming is the process of reducing a word to its stem or root form. It allows documents in which a term is expressed using a different morphological form from the query, to be found and matched.

Although experiments with English data show mixed results [9,11,14], retrieval performance for morphologically more complex languages (e.g., Hungarian, Czech and Bulgarian [17], German [20,3], Dutch and Italian [20], and Arabic [33]) has benefited consistently and significantly from stemming.

The Kurdish language is an Indo-European language spoken in Turkey, Iran, Iraq and Syria. Despite having a large number of speakers, Kurdish is considered a less-resourced language for which –among other basic tools– no stemmer has been developed. Apart from the resource-scarcity problem, diversity –in both dialect and writing systems– is another primary challenge in Kurdish language processing. In fact, Kurdish

R.E. Banchs et al. (Eds.): AIRS 2013, LNCS 8281, pp. 272–283, 2013.
© Springer-Verlag Berlin Heidelberg 2013

is considered a *bi-standard* language [7,10]: the Sorani dialect written in an Arabic-based alphabet and the Kurmanji dialect written in a Latin-based alphabet. The features distinguishing these two dialects are phonological, lexical, and morphological.

This paper reports on our efforts in building stemmers for the two main dialects of the Kurdish language and investigate their effectiveness on Kurdish IR. The main contributions of this work are:

- we build *Jedar*, a rule-based stemmer for both Sorani Kurdish and Kurmanji Kurdish,
- we implement *GRAS* –a state-of-the-art statistical stemming technique– and apply it to both of the Kurdish dialects,
- we conduct a comprehensive experimental study to compare the effectiveness of these stemmers (including sensitivity analysis to fine-tune their parameters), and
- we carry out a detailed analysis of the results to obtain insights about the behavior of each configuration.

Additionally, our source codes for the Jedar and GRAS implementations along with the list of Kurmanji and Sorani suffixes used in our experiments are freely accessible and can be obtained from [12]. We hope that making these resources publicly available, would bolster further research on Kurdish IR.

The rest of the paper is organized as follows. We first, in Section 2, give a little bit of background on stemming in IR and also on the Kurdish language and dialects. Then in Section 3 we present the Kurdish suffixes and show how we used them to build Jedar, our rule-based stemmer. In Section 4, we briefly explain the GRAS statistical stemming algorithm [22] as well as our implementation of this algorithm. The details of our experimental study and analysis are reported in Section 5. Finally, we conclude the paper in Section 6.

2   Background

In this section we first give an overview of stemming in IR and then briefly introduce the Kurdish language and dialects.

2.1   Stemming for Information Retrieval

In an IR system, stemming is used to reduce variant word forms to common roots, and thereby improve the ability of the system to match query and document vocabulary. The variety in word forms comes from both inflectional and derivational morphology [32]. Inflection characterizes the changes in word form that accompany case, gender, number, tense, person, mood, or voice. Derivational analysis reduces surface forms to the base form from which they were derived, and includes changes in the part of speech [11].

All stemming algorithms can be roughly classified as rule-based (a.k.a affix removing) or statistical. Below we give a brief overview of each of these classes.

Rule-Based Stemmers. Rule-based stemmers apply a set of transformation rules to each word, trying to strip its suffixes[1]. Two of the most popular algorithms in English IR, the Lovins stemmer and the Porter stemmer, are based on suffix removal.

Lovins' paper [15] was the first published description of a stemmer. It defines 294 endings, each linked to one of the 29 conditions, and the 35 transformation rules. For a word being stemmed, an ending with a satisfying condition is found and removed. The algorithm is fast but misses certain endings.

Porter's algorithm [23] defines five successively applied steps of word transformation. Each step consists of set of rules. The algorithm is concise (about 60 rules) and efficient. The main flaws and errors are well-known and can mostly be corrected with a dictionary. The idea of Porter algorithm was later generalized into a stemmers framework called Snowball [24].

The major drawback of the rule-based approach is its dependency on a priory knowledge of the concerned language's morphology.

Statistical Stemmers. In contrast to the rule-based stemmers, statistical stemmers are language-independent and only require a corpus or a lexicon. In following we briefly summarize three important statistical stemmers.

The authors of the YASS stemmer [18] viewed stemming as a clustering problem in which the resulting clusters are considered as equivalence classes and their centroids as stems. Based on their implementation and experiments, they conclude that YASS' performance is comparable to rule-based stemmers like Porter or Lovins for English. For more morphologically-complex languages such as Bengali and French, YASS provides substantially improved performance as compared to using no stemming [18] .

Bacchin et al. [1] described a probabilistic model which relies on the mutual reinforcement relationship between stems and suffixes. Once the prefix and suffix scores are computed over a subset of documents from the corpus, the algorithm estimates the most probable split (into stem and suffix pair) for each word in the full corpus. A set of experiments with several languages produced equally good results as those produced by rule-based stemmers [1].

The main disadvantage of the aforementioned statistical stemming algorithms is that they are computationally expensive. In contrast, the recently-proposed GRAS algorithm [22] has been shown to be an efficient alternative. In experiments with seven languages of very different language families and varying morphological complexity, the authors showed that GRAS outperforms rule-based stemmers, three statistical methods (including YASS [18]), and the baseline strategy that did not use stemming.

Hence, we consider GRAS as the state-of-the-art solution for statistical stemming and use it in our experiments. We will describe the GRAS algorithm in more details later in Section 4.

2.2 The Kurdish Language and Dialects

Kurdish belongs to the Indo-Iranian family of Indo-European languages. Its closest better-known relative is Persian. Kurdish is spoken by 20 to 30 million people [8,10]

---

[1] Deletion of prefixes is not generally helpful for a stemming algorithm [11,21].

in Kurdistan, a large geographical area spanning the intersections of Turkey, Iran, Iraq, and Syria. It is one of the two official languages of Iraq and has a regional status in Iran.

Kurdish is a dialect-rich language, however, in this paper we focus on Sorani and Kurmanji which are the two closely-related and widely-spoken dialects of the Kurdish language [8]. Together, they account for more than 75% of native Kurdish speakers [31].

As summarized below, these two dialects differ not only in some linguistics aspects, but also in their writing systems.

Morphological Differences. Some of the important morphological differences are [16,8]:

- Kurmanji is more conservative in retaining both gender (feminine:masculine) and case opposition (absolute:oblique) for nouns and pronouns. Sorani has largely abandoned this system and uses the pronominal suffixes to take over the functions of the cases,
- the definiteness suffix -aka appears only in Sorani,
- in the past-tense transitive verbs, Kurmanji has full ergative alignment but Sorani, having lost the oblique pronouns, resorts to pronominal enclitics.

Scriptural Differences. Due to geopolitical reasons, each of the two dialects uses its own writing system: Sorani is almost-exclusively written in an Arabic-based alphabet and Kurmanji is almost-exclusively written in a Latin-based alphabet. Figure 1 shows the two standard alphabets and the mappings between them [5].

	1	2	3	4	5	6	7	8	9	10	11	12	13	14	15	16	17	18	19	20	21	22	23	24
Arabic-based	ا	ب	ج	چ	د	ئ	ف	گ	ژ	ک	ل	م	ن	ڤ	پ	ق	ر	س	ش	ت	وو	ڤ	خ	ز
Latin-based	A	B	C	Ç	D	Ê	F	G	J	K	L	M	N	O	P	Q	R	S	Ş	T	Û	V	X	Z

(a) One-to-One Mappings

	25	26	27	28
Arabic-based	/ ئ	و	ی	ه
Latin-based	I	U / W	Y / Î	E / H

(b) One-to-Two Mappings

	29	30	31	32	33
Arabic-based	ڕ	ڵ	ع	غ	ح
Latin-based	(RR)	-	(E)	(X)	(H)

(c) One-to-Zero Mappings

Fig. 1. The Two Standard Kurdish Alphabets [5]

As we will explain in Section 3, these differences have direct implications on designing Kurdish stemmers.

3   Kurdish Stemming: Rule-Based Approach

In the following, we first present the main Kurdish suffixes and then introduce our rule-based suffix-removing stemmer.

3.1 Main Suffixes in Kurdish

Kurdish has a complex morphology [26,29,5] and one of the main driving factors behind this complexity is the wide use of inflectional and derivational suffixes [6]. In general, Sorani and Kurmanji share a large proportion of suffixes. However, there is a small, but very important, set of Sorani-specific suffixes. Below, we elaborate more on each of these two groups.

<table>
<tr><td colspan="3">Suffix Group</td><td>Sorani</td><td>Kurmanji</td></tr>
<tr><td rowspan="8">Inflectional</td><td rowspan="4">Izafe Construction Markers</td><td rowspan="2">Masculine</td><td>Absolute</td><td>ێ</td><td>(y)ê</td></tr>
<tr><td>Oblique</td><td>ی</td><td>(y)î</td></tr>
<tr><td rowspan="2">Feminine</td><td>Absolute</td><td>ی</td><td>(y)a</td></tr>
<tr><td>Oblique</td><td>ێ</td><td>(y)ê</td></tr>
<tr><td rowspan="2">Plural Markers</td><td colspan="2">Absolute</td><td>ان</td><td>(y)ên</td></tr>
<tr><td colspan="2">Oblique</td><td>ان</td><td>(y)an</td></tr>
<tr><td colspan="3">Definiteness Makers</td><td>ەك</td><td>ek</td></tr>
<tr><td rowspan="6">Derivational</td><td colspan="3" rowspan="3">Professional Nouns</td><td>وان</td><td>van</td></tr>
<tr><td>کار</td><td>dar</td></tr>
<tr><td>دار</td><td>kar</td></tr>
<tr><td colspan="3" rowspan="3">Locational Nouns</td><td>خانه</td><td>xane</td></tr>
<tr><td>ستان</td><td>stan</td></tr>
<tr><td>گه</td><td>geh</td></tr>
</table>

<table>
<tr><td colspan="2">Suffix Group</td><td>Sorani</td><td>Kurmanji</td></tr>
<tr><td rowspan="6">Personal Verb Endings & "To Be"</td><td>1st Person Singular</td><td>م</td><td>(i)m</td></tr>
<tr><td>2nd Person Singular</td><td>ی</td><td>î</td></tr>
<tr><td>3rd Person Singular</td><td>ێ/ئە</td><td>e</td></tr>
<tr><td>1st Person Plural</td><td>ین</td><td>in/ne</td></tr>
<tr><td>2nd Person Plural</td><td>ن</td><td>in/ne</td></tr>
<tr><td>3rd Person Plural</td><td>ن</td><td>in/ne</td></tr>
<tr><td rowspan="9">Helper Verbs</td><td rowspan="6">Used in Infinitive Form</td><td>گرتن</td><td>girtin</td></tr>
<tr><td>کردن</td><td>kirin</td></tr>
<tr><td>بوون</td><td>bûn</td></tr>
<tr><td>بردن</td><td>birin</td></tr>
<tr><td>بوو</td><td>bû</td></tr>
<tr><td>کرد</td><td>kir</td></tr>
<tr><td rowspan="3">Used in Conjugated Form</td><td>کراو/کردوو</td><td>kirî/kiri</td></tr>
<tr><td>دەکەن</td><td>dikin</td></tr>
<tr><td>دەکات</td><td>dike</td></tr>
</table>

(a) Noun Suffixes   (b) Verb Suffixes

Fig. 2. Common Suffix Groups in Sorani Kurdish and Kurmanji Kurdish

Common Suffixes. An essential subset of common suffixes between Sorani and Kurmanji is depicted in Figure 2. The complete set can be downloaded from [12]. It should be noted that for some pairs, the Sorani and the Kurmanji strings are not complete transliteration-equivalents (based on the char-level mappings of Figure 1). The left side of Figure 2 (part a) contains the common *noun* suffixes. A few important remarks regarding this list are:

- the Izafe Construction is a shared feature of several Western Iranian languages [25]. It approximately corresponds to the English preposition *of* and is added between prepositions, nouns and adjectives in a phrase. The Kurmanji Izafe marker agrees in gender and in case with the head noun [30], thus giving rise to various forms,
- the impact of case in Kurmanji is also evident in the plural noun marker [30], for which two different forms exist,
- in the Kurmanji writing system, if suffixing results in two consecutive vowels, an extra *y* is inserted between them.

The right side of Figure 2 (part b) represents the common *verb* suffixes. There are two important notes here:

- in Sorani and Kurmanji while conjugating a verb in past or present tense, personal endings are added to the verb root. These endings –except in the past transitive tense– are identical to the present forms of the verb *to be* in Kurdish (بوون/ "bûn") [27].

- Kurdish resembles most Iranian languages in the fact that it possesses only a limited amount (around 300) of synthetic verbal lexemes [16,2]. Most verbal meanings in Kurdish are expressed through complex compositions. One important class of composition elements is auxiliary verbs which can be used in their infinitive form to build new nouns, or in conjugated form to build different tenses.

Sorani-Specific Suffixes. Compared to Kurmanji, Sorani has a richer set of suffixes. A small, but nonetheless very crucial, set of Sorani-specific suffixes is listed in Figure 3. As described below, the existence of these suffixes is due to Sorani's inherent

Suffix	Translit.	Description
م	m	1st Person Singular
ت	t	2nd Person Singular
ی	i	3rd Person Singular
مان	maan	1st Person Plural
تان	taan	2nd Person Plural
یان	yaan	3rd Person Plural

Suffix	Translit.	Description
هکه	aka	Definite Marker Singular
هکان	akaan	Definite Maker Plural
دا	daa	A Common Postposition
ش	sh	A Common Conjunction

(a) MPM/Possessive Pronouns   (b) Others

Fig. 3. Sorani-Specific Suffixes

morphological properties as well as its script and system of writing:

- Sorani uses the pronominal suffixes to take over the functions of the cases (see Section 2.2). The two principal uses of such suffixes are: (i) the mobile person markers (MPMs) [27,29] which are used as pronominal enclitics in past-tense transitive verbs (Kurmanji, in contrast, has full ergative alignment), and (ii) the possessive pronouns (Kurmanji, instead, uses the oblique form of the personal pronouns). As reflected in Figure 3a, these two suffix sets have identical representations.
- the definite markers (هکه *aka* and هکان *akaan* for singular and plural nouns, respectively) only exist in Sorani,
- there is a general tendency in Sorani's writing system to join suffixes to their preceding noun [5]. Its most prominent example is the verb بوون *boon* "to be" (presented in Figure 2b). Two other widely-used instances are the postposition دا *daa* –which is in fact the closing part of some commonly-used circumpositions and therefore has no independent meaning– and the conjunction یش *ish* "too".

3.2 Jedar

In this section we introduce **Jedar**[2], the first rule-based stemmer for the Kurdish language. Kurdish stems are often followed by multiple suffixes, hence, Jedar adopts a recursive approach to handle nested suffixes. Moreover, we have devised two techniques to decrease Jedar's over-stemming error[3]. The first technique –adopted from [15]– is to prevent over-stemming by setting a minimum stem length parameter, denoted by L.

---

[2] A Kurdish word (in Sorani: ژێدەر , in Kurmanji: *Jêder*) meaning "origin" in English.
[3] A common error in rule-based stemmers caused by blindly removing substrings that belong to the word's stem.

The second technique is to exploit the inherent suffixing properties of the Kurdish language. Below, we give a brief description of some of these properties:

- the nominal suffixes appear in a certain pre-defined order. To demonstrate this order, we analyze the example word كتێوهكانيشتاندا *ktewakaanishtaandaa* "[in] your books too" which consists of a stem (كتێو *ktew* "book") and four different suffixes:

دا	+	تان	+	يش	+	هكان	+	كتێو	=	كتێوهكانيشتاندا
daa	+	*taan*	+	*ish*	+	*akaan*	+ *ktew*	=	*ktewakaanishtaandaa*
postpos.	+	poss. pron.	+	conjunc.	+	def. marker	+ stem	=	word

- in any given word, only one instance of each suffix type can appear. For example, although the word كلينيكهكه *klinekaka* "the clinic" contains both the indefinite marker (ێک *ek*) and the definite marker (هكه *aka*), only the second one is a valid suffix and the first one should be left untouched. One important exception to this rule is MPMs/possessive pronouns (Figure 3a), which have identical representations but different roles.

- under some circumstances, the minimum length constraint can be relaxed. For example if a word ends in بوو *boo* "was", this string can be removed, as it is solely used to build the past perfect form of the verbs.

Jedar has been implemented as a single Java class (for both Sorani and Kurmanji) that takes a list of dialect-specific suffixes as input. For each input word, Jedar recursively removes the best matching suffix, taking into account a set of rules including those explained above.

4   Kurdish Stemming: Statistical Approach

As explained in Section 2.1, the GRAph-based Stemming (GRAS) algorithm has been shown to outperform a number of other existing statistical stemmers. Hence we chose this algorithm to compare with Jedar. The GRAS algorithm, in essence, consists of three steps [22]:

Step 1: Frequent Suffix Pair Identification. GRAS starts with a lexicon, a list of the distinct words of the concerned language (usually extracted from a corpus). The words in this lexicon are partitioned into a number of groups such that each pair of words drawn from a group has a common prefix of length at least λ, a pre-defined threshold. Within each group, all possible word pairs are enumerated and suffix pairs are extracted. For example, since the word pair $(w_1 = p||s_1, w_2 = p||s_2)$ share a common prefix p, then s_1 and s_2 constitute a candidate suffix pair. When all groups are exhausted, the total frequency of each suffix pair is computed and the non-frequent pairs (fewer occurrences than α, a cutoff threshold) are discarded.

Step 2: Graph Construction. Having built a list of frequent suffix pairs, this list is then used to construct a weighted undirected graph $G = (V, E)$ as follows. Each word in the lexicon is represented by a vertex in G. In this graph, the edge weight, $w(u, v)$, is the frequency of the suffix pair induced by the word pair represented by u and v. Needless to say, if $w(u, v) < \alpha$, there is no edge between u and v.

Step 3: Graph Decomposition. Once the graph G is constructed, the next step is to decompose it. The decomposition algorithm first chooses a pivotal node (say p) from the remaining vertices, such that its degree is maximized. Next, it considers the vertices adjacent to the pivotal node p one-by-one and measures the *cohesion* between p and v using the formula:

$$cohesion(p, v) = \frac{1 + |Adjacent(p) \cap Adjacent(v)|}{|Adjacent(v)|}$$

The value of cohesion lies between 0 and 1. If the cohesion value exceeds a certain threshold (δ), the vertex v is assumed to be morphologically related with the pivot p and is put in the same class as p. Otherwise, the edge (p, v) is deleted immediately to mark that p and v are not related.

As highlighted by the authors, the choices of the three main parameters –namely the minimum length of the common prefix λ, the suffix frequency cutoff α, and the cohesion threshold δ– are important for the performance of the algorithm. Although they provide some clues, but as shown later, more precise values can be found empirically.

The original implementation of GRAS is unfortunately not open source. Therefore, we built our own implementation from scratch by closely following the descriptions given in [22]. Our Java implementation of the GRAS algorithm (along with Jedar's implementation) can be obtained from [12].

5 Experiments

In our experiments, we used Pewan, a publicly-available Kurdish test collection [13] which contains two separate text corpora (one Sorani one Kurmanji) and a set of queries available in both dialects. The main properties of the Pewan collection are summarized in Table 1.

Table 1. The Pewan Test Collection [6]

	Number of Documents	Number of Queries	Average QRel Length
Sorani	115,340	22	42
Kurmanji	25,572	22	12.5

For the IR engine, we chose **MG4J** [19], an open-source Java retrieval system which has been shown [4,6] to be the best performing system for Kurdish IR among a number of systems.

In the following, we first report on the sensitivity analysis that we carried out to fine-tune Jedar's and GRAS' parameters. Then we provide more insights about the outcomes through a detailed analysis of the results.

5.1 Parameter Tuning

In these experiments we vary the stemming parameters and compare the results based on Mean Average Precision (MAP) values. Additionally, we also report the size of the resulting lexicon, that is the total number of distinct strings in Pewan after applying stemming.

Jedar's Parameter. We performed a sensitivity analysis on Jedar by varying the minimum stem length parameter, L, from 3 to 6 (according to Lovins [15], any useful stem often consists of at least three or four characters). The results are shown in Table 2. In this table, *Baseline* denotes the case in which no stemming was applied. Based on these numbers, two important conclusions can be drawn: (i) our rule-based stemming solution generally improves the retrieval performance, (ii) for both Sorani and Kurmanji, the best result is achieved for $L = 3$ (the gains are 25% and 35% respectively).

Table 2. Tuning Jedar's Minimum Stem Length Parameter

Parameter		Sorani		Kurmanji	
Minimum Stem Length (L)	MAP	Lexicon Size	MAP	Lexicon Size
3	**0.440**	217522	**0.340**	55920
4	0.435	228526	0.285	64488
5	0.433	248692	0.312	71971
6	0.438	274378	0.308	84576
Baseline	0.352	483846	0.251	121625

GRAS' Parameters. One of the important steps in building statistical stemmers is find the best of set of values for the parameters [28]. For GRAS, although the authors provide some general hints in [22] (i.e., λ to be the average word length for the language concerned, $\alpha = 4$ and $\delta = 0.8$), but we decided to run a set of experiments to empirically identify the best vales for the these parameters.

From the computational complexity perspective, λ is the most important parameter, as it directly affects the complexity of the graph decomposition step. In our experiments, we varied the value of λ from 3 to 7 (Sorani's average word length is 5.6; for Kurmanji it is 4.8 [5]). Moreover, since running the algorithm with $\lambda = 3$ and $\lambda = 4$ on the full version of our Sorani lexicon (generated from all documents in Pewan's Sorani corpus) exhausted our computational resources, for these cases we used reduced lexicons (generated from 10% and 25% of the documents, accordingly).

The results of this study is shown in Table 3. We would like to note that in the interest of space and due to its inferior performance, the results for $\lambda = 7$ are not included in this table.

Based on these numbers, the following observations can be made: (i) our implementation of the GRAS statistical stemmer generally improves the retrieval performance, (ii) while for Kurmanji the best outcome is achieved for $(\lambda = 3, \alpha = 2, \delta = 0.7)$, Sorani's peak is reached at $(\lambda = 4, \alpha = 6, \delta = 0.9)$.

5.2   Analysis

The MAP measure is useful to compare the *overall* performance of different IR systems. In order to better understand the behavior of these systems, a detailed analysis of the results is required. To this end, in the following we present a drill-down comparison of Jedar's and GRAS' outputs at their best-performing configuration.

Detailed Comparison. Figure 4 depicts the precision curves at the standard 11 recall points. It clearly demonstrates the facts that (i) both Jedar and GRAS improve the IR performance at all recall levels, (ii) the gains from Jedar and GRAS are comparable.

Table 3. Tuning GRAS' Parameters

Parameters			Sorani		Kurmanji	
λ	α	δ	MAP	Lexicon Size	MAP	Lexicon Size
3	2	0.7	0.356	393631	**0.341**	43704
		0.8	0.387	395257	0.280	15290
		0.9	0.400	404448	0.280	15290
	4	0.7	0.422	404137	0.280	15290
		0.8	0.387	395257	0.280	15290
		0.9	0.400	404448	0.280	15290
	6	0.7	0.356	393631	0.280	15290
		0.8	0.387	395257	0.280	15290
		0.9	0.407	412398	0.280	15290
4	2	0.7	0.445	343658	0.305	63316
		0.8	0.364	315986	0.313	63563
		0.9	0.364	315986	0.304	66333
	4	0.7	0.364	315986	0.300	70634
		0.8	0.364	315986	0.300	70894
		0.9	0.364	315986	0.319	72642
	6	0.7	0.427	361278	0.300	73678
		0.8	0.432	352719	0.305	73943
		0.9	**0.448**	352523	0.314	75597
5	2	0.7	0.440	198860	0.296	79240
		0.8	0.415	161743	0.296	79324
		0.9	0.415	161743	0.301	80177
	4	0.7	0.415	161743	0.294	83627
		0.8	0.415	161743	0.296	83714
		0.9	0.415	161743	0.308	84436
	6	0.7	0.415	161743	0.294	85466
		0.8	0.415	161743	0.298	85529
		0.9	0.415	161743	0.314	86343
6	2	0.7	0.409	232014	0.292	93144
		0.8	0.409	231975	0.293	93197
		0.9	0.409	231975	0.294	93543
	4	0.7	0.409	231975	0.305	95794
		0.8	0.409	231975	0.308	95805
		0.9	0.409	231975	0.308	96224
	6	0.7	0.409	231975	0.306	97002
		0.8	0.409	231975	0.306	97047
		0.9	0.409	231975	0.304	97488
Baseline			0.352	483846	0.251	121625

Given GRAS' reasonable computational cost and its language-independent nature, this can mean that GRAS is the favorable option.

Query-Level Analysis. We also carried out a query-level examination of the results and identified three distinct groups among the queries. Below, we enumerate these groups and present an example for each one:

- *GRAS outperforming Jedar*: for example for Q_{21} in the Sorani experiments, while GRAS correctly puts the words سووریه *Soorya* and سووریا *Sooryaa* (different variations of the country name "Syria") in one cluster, Jedar over-stems the word سووریه *Soorya* to سوور *Soor* (the color name "red") which is obviously irrelevant and entails ambiguity.
- *Jedar outperforming GRAS*: for instance in the Sorani version of Q_{22}, GRAS puts the named entity تووڕج *Tooraj* (first name of a local photographer) into an irrelevant cluster with the stem تووڕەبوون *Toorraboon* "resent".

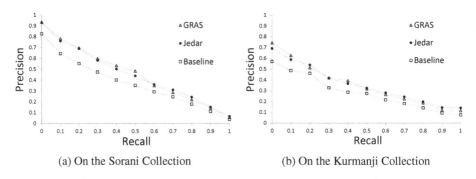

(a) On the Sorani Collection   (b) On the Kurmanji Collection

Fig. 4. PR-Graphs for the Best-Performing Configurations of Jedar and GRAS

– *Stemming unhelpful*: e.g., for query Q_{10} in the Kurmanji experiments, both stemming approaches result in performance degradation, compared to the baseline approach in which no-stemming is applied. This is because both Jedar and GRASS consider the composite named entity Hikûmeta Herêma Kurdistanê (*Kurdistan Regional Government*) to be three independent words and stem them separately, leading to retrieval of irrelevant documents.

6   Conclusions and Future Work

In this paper we presented Jedar, the first rule-based stemmer for Sorani Kurdish and Kurmanji Kurdish. We also introduced our implementation of GRAS [22], a recent proposal for statistical stemming. After fine-tuning their parameters, these stemmers were used to empirically study the effectiveness stemming for Kurdish IR.

Our results show that: (i) both Jedar and GRAS can significantly improve the performance of Kurdish IR systems, (ii) the rule-based approach and the the statistical stemmer approach perform comparably well, (iii) overall, the shorter stem lengths (i.e., 3,4) seem to be more effective.

In future, we plan to propose solutions to fix some of the systematic stemming errors that we highlighted in the analysis section (e.g., over-stemming and mishandling of named entities). Comparing the performance of these stemmers against N-grams is another avenue for future work.

References

1. Bacchin, M., Ferro, N., Melucci, M.: A Probabilistic Model for Stemmer Generation. Information Processing and Management 41(1), 121–137 (2005)
2. Blau, J.: Méthode de Kurde: Sorani. Harmattan (2000)
3. Braschler, M., Ripplinger, B.: How Effective is Stemming and Decompounding for German Text Retrieval? Information Retrieval 7(3-4), 291–316 (2004)
4. Esmaili, K.S., et al.: Building a Test Collection for Sorani Kurdish. In: Proceedings of IEEE AICCSA (2013)
5. Esmaili, K.S., Salavati, S.: Sorani Kurdish versus Kurmanji Kurdish: An Empirical Comparison. In: Proceedings of the 51st Annual Meeting of ACL (2013)

6. Esmaili, K.S., Salavati, S., Datta, A.: Towards Kurdish Information Retrieval. ACM TALIP (to appear, 2013)
7. Gautier, G.: Building a Kurdish Language Corpus: An Overview of the Technical Problems. In: Proceedings of ICEMCO (1998)
8. Haig, G., Matras, Y.: Kurdish Linguistics: A Brief Overview. Language Typology and Universals 55(1) (2002)
9. Harman, D.: How Effective is Suffixing? JASIS 42(1), 7–15 (1991)
10. Hassanpour, A., et al.: Introduction. Kurdish: Linguicide, Resistance and Hope. International Journal of the Sociology of Language 217, 1–8 (2012)
11. Hull, D.A.: Stemming Algorithms: A Case Study for Detailed Evaluation. Journal of the American Society for Information Science 47(1), 70–84 (1996)
12. KLPP. Kurdish Language Stemmers, http://klpp.github.io/
13. KLPP. The Pewan Test Collection, http://klpp.github.io/
14. Krovetz, R.: Viewing Morphology as an Inference Process. In: Proceedings of ACM SIGIR 1993, pp. 191–202 (1993)
15. Lovins, J.B.: Development of a Stemming Algorithm. MIT Information Processing Group, Electronic Systems Laboratory (1968)
16. MacKenzie, D.N.: Kurdish Dialect Studies. Oxford University Press (1961)
17. Majumder, P., Mitra, M., Pal, D.: Bulgarian, hungarian and czech stemming using YASS. In: Peters, C., Jijkoun, V., Mandl, T., Müller, H., Oard, D.W., Peñas, A., Petras, V., Santos, D. (eds.) CLEF 2007. LNCS, vol. 5152, pp. 49–56. Springer, Heidelberg (2008)
18. Majumder, P., Mitra, M., Parui, S.K., Kole, G., Mitra, P., Datta, K.: YASS: Yet Another Suffix Stripper. ACM TOIS 25(4), 18 (2007)
19. MG4J. Managing Gigabytes for Java, http://mg4j.dsi.unimi.it/
20. Monz, C., De Rijke, M.: Shallow Morphological Analysis in Monolingual Information Retrieval for Dutch, German, and Italian. In: Evaluation of Cross-Language Information Retrieval Systems, pp. 262–277 (2002)
21. Paice, C.D.: An Evaluation Method for Stemming Algorithms. In: Proceedings of ACM SIGIR 1994, pp. 42–50 (1994)
22. Paik, J.H., Mitra, M., Parui, S.K., Järvelin, K.: GRAS: An Effective and Efficient Stemming Algorithm for Information Retrieval. ACM TOIS 29(4), 19 (2011)
23. Porter, M.F.: An algorithm for suffix stripping, pp. 313–316. Morgan Kaufmann Publishers Inc. (1997)
24. Porter, M.: Snowball: A Language for Stemming Algorithms (2001)
25. Samvelian, P.: When Morphology Does Better Than Syntax: The Ezafe Construction in Persian. Ms., Université de Paris (2006)
26. Samvelian, P.: A Lexical Account of Sorani Kurdish Prepositions. In: Proceedings of International Conference on Head-Driven Phrase Structure Grammar, pp. 235–249 (2007)
27. Samvelian, P.: What Sorani Kurdish Absolute Prepositions Tell Us about Cliticization. Texas Linguistic Society IX, p. 265 (2007)
28. Smirnov, I.: Overview of Stemming Algorithms. Mechanical Translation (2008)
29. Walther, G.: Fitting into Morphological Structure: Accounting for Sorani Kurdish Endoclitics. In: The Proceedings of the Eighth Mediterranean Morphology Meeting (2011)
30. Walther, G., et al.: Fast Development of Basic NLP Tools: Towards a Lexicon and a POS Tagger for Kurmanji Kurdish. In: Proceedings of the 29th International Conference on Lexis and Grammar (2010)
31. Walther, G., Sagot, B.: Developing a Large-scale Lexicon for a Less-Resourced Language. In: SaLTMiL's Workshop on Less-resourced Languages (LREC) (2010)
32. Xu, J., Croft, B.: Corpus-based Stemming Using Cooccurrence of Word Variants. ACM TOIS 16(1), 61–81 (1998)
33. Xu, J., Fraser, A., Weischedel, R.: Empirical Studies in Strategies for Arabic Retrieval. In: Proceedings ACM SIGIR 2002, pp. 269–274 (2002)

The Utility of Discourse Structure
in Forum Thread Retrieval

Li Wang[1,2], Su Nam Kim[3], and Timothy Baldwin[1,2]

[1] Department of Computing and Information Systems, The University of Melbourne
[2] NICTA Victoria Research Laboratory
[3] Faculty of Information Technology, Monash University
li@liwang.info, sunamkim@gmail.com, tb@ldwin.net

Abstract. Web user forums are a valuable means for users to resolve specific information needs, both interactively for the participants and statically for users who search/browse over historical thread data. However, the complex structure of forum threads can make it difficult for users to extract relevant information. Information retrieval (IR) over forum threads is one important way to obtain useful information on questions asked by others. In this paper, we investigate the task of IR over web user forums by utilising the discourse structure of forum threads. Experimental results show that exploiting the characteristics of discourse structure of forum threads can benefit IR, when compared to previously-published results.

Keywords: Discourse Structure, Web User Forum, Information Retrieval, Social Media, Dialogue Act.

1 Introduction

Web user forums (or simply "forums") are online platforms for people to discuss information and obtain information via a text-based threaded discourse, generally in a pre-determined domain (e.g. IT support or DSLR cameras). With the advent of Web 2.0, there has been an explosion of web authorship in this area, and forums are now widely used in various areas such as customer support, community development, interactive reporting and online eduction. In addition to providing the means to interactively participate in discussions or obtain/provide answers to questions, the vast volumes of data contained in forums make them a valuable resource for "support sharing", i.e. looking over records of past user interactions to potentially find an immediately applicable solution to a current problem. On the one hand, more and more answers to questions over a wide range of domains are becoming available on forums; on the other hand, it is becoming harder and harder to extract and access relevant information due to the sheer scale and diversity of the data.

One potential way to enhance information access and support sharing in forums is to improve information retrieval (IR) effectiveness over forum threads. To this end, Elsas [1] amassed a forum dataset for forum thread retrieval and

R.E. Banchs et al. (Eds.): AIRS 2013, LNCS 8281, pp. 284–295, 2013.
© Springer-Verlag Berlin Heidelberg 2013

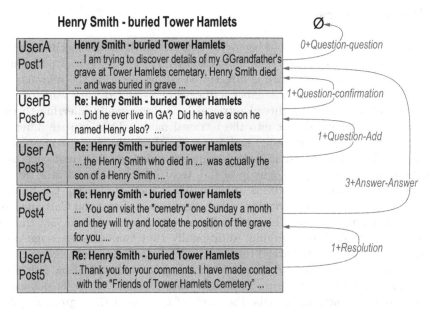

Fig. 1. A snippeted and annotated **Ancestry** thread

conducted initial experiments. We build on this earlier work, in exploring the hypothesis that incorporating thread discourse structure [2,3] into the IR model can improve retrieval effectiveness.

The discourse structure of a thread is modelled as a rooted directed acyclic graph (DAG), with the posts in the thread represented as nodes in the DAG. The reply-to relations between posts take the form of directed edges (Links) between nodes in the DAG, and dialogue acts (DAs) are used to label the edges. For the purposes of illustration, we use an annotated example thread from Elsas' **Ancestry** dataset [1], made up of 5 posts from 3 distinct participants, as shown in Fig. 1. In this example, UserA initiates the thread with a question (DA = Question-question) in the first post, seeking information about his/her great-grandfather. In response, UserB asks for more details about the question (DA = Question-confirmation). Then UserA responds to UserB to add extra information to his/her original question (DA = Question-add). Finally, UserC proposes a solution to the original question (DA = Answer-answer), and UserA confirms that this answer is correct (DA = Resolution). It should be noted that the discourse structure of most threads actually takes the form of a tree, as shown in Fig. 1. However, in some rare cases, a given post can reply to two or more previous posts, producing a DAG structure.

Specifically in this paper, we automatically infer the thread discourse structure of a target forum dataset by using a discourse parser that is trained over out-of-domain annotated data. We then incorporate information derived from this thread discourse structure into a state-of-the-art IR model for forum retrieval, and find that thread discourse structure can, indeed, benefit thread retrieval. We also investigate the reason behind the improvements.

2 Related Work

As far as we are aware, there has been very little IR work that is specifically targeted at web user forum data. The most closely-related work is that performed by Elsas [1], on which this work is directly based; we describe the relevant details of Elsas' work later in this paper. Other closely-related work was done by Seo et al. [4], in improving thread retrieval by automatically inferring thread structure and incorporating it into the retrieval model. They explore different thread document representations, such as at the thread-level (i.e. concatenate all the posts in a thread into a single document), pair-level (i.e. treat each pair of posts as a document), dialogue-level (i.e. treat each sub-thread in a thread as a document), and combinations of these. They show that using the linking structure of threads boosts thread retrieval effectiveness. Elsas and Carbonell [5] conducted preliminary research on thread retrieval and also showed that thread structure is useful in thread ranking. Additionally, they found that message/post selection can contribute to thread retrieval.

Research on thread discourse structure analysis and classification over user forums has gained in momentum in recent years. Fortuna et al. [6] defined 5 post-level dialogue acts to describe the levels of agreement (i.e. agreement, disagreement, insult) and identify questions and answers (i.e. question and answer) in forum posts. Xi et al. [7] defined 5 prevalent types of post-level dialogue acts in forum threads. This set of dialogue acts was then adapted and extended by us in earlier work [2] to describe possible types of posts in troubleshooting-oriented online forums. Specifically, we devised a post-level dialogue act set and annotated a set of threads from forums.cnet.com In this work, we proposed a set of novel features, which they applied to the separate tasks of post link classification and dialogue act classification. We later applied the same basic methodology to dialogue act classification over one-on-one live chat data with provided message dependencies [8], demonstrating the generalisability of the original method. In both cases, however, we tackled only a single task, either link classification (optionally given dialogue act tags) or dialogue act classification, but never the two together.

In later work, we delved into the task of thread discourse structure parsing further [3]. We used the same features as [2], but different parsing approaches. Specifically, we approached thread discourse structure parsing as a joint link and dialogue act classification task, using conditional random fields [9] and dependency parsing [10]. We also demonstrated that our discourse structure parsing method was able to perform equally well over partial threads as complete threads, by experimenting with "in situ" classification of evolving threads.

There has also been research focusing on particular types of dialogue acts, such as question–answer pairs in emails [11] and forum threads [12], question–context–answer in forum threads [12], initiation–response pairs (e.g. question–answer, assessment–agreement, and blame–denial) in forum threads [13], as well as request and commitment in emails [14].

Thread discourse structure can be used to facilitate different tasks in web user forums. For example, we demonstrated that the information extracted from thread discourse structure can be used to improve Solvedness (i.e. whether the problem presented in the thread is solved or not) classification of forum threads [15]. Additionally, threading information has been shown to enhance retrieval effectiveness for post-level retrieval [7,4], thread-level retrieval [4,5], sentence-level shallow information extraction [16], and near-duplicate thread detection [17]. Moreover, Wang and Rose [13] demonstrated that initiation–response pairs (e.g. question–answer, assessment–agreement, and blame–denial) from online forums have the potential to enhance thread summarisation and automatically generate knowledge bases for Community Question Answering (cQA) services such as Yahoo! Answers. Furthermore, Kim et al. [18] showed that dialogue acts can be used to classify student online discussions in web-enhanced courses. Specifically, they use dialogue acts to identify discussion threads that may have unanswered questions and need the attention of an instructor.

3   Dataset Description

3.1   The Ancestry Forum Dataset

The Ancestry.com Forum Dataset (Ancestry) was created by Jonathan Elsas and Ancestry.com, a website which supports historical genealogical research. The Ancestry dataset contains a full snapshot of the Ancestry.com online forum (boards.ancestry.com) from December 1995 to July 2010. The dataset includes $22,054,728$ posts spanning $9,040,958$ threads, from $165,358$ sub-forums. The total number of unique users is $3,775,670$. The Ancestry dataset is presented at the post-level, and information associated with each post includes: post identifiers, the subforum name, thread identifier, author name/identifier, timestamp (at the day level), URL of the original post, post title and post body. The inter-post link structure of each thread, in terms of the reply-to structure generated by users when posting to the thread, are also provided.

The Ancestry dataset also comes with a selected set of 191 queries from Ancestry.com's query log, and pairwise preference relevance judgements for each query over the Ancestry.com forum data.

To create the pairwise preference relevance judgements annotation, a document pool is simulated as the first step. Firstly, Indri (lemurproject.org), Terrier (terrier.org), Zettair (www.seg.rmit.edu.au/zettair) and Ancestry.com's ranked boolean system are applied over the whole dataset to produce post rankings, with each ranking containing 1000 posts. Then, three aggregation methods, namely Mean, Max and Pseudo-Cluster Selection (PCS) [19], are used to convert each post ranking to a thread ranking. Lastly, the document pool is created by combining the top 100 threads of each thread ranking. The document pool contains 374 unique threads per query on average.

Relevance assessment is conducted by Ancestry.com, by collecting document-pair preferences [20]. This approach presents side-by-side document pairs (L, R) and collects judgements: L is preferred to R, R is preferred to L, L and R are duplicates, L is bad or R is bad. During the assessment process, a document pair selection algorithm, which is described in detail in [1], is used to reduce the number of assessments.

Out of the 191 queries, 50 queries were first selected for a pilot assessment, with each query annotated by two assessors. The results of the pilot assessment were analysed and used as a guide to set the parameters of the document pair selection algorithm, as well as adjust assessor training and assessment guidelines. Then, each of the remaining 141 queries was assessed by one assessor, with the adjusted parameters of the pair selection algorithm.

3.2   The CNET Forum Dataset

The CNET forum dataset of Kim et al. [2][1] contains 1332 annotated posts spanning 315 threads, collected from the Operating System, Software, Hardware and Web Development sub-forums of CNET.[2] Each post is labelled with one or more links (including the possibility of null-links, where the post doesn't link to any other post), and each link is labelled with a dialogue act. The dialogue act set is made up of 5 super-categories: Question, Answer, Resolution (confirmation of the question being resolved), Reproduction (external confirmation of a proposed solution working) and Other. The Question category contains 4 sub-classes: question, add, confirmation and correction. Similarly, the Answer category contains 5 sub-classes: answer, add, confirmation, correction and objection. For example, the label Question-add signifies the Question superclass and add subclass, i.e. addition of extra information to a question.

3.3   The ILIAD Forum Dataset

The ILIAD (Improved Linux Information Access by Data Mining) dataset [21] contains 1158 posts spanning 250 threads, collected from Linuxquestions[3] and Debian mailing lists.[4] We hand-annotated the discourse structure of the ILIAD dataset [15], based on a slightly modified version of the dialogue act set from our earlier work [2]. As part of this annotation, we proposed an additional Question-information dialogue act, for posts which provide information in non-troubleshooting threads. We also slightly adjusted the definition of the Resolution dialogue act. For full details of the ILIAD dataset and the annotations over it, see [21] and [15], respectively.

---

[1] Available from http://www.csse.unimelb.edu.au/research/lt/resources/conll2010-thread/

[2] http://forums.cnet.com/

[3] http://www.linuxquestions.org

[4] http://lists.debian.org/completeindex.html

Table 1. Summary of Elsas' [1] experimental setup

IR Systems	
System	Configuration Used
Indri	Bag-of-words (BoW) queries
Indri	Dependence Model (DM) queries [23], with suggested model weights
Indri	Fielded query with linear combination
Indri	Fielded query with loglinear combination
Terrier	*PL2* with default parameters
Terrier	*InL2* with default parameters
Zettair	Default Okapi BM25 ranking algorithm
Ancestry.com	The ranked boolean system used by Ancestry.com
Aggregation Methods	
Name	Description
Mean	Thread score is the mean of retrieved posts' scores
Max	Thread score is the max score of the retrieved posts
Pseudo-Cluster Selection (PCS)[19]	Thread score is the geometric mean of the top-k retrieved posts' scores ($k = 5$ is used)

4 Pairwise Preference Evaluation

As explained in Section 3.1, the relevance judgements in the Ancestry dataset are pairwise preferences, rather than traditional absolute preferences (judgements). As analogues to absolute evaluation measures such as Precision at a cutoff ($P@k$) and Average Precision (AP), Elsas [1] uses Precision of Preferences at a cutoff ($ppref@k$) and a modified version of Average Precision of Preferences ($mAPpref$), which was originally proposed by Carterette [22]. $ppref@k$ represents the proportion of correctly ordered preferences to ordered preferences, where at least one document/thread in the pair is ranked above k. $mAPpref$ is the average of $ppref$ values over the ranks (i.e. k) of all documents which have ever been preferred to any other documents. While $ppref$ used by Elsas [1] is unchanged, the original $APpref$ proposed by Carterette [22] is the average of $ppref$ values over the ranks (i.e. k) at which the recall of preferences ($rpref$) increases. $rpref$ is the proportion of correctly ordered preferences to the total number of preferences made by assessors.

For comparability, the primary evaluation metrics used in this paper are $ppref@10$ and $mAPpref$, based on the evaluation script provided by Elsas [1].[5]

5 Baseline Systems

Elsas [1] conducted a series of IR experiments over the Ancestry dataset, using 4 retrieval systems with various configurations. The retrieval was done at the post-level, and 3 different aggregation methods were used to convert the post-level

---

[5] Available at https://github.com/jelsas/Pairwise-Preference-Evaluation

Table 2. Elsas' [1] IR results (Original) and our reproduced results (Reproduced) over the Ancestry dataset. Retrieval is performed at the post-level, and evaluation is conducted at the thread-level. Three aggregation methods are used for each system to transform post-level scores to thread-level scores. The best results for each column are **bold-faced**.

System	Aggregation Method	*mAPpref*		*ppref*@10	
		Orginal	Reproduced	Orginal	Reproduced
Indri-BoW	Mean	.542	.533	.492	.501
	Max	.599	.591	.561	.556
	PCS	.656	.650	.640	.633
Indri-DM	Mean	.549	.536	.506	.510
	Max	.608	.597	.571	.568
	PCS	**.661**	**.657**	**.646**	**.664**

rankings to thread-level rankings. A summary of the retrieval systems with the configurations used, as well as the aggregation methods, is presented in Table 1.

According to the experiments of Elsas [1], Indri with bag-of-words (BoW) and dependence model (DM: [23]) query formulation perform the best; our experiments support this conclusion. The DM used is a full dependency variant of a Markov Random Field, which assumes that all query terms are in some way dependent on each other. It considers the BoW representation (with weight 0.8) of the whole query, as well as ordered representation (with weight 0.1) and unordered representation (with weight 0.1) of the subsets of the query.

We tried to reproduce the results presented in [1] using Indri-BoW and Indri-DM for post-level retrieval with three different aggregation methods: Mean, Max and Pseudo-Cluster Selection (PCS). Our experimental results are displayed alongside the results reported in [1] in Table 2. Although there are slight differences between our results and Elsas' [1] results, the overall results are comparable. Because Indri-DM with PCS (Indri-DM-PCS) obtains the best results for both *mAPpref* and *ppref*@10, it will be used as our baseline IR method.

Following the work of Seo et al. [4], we also experimented with retrieval based on contexts of differing size, such as the thread-level, pair-level, dialogue-level, and various combinations of these. None of these experiments resulted in better results than the Indri-DM-PCS baseline, and the results are omitted from the paper.

6   Discourse Structure Parsing for Thread Retrieval

It is not practical for us to manually annotate the discourse structure of the whole Ancestry dataset nor just the portion of the dataset retrieved by the different IR systems. Rather, we opt to use automatically-predicted discourse structure. To build a discourse parser for Ancestry threads, we randomly selected and annotated 50 threads from the whole dataset to use for parameter tuning.

Table 3. Discourse structure parsing F-scores by applying CRFSGD with Initiator feature using the Combine approach over different training dataset setups. (The best result for each column is **bold-faced**.)

Train dataset setup	LD	Link	DA
Ancestry	.513	**.842**	.530
CNET	.359	.681	.435
ILIAD	.529	.801	**.569**
Ancestry+CNET	.427	.711	.501
Ancestry+ILIAD	**.539**	.827	**.569**
CNET+ILIAD	.406	.688	.478
Ancestry+CNET+ILIAD	.488	.730	.563

Discourse structure parsing, as discussed in [3], can be addressed in several ways. If a structured classification approach, such as a conditional random field (CRF), is used, we can either classify the links (Link) and dialogue act (DA) separately and compose them afterwards (denoted as Composition), or classify the combined Link and DA (e.g. treat 0+Question-question as a single label) directly (denoted as Combine). Another approach is to treat discourse parsing as a dependency parsing problem. Dependency parsing [24] is the task of automatically predicting the dependency structure of a token sequence, in the form of binary asymmetric dependency relations with dependency types. The joint classification task of Link and DA is a natural fit for dependency parsing, in that the task is intrinsically one of inferring labelled dependencies between posts.

For discourse parsing, we follow our earlier work [3]. All experiments were carried out based on stratified 10-fold cross-validation, stratifying at the thread level to ensure that all posts from a given thread occur in a single fold. Additionally, we augment the training data with the CNET and ILIAD datasets. The results are evaluated using post-level micro-averaged F-score ($\beta = 1$). All three discourse parsing methods described above were tested in our experiments, using CRFSGD [25] and MaltParser [10]. For features, we experimented with all the features proposed in our earlier work [3], as well as many of our own features. We found that using CRFSGD with a simple feature indicating whether a post's author is the initiator of the thread and the Combine approach achieves the highest Link and DA joint (LD) F-scores, as shown in Table 3. Because the availability of annotated discourse structure data cannot always be assumed, we decided to use only out-of-domain data to train the discourse parsers. Therefore, only the configurations of CNET, ILIAD and CNET+ILIAD are used in later experiments.

7 Augment Thread Retrieval with Discourse Structure

The basic idea of using the discourse structure to enhance existing IR systems is to use either links (Links) or dialogue acts (DAs) to modify the document ranking. For example, in the framework of Pseudo-Cluster Selection (PCS), one could imagine that a retrieved Answer-answer (i.e. an independent answer to a question) post should be weighted higher than Other posts (including irrelevant posts), and thus contribute more to the thread ranking score. Under this assumption, we examined all the correctly predicted instances from the parsers described in Section 6 over our Ancestry development set, and found that the correctly predicted set only contains 5 dialogue acts, namely: Question-question (Qq), Question-add (Qadd), Answer-answer (Aa), Answer-add (Aadd), and Resolution (Res). Therefore, only predictions for these 5 dialogue acts are considered. Build on the Indri-DM-PCS system, our system (Indri-DM-LD) modifies the post-level rankings based on the predicted DA types of the posts. If a post's predicted DA type belongs to the selected DA subset (DASubset), it is considered to be more important than other posts and its score is increased/promoted by a certain factor. In addition to the 5 dialogue acts (DAs+ALL), we experimented with omitting one DA at a time (e.g. DAs-Qq = the five DAs minus Question-question predictions), to gauge the impact of each DA on the overall results.

Furthermore, in the model of PCS, one crucial parameter is the k which governs the number of retrieved posts that are used to calculate the thread-level ranking scores. Because of the potential interaction between this parameter k and our DA promotion model Indri-DM-LD, we also examined the effect of k in the baseline system Indri-DM-PCS as well as in our system Indri-DM-LD. We found that while $k = 5$ produces the best results for Indri-DM-PCS, $k = 4$ is the best setting for our Indri-DM-LD system. All experimental results reported in this paper are based on these respective k settings.

Table 4 presents the $mAPpref/ppref@10$ results for our Indri-DM-LD system with different DASubset configurations and promotion factors (i.e. 30%–70%). We test for statistical significance over the Indri-DM-PCS baseline with the two-tailed t-test ($p < 0.05$).

From Table 4 we can see that our system outperforms the Indri-DM-PCS baseline system ($mAPpref = .657$ and $ppref@10 = .664$) in most cases, demonstrating the superiority of our method. Our best results ($mAPpref = .674$ and $ppref@10 = .678$) are achieved using the combined CNET and ILIAD datasets for discourse parser training, the DASubset of DAs-Qq, and a DA promotion factor of 50%. The intuition behind Question-question posts not warranting promotion is that they contain question and not answer data, and are less likely to contain information relevant to the resolution of a query. It is important to reinforce that the discourse structure information used in these experiments was derived automatically based on out-of-domain data.

To investigate the mechanics behind our system, we conducted error analysis over Indri-DM-PCS vs. Indri-DM-LD. In one case, there are two threads, namely Thread1 and Thread2, which relate to Query 38 (*jacob lazarus; great synagogue, dukes place, london*). In the gold-standard annotation, Thread1 is preferred to Thread2. The posts retrieved by Indri-DM system are posts 3, 4 and 9 for Thread1 and posts 2, 7 and 12 for Thread2. Under the Indri-DM-PCS baseline system, Thread2 is ranked higher than Thread1. However, with Indri-DM-LD and DAs-Qq, the correct ordering of Thread1 and Thread2 is predicted, as the DA of post 12 in Thread2 is Question-question while the DA of all other posts is

Table 4. The *mAPpref/ppref*@10 scores from `Indri-DM-LD` when training the discourse parser over different training data sets (`CNET`, `ILIAD` or `CNET+ILIAD`), and with different promotion factors for the selected DAs; **boldface** signifies a better result than the `Indri-DM-PCS` baseline at a level of statistical significance ($p < 0.05$)

DA training	DASubset	mAPpref					ppref@10				
		30%	40%	50%	60%	70%	30%	40%	50%	60%	70%
	DAs +ALL	**.667**	**.668**	**.668**	**.669**	**.670**	.668	.673	.672	.664	.664
	−Qq	**.670**	**.673**	**.673**	**.674**	**.674**	**.674**	.673	**.678**	.671	.666
	−Qadd	**.667**	**.669**	**.670**	**.670**	**.671**	.667	.673	.673	.665	.666
CNET	−Aa	.656	.655	.654	.654	.654	.660	.659	.658	.660	.657
	−Aadd	**.667**	**.668**	**.668**	**.669**	**.670**	.668	.673	.671	.664	.664
	−Res	**.666**	**.667**	**.667**	**.668**	**.670**	.666	.669	.669	.661	.661
	DAs +ALL	**.666**	**.668**	**.668**	**.669**	**.669**	.668	.673	.671	.664	.664
	−Qq	**.670**	**.673**	**.673**	**.674**	**.674**	.672	.673	.673	.666	.666
	−Qadd	**.667**	**.668**	**.669**	**.671**	**.671**	.666	.668	.671	.667	.668
ILIAD	−Aa	**.666**	**.666**	**.667**	**.667**	**.668**	.670	.669	.669	.668	.668
	−Aadd	.661	.661	.661	.659	.658	.660	.661	.660	.657	.657
	−Res	**.666**	**.668**	**.668**	**.669**	**.669**	.668	.673	.672	.663	.663
	DAs +ALL	**.667**	**.668**	**.668**	**.669**	**.670**	.669	.673	.672	.663	.665
	−Qq	**.670**	**.673**	**.674**	**.674**	**.674**	**.674**	.673	**.678**	.671	.671
	−Qadd	**.667**	**.669**	**.669**	**.670**	**.671**	.664	.669	.672	.668	.663
CNET+ILIAD	−Aa	.657	.655	.655	.654	.654	.661	.659	.658	.660	.657
	−Aadd	**.667**	**.668**	**.668**	**.669**	**.670**	.669	.673	.671	.663	.664
	−Res	**.666**	**.668**	**.667**	**.669**	**.670**	.667	.671	.669	.662	.663

in DAs–Qq. As a consequence, the relative promotion of Thread1 is greater than Thread2, and the correct ranking is derived.

During our experiments, we demonstrated that making use of discourse structure of forum threads can boost retrieval effectiveness. As an alternative to full discourse parsing, we experimented with simply promoting all non-first posts (under the assumption that first posts are most likely to be Question-question posts). The best results achieved for this simple method are *mAPpref* = .667 and *ppref*@10 = .670. Although the *mAPpref* score is significantly better than the baseline, the *ppref*@10 is not (and both results are slightly below the best results achieved with discourse parsing, of *mAPpref* = .674 and *ppref*@10 = .678). Nevertheless it shows the potential of using a lighter-weight version of discourse structure to improve IR effectiveness. We will explore this line of research further in future work.

8   Conclusion

In this research, we have explored the hypothesis that IR over forum threads can be improved by incorporating thread discourse structure in the form of a rooted DAG over posts, with edges labelled with dialogue acts. When compared to previous research conducted over the `Ancestry` dataset, we achieved significantly better results using automatically-predicted thread discourse structure.

In future work, we plan to firstly investigate more ways to capture thread discourse structure information. Furthermore, we intend to look into means of exploiting the structural information of threads for the purpose of IR, and their interaction with thread discourse structure. For example, the same dialogue act of Answer-answer may contribute to the thread ranking differently if it appears at different positions in a thread (e.g. second post vs. last post).

Acknowledgements. NICTA is funded by the Australian government as represented by Department of Broadband, Communication and Digital Economy, and the Australian Research Council through the ICT centre of Excellence programme.

References

1. Elsas, J.: The Ancestry.com forum dataset. CMU LTI Tech. Report CMU-LTI-017 (2011), http://www.cs.cmu.edu/~jelsas/data/ancestry.com/Ancestry_TR.pdf
2. Kim, S.N., Wang, L., Baldwin, T.: Tagging and linking web forum posts. In: Proceedings of the 14th Conference on Computational Natural Language Learning (CoNLL 2010), Uppsala, Sweden, pp. 192–202 (2010)
3. Wang, L., Lui, M., Kim, S.N., Nivre, J., Baldwin, T.: Predicting thread discourse structure over technical web forums. In: Proceedings of the 2011 Conference on Empirical Methods in Natural Language Processing, Edinburgh, UK, pp. 13–25 (2011)
4. Seo, J., Croft, W.B., Smith, D.A.: Online community search using thread structure. In: Proceedings of the 18th ACM Conference on Information and Knowledge Management (CIKM 2009), Hong Kong, China, pp. 1907–1910 (2009)
5. Elsas, J.L., Carbonell, J.G.: It pays to be picky: An evaluation of thread retrieval in online forums. In: Proceedings of 32nd International ACM-SIGIR Conference on Research and Development in Information Retrieval (SIGIR 2009), Boston, USA, pp. 714–715 (2009)
6. Fortuna, B., Rodrigues, E.M., Milic-Frayling, N.: Improving the classification of newsgroup messages through social network analysis. In: Proceedings of the 16th ACM Conference on Information and Knowledge Management (CIKM 2007), Lisbon, Portugal, pp. 877–880 (2007)
7. Xi, W., Lind, J., Brill, E.: Learning effective ranking functions for newsgroup search. In: Proceedings of 27th International ACM-SIGIR Conference on Research and Development in Information Retrieval (SIGIR 2004), Sheffield, UK, pp. 394–401 (2004)
8. Kim, S.N., Cavedon, L., Baldwin, T.: Classifying dialogue acts in one-on-one live chats. In: Proceedings of the 2010 Conference on Empirical Methods in Natural Language Processing (EMNLP 2010), Boston, USA, pp. 862–871 (2010)
9. Lafferty, J., McCallum, A., Pereira, F.: Conditional random fields: Probabilistic models for segmenting and labeling sequence data. In: Proceedings of the 18th International Conference on Machine Learning, Williamstown, USA, pp. 282–289 (2001)
10. Nivre, J., Hall, J., Nilsson, J., Chanev, A., Eryigit, G., Kübler, S., Marinov, S., Marsi, E.: MaltParser: A language-independent system for data-driven dependency parsing. Natural Language Engineering 13(02), 95–135 (2007)

11. Shrestha, L., McKeown, K.: Detection of question-answer pairs in email conversations. In: Proceedings of the 20th International Conference on Computational Linguistics (COLING 2004), Geneva, Switzerland, pp. 889–895 (2004)

12. Cong, G., Wang, L., Lin, C.Y., Song, Y.I., Sun, Y.: Finding question-answer pairs from online forums. In: Proceedings of 31st International ACM-SIGIR Conference on Research and Development in Information Retrieval (SIGIR 2008), Singapore, pp. 467–474 (2008)

13. Wang, Y.C., Rosé, C.P.: Making conversational structure explicit: identification of initiation-response pairs within online discussions. In: Human Language Technologies: The 2010 Annual Conference of the North American Chapter of the Association for Computational Linguistics (NAACL HLT 2010), pp. 673–676 (2010)

14. Lampert, A., Dale, R., Paris, C.: Detecting emails containing requests for action. In: Human Language Technologies: The 2010 Annual Conference of the North American Chapter of the Association for Computational Linguistics (NAACL HLT 2010), Los Angeles, California, pp. 984–992 (2010)

15. Wang, L., Kim, S.N., Baldwin, T.: The utility of discourse structure in identifying resolved threads in technical user forums. In: Proceedings of the 24th International Conference on Computational Linguistics (COLING 2012), Mumbai, India, pp. 2739–2756 (2012)

16. Sondhi, P., Gupta, M., Zhai, C., Hockenmaier, J.: Shallow information extraction from medical forum data. In: Proceedings of the 23rd International Conference on Computational Linguistics (COLING 2010), Posters Volume, Beijing, China, pp. 1158–1166 (2010)

17. Muthmann, K., Barczyński, W.M., Brauer, F., Löser, A.: Near-duplicate detection for web-forums. In: Proceedings of the 2009 International Database Engineering & Applications Symposium (IDEAS 2009), Cetraro, Italy, pp. 142–151 (2009)

18. Kim, J., Chern, G., Feng, D., Shaw, E., Hovy, E.: Mining and assessing discussions on the web through speech act analysis. In: Proceedings of the ISWC 2006 Workshop on Web Content Mining with Human Language Technologies, Athens, USA (2006)

19. Seo, J., Croft, W.B., Smith, D.A.: Online community search using conversational structures. Information Retrieval 14(6), 547–571 (2011)

20. Carterette, B., Bennett, P.N., Chickering, D.M., Dumais, S.T.: Here or there: Preference judgments for relevance. In: Macdonald, C., Ounis, I., Plachouras, V., Ruthven, I., White, R.W. (eds.) ECIR 2008. LNCS, vol. 4956, pp. 16–27. Springer, Heidelberg (2008)

21. Baldwin, T., Martinez, D., Penman, R.B.: Automatic thread classification for Linux user forum information access. In: Proceedings of the 12th Australasian Document Computing Symposium (ADCS 2007), Melbourne, Australia, pp. 72–79 (2007)

22. Carterette, B., Bennett, P.N.: Evaluation measures for preference judgments. In: Proceedings of the 31st Annual International ACM SIGIR Conference on Research and Development in Information Retrieval (SIGIR 2008), Singapore, pp. 685–686 (2008)

23. Metzler, D., Croft, W.B.: A markov random field model for term dependencies. In: SIGIR 2005, Salvador, Brazil, pp. 472–479 (2005)

24. Kübler, S., McDonald, R., Nivre, J.: Dependency parsing. Synthesis Lectures on Human Language Technologies 2(1), 1–127 (2009)

25. Bottou, L.: CRFSGD software (2011), http://leon.bottou.org/projects/sgd

A Conceptual Model for Word Sense Disambiguation in Medical Image Retrieval

Karim Gasmi, Mouna Torjmen Khemakhem, and Maher Ben Jemaa

ReDCAD Laboratory, ENIS Soukra km 3,5, University of Sfax
B.P.:w 1173-3000 Sfax TUNISIA
gasmikarim@yahoo.fr,
torjmen.mouna@redcad.org,
maher.benjemaa@enis.rnu.tn
http://www.redcad.org

Abstract. Word sense disambiguation (WSD) is the task of determining the meaning of an ambiguous word. It is an open problem in natural language processing because effective WSD can improve the quality of related fields such as information retrieval. Although WSD systems achieve sufficiently high levels of accuracy thanks to several technologies, it remains a challenging problem in the medical domain. In this paper, we propose a conceptual model to resolve the word sens ambiguity problem using the semantic relations between extracted concepts, through MetaMap tool and UMLS Metathesaurus. The evaluation of our disambiguation model is done through the use of information retrieval domain. Results carried out with Clef medical image retrieval 2009 show that our WSD model improves the results that are obtained by the MetaMap WSD model.

Keywords: medical image retrieval, semantic graph, word sense disambiguation and concept mapping.

1 Introduction

In natural language processing (NLP), word-sense disambiguation (WSD) is an open problem which governs the task of automatically assigning the appropriate meaning to an ambiguous word (i.e. having multiple meanings). The solution to this problem [1] [6][13][14] impacts other computer-related domains, such as information retrieval, machine translation and summarization.

In medical domain, several studies [5][19] have shown that medical text is extremely ambiguous: a word can have several connotations depending on the context in which it belongs.

For example, the word "cold" is ambiguous as it has several senses[1] [15]. It may refer to a disease ("I am taking aspirin for my cold"), a temperature sensation ("Let's go inside, I'm cold"), or an environmental condition ("It's cold today, only 2 degrees").

---

[1] http://wsd.nlm.nih.gov/

R.E. Banchs et al. (Eds.): AIRS 2013, LNCS 8281, pp. 296–307, 2013.
© Springer-Verlag Berlin Heidelberg 2013

In addition to the word ambiguity, we note also the abbreviation ambiguity. For example, the "AAO" abbreviation stands for multiple health-related organizations including the "American Association of Ophthalmology", the "American Association of Orthodontists" and the "American Academy of Otolaryngology". Most of works for WSD in medical domain propose to map textual information into concepts using external semantic resources such as WordNet like in [10] or Unified Medical Langage System (UMLS[2]). The basic idea behind the text mapping into concepts is that the whole sentence and the context of each word is used to choose the appropriate concepts. Nevertheless, it is possible to find different concepts for the same word or the same sentence. For example, using the MetaMap tool, the sentence "tx" is mapped into 7 concepts (Texas, Turkmenistan, Therapeutic procedure, Tumor stage TX, CASP4 gene,CASP4 protein, CASP4 wt Allele). A new problem appears: using erroneous concepts to map the medical text can negatively affects the WSD methods. Consequently, mapping medical text to medical concepts resolves partially the word sens ambiguity. The problem becomes, thus, the concept sens desambiguation (CSD). Some solutions are proposed by using other external resources as Medline and MESH [11], to choose relevant concepts through all candidates concepts, but in our knowledge and as mentioned in [12], semantic relations between extracted concepts are not used in CSD.

In this paper, we present a conceptual model to solve the word sens ambiguity problem using the semantic relations between extracted concepts through MetaMap tool, using UMLS Metathesaurus. More precisely, we compute semantic relations between UMLS candidates concepts using two semantic measures. Then, we build a semantic graph by removing isolated (not related) concepts. To evaluate our model, we have used medical image collection[3] for two reasons: (1) only few textual information as image caption and document title will be mapped into concepts. So, in the most of cases, candidates concepts are few and consequently ambiguous: the more we have information, the lesser we have ambiguity. (2)Medical image collection is less time consuming than medical document collection. Several experiments are carried out using the Medical Image CLEF 2009 collection, and results show that our method outperforms the WSD solution of MetaMap tool.

The rest of the paper is organized as follows. In the next section, we discuss the literature works related in medical WSD. Section 3 explains our method, while section 4 describes our experiments and results. Finally, section 5 provides a conclusion and some future works.

2   Related Work

In this section, we review some WSD works in medical domain. Authors in [7] propose a context-based method to disambiguate gene/protein name in biomedical documents. More precisely, instead of directly using all of a word's surrounding

[2] http://www.nlm.nih.gov/research/umls/
[3] Nonetheless, our model can be used in any medical collection.

words, they propose only the selection of certain words with high "discriminating" capabilities as features. These features are then used to represent each instance of the word. This method is based on machine learning and can be viewed as a context-based classification approach. Results show the effectiveness of the method in achieving impressive accuracy, precision and recall rates.

Several studies investigate the use of external resources such as UMLS Metathesaurus to solve the WSD problem [8] [3] [2]. The idea is to map text into concepts using, for example, the MetaMap tool with a medical semantic ontology as UMLS or MESH[4]. MetaMap tool proposes also a dataset for WSD [11] in medical domain called MSH WSD Test Collection[5]. This latter contains both biomedical words and abbreviations and it is automatically created using the UMLS Metathesaurus and the manual MeSH indexing of MEDLINE. Authors in [11] note that this technique does not cover all the meanings of the words and that more work is needed to solve this problem.

To summarize, Word Sens Disambiguation remains a challenging problem in medical domain, and the most of recent works use external resources to solve this problem as UMLS Metathesaurus. However, semantic relations between extracted concepts are not outright (or enough) used to resolve WSD.

3   Conceptual Model for WSD

In this section, we present our conceptual model for medical WSD. As many literature works, we propose the use of concepts instead of words to represent textual information. However, erroneous concepts could be selected and consequently the document meaning will be affected. To overcome this problem, we propose the calculation of relations between concepts, and only related concepts will be selected. In fact, isolated concepts will be considered as erroneous concepts and should not be selected to represent the text information. To map text into concepts, we use the MetaMap tool using UMLS Metathesaurus, and to compute relations between candidate concepts, a semantic and a contextual measures are used. Then, we build a semantic graph where concepts are nodes and relations are edges. Finally, concepts that are not related to the graph are removed. An overview of our WSD model, in information retrieval context, is done in Figure 1.

3.1   Mapping Text to Concepts

The aim of this step is to map text into concepts. For this purpose, we start by preprocessing the collection in order to keep only significant words. Then, we use the MetaMap [6] tool to map words into concepts. Concept extraction steps using MetaMap are the following:

---

[4] ww.nlm.nih.gov/mesh

[5] http://wsd.nlm.nih.gov/collaboration.shtml#MSH_WSD

[6] http://metamap.nlm.nih.gov/

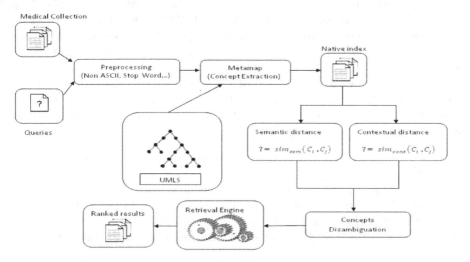

Fig. 1. Overview of our WSD model in information retrieval context

1. Parse the text into noun phrases;
2. Produce noun phrase variants wherever a variant consists of one or more noun phrase terms, all with the whole of its spelling variants, abbreviations, acronyms, synonyms, inflectional and derivation variants, or meaningful combinations of these.
3. Look for different candidate concepts from all metathesaurus containing one of the variants found in step 2.
4. Use an evaluation function to compute the mapping strength from the noun phrase. This step is performed for each candidate concept. The evaluation function computes a quality score of the matching between a phrase and a Meta candidate. This function is based on four components: (1) *centrality* which equals 1 if the Meta candidate involves the head of the phrase and 0 otherwise, (2) *variation* which estimates how much the variants in the Meta candidate differ from the corresponding words in the phrase, (3) *coverage* which indicates how much the Meta candidate and the phrase are involved in the match, and (4) *cohesiveness* which is similar to the coverage value but emphasizes the importance of connected component. More details about the evaluation function and its components are given in [4].
5. Combine candidate concepts involved with disjoint parts of the noun phrase, re-compute the match strength based on the combined candidates, and select those having the highest score to form a set of best Metathesaurus mappings for the original noun phrase.

For exemple the mapping of the phrase *"heart attack trial"* give a sets of condidate concepts (meta condidates), each candidate is represented by its MetaMap score, its concept name in the Metathesaurus and its semantic type in the Semantic Network, whereas the second section (meta mapping) give as a result the highest scoring candidates. For the example of *"heart attack trial"* MetaMap tool generates the concepts ID *C0027051* and *C0008976*, which represent respectively *"heart attack"* from the semantic type *"Disease or Syndrome"* and *"Trial"* from the semantic type *"Research Activity"*, as the best results between the eight meta-condidates.

Authors in [9] reveale that a total of 17 022 (24.3%) of associations (parent-child) between UMLS notions can not be justified according to the semantic categories of concepts. Among several cases that can produce artificial relations, we cite:

- Cases where the semantic category of the child is very broad whereas the parent's semantic type is too specific;
- Situations where the parent-child relationship is erroneous;
- Cases where a parent-child relationship is lacking and have to be added to the UMLS semantic network;
- Conditions where the parent or the child is missing a semantic category;

To avoid these problems, we propose the selection of the most relevant concepts, which are close to the significant meaning of the image. Therefore, candidate concepts extracted through the MetaMap tool will be the input of the semantic graph building described in the next section.

3.2 Semantic Graph Building

Having a set of candidate concepts for each image description, a semantic distance is computed between each pair of concepts, after this step we remove every concepts that are not related to the graph and not related to any other concept. We construct, thus, a graph: concepts are considered vertexes and relations are considered edges. Relations between two concepts i and j are determined as follows:

$$Rel_{i,j} = dist(C_i, C_j) \tag{1}$$

Semantic similarity measures are classified into three different categories:

- The similarity measure that is based on the number of edges, is called in this paper "Semantic Distance".
- The similarity measure that is based on the information content, is called in this paper "Contextual Distance"
- The hybrid similarity measure (information content and number of edges), is called in this paper "Hybrid Distance"

Semantic Distance
The concept selection is based on the similarity measure through the number of edges between two concepts using the hierarchical structure "is-a" of UMLS. One of the most noticeable ways to estimate semantic similarity in a category is to determine the distance between notions, using the shortest path as a unit.

Computing the similarity based on the number of edges restricting the "is-a" relation has two difficulties:

- Granularity: concepts lay down the thesaurus and then the more specific the concepts are, the more similar they are;
- Density: a concept having many children is more similar to its children than the other that do not. Consequently, the similarity should be increased in the densest elements of the thesaurus.

$$Dist_{sem}(C1, C2) = \frac{1}{Path(C1, C2)} \tag{2}$$

Figure 2 illustrates an example of using the semantic measure to construct the semantic graph.

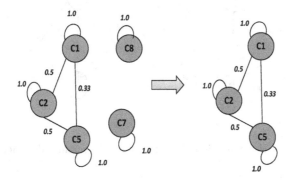

Fig. 2. Building graph based on the semantic measure

According to this figure, D1 is a document presented by C1, C2, C5, C7 and C8. After the weighting step, D1 is presented only by C1, C2 and C5. C7 and C8 are removed because they do not have any relationship with other concepts.

Contextual Distance

To correct the lack of every relationship in the UMLS, we propose the hybridization of the semantic distance with the contextual distance which is computed between two concepts, using their definition according to UMLS.

We choose to apply the cosine measure to compute the similarity between the two concepts definitions. Words of both definitions def1 and def2 are presented in vectors A and B. Each word in the definition presents a dimension in the Euclidean space and the frequency of each word corresponds to the value in the dimension. Then, the cosine similarity measure is used as follow:

$$Dist_{con}(C1, C2) = \frac{A.B}{||A||.||B||} \tag{3}$$

where $||A||$ and $||B||$ are respectively the length of the vector A and the vector B.

Combination of Semantic and Contextual Distances

For the UMLS, some relationships are missing between concepts, so using only semantic measure is not sufficient. Consequently, the use of a hybridization between contextual and semantic distance is appreciated. The distance measure becomes as follows :

$$Dist(C1, C2) = \frac{A.B}{||A||.||B||} + \frac{1}{Path(C1, C2)} \tag{4}$$

Using the example of Figure 2, Figure 3 shows the hybridization step.

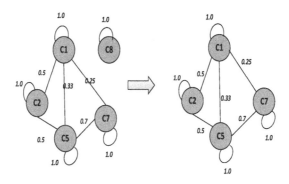

Fig. 3. Hybridization of contextual and semantic distances

Using both distances, D1 is presented by C1, C2, C5, and C7, since C7 has a contextual relationship with C2 and C5.

So as it is shown in the figure, we remove all the concepts that are not related to either the graph, or any other concept.

From Weighted Graph to Binary Graph

Taking into account the problems mentioned in section 3.1, the semantic weight between two concepts is not always efficient and do not reflect always the real semantic matching between two concepts. For example, if a child-parent relation between two concepts is missed, similarity measures that are based on edges, such as the path length, will be affected and consequently the semantic distance weight will be incorrect.

Moreover, when using similarity measures based on the information content of the concepts, the weight can be affected, due to the term ambiguity problem of concept definitions.

For these reasons, we propose the translation of the obtained weighted graph into a binary graph, without taking into account the relation weights. Figure 4 gives an example of transforming a weighted graph to a binary one.

Using the binary graph, we take into account the existence of a semantic relation between two concepts, but neglecting the percentage of this semantic matching.

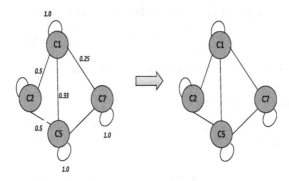

Fig. 4. From weighted graph to binary graph

3.3 Retrieval Model

We use the semantic vector model to compute the similarity between documents and queries. This model is an extension of the vector space model (SVM) [17] [16], in which, each dimension represents an ontology concept instead of a term. Documents and queries are represented by a vector with n dimensions where n is the number of the ontology concepts [18].

The vector space has N dimension (N is the number of concepts of the collection). Each document D_j is represented by a vector of concepts :
$D_j = (w_{1j}, w_{2j}, w_{3j}, ..., w_{Nj})$.
Each query Q is represented by a vector of concepts:
$Q = (wq_1, wq_2, wq_3, ..., cq_N)$,
with:

- w_{ij} is the weight of the concept C_i in the document D_j;
- wq_i is the weight of the concept C_i in the query Q.

The value of system relevance is calculated using a similarity function called $RSV(Q, d)$ (Retrieval Status Value) where Q is a query and a document D_j base. The RSV measure is the following:

$$RSV\left(Q, D_j\right) = \frac{\sum_{i=1}^{N} wq_i . w_{ij}}{\left(\sum_{i=1}^{N} wqi^2\right)^{\frac{1}{2}} \cdot \left(\sum_{i=1}^{N} w_{ij}^2\right)^{\frac{1}{2}}} \quad (5)$$

We propose to use two formulas to compute each concept weight:

- The concept frequency as shown in the following:

$$w_{ij} = cf_{ij} \quad and \quad wq_i = cf_{qi} \quad (6)$$

Where cf_{ij} (respectively cf_{qi}) is the number of occurrences of the concept C_i in the document D_j (respectively the query q);

– The inverse document frequency as shown in the following:

$$w_{ij} = cf_{ij} * idf_{ij} \quad and \quad wq_i = cf_{qi} * idf_{qi} \tag{7}$$

Where idf_{ij} that stands for the inverse document frequency, is equal to devide the number of documents containing the concept i, by the number of all documents in the collection.

In order to integrate the semantic distance in the RSV function, we propose the following formula:

$$RSV(Q, D_j) = \sum_{i=1}^{N} \sum_{j=1}^{k} w_{iQ}.w_{jD}.Dist(C_{iQ}, C_{jD}) \tag{8}$$

with:

– N and k are respectively the number of query concepts and document concepts.
– $Dist(C_{iQ}, C_{jD})$ is the distance between the document concept and the query concept.

4   Experiments and Results

4.1   Dataset and Tools

To evaluate our approach, we use the 2009 ImageCLEF[7] collection composed of 74,902 medical images and annotations associated with them. This collection contains images and captions from Radiology and Radiographic, two Radiological Society of North America (RSNA)[8] journals. The number of queries is 25.

The evaluation measures to use are P@5, P@10 and Mean Average Precision MAP.

4.2   Results

In this section, we will present the different results obtained by our WSD model.

Comparison between Distance Measures
Table 1 compares results obtained by real distance (Eq. 8) with semantic, contextual distance and hybridization of both, according to cf and cf*idf. According to this table, the Cf*idf weight improves the results obtained by the Cf weight. This can be justified by the fact that the Cf*idf model does not take into account the concepts which are very common thorough the collection. For example the term "medical" presented by the ID C0205476, it is very common in our area of research, the use of cf*idf will reduce its importance in the retrieval process.

---

[7] http://www.imageclef.org/
[8] http://www.rsna.org/

Table 1. Comparison between distance measures with real distance

	CF			CF*IDF		
	Semantic	Contextual	Hybrid distance	Semantic	Contextual	Hybrid distance
P@5	0.1905	0.1917	0.1917	0.2720	0.1520	**0.3619**
P@10	0.1524	0.1667	0.1625	0.2240	0.1440	**0.3619**
MAP	0.1157	0.1341	0.1355	0.1222	0.0916	**0.1958**

Also, we note that the use of hybrid distance help to correct the lack of relationship in the UMLS. However, despite attempts to improve performance by hybridization, the results obtained by the real distance are outstanding need for improvement, this can be justified by the fact that the semantic relations between concepts are not of hight quality, and further researchs are needed to improve the impact of the relations between the two concepts.

We made same experiences by binary distance instead of the real distance. We note that the contextual distance improves slightly the results obtained, and even by the binary distance, the hybridization between the two distances improves the results.

Table 2 compares best results obtained by real distance (Eq. 8) and binary distance (Eq. 5) with the hybridization between the contextual and semantic distance. We note that the use of binary distance is better than the use of real

Table 2. Comparison between binary and real distance

	Real Distance (Eq. 8)	Binary Distance (Eq. 5)
P@5	0.3429	**0.4833** (+41%)
P@10	0.3619	**0.4542** (+25%)
MAP	0.1958	**0.2647** (+35%)

distance (improvement of 35 % according to the MAP measure). This can be justified by the fact that conceptual measures between concepts are not of hight quality, more work is needed to reach more better results.

Comparison of our Approach with Other WSD Methods

Table 3 compares our model with Metamap tool (i.e. without WSD) and WSD MetaMap (i.e. WSD method proposed by MetaMap). In this comparison, we use the hybrid distance, the $cf * idf$ weighting schema and the binary graph.

According to this table, we note that WSD MetaMap and our model results are better than MetaMap ones. This observation affirms that the use of a WSD solution improves the retrieval accuracy. These results are justified by the presence of the terms that are out of context, in a model that does not use a method of WSD, these terms can guide the retrieval model to erroneous results.

Additionally, cancerning the P@5 measure, our WSD model outperforms WSD MetaMap model by 9.8%. As for the MAP measure, our WSD model outperforms the WSD MetaMap model by 22.5% . Consequently, we can conclude that the use of concept relations to disambiguate concepts is a good solution. These results are justified by the presence of the concepts that are out of context,

Table 3. Comparison between the proposed approach and other approaches

	P_5	Improvement rate		P_10	Improvement rate		Map	Improvement rate	
		MetaMap	WSD MM		MetaMap	WSD MM		MetaMap	WSD MM
MetaMap	0.3920	–	–	0.3440	–	–	0.2163	–	0.2%
WSD MetaMap	0.4400	12%	–	0.428	24%	–	0.2160	–	–
Proposed method	**0.4833**	**23%**	**9.8%**	**0.4542**	**32%**	**6.1%**	**0.2647**	**22.3%**	**22.5%**

in WSD MetaMap model, on the other hand, with our method we removed these erroneous concepts.

5 Conclusion and Future Works

We have proposed a conceptual model for word sens disambiguation in medical domain. The main finding is that using the semantic relations between medical concepts allows for an efficient disambiguation.

We have also discovered that the use of binary distance (weight is either 1 or 0) between concepts gives better results than the use of real distance. This observation shows that more studies are needed in the semantic distance measures to really compute the semantic similarity between two concepts.

In future work, we plan to solve the relation weight problem and to propose a semantic similarity distance to calculate a disambiguation degree that can be included in our WSD model.

References

1. Agirre, E., Rigau, G.: Word sense disambiguation using conceptual density. In: Proceedings of the 16th Conference on Computational Linguistics, COLING 1996, vol. 1, pp. 16–22. Association for Computational Linguistics, Stroudsburg (1996)
2. Agirre, E., Soroa, A., Stevenson, M.: Graph-based word sense disambiguation of biomedical documents. Bioinformatics 26(22), 2889–2896 (2010)
3. Andreopoulos, B., Alexopoulou, D., Schroeder, M.: Word sense disambiguation in biomedical ontologies with term co-occurrence analysis and document clustering. Int. J. Data Min. Bioinformatics 2(3), 193–215 (2008)
4. Aronson, A.R.: Metamap: Mapping text to the umls metathesaurus (1996), http://ii.nlm.nih.gov/resources/metamap.pdf
5. Aronson, A.R.: Effective mapping of biomedical text to the umls metathesaurus: the metamap program. In: Proc. AMIA Symp., pp. 17–21 (2001)
6. Boyd-Graber, J., Blei, D., Zhu, X.: A Topic Model for Word Sense Disambiguation (2007)
7. Chen, P., Al-Mubaid, H.: Context-based term disambiguation in biomedical literature. In: Proceedings of the Nineteenth International Florida Artificial Intelligence Research Society Conference, FLAIRS 2006, pp. 62–67 (2006)
8. Chevallet, J., Lim, J., Le, D.T.H.: Domain knowledge conceptual inter-media indexing: application to multilingual multimedia medical reports. In: Proceedings of the Sixteenth ACM Conference on Information and Knowledge Management, CIKM 2007, pp. 495–504. ACM, New York (2007)

9. Cimino, J.J., Min, H., Perl, Y.: Consistency across the hierarchies of the umls semantic network and metathesaurus. Journal of Biomedical Informatics 36(6), 450–461 (2003)
10. Hwang, M., Choi, C., Kim, P.: Automatic enrichment of semantic relation network and its application to word sense disambiguation. IEEE Trans. Knowl. Data Eng. 23(6), 845–858 (2011)
11. Jimeno-Yepes, A.J., McInnes, B.T., Aronson, A.R.: Exploiting mesh indexing in medline to generate a data set for word sense disambiguation. BMC Bioinformatics 12, 223 (2011)
12. Joshi, M., Pedersen, T., Maclin, R.: A comparative study of support vector machines applied to the supervised word sense disambiguation problem in the medical domain. In: Proceedings of the 2nd Indian International Conference on Artificial Intelligence, IICAI 2005, pp. 3449–3468 (2005)
13. Li, L., Roth, B., Sporleder, C.: Topic models for word sense disambiguation and token-based idiom detection. In: Proceedings of the 48th Annual Meeting of the Association for Computational Linguistics, ACL 2010, pp. 1138–1147. Association for Computational Linguistics, Stroudsburg (2010)
14. Magnini, B., Pezzulo, G., Gliozzo, A.: Using domain information for word sense disambiguation. In: Proc. of SENSEVAL2 (2001)
15. Plaza, L., Stevenson, M., Díaz, A.: Resolving ambiguity in biomedical text to improve summarization. Inf. Process. Manage. 48(4), 755–766 (2012)
16. Salton, G.: The smart retrieval system: Experiments in automatic document processing (1970)
17. Salton, G., McGill, M.: Introduction to modern information retrieval (1983)
18. Ventresque, A., Cazalens, S., Lamarre, P., Valduriez, P.: Improving interoperability using query interpretation in semantic vector spaces. In: Bechhofer, S., Hauswirth, M., Hoffmann, J., Koubarakis, M. (eds.) ESWC 2008. LNCS, vol. 5021, pp. 539–553. Springer, Heidelberg (2008)
19. Weeber, M., Mork, J., Aronson, A.: Developing a test collection for biomedical word sense disambiguation. In: Proceedings of AMIA Annual Symposium, pp. 746–750 (2001)

Disambiguation to Wikipedia: A Language and Domain Independent Approach

Truc-Vien T. Nguyen

University of Lugano,
via Giuseppe Buffi 13,
CH-6900 Lugano, Switzerland
thi.truc.vien.nguyen@usi.ch

Abstract. Disambiguation to Wikipedia ($D2W$) is the task of linking mentions of concepts in text to their corresponding Wikipedia articles. Traditional approaches to $D2W$ has focused either in only one language (e.g. English) or in formal texts (e.g. news articles). In this paper, we present a multilingual framework with a set of new features that can be obtained purely from the online encyclopedia, without the need of any natural language specific tool. We analyze these features with different languages and different domains. The approach shows as fully language-independent and has been applied successfully to English, Italian, Polish, with a consistent improvement. We show that only a sufficient number of Wikipedia articles is needed for training. When trained on real-world data sets for English, our new features yield substantial improvement compared to current local and global disambiguation algorithms. Finally, the adaption to the Bridgeman query logs in digital libraries shows the robustness of our approach even in the lack of disambiguation context. Also, as no natural language specific tool is needed, the method can be applied to other languages in a similar manner with little adaptation.

1 Introduction

The possibility to understand multilingual content can facilitate better several natural science applications, such as information extraction, information retrieval, web search, and web mining, where popular systems can provide enough accuracy just for the languages of interest. Due to the lack of systems and resources, the adaptation of one method to other languages often create problems. This problem is even worse with low-resource languages. Therefore, a general method for multilingual processing is very essential.

The ability to identify entities (such as people, locations and organizations) has been placed as an important task and has been considered as a valuable preprocessing step for many types of language analysis, including question answering, machine translation, and information retrieval. Its goal is the detection of entities and mentions in text, and labelling with one of several categories (PERSON or LOCATION). An entity (such as George W. Bush) can be refered

R.E. Banchs et al. (Eds.): AIRS 2013, LNCS 8281, pp. 308–319, 2013.
© Springer-Verlag Berlin Heidelberg 2013

to multiple surface forms (e.g. "George Bush" and "Bush") and a surface form can refer to multiple entities (e.g. two U.S presidents or the pianist Alan Bush).

We purpose the automatic construction of a large-scale, multilingual system that can recognize and disambiguate entities from a text for a general domain. As these texts can be in multiple languages, we target a method that can perform well in a multilingual environment. Also, when the query input is taken from the Bridgeman Art Library[1], they are short texts which are informally written. They suffer from spelling mistakes, grammatical errors and the usually do not form a complete sentence. Our approach takes advantage of the human knowledge created through Wikipedia, a large-scale, collaborative web-based resource with collective efforts of millions of contributors.

Our work differs from that of previous researchers is that we have focused primarily on multilingual aspects as opposed to one single language, observed in all previous works [1–4]. We propose a framework in which dictionary and structures are extracted from the online encyclopedia and are employed to derive statistical measures which are then placed in a machine learner for disambiguation. Ours is a unsupervised approach, without requiring any human effort. To the best of our knowledge, it is the first attempt trying to adapt and apply disambiguation to Wikipedia to multiple languages and general domain, which is more difficult than previous wokrs on only English.

In this work, we revisit previous work and propose two sets of new features: semantic relatedness and contextual features, experimented in different languages (English, Italian, Polish). The relatedness features are computed from the set of incoming links, commonness and keyphraseness in different formulations, while contextual features are adapted from previous work [1], combined, weighted and averaged with our new relatedness features. Both kinds of features yield improvement in all three languages, both when injected separately and when used in combination together. In addition, we evaluate the contribution of these novel features in different domains (Wikipedia, newswire, query logs).

The structure of the paper is as follows. In Section 2 we discuss previous work on using Wikipedia for entity disambiguation and linking. In Section 3 we present our framework, the knowledge and statistical measures extracted from Wikipedia. In Section 4 we present the adaptation of the traditional *D2W* to other languages and domains; the experimental setting used to evaluate these methods and the dataset. The results we obtained and future works are discussed in Section 5 and 6.

2   Related Work

2.1   Disambiguation to Wikipedia

Entity disambiguation refers to the detection and association of text segments with entities defined in an external repository. Disambiguation to Wikipedia (*D2W*) refers to the task of detecting and linking expressions in text to their

---

[1] http://www.bridgemanart.com/

referent Wikipedia pages. In the last decade, substantial consideration has been given to the use of encyclopedic knowledge for disambiguation. Using encyclopedic knowledge for entity disambiguation has been pioneered by [5]. Subsequent works have been intensively exploited Wikipedia link structures and made use of natural annotations as the source for learning [1–4].

For example, given a text "John McCarthy, 'great man' of computer science, wins major award.", a *D2W* system can detect the text "John McCarthy" and link to the correct Wikipedia page *John_Mc_Carthy_(computer_scientist)*[2], instead of other *John McCarthy* who are ambassador, senator or linguist.

2.2   Previous Work

One of the shortcoming of previous studies on *D2W* is that they have mainly focused on only one language. For instance, [5] has focused on linking only named entities in Wikipedia articles. The author first propose some heuristics to define if a Wikipedia title correspond to a named entity or not, then exploits the redirect pages and disambiguation pages to collect other ambiguous names to build the dataset. Overlapping categories between pages with traditional *bag-of-words* and *TF-IDF* measures are lastly employed in a kernel function for name disambiguation. This work, however, targets only named entities and uses only a small subset of Wikipedia articles (roughly half of a million).

[3] presents a method for named entity disambiguation based on Wikipedia. They first extract resources and context for each entity from the whole Wikipedia collection, then use named entity recognizer in combination with other heuristics to identify named entity boundaries in the articles. Finally, they employ a vector space model which includes context and categories for each entity for the disambiguation process. The approach works very well with high disambiguation accuracy. However, note that the use of many heuristics and named entity recognizer shows one weakness of the method that is difficult to adapt to other languages as well as other content types such as noisy text.

[1] proposes a general approach for *D2W*. First, they process the whole Wikipedia and collect set of incoming/outgoing links for each page. They employ a statistical method for detecting links by gathering all *n-gram* in the document and retaining those whose probability exceeds a threshold. For entity disambiguation they use machine learning with a few features, such as the commonness of a surface form, its relative relatedness in the surrounding context and the balance of these two features. However, note that they have never tried to adapt this method to other kinds of text or other languages.

[4] tries to combines local and global approaches for the *D2W* task with a set of local features in combination with global features. Based on traditional *bag-of-words* and *TF-IDF* measures, semantic relatedness, they implement a global approach for *D2W*. However, their system makes use of many natural

---

[2] We use the title *John_Mc_Carthy_(computer_scientist)* to refer to the full address `http://en.wikipedia.org/wiki/John_Mc_Carthy_(computer_scientist)`.

language specific tool, such as named entity recognition, chunking and part-of-speech tagging. Thus, it is very difficult to apply the method to noisy text as well as to adapt to other languages.

Recently [6] adapted the *D2W* to microblogs in Twitter. To cope with the lack a rich disambiguation context, they proposed two context expansion methods based on tweet authorship and topic-based clustering. Still this work was focused on only English and have to heavily adapt since it makes use of [4] and popular natural language software which are very difficult to find for other languages.

Previous approaches to *D2W* differ with respect to the following aspects: 1. the corpora they address; 2. the type of the text expression they target to link; 3. the way they define and use the disambiguation context for each entity. For instance, some methods focus on linking only named entities, such as [3, 5]. In [3], the author defines the disambiguation context by using some heuristics such as entities mentioned in the first paragraph and those for which the corresponding pages refer back to the target entity. [1] utilizes entities which have no ambiguous names as local context and also to compute semantic relatedness. A different method is observed in [4] where they first train a local disambiguation system and then use the prediction score of that as disambiguation context.

It is worth noting that all of the aforementioned methods have been proposed and tested in only English. In the previous work [7], we have implemented a baseline for *D2W* in English, tested with a standard dataset and with query blogs. In this work, we revisit previous work and propose two sets of new features: semantic relatedness and contextual features. The relatedness features are computed from the set of incoming links, commonness and keyphraseness, while contextual features are adapted from previous work [1], combined, weighted and averaged with our new relatedness features. Both kinds of features yield improvement in all three languages, both when injected separately and when used in combination together.

An example of disambiguation context is shown in figure 1. The disambiguation context of the surface form *human* may includes other unambiguous surface forms (which is linked to only one target article), which is a subset of *communication, linguistics, dialects, Natural languages, spoken, signed*, etc.

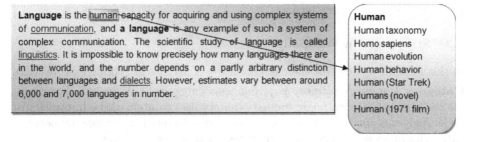

Fig. 1. Disambiguation context

3   Resource and System Overview

3.1   Datasets

We evaluate our *D2W* on seven datasets, in which four are from previous work. The first three datasets, from [4], are constructed using Wikipedia itself. [4] used a sample of 10,000 paragraphs from Wikipedia pages. Mentions in this data set correspond to existing hyperlinks in the Wikipedia text. However, in our work, we derive three datasets from that, samples of 500/1,000/1,500 paragraphs, respectively. We prove that a data of only about 500 paragraphs is sufficient for training, other datasets of increasing size yield similar results.

The fourth dataset, from [1], is a subset of the AQUAINT corpus of newswire text that is annotated to mimic the hyperlink structure in Wikipedia. The fifth dataset is a sample of 500 Italian Wikipedia articles. The sixth dataset is a sample of 500 Polish Wikipedia articles. To evaluate our approach on noisy text, we use the seventh dataset, a collection of 1000 queries. The annotators are asked to link the first five nominal mentions of each co-reference chain to Wikipedia, if possible.

In the last dataset, we used a corpus of query logs provided by the Bridgeman Art Library (BAL). Bridgeman Art library contains a large repository of images coming from 8000 collections and representing more than 29.000 artists. From 6-month query logs, we sample 1000 queries containing around 1,556 tokens. Queries are typed by users of the art library, using Bridgeman query language constructions. Each query is a text snippet containing some name of an artist, a painter, a painting, or an art movement. These texts often present spelling errors, capitalization mistakes, abbreviations, and non-standard words. The length of each query varies from 1 to 10 words; in average, there are 3 words per query. Some examples of the queries are shown in table 1.

Table 1. Examples of queries

calling of st. matthew, friedrich and dresden, piazzetta giambattista, charles the bold, herbert james draper lamia, rembrandt crosses, order of malta, man with scythe, buddha tang guimet, lady%27s maid, cagnes-sur-mer, segovia cathedral, san francesco assisi italy, tour eiffel, guy fawkes before king james, napoleon%27s retreat, ruins wwi, v-j day, napoleon crossing the alps, princes in the tower, jean-etienne liotard, corinium museum cirencester gloucestershire

3.2   Structures in Wikipedia

In this section, we describe the categorization of articles in Wikipedia collection.

Category Pages. A *category page* defines a category in Wikipedia. For example the article *Category:Impressionist_painters* lists painters of the Impressionist style. As it contains subcategories, one can use it to build the taxonomy between categories or to generalize a specific category to its parent level.

Disambiguation Pages. A *disambiguation page* presents the problem of polysemy, the tendency of a surface form to relate to multiple entities. For example, the surface form *tree* might refer to a woody plant, a hierarchical data structure in a graphical form, or a computer science concept. The correct sense depends on the context of the surface form to which we are comparing it to; consider the relatedness of *tree* to *algorithm*, and *tree* to *plant*.

List_of Pages. A *list_of page*, as its name indicates, lists all articles related to the specific domain. It is useful when we want to build some domain-dependent applications. For example one can employ the article *Lists_of_painters* to take the information of all popular painters and build an entity disambiguator.

Redirect Pages. A *redirect page* exists for each alternative name to refer to an entity in Wikipedia. The name is transformed into a title whose article contains a redirect link to the actual article for that entity. For example, *Da Vinci* is the surname of *Leonardo da Vinci*. It is therefore an alternative name for the artist, and consequently the article *Da_Vinci* is just a pointer to the article *Leonardo_da_Vinci*.

Relevant Pages. A *relevant page* is remained after scanning over the whole Wikipedia collection and excluding category pages, disambiguation pages, list_of pages, redirect pages, and pages used to provide help, define template and Wikipedia definitions.

Unrelevant Pages. *Unrelevant pages* are those used to define some terms, some templates or provide some help (*Template:Periodic_table* and *Help:Editing* for example).

3.3   Parsing Wikipedia Dump

As parsing the Wikipedia dump we perform a structure analysis of running text. We use the *pages-articles.xml* that contains current version of all article pages, templates, and other pages. The parser takes as input the Wikipedia dump file and analyzes the content enclosed in the various XML tags. We use the Wikipedia dump in July 2011. In the first running parse, it builds the set of redirection pairs (i.e., one article is a pointer to some actual one), list_of pages, disambiguation pages, and set of titles of all articles in that Wikipedia edition.

In the second parse, the system scans over all Wikipedia articles and construct list of links (i.e., surface form and target article for each link, number of times one surface form is linked to the target article), list of incoming and outgoing links of each article. Note that we use the set of redirection pairs to keep everything related to links only as the actual article and not as the redirected article. For example, in the example above, if the title *Da_Vinci* appears in one link, we will change it to *Leonardo da Vinci*. This process makes the statistical measures derived from links more accurate.

The third parse focuses mainly on individual pages. It scans over all Wikipedia articles and construct for each article: ID, title, set of links (with surface form and target article), set of categories, set of templates. Note that in all three times of parsing, we exclude the category pages, disambiguation pages, file pages, help pages, list_of pages, pages refering to templates and Wikipedia itself. As a result, we keep only the most relevant pages with textual content.

---

[2] http://dumps.wikimedia.org/

3.4   Extracting Dictionaries and Structures

The set of Wikipedia titles and surface forms are preprocessed by casefolding. After scanning over all Wikipedia articles, we construct a set of titles, set of surface forms (i.e., words or phrases that are used to link to Wikipedia articles), set of files (i.e., a Wikipedia article but does not have textual content, *File:The_Marie_Louise's_diadem.JPG* for example), and set of links (with surface form and target article for each link). We use the term *surface form* to denote the occurence of a mention inside a Wikipedia article and the term *target article* to denote the target Wikipedia article that surface form linked to.

Table 2. Wikipedia statistics of the three languages

Type/Number	English	Italian	Polish
Redirect	4,466,270	323,591	134,148
List of	138,614	836	5,021
Disambiguation	177,483	6,193	4,553
Relevant	4,208,917	917,354	920,486
Total	11,459,639	1,654,258	1,200,313

Table 3. Dictionaries derived from Wikipedia

Dictionary	Size	Italian	Polish
Titles	3,742,663	917,354	920,486
Surface forms	8,829,624	2,484,045	2,482,104
Files	745,724	72,126	n/a
Links	10,871,741	2,917,235	2,937,981

Table 4. Links derived from Wikipedia

Surface form	Target article
human	Human
communication	Communication
linguistics	Linguistics
dialects	Dialects
Natural languages	Natural_language

Table 3 shows the dictionaries we extracted with corresponding size. Table 4 depicts links with corresponding surface forms and target articles derived from the Wikipedia paragraph in figure 1. We use the dictionaries of titles, surface forms, and files to match with the textual content and detect entity/mention boundaries, whereas set of links are used to compute statistical measures for our learning framework.

3.5   Statistical Measures

Following previous work [1, 4], we develop a machine learning approach for disambiguation, based on the links available in Wikipedia articles for training.

For every surface form in an article, a Wikipedian has manually selected the correct destination to represent the intended sense of the anchored text. This provides millions of manually defined ground-truth examples (see table 3) to learn from.

From the dictionaries and structures extracted from Wikipedia, we derive statistical measures. We now describe the primitives for our statistical measures and learning framework.

- s: a surface form (anchor text)
- t: a target (a link)
- W: the entire Wikipedia
- t_{in}: pages that link to t ("incoming links")
- t_{out}: pages going from t ("outgoing links")
- $count(s_{link})$: number of pages in which s appears as a link
- $count(s)$: total number of pages in which s appears
- $p(t|s)$: number of times s appears as a link to t
- $p(s)$: number of times s appears as a link
- $|W|$: total number of pages in Wikipedia

Keyphraseness. *Keyphraseness* is the probability of a phrase to be a potential candidate to link to a Wikipedia article. Similarly as [8], to identify important words and phrases in a document, we first extract all word n-grams. For each n-grams a, we compute its probability of being a potential candidate.

$$Keyphraseness(s) = \frac{count(s_{link})}{count(s)}$$

Commonness. *Commonness* is the probability of a phrase s to link to a specific Wikipedia article t.

$$Commonness(s, t) = \frac{p(t|s)}{p(s)}$$

Relatedness. To measure the similarity between two terms, we consider each term as a representative Wikipedia article. For instance, the term *exhibition* is represented by the Wikipedia page $http://en.wikipedia.org/wiki/Exhibition$. We used the Normalized Google Distance [9], where the similarity judgement is based on term occurrence on web pages. The method was employed in [10] to compute relatedness between Wikipedia articles. In this method, pages that link to both terms suggest relatedness.

$$Relatedness(a, b) = \frac{log(max(|A|, |B|)) - log(|A \cap B|))}{log(|W|) - log(min(|A|, |B|))}$$

where a and b are the two articles of interest, A and B are the sets of all articles that link to a and b, respectively, and W is the entire Wikipedia.

4 Disambiguation Method

We follow a two-phase approach for disambiguation algorithm: first recognize mentions (i.e. surface forms) in a document with potential candidates, then generate features for each candidate and apply a machine learning approach.

4.1   Disambiguation Candidate Selection

The first step is to extract all mentions that can refer to Wikipedia articles, and to construct, for each recognized mention, a set of disambiguation candidates. Following previous work [1, 4], we use Wikipedia hyperlinks to perform these steps.

To identify important words and phrases in a document, we first extract all word n-grams. For each n-grams a, we use its keyphraseness– the probability of being a potential candidate to recognize potential n-grams that are candidates to link to an Wikipedia article. We retain n-grams whose keyphraseness exceeds a certain threshold. Preliminary experiments on a validation set showed that the best performance for mention detection is achieved with $keyphraseness = 0.01$.

The next step is to identify potential candidate links. For that we employ commonness– the probability of an n-gram to link to a specific Wikipedia article. The result is a set of possible mappings $(surface form, link_i)$. For computational efficiency, we use the top 10 candidates with highest commonness.

4.2   Learning Method

As illustrated, disambiguation deals with the problem that the same surface form may refer to one or more entities. The links $(surface form/target article)$ derived from Wikipedia provide a dataset of disambiguated occurences of entities. Table 5 shows examples of positive and negative examples in the dataset, created for the six separate concepts of the surface form *human*.

Table 5. Disambiguation dataset

δ	Text	Target article
1	Language is the **human** capacity	Human
0	Language is the **human** capacity	Human_taxonomy
0	Language is the **human** capacity	Homo_sapiens
0	Language is the **human** capacity	Human_evolution
0	Language is the **human** capacity	Human_behavior
0	Language is the **human** capacity	Humans_(novel)

Given a surface form with its potential candidates, the entity disambiguation problem can be cast as a ranking problem. Assuming that an appropriate scoring function $score(s, t_i)$ is available, the link corresponding to surface form s is defined to be the one with highest score:

$$\hat{t} = \arg \max_{t_i} score(s, t_i)$$

4.3   Baseline and Features

Baseline. As a baseline we use the commonness, which is the fraction of times the title t is the target page for a surface form s. This single feature is a very reliable indicator of the correct disambiguation [1, 4], and we use it as a baseline in our experiments.

Relatedness and **Contextual Features.** As ranking algorithm for disambiguation, we use three kinds of features: the commonness of each candidate link, its average relatedness in the surrounding context, and the disambiguation context measure. We follow a global approach where the disambiguation context is measured by taking every n-grams that have only one candidate, and thus, is unambiguous. Here we use the term 'candidate sense' to refer to a potential candidate and 'context article' as a unambiguous candidate.

The relatedness of each candidate sense is the weighted average of its relatedness to each context article. To weight context articles, we use the two measure mentioned previously. First, *keyphraseness* can help to identify how often a surface word is used as a link. Second, *commonness* can help to test how often a surface word is linked to that context article.

$$score(s,t) = \frac{\sum_{c \in C} relatedness(t,c)}{|C|} \times commonness(s,t)$$

where $c \in C$ are the context articles of t. The target with the highest score will be chosen as the final answer.

To balance commonness and relatedness, we need take into account both how frequent a surface form is and how good the context is. To measure disambiguation context, [1] used the sum of the weights that were previously assigned for each unambigous surface form. In our approach, we use the weight as defined previously and compute the average weighted of every context article. The data and experiments in this paper are based on a version of Wikipedia that was released in July 2011. For the learning machine we use LibSVM[3] [11] as our disambiguation classifier.

5   Experiments and Results

The results are shown from tables 6 to 9. First, the results achieved with standard datasets in table 6 prove that ours are competitive to those of state-of-the-art systems [1, 4] and with the AQUAINT dataset it achieves highest performance. To test if a larger dataset is more effective for learning a *D2W* system, we experiment with datasets in increasing size, from 500 to 1,000 and 1,500 Wikipedia paragraphs, respectively. As shown in table 7, more data provide similar accuracy. It means that only a sufficient amount of data is needed for *D2W* training.

Table 8 shows our results in three datasets with the baseline, when injected with only the relatedness and when all features are used. In all datasets, the average relatedness proves very effective with consistent improvement across different datasets and languages. Whereas table 9 show the Wikification results in three languages and with query logs. Both Italian and Polish are about 22% of size of English Wikipedia (regarding the number of pages, as seen in table 2), but the decrease in performance is very large for Polish. The reason may lie in the accents and special characters in Polish. Also, we observe that Polish Wikipedia

---

[3] http://www.csie.ntu.edu.tw/~cjlin/libsvm/

contains much shorter texts with less structured information (number of links) and still some information is missing in Polish Wikipedia pages (e.g. file and image information). Lastly, the results with query logs show that a statistical approach is useful for entity recognition and disambiguation on noisy text such as query logs and the exploitation of large-scale resource can compensate for the lack of language context.

Table 6. Comparison with previous works on English datasets

System	AQUAINT	Wikipedia
Ours	86.16	84.37
Milne-Witten:2008b	83.61	80.31
Ratinov-Roth:2011	84.52	90.20

Table 7. Effect of size

System	500	1,000	1,500
Baseline	82.57	83.02	82.74
All features	84.37	84.61	84.73

Table 8. Effect of features

System	AQUAINT	Wikipedia	Italian
Baseline	84.32	82.57	77.37
W. relatedness	85.92	83.76	78.92
All features	86.16	84.37	79.64

Table 9. Results with multiple languages and domains

System	Baseline	All features
English	82.57	84.37
Queries	54.23	56.22
Italian	77.37	79.64
Polish	58.53	60.81

6   Conclusion

The results show that a statistical approach is useful for semantic disambiguation on multiple languages (English, Italian, Polish) and on different genres (Wikipedia, newswire, query logs). Results show that the exploitation of large-scale resource can help for noisy text whereas a language-independent approach is still feasible. Note that we achieve competitive performance with previous works [1, 4] with standard datasets in English. Our approach does not make use of any natural language specific tool, such as named entity recognition, POS tagger and can easily adapt to other languages in the same manner, with very little adaptation.

Acknowledgements. This work is supported by State Secretariat for Education, Research and Innovation (SERI) project nr. C11.0128 title "Automatic Web data collection from non-reactive sources by means of normative systems and Semantic Web Technologies", which is connected to the COST Action IS1004 WEBDATANET (http://webdatanet.eu). We would like to thank Massimo Poesio for useful discussions.

References

1. Milne, D., Witten, I.H.: Learning to link with wikipedia. In: Proceedings of the 17th ACM Conference on Information and Knowledge Management, pp. 509–518. ACM, New York (2008)
2. Mihalcea, R., Csomai, A.: Wikify!: linking documents to encyclopedic knowledge. In: Proceedings of the 16th ACM Conference on Conference on Information and Knowledge Management, pp. 233–242. ACM, New York (2007)
3. Cucerzan, S.: Large-scale named entity disambiguation based on Wikipedia data. In: Proceedings of the Joint Conference on Empirical Methods in Natural Language Processing and Computational Natural Language Learning (EMNLP-CoNLL), pp. 708–716. Association for Computational Linguistics, Prague (2007)
4. Ratinov, L., Roth, D., Downey, D., Anderson, M.: Local and global algorithms for disambiguation to wikipedia. In: Proceedings of the 49th Annual Meeting of the Association for Computational Linguistics: Human Language Technologies, pp. 1375–1384. Association for Computational Linguistics, Portland (2011)
5. Bunescu, R., Pasca, M.: Using encyclopedic knowledge for named entity disambiguation. In: Proceesings of the 11th Conference of the European Chapter of the Association for Computational Linguistics, Trento, Italy, pp. 9–16 (2006)
6. Cassidy, T., Ji, H., Ratinov, L.A., Zubiaga, A., Huang, H.: Analysis and enhancement of wikification for microblogs with context expansion. In: Proceedings of COLING 2012, Mumbai, India, pp. 441–456 (December 2012)
7. Nguyen, T.V.T., Poesio, M.: Entity disambiguation and linking over queries using encyclopedic knowledge. In: Proceedings of the 6th Workshop on Analytics for Noisy Unstructured Text Data. AND 2012 (December 2012)
8. Medelyan, O., Witten, I.H., Milne, D.: Topic indexing with wikipedia. In: Proceedings of the first AAAI Workshop on Wikipedia and Artificial Intelligence (2008)
9. Cilibrasi, R.L., Vitanyi, P.M.B.: The google similarity distance. IEEE Transaction on Knowledge and Data Engineering 19(3), 370–383 (2007)
10. Milne, D., Witten, I.H.: An effective, low-cost measure of semantic relatedness obtained from wikipedia links. In: Proceedings of the 22nd Conference on Artificial Intelligence (2008)
11. Chang, C.C., Lin, C.J.: LIBSVM: A library for support vector machines. ACM Transactions on Intelligent Systems and Technology 2, 27:1–27:27 (2011) Software available at, http://www.csie.ntu.edu.tw/~cjlin/libsvm

Open Relation Mapping Based on Instances and Semantics Expansion

Fang Liu, Shizhu He, Shulin Liu, Guangyou Zhou, Kang Liu, and Jun Zhao

Institute of Automation, Chinese Academy of Sciences
{fliu,szhe,shulin.liu,gyzhou,kliu,jzhao}@nlpr.ia.ac.cn

Abstract. Mining the semantics of open relations is an important task in open information extraction (Open IE). For this task, the difficulty is that the expressions of a specific semantic in free texts are always not unique. Therefore, it needs us to deeply capture the semantics behind the various expressions. In this paper, we propose an open relation mapping method combining the instances and semantic expansion, which maps the open relation mentions in free texts to the attribute name in knowledge base to find the real semanics of each open relation mentions. Our method effectively mines semantic expansion beyond the text surface of relation mentions. Experimental results show that our method can achieve 74.4% average accuracy for open relation mapping.

Keywords: open relation mapping, semantic mining, relation paraphrase.

1 Introduction

In open information extraction, the expressions of a specific semantic relation between two entities are various. For example, we use "X was born in Y", "X's hometown Y" or "X's birth in Y" to express a semantic relation "birthPlace", where X and Y are two named entities. These expressions, like "was born in", " 's hometown" and "'s birth in" are called relation phrases [1,2,3] or relational patterns [1] (we call them open relations or relation mentions in this paper). We notice that there are textual mismatches between relation mentions and the corresponding semantic, which is a big obstacle for semantic discovery in many applications, like natrual language understanding, ontology-based question answering etc. For example, when we ask "Where is the hometown of Yao Ming?", question answering system can give the right answer if it knows the target semantic relation is "birthPlace", then the system will match the attribute value of "birthPlace" for "Yao Ming" from knowledge base. However, if the relation words in question is aforementioned "hometown", and the attribute name stored in knowledge base is "birthPlace", it's difficult to obtain the correct answers since that they are mismatched on the surface forms (detailedly illustrated in Tab.1). Therefore, constructing the mapping between relaion mentions and the semantic relation names stored in KB (shortly named as Open Relation Mapping) is very important and meaningful, which is the focus of this paper.

Formally, the source of open relation mapping is the relation mentions in free texts, and the target is the relations in knowledge base, which are usually human edited attributes (we call it attribute relation later in this paper). Intuitively, a relation mention

R.E. Banchs et al. (Eds.): AIRS 2013, LNCS 8281, pp. 320–331, 2013.

and an attribute can be directly linked if they share the common entity pairs (which are called relation instances). Unfortunately, this assumption is not always correct. As illustrated in Fig.1, ⟨ Yao Ming, fly back to, Shanghai⟩ is mapped to "birthPlace" according to the common instance (⟨ Yao Ming, Shanghai⟩ in Fig.1) assumption, which is obviously incorrect.

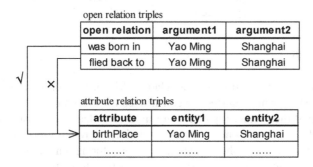

Fig. 1. An example of coincidental match in open relation mapping

Therefore, beside the relation instances, we must further consider the semantic similarity between relation mentions and relation names (attributes) in KB. For example, if we know that "hometown" has the similar semantic with "birthplace", it's easily to construct a mapping between them. However, simply computing this similarity based on surface texts, like edit distance, is insufficient. Tab.1 lists some examples of relations mappings, majority of which are mismatched by simply using surface textual. For example, "received degree in" has not any common words with attribute "yago:graduatedFrom", but they actually should be mapped. Thus, we must mine the deeper semantics behind the texts.

For this aim, we propose a novel method for open relation mapping which considers both of the semantics of relation mentions and relation instances. Our method mainly contains two steps. First, we use relation instances to generate mapping candidates. Second, we compute the semantic similarity between each candidates and the target relation mention. The candidate with similarity score above a threshold will be linked to the relation mention. In specific, we explore external resources of knowledge, like Wikipedia, to mine concepts for the semantic representation. Then, the semantic similarity of relation mention and attribute candidate is computed on this semantic space. We further make semantic expansion for each attribute to improve the mapping performance by using WordNet synset. The behind reason is that directly mining the similarity between attribute candidates and relation mentions may miss much useful information. To demonstrate the effectiveness of the proposed method, we use YAGO [4] as knowledge base, PATTY [1] as open relation dataset. Experimental results on five kinds of relations show that our method can achieve 74.4% average accuracy for open relation mapping, and the proposed semantic expansion method can effectively improve the mapping performance.

Table 1. Some mismatch examples of open relations and attributes

ID	Relation Name in KB (Attribute)	Open Relation
1	yago:wasBornIn	was born in
2	yago:wasBornIn	's hometown
3	yago:wasBornIn	's birth in
4	yago:created	creator of
5	yago:graduatedFrom	received degree in
6	yago:actedIn	played role in films

2 Related Work

In the early days, relation extraction (RE) is relation-driven. Target relations are predefined according to task, then instances are constructed for every target relation to gain relation patterns, and then relation patterns are used to collect more instances which share the same relation. The number of target relations in relation-driven extraction is limited and predefined. With the invention of open information extraction, RE became data-driven. Data-driven RE extracts relation triples from free texts whenever two entities are detected associated by a relation by a trained classifier. The number of relations in data-driven RE is unbounded and the target relations are not known in advance. The data-driven extraction is regarded as "Open Information Extraction"(Open IE) [1,5,6,7,8]. As the relation is not known, additional mapping processing is required to mine the semantics of relation expressions.

Semi-supervised mapping methods like active learning are used to match relation phrases or mentions to domain-specific relations, like NFL-scoring [9] or nutrition domain [10]. Active learning method still requires some human labeling. Later distant supervision [11,12,13] is proposed, and the target domain of mapping is extended to more general domains covered by knowledge base such as YAGO [4], DBpedia [14] etc. Then knowledge-base-supervised method is exploited to map open relations. Takamatsu etc. [12] and Surdeanu etc. [13] present a generative model to model the labeling process of distant supervision according to statistical feature of instances. Semantics is the key to avoid some wrong mapping, like coincidental match where mapping open relation "flied back to" to attribute "wasBornIn" in light of the provenance of "Yao Ming flied back to Shanghai".

Research about open relations has attracted increasing attentions, as open relation getting more important. Yates and Etzioni [2], Kok and Domingos [15] cluster relation phrases and entities at the same time, further Min et al. [3] loose the constraint that each entity or relation phrase belongs to one cluster to handle polysemy relations. But the above work group synonymy relation phrases into clusters without explicit semantics of each cluster. PATTY [1] constructs a WordNet-style hierarchical taxonomy for binary relation patterns (phrases). It also paraphrases canonical relations in DBpedia and YAGO knowledge bases with relation patterns according to common instances assumption. They did not validate the correctness of the semantics of paraphrases, there are too many noisy mappings and cannot be used directly in applications. For example, "died just""buried in""[[con]] graduated in" are regarded as paraphrase for "yago:wasBornIn".

3 Our Method

In this section, we describe our method in detail. The main framework is illustrated in Fig. 2.

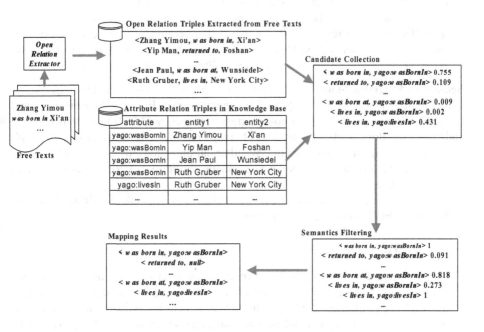

Fig. 2. Flowchart of proposed mapping algorithm

There are two parts of input data. One is relational triples stored in knowledge base taking the form of $\langle$ attr, ent1, ent2$\rangle$. where *attr* is the attribute relationship holds between the first entity *ent1* and the second entity *ent2*. Such as $\langle$ yago:wasBornIn, Zhang Yimou, Xi'an$\rangle$ etc. The other is relation triples extracted from free text taking the form of $\langle$ arg1, open, arg2$\rangle$. *open* is an open relation expressing the relation between the first argument *arg1* and the second argument *arg2*. Such as $\langle$ Zhang Yimou, was born in, Xi'an$\rangle$ etc.

The output is the explicit semantics of open relations which is called mapping pair. For example, mapping pair $\langle$ was born at, yago:wasBornIn$\rangle$ means "was born at" expresses the semantics of "yago:wasBornIn"; mapping pair $\langle$ returned to, null$\rangle$ means "returned to" expresses no semantics defined in knowledge base.

It takes two steps to implement our mapping algorithm: candidate collection and semantics filtering.

Candidate Collection. There are thousands of attributes recorded in knowledge base, YAGO[4] has 72[1] attributes , DBpedia[14] has 48,293[2] . It is time consuming, and also unnecessary to compare every attribute with open relations to eliminate unrelated

---

[1] http://www.mpi-inf.mpg.de/yago-naga/yago/statistics.html
[2] http://wiki.dbpedia.org/Datasets/DatasetStatistics

candidate attributes. Hence, we use common instances assumption to find candidate attributes as the semantics of every open relation. This process was shown at the upper part in Fig. 2. From the fact that entity pair ⟨ Ruth Gruber, New York City⟩ is shared by open relation " lives in" (Row 5 in open extracted triples in Fig. 2) and two attributes: "yago:wasBornIn" and "yago:livesIn" (Row 4 and 5 in knowledge base triples in Fig. 2), we infer that "yago:wasBornIn" and "yago:livesIn" are candidate attributes for open relation "lives in". We regard attributes which share common instances with open relations as candidate semantics. This assumption may lead to coincidental match error, therefore next we mine semantics similarity to filter out irrelevant attributes.

Semantics Filtering. Statistical features alone, that is the co-occurrence frequency of open relations and attributes may lead to mapping error. In Fig. 2 "returned to" and "yago:wasBornIn" have a higher co-occurrence frequency (0.109) than "was born at" and "yago:wasBornIn" (0.009), but "was born at" has much more closer meaning with "yago:wasBornIn" than "returned to". We filter out unrelated attributes to mitigate this kind of mapping problem by computing semantic similarity between relation mention and its candidates.

After explaining the function of the two steps in our mapping algorithm above, we will give the details of the implementation.

3.1   Candidate Collection

Generating candidate attribute is based on common instances assumption, which requires matching the aforementioned entity1 and entity2 in the relation triple simultaneously. It takes two phrases to collect attribute candidates for every open relation. First is to put binary relations into database, and make index to facilitate subsequent searching. Second is online searching and matching, which read each open extracted relation triples, then search entity1 and entity2 in prepared database. If finding attrib-ute relation triples that have arguments are also entity1 and entity2, we should then save returned attributes as candidate semantics of open relation.

After the above mapping, a series of mapping pairs ⟨open relation, candidate attribute⟩ are collected. As every mapping pair shares at least one common entity pair, we can make a statistics about the number of common instances for every mapping pair and compute the confidence as Eq.1.

$$confidence_{<open,attr>} = \frac{N_{open \cap attr}}{N_{attr}} \tag{1}$$

Where, N_{attr} is the occurrence times of attribute attr in mapping set. $N_{open \cap attr}$ is the occurrence times of mapping pair ⟨open, attr⟩ in mapping set. As shown in Fig. 2, the mapping pair ⟨ was born in, yago:wasBornIn⟩ in first step has a confidence of 0.755, meaning that the probability is 0.755 when an entity pair associated by semantic relation "yago:wasBornIn" is expressed by "was born in".

3.2   Semantics Filtering

In the second step, we compute the semantic similarity between candidate attributes retrieved in the first step and the extracted relation mentions to make filtering. We exploit empirical threshold to make decisions on whether an open relation can be mapped to an attribute. If similarity value is above a threshold, two strings have mapping relation. Otherwise, they do not. This strategy can map one open relation to multiple semantic relations and map unrelated open relations to null.

We notice *open* in open relation triples and *attr* in relational database are both tokens. For example, relation in knowledge bases is defined like "YAGO:wasBornIn", relation phrases openly extracted are like "'s hometown of" etc. Therefore token-based strings similarity method is required to accumulate the similarity between every two tokens from attribute and relation mention respectively. In our observation, when phrases contains head words of relation, like phrase "' birth in" containing common head word "birth" of "birthPlace", we have very great confidence that "' birth in" indicating relation "birthPlace". According to this feature, we prefer Generalized Mongue-Elkan (GME) proposed by Jimenez et al. [16] as our external similarity, which is computed as follows:

$$sim(A, O) = \left[\frac{1}{|A|} \sum_{\{a_i\} \in A} \left(\max_{\{o_j\} \in O} sim'(a_i, o_j) \right)^m \right]^{\frac{1}{m}} \tag{2}$$

Where, A stands for attribute, O for open relation. When m>2, GME gives greater importance to those pairs of tokens $[a_i, o_j]$ that are more similar, which is the exact feature we need. In our experiment later, m is set to 2. Then the next problem becomes choose internal similarity sim' to meet our mapping requirement which is to capture semantic similarity and immunize to expressions variations.

Semantics Filtering Based on Text Surface. Edit-based string similarity method (like Levenshtein Distance [17] etc.) finds the similarity from textual surface forms in which words share common substrings, like "yago:wasBornIn" and "was born in" in Tab.1-1. It cannot handle different expressions to the same semantics, like "'s hometown" expresses the meaning of "yago:wasBornIn" as shown in Tab.1-2. This method is not fit to open relation mapping.

Semantics Filtering by Using Semantics. Alternately, we employ some lexical resources like experts generated WordNet [18], crowdsources generated Wikipedia etc., which expand the extensional meaning of words to mine implicature. As WordNet labels the semantics relations among words, WordNet-based method could find some morphological changes, such as "born" is synonymous to "birth" (Tab.1-3). It is unable to compute the similarity between words with different part-of-the-speech (POS). The similarity score of "created" and "creator" (example shown in Tab1-4) computed by Jiang&Conarth [19] or Lin [20] methods which exploit the taxonomy of WordNet is all zero. Wikipedia-based methods (WikiMiner [21], WikiRelate! [22], Explicit Semantics Analysis (ESA) [23] etc.) taking advantage of the vast amounts of highly organized knowledge encoded in Wikipedia could mine the similarity between words according to their linkage, hierarchy or co-occurrence information in Wikipedia. However, WikiMiner [21] compares proper nouns, like person or organization name, which share common inner-linked pages. WikiRelate! [22] compares words that occur in titles of Wikipedia articles. ESA [23] compares words appeared within the text of Wikipedia articles. For our task, ESA is much more reasonable methods, as open relations are textual form of attributes. However, the text relatedness computed by ESA is not specified for open relation mapping. In the Wikipedia Concept space, "graduated from" is more related to "degree" than "received degree in", as "received" introduced a dilution.

Semantics Filtering by Using Semantic Expansion. As existing string similarity methods, like edit/character-based, WordNet-based and Wikipedia- based methods, have their limits in open relation mapping. Therefore, we proposed a semantic similarity computation method combining two lexical resources WordNet and Wikipedia under the strategy of GME [16]. In which, WordNet is used to expand the meaning of attributes words to adapt to various changes of open relations. Wikipedia is used to construct a semantic space which is defined as Wikipedia Concepts. Then the similarity of attribute candidates and relation mentions are computed under that semantic space by ESA tool. ESA stems [24] all substantivals in Wikipedia texts, and then maps them to Wikipedia Concepts. Take "acted" and "played role in films" as an example to illustrate the procedure of our proposed se-mantic similarity computation method (shown in Fig.3).

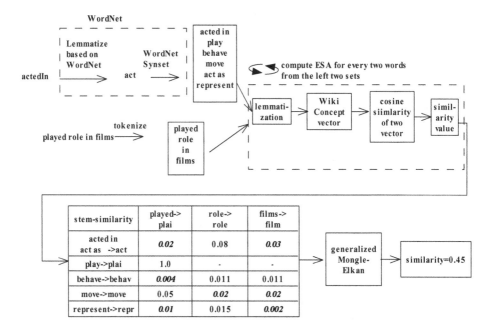

Fig. 3. Take "acted" and "played role in films" as an example to illustrate the flowchart of proposed semantics similarity computation method

The procedure is as follows:

First, tokenize attribute, delete stop words, lemmatize remain words, expand lemmatized words using WordNet synset, construct a string set by adding attribute to WordNet synset. As shown in top left of Fig.3, the yago attribute "actedIn" is lemmatized by WordNet to be "act". Then a synset of the lemmetized word is collected from WordNet as acted in, play, behave, move, act as, represent. Meanwhile, tokenize the compared open relation, and regard tokenized words as a string set. As we can see from left center of Fig.3, open relation "played role in films" is tokenized to be played, role, in, films.

Second, compute the word similarity by ESA for every pair word from the two string set, then get a matrix of similarity value. We iteratively pick one word from expanded attribute string set, compare it with every word in tokenized open relation string set using ESA. For example, ESA first stems "played" to "plai", "acted in" to "act", and retrieve the Wikipedia Concept vector corresponding to "plai" and "act" respectively. Then compute the cosine similarity between the retrieved vector to ob-tain the semantic relatedness of "played" and "acted in". Repeat the above process to get a matrix of stem-similarity as shown is lower left.

Third, put the value in matrix into GME [16] (Eq.3), then get a similarity of the two relations. Finally, store the mapping from open relation to attribute when the similarity of the two is larger than the threshold. In our example, substitute the value in matrix into Eq.2, we get the similarity value between "played role in films" and "actedIn" is 0.45.

4   Experiments

We use PATTY[3] as open relation triples input and attribute relation triples in YAGO2[4] as static relation input. The open relations of PATTY are extracted from the New York Times archive (NYT) which includes about 1,800,000 newspaper articles from the years 1987 to 2007. YAGO contains 72 attributes, 10 million entities and 120 million relation facts. The Wikipedia (WKP) data used to train ESA[5] is the English version, which contains about 3,800,000 articles (as of August 3, 2011). All relational triples are stored in a MySQL database. We evaluated mapping quality along five representative attributes: actedIn (who appeared in which show), created(who created which novel thing), graduatedFrom(who graduated from which school), hasAcademicAdvisor(who got academic guidance from who), wasBornIn(who was born in where). "wasBornIn" is the most noisy relation type. "created" has the most transformations of lexicon. "hasAcademicAdvisor" is a much ambiguous and noisy relation. "actedIn" has an acceptable quality only with instance mapping. "graduatedFrom" does not have many changes in surface form without much ambiguity.

To assess the quality of relations mapping, we ranked the open relations mapped to the above mentioned attributes and evaluated the precision of the top 100. Human judgment stated whether an open relation indicated the semantics of its mapped attribute. If so, the mapping pair was labeled as 1. If not, labeled 0. If not sure labeled 0.5.

---

[3] http://www.mpi-inf.mpg.de/yago-naga/patty/
[4] http://www.mpi-inf.mpg.de/yago-naga/yago/
[5] http://ticcky.github.io/esalib/

To compare the effect of different semantics mining methods, we used the results of Candidate Collection as baseline, adding edit-based analysis, WordNet[6] lexical resource, Wikipedia resource and our proposed method respectively.

1. **Baseline:** This method ranks the mapping results according to the confidence computed by Equation 1. This is to evaluate the quality of mapping using only instances without semantics, which is an re-implement of mapping method of PATTY[1].
2. **Edit-based Semantics Mining:** Add edit-based string similarity filtering method to baseline. This method computes the edit distance [17] between open relation and attribute, then transform the distance into a normalized similarity value. The threshold is 0.5.
3. **WordNet-based Semantics Mining:** Add WordNet-based string similarity filtering method to baseline. First, we lemmatize two comparing strings using WordNet, pick the every same POS from their lemmas then compute the similarity using Jiang&Conrath[19], we take the maximum similarity from the similarity set. The threshold is set to 0.5
4. **Wikipedia-based Semantics Mining:** Add Wikipedia-based string similarity filtering method to baseline. Computes the similarity of open relation and attribute by ESA[23]. The threshold is set to 0.05.
5. **Our Combining method:** Our method computes the similarity of two strings by our method combining WordNet and Wikipedia. The threshold is set to 0.05.

Table 2. The precision of top100 results under different methods

precision	actedIn	created	graduated From	hasAcademic Advisor	wasBornIn	average
Baseline	0.725	0.67	0.57	0.31	0.22	0.499
EditDistance	0.66	**0.915**	0.95	0.195	0.42	0.628
WordNet	0.865	0.61	**0.99**	0.485	0.545	0.699
Wikipedia	0.91	0.775	0.825	0.495	0.485	0.698
Proposed	**0.965**	0.815	0.855	**0.575**	**0.51**	**0.744**

As shown in Tab. 2, we can see that for "actedIn", "hasAcademicAdvisor" these two attributes with various lexical changes in their open relations, adding edit-based semantics mining method decreases the performance with lower precision than baseline. However, adding resources boosts the performance to reach higher precision than baseline, in which our combining method is better than adding single resource methods. For attribute "graduatedFrom" and "created" , there are no much lexical changes in their open expressions, meanwhile, headwords of attributes , like "graduated" for "graduatedFrom", "created" for attribute "created", strongly indicate the semantics of attributes. For these kinds of attributes, adding edit-based methods can significantly improve the relation performance mapping precision. Resource-based methods are not as good as edit-based method under top100 precision assessment, but still achieve better quality

---

[6] http://wordnet.princeton.edu/

than baseline for these attributes. For noisy attribute like "wasBornIn", the precision of mapping with only instances is quite low. When adding different semantics mining resource, the quality will get improvement by different degrees.

From the average performance (Col. 7 in Tab. 2), we can see that relation mapping adding semantics is better than mapping with only instances. Resource-based semantics mining method is better than edit-based method. WordNet-based semantics mining method has a comparable quality with Wikipedia-based method. Our combining method outperforms the other semantic mining methods. The average accuracy of our method for open relation mapping achieves 74.4% which is 20% higher than the baseline.

To further evaluate the effectiveness of our proposed method, we compare the top 5 results between PATTY and our method for YAGO attribute "wasBornIn", "created", "actedIn" shown in Tab. 3. From this table, we can see that the semantics filtering strategy of our method can better reduce the coincidental matching error.

Table 3. The top5 results of PATTY and our method for some attributes

	Attribute	PATTY	Our
1		[[con]] grew up	born in
2		died just	was born [[con]]
3	wasBornIn	buried in	is born to
4		was born [[con]] was raised in	[[adj]] was born in
5		[[con]] graduated in	been born
1		s album [[num]]	also created for
2		released	in creating
3	created	released [[prp]] debut album [[det]]	also created
4		[[adj]] studio album [[adj]]	[[det]] created
5		[[adj]] song in	[[mod]] create
1		also starred in	also played supporting roles in films [[adj]]
2		starred in [[det]] film	played supporting roles as
3	actedIn	twice won [[det]]	played supporting [[con]] [[adj]] roles in
4		appeared in [[adj]] film	played supporting roles in
5		also acted [[con]]	played supporting roles

5   Conclusion and Future Work

In order to reduce noisy mappings, we propose a novel open relation mapping method, which combines the instances and semantics, to mine the explicit semantics of open relations, such as hand-editing attribute names in knowledge base. We mine semantics in two steps. In the first step, we use instance information to collect candidate attributes. And in the second step, we filter out the unrelated attributes using our novel semantic similarity method which takes advantage of WordNet and Wikipedia resources. Experimental results show that our method can achieve 74.4% average accuracy for open

relation mapping and the proposed semantic expansion method can effectively improve the mapping performance.
Our future works include two aspects:

1. Handling redirection of entities. There may be more than one spelling of a certain entity in texts. We can get more semantic information by recognizing various mentions to same entity.
2. Trying to find other methods to combine various features. Our present method considers the entity pairs and semantics separately. In the future, we will consider other methods which can capture interaction effects between entity pairs and semantics.

Acknowledgments. This work was supported by the National Natural Science Foundation of China (No. 61070106, No. 61272332 and No. 61202329), the National High Technology Development 863 Program of China (No. 2012AA011102), the National Basic Research Program of China (No. 2012CB316300) and the Opening Project of Beijing Key Laboratory of Internet Culture and Digital Dissemination Research (ICDD2 01201).

References

1. Nakashole, N., Weikum, G., Suchanek, F.: Patty: a taxonomy of relational patterns with semantic types. In: Proceedings of the 2012 Joint Conference on Empirical Methods in Natural Language Processing and Computational Natural Language Learning, pp. 1135–1145. Association for Computational Linguistics (2012)
2. Yates, A., Etzioni, O.: Unsupervised resolution of objects and relations on the web. In: Proceedings of NAACL HLT, pp. 121–130 (2007)
3. Min, B., Shi, S., Grishman, R., Lin, C.Y.: Ensemble semantics for large-scale unsupervised relation extraction. In: Proceedings of the 2012 Joint Conference on Empirical Methods in Natural Language Processing and Computational Natural Language Learning, pp. 1027–1037. Association for Computational Linguistics (2012)
4. Suchanek, F.M., Kasneci, G., Weikum, G.: Yago: A large ontology from wikipedia and wordnet. Web Semantics: Science, Services and Agents on the World Wide Web 6(3), 203–217 (2008)
5. Zeng, D., Lai, S., Zhang, Y.: Open entity attribute-value extraction from unstructured text. In: Proceedings of the 2012 China Conference on Information Retrieval. Jiangxi Normal University (2012)
6. Zhao, J., Liu, K., Zhou, G., Cai, L.: Open information extraction. Journal of Chinese Information Processing 25(6), 98–110 (2011)
7. Yates, A., Cafarella, M., Banko, M., Etzioni, O., Broadhead, M., Soderland, S.: Textrunner: open information extraction on the web. In: Proceedings of Human Language Technologies: The Annual Conference of the North American Chapter of the Association for Computational Linguistics: Demonstrations, pp. 25–26. Association for Computational Linguistics (2007)
8. Fader, A., Soderland, S., Etzioni, O.: Identifying relations for open information extraction. In: Proceedings of the Conference on Empirical Methods in Natural Language Processing, pp. 1535–1545. Association for Computational Linguistics (2011)
9. Soderland, S., Roof, B., Qin, B., Xu, S., Etzioni, O., et al.: Adapting open information extraction to domain-specific relations. AI Magazine 31(3), 93–102 (2010)

10. Soderland, S., Mandhani, B.: Moving from textual relations to ontologized relations. In: Proc. AAAI Spring Symposium on Machine Reading (2007)
11. Mintz, M., Bills, S., Snow, R., Jurafsky, D.: Distant supervision for relation extraction without labeled data. In: Proceedings of the Joint Conference of the 47th Annual Meeting of the ACL and the 4th International Joint Conference on Natural Language Processing of the AFNLP, vol. 2, pp. 1003–1011. Association for Computational Linguistics (2009)
12. Takamatsu, S., Sato, I., Nakagawa, H.: Reducing wrong labels in distant supervision for relation extraction. In: Proceedings of the 50th Annual Meeting of the Association for Computational Linguistics: Long Papers, vol. 1, pp. 721–729. Association for Computational Linguistics (2012)
13. Surdeanu, M., Tibshirani, J., Nallapati, R., Manning, C.D.: Multi-instance multi-label learning for relation extraction. In: EMNLP-CoNLL 2012, pp. 455–465 (2012)
14. Auer, S., Bizer, C., Kobilarov, G., Lehmann, J., Cyganiak, R., Ives, Z.G.: DBpedia: A nucleus for a web of open data. In: Aberer, K., et al. (eds.) ASWC 2007 and ISWC 2007. LNCS, vol. 4825, pp. 722–735. Springer, Heidelberg (2007)
15. Kok, S., Domingos, P.: Extracting semantic networks from text via relational clustering. In: Daelemans, W., Goethals, B., Morik, K. (eds.) ECML PKDD 2008, Part I. LNCS (LNAI), vol. 5211, pp. 624–639. Springer, Heidelberg (2008)
16. Jimenez, S., Becerra, C., Gelbukh, A., Gonzalez, F.: Generalized mongue-elkan method for approximate text string comparison. In: Gelbukh, A. (ed.) CICLing 2009. LNCS, vol. 5449, pp. 559–570. Springer, Heidelberg (2009)
17. Levenshtein, V.I.: Binary codes capable of correcting deletions, insertions and reversals. Soviet Physics Doklady 10, 707 (1966)
18. Fellbaum, C.: Wordnet: an electronic lexical database (1998/2010) WordNet is available from, http://www.cogsci.princeton.edu/wn
19. Jiang, J.J., Conrath, D.W.: Semantic similarity based on corpus statistics and lexical taxonomy. arXiv preprint cmp-lg/9709008 (1997)
20. Lin, D.: An information-theoretic definition of similarity. In: Proceedings of the 15th International Conference on Machine Learning, San Francisco, vol. 1, pp. 296–304 (1998)
21. Milne, D.N., Witten, I.H.: Learning to link with wikipedia. In: CIKM 2008, pp. 509–518 (2008)
22. Strube, M., Ponzetto, S.P.: Wikirelate! computing semantic relatedness using wikipedia. In: AAAI 2006, p. 1 (2006)
23. Gabrilovich, E., Markovitch, S.: Computing semantic relatedness using wikipedia-based explicit semantic analysis. In: Proceedings of the 20th International Joint Conference on Artificial Intelligence, vol. 6, p. 12 (2007)
24. Porter, M.F.: An algorithm for suffix stripping. Program: electronic library and information systems 14(3), 130–137 (1980)

A Wikipedia Based Hybrid Ranking Method for Taxonomic Relation Extraction

Xiaoshi Zhong

Department of Industrial Engineering and Logistics Management,
The Hong Kong University of Science and Technology, Clear Water Bay, Kowloon,
Hong Kong, China
zhongxiaoshi@gmail.com

Abstract. This paper proposes a hybrid ranking method for taxonomic relation extraction (or select best position) in an existing taxonomy. This method is capable of effectively combining two resources, an existing taxonomy and Wikipedia, in order to select a most appropriate position for a term candidate in the existing taxonomy. Previous methods mainly focus on complex inference methods to select the best position among all the possible position in the taxonomy. In contrast, our algorithm, a simple but effective one, leverage two kinds of information, the expression of and the ranking information of a term candidate, to select the best position for the term candidate (the hypernym of the term candidate in the existing taxonomy). We conduct our approach on the agricultural domain and the experimental result indicates that the performances are significantly improved.

Keywords: taxonomic relation extraction, select best position, hybrid ranking method, Wikipedia.

1 Introduction

Applications of semantic network and knowledge bases (KB) are often required to organize and manage data (e.g., webpages, musices and images) from a wide variety of sources regarding the knowledge representation in some specific taxonomies. Most existing taxonomies are manually created at great deal of time and labor consuming, and it is not always possible to manually maintain these existing taxonomies for rapidly changing or new coming domains. Therefore, such kinds of taxonomies are rarely complete that they fail to satisfy practical applications. Taxonomic relation extraction is a fundamental step toward automatic taxonomy construction, which is a practical solution to build a semantic web or knowledge ontology.

In general, taxonomic relation extraction based on an existing taxonomy can be treated as *term organization*, in which the goal is to posit term candidates in the existing taxonomy. The research issue in term organization is demonstrated by the following example in the agricultural taxonomic relation extraction.

R.E. Banchs et al. (Eds.): AIRS 2013, LNCS 8281, pp. 332–343, 2013.

Suppose that the term candidate "almond" is extracted from an existing taxonomy and the three hypernym relation triplets are extracted from Wikipedia <almond, *is-a*, plant products>, (<almond, *is-a*, nuts>, and <almond, *is-a*, trees>). From these three relation triplets, the corresponding taxonomic term candidates of the term candidate ("almond") are "plant products", "nuts" and "trees". Here, *taxonomic terms* are the nodes in the existing taxonomy, *term candidates* are the nodes which will be posited to the existing taxonomy, and *taxonomic term candidates* refer to the terms which are the potential parent nodes (hypernyms) for the given term candidate.

Among these three taxonomic term candidates, the best one is "nuts" in the agricultural taxonomy. There are two main issues in term organization. First, generally people construct taxonomies for particular purposes according to specific taxonomic criterions. Most basic concepts are of multiple perspectives, but each taxonomy mainly focuses on one or two [1]. Thus, only "plant products" and "nuts" are selected as the possible parent of "almond". Second, positing the term candidate "almond" in the agricultural taxonomy require the most concrete or specific hypernym of "almond". Therefore, only "nuts" is finally selected in this example. Overall, the goal of term organization is to select the best taxonomic term candidate which mush be taxonomy-oriented and most specific.

In terms of term organization, most of previous work proposed complicated inference methods to select the best one among all the taxonomic term candidates [2][3][4]. In this paper, we propose a ranking-based term organization that attempt to effectively leverage information from Wikipedia and an existing taxonomy for taxonomic relation extraction. Our method is a simple two-stage process: taxonomy-oriented taxonomic term candidate extraction and ranking-based term organization.

Firstly, we implement a taxonomy-oriented process for taxonomic term candidate extraction. In other words, our taxonomic term candidate extraction is oriented by the existing taxonomy. Wikipedia-based term extraction has been intensively researched in the recent years, but most of them restrict their work only to Wikipedia and neglect the goal - taxonomic relation extraction in the existing taxonomy. In fact, the existing taxonomy plays an important role in taxonomic relation extraction. For instance, although "almond" is a kind of "trees" in biology and is a kind of "nuts" in agriculture, only "nuts" needs to be extracted for the agricultural taxonomic relation extraction. Therefore, the taxonomic term candidate extraction should be guided by the focus taxonomy. When taking the existing taxonomy into account, the techniques of taxonomic term candidate extraction become much simple. In this paper, we propose a head-matching method for taxonomic term candidate extraction.

Secondly, after taxonomic term candidate extraction, term organization needs only to focus on selecting the most concrete or specific taxonomic term candidates. First, a modifier-graph based ranking method is used to distinguish the taxonomic term candidates. Second, based on our data analysis, a hybrid ranking method is proposed, which uses different ranking strategies to select the most specific taxonomic term candidate for word-based term candidates (including one and only one token) and phrase-based term candidates (including at least two tokens).

We conduct our method on the agricultural domain, and experimental result indicates that such taxonomic relation extraction method achieves significant improvement. Of course, our method is almost domain independent, and is easy to transfer to other domains.

The rest of the paper is organized as follows. Section 2 describes our taxonomy-oriented taxonomic term candidate extraction and ranking-based term organization. Section 3 introduces our experimental data and experiment design, and then presents performances. Section 4 discusses the related work on term organization. Section 5 draws conclusion.

2 Methodology

We first introduce terminologies used in this paper. A taxonomy can be treated as a graph where a node is a concept (or an instance) and the edge denotes a semantic relation (*hypernym-hyponym*) between two nodes. In the graph, conceptes/instances are non-leaf/leaf nodes. The goal, in this paper, is to extract such semantic relation in order to select a best position for a term candidate in a taxonomy.

There are two main steps in our taxonomic relation extraction system: taxonomy-oriented taxonomic term candidate extraction and ranking-based term organization. In the first step, for each term candidate (i.e., a node) in the existing taxonomy, all corresponding taxonomic term candidates are identified with the help of the information in Wikipedia (including unstructured text, infobox, and category structure). In ranking-based term organization, the best taxonomic term candidate that is the most specific hypernym of the term candidate in the existing taxonomy is selected.

2.1 Taxonomy-Oriented Taxonomic Term Candidate Extraction

There are four steps in our taxonomy-oriented taxonomic term candidate extraction: 1) selection of target Wikipedia articles, 2) preprocessing, 3) grouping of taxonomic term candidates, and 4) extraction of taxonomic term candidates.

Selection of Target Wikipedia Articles: Wikipedia is a comprehensive corpus and experiments in this paper are conducted in the agricultural domain, therefore, Wikipedia articles that relevant to plant according to the infoboxes are selected. These articles are denoted by $WA = \{wa_i, i = 1, ..., n\}$.

Preprocessing: A series of preprocesses are done for both Wikipedia articles and term candidates. For a Wikipedia article, for the unstructured text, sentence segmentation, tokenization, and stemmer are used. For the infobox names and category names, tokenization and stemmer are firstly used, and then the head extraction tool [5] is applied to extract the heads.

For the term candidate in the taxonomy, tokenization and stemmer are firstly used. The head extraction [5] is then applied to extract the head and the list of taxonomic head is denoted by $TH = \{th_j, j = 1, ..., m\}$.

Grouping of Taxonomic Term Candidates: For each selected Wikipedia article wa_i, any string which matches to any term candidates in the existing taxonomy is extracted and all such strings are grouped into a set of taxonomic term candidates, denoted by ttc_i. With this simple grouping strategy, each taxonomic term candidate can be mapping to a node of the existing taxonomy. All the selected Wikipedia articles are represented as $TTCSet = \{ttc_i, i = 1, ..., n\}$ and their corresponding Wikipedia articles are $WA = \{wa_i, i = 1, ..., n\}$.

Extraction of Taxonomic Term Candidates: For each set of taxonomic term candidate $ttc_i \in TTCSet$ (the corresponding Wikipedia article is $wa_i \in WA$), the adapted head-matching approach used in the paper [6] is applied to extract its corresponding taxonomic term candidates from the Wikipedia article wa_i.

Because Wikipedia articles are directly opened to general users, their expressions often prefer to be colloquial than be technical. In order to capture the colloquial terms when corresponding technical terms are missing in Wikipedia, we choose the head-matching method.

There are three types of taxonomic term candidates ($TTC@UnText$, $TTC@CaName$ and $TTC@InBox$) which are derived from the unstructured texts, the category names and the infoboxes in the Wikipedia article wa_i separately.

1) *Taxonomic term candidate from unstructured texts* ($TTC@UnText$): there are four steps to examine whether a term is a taxonomic term candidate based on the unstructured texts in the Wikipedia article.

(a) *Initialization*: Initialize the head set $HSet@UnText$ to be empty.

(b) *Taxonomic head extraction*: for each taxonomic head $th_j \in TH$, if it occurs in the unstructured texts of the Wikipedia article wa_i, there seems a relation between the taxonomic head th_j and the taxonomic term candidate ttc_i. Thus, the taxonomic head th_j and its occurring frequency are incorporated into $HSet@UnText$.

(c) *Taxonomic head selection*: since taxonomic heads in $HSet@UnText$ are noisy, it needs the filtering processing. Firstly, the taxonomic heads in $HSet@UnText$ are sorted according to their occurring frequencies. Secondly, given a frequency threshold Fq, the taxonomic heads in $HSet@UnText$ whose occurring frequency is less than Fq are discarded. This is because the unstructured texts of a Wikipedia article often too noisy, only some taxonomic heads remains.

(d) *Taxonomic term candidate extraction*: set $TTC@UnText$ is the set of terms whose taxonomic heads remained in $HSet@UnText$ after the step(c).

2) *Taxonomic term candidates from category names* ($TTC@CaName$): Step (a)-(b) of the aforementioned approach is applied to the heads of the category names of the Wikipedia article wa_i, to get the

head set $HSet@CaName$. Since there are few category names in the Wikipedia article wa_i and filtering processing is not necessary, Step (c) is skipped. Lastly, Step (d) is that $TTC@CaName$ is the collection of the taxonomic terms whose head in $HSet@CaName$.

3) **Taxonomic term candidates from infoboxes** ($TTC@InBox$): The approach for $TTC@CaName$ is applied to the heads of the infoboxes of the Wikipedia article wa, and get $TTC@InBox$.

2.2   Ranking-Based Term Organization

For a given term candidate, we can still obtain hundreds of taxonomic term candidates from $TTC@UnText$, $TTC@CaName$ and $TTC@InBox$. In order to recognize the most appropriate (or best) taxonomic term candidate, we propose a ranking-based method to further selection.

Our ranking-based method involves two components: graph-based ranking approach and hybrid ranking approach. The graph-based ranking approach attempts to distinguish taxonomic term candidates in $TTC@CaName$, and the hybrid ranking makes a final selection according to that which the given term candidate belongs to, either word-based or phrase-based and that the ranking information in $TTC@UnText$, $TTC@CaName$ and $TTC@InBox$. In what follows, we will first illustrate the graph-based ranking approach and then describe the hybrid ranking approach.

Graph-Based Ranking: Since the taxonomic term candidates in $TTC@CaName$ often are noisy, we attempt to rank them by using their modifiers. In this paper, we choose a adapted version of the modifier-graph based ranking approach proposed in the paper [2]. In the rest of the section, we first briefly introduce the modifier-graph based ranking approach used in [2] and then adapt the modified graph-based ranking approach for our taxonomic relation extraction.

First, for the given term candidate B, the paper [2] constructs a modifier graph, which can examine whether or not a relation <A, *is-a*, B> in Wikipedia's category structures is true. There are five main steps shown as follows.

(a) construct a modifier graph. It is a directed graph where each node denotes each token inside $U(B, n)$, and each edge denotes a co-occurrence as modifier-head relation inside each term of $U(B, n)$. Here, $U(B, n)$ is defined as the set of upper concepts of B up to n step in Wikipedia's category structures.

(b) A adapted version of the HITS algorithm [7] is applied to calculated the score for the nodes in that graph.

(c) The score of A for the relation <A, *is-a*, B> is calculated as Eq(1).

(d) All relations associated with term B are sorted according to their scores.

(e) The top k terms are selected as the truly *is-a* relations for B in Wikipedia's category structures.

$$Score(A, B) = score(head) + \sum_{a \in mod(A)} score(a) \tag{1}$$

where *head* is the head of A, and $mod(A)$ is the set of modifiers of A (e.g., the phrase "plant product", "product" is the head, $mod(product) = \{plant\}$).

When takeing a close look at the data, we find that there are two main issues for the adaptation of the modifier-graph based ranking approach to our task.

Firstly, although the paper [2] provides theoretical measure for confirming *is-a* relation for term B, their experimental corpus actually rely on the agreements of two annotators. But, we work on taxonomic relation extraction in an existing taxonomy and the existing taxonomy actually involves the specific taxonomic criteria. Therefore, rather than Wikipedia's category structure, we use the existing taxonomy to get $U(B, n)$ (see step (a)).

Secondly, our task if different from the work in [2]. The work [2] attempts to recognize term A which contains the intrinsic (essential) property of term B while our task attempt to recognize the term A which is the most specific hypernym of term B. Therefore, we transform Eq(1) as to Eq(2). The score calculated by Eq(2) actually is the inverse of the score by Eq(1).

$$Score(A, B) = \frac{1}{score(head) + \sum_{a \in mod(A)} score(a)} \qquad (2)$$

Hybrid Ranking: The hybrid ranking approach leverages different ranking strategies to select the best taxonomic term candidate according to which the given term candidate belongs to, either word-based or phrase-based. The input data are the three kinds of taxonomic term candidates ($TTC@UnText$, $TTC@CaName$ and $TTC@InBox$) from taxonomic term candidate extraction.

1) **Word-based term candidates:** There are four steps in the ranking strategy which solves the problem of term organization for word-based term candidates, illustrated as follows.

(a) *Initialization:* initialize the set $BestTTC$ to be empty. $BestTTC$ is the set of the potential best taxonomic term candidates;

(b) *Graph-based ranking:* the modifier-graph based ranking approach is applied to rank the taxonomic term candidates in $TTC@CameN$, and then only top k terms are selected (denoted by $TTC@Graph$);

(c) *Multi-resource based re-ranking:* for any taxonomic term candidate in $TTC@Graph$, $TTC@UnText$ or $TTC@InBox$, the final score is defined as Eq(3). $Score(A, @Graph)$ is 1 if term A occurs in $TTC@Graph$; Otherwise, it is 0. So does to $Score(A, @CaName)$ and $Score(A, @InBox)$.

(d) *Extraction of the best taxonomic term candidate:* firstly, for any taxonomic term candidate in $TTC@Graph$, $TTC@UnText$ or $TTC@InBox$, if its new score (defined as Eq(3)) is greater than 1, add it into $BestTTC$; Secondly, if $BestTTC$ is empty, add the top one term of $TTC@Graph$ into $BestTTC$.

$$Score(A) = Score(A, @Graph) + Score(A, @UnText) + Score(A, @InBox) \qquad (3)$$

We should note that from the strategy of grouping taxonomic term candidates, as mentioned before, each the taxonomic term candidates can be mapping to a node of the existing taxonomy. This indicates that when the best taxonomic term candidate of a term candidate is successfully extracted, the hynpernym of the term candidate is found, so does the best position of the term candidate.

2) *Phrased-based term candidates*: According to our data analysis, if the term candidate is phrase-based, the best taxonomic term candidate is usually one of the tokens in the term candidate. However, there is no measure to point out which token is the correct one. For example, the best taxonomic term candidate for "plant products" is "products", while the one for "abies alba" is "abies".

In this paper, we use the following strategy for a phrase-based term B:

(a) If there are several tokens in term B occurring in $HSet@UnText$ (see Section 2.1), the top one which is with highest occurring frequency is selected as the best taxonomic term candidate.

(b) Else, utilize the ranking strategy for word-based term candidates.

3   Experiments

In this section, we first introduce the experimental data and the experiment design, and then describe our performance analysis.

3.1   Experimental Data

Data Description. There are two types of data in our experiments: $AGROVOC^1$ and $TTCSet$ (see Section 2.1). $AGROVOC$, an agricultural taxonomy provided by Food and Agriculture Organization of the United Nations, contains 31,817 nodes, and the plant $TTCSet$ includes 39,859 terms.

In our experiment, to avoid human annotation (which requires much domain knowledge and at great cost), we leverage the overlapping terms between $AGROVOC$ and the plant $TTCSet$ as the experimental data, totally 2,132 term candidates. Among them, 500 terms are randomly selected as the development data and the rest serve as the test data in our experiment.

Data Analysis. In this section, we carry on two series of data analysis to support our design of the taxonomic relation extraction.

Table 1. The statistics of the term candidates in $AGROVOC(\%)$

	Instance	Concept
Word-based	23.55	34.15
Phrase-based	42.21	0.09

Firstly, Table 1 shows the statistics of our experiment data according to word/phrase and instance/concept in $AGROVOC$. From Table 1, we can observe that the number of the word-based term candidates and of the phrase-based term candidates are comparable (57.70% v.s. 42.30%). Thus, we should design different strategies for these two kinds of term candidates respectively.

---

[1] http://aims.fao.org/standards/agrovoc/about

Secondly, in our graph-based ranking approach, we choose an existing taxonomy (i.e., $AGROVOC$) instead of Wikipedia's category structure. Here, we compare $AGROVOC$ and Wikipedia's category structure in Table 2. Table 2 shows the statistics of $U(B, 2)$ (defined in Section 2.2, Graph-based ranking) in these two corpora, where B is a term in the $TTCSet$.

Table 2. The statistics of $U(B, 2)$

	Wikipedia	AGROVOC
#Average term	17.4	4.2
#Average modifier	3.93	0.67

From Table 2, we find that the two taxonomies are much different. Wikipedia's category structure involves more terms (17.4 v.s. 4.2). This indicates that Wikipedia's category structure is more divergent than our existing taxonomy. The terms in $U(B, 2)$ of Wikipedia's category structure seems more likely to be phrase (i.e., having modifiers) (3.93 v.s. 0.67). This indicates that the modifier-graph based ranking approach should take more roles in Wikipedia's category structure than in our existing taxonomy. Overall, the graph-based ranking approach used in [2] should not be directly applied to our work.

3.2 Experiment Design

During the test, we test only one term candidate at each time. In other words, only the focus term candidate is missing and other terms are still in the taxonomy. For instance, when testing term candidate B, the input taxonomy is $AGROVOC$ without term B and its edges. Our test data contains 1,632 term candidates, thus our system runs 1,632 times during test. The final performances are the average measures of the 1,632 term candidates.

In the experiments, five approaches used to our taxonomic relation extraction are as follows: $TTC@UnText$, $TTC@CaName$, $TTC@InBox$, $TTC@Graph$ and $HyRank$. For the given term candidate, each approach ranks its corresponding taxonomic term candidates and selects only the top one as the best taxonomic term candidate. The parameter setting for each approach is learned from the development data.

3.3 Experiment Result

Firstly, we show the overall performance for the aforementioned approaches in Table 3. In this paper, the three measures which are used to evaluate the taxonomic relation extraction are the three traditional metrics, namely precision, recall and F-score.

From Table 3, we can see that $TTC@UnText$, $TTC@CaName$ and $TTC@InBox$ perform poor. This indicates that the simple information derived

Table 3. The overall performances of different approaches on the test data

	Precision	Recall	F-score
$TTC@UnText$	23.79	25.25	24.50
$TTC@CaName$	11.16	23.53	15.14
$TTC@InBox$	12.34	57.66	20.33
$TTC@Graph$	36.88	36.88	36.88
$HyRank$	65.66	80.34	72.26

from unstructured texts, category names or infoboxes in Wikipedia cannot completely solve the problem of taxonomic relation extraction by itself. That means the information in Wikipedia is much noisy and need more exploration. The graph-based ranking approach ($TTC@Graph$) achieves improvements, but not much, maybe because these two corpora ($AGROVOC$ and Wikipedia) are much more different (see Section 3.1, Data Analysis). Finally, our hybrid ranking approach ($HyRank$) achieves significant improvement in all the three metrics. This indicates that taxonomic relation extraction needs some way which can effectively combine different information in Wikipedia.

Secondly, we show the comparison of the performances of $TTC@Graph$ and $HyRank$ in Table 4. From Table 4, we have following observations.

Table 4. The comparison of $TTC@Graph$ and $HyRank$ on the test data

		Precision	Recall	F-score
$TTC@Graph$	Phrase-based	63.64	63.64	63.64
	Word-based	16.87	16.87	16.87
$HyRank$	Phrase-based	95.04	96.30	95.67
	Word-based	45.46	65.54	53.69

1) Compared to $TTC@Graph$, $HyRank$ achieves much better performances in both of phrase-based term candidates and word-based term candidates. In terms of word-based term candidates, besides $TTC@Graph$, the additional processing which incorporates other *information* in Wikipedia (category names and infoboxes) is done in $HyRank$. The significant differences in performances indicates that the top one term in $TTC@Graph$ are very noisy, and the additional information used in $HyRank$ can effectively move the best taxonomic term candidates as top as possible.

2) For $HyRank$, the performances for phrase-based term candidates are significantly better than the ones for word-based term candidates. This indicates that the difficulty of taxonomic relation extraction is the insertion of rather abstract concepts (word-based term candidates). More efforts should be done for

word-based term candidates. Moreover, for phrased-based term candidates, we observe that 95% of them are solved in Step 1 (see Section 2.2, Phrase-based term candidates). This indicates our approach is very effectively for phrase-based term candidates.

4   Related Work

For taxonomic relation extraction, there has been a variety of studies on taxonomic term candidate extraction, and few studies have explored term organization. We briefly introduce them as follows.

4.1   Taxonomic Term Candidate Extraction

Methods for taxonomic term candidate extraction can be grouped into two broad categories according to the format of input text: unstructured and structured.

In terms of unstructured text, taxonomic term candidate extraction mainly leverages pattern-based and clustering-based approaches [1][8][9][10].

Pattern-based approaches: Firstly, Hearst [10] propose to use bootstrapping to discover *is-a* relation with a list of manual hyponym patterns. From then on, many methodes explore Hearst-style patterns to extract different kinds of semantic relations [3][8][11]. In recent years, the pattern-based approaches are applied to unstructured text in Wikipedia [12][13][14]. Although pattern-based approach plays an important role in taxonomic term candidate extraction due to their simplicity and high accuracy, it suffers from the problems of low coverage.

Clustering-based approaches: Usually, context are represented in a vector space which involves different kinds of information (such as contextual feature, syntactic dependency, co-occurrence), and clustered depending on similarities of the vectors [3][4]. Clustering-based approaches can disclose implicit relations, but they require large corpora. Moreover, clustering-based approaches can solve only *is-a* and sibling relations.

In terms of structured text, most previous work on Wikipedia focus on the three kinds of information: infoboxes, category structure and inter-article links.

(a) *Infoboxes*: Suchanek et al. [15][16] applies a set of heuristic rules to Wikipedia's infoboxes to extract the instances of 92 relations for their *YAGO* taxonomy. *KOG* system is automatically refined the Wikipedia's infobox structure and then integrated WordNet into Wikipedia's infobox-class schemata [17].

(b) *Category structure*: Category structure of Wikipedia is a rich online resource for taxonomic relation extraction. With the help of WordNet, Suchanek et al.[16] construct a taxonomy through combining entities and relations in Wikipedia's category structure. Choi et al. [2] construct a high-quality taxonomy through examining whether or not a *hypernym-hyponym* relation in the Wikipedia's structure is true.

(c) *Inter-article links*: Most relations between terms are reliable if there are inter article links between them in Wikipedia [18]. Moreover, taxonomic term candidate extraction depending on Wikipedia's inter-article links can achieve a high accurate performance despite of using little linguistic analysis [18][19][20].

4.2 Term Organization

For term organization, most of previous work explored complicated inference methods [3][4][21]. Snow et al. [3] maximize the conditional probability of *hypernym-hyponym* relations with certain evidence. The work in [4] maximizes a metric-based ranking formula which combines heterogeneous features like context, co-occurrence, and surface patterns. The work in [21] maximizes a scoring function for each term network which considers a set of relational constraints.

5 Conclusion

In this paper, we examine the taxonomic relation, and propose a taxonomy-oriented approach for taxonomic term candidate extraction and a ranking-based approach for term organization. Both of two approaches can effectively leverage the two kinds of resources, Wikipedia and an existing taxonomy. We conduct our experiments on the agricultural domain, and achieve significant improvement. We believe that the present research should provide the foundation for future research on taxonomic relation extraction.

References

1. Kozareva, Z., Riloff, E., Hovy, E.: Semantic Class Learning from the Web with Hyponym Pattern Linkage Graphs. In: Proceedings of ACL 2008:HLT, pp. 1048–1056 (2008)
2. Choi, D., Kim, E.K., Shim, S.A., Choi, K.S.: Intrinsic Property-based Taxonomic Relation Extraction from Category Structure. In: Proceedings of the 23rd International Conference on Computational Linguistics, p. 48 (2010)
3. Snow, R., Jurafsky, D., Ng, A.Y.: Learning syntactic patterns for automatic hypernym discovery. Advances in Neural Information Processing Systems (2004)
4. Yang, H., Callan, J.: A Metric-based Framework for Automatic Taxonomy Induction. In: Proceedings of the Joint Conference of the 47th Annual Meeting of the ACL and the 4th International Joint Conference on Natural Language Processing of the AFNLP, pp. 271–279 (2009)
5. Collins, M.: Head-Driven Statistical Models for Natural Language Parsing. Computational Linguistics 29(4), 589–637 (2003)
6. Nagata, M., Shibaki, Y., Yamamoto, K.: Using Goi-Taikei as an Upper Ontol-ogy to Build a Large-Scale Japanese Ontology from Wikipedia. In: Proceedings of the 6th Workshop on Ontologies and Lexical Resources, Beijing, pp. 11–18 (August 2010)
7. Jon, K.: Authoritative sources in a hyperlinked environment. Journal of the ACM, JACM (1999)
8. Etzioni, O., Cafarella, M., Downey, D., Popescu, A., Haked, T., Soderland, S., Weld, D., Yates, A.: Unsupervised named-entity extraction from the web: an experimental study. Artificial Intelligence 165(1), 91–134 (2005)
9. Girju, R., Badulescu, A., Moldovan, D.: Automatic Discovery of Part-whole Relations. Computational Linguistics 32(1), 83–135 (2006)

10. Hearst, M.A.: Automatic acquisition of hyponyms from large text corpora. In: Proceedings of the 14th Conference on Computational Linguistics, vol. 2, pp. 539–545 (1992)
11. Mann, G.S.: Fine-Grained Proper Noun Ontologies for Question Answering. In: Proceedings of SemaNet 2002 Building and Using Semantic Network (2002)
12. Erp, M.V., Bosch, A.V.D., Wubben, S., Hunt, S.: Instance-driven Discovery of Ontological Relation Labels. In: Proceedings of the EACL 2009 Workshop on Language Technology and Resources for Cultural Heritage, Social Sciences, Humanities, and Education, pp. 60–68 (2009)
13. Nakayama, K., Hara, T., Nishio, S.: Wikipedia link structure and text mining for semantic relation extraction towards a huge scale global web ontology. In: Proceedings of Sem-Search 2008 CEUR Workshop, Tenerife, Spain, pp. 59–73 (2008)
14. Nguyen, D.P.T., Matsuo, Y., Ishizuka, M.: Exploiting syntactic and semantic information for relation extraction from Wikipedia. In: Proceedings of Workshop on Text-Mining and Link-Analysis(TextLink 2007) at IJCAI (2007)
15. Suchanek, F.M., Kasneci, G., Weikum, G.: YAGO: A Core of Semantic Knowledge. In: Proceedings of the 16th International Conference on World Wide Web (2007)
16. Suchanek, F.M., Kasneci, G., Weikum, G.: YAGO: A Large Ontology from Wikipedia and WordNet. Web Semantics: Science, Services and Agents on the World Wide Web 6(3), 203–317 (2008)
17. Wu, F., Weld, D.S.: Automatically refining the Wikipedia Infobox Ontology. In: Proceedings of the 17th International Conference on World Wide Web, pp. 635–644. ACM (2008)
18. Kamps, J., Koolen, M.: The importance of link evidence in wikipedia. In: Macdonald, C., Ounis, I., Plachouras, V., Ruthven, I., White, R.W. (eds.) ECIR 2008. LNCS, vol. 4956, pp. 270–282. Springer, Heidelberg (2008)
19. Blohm, S., Cimiano, P.: Using the web to reduce data sparseness in pattern-based information extraction. In: Kok, J.N., Koronacki, J., Lopez de Mantaras, R., Matwin, S., Mladenič, D., Skowron, A. (eds.) PKDD 2007. LNCS (LNAI), vol. 4702, pp. 18–29. Springer, Heidelberg (2007)
20. Tamagawa, S., Sakurai, S., Tejima, T., Morita, T., Izumi, N., Yamaguchi, T.: Learning a Large Scale of Ontology from Japanese Wikipedia. In: Web Intelligence and Intelligent Agent Technology (WI-IAT). IEEE (2010)
21. Do, Q.X., Roth, D.: Constraints based Taxonomic Relation Classification. In: Proceedings of the 2010 Conference on Empirical Methods in Natural Language Processing, pp. 1099–1109 (2010)

Exploring Distinctive Features in Distant Supervision for Relation Extraction

Yang Liu, Shulin Liu, Kang Liu, Guangyou Zhou, and Jun Zhao

National Laboratory of Pattern Recognition
Institute of Automation, Chinese Academy of Sciences
{yang.liu,shulin.liu,kliu,gyzhou,jzhao}@nlpr.ia.ac.cn

Abstract. Distant supervision (DS) for relation extraction suffers from the noisy labeling problem. Most solutions try to model the noisy instances in the form of multi-instance learning. However, in the non-noisy instances, there may be noisy features which would harm the extraction model. In this paper, we employ a novel approach to address this problem by exploring distinctive features and assigning distinctive features more weight than the noisy ones. We make use of all the training data (both the labeled part that satisfies the DS assumption and the part that does not), and then employ an unsupervised method by topic model to discover the distribution of features to latent relations. At last, we compute the distinctiveness of features by using the obtained feature-relation distribution, and assign features weights based on their distinctiveness to train the extractor. Experiments show that the approach outperforms the baseline methods in both the held-out evaluation and the manual evaluation significantly.

Keywords: Relation Extraction, Distant Supervision, Distinctive Features.

1 Introduction

Relation Extraction is the task of extracting semantic relations between entity pairs given a set of sentences containing both entities. It gains much interest for its potential effects on constructing large scale knowledge bases and supporting many other applications like question answering [12], textual entailment [15] etc. Traditional supervised approaches for relation extraction [7][22] need to label training data, which is expensive and biased towards the domain of labeled data. Due to the problems of supervised approaches, an attractive paradigm called distant supervision (DS) [10] is employed. It automatically produces labeled training data by aligning entities in a knowledge base with relation facts (such as Freebase[1]) to sentences. However, it suffers from noisy labeled data which will bring poor extraction results. For example, in Figure 1, $r(e1, e2) =$ "$BornIn(Yao\ Ming, Shanghai)$" is a relation in the knowledge base. After automatic labeling, we get the sentences containing both $e1 =$ "$Yao\ Ming$" and $e2 =$ "$Shanghai$". The upper sentence truly express the relation $r =$ "$BornIn$" between two entities. However, the lower one does not. It is a noisy labeled sentence. In this paper, we focus to address the noisy labeling problem in DS for relation extraction.

---

[1] http://www.freebase.com/

R.E. Banchs et al. (Eds.): AIRS 2013, LNCS 8281, pp. 344–355, 2013.

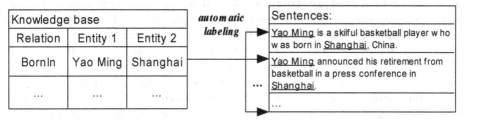

Fig. 1. Noise in training data by distant supervision. The first sentence is the correct labeling and the second one is incorrect.

To overcome the problem of noisy labeled data in DS, work in [13][9][14] attempted to model the noisy data with multi-instance learning methods. They assume that at least one of the sentences containing both $e1$ and $e2$ expresses $r(e1, e2)$. However, this at-least-one assumption can fail, for that Takamatsu et al. [16] showed 91.7% of entity pairs only have one labeled sentence in Wikipedia articles which do not fit for the multi-instance learning assumption. Moreover, they used binary features in their model. This setting will enforce some frequent indistinctive features. For example, labeled sentence "*Life of Pie, by Ang Lee, can be said to be the best...*" for $r(e1, e2) = $ "*DirectorOf(Ang Lee, Life Of Pi)*" has one lexical feature "*e2 by e1*" where $e1$ and $e2$ are placeholders for two entities. However, it can also be found in the "*AuthorOf*" relation like the sentence "*One Hundred Years of Solitude, by Gabriel Garcia Marquez, is a novel that tells...*" for "*AuthorOf(Gabriel Garcia Marquez, One Hundred Years of Solitude)*". As a result, entity pairs of *AuthorOf* are probably mistaken for relation *DirectorOf*. Although the feature is from a positive sentence, it is still noisy. Binary features can not discriminate between the distinctive features and noisy ones.

In the paper, due to the deficiencies of the at-least-one assumption and the binary feature setting, we propose a novel approach to solve the noisy labeling problem. Instead of using binary features which take no difference to all features, we explore the distinctive features and assign distinctive features higher weight than the noisy ones. In this way, we do not use the at-least-one assumption as the multi-instance learning does and can solve the noisy feature problem in the non-noisy sentences that indeed express the target relations caused by the binary feature setting mentioned above.

Specifically, we employ a new method to calculate the distinctiveness of each feature. Our intuition is that the noisy features tend to appear in several different relations. It means that if a feature is used to indicate several different relations, it would be less distinctive. To obtain the feature-relation distribution, instead of only using the sentences labeled by a knowledge base with the DS assumption (**KB-matched instances**[2]) like previous work, we use the **united instances** that combine the KB-matched instances with the instances generated by entity pairs in training data but not in the knowledge base (**KB-not-matched instances**). For that, the KB-matched instances are only a small part of the training data, instances in which are biased to the relations used as labeling

---

[2] An instance consists of features of an entity pair extracted from all its labeled sentences.

sources and not sufficient to discover the distribution of features to latent relations. And then we employ a topic model to model the generating process of instances in united instances where the feature can be considered as "word", instances as "documents" and relations as "topics". After estimating the parameters, We can get the feature-relation distribution (or the "word-topic" distribution) via this model. After that, we compute the distinctiveness of each feature based on the feature-relation distribution, and assign features different weights according to their distinctiveness. Finally, we use these weighted features to train a classifier for discovering relations in new instances.

This paper mainly makes the following contributions:

– To solve the noisy training data problem, we propose a method to assign features different values according to features' distinctiveness to latent relations. We avoid the "at-least-one" assumption in multi-instance learning and can solve the noisy features extracted from positive labeled sentences such as "$e2$ by $e1$" in "*Life of Pie, by Ang Lee, can be said to be the best...*". To our best knowledge, little work has considered to weigh features for solving the noisy labeling problem in DS for relation extraction.
– To discover the probabilities of features belonging to latent relations, we model united instances combined KB-matched instances with KB-not-matched instances via a topic model and obtain the feature-relation distribution. Previous work mainly focused on the KB-matched instances, little work has tried to make use of unlabeled data (KB-not-matched instances), which do not satisfied the DS assumption.
– We conduct experiments to evaluate our method with Wikipedia articles and Freebase as the knowledge base. We compare our method with Mintz et al. [10] and the multi-instance learning approach of MULTIR [9]. The experimental results show that our method outperforms both methods.

The remainder of the paper is organized as follows. Section 2 introduces the related work. Section 3 describe the relation topic model. Section 4 introduces the method to weigh features. Section 5 illustrates our experiments and evaluation. Finally, we conclude our paper with the future work.

2   Related Work

Distant supervision (also known as weak supervision or self supervision) is used to a broad class of methods in information extraction which aims to automatically generate labeled data by aligning with data in knowledge bases. It is introduced by Craven and Kumlien [4] who used the Yeast Protein Database to generate labeled data and trained a naive-Bayes extractor. Bellare and McCallum [2] used BibTex records as the source of distant supervision. The KYLIN system in [18] used article titles and infoboxes of Wikipedia to label sentences and trained a CRF extractor aiming to generate infoboxes automatically. The Open IE systems TEXTRUNNER [21] and WOE [19] trained their extractors with the automatic labeled data from Penn Treebank and Wikipedia infoboxes respectively. Yao et al. [20] trained a CRF considering selectional preference constraints of entity types with weak supervision.

Our work was inspired by [10] which performed distant supervision for relation extraction. It used Freebase as the knowledge base to label sentences in Wikipedia as training data and trained a logistic regression classifier to extract relations between entities. Distant supervision supplied a method to generate training data automatically, however it also bring the problem of noisy labeling. After their work, a variety of methods focused to solve this problem. Work in [16] predicted negative patterns using a generative model and remove labeled data containing negative patterns to reducing noise in labeled data. In [13][9][14], they proposed multi-instance learning methods with the assumption that at least one of the labeled sentences truly expressed their relation. However, this assumption does not fit for the entity pair with only one labeled sentence. We employ an alternative approach without the mentioned assumptions. Different from the previous work using binary features, we assign different weight to features according to their distinctiveness to target relations.

Algorithm 1. Unite KB-matched instances with KB-not-matched instances

Input:
The feature set of KB-mathced instances: $feat\_set(KB\_matched)$
KB-mathced instances: $Instances(KB\_matched)$
KB-not-mathced instances: $Instances(KB\_not\_matched)$

Output:
United instances: $Instances(U)$

1 $tmpset=feat\_set(KB\_Matched)$
2 $pre\_set\_size = tmpset.size()$
3 $cur\_set\_size = pre\_set\_size$
4 $Instances(U) = Instances(KB\_matched)$

5 **while** $pre\_set\_size \mathrel{!=} cur\_set\_size$ **do**
6   **for** $each\ instance\ in\ Instances(KB\_not\_matched)$ **do**
7   **for** $each\ feature\ in\ instance$ **do**
8   **if** $feature\ in\ tmpset$ **then**
9   add $instance$ to $Instances(U)$
10   add $features$ in $instance$ to $tmpset$
11   break
12   **end**
13   **end**
14   **end**
15    $pre\_set\_size=cur\_set\_size$
16    $cur\_set\_size = tmpset.size()$
17 **end**
18 remove features with frequency below 5 from $Instances(U)$
19 **return** $Instances(U)$;

---

3   Relation Topic Model

Aiming to discover the distribution of features to latent relations and due to , in this section, we first use features of KB-matched instances to combine with KB-not-matched instances, and then use a topic model for modeling features in united instances. At last we obtain the feature-relation distribution.

3.1 Generating United Instances

Given the training data set, previous work trained their models only using the sentences labeled by a knowledge base with the DS assumption (KB-matched instances2). However the KB-matched instances are only a small part of the training data, instances in them are biased to the relations used as labeling sources and not sufficient to discover the distribution of features to latent relations. As a result, we employ a method to unite KB-matched instances and KB-not-matched instances:

(a) First, after labeling with the DS assumption, we extract features for each entity pair from the matched sentences to obtain KB-matched instances[3]. The types of features are the same with the work [10].
(b) Second, we collect all entity pairs in training data except those generating KB-matched instances. The entity pairs are used as a source to match sentences from the training data with the DS assumption. And then we extract their features to obtain KB-not matched instances.
(c) Third, we united the two part of instances by features of KB-matched instances. We use the features of KB-matched instances to form a feature set, and then collect instances in KB-not-matched instances which contain at least one feature in the feature set. New features in the collected instances are added to the feature set. We iteratively do these steps until no new features can be found. The united instances consist of the KB-matched instances and the instances collected from KB-not matched instances(see Algorithm 1. for details).
(d) At last, we remove the features with frequencies below 5, for two reasons, one is that we consider features with low frequencies are distinctive so that we assign them high value directly, and the other is that their frequencies are too low to help discriminating the distinctiveness of frequent features by the topic model to be introduced next.

3.2 Modeling United Instances with Topic Model

Topic model (or LDA) [3] is a generative graphical model. It has achieved great success in finding the latent topic for documents. In this paper, we use it to model the generative process of each instance which has a set of features (Figure 2). We can consider a instance as an "document", features f in the "document" as "words" and latent relations r as latent "topics".

The generation process of topic model for each instance is as following:

1. Choose $N \sim$ Poisson(ξ).
2. Choose $\theta \sim$ Dirichlet(α).
3. Choose $\phi \sim$ Dirichlet(β).
4. For each of the N features f_n:
   (a) Choose a relation $r_n \sim$ Multinomial(θ)
   (b) Choose a feature f_n from $p(w_n | r_n, \phi_{r_n})$, a multinomial probability conditioned on the relation r_n.

---

[3] We mean the KB-matched instances as both the labeled positive instances and the negative instances (See Section 5.1).

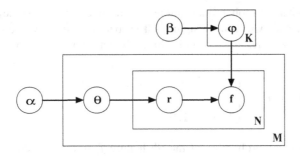

Fig. 2. Graphical model representation of topic model

Based on the generative graphical model depicted in Figure 2, the joint distribution of θ, $\mathbf{r}$ and $\mathbf{f}$ is given by:

$$p(\theta, \mathbf{r}, \mathbf{f}, \Phi | \alpha, \beta) = p(\Phi | \beta) \prod_{n=1}^{N} p(f_n | \phi_{r_n}) p(r_n | \theta) p(\theta | \alpha) \tag{1}$$

And the likelihood of an instance:

$$p(\mathbf{f} | \alpha, \beta) = \int \int p(\theta | \alpha) p(\Phi | \beta) \cdot \prod_{n=1}^{N} p(r_n | \theta, \Phi) d\Phi d\theta \tag{2}$$

Finally, taking the product of the likelihood of each instance, we get the probability of a relation corpus:

$$p(R | \alpha, \beta) = \sum_{m=1}^{M} p(\mathbf{f} | \alpha, \beta) \tag{3}$$

We estimate its parameters with Gibbs Sampling [8][11] and set number of relations as 50 and iteration times as 2000 in our experimetns. After estimation, we obtain a matrice $\Phi_{K \times N}$ representing the feature-relation distribution. The probability $p(f_i | r_k)$ of a feature f_i conditioned on a target relation r_k in $\Phi_{K \times N}$ is computed as follows:

$$p(f_i | r_k) = \phi_{k,i} = \frac{n_k^{(i)} + \beta_i}{\sum_{v=1}^{V} n_k^{(v)} + \beta_v} \tag{4}$$

Where $n_k^{(i)}$ is the number of times that the ith feature is assigned to the kth relation. V is the size of features.

We will use the distribution to compute the distinctiveness of features in the next section.

4 Weighing Features by Their Distinctiveness

In this part, we use the obtained feature-relation distribution $\Phi_{K \times N}$ and the feature distribution in united instances to compute features' distinctiveness. Intuitively, if features has equivalent probabilities among several latent relations, they are less distinctive than the ones which have significant probabilities in only one latent relation. We call it *clarity*. We measure the clarity for each feature by the following equation:

$$Clarity_{f_i} = \begin{cases} log_2 \frac{K \cdot max_{k \in \{1...K\}} p(f_i|r_k)}{\sum_{k=1}^{K} p(f_i|r_k)} \cdot \frac{1}{log_2 K}, & K > 1 \\ 1, & K = 1, 0 \end{cases} \tag{5}$$

Where $p(f_i|r_k)$ is the probability of the ith feature f_i in the kth relation r_k from the relation-feature distribution $\Phi_{K \times N}$. If a feature is only observed once, its *clarity* is 1. If a feature can not be observed in features of the relation-feature distribution, its *clarity* is also 1. The reason is that the unobserved features are those with low frequencies, we consider they are less likely belonging to several relations.

Besides the clarity, intuitively, we think features with more information will tend to be less noisy. Our features are composed of lexical and syntactic pathes between two entities the same with [10]. More words in the pathes, more information the features will contain. For example, two feature "e2 *by* e1" and "e2 *directed by* e1" for the relation "*DirectorOf(Ang Lee, Life Of Pi)*", the latter one is more informative than the former one and it can better predict the target relation. And more, if a feature has a low frequency in united instances, it tends to be more specific to the relation containing this feature and be more predictable to this relation. As a result, less frequent features are more informative than more frequent ones. We measure features' *informativeness* with the following equation considering both the length and frequency mentioned above:

$$Informativeness_{f_i} = (\frac{len(f_i)}{max_{j \in \{1...n\}} len(f_j)})^\alpha \cdot (\frac{1}{freq(f_i)})^\alpha \tag{6}$$

In it, $len(f_i)$ denotes the number of words in feature f_i. $max_{j \in \{1...n\}} len(f_j)$ means the max number of words in features, $freq(f_i)$ is the frequency of the feature f_i in united instances. We use α $(0 < \alpha < 1)$ to avoid values of features with high frequency or short length being too small. In the experiments, we set α as 0.25.

We compute the *distinctiveness* of a feature by combining *clarity* and *informativeness*. Based on the theory of Discriminative Category Mathcing (DCM) [6][1], we have the following equation, where $\sqrt{2}$ is a normalization factor:

$$Distinctiveness_{f_i} = \frac{Clarity_{f_i}^2 \cdot Informativeness_{f_i}^2}{\sqrt{Clarity_{f_i}^2 + Informativeness_{f_i}^2}} \cdot \sqrt{2} \tag{7}$$

We assign the *distinctiveness* to each feature in KB-matched instances as its feature value, and then train a multi-class logistic classifier with Gaussian regularization as the extractor. Our extractor takes an entity pair and its feature vector as in put, and

Table 1. Nine relation types and their number of entity pairs in training and testing data labeled with the DS assumption

Relation Type	♮ in training data	♮ in testing data
location.country.administrative_divisions	1892	1441
location.location.contains	77120	50795
location.location.events	490	301
people.deceased_person.place_of_death	3591	1994
people.person.nationality	9717	5592
people.person.place_of_birth	7670	3785
film.film.directed_by	1501	856
film.film.written_by	1007	582
film.film.country	1404	873

return a relation name and its corresponding confidence score based on the probability it belongs to that relation. At last, we rank the extracting result based on their confidence to generate n most likely new relation instances and evaluate our method comparing to previous methods.

5 Experiments

5.1 Data

We conduct our experiments on articles of Wikepedia with Freebase as the knowledge base. We randomly sample 900,000 Wikipedia articles from Freebase Wikipedia Extraction (WEX)[4] data dump of 2012. In them, 600,000 articles are used as training data, and 300,000 are used as testing.

For preprocessing, we segment each article to sentences by XML tags in the WEX dump. To find entities in sentences, we first do NER tagging with Stanford NER [5]. We tag tokens into 5 categories: PERSON, ORGANIZATION, LOCATION, MISC and NONE where MISC means name entities not belonging to the first three categories. Adjacent name entities with the same NER tag are combined to one name entity. Then for entity pairs in sentences, we extract their features (see Section 3). The feature types are the same with [10] which mainly consist of lexical Part-Of-Speech (POS), name entity and syntactic features (paths between two entities in the dependency parsing tree). We use the Stanford POS tagger [17] to assign the Pos tags and Stanford parser[5] to parse the sentences. .

To distant supervision for relation extraction, we evaulate 9 of the most frequent relations in Freebase from three categories: people, location and film (see Table 1). To train our extractor, we need negative instances. As a result, we randomly sample 10% of the entity pairs that appear in the same sentence labeled by the DS assumption but are not contained in Freebase, and then use them to label negative instances.

---

[4] http://wiki.freebase.com/wiki/WEX
[5] http://nlp.stanford.edu/software/stanford-dependencies.shtml

5.2 Baselines

We compare our method ($PROP$) against two methods:

- $Mintz$: this method is implemented based on [10]. We use their aggregate feature setting to train a multi-class logistic regression classifier.
- $MULTIR$: this is the "at-least-one" model (a form of multi-instance learning) reported in [9]. It learns using a Perceptron algorithm. We use its released code[6] for our experiment.

5.3 Evaluation

Following the work in [10][9], we evaluate our method in two ways: the held-out evaluation and the manual evaluation. The held-out evaluation only compared the newly discovered relation instances against Freebase relation data, it would suffer from false negatives. Thus, besides the held-out evaluation, we further conduct the manual evaluation.

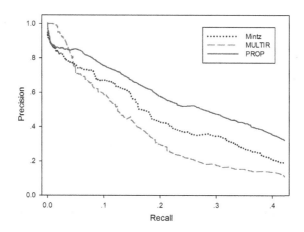

Fig. 3. Precision-recall curves in the held-out evaluation for three method: $Mintz$, $MULTIR$ and $PROP$

Held-Out Evaluation. In held-out evaluation, the extracted relation instances from testing data are automatically compared with those in Freebase. We rank the predicted relation instances by their confidences. Then we traverse this ranked list from high to low and measure precision and recall at each position.

Figure 2 shows the precision and recall curves for $Mintz$, $MULTIR$ and our proposed method $PROP$. At the head of the curves, $MULTIR$ outperforms the other two methods. However, it drops quickly below other two curves. $PROP$ is consistently outperforming $Mintz$ and it also achieve a better curve than $MULTIR$.

---

[6] http://raphaelhoffmann.com/mr/

Manual Evaluation. In manual evaluation, we remove the relation instances existing in Freebase and pick the top ranked 50 relation instances for each of the 9 relations. We manually label instances whether the relations indeed holds.

Table 2 shows the top 50 precisions of the 9 relations. Our approach $PROP$ outperforms $Mintz$ in 8 relations and outperforms $MULTIR$ in 4 relations. All the three methods fail in extracting the $film.film.country$ relation with no correct instance in its top 50 instances. Among the three methods, $PROP$ achieve the best average precision.

Table 2. Precision of manual evaluation of the top 50 ranked results for each relation

Relation Type	Precision		
	$Mintz$	$MULTIR$	$PROP$
location.country.administrative_divisions	0.82	0.64	**0.90**
location.location.contains	0.50	**0.98**	0.70
location.location.events	0.56	**0.64**	0.62
people.deceased_person.place_of_death	0.68	0.36	**0.72**
people.person.nationality	0.66	**0.92**	0.90
people.person.place_of_birth	0.68	0.90	**0.92**
film.film.directed_by	0.40	0.40	**0.58**
film.film.written_by	0.52	**0.74**	0.56
film.film.country	0	0	0
Average	0.54	0.62	**0.66**

Analysis. The experiment results show the advantage by exploring distinctive features and weighing features based on their distinctiveness. $Mintz$ used aggregate features which aggregates sentential binary faetures and $MULTIR$ used binary features. Their feature settings enforces some frequent noisy features in the labeled data generated with the distant supervision assumption like "$e2$ by $e1$" for the $DirectorOf$ relation. Our method overcomes this problem.

$MULTIR$ learns a model driven by sentence-level features and aggregated sentence-level extracting results as a form of multi-instance learning. It alleviates the noisy labeling problem to some extent and achieves better results in some relations. However, because of the problem caused by the binary feature setting mentioned above, it performs quit bad in several relations. Taking the relation $people.deceased\_person.place\_of\_death$ as an example. We inspect its extracting result, it emphasizes the feature "$e1$ of $e2$" like "$Barack$ $Obama$ of $Illinois$" which hurts its precision much.

The three methods failed in extracting the $film.film.country$ relation. The reason is that its automatically labeled data are in bad qualities. There are little specific information that can predicate this relation. The mistaken sentences are as follows: "$...to$ $unite$ $with$ $[Czechoslovakia]_{e2}, [Harvard$ $Ukrainian$ $Research$ $Institute]_{e1}$." and "$[Mohatta$ $Palace]_{e1} - ([Karachi]_{e2})$." etc.

6   Conclusion

In this paper, we propose a new approach to address the noisy labeling problem in DS for relation extraction. Our method does not use the at-least-one assumption which can fail when there is only one labeled sentence, and it is able to handle the problem of noisy features in non-noisy instances. We explore distinctive features and assign distinctive features more weight than the noisy ones. We employ unsupervised topic model to discover feature-relation distribution in both KB-matched instances and KB-not-matched instances (united instances). And the feature-relation distribution are used to compute features' distinctiveness for weighing features. At last, we use the weighed features to train a classifier to discover relations of new instances.

In the future work, we will try to explore the features in all the training data that related to the labeled part of training data but not appeared in them. We expect they can help to improve the extracting performance.

Acknowledgments. This work was supported by the National Natural Science Foundation of China (No. 61070106, No. 61272332 and No. 61202329), the National High Technology Development 863 Program of China (No. 2012AA011102), the National Basic Research Program of China (No. 2012CB316300) and the Opening Project of Beijing Key Laboratory of Internet Culture and Digital Dissemination Research (ICDD2 01201).

References

1. Akbik, A., Visengeriyeva, L., Herger, P., Hemsen, H., Löser, A.: Unsupervised discovery of relations and discriminative extraction patterns. In: Proceedings of the 24th International Conference on Computational Linguistics, pp. 17–32 (2012)
2. Bellare, K., McCallum, A.: Learning extractors from unlabeled text using relevant databases. In: Sixth International Workshop on Information Integration on the Web (2007)
3. Blei, D.M., Ng, A.Y., Jordan, M.I.: Latent dirichlet allocation. The Journal of Machine Learning Research 3, 993–1022 (2003)
4. Craven, M., Kumlien, J., et al.: Constructing biological knowledge bases by extracting information from text sources. In: Proceedings of the Seventh International Conference on Intelligent Systems for Molecular Biology, Heidelberg, Germany, pp. 77–86 (1999)
5. Finkel, J.R., Grenager, T., Manning, C.: Incorporating non-local information into information extraction systems by gibbs sampling. In: Proceedings of the 43rd Annual Meeting on Association for Computational Linguistics, pp. 363–370. Association for Computational Linguistics (2005)
6. Fung, G.P.C., Yu, J.X., Lu, H.: Discriminative category matching: Efficient text classification for huge document collections. In: Proceedings of the 2002 IEEE International Conference on Data Mining, ICDM 2003, pp. 187–194. IEEE (2002)
7. GuoDong, Z., Jian, S., Jie, Z., Min, Z.: Exploring various knowledge in relation extraction. In: Proceedings of the 43rd Annual Meeting on Association for Computational Linguistics, pp. 427–434. Association for Computational Linguistics (2005)
8. Heinrich, G.: Parameter estimation for text analysis (2005),
http://www.arbylon.net/publications/text-est.pdf

9. Hoffmann, R., Zhang, C., Ling, X., Zettlemoyer, L., Weld, D.S.: Knowledge-based weak supervision for information extraction of overlapping relations. In: Proceedings of the 49th Annual Meeting of the Association for Computational Linguistics: Human Language Technologies, vol. 1, pp. 541–550 (2011)

10. Mintz, M., Bills, S., Snow, R., Jurafsky, D.: Distant supervision for relation extraction without labeled data. In: Proceedings of the Joint Conference of the 47th Annual Meeting of the ACL and the 4th International Joint Conference on Natural Language Processing of the AFNLP, vol. 2, pp. 1003–1011. Association for Computational Linguistics (2009)

11. Phan, X.-H., Nguyen, L.-M., Horiguchi, S.: Learning to classify short and sparse text & web with hidden topics from large-scale data collections. In: Proceedings of the 17th International Conference on World Wide Web, pp. 91–100. ACM (2008)

12. Ravichandran, D., Hovy, E.: Learning surface text patterns for a question answering system. In: Proceedings of the 40th Annual Meeting on Association for Computational Linguistics, pp. 41–47. Association for Computational Linguistics (2002)

13. Riedel, S., Yao, L., McCallum, A.: Modeling relations and their mentions without labeled text. In: Balcázar, J.L., Bonchi, F., Gionis, A., Sebag, M. (eds.) ECML PKDD 2010, Part III. LNCS, vol. 6323, pp. 148–163. Springer, Heidelberg (2010)

14. Surdeanu, M., Tibshirani, J., Nallapati, R., Manning, C.D.: Multi-instance multi-label learning for relation extraction. In: Proceedings of the 2012 Joint Conference on Empirical Methods in Natural Language Processing and Computational Natural Language Learning, pp. 455–465. Association for Computational Linguistics (2012)

15. Szpektor, I., Tanev, H., Dagan, I., Coppola, B., et al.: Scaling Web-based aquisition of entailment relations. PhD thesis, Tel Aviv University (2005)

16. Takamatsu, S., Sato, I., Nakagawa, H.: Reducing wrong labels in distant supervision for relation extraction. In: Proceedings of the 50th Annual Meeting of the Association for Computational Linguistics: Long Papers, vol. 1, pp. 721–729. Association for Computational Linguistics (2012)

17. Toutanova, K., Klein, D., Manning, C.D., Singer, Y.: Feature-rich part-of-speech tagging with a cyclic dependency network. In: Proceedings of the 2003 Conference of the North American Chapter of the Association for Computational Linguistics on Human Language Technology, vol. 1, pp. 173–180. Association for Computational Linguistics (2003)

18. Wu, F., Weld, D.S.: Autonomously semantifying wikipedia. In: Proceedings of the sixteenth ACM Conference on Conference on Information and Knowledge Management, pp. 41–50. ACM (2007)

19. Wu, F., Weld, D.S.: Open information extraction using wikipedia. In: Proceedings of the 48th Annual Meeting of the Association for Computational Linguistics, pp. 118–127. Association for Computational Linguistics (2010)

20. Yao, L., Riedel, S., McCallum, A.: Collective cross-document relation extraction without labelled data. In: Proceedings of the 2010 Conference on Empirical Methods in Natural Language Processing, pp. 1013–1023. Association for Computational Linguistics (2010)

21. Yates, A., Cafarella, M., Banko, M., Etzioni, O., Broadhead, M., Soderland, S.: Textrunner: open information extraction on the web. In: Proceedings of Human Language Technologies: The Annual Conference of the North American Chapter of the Association for Computational Linguistics: Demonstrations, pp. 25–26. Association for Computational Linguistics (2007)

22. Zhou, G., Zhang, M., Ji, D.H., Zhu, Q.: Tree kernel-based relation extraction with context-sensitive structured parse tree information (2007)

User-Centered Social Information Retrieval Model Exploiting Annotations and Social Relationships

Chahrazed Bouhini, Mathias Géry, and Chritine Largeron

Université de Lyon, F-42023, Saint-Étienne, France
CNRS, UMR 5516, Laboratoire Hubert Curien, 42023, Saint-Étienne, France
Université de Saint-Étienne, Jean-Monnet, F-42023, Saint-Étienne, France
{Chahrazed.Bouhini,Mathias.Gery,Christine.Largeron}@univ-st-etienne.fr

Abstract. Social Information Retrieval (SIR) has extended the classical information retrieval models and systems to take into account social information of the user within his social networks. We assume that a SIR system can exploit the informational social context (ISC) of the user in order to refine his retrieval, since different users may express different information needs as the same query. Hence, we present a SIR model that takes into account the user's social data, such as his annotations and his social relationships through social networks. We propose to integrate the user's ISC into the documents indexing process, allowing the SIR system to personalize the list of documents returned to the user. Our approach has shown interesting results on a test collection built from the social collaborative bookmarking network *Delicious*.

Keywords: Social information retrieval model, social test collection, annotations, relationships, indexing.

1 Introduction

The participants of social networks are not only allowed to share Web documents but also to annotate, to evaluate and to comment them [19]. Social tagging data, known as *folksonomies*, create social association between the users and the Web pages through the social annotations [20]. Social annotation is a set of tags (keywords) freely assigned by a user to describe the content of a Web document. To this end, annotations are widely considered as an effective means of enriching content with meta-data. *Folksonomies* can be considered as a fairly accurate source to discover user interests [18]. In this context, Social Information Retrieval (SIR), defined as the incorporation of information related to social networks and relationships into the information retrieval process [8], attempts to extend classical IR by taking into consideration the user's ISC within his social network. Indeed, social networks users may be seeking different informations expressed by the same queries. Thus, SIR systems can exploit the user's ISC to refine the user's retrieval. Hence, one aim of SIR consists in adapting usual IR models and systems in order to deal with this user's social data (user's annotations and

R.E. Banchs et al. (Eds.): AIRS 2013, LNCS 8281, pp. 356–367, 2013.
© Springer-Verlag Berlin Heidelberg 2013

social relationships). We propose a SIR model, called $BM25F_S$, which integrates user's ISC during the indexing step. More specifically, the user's ISC is generated out of his annotations. Then, we benefit from social relationships of the user, that we call neighborhood, to enrich the user's ISC with the annotations of his neighborhood. Once the user's ISC generated, we investigate the way to integrate this social information into the SIR model.

This paper is organized as follows: we discuss some related works in Section 2 and we explain the motivations of our work in Section 3. In Section 4, we present our methodological framework by describing the approach that we used to generate the user's ISC and we detail the main contribution of our work which consists in integrating the user's ISC in the documents indexing step in order to build a personalized documents index. Further, we present some results of experiments done on a test collection generated from the collaborative bookmarking network **Delicious**[1] in Section 5, and we conclude with some perspectives.

2   Related Work

Social networks provide valuable additional information which have been used to improve the results of recommendation systems [6], collaborative filtering [5], or information retrieval [7]. Much related works use social informations for query expansion and disambiguation [15],[9],[4].

In this paper, we focus on the use of these social annotations and relationships in the SIR models for IR personalization. For example, with the aim to improve Web search, Bao et al. [2] propose two methods: SocialSimRank and SocialPageRank. The former allows to find the latent semantic association between queries and annotations, while the latter takes into account the popularity of web pages [2].

The first step of the IR personalization aims at modeling the user's profile and social context [1],[3],[18],[20],[17]. Indeed, several studies have proven that user's ISC can be effectively harvested from the social bookmarking systems [1],[17]. These works assume that the documents and the tags posted by users depend highly on their interests and provide rich information for building user profiles [3],[18],[20].

The second step aims at integrating the user's ISC into the SIR model by combining different weighting function. Authors in [3],[18],[20],[11], propose to personalize the user's search by ranking the resource based on, a matching between the user's interests and the documents' topics [20], or between the user's profile and the resource's profile [18],[3]. Rather than considering the resource's content, authors in [3],[18],[11] propose to build a *resource's profile* through the resource's annotations and compute a matching function between this resource's profile and the query terms, on the one hand and between the resource's profile and the user's profile, on the other hand.

Unlike in [3],[18] and [11], Xu et al., consider to match the document's content instead of matching only the document's profile over the query terms and the

---

[1] https://delicious.com/

user's profile. The success they achieved is a strong support for our work [20]. Although, Cai et al., [3] discuss the limits of the weighting functions used in the previous cited works [18][20],[11] as for a case study based only on a set of tags for resource recommendation, they propose a normalized term frequency to indicate the preference degree of a tag for the user and the representative degree of a tag for the resource [3]. We note that the user's profile generated in these works is based only on the user's annotations without exploring his relationships.

In our approach, we assume that the document content is useful for IR. Thus, using only the document profile is not enough. We assume also that it is important to exploit the social annotations of the user's relationships (neighborhood) in addition to his own social annotations. As Stoyanovich et al. [16] show, the predicted relevance of documents may be enhanced by exploiting the user neighbors' tagging actions [16]. Finally, we think that combining the document content with this ISC requires IR techniques that are able to handle large textual documents. This led us to introduce an original approach presented in the following sections.

3   Personalized IR Exploiting Folksonomies

3.1   Ambiguous Queries

Almost all test collections, in IR research, assume that queries have a single interpretation representing the information need expressed by one user, which is implicitly defined in his relevance judgments [14]. However, in practice this is not necessary the case. For this reason, in this paper we propose a framework for personalized information retrieval based on folksonomies. Such a system should be able to handle ambiguous queries, i.e. queries having potentially several interpretations representing different information needs.

For example, suppose that two users u_1 and u_2 have the same query $q =$ "smartphone android" (cf. Table 1). We consider two documents d_1 and d_2; each document contains one query term, but *smartphone* is more important than *android* in the first document since d_1 contains only *smartphone*, and *android* is more important than *smartphone* in the second one since d_2 contains only *android*. Assuming that the two query terms have the same importance, a classical IR system should estimate that d_1 is equally relevant as d_2 for the query "*smartphone android*". However, depending on the user and his personal interests, the information need behind this query may focus either on the term *smartphone* or on the term *android*. The user u_1 is mainly interested in smartphone devices, then his information need is probably centered around smartphones with an opening on Android, and thus the query term *smartphone* should be more important than the query term *android*. On the other hand, the user u_2 is mainly interested by the Android operating system, consequently his information need is probably centered around Android, and thus the query term *android* should be more important than the query term *smartphone*.

Table 1. Example: query, documents and user's profiles

	t_1 = smartphone	t_2 = android	t_3 = features
Query q	1	1	0
Document d_1	1	0	0
Document d_2	0	1	1
User u_1	2	1	0
User u_2	1	2	0

3.2   Personalized Information Retrieval

A personalized information retrieval system should be able to identify the user's personal interests, in order to better interpret the information need behind his queries, and returns lists of relevant documents to the users depending on their personal interests. In our example, a personalized IR system should consider d_1 as more relevant than d_2 for u_1, and the opposite for u_2.

3.3   Folksonomies and User's Informational Social Context (ISC)

We assume that folksonomies may be exploited in order to build the informational social context of the user that could represent the user's interests and that could help the system to handle ambiguous queries return personalized results to the user.

As pointed out in related literature, the user's profile can be inferred from his social annotations ([1],[17]). The neighborhood's profile is defined by the annotations of his neighborhood. We assume that the user's profile can be enriched by the annotations of his neighbors to build the user's ISC.

3.4   Integrating User's ISC within the IR Model

Since we exploit the social information about the user and his neighborhood to generate his ISC, we assume that the important terms representing the user's interests should appear in this ISC. Thus, reweighting such important terms when they are found within the document, should improve the document relevance score and allows to return the personalized relevant documents. We think that the integration of the user's ISC within the IR model is an important part of the personalization. One aim of this work is to handle textual documents containing thousands of terms, unlike most related work which only handle small sets of tags describing the document. Combining the user's ISC with this kind of textual data raises different issues than combining two sets of tags, like for instance in the work of Cai et al. [3]. Our work attempts to deal with this issue.

4   Social Information Retrieval Model

We present a SIR model, called $BM25F_S$, that takes into account the user's ISC, to better describe the documents with respect to the user viewpoint.

4.1   Notations

We represent the "social tagging data", also known as *Folksonomies* [18], by a tuple $< U,\ Rel,\ T,\ D,\ A >$, where:

- $U = \{u_1, u_2, ..., u_x, ..., u_{|U|}\}$ is a set of social network users.
- $Rel \subseteq U \times U$ is a set of relationships between pairs of users, such that $(u_x, u_y) \in Rel$ iff there is a social relationship between a user u_x and another user u_y. The users related to u_x are typically those declared explicitly by u_x as his *neighbors* where $neighborhood(u_x) = \{u_y\ /\ (u_x, u_y) \in Rel\}$.
- $T = \{t_1, t_2, ..., t_j, ..., t_{|T|}\}$ is a set of index terms.
- $D = \{d_1, d_2, ..., d_i, ..., d_{|D|}\}$ is a set of documents on the Web (images, videos, Webpages, etc.). A document d_i is represented by a set of terms $(t_j \in T)$ and a term t_j may appear one or several times in a document d_i. We denote by tf_{ij} the term frequency of t_j in d_i. A weight w_{ij} of a term t_j for a document d_i is computed using this term frequency tf_{ij} of t_j in d_i.
- $A = \{a_1, a_2, ..., a_z, ..., a_{|A|}\}$ is a set of social annotations, i.e., $a_z = < d_i, u_x, T_z >$ is the annotation of the user u_x for the document d_i using a subset of terms $T_z \subset T$.

We define also:

- $Q = \{q_1, q_2, ..., q_l, ..., q_{|Q|}\}$, a set of users' queries, where each query q_l is represented by a set of terms.
- $Qrels = \{qrels_1, qrels_2, ..., qrels_l, ..., qrels_{|Q|}\}$, a set of global relevance judgments, where $qrels_l \subset D$ denotes the set of relevant documents for q_l.
- $Q_{UC} = \{(q_l, u_x) \subset Q \times U\}$, a set of couples (q_l, u_x) where the query q_l is issued by the user u_x to express his information needs.
- $Qrels_{UC} = \{qrels_{1,1}, qrels_{1,2}, ..., qrels_{l,x}, ..., qrels_{|Q|,x}\}$, a set of user-centered relevance judgments, where $qrels_{l,x} \subset D$ denotes the set of relevant documents for the query q_l and the user u_x.

4.2   Information Retrieval Model: BM25

We choose as baseline the IR weighting function BM25 [13], which is one of the most used indexation models in the IR research benchmarks such as INEX[2], TREC[3], etc. In this IR weighting function, the weight of a term t_j within a document d_i is computed according to the formula (1):

$$w_{ij} = \frac{(k_1 + 1) \times tf_{ij}}{k_1 \times ((b-1) + b \times (\frac{dl_i}{avgdl})) + tf_{ij}} \times log(\frac{N - df_j + 0.5}{df_j + 0.5}) \qquad (1)$$

where:

- dl_i is the document length of d_i and $avgdl$ is the average documents length.
- tf_{ij} is the term frequency of t_j within the document d_i.

---

[2] INEX (INitiative for the Evaluation of XML-Retrieval):
https://inex.mmci.uni-saarland.de/
[3] TREC (TExt Retrieval Conference): http://trec.nist.gov/

- k_1 is the saturation parameter of tf_{ij}.
- b is the length normalization factor.
- N is the total number of documents in the corpus.
- df_j is the number of documents containing the term t_j.

In the $BM25$ model, the global score of a document d_i for a query q_l is computed as follows:

$$BM25(q_l, d_i) = \sum_{t_j \in q_l \cap d_i} w_{ij} \tag{2}$$

4.3   User Informational Social Context (ISC)

The user's informational social context may contain different information types (annotations, comments, citations, social relationships, etc.). In this work we generate the user's ISC from the terms in his annotations and those of his neighbors. We present two variants of the user's ISC: $ISC_u(u_x)$, called "the user's profile" and $ISC_n(u_x)$, called "the neighborhood's profile":

The user's profile $ISC_u(u_x)$ is the set of terms which occur within the social annotations of the user.

$$ISC_u(u_x) = \{t_j \in T_z \ / \ a_z = \ <d_i, u_x, T_z> \ \in A_{u_x}\} \tag{3}$$

where: A_{u_x} is the set of social annotations of u_x.

The user's profile may contain several occurrences of the same term. Thus we can compute the term frequency tfu_{xj} for a given term t_j that has been used by u_x to annotate the documents. In the example provided in Table 1, the user profiles with the tfu_{xj} associated are represented as follows: $ISC_u(u_1) = ISC_u(u_2) = \{"smartphone", "android"\}$ and the tfu_{xj} associated are (2,1) for u_1 and (1,2) for u_2.

The neighborhood's profile $ISC_n(u_x)$ is the set of terms which occur within the user neighborhood's annotations.

$$ISC_n(u_x) = \cup_{u_y \in U \ / \ (u_x, u_y) \in Rel} ISC_u(u_y) \tag{4}$$

Like previously, the neighborhood's profile may also contain several occurrences of the same term t_j, and we can compute the term frequency tfn_{xj} for a given term t_j that has been used by the neighborhood of u_x to annotate the documents. In our example, the $neighborhood(u_1)$ is composed of u_3 and the $neighborhood(u_2)$ is composed of u_4, with the user's profiles for u_3 and u_4. Then, we can compute the neighborhood's profiles for u_1 and u_2, given in Table 1.

4.4   Personalized Index

Now, our aim is to take into account the user's ISC during the indexing step, in order to personalize the documents index.

Table 2. Example: term frequencies of the user's ISC

	$t_1 =$ smartphone	$t_2 =$ android	$t_3 =$ features
Query q	1	1	0
tf_{1j}	1	0	0
tf_{2j}	0	1	1
tfu_{1j}	2	1	0
tfu_{2j}	1	2	0
tfu_{3j}	2	3	0
tfu_{4j}	3	3	1
tfn_{1j}	2	3	0
tfn_{1j}	3	3	1

We combine the content of the document d_i, represented by a vector of term frequencies tf_{ij}, with the user's ISC, composed of two vectors of term frequencies tfu_{xj} and tfn_{xj}. Each document is indexed by a vector of weights ws_{xij}, with ws_{xij} the weight of the term t_j in the document d_i for the user u_x. The term weight ws_{xij} is a personalized version of w_{ij} for the user u_x.

We propose to combine the document's content and the user's ISC as three different fields of information (i.e. 3 vectors). As it has been shown more coherent than combining the score of each vector computed independently, in [12]. Thus, we built a personalized documents index based on these three fields:

- the *content of d_i*, represented by a vector of *field term frequencies* ftf_{xij} is equal to the classical tf_{ij}:

$$ftf_{xij} = tf_{ij} \tag{5}$$

- the *user's profile $ISC_u(u_x)$*, represented by a vector of *field term frequencies* $ftfu_{xij}$. Only the weights of the terms appearing both in the content of the document and in the user's profile should be considered:

$$ftfu_{xij} = \begin{cases} tfu_{xj} & \text{if } tf_{ij} > 0 \\ 0 & \text{else.} \end{cases} \tag{6}$$

where tfu_{xj} is the term frequency of t_j used by u_x in his annotations.
- the *neighborhood's profile $ISC_n(u_x)$*, represented by a vector of *field term frequencies* $ftfn_{xij}$. Similarly, only the weights of the terms appearing both in the content of the document and in the neighborhood's profile should be considered:

$$ftfn_{xij} = \begin{cases} tfn_{xj} & \text{if } tf_{ij} > 0 \\ 0 & \text{otherwise.} \end{cases} \tag{7}$$

where tfn_{xj} is the term frequency of t_j used by the neighborhood of u_x to annotate documents.

The BM25F weighting function has been proposed by [12] in order to index structured documents composed of several *fields* (e.g. *title, abstract, body,* etc.). $BM25F$ seems to be suitable for indexing our three fields-documents. This function was extended by [21] in order to optimize the length normalization field-by-field. We chose to use this latter BM25F variant. Then, like Zaragoza et al., the first step of the BM25F function normalizes the term frequencies of each field by the field length [21]:

$$\overline{ftf}_{xij} = \frac{ftf_{xij}}{1 + b_d \times (\frac{dl}{avgdl} - 1)} \tag{8}$$

$$\overline{ftfu}_{xij} = \frac{ftfu_{xij}}{1 + b_{ux} \times (\frac{ul}{avgul} - 1)} \tag{9}$$

$$\overline{ftfn}_{xij} = \frac{ftfn_{xij}}{1 + b_{nx} \times (\frac{nl}{avgnl} - 1)} \tag{10}$$

where:

- b_d, b_{ux} and b_{nx} are some field-dependent parameters, similar to b (in BM25), for the d_i content field, the user's profile field and the neighborhood's profile field, respectively,
- ul and nl are the length of the user's profile field and the length of the neighborhood's profile field, respectively,
- $avgul$ and $avgnl$ are the average length of the user's profile field over the collection and the average length of the neighborhood's profile field over the collection.

Then, following Zaragoza's BM25F [21], we compute the term weight ws_{xij} for t_j within the document d_i for the user u_x using the weighting function in formula 11:

$$ws_{xij} = \frac{ctf_{xij}}{k_1 + ctf_{xij}} \times log\left(\frac{N - df_j + 0.5}{df_j + 0.5}\right) \tag{11}$$

where:

- ctf_{xij} is the combined term frequency of the three fields:

$$ctf_{xij} = w_d.\overline{ftf}_{xij} + w_{ux}.\overline{ftfu}_{xij} + w_{nx}.\overline{ftfn}_{xij} \tag{12}$$

- w_d, w_{ux} and w_{nx} are three field-dependent parameters used to tune the importance of the user's profile field and the neighborhood's profile field in relation to the importance of the document content field.

Finally, the personalized relevance score of a document d_i for the query q_l and the user u_x is given by equation 13:

$$BM25F_S(q_l, d_i, u_x) = \sum_{t_j \in q_l \cap d_i} ws_{xij} \tag{13}$$

Table 3 shows the field term frequencies for the example given in Table 1 and the relevance scores obtained using $BM25$ and $BM25F_S$. These scores have

Table 3. Impact of the user's ISC on the indexing process

U	D	ftf	T			$BM25(q_l, d_i)$	$BM25F_S(q_l, d_i, u_x)$
			t_1	t_2	t_3		
u_1	d_1	$ftfu_{11j}$	2	0	0	1.681	1.983
		$ftfn_{11j}$	3	0	0		
		ftf_{11j}	1	0	0		
	d_2	$ftfu_{12j}$	0	1	0	1.681	1.898
		$ftfn_{12j}$	0	3	0		
		ftf_{12j}	0	1	1		
u_2	d_1	$ftfu_{21j}$	1	0	0	1.681	1.898
		$ftfn_{21j}$	2	0	0		
		ftf_{21j}	1	0	0		
	d_2	$ftfu_{22j}$	0	2	0	1.681	1.983
		$ftfn_{22j}$	0	3	1		
		ftf_{22j}	0	1	1		

been computed using the formula 11, with usual BM25 parameters values: $b_d = b_{ux} = b_{nx} = 0.75$ and $k = 1.2$.

The document relevance score increases when the frequencies of the user's profile terms are combined to those of the document terms. Furthermore, for two different user's ISCs with the same query terms, the ranking of the documents could vary according to the ISC of each user. For instance, when the user's ISC is considered, the document d_1 is more relevant than d_2 for u_1 (1.983 vs 1.898), whereas d_2 is more relevant than d_1 for u_2.

5   Experiments

Experiments have been carried out to evaluate the SIR model that considers the user's ISC compared to the classical IR model. Using the social test collection (Del_{SIR}) described bellow, and the evaluation measures MAP (Mean Average Precision) and $P[0.1]$ (the precision at 10% of recall) [10], we evaluated the rankings produced:

- by a classical IR model with two kinds of data: the first one is composed of 79 global queries (Q) and their global relevance judgments ($Qrels$), the second one is composed of 244 user-centered queries (Q_{UC}) and corresponding user-centered relevance judgments ($Qrels_{UC}$).
- by our SIR model ($BM25F_S$) with only user-centered data (Q_{UC} and $Qrels_{UC}$), since the SIR model is not suited to handle global queries.

5.1   Social Test Collection

To the best of our knowledge, no SIR test collection exists providing a list of relevant documents for each user. So, we built a test collection Del_{SIR} based on Web documents and user annotations extracted from the social collaborative book-marking network *Delicious*. We collected 30,224 documents annotated by 370 users with 21,284 terms. To complete the social dataset with the user-centered data composed of pairs (*query, user*) and user-centered relevance judgments, we created automatically 79 queries. Each query is composed by 2 terms occuring frequently together [4] in the annotations collected from Delicious. Then we generated 4,685 global relevance judgments and user-centered relevance judgments. A document is globally relevant if it has been annotated by any user with the 2 query terms in the same annotation. A document is user-relevant if it has been annotated by the user with the 2 query terms in the same annotation.

We kept only the pairs (*query, user*) with at least 10 relevant documents ($|qrels_{l,x}| \geq 10$) so that we obtained 244 pairs (q_l, u_x) in the set Q_{UC}. This led to a reduction of the number of users (70 users left).

5.2   Evaluation Results with the Classical IR Model $BM25$

For each given query, the classical IR model returns the same relevant documents whoever the user is. The results quality obtained with the $BM25$ decreases for both the MAP (0.0308 vs 0.1012) and the $P[0.1]$ (0.0521 vs 0.1775) when the user-centered relevance judgments $Qrels_{UC}$ are considered. This confirms our expectations that the classical IR system has to adapt its models in order to deal with the user-centered data (Q_{UC} and $Qrels_{UC}$).

5.3   Evaluation Results with the SIR Model $BM25F_S$

In our experiments we have tuned in the same way as in [21], using the grid-based 2D optimization, the b and k parameters for BM25 and for each field of $BM25F_S$. Table 4 shows results obtained with two fields-weight settings:

- $BM25F_S$, *settings*$_1$: $w_d = 1$, $w_{ux} \in]0..1]$ and $w_{nx} = 0$
- $BM25F_S$, *settings*$_2$: $w_d = 1$, $w_{ux} \in]0..1]$ and $w_{nx} \in]0..1]$

We selected the users having at least 5 queries and obtaining with classical IR a *MAP* result between 0.5% and 50%. We obtain a set of 10 users, corresponding to a set of 60 pairs (query, user) The results of our SIR model $BM25F_S$ compared to the baseline $BM25$ are shown in Table 4.

Considering the precision at 10% of recall (P[0.1]), the SIR model provides less good results than the baseline. While, using the Mean Average Precision measures (MAP), the SIR model $BM25F_S$ results (MAP = 0.0297 and MAP = 0.0293) are statistically better than the baseline (MAP = 0.0257). The significance has been checked by using statistical tests based on Wilcoxon matched-pairs signed-rank test at the 0.05 level, i.e. the improvement is significant when the p-value is less than 0.05. These results, obtained on a set of 60 pairs (q_l, u_x) for the 10 users in Table 4, confirm that a SIR model which takes into account the user's ISC, with or without neighborhood, enhance the relevance score results using the MAP measure which is considered as a global evaluation metric.

---

[4] In fact, the 79 couples of terms having the highest Jaccard Index.

Table 4. $BM25F_S$ evaluation results

	BM25		$BM25F_S$			
			$settings_1$		$settings_2$	
	MAP	$P[0.1]$	MAP	$P[0.1]$	MAP	$P[0.1]$
u_1	0.0614	0.1310	0.0816	0.1426	**0.0819**	**0.1503**
u_2	0.0404	**0.2614**	0.0402	0.1265	**0.0416**	0.1203
u_3	0.0358	0.1076	**0.0486**	0.1438	0.0483	**0.1438**
u_4	0.0262	0.0922	**0.0278**	**0.0956**	0.0275	0.0948
u_5	**0.0287**	0.0569	0.0253	0.0484	0.0284	**0.0688**
u_6	0.0174	0.0529	**0.0199**	**0.0568**	0.0197	0.0550
u_7	**0.0183**	0.0207	0.0173	0.0298	0.0148	**0.0391**
u_8	0.0138	0.0296	0.0148	0.0316	**0.0156**	**0.0319**
u_9	0.0074	**0.0221**	**0.0093**	0.0215	0.0091	0.0188
u_{10}	0.0077	0.0095	0.0085	**0.0115**	**0.0103**	0.0101
Average	0.0257	**0.0784**	0.0293	0.0708	**0.0297**	0.0733

6   Conclusion

We presented an approach that integrates the user's ISC into the documents. The user's ISC has been built using the user's annotations and those of his relationships. The aim is to personalize the user's search by considering his preferences and interests. Our approach allows to highlight and reweight the important terms of the user's ISC when they are found in the document content. As we consider textual documents containing thousands of terms, we proposed to combine the user's ISC with textual content, in the weighting function. The SIR model, that considers the user's ISC, allows to better find the relevant documents for the user query than the IR model which does not consider the user's ISC. As future works, we plan to extend the user's ISC with further social data including the neighborhood of neighborhood's (friends of friends) annotations and build a bigger social test collection from *Delicious'* bookmarks. We would also like to study different parameters with further experiments to evaluate our SIR model.

References

1. Au-Yeung, C.M., Gibbins, N., Shadbolt, N.: A study of user profile generation from folksonomies. In: Workshop on Social Web and Knowledge Management. SWKM (2008)
2. Bao, S., Xue, G., Wu, X., Yu, Y., Fei, B., Su, Z.: Optimizing web search using social annotations. In: World Wide Web, WWW 2007, pp. 501–510 (2007)
3. Cai, Y., Li, Q.: Personalized search by tag-based user profile and resource profile in collaborative tagging systems. In: 19th Conference on Information and Knowledge Management, CIKM 2010, pp. 969–978 (2010)
4. Chirita, P.A., Firan, C.S., Nejdl, W.: Personalized query expansion for the web. In: 30th Conference on Research and Development in Information Retrieval, SIGIR 2007, pp. 7–14 (2007)

5. Ferrara, F., Tasso, C.: Improving collaborative filtering in social tagging systems. In: 14th Conference on Advances in Artificial Intelligence: Spanish Association for Artificial Intelligence, CAEPIA 2011, pp. 463–472 (2011)
6. Guy, I., Zwerdling, N., Ronen, I., Carmel, D., Uziel, E.: Social media recommendation based on people and tags. In: 33rd Conference on Research and Development in Information Retrieval, SIGIR 2010, pp. 194–201 (2010)
7. Hotho, A., Jäschke, R., Schmitz, C., Stumme, G.: Information retrieval in folksonomies: Search and ranking. In: Sure, Y., Domingue, J. (eds.) ESWC 2006. LNCS, vol. 4011, pp. 411–426. Springer, Heidelberg (2006)
8. Kirsch, S.M.: Social Information Retrieval. Ph.D. thesis, Rheinische Friedrich-Wilhelms-Universitat Bonn (2005)
9. Lin, Y., Lin, H., Jin, S., Ye, Z.: Social annotation in query expansion. In: 34th Conference on Research and Development in Information Retrieval, SIGIR 2011, pp. 405–414 (2011)
10. Manning, C.D., Raghavan, P., Schutze, H.: Introduction to Information Retrieval, 1st edn. Cambridge University Press (2008)
11. Noll, M.G., Meinel, C.: Web search personalization via social bookmarking and tagging. In: Aberer, K., et al. (eds.) ASWC 2007 and ISWC 2007. LNCS, vol. 4825, pp. 367–380. Springer, Heidelberg (2007)
12. Robertson, S., Zaragoza, H., Taylor, M.: Simple BM25 extension to multiple weighted fields. In: 13th Conference on Information and Knowledge Management, CIKM 2004, pp. 42–49 (2004)
13. Robertson, S.E., Walker, S.: Some simple effective approximations to the 2-poisson model for probabilistic weighted retrieval. In: 17th Conference on Research and Development in Information Retrieval, SIGIR 1994, pp. 232–241 (1994)
14. Sanderson, M.: Ambiguous queries: test collections need more sense. In: 31st Conference on Research and Development in Information Retrieval, SIGIR 2008, pp. 499–506 (2008)
15. Schenkel, R., Crecelius, T., Kacimi, M., Michel, S., Neumann, T., Parreira, J.X., Weikum, G.: Efficient top-k querying over social-tagging networks. In: 31st Conference on Research and Development in Information Retrieval, SIGIR 2008, pp. 523–530 (2008)
16. Stoyanovich, J., Amer-Yahia, S., Marlow, C., Yu, C.: Leveraging tagging to model user interests in del.icio.us. In: AAAI Spring Symposium: Social Information Processing, pp. 104–109 (2008)
17. Szomszor, M., Alani, H., Cantador, I., O'Hara, K., Shadbolt, N.R.: Semantic modelling of user interests based on cross-folksonomy analysis. In: Sheth, A.P., Staab, S., Dean, M., Paolucci, M., Maynard, D., Finin, T., Thirunarayan, K. (eds.) ISWC 2008. LNCS, vol. 5318, pp. 632–648. Springer, Heidelberg (2008)
18. Vallet, D., Cantador, I., Jose, J.M.: Personalizing web search with folksonomy-based user and document profiles. In: Gurrin, C., He, Y., Kazai, G., Kruschwitz, U., Little, S., Roelleke, T., Rüger, S., van Rijsbergen, K. (eds.) ECIR 2010. LNCS, vol. 5993, pp. 420–431. Springer, Heidelberg (2010)
19. Volkovich, Y., Kaltenbrunner, A.: Evaluation of valuable user generated content on social news web sites. In: WWW (Companion Volume), pp. 139–140 (2011)
20. Xu, S., Bao, S., Fei, B., Su, Z., Yu, Y.: Exploring folksonomy for personalized search. In: 31st Conference on Research and Development in Information Retrieval, SIGIR 2008, pp. 155–162 (2008)
21. Zaragoza, H., Craswell, N., Taylor, M., Saria, S., Robertson, S.: Microsoft cambridge at TREC 13: Web and hard tracks. In: TExt Retrieval Conference, TREC 2004 (2004)

A Diversity-Dependent Measure for Discovering Influencers in Social Networks

Pei-Ying Huang, Hsin-Yu Liu, Chun-Ting Lin, and Pu-Jen Cheng

Department of Computer Science and Information Engineering
National Taiwan University, Taiwan
{d96004,b98013,r99044,pjcheng}@csie.ntu.edu.tw

Abstract. In this paper, a diversity-dependent influence measure, considering social diversity and transition probability, is proposed for detecting the influencers by evaluating the influence of users across the social networks. Two models are then proposed to evaluate this measure. Comparative analyses on synthetic social networks and a real Twitter data suggest that the social diversities of the influenced people may play an important role in the identification of various influence levels of influencers. Comparative analysis between our proposed methods shows that the weighted spread strategy performs best. It implies that the pattern of the influence propagation would be beneficial to discover influencers. Our proposed scheme is therefore practical and feasible to be deployed in the real world.

Keywords: influencers, social diversity, influence propagation, social networks.

1   Introduction

Owing to the real-time and fast growing features, social network becomes a new media for advertising companies, politicians and even government to spread of information and influence for target marketing, election and policy execution. It has been believed that target influencers usually lead to a vast propagation of information across the social networks. In viral marketing, advertisers target these influencers and hope they can influence their friends to use the product. And then through word of mouth effect, they finally trigger a huge cascade of influence so that many people will use the product. In politics, parties nominate influencers will be most likely to win the election. Besides, everyone has different influence level. As for viral marketing, if advertisers target top influencers, the company needs to pay more money to promote their product. By knowing the influence level, the company can choose the proper target influencers based on their budget to maximize their profit. As for politics, party nominates a person of local influence to president would most likely lose the game. It is thus important to discover and discriminate the influence level of users.

Several studies in social network focus on the issue of social influence. Considering the impact of social influence, Agarwal et al. [1] addressed the problem on identifying the influential bloggers in blogosphere. Ye et al. [2] evaluated different social influences by considering their stabilities, assessments, and correlations. Bakshy et al. [3]

R.E. Banchs et al. (Eds.): AIRS 2013, LNCS 8281, pp. 368–379, 2013.
© Springer-Verlag Berlin Heidelberg 2013

reported that weak ties, responsible for the propagation of novel information, may play a more dominant role in the dissemination of information than currently believed.

Identification of influencers by using Twitter follower graph has caught much attention from recent research studies. Many approaches are proposed to solve this problem by considering different influence measures. Lee et al. [4] proposed a method to find influencers based on both the temporal order of information adoption and the link structure. Kwak et al. [5] compared three different measures of influence, namely followers, page-rank and retweets and found that the ranking of the influencers differed by these three measures. And the analysis of network topology showed low reciprocity. Besides, a consistent argument of low reciprocity was found by Cha et al. [6]. They also made a comparative analysis of three different measures of influence, namely followers, retweets and user mentions, which were used to evaluate the social influence. Their results presented that the number of followers may not be the best measure of the influence. However, Weng et al. [7] contradicted the observation by Cha et al. [6] and reported that their study exhibited the phenomenon of high reciprocity which can be explained by homophily. Moreover, based on this finding, they proposed a TwitterRank measure, similar to the work by Haveliwala [8] to find topic-sensitive influential twitterers. Bakshy et al. [9] uncovered an interesting observation that the ordinary influencers would be the most cost-effective in many circumstances, only under some circumstances the most influential users are the most cost-effective. Note that the ordinary influencers are defined by them as individuals who exert average or even less-than-average influence. The above researches have been proposed different measures to find the influencers. However, there is no researches tackle this issue from the perspective of social diversities of the influenced people. Our basic idea is that if a user influences more diverse people, he/she will gain more influence. Since each of these diverse people would contribute to an independent information flow and lastly trigger a large cascade effect to make propagation disperse further and faster. On the contrary, exert influence on people with less diversity might bring a looping effect which renders the information propagation end within the cluster of people without dispersing outside the loop.

In the previous studies, they consider a user will have more influence potential if he/she influences more people. However, they don't consider the degree of difficulty in influence spread. We believe that a user needs to exert more influence to target people with high social diversity than those with low social diversity. People with similar attributes are believed to have more frequent interaction and are prone to influence each other so that speed the influence spread. By contrast, diverse people have less connections and a user, at the worst case, needs to influence them one by one without getting any benefit from social similarity. So such influence spread is more difficult. Social diversities of the influenced people are thus hypothesized to have a great impact on the influence of a user.

As mentioned above, we conjecture that the social diversities of the influenced people may play an important role in identifying influencers. However, to the best of our knowledge, there are no previous research studies targeted to this issue in detection of influencers. Thus, it remains unclear to what extent and in what way the effect of the social diversities of the influenced people would be imposed on the detection of influencers. In this paper, we therefore focus on understanding the impact of social diversities of the influenced people on the detection of influencers by aggregating Twitter retweet-follower graph. Our study provides clear evidences that the social diversity feature is an essential factor in detection of influencers.

2   Twitter Dataset

For the purpose of this study, a set of Twitter data was prepared over the two weeks, from December 4 2012 to December 17 2012. First, 600 out of top 1000 users and their two levels of followers, covering 5,894 users, were obtained from http://twitaholic.com/ as seeds to construct a retweet graph of 75, 042 tweets and of 400,967 retweets. Second, we crawled all followers of every user. Subsequently, we placed those followers in a queue to be crawled, thereby finding their followers, who were then also placed in the queue, and so on. A follower graph is then constructed. The retweet and follower graph are combined to further construct a retweet-follower graph of 152,119 users, of 169,942 edges, of 192,437 message propagations. To eliminate ambiguity in our analysis, we removed the users who published excessive tweets. As a result, we had a total of 151,305 users for later analysis.

3   Influencers Identification

3.1   Kernel Ideas

Twitter user (twitterer) is followed by his/her followers who can read and even share the tweet published by him with their friends via retweeting. We call these followers who are influenced by the twitterer to share information with their friends as mediators. The basic idea of our work is that the twitterer inherits influence from his/her mediators and thereby we made the following assumptions. The twitterer will gain higher influence if his/her mediators have higher influence. The mediators have higher influence if they have higher social diversity. That is to say, the twitterer will exert more influence if his/her followers have higher social diversity. The goal of this paper is to find such influential users (influencers) in a social network via considering the social diversities from the mediators to evaluate their corresponding influence scores. To achieve this goal, we extend PageRank to propose three diversity-dependent approaches, incorporating concepts of transition probability and social diversity, to measure the influence of twitterers. Notice that, to the best of our knowledge, we are the first one to introduce the concept of social diversities from the mediators to identify influencers in a social network.

3.2   Transition Probability

Transition probability is measured as how much attention the twitterer could draw from his/her mediators? As shown in Fig. 1, a user u_g receive messages from five other users besides u_a while a user u_h is the only message receiver of u_a. The transition probability from u_a to u_g is thus measured as 1/6 while that from u_a to u_h is measured as one. Note that, in this case, only one message propagation in each of directed edges. The transition probability $TP(i, j)$ for a directed edge $e(i, j)$ is defined as follows.

The transition probability of the message propagated from u_i to u_j is defined as:

$$TP(i, j) = \frac{mp_{ij}}{\sum\limits_{k:\, u_j \text{ retweet } u_k} mp_{kj}} \qquad (1)$$

mp_{ij} is number of messages propagated from u_i to u_j, and $\sum\limits_{k:\, u_j \text{ retweet } u_k} mp_{kj}$ sums up the number of messages u_j received.

Although this concept is similar to the work by Weng et al. [7], there is a major difference between our work and theirs. They take following relationship into account, when measuring the transition probability, while we consider the retweeting relationship.

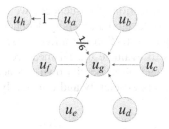

Fig. 1. Example of transition probability caculation

3.3   Social Diversity

Our idea is that if a user exerts influence on people with high diversity, diverse people would contribute to independent information flows and trigger a large cascade effect to make propagation disperse further and faster. As shown in Fig. 2b, u_a influences u_e, u_f and u_g to produce three independent information flows and eventually trigger a large cascade of information propagation. On the contrary, exert influence on people with less diversity might bring a looping effect which renders the information propagation end within the cluster of people without dispersing outside the loop. As shown in Fig. 2a, u_a propagates message to u_b, u_c and u_d and the information finally terminate within the cluster form by u_b, u_c and u_d. Furthermore, we believe that a user needs to exert more influence to target his/her mediators in Fig. 2b than in Fig. 2a. User u_a needs to influence one by one to reach all of his/her mediators, as shown in Fig. 2b while u_a may only need to influence one of them and finally reach all of them via the effect of social similarity. Social diversities of user's mediators are thus hypothesized to have a great impact on the influence of a user.

Social diversity is measured as one divided by the size of cluster. As for the case in Fig. 2a, social diversities for u_b, u_c and u_d are all 1/3 while, in Fig. 2b, social diversities of u_e, u_f and u_g are all one.

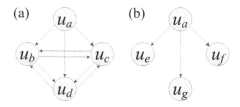

Fig. 2. Illustration of social diversity (a) low diversity (b) high diversity

4   Diversity-Dependent Algorithms

To solve the problem of identification of influencers, we consider the transition propagation and social diversity to develop a diversity-dependent influence (DI) measure. Our goal aims to use DI measure to find the influencers. We then extend PageRank [10] to propose two models to evaluate the DI measure, including prior model and propagation model. Each model possesses its own physical meaning and is able to determine the influence of users efficiently and effectively. We describe and discuss each of them in the following.

4.1   The Prior Model

We first describe the processing on finding social diversity for prior model. The social diversity SD_i^{prior} is estimated by the community structure. If the nodes in the community formed by node v_i and its descendants are more dense connections, node v_i would get less social diversity such that less influence node v_i could exert. SD_i^{prior} is defined as follows:

$$SD_i^{prior} = \frac{Des_i}{L_i} \qquad (2)$$

Des_i is the number of descendants of node v_i, and L_i is the number of links between node v_i and its descendants.

With the transition probability and social diversity, the diversity-dependent influence score, denoted as DIS, for each node v_i associated with v_j ($(i, j) \in E$) can be calculated iteratively as transition probability T_i^{prior} linearly combines with social diversity SD_i^{prior} is defined as follows:

$$DIS_i^{prior} = \alpha * T_i^{prior} + (1-\alpha) * SD_i^{prior} \tag{3}$$

where α is a parameter between 0 and 1 to control the weight of social diversity. The lower α is, the higher weight the social diversity will have, and vice versa. The calculation of T_i^{prior} is similar to PageRank [10], but with a small change, defined as

$$T_i^{prior} = \begin{cases} \dfrac{(1-d)}{n} + d*(\sum_j \dfrac{X}{Y}) + Z, & \text{if } v_i \text{ with outbound links} \\ \dfrac{(1-d)}{n} + d*Z & , \text{otherwise} \end{cases} \tag{4}$$

where n is the number of nodes in G, d is a damping factor set around 0.85, $X = TP(i,j)*DIS_j^{prior}$, $Z = \dfrac{\left(\sum_k DIS_k^{prior}\right)}{n}$ where v_k without inbound links, and $Y = \sum\limits_{m:(m,j)\in E} TP(m,j)$.

4.2   The Propagation Model

Social diversity is determined by the community structure for the prior model. However, it might be more reasonable in real-world to take the flow of influence propagation into account on estimating the social diversity. To account for the relative effects of influence propagation on calculating social diversity, thus, we propose two variants of propagation matrices, then star algorithm [11] is employed to do the clustering, according to the clustering, social diversity is finally evaluated. Calculation of social diversities of mediators, considering true influence propagation or not, for two proposed algorithms (zero-one spread and weighted spread) are described as follows.

Social Diversity Calculation with Static Propagation Matrix: Different from prior model, the main concept of these two methods is to calculate social diversity by considering a static propagation matrix, not simply by community structure.

Static propagation matrix: zero-one spread first construct a propagation matrix $T_{n\times n}$, where $T_{ij} = 1$ if $e(i,j)\in E$, otherwise $T_{ij} = 0$. The propagation matrix of zero-one spread T^k is then calculated by T multiplied by T k-1 times. Contrast to zero-one spread, weighted spread considers the real number of message propagation and calculates $T_{ij} = TP(i,j)$ in the initial propagation matrix.

Clustering: Star algorithm is employed to calculate the similarity of the pattern of influence propagation between descendants of v_i. If the similarity of two nodes (T_j^k, T_k^k) higher than a threshold $(\theta = 0.5)$, edge $e(j,k) \in E_\theta$. A cluster is then constructed, from G_θ, by the node with highest degree and its associated nodes.

Social diversity calculation: After clustering, the social diversity of node v_i associated with v_j ($e(i, j) \in E$) defined as follows is based on the size of the cluster it belongs to.

$$SD_{ij} = \frac{1}{g_{ij}} \tag{5}$$

where g_{ij} is the size of the cluster v_j belongs to.

DI Measure for Propagation Model: Considering the transition probability and social diversities of mediators, the DI measure can be calculated iteratively for zero-one spread and weighted spread, respectively by

$$DIS_i = \begin{cases} \dfrac{0.15}{n} + 0.85 * (\sum_j \dfrac{X}{Y}) + Z, \text{ if } v_i \text{ with outbound links} \\ \dfrac{0.15}{n} + 0.85 * Z \qquad\qquad , otherwise \end{cases} \tag{6}$$

where $X = TP(i, j) * SD_i * DIS_j, Y = \sum_{m=1}^{n}\left(TP(m, j) * SD_j \right)$, $Z = \dfrac{\left(\sum_k DIS_k \right)}{n}$, v_k without outbound link, and n is the number of nodes in G.

5   Results and Discussion

5.1   Discrimination of Influencers of Different Influence Levels

In order to evaluate our approaches, we conducted an experiment in which results from our models were compared to those from PageRank. BA model [12] was then employed to generate a synthetic social network in which node A was connected to five independent groups of 1000 nodes while node B only connected to one of them, as shown in Figure 3. These two nodes have the same number of out-degree nodes and their out-degree nodes got similar rankings by PageRank. Since node A has the same number but more diverse out-degree nodes compared to node B, the influence level by node A is thus higher than node B. Table 1 presented the scores and ranks of node A and node B calculated by our methods and PageRank. These two nodes have the similar scores and ranks by PageRank since they have the same number and similar ranking of out-degree nodes. Compared to PageRank, our methods all showed that there was a significant difference from scores and ranks of these two nodes. Our methods performed better and successfully discriminate the influence level via considering the social diversity of out-degree nodes (the influenced people).

Fig. 3. Nodes with different influence levels

Table 1. Scores and ranks for node A and node B

	PageRank		Prior		Zero-one spread		Weighted spread	
Node	A	B	A	B	A	B	A	B
Score	1.099e-03	1.053e-03	1.009e-03	9.571e-04	1.521e-03	9.775e-04	1.270e-03	1.062e-03
Rank	117	126	118	133	91	194	110	152

5.2   Effect of Social Diversities from Children

A comparative analysis was then performed in order to clarify the performance of our approaches. BA model was then employed to generate a synthetic social network in which node A was connected to five independent groups of 1000 nodes, denoted as G_0. Additional three social networks, named G_1 to G_3, were subsequently generated by adding 5000, 10000, 15000 links among five groups, as shown in Figure 4.

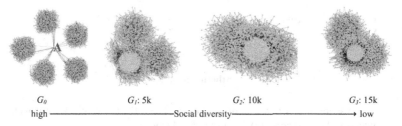

G_0	G_1: 5k	G_2: 10k	G_3: 15k

high ————————————————Social diversity———————————————→ low

Fig. 4. Synthetic social networks with various social diversities of mediators

The independence level of five groups decreased from G_0 to G_3, that is, the social diversity of nodes within the groups decreased with the adding links. Five groups might eventually be clustered into one by adding more enough links. In a real-world, the denser group means people within the group interact to each other frequently. This clustering effect is often driven by the social similarity, to a certain extent, loses social diversity. The influence scores in our methods fall when the social diversities of children decrease (Fig. 5a), but a similar relationship is also presented in PageRank.

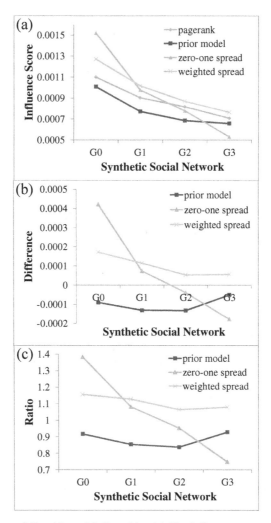

Fig. 5. Influence score falls with social diversities (a) The influence scores for our methods (b) The difference of influence scores (c) The ratio of influence scores

In order to measure the effect of our methods relative to PageRank, computed as either the difference or ratio between the influence score by our methods and Page-Rank (Fig. 5bc). The difference in influence score falls with the decrease of social diversities of children of node A, the relative ratio shows the similar results. This finding suggests that social diversity of child in our methods is most likely to make an impact on influence score of node A. The relative impact on the influence is highest for social network with child of high social diversity. That is, changes in the social diversities of out-degree nodes could alter the influence level of node A. Our methods all could better capture the variances in social diversities of children to discover and discriminate the influencers of different influence level.

The weighted spread scheme performs best. The zero-one spread scheme did not consider the actual number of message propagations and it treats as one message propagation no matter how many times the message being propagated. The calculation of child's social diversity in prior model is based on the network structure and not to consider the distribution of influence propagation. Thus, zero-one spread and prior model might underestimate the effect of child's social diversity and not to reflect the real ranking level.

6   Case Study

To give a sense of how well our approach works, we further compare the users which fall into the class of media. The difference between the ranks computed by weighted spread and by PageRank was measured, as shown in Table 2. Reuters Top News and The Washington Post are international media. Since the impact of their name value, they often draw attention from numbers of followers from all walks of life to read and share their published tweets with friends and make the information propagation quick and far. Thus, our method and PageRank obtained a similar ranking.

Table 2. Variation of the ranks for media

Media				
Screen name	Description	PageRank	Weighted	Var.
Sky Sports News	Sports news channel	346	349	3
Reuters Top News	International news agency	386	387	1
The Washington Post	American daily newspaper	466	464	-2
SportsNation	Sports-related television program	454	469	15
TMZ	Celebrity news website	470	483	13
NPR News	Public radio network	540	552	12
TODAY	American morning television show	595	622	27
Entertainment Weekly	American entertainment magazine	739	765	26
BBC Click	BBC television program	809	783	-26
Gossip Girl	American teen drama television series	803	793	-10
Digg	Social news website	829	853	24
Teen Vogue	Vogue magazine for teenage girls	1064	1156	92
NPR Politics	Political podcast	1383	1487	104
Newsweek	American weekly news magazine	1847	2014	167
ELLE Magazine (US)	Worldwide lifestyle magazine	1938	2120	182
The New Yorker	American magazine	2455	2583	128
Vogue Magazine	American fashion and lifestyle magazine	2609	2681	72

As for The New Yorker, Newsweek, NPR Politics and ELLE Magazine, their ranks dropped a lot when compared to those by PageRank. Take a further examination, we can find The New Yorker is a local medium and both NPR Politics and ELLE Magazine talked about specific subjects (*i.e.,* politics and lifestyle). They might appeal to a group of people of the same interests, clustered by social similarity, and thus less effect of social diversities from their influenced people will be imposed on their influence score, leading to worse ranks.

7   Conclusion

In this paper, we address the problem of identification of influencers in social networks by introducing the concepts of social diversities of the influenced people and influence propagation. We believe that this is the first study to use social diversities of the influenced people to measure the influence of users. We then proposed three diversity-dependent schemes to identify influencers via measuring the influence scores of users. The prior model is based on the network structure while the propagation model considers the pattern of influence spread.

Comparative analyses on synthetic social networks suggest that the social diversities of the influenced people may play an important role in the identification of various influence levels of influencers. Comparative analysis between our methods shows that weighted spread is superior to the others. We also apply weighted spread to Twitter data and compare with PageRank. Our results show that our strategy performs better. It implies that the pattern of the influence propagation could be beneficial to discriminate the influencers. Our proposed scheme is therefore practical and feasible to be deployed in the real world.

References

1. Agarwal, N., Liu, H., Tang, L., Yu, P.S.: Identifying the influential bloggers in a community. In: Proceedings of the 2008 International Conference on Web Search and Data Mining, pp. 207–218. ACM, Palo Alto (2008)
2. Ye, S., Wu, S.F.: Measuring message propagation and social influence on twitter.com. In: Bolc, L., Makowski, M., Wierzbicki, A. (eds.) SocInfo 2010. LNCS, vol. 6430, pp. 216–231. Springer, Heidelberg (2010)
3. Bakshy, E., Rosenn, I., Marlow, C., Adamic, L.: The role of social networks in information diffusion. In: Proceedings of the 21st International Conference on World Wide Web, pp. 519–528. ACM, Lyon (2012)
4. Lee, C., Kwak, H., Park, H., Moon, S.: Finding influentials based on the temporal order of information adoption in twitter. In: Proceedings of the 19th International Conference on World Wide Web, pp. 1137–1138. ACM, Raleigh (2010)
5. Kwak, H., Lee, C., Park, H., Moon, S.: What is Twitter, a social network or a news media? In: Proceedings of the 19th International Conference on World Wide Web, pp. 591–600. ACM, Raleigh (2010)
6. Cha, M., Haddadi, H., Benevenuto, F., Gummadi, K.P.: Measuring user influence in Twitter: The million follower fallacy. In: Proceedings of international AAAI Conference on Weblogs and Social, ICWSM 2010 (2010)
7. Weng, J., Lim, E.-P., Jiang, J., He, Q.: TwitterRank: finding topic-sensitive influential twitterers. In: Proceedings of the third ACM International Conference on Web Search and Data Mining, pp. 261–270. ACM, New York (2010)
8. Haveliwala, T.H.: Topic-sensitive PageRank. In: Proceedings of the 11th International Conference on World Wide Web, pp. 517–526. ACM, Honolulu (2002)
9. Bakshy, E., Hofman, J.M., Mason, W.A., Watts, D.J.: Everyone's an influencer: quantifying influence on twitter. In: Proceedings of the Fourth ACM International Conference on Web Search and Data Mining, pp. 65–74. ACM, Hong Kong (2011)

10. Page, L., Brin, S., Motwani, R., Winograd, T.: The PageRank Citation Ranking: Bringing Order to the Web. Technical Report, Stanford InfoLab (1999)
11. Aslam, J.A., Pelekhov, E., Rus, D.: The Star Clustering Algorithm For Static And Dynamic Information Organization. Journal of Graph Algorithms and Applications 8, 95–129 (2004)
12. Albert, R., Barabási, A.-L.: Statistical mechanics of complex networks. Reviews of Modern Physics 74, 47–97 (2002)

Characterizing Expertise of Search Engine Users

Qianli Xing*, Yiqun Liu, Min Zhang, Shaoping Ma, and Kuo Zhang

State Key Laboratory of Intelligent Technology and Systems
Tsinghua National Laboratory for Information Science and Technology
Department of Computer Science and Technology, Tsinghua University, Beijing 100084, China
xingqianli@gmail.com, {yiqunliu,z-m,msp}@tsinghua.edu.cn,
zhangkuo@sogou-inc.com

Abstract. Search engine click-through data is a valuable source of implicit user feedback for relevance. However, not all user clicks are good indication of relevance. The clicks from search experts, who are more successful searching a query, tend to be more reliable in indicating document relevance than those of the non-experts. Therefore, knowing the expertise of search users is helpful to better understand their clicks. In this paper, we propose two probabilistic modelings of user expertise in the environment of web search. Inspired by the idea of evaluation metrics in classification, search users are treated as classifiers and result documents are viewed as the data samples to classify in our models. A click implies that the document is classified as relevant by the user. Therefore, the expertise of a user can be measured by how well he/she classifies the documents. We carry out experiments on a real-world click-through data of a Chinese search engine. The results show that modeling user expertise helps the click models with relevance inference, which also implies that our models are effective in identifying the user expertise.

Keywords: User expertise, Click-through data, web search.

1 Introduction

Search engines collect a large amount of user interaction logs everyday when people search the Web. Among these logs, click-through data has drawn a lot of attention because of the relevance information embedded in it. Although the click data might be noisy, it can still reflect users' relevance judgments towards the documents to certain extent. Previous studies [8, 1] have presented that the relevance preferences can be extracted from the click-through data and the quality of the extracted result is even comparable to human annotations. Such implicit relevance information in click logs can be used to evaluate and improve the search engine performance. A big advantage of using user clicks for relevance is that they can be collected at low costs and the scale is far big than that the human annotation can do. Therefore, a lot of methods are proposed in an attempt to mine relevance from clicks [5–7, 2]. The core idea of these methods is to use the wisdom of the crowd in the clicks.

---

* This work was supported by Natural Science Foundation (60903107, 61073071) and National High Technology Research and Development (863) Program (2011AA01A205) of China.

R.E. Banchs et al. (Eds.): AIRS 2013, LNCS 8281, pp. 380–391, 2013.

However, not every click is equally informative to indicate relevance for various reasons. During a search, some users may used to click multiple documents at a time without careful selection; some users are bad at making relevance judgment so their clicked documents may not be as relevant as they thought. Generally, the experienced search users are more likely to accomplish a successful search while the novices may have trouble finding the relevant documents. White et al. [13] investigated the behavioral variability among search users. The results showed that the users had considerable differences in some key aspects of search, such as querying, browsing and clicking. It is also reported that the users with domain knowledge have larger percentage of successful in-domain search sessions [14]. Being aware of the diversity of search users, it is essential to take user expertise into consideration to better understand the clicks.

It is a big challenge to characterize the expertise of a search user because it is hard to define an expert in the Web search scenario. The previous studies used some simple ways to identify search experts. For example, White et al. [12] considered advanced users in Web search to be those who had issued queries with advanced syntax. As to domain search experts, the proportion of expert sites (assessed by domain experts) that a user visited was used to approximate the expertise [14]. However, these methods are neither accurate nor formal enough to be widely adopted.

In this paper, we propose two probabilistic methods to define and model the search expertise for search users. Our models assume that a click event depends on both the document relevance and the user's expertise, which most click models usually ignore. The process that a user makes relevance judgment documents is viewed as a classification task. User is the classifier and the documents are data samples to classify. The expertise of a search user can be then measured by the classifying performance. In our experiment, the parameters of expertise and relevance are estimated with a large-scale click log from a Chinese search engine. We also carry out a series of experiments to evaluate the effectiveness of the proposed models.

2 Related Work

Previous studies have shown that the click-through data are useful but meanwhile noisy. Clicks from different search users may not be equally informative in relevance indication. Search users who issued queries with advanced syntax were reported to be more successful in their search sessions by [12]. In that study, the expertise of a user is viewed as the percentage of his/her queries that include advanced syntax. The experiment results showed that the average relevance of the clicked documents by the advanced users (i.e. users that issued queries with advanced syntax) are higher than that of the non-advanced users. And the more advanced syntax one uses, the more successful his/her searches are. Although this definition for user expertise was simple, it revealed the connection between user expertise and quality of the clicks.

Besides search expertise, it was reported that domain expertise also has impact on user clicks [14]. In their work, the affection of domain expertise to users' search behavior was studied in four specific domains (medicine, finance, law and computer science). In each domain, the users were separated into experts and non-experts based on whether they had visited one or more of the pre-defined expert sites. The results showed notable difference between domain experts and non-experts with respect to search behavior. More concretely, domain experts were found to be more successful when searching in-domain queries; the pages visited by domain experts had deeper technical depth than those visited by non-experts and so on. Building upon the analysis, a classifier was trained to predict whether a user is domain expert using his/her search interaction features. In their work, domain expertise was defined to be binary and it did not study how the expertise is related to the relevance of clicks.

There are also studies on personalized click model that treat users differently when inferring document relevance. For example, Shen et al. [10] used collaborative filtering technique to capture users' interested domains. In their personalized click model, it was assumed that the users have different domains of interests and latent factors were used to represent one's interests. The better the topics of a document match a user's interested domains, the higher the click probability. Another noise-aware click model [3] was proposed to measure the probability of a click being noisy by using both user class features and context class features. A variable N was introduced into the model, indicating whether the context is noisy. Then they made different click assumptions for different value of N. These two studies have considered the user level features when modeling clicks, but the influence of search expertise was still not taken into account.

3   Models

Our aim of introducing search expertise into click modeling is to help improve the relevance inference. Thus, the search expertise of a user should be able to reflect how well the user can make the right relevance judgment of a given document. When a user searches a query, a click indicates that he/she thinks the document is relevant and a skip (no click after examination) indicates an irrelevant judgment. If we view the this process of user making relevance judgments as a classification task, then the documents are the data samples to classify and the user is the classifier. Relevant documents correspond to positive samples and irrelevant documents correspond to negative samples. The click on a document indicates that the user classifies this document as relevant. Therefore, the expertise of a user is actually the performance of the classifier. There are many evaluation metrics for classifiers and we use *accuracy* and *confusion matrix* to measure the expertise in this paper.

3.1   Accuracy Model

Accuracy is a widely used evaluation metric in classification. It is calculated as the proportion of the correctly classified samples. In our application scenario, let a_u be the accuracy of user u making the right relevance judgment, which is a real-valued parameter ranging from 0 to 1. For the ith document in the search result page, u will make the right relevance judgment with probability a_u. It can be formally denoted as:

$$a_u = P(C_i = 1 | R_i = 1, E_i = 1, u)$$
$$= P(C_i = 0 | R_i = 0, E_i = 1, u) \tag{1}$$

where C_i, R_i, and E_i are binary variables. C_i indicates whether the document is clicked; R_i indicates whether the document is relevant; and E_i indicates whether the document is examined by u. Thus, if u has examined the ith document, the probability of the document being clicked can be written as:

$$
\begin{aligned}
& P(C_i = 1 | E_i = 1, u) \\
& = \sum_{R_i \in \{0,1\}} P(R_i) P(C_i = 1 | R_i, E_i = 1, u) \\
& = r_i a_u + (1 - r_i)(1 - a_u)
\end{aligned}
\tag{2}
$$

where r_i is the probability that the ith document is relevant. It means that a click happens under two situations: (1) the document is relevant and the user makes right relevance judgment; (2) the document is irrelevant and the user makes wrong relevance judgment. We call this model the accuracy model and a_u is the expertise of user u.

3.2 Confusion Matrix Model

Confusion matrix is another popular evaluation metric in classification. Unlike accuracy, it measures the classification accuracy for positive samples and negative samples separately. It is presented in the form of a matrix called the confusion matrix, as shown in Eq. 3. The element p_{ij} in the matrix is the probability that class i being classified as class j by the classifier. In our problem setting, p_{11} denotes the probability that a relevant document being classified as relevant (clicked) and p_{00} is the probability that an irrelevant document being classified as irrelevant(skipped). Therefore, in this confusion matrix model, the expertise of user u is represented by the matrix $\mathbf{M_u}$. The larger the values on the diagonal, the higher the user's expertise.

$$
\mathbf{M_u} = \begin{bmatrix} p_{00}^u & p_{01}^u \\ p_{10}^u & p_{11}^u \end{bmatrix}
\tag{3}
$$

The values in each row of the matrix sum up to 1. Therefore, one's expertise can be represented by the following two parameters instead of the whole matrix.

$$
\begin{aligned}
p_{11}^u &= P(C_i = 1 | R_i = 1, E_i = 1, u) \\
p_{00}^u &= P(C_i = 0 | R_i = 0, E_i = 1, u)
\end{aligned}
\tag{4}
$$

For user u, the click probability of the ith document after examination becomes

$$
P(C_i | E_i = 1, u)^T = \begin{bmatrix} r_i \\ 1 - r_i \end{bmatrix}^T \mathbf{M_u}
\tag{5}
$$

As there are two expertise parameters, p_{00}^u and p_{11}^u, for each user. This confusion matrix model is more flexible than the accuracy model. And it can degenerate to the accuracy model if we let $p_{11} = p_{00}$.

3.3 Baseline Model

To evaluate the performance of the above two proposed models, we use a baseline model for comparison. Like most of the existing click models, this baseline model does

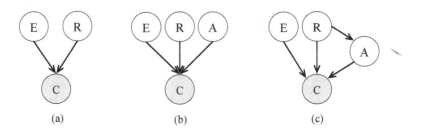

Fig. 1. The graphical representations of the models. (a) is the baseline model; (b) is the accuracy model and (c) is the confusion matrix model. R is the hidden variable for relevance; E is the hidden variable for examination; A is the hidden variable for expertise and C denotes click.

not take user expertise into consideration. Thus the click probability of a document after examination only depends on the document relevance.

$$P(C_i = 1 | E_i = 1, u) = P(R_i = 1) \tag{6}$$

This assumption is widely used in click models such as [5, 7, 6]. It treats all the clicks as relevance indication.

3.4 Graphical Representations

In the baseline model, R and E are the hidden variables and C can be observed from the data. The difference between our models and the baseline model is the hidden variable A which indicates whether the user made the right relevance judgment. Our models treat a click as relevance indication only when the user made the right judgment on this document. We can demonstrate the idea of the three models more clearly with the graphical representation in Figure 1. Figure 1(a) is the baseline model with the dependencies of a regular click model. (b) represents the accuracy model in which A is added as a dependent factor of C. (c) denotes the confusion matrix model in which another dependency is added from A to R, indicating that users behave differently on the relevant documents and the irrelevant documents. All these models are in probabilistic framework and can be solved in an efficient way.

4   Parameter Estimation

Having the different search expertise modelings proposed above, we now introduce how the parameters are estimated in these models. As the probability $P(C_i | E_i, u)$ has been derived for each model, we can compute the likelihood of the observed click-through data. For a search session[1], the commonly used *linear traversal hypothesis* in click models assume that users examine the documents one by one from top to bottom of a

---

[1] Here a session is defined as the activities of a user searching a query in a short period of time. In this paper, we set the interaction timeout to 30 minutes.

search result page. The *examination hypothesis* [4] assumes that users have to examine a document before clicking on it. These two hypotheses together implies that all the documents before a click have been examined. But for the documents after the last click in a session, we do not know whether they have been examined or not. Some click modes, such as [5, 6], use more complex assumptions to model the examination probabilities of the documents in all positions. However, considering that the focus of this paper is the influence of user expertise in modeling clicks, we decide to use the simplest examination hypothesis to reduce the influence of the other affecting factors. Therefore, we assume that in a search session, the user examined all the documents that ranked before the last clicked position. The likelihood of a search session s is then calculated as:

$$L(s) = \prod_{i=1}^{N_s} P(C_i = 1 | E_i = 1, u_s)^{C_i} \times P(C_i = 0 | E_i = 1, u_s)^{1-C_i} \tag{7}$$

where N_s is the last clicked position in session s and u_s is the user that conducted the session. The log-likelihood of the whole session observations is:

$$l(S) = \sum_{s \in S} \log L(s) \tag{8}$$

where S is the set of all sessions. To estimate the unknown parameters, we maximize the log-likelihood in Eq. 8 for each model.

Baseline Model. The baseline model has no expertise parameters. The only parameters to estimate are the relevance parameter $\{r\}$. By maximizing Eq. 8, the relevance of document d can be estimated as:

$$r_d = \frac{\#\text{Click on } d}{\#\text{Impression of } d \text{ before position } l} \tag{9}$$

where l is the position of the last click of each session that includes document d. The denominator calculates how many times d has appeared before a clicked document in all related sessions. r_d can be computed very efficiently by scanning the click-through data only once. In fact, this estimated relevance is exactly the same as that in the dependent click model proposed by Guo et al.[7], which was reported to be a very effective and efficient model in estimating relevance.

Accuracy Model. In the accuracy model, C is dependent on two hidden variables A and R. The click probability $P(C_i = 1 | E_i = 1, u)$ becomes a sum of several parts and the MLE method can no longer lead to closed form solution in parameter estimation. Therefore, the expectation-maximization algorithm (EM) is used here. In order to have a better control on the value of the estimated expertise parameters, beta distribution is used as conjugate prior for the expertise parameters. In an EM iteration, the parameters are updated in the following way:

$$r_d^{new} = \frac{1}{|S_d|} \sum_{s \in S_d} I_{C=1} \frac{r_d a_u}{1 - r_d - a_u + 2r_d a_u} + I_{C=0} \frac{r_d(1 - a_u)}{a_u - r_d a_u + r_d - r_d a_u}$$

$$a_u^{new} = \frac{1}{\sum_{s \in S_u} N_s(\alpha + \beta - 1)} \sum_{s \in S_u} \sum_{i=1}^{N_s} I_{C_i=1} \frac{\alpha r_d a_u + (\beta - 1)(1 - r_d)(1 - a_u)}{1 - r_i - a_u + 2r_i a_u} +$$

$$I_{C_i=0} \frac{\alpha(1 - r_d)a_u + (\beta - 1)r_d(1 - a_u)}{a_u - r_i a_u + r_i - r_i a_u}$$

$$(10)$$

where S_d is the set of sessions that include document d; S_u is the set of sessions of user u and N_s is the number of the examined documents in session s; I is the indicator function; α and β are the parameters of the beta prior. When $\alpha = 1$, $\beta = 1$, the pdf of beta distribution becomes a constant value (i.e. equal to using no prior).

Confusion Matrix Model. For the confusion matrix model, the capacity of a user making the right relevance judgment is represented by two parameters p_{11} and p_{00}, while in the accuracy model we only use one parameter. p_{11} and p_{00} are independent from each other. The estimation of the parameters using EM algorithm is similar to that in the accuracy model so the details are not listed here due to the space limitation. For simplicity, we let p_{11} and p_{00} share the same beta prior.

During the training of accuracy model and confusion matrix model, we run the EM algorithm for a fixed number of 20 iterations. The EM algorithm has a fast convergency speed so that after 20 iterations, the change ratio of the objective function is smaller than 0.1%, which is regarded as a signal of convergence.

5   Experiments

5.1   Experimental Settings

A sampled click log of a commercial Chinese search engine in November 2011 is used for our experiments. The click log records the interaction information of users with the search engine, such as user's cookie ID, session ID, query string, presented documents, clicked documents and timestamps. For the protection of users' privacy, all sensitive attributes are processed into numbers. A user is identified by cookie ID. As some users might have cleaned the cookie during the period that the data was collected, we removed the users who have fewer than 10 distinct queries to avoid noise when estimating the parameters of user expertise. After that, we finally obtain 23,534 unique users, 253,045 unique queries, 1,034,598 query sessions, 1,173,426 clicks and 476,737 skips. For each user, all his/her sessions are sorted by timestamp and we split them into two parts at the ratio of 4:1 for training and testing respectively.

For the prior, α and β together control the shape of beta distribution. In the training phase, we try different combinations of α and β and the best performance is obtained when $\alpha = 2$, $\beta = 2$ with respect to the estimated relevance. Therefore, we only use the results of $\alpha = 2$, $\beta = 2$ for demonstration in this section.

5.2 Perplexity

Perplexity is an evaluation metric often used by click models [4]. It measures how well the predicted probabilities fit the real data. Smaller perplexity means better performance and the ideal value for perplexity is 1. We calculate the perplexity for all models on both training set and test set. Table 1 shows the results. The accuracy model (AM) without prior and the confusion matrix model (CMM) without prior have close perplexity together with the baseline model on test set. We notice that the models with prior have worse perplexity. The reason is that perplexity is very similar to likelihood, which is the optimization objective of the models without prior. When the posterior becomes the optimization objective for the models with prior, the perplexity is no longer optimized. Therefore, it is not surprising that CMM without prior obtains the best perplexity given that CMM has greater flexibility than AM. Although the models without prior perform better in perplexity, it does not mean they are better in inferring relevance. In fact, perplexity can not directly reflect the quality of the estimated relevance. Wang et al. have pointed out that perplexity might not be a trustable metric for click models because it is defined based on the absolute value of the predicted probabilities and thus is sensitive to scaling [11]. Therefore, we use perplexity as a reference but it is not the main evaluation metric in this paper. For the evaluation, we will focus on the quality of the estimated relevance, which is the aim of modeling the clicks.

Table 1. Perplexity of different models

	Training set			Test set		
	all	click	skip	all	click	skip
	1,339,912	950,934	388,978	222,275	165,758	56,517
Baseline	1.203	1.934	1.380	1.302	2.779	1.579
AM(no prior)	1.206	1.911	1.379	1.304	2.795	1.583
AM($\alpha = 2, \beta = 2$)	1.760	2.044	1.838	1.752	2.085	1.831
CMM(no prior)	1.201	1.900	1.372	1.299	2.795	1.576
CMM($\alpha = 2, \beta = 2$)	1.710	2.141	1.825	1.703	2.208	1.820

5.3 Effectiveness of the Estimated Relevance

To evaluate the effectiveness of the estimated relevance, we use the manually labeled relevance as ground truth. To create the relevance labels, we first divide all queries into seven groups according to log-frequency of the query and randomly select 30 queries from each group. For the 210 selected queries, the related documents (clicked or skipped in a session) are then extracted from the click log, which gives us 1,133 unique query-document pairs. We manually label all the query-document pairs with three relevance scales: 2=*very relevant*, 1=*relevant*, 0=*irrelevant*.

As the estimated relevance is supposed to help improve the search engine ranking performance, the relative order of relevance of document pair can be used to evaluate the effectiveness of the estimated relevance [1]. The idea is that for a document pair (d_i, d_j) under a query, if d_i is more relevant than d_j, the estimated relevance of d_i should be higher than the estimated relevance of d_j as well. With the relevance labels, we investigate the agreement between the estimated relevance preference pairs and the labeled relevance preference pairs. Let r_i be the estimated relevance of d_i and l_i be the labeled relevance of d_i. A concordant pair means that $r_i > r_j, l_i > l_j$ or $r_i < r_j, l_i < l_j$. If $r_i > r_j, l_i < l_j$ or $r_i < r_j, l_i > l_j$, it is a discordant pair. Otherwise, it is neither a concordant nor a discordant pair. The more concordant pairs a model obtains, the better the model is in estimating relevance.

Table 2. Relevance preference pairs

	#concordant pair	#discordant pair	precision	%improve over baseline
baseline	780	449	63.5%	-
AM(no prior)	778	451	63.3%	-0.3%
AM($\alpha = 2, \beta = 2$)	**862**	**367**	**70.1%**	**10.5%**
CMM(no prior)	767	462	62.5%	-1.6%
CMM($\alpha = 2, \beta = 2$)	**817**	**412**	**66.5%**	**4.74%**

Table 2 shows the number of concordant and discordant relevance preference pairs obtained by each model. Precision is defined as the proportion of concordant pairs. We observe that without prior, AM and CMM are even worse than the baseline model which does not consider user expertise at all. It indicates the necessity of introducing prior. With a proper beta prior $\alpha = 2, \beta = 2$, both AM and CMM gain good precision. The precision of the accuracy model even reaches 70.1%, which improves the baseline by 10%. The confusion matrix model also improves the baseline by 4.7%. This fact verifies the effectiveness of our models in estimating relevance. We notice that the confusion matrix model, which has more modeling flexibility, fails to outperform the accuracy model. We will analyze the reason in next section by investigating the estimated user expertise parameters.

The inferred relevance preference pairs are useful in improving the search engine ranking performance. They can either be used as training samples in the pairwise learning algorithms, or they can be used directly to re-rank the search results. When used as training samples, the automatically generated preference pairs are of particular advantage because they are faster and easier to get compared to manual relevance labeling.

5.4   Effectiveness of the Estimated User Expertise

Besides document relevance, our models estimate the expertise of users as well. In this section, we evaluate how close the estimated expertise parameters are to the ground truth. Before the evaluation, we first need to obtain the ground truth of a user's expertise. With the labeled relevance in the previous section, we can calculate the ground truth of the expertise parameters using their definitions. Let L be the set of labeled query-document pairs, for a user u, the ground truth of a_u in the accuracy model is calculated as the proportion of correct click/skip decisions made by u on the all documents in L; the ground truth of p_{11} and p_{00} are also calculated in L according to their own definitions. To avoid noise, we do not evaluate the users with fewer than ten query-document pairs in L. We note that the calculated ground truth will be unavoidably biased to certain extent because of the limited size of L. However, this has been the best ground truth we can obtain with the data we have.

For each user u, we now have the estimated a_u, p_{11}^u, p_{00}^u and the calculated ground truth. We use multiple metrics to measure the gap between the estimated value and the ground truth, such as correlation, Kendall's τ, mean absolute error (MAE) and rooted mean square error (RMSE). Table 3 shows the results.

Table 3. Comparing the estimated expertise parameters with the ground truth

	Kendall's τ	correlation	MAE	RMSE
AM-$a_u(\alpha = 2, \beta = 2)$	0.425	0.609	0.277	0.298
AM-a_u(no prior)	0.413	0.407	0.129	0.201
CMM-$p_{11}(\alpha = 2, \beta = 2)$	0.395	0.591	0.280	0.299
CMM-p_{11}(no prior)	0.419	0.512	0.113	0.182
CMM-$p_{00}(\alpha = 2, \beta = 2)$	0.272	0.540	0.162	0.201
CMM-p_{00}(no prior)	0.321	-0.077	0.516	0.556

Kendall's τ [9] measures the similarity of the orderings of the data ranked by two quantities. We find that all the models obtain a positive τ. The correlation coefficient measures the dependence between two variables. Except for p_{00} in CMM without prior, all the estimated parameters have a relatively high correlation coefficient with the ground truth, especially for the models with prior. For the accuracy model with prior $\alpha = 2, \beta = 2$, which is the best performing model in relevance estimation, the estimated parameter a_u obtains the largest τ and correlation coefficient with the ground truth among all the models. MAE and RMSE reflect the distance of the absolute values. It is not surprising to find that for a_u and p_{11}, the models with prior have larger MAE and RMSE than the models without prior, which is not consistent with the result of τ and correlation. One explanation is that adding prior helps the models do better with the relative order of the estimate parameters rather than the absolute value, which we care more in the evaluation. We notice that the result of p_{00} in Table 3 is quite noisy. After investigation, we find that the number of users who have ground truth calculated for p_{00} is much smaller than that for a_u and p_{11} (i.e. the relevant query-document pairs in L are more accessed than the irrelevant pairs by users).

Since the calculated ground truth of expertise for individual users can be noisy due to the lack of data. We now evaluate the expertise of user groups. In this evaluation, we first divide users into ten user groups according to estimated expertise in descending order such that each user group has the same number of users. Then we treat each user group as a single unit and compute its ground truth of expertise on set L. As a user group is supposed to have sufficient amount of data, the calculated ground truth is more reliable than that calculated for individual users. Figure 2 shows the performance of different user groups.

From Figure 2(a) we see that for the accuracy model with prior, the ground truth of a_u strictly decreases as the group number increases. It indicates that the estimated a_u is very effective in ordering the users such that the group expertise reflects the ground truth very well. If we let the estimated expertise of user group i be $(1 - i/10)$, the

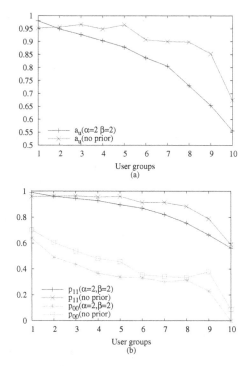

Fig. 2. The ground truth of expertise for different user groups. (a) shows the ground truth of a_u in the accuracy model. (b) shows the ground truth of p_{11} and p_{00} in the confusion matrix model. Smaller group number indicates higher estimated expertise.

group level correlation coefficient between the estimated expertise and the ground truth reaches as high as 0.949, which is much higher than the values reported in Table 3 for individual users. And the Kendall's τ even reaches the optimal value 1, which means perfect ranking for the user groups. This result validates the effectiveness of estimated expertise in the accuracy model. For the confusion matrix model with prior, we also observe the similar trend for p_{11} in Figure 2(b); the trend for p_{00} is basically consistent but not as clear as that of p_{11}. It indicates that the estimated p_{00} in the confusion matrix model does not reflect the ground truth well as p_{11}. And this may be the reason that the confusion matrix model failed to outperform the accuracy model in relevance estimation. In Figure 2, we also plot the result for the models without prior, which shows more inconsistency and weaker correlation with the ground truth. This fact again verifies the advantage of using prior in our models.

To conclude, we find that the accuracy model with beta prior achieves the best performance in inferring relevance and user expertise. It implies that the assumption of the accuracy model is more suitable to the real situation. We also find that the estimated expertise can better reflect the ground truth when used in level of user groups.

6   Conclusion and Future Work

Clicks from different search users in Web search are not equally informative in indicating relevance. Search experts are supposed to be more likely to find relevant documents than the others so their clicks are more reliable in inferring relevance. In this paper, we propose two probabilistic modelings for users' search expertise which are inspired by the evaluation metrics of classification. The experimental results on a real-world click-through data show that our models are effective in estimating both the relevance and the user expertise. Our best performing model improves the baseline by 10% in inferring relevance preference pairs. And the estimated expertise is highly consistent with the ground truth, especially when used in group level. The user expertise information can be useful in helping the search engine improve personal search experience, which is the direction of our future work.

References

1. Agichtein, E., Brill, E., Dumais, S.: Improving web search ranking by incorporating user behavior information. In: Proceedings of SIGIR 2006, pp. 19–26 (2006)
2. Chapelle, O., Zhang, Y.: A dynamic bayesian network click model for web search ranking. In: Proceedings of WWW 2009, pp. 1–10 (2009)
3. Chen, W., Wang, D., Zhang, Y., Chen, Z., Singla, A., Yang, Q.: A noise-aware click model for web search. In: Proceedings of WSDM 2012, pp. 313–322 (2012)
4. Craswell, N., Zoeter, O., Taylor, M., Ramsey, B.: An experimental comparison of click position-bias models. In: Proceedings of WSDM 2008 (2008)
5. Dupret, G., Piwowarski, B.: A user browsing model to predict search engine click data from past observations. In: Proceedings of SIGIR 2008 (2008)
6. Guo, F., Liu, C., Kannan, A., Minka, T., Taylor, M., Wang, Y., Faloutsos, C.: Click chain model in web search. In: Proceedings of WWW 2009, pp. 11–20 (2009)
7. Guo, F., Liu, C., Wang, Y.: Efficient multiple-click models in web search. In: Proceedings of WSDM 2009, pp. 124–131 (2009)
8. Joachims, T., Granka, L., Pan, B., Hembrooke, H., Gay, G.: Accurately interpreting click-through data as implicit feedback. In: Proceedings of SIGIR 2005 (2005)
9. Kendall, M.G.: A new measure of rank correlation. Biometrika 30(1/2), 81–93 (1938)
10. Shen, S., Hu, B., Chen, W., Yang, Q.: Personalized click model through collaborative filtering. In: Proceedings of WSDM 2012 (2012)
11. Wang, H., Zhai, C., Dong, A., Chang, Y.: Content-aware click modeling. In: Proceedings of the 22nd international conference on World Wide Web, WWW 2013, Republic and Canton of Geneva, Switzerland, pp. 1365–1376. International World Wide Web Conferences Steering Committee (2013)
12. White, R., Morris, D.: Investigating the querying and browsing behavior of advanced search engine users. In: Proceedings of SIGIR 2007, pp. 255–262 (2007)
13. White, R.W., Drucker, S.M.: Investigating behavioral variability in web search. In: Proceedings of WWW 2007, pp. 21–30 (2007)
14. White, R.W., Dumais, S.T., Teevan, J.: Characterizing the influence of domain expertise on web search behavior. In: Proceedings of WSDM 2009, pp. 132–141 (2009)

Understanding and Exploiting User's Navigational Intent in Community Question Answering

Long Chen, Dell Zhang, and Mark Levene

DCSIS, Birkbeck, University of London
Malet Street, London WC1E 7HX, UK
long@dcs.bbk.ac.uk, dell.z@ieee.org, mark@dcs.bbk.ac.uk

Abstract. Verbose or colloquial queries take up a small but non-negligible proportion in the modern searching paradigms, and are commonly used in other platforms such as Community Question Answering (CQA), where answerers often include URLs as part of answers to provide further information. To begin with, we define questions resolved (or largely explained) by the linked web pages (i.e., in the corresponding answers) as navigational question, which are simulated as verbose queries to evaluate the performance of search engines (i.e., by considering the associated linked web pages as relevant documents). Then we experiment with the process of identifying new navigational questions from CQA, from which we demonstrate that navigational intent detection can be effectively automated by using textual features and a set of metadata features. Lastly, to effectively identify relevant navigational questions, we present a hybrid approach which blends several language modelling techniques, namely, the classic (query-likelihood) language model, the state-of-the-art translation-based language model, and our proposed intent-based language model. Our experiments on two real-world datasets show that the proposed mixture language model leads to a significant performance boost compared to that of the state-of-the-art language modelling approach.

Keywords: Navigational Intent, Search Engine, Query Refinement, Community Question Answering, Language Model.

1   Introduction

A vast majority of queries in search engine are short ones. For example, the average query length of MSN search is 2.4 words [6]. However, there are also a non-negligible proportion of long queries — about 10% of queries are 5 words or longer [6]. Current search engines present convincing performance over short keywords queries but usually fail to handle verbose or colloquial queries competently [8].

On the other hand, verbose queries can be found in Community Question Answering services (CQA), which has been proven as an amenable form to social media for allowing anyone in the community to ask and answer questions

R.E. Banchs et al. (Eds.): AIRS 2013, LNCS 8281, pp. 392–403, 2013.

in natural language. It is difficult to encourage users to answer unattractive questions in CQA, especially for those information-driven ones, since answering informational questions requires certain in-depth knowledge that only a small proportion of the population have the capacity of resolving it. Enabling search engines to answer verbose queries efficiently and effectively can thus remove the needs of submitting navigational questions to CQA services.

In this paper, we endeavor to address the following three questions:

- *What's the performance for current search engines in handling navigational questions?*
- *Can we identify navigational question from CQA services automatically?*
- *Given a navigational question from CQA, how can we identify the most relevant questions from the CQA repository?*

We define questions resolved (or largely explained) by the linked web pages (i.e., in the corresponding answers) as navigational question, which are simulated as verbose queries for evaluating search engine performance. The rationale is that queries from CQA services are less artificial when compared with TREC QA queries and less constraint when compared to search queries, where users are prone to generate queries in a simple keyword style. However, due to the inhomogeneous nature of the CQA services, questions cannot be treated as navigational questions straight away. For example, as revealed by Chen [5], that 43% of questions in CQA are subjective intent and 10.2% are social intent. To solve this problem, Huston et al. [8] use a method in which they consider queries from certain categories as verbose queries, which is then submitted to search engines. This method is effective in filtering short web-style queries, however, it may fail to remove the question with subjective (sentiment-based) opinions or social interactions intent. In this paper, we use the dichotomy of navigational vs. non-navigational, in which navigational questions can be resolved by (or at least largely explained by) web information while non-navigational questions usually require participants in the community to answer manually.

Automatically identifying navigational intent of a new question is not an easy task since it is hard to recognize navigational intent by textual features. For example, the question "Can anybody recommend decent free music creation software?" with a survey style seems to be a transactional intent , but it is actually a navigational question with the best answer like "Hyrogen is ok, http://www.hydrogen-music.org." This implies that navigational intent is not always easy to be inferred solely based on textual features. Rather, metadata features, such as asker's asking experience or the category from which the question corresponds to, is crucial for the intent deduction. Thus we build a predictive model through machine learning based on both text and metadata features.

The rest of this paper is organised as follows. In Section 2, we review the related work. In Section 3, we evaluate the performance of current search engines for handling verbose queries. In Section 4, we investigate the usefulness of text and metadata features for identifying the user intent of questions. In Section 6, we make conclusions and discuss the future work.

2   Related Work

This paper is related to a series of techniques, spanning from search evaluation, question classification to retrieval models.

The current search engines have been evaluated in various ways. Liu [1] assesses the effectiveness of Google, Bing, and Blekko by surveying 35 undergraduate students in Computer Science, from which he concludes that Google and Bing share a comparable performance in 2011. Liu et al. [12] provide a comprehensive study on predicting user satisfaction in CQAs and discuss how to evaluate it through machine learning. The work most similar to ours is [8] in which Huston et al. use Yahoo! Answers questions to evaluate search engine performance with Yahoo! API and Bing API respectively, and they find Bing is slightly better than Yahoo in 2011. Our approach is somewhat similar to these works but instead of evaluating relevance documents with human judgment, we propose to automate the evaluation process by matching between the associated URLs in the answers and the search engine results. It may be not as accurate as human judges — since not all the associated URLs are good answers, and since large amount of relevant web pages may be omitted. But our approach wins by sheer weight of numbers (especially when we can obtain virtually unlimited number of questions from CQA sites), which cancels out the side-effects of the incomplete judgment.

With regard to the task of navigational intent identification, Broder's seminal work [2] puts the intent of web search queries into three categories: informational, navigational, and transactional. Uichin et al. [11], later on, proposed a framework to automate the process of navigational intent identification in web search, in which *user-click behavior* and *anchor-link distribution* features are found to be useful for detecting navigational intent. Sadikov et al. [16] model user's navigational intent by clustering document click and session co-occurrence information. However, all these taxonomies cannot be directly applied to CQA due to the different expectations within people's mind-sets: in CQA users normally ask natural language questions which are addressed to human beings, whereas in Web search users submit keyword queries which are addressed to automated search engines. To the best of our knowledge, this is the first work which attempts to understand user's navigational intent in CQA.

3   Search Engines Evaluation

Google is arguably the most powerful search engine in the world, and Bing has been rising up enormously recently, both of which are proven to be viable searching paradigms. Which one is a better choice is still one of the most controversial topics in the IR community. In light of this, we conduct a experiment which test search engine's ability to answer navigational questions of Yahoo! Answers.

3.1   Setup

Vast amount of navigational questions (see Section 1) are available on CQA services. Indeed, in 2005, 11.5% of questions in Yahoo! Answers have at least

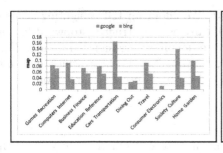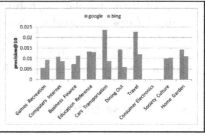

Fig. 1. The performance comparison between Bing and Google for dealing with verbose questions over top 10 yahoo navigational categories

one URL in one of the answers and 5.5% of questions include at least one URLs in the corresponding best answer. Users cannot access the linked page themselves either because they don't have the necessary search optimization skill or they prefer communicating with people rather than the texts produced by search engines.

The following examples illustrate navigational questions that askers currently post in Yahoo! Answers:

- **Navigational:** What is the best free online photography portfolio website? *I want to get into photography. is there a free online portfolio that prevents people from being able to right click and save the pictures?*
- **Non-navigational:** How much should you tip a pizza delivery man?

The search engine evaluation experiment is derived from a dataset crawled by ourselves, which is collected from Yahoo! Answers [1] dating from 2013/03/15 to 2013/04/01, contains a total of 54483 questions (note that after data cleansing, this is only a subset and cannot cover all the questions during that period of time). We adopt this dataset for the search engine evaluation task because they are collected fairly new and should have been well indexed by both Google and Bing. There are 5747 navigational questions in this dataset, from which 3752 ones are from top 10 categories which are then simulated as testing data to evaluate search engines.

Google API [2]and Bing API [3] are employed for evaluation because we noticed that "black box" approach has been extensively used in many recent works [7,8] and is becoming more and more important for commercial purposes.

3.2 Stopword Removal

There are many stopword lists available in the IR community, but we chose to create a new stopword list since the language that used in the test questions is

---

[1] http://answers.yahoo.com/
[2] https://developers.google.com/web-search/
[3] http://datamarket.azure.com/dataset/bing/search

more noisy than the regular English text. We adopt an IDF-weighting scheme to the Yahoo! Answers repository. Specifically, we construct a stopword list by taking the top 100 words from the inverse document frequency ranking. This process identified words such as "help", "anyone," and "what" which may not appear in the standard stopword list, but are usually useless search words.

3.3 Noun Phrase Detection

Learning from the previous work that noun phrases from the query can help identify the key concepts within the query, we used the Standford parser toolkit [10,15] to automatically extract those potential noun phrases. Considering that we are using a search engine as a black box, the usage of the noun phrase technique is restrictive from the query: it is impossible to assign weights to terms in terms of condence or priority. There are many ways to enable the search engine to communicate with the extracted noun phrases, we report two such methods:

- The first method put each of the extracted noun phrases in the query in quotation marks, removing no words in the query.
- The second method only keep the extracted noun phrases and quotation marks are not used.

For example, 2 noun phrases: "the website" and "American eagle" are detected in the query:
"what is the website for American eagle?"
Using the first method, we would generate the query:
what is "the website" for "American eagle"?
Using the second method, we would generate the query:
"the website" "American eagle"

3.4 Search Results

The retrieval performances, measured by *Precision at 10* (P@10) [13] and *Mean Average Precision* (MAP) [13], are reported in Table 1 and Figure 1. *For relevance judgement, only URLs appeared in the answers are regarded as relevant web pages.* Note that we employ MAP instead of MRR (Mean reciprocal rank) because there are often several URLs appear in the answers such that the number of relevant web pages is usually uncertain. Even though the relevance judgments for the verbose queries are incomplete and the absolute retrieval performance is relatively low (which is expected because of the sparseness of the relevance judgment), our approach is probably more reasonable to traditional ones — it has been demonstrated by Carterette [3,4] that evaluation over more queries with fewer or noisier judgments is preferable to evaluation over fewer queries with more judgments. The large number of the testing data compensates for the incompleteness of the judgment. Another concern is that the searching results may be time-sensitive since most search engines are regularly updated on a hourly basis. In order to reduce this risk, we submitted all queries of the above approaches to search engines within a short time session, spanning from 26/03/2013 to 30/03/2013. One should also note that search engines often return the Yahoo! Answers original web pages, which are removed from the results to allow an impartial judgment.

Table 1. Summary of the search engines evaluation for dealing with verbose queries (statistical significance using Paired t-tests were performed between each result shown and the Original: ** indicates p-value < 0.01 while * indicates p-value < 0.05).

	Google API		Bing API	
	map	precision@10	map	precision@10
original	0.0687	0.0112	0.0452	0.0101
stopwords removal	0.071*	0.0124*	0.0467*	**0.0115****
quoted noun phrases	0.0457	0.0089	0.0372	0.0075
only noun phrases	0.0715*	**0.012****	0.0475*	0.011*
quoted noun phrases - stopwords	0.0472	0.0109	0.0412	0.0083
only noun phrases - stopwords	**0.0732****	**0.013****	**0.0476****	**0.0114****

Table 1 reports the retrieval results for all of the query processing techniques when applied to Yahoo! Answer testing data using the Google and Bing search engines. The results from the two search engines are very similar in terms of precision@10; when it comes to *MAP(Mean Average Precision)*, however, Google overwhelms Bing with almost 50% improvement. This suggest that Google and Bing have a comparable ability to capture the desired documents, but Google is superior to Bing when ranking user's desired documents. Also the use of quotations of the noun phrases(method one) for the query reformulation is clearly not effective. But both noun phrase(method two) and stopword removal produce significant improvements. The most effective technique, however, is the combination of the above two.

Some users may be curious about which search engine advances in which topics (especially for those working in advertisement industry such that people can strategize their investment more smartly). For that reason, we also present a separate performance comparison under each top 10 Yahoo! Answers navigational categories. Although most of the categories share a comparable performance in Figure 1, it is clear that Google excels in *Car Transportation, Travel,* and *Home Gardens* categories, whereas Bing can hardly beat Google for any categories (some categories show inconsistent results over *precision@10* and *MAP*, such as *Bossiness Finance*).

4   Question Classification

To address the task of navigational question prediction in CQA, a variety of personal information and social relationship features are collected and exploited to model users' social behaviors behind their search intent.

4.1   Setup

The classification experiment is based on Yahoo! Answers dataset which is derived from Yahoo! Answers Comprehensive Questions and Answers (v1.0), a dataset kindly provided by Yahoo Research Group [4]. It consists of 4483032 questions and respect answers from 2005/01/01 to 2006/01/01. We use this dataset for question classification task since there is a rich metadata features set available for understanding user's asking behaviors.

4.2   Classification Performance Measure

Since the class sizes are imbalanced in this problem, we use the F_1 score [13] instead of accuracy to measure the performance of question classification. The F_1 score is the harmonic mean of precision P and recall R: $F_1 = \frac{2PR}{P+R}$, where $P = \frac{\text{true positive}}{\text{true positive + false positive}}$, $R = \frac{\text{true positive}}{\text{true positive + false negative}}$. Note that there are two versions of F_1 score namely, micro-averaged F_1 (miF_1) and macro-averaged F_1 (maF_1) [5]. The former carries out averaging over all test questions while the latter over all question categories, therefore the former is dominated by performance on major question categories while the latter treats all question categories equally. The results reported in the next section are all predicated on (maF_1).

4.3   Classification Results

We use the SVM implemented by Platt et al. [14] with a probabilistic output and adopt a linear kernel in this task — we find that linear kernel generally outperform non-linear ones. We use 5-fold cross-validation to get a good value of C and ξ: Choosing C with the range of $0.01 < C < 0.1$ is good for all configurations across different datasets; Similarly, ξ between 1×10^{-8} to 1×10^{-16} gives a good performance. The parameters used in our experiment is $C = 0.5$ and $\xi = 1\times10^{-12}$. The parameter for the class weights is set as *navigational* : *non − navigational* $= 0.9 : 0.1$ since the classification task is an imbalance problem in nature.

Table 2 depicts the performance (maF_1) of [binary] question classification through supervised learning (linear SVM) with different sets of features, by using 10-cross validation. It's quite surprising to us that metadata features are even more important than textual features by giving insight of user's asking behaviors.

---

[4] http://webscope.sandbox.yahoo.com/

Table 2. The performance of supervised learning with different sets of features

features	non-navigational	navigational
text	0.873	0.363
metadata	0.934	0.883
text+metadata	0.936	0.893

However, the mixture classifier with both text features and metadata features works better than textual features classifier or metadata features classifier alone that only looks at one perspective of the user intent.

5 Question Retrieval

Given a question is navigational intent, we experimented with various language modelling techniques for question retrieval. The following language models are incorporated into our framework:

5.1 Classic Language Model

Using the classic (query-likelihood) language model [18] for information retrieval, we can measure the relevance of an archive question d with respect to the query question q as:

$$P_{cla}(q|d) = \prod_{w \in q} P_{cla}(w|d) \tag{1}$$

assuming that each term w in the query q is generated independently by the unigram model of document d. The probabilities $P_{cla}(w|d)$ are estimated from the bag of words in document d with Dirichlet prior smoothing.

5.2 Translation-Based Language Model

It has been demonstrated that the lexical gaps between a query question and archive questions could be addressed by the translation-based language model [9,17]:

$$P_{tra}(q|d) = \prod_{w \in q} P_{tra}(w|d) \tag{2}$$

$$P_{tra}(w|d) = \sum_{t \in d} P(w|t)P(t|d) \tag{3}$$

where $P(w|t)$ represents the probability of a document term t being translated into a query term w. As in [17], we estimate such word-to-word translation probabilities $P(w|t)$ on a parallel corpus that consists of 200,000 archived question-answer pairs from Yahoo! Answers.

5.3   Intent-Based Language Model

We propose to take user intent into account for question retrieval in the language modelling framework:

$$P_{int}(q|d) = \prod_{w \in q} P_{int}(w|d) \tag{4}$$

$$P_{int}(w|d) = \sum_{k=1}^{N} P(w|C_k)P(C_k|d) \tag{5}$$

where C_k represents a category, $P(w|C_k)$ is its corresponding unigram language model 5.3 and $P(C_k|d)$ is the probability that the document d belongs to that category (see Section 4).

Estimating Unigram Models for User Intent. Given the probabilistic classification results on all archive questions, we can obtain the unigram language model for each user intent category C_k through maximum-likelihood estimation:

$$P(w|C_k) = \frac{\sum_{d \in C_k} tf(w,d)P(C_k|d)}{\sum_{w' \in d} \sum_{d \in C_k} tf(w',d)P(C_k|d)} \tag{6}$$

where $tf(w,d)$ is the term frequency of word w in document d. It is possible to employ more advanced estimation methods, which is left for future work.

5.4   Mixture Model

To exploit evidences from different perspectives for question retrieval, we can mix the above language models via linear combination:

$$P_{mix}(q|d) = \alpha P_{cla}(q|d) + \beta P_{tra}(q|d) + \gamma P_{cat}(q|d) \tag{7}$$

where α, β, and γ are three non-negative weight parameters satisfying $\alpha + \beta + \gamma = 1$. When $\gamma = 0$, the complete mixture model backs off to the current state-of-the-art approach, i.e., the combination of the classic language model and the translation-based language model only [17].

5.5   Experimental Setup

We conducted question retrieval experiments on two real-world CQA datasets. The first dataset, YA, comes from Yahoo! Answers. It is part of Yahoo! Labs' Webscope[5] L6 dataset that consists of 4,483,032 questions with their answers from 2005-01-01 to 2006-01-01. The second dataset, WA, comes from WikiAnswers. It contains 824,320 questions with their answers collected from WikiAnswers[6] from 2012-01-01 to 2012-05-01.

---

[5] http://webscope.sandbox.yahoo.com/
[6] http://wiki.answers.com/

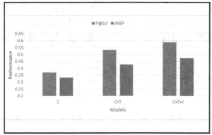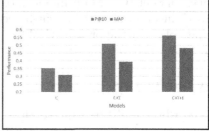

Fig. 2. The experimental results on Yahoo! Answers (left) and WikiAnswers (right) respectively

Table 3. The model parameters for different question retrieval approaches

	C	C+T	C+T+I
α	1	0.3	0.18
β	0	0.7	0.42
γ	0	0.0	0.40

We experimented with question retrieval using a similar set-up as in [17]: 50 questions were randomly sampled from the YA and WA datasets respectively for testing (which were excluded from the CQA retrieval repositories to ensure the impartiality of the evaluation), and the top archive questions (i.e., search results) returned for each test query question were manually labelled as either relevant or not.

5.6 Experimental Results

In order to see whether intent relevance can improve the search performance, we compared the following three approaches:

- the baseline approach which only employs the classic language model (C);
- the state-of-the-art approach which combines the classic language model and the translation-based language model (C+T) [17];
- the proposed hybrid approach which blends the classic language model, the translation-based language model, and the Intent-based language model (C+T+I).

The model parameters were tuned on the training data to achieve optimal results, as shown in Table 3. In the mixture models (C+T) and (C+T+I), the ratio between parameter values α and β was same as that in [17].

In accordance with the observation in [17], adding the translation-based language model (C+T) brings substantial performance improvement to the classic language model (C). More importantly, it is clear that our proposed hybrid approach incorporating the intent-based language model (C+T+I) outperforms the state-of-the-art approach (C+T) significantly, according to both P@10 and MAP on YA and WA.

6   Conclusions

The contribution of this paper is three fold. First, this is the first work which attempts to understand user's navigational intent in CQA — to the best of our knowledge. Second, we propose a novel evaluating method which automates the verbose query evaluation process by matching between the associated URLs in the answers (of the navigational question) and the search engine results. The current best search engines, namely Google and Bing, are evaluated with navigational questions (act as verbose queries), from which we show that Google is still the best search engine. In addition, we find that the best way of query refinement for the current search engines is to combine both noun phrase(method two) and stopword removal techniques. Third, we present a intent-based language model which supersedes that of the existing category-based language model, since one question can belong to multiple (user intent) categories to different degrees, and since a probabilistic question classifier is built automatically by taking into consideration of both textual features and metadata features.

For future work will answer what's the best way for query refinement in search engine(query expansion or query reduction), for which this work is the foundation for future research of utilizing phrases/concepts detection techniques for query expansion.

References

1. Bing, L.: User personal evaluation of search engines,
   http://www.cs.uic.edu/~liub/searchEval/
   Search-Engine-Evaluation-2011.pdf
2. Broder, A.: A taxonomy of web search. SIGIR Forum 36, 3–10 (2002)
3. Carterette, B., Pavlu, V., Kanoulas, E., Aslam, J.A., Allan, J.: Evaluation over thousands of queries. In: Proceedings of the 31st Annual International ACM SIGIR Conference on Research and Development in Information Retrieval, SIGIR 2008, pp. 651–658. ACM, New York (2008)
4. Carterette, B., Smucker, M.D.: Hypothesis testing with incomplete relevance judgments. In: Proceedings of the Sixteenth ACM Conference on Information and Knowledge Management, CIKM 2007, pp. 643–652. ACM, New York (2007)
5. Chen, L., Zhang, D., Levene, M.: Understanding user intent in community question answering. In: Proceedings of the 21st International Conference Companion on World Wide Web, WWW 2012 Companion, pp. 823–828. ACM, New York (2012)
6. Elsayed, T.M.: Identity resolution in email collections. PhD thesis, College Park, MD, USA, AAI3372840 (2009)
7. Guo, J., Xu, G., Li, H., Cheng, X.: A unified and discriminative model for query refinement. In: Proceedings of the 31st Annual International ACM SIGIR Conference on Research and Development in Information Retrieval (SIGIR), pp. 379–386 (2008)

8. Huston, S., Croft, W.B.: Evaluating verbose query processing techniques. In: Proceedings of the 33rd International ACM SIGIR Conference on Research and Development in Information Retrieval, SIGIR 2010, pp. 291–298 (2010)
9. Jeon, J., Croft, W.B., Lee, J.H.: Finding similar questions in large question and answer archives. In: Proceedings of the 14th ACM International Conference on Information and Knowledge Management (CIKM), Bremen, Germany, pp. 84–90 (2005)
10. Klein, D., Manning, C.D.: Accurate unlexicalized parsing. In: Proceedings of the 41st Annual Meeting on Association for Computational Linguistics, ACL 2003, vol. 1, pp. 423–430. Association for Computational Linguistics, Stroudsburg (2003)
11. Lee, U., Liu, Z., Cho, J.: Automatic identification of user goals in web search. In: Proceedings of the 14th International Conference on World Wide Web, WWW 2005, pp. 391–400. ACM, New York (2005)
12. Liu, Y., Bian, J., Agichtein, E.: Predicting information seeker satisfaction in community question answering. In: Proceedings of the 31st Annual International ACM SIGIR Conference on Research and Development in Information Retrieval, SIGIR 2008, pp. 483–490. ACM, New York (2008)
13. Manning, C.D., Raghavan, P., Schtze, H.: Introduction to Information Retrieval. Cambridge University Press (2008)
14. Platt, J.C.: Probabilistic outputs for support vector machines and comparisons to regularized likelihood methods. In: Advances in Large Margin Classifiers, pp. 61–74. MIT Press (1999)
15. Rafferty, A.N., Manning, C.D.: Parsing three german treebanks: lexicalized and unlexicalized baselines. In: Proceedings of the Workshop on Parsing German, PaGe 2008, pp. 40–46. Association for Computational Linguistics, Stroudsburg (2008)
16. Sadikov, E., Madhavan, J., Wang, L., Halevy, A.: Clustering query refinements by user intent. In: Proceedings of the 19th International Conference on World Wide Web, WWW 2010, pp. 841–850. ACM, New York (2010)
17. Xue, X., Jeon, J., Croft, W.B.: Retrieval models for question and answer archives. In: Proceedings of the 31st Annual International ACM SIGIR Conference on Research and Development in Information Retrieval (SIGIR), Singapore, pp. 475–482 (2008)
18. Zhai, C.: Statistical language models for information retrieval a critical review. Found. Trends Inf. Retr. 2(3), 137–213 (2008)

Are Most-Viewed News Articles Most-Shared?

Yangjie Yao and Aixin Sun

School of Computer Engineering
Nanyang Technological University, Singapore
{yyao002,axsun}@ntu.edu.sg

Abstract. Despite many users get timely information through various social media platforms, news websites remain important mainstream media for high-quality news articles and comprehensive news coverage. Moreover, news websites are becoming well connected with the social media platform by enabling one-click sharing, allowing readers to comment on the articles, and pushing news update to social media through dedicated accounts. In this paper, we make the first step to analyze user behavior for news viewing, news commenting, and news sharing. Specifically, we focus on the sets of most-viewed, most-shared, and most-commented news published by a major news agency for about two months. Through topic modeling and named entity analysis, we observe that economy news is more likely to be shared and sports news is less likely to be shared or commented. News about health has higher chance of being shared, but does not attract large number of comments. Lastly, users are more likely to comment on than to share politics news.

Keywords: User behavior, News sharing, News commenting, News viewing, Popular news.

1 Introduction

The popularity of social networking platforms (*e.g.*, Twitter and Facebook) is redefining the roles of information provider and information consumer and changing the way people access and receive information online. On the one hand, more users receive information pushed by other users through social platforms, which potentially reduces the number of direct visits to news websites. On the other hand, news websites remain important mainstream media for providing high-quality news articles written by professionals and offering comprehensive news coverage.

To be better connected with users and attract more visits, most news websites facilitate social interactions among their readers in at least three forms. One form of social interaction is to enable user discussion through comments to the news articles. Comments received from readers are maintained by the news websites and are often presented together with the news articles to the next readers [6]. Another form of social interaction is to minimize the effort for users to share a news article to her social networks. Many news websites provide a list of buttons; sharing a news article to Facebook, Twitter or other social networks

R.E. Banchs et al. (Eds.): AIRS 2013, LNCS 8281, pp. 404–415, 2013.
© Springer-Verlag Berlin Heidelberg 2013

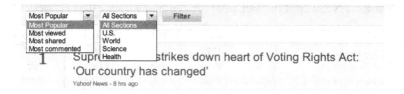

Fig. 1. The 4 categories and the 5 sections in most popular headlines

becomes a single click of a button. The last form of social interaction is to directly push news articles to the social networks through the news providers' accounts registered with the social networks. It is observed that mass media accounts (*e.g.,* CNN Breaking News, the New York Times, TIME) gain large followership in Twitter [9]. The link (often with a short description) of a news article then reaches more users in a social network though user re-sharing. The next question is: to what extent the user commenting and sharing mechanism influence news article viewership?

In this paper, we take the very first step and report a preliminary study on the most-popular news articles from a major news provider and try to answer the following questions: (i) are the most-viewed news articles most-shared, and vice versa? and (ii) are the most-viewed news articles most-commented, and vice versa? The answers to the above questions would help the news providers to better understand users' news reading behavior, so as to improve the effectiveness of news delivery to users through all possible channels including social platforms and news personalization or recommendation [4, 11, 12].

In the following, we first present the data collected for this study and then report the analysis based on topic modeling and named entity extraction.

2   Dataset

We collected the most-popular headlines published by Yahoo! News[1] for about two months from 15 April 2013 to 13 June 2013. Illustrated in Figure 1, the popular news headlines are categorized into most-popular, most-viewed, most-shared, and most-commented, for five sections: All, U.S., World, Science, and Health. For each kind of popular news (*e.g.,* most-viewed) in each section, maximum 100 news headlines are listed. We crawled the popular headlines and the full content of the news articles on daily basis at a fixed time. The number of distinct news articles collected for most-viewed/-commented/-shared in each section is listed in Table 1. We do not include the category "most-popular" in our following study because the meaning of popular here is not clearly defined. Observe from Table 1, the number of news falling under Health and Science sections is much smaller compared to the other three sections probably due to topic specificity.

---

[1] http://news.yahoo.com/popular/. Accessed on 20 June 2013.

Table 1. Number of distinct news articles under each category/section

Category	All	World	U.S.	Health	Science
Most-viewed	5472	4772	4901	1259	1435
Most-commented	5526	4897	4843	1188	1420
Most-shared	5034	4708	4503	1222	1403

Table 2. The conditional probability of news being most-viewed/-commented/-shared

Category	All	World	U.S.	Health	Science
$P(\text{most-viewed}\vert\text{most-commented})$	0.67	0.86	0.84	0.98	0.97
$P(\text{most-commented}\vert\text{most-viewed})$	0.68	0.89	0.83	0.92	0.96
$P(\text{most-viewed}\vert\text{most-shared})$	0.69	0.82	0.84	0.98	0.98
$P(\text{most-shared}\vert\text{most-viewed})$	0.63	0.81	0.75	0.95	0.96

The first row in Table 2 reports the conditional probability of a news article being most-viewed provided it is one of the most-commented articles in one of the five sections. Similarly, the conditional probabilities of being most-commented/most-shared are reported in the table. Observe that, the conditional probabilities reported under the Health and Science sections are above 90%. That is, for a news article, reporting a new finding in Health or Science area, if it is one of the most-viewed, very likely, it is one of the most-commented and the most-shared, and vice versa. One possible reason is that Health and Science are relatively topic-specific and the news articles are often about advices or new findings in these two areas with good support from scientific studies. Most users are not experts in Health or Science. Thus users have common background or common context in understanding the news. In other words, users' self-interests and inter-subjective interests[2] are likely to be the same.

For news articles falling under World and U.S. sections, the conditional probabilities are mostly over 80%. Under All section, the chance of a news article being most-viewed is below 70% even if it is one of the most-shared or most-commented article. That is, for a news article under this section, a good number of users read the article but do not share or comment it. A most-shared article in this section may not attract enough viewership to make it one of the most-viewed article. Compared with World and U.S., news articles in All section cover all happenings worldwide and cover various diverse topics. The diverse topics may affect users' behavior in viewing, commenting, and sharing the news articles. We therefore conduct our analysis mainly on the news articles in All section.

3   Analysis

We now analyze the news articles under All section and try to understand why not all most-viewed articles are not among most-shared/-commented or the most-shared/-commented articles are not among the most viewed. To begin with, we make the following assumptions.

---

[2] Inter-subjective interest refers to one user's prediction of other users' interest.

- A news article's viewership consists of two groups of users: (i) users who discover the URL by themselves (*e.g.*, visiting the news website, news search), and (ii) users who click the URL from their social networks' feeds (*i.e.*, the URL is shared in the social networks).
- After reading a news article, a user may: (i) leave a comment on the news website, (ii) share the link in her social network with her description/comment of the link, and (iii) leave the page without commenting or sharing.
- Because we cannot access the exact number of views, number of shares, and number of comments each news article receives, all our analysis will be based on relative ranking. For example, if news article a_v is listed under most-viewed but not most-commented, and news article a_c is listed under most-commented but not most-viewed, we assume that a_v receives more views than a_c, and a_c receives more comments than a_v.

Let V, S, and C be the sets of news articles that are most-viewed, most-shared, and most-commented, respectively, in the All section. Next we perform topic modeling to analyze the topic distributions of the documents in All section.

3.1 Analysis by Topic Modeling

Topic modeling has demonstrated promising results in understanding the topic distribution of documents as well as in many prediction tasks [2]. Here, we are interested in finding out whether the topics of the news articles influence the viewing, commenting, and sharing behavior. More specifically, we are more interested in finding the topics for which the news articles are most-viewed but are less likely to be most-shared (or -commented), or the news articles are most-shared (or -commented) but are less likely to be most-viewed.

We adopt latent Dirichlet allocation (LDA) in our analysis. In LDA, a document in the collection is a distribution over a set of topics, and each topic is a probabilistic distribution over words. Given all the most-viewed/-shared/-commented documents in All section, we applied standard LDA model with following parameter setting: number of topics is set to 100^3, the Dirichlet prior on the per-document topic distribution $\alpha = 0.5$, the Dirichlet prior on the per-topic word distribution $\beta = 0.01$, the number of iteration is 1000.

Viewing vs Sharing. With the result of topic modeling, each news article has a distribution over the 100 topics inferred from the news collection. For easy analysis, we assign each news article one topic (*i.e.*, the topic with the highest probability among the 100 topics for this news article)[4]. With the topic assignment, we get the number of documents for each topic in the set V (most-viewed news articles) and in the set S (most-shared news articles) respectively.

---

[3] Similar results were observed by setting the number of topics to 50 or 200 in our experiments.

[4] We have also conducted analysis by assigning multiple topics to each news article weighted by the LDA results and similar results were observed.

Table 3. Topics and user preference of sharing and viewing

R_s	[Topic] and words for topics with higher user preference of sharing than viewing
0.81	[**economy**] company, million, percent, sales, billion, business, year, market, shares, price
0.75	[**economy**] percent, economy, year, market, rate, growth, month, price, job, economic
0.74	[**economy**] bank, europe, germany, eu, government, euro, switzerland, country, financial, greece
0.72	[**health**] study, research, drug, people, risk, health, patient, disease, blood, weight
0.71	[**energy**] oil, energy, gas, plant, water, company, power, industry, environmental, production
0.70	[**unknown**] france, italy, spain, paris, europe, beat, australia, britain, brazil, de
0.67	[**economy/politics**] worker, job, time, employee, union, company, labor, hire, pay, business
0.64	[**health**] restaurant, add, food, calorie, cup, cheese, fat, salt, minutes, pepper
0.63	[**economy/politics**] loan, student, rate, pay, debt, detroit, interest, financial, plan, payment
0.61	[**health**] virus, disease, health, infection, hospital, people, case, antibiotic, patient, infect

R_v	[Topic] and words for topics with higher user preference of viewing than sharing
0.77	[**crime**] castro, women, cleveland, berry, police, house, home, dejesu, knight, kidnap
0.76	[**sports**] final, match, nadal, set, title, champion, win, play, year, open
0.75	[**sports**] wood, shot, hole, garcia, tour, birdie, golf, play, par, putt
0.74	[**celebrity**] jackson, bieber, lohan, justin, virginia, rehab, aeg, lindsay, paris, cuccinelli
0.71	[**sports**] game, team, play, season, miami, james, points, final, nba, player
0.71	[**unknown**] reuter, edit, report, states, united, told, additional, writing, david, washington
0.71	[**celebrity**] dear, abby, husband, married, box, wedding, couple, phillip, mother, wife
0.70	[**politics**] sanford, colbert, carolina, south, busch, weiner, mark, campaign, politics, district
0.69	[**crime**] colorado, holmes, witherspoon, denver, arrest, trooper, driving, police, toth, insanity
0.69	[**crime**] trial, case, sentence, judge, prosecutor, defense, murder, death, prison, jury

For each topic, we then compute its *user preference of sharing*. Let t_s be the number of news articles under topic t in set S, and let t_v be the number of news articles under the same topic in set V. The user preference of sharing for topic t is computed as the ratio $R_s = \frac{t_s}{t_s+t_v}$. The user preference of viewing for the topic t is computed in a similar manner $R_v = \frac{t_v}{t_s+t_v}$. Note that, if a news article is among both most-viewed and most-shared, the news article is counted in both t_s and t_v for its assigned topic t.

Table 3 reports the topics selected by the user preference of sharing and viewing. The upper half of the table lists the topics with higher user sharing preference than viewing ranked by R_s in descending order; the lower half of the table lists the topics of higher user preference of viewing than sharing ranked by R_v in descending order. For each topic, the top-10 most relevant words are listed by their probabilities of belonging to that topic. The topic labels, in boldface in Table 3, are manually assigned based on the topical words and the content of the news articles in the topic. From Table 3, we make the following observations:

- The top-10 topics with higher preference of sharing and the top-10 topics with higher preference of viewing are significantly different.
- Users are more willing to share news articles under topics of economy (5 out of 10) and health (3 out of 10). The economic topics are about employment environment, European economics, and policies related to economic problems including worker rights and student loan.
- Users are less likely to share news articles under topics of sports (3 out of 10), crime (3 out of 10), and celebrity (2 out of 10). News articles under the three sports topics are about tennis match, golf match and NBA match respectively. The three crime cases are widely reported in newspapers.

Usefulness is one of the key motivations users use social networks [10]. A user in a social network therefore carefully selects who to make friend with and/or who to follow so as to receive useful information from the selected friends/followees. On the other hand, to be able to maintain or increase one's social capital [5,7], it is important for a user to provide useful information to her friends or followers. After reading a news article, a user shares this article to her friends/followers if she believes that this piece of information is useful to others. A piece of useful information in a social network feed has the potential to catch attention, attract new friends/followers, or strength social bonding with other users by initiating a conversation. From this point of view, it becomes reasonable that users are more willing to share news articles under topics of health and economy which are perceived to be more relevant to everyone's daily life or have impact to everyone's daily life in short term (*e.g.*, news about worker's right and employment environment).

A user's friends/followers in social networks usually have diverse interests. For example, to users who are not interested in sports, news updates on sports become less relevant or even spam to them. In particular, followee's informativeness is a major factor affecting the decision to unfollow in Twitter [8]. Sports news and crime news, in this sense, might not be useful to most other users in a social network unless in a domain-specific community formed by many users sharing the same interest. Another key issue a user has to consider before sharing a news article in social network is that the action of sharing reveals what she reads to all her friends/followers. Depending on her social status, a user may not share news about celebrity gossips for example.

Viewing vs Commenting. Table 4 lists the top-10 topics with higher user preference for commenting and top-10 topics with higher user preference for viewing respectively, computed in a similar manner as that for Table 3. Note that, the topics listed in the lower parts of Table 3 and 4 are different because the user preference for viewing R_v is computed differently, one is for viewing against sharing (Table 3) and the other is for viewing against commenting (Table 4).

Table 4. Topics and user preference of topic-commenting and topic-viewing

R_c	[Topic] and words for topics with higher user preference of commenting than viewing
0.73	[**politics**] united, states, country, meeting, mexico, talks, president, kerry, plan, amer-ica
0.71	[**politics**] tax, budget, cut, house, spend, bill, billion, government, republican, year
0.70	[**economy**] percent, economy, year, market, rate, growth, month, price, job, eco-nomic
0.70	[**politics**] sanford, colbert, carolina, south, busch, weiner, mark, campaign, politics, district
0.69	[**politics**] state, law, states, federal, bill, group, government, require, policy, pass
0.67	[**politics**] immigrate, bill, immigrant, senate, reform, republican, border, illegal, legislation, house
0.67	[**politics**] israel, iran, palestinian, nuclear, netanyahu, jerusalem, west, state, gaza, arab
0.66	[**politics**] gay, marriage, sex, rights, vote, bill, support, couple, state, lesbian
0.65	[**politics**] obama, president, house, white, bush, barack, administration, washington, america, republican
0.65	[**politics/economy**] loan, student, rate, pay, debt, detroit, interest, financial, plan, payment
R_v	[Topic] and words for topics with higher user preference of viewing than commenting
0.86	[**sports**] final, match, nadal, set, title, champion, win, play, year, open
0.79	[**sports**] wood, shot, hole, garcia, tour, birdie, golf, play, par, putt
0.76	[**science**] solar, moon, sun, space, photo, comet, image, planet, eclipse, earth
0.72	[**disaster**] river, water, flood, rain, snow, inch, people, area, weather, dam
0.71	[**health**] study, research, drug, people, risk, health, patient, disease, blood, weight
0.71	[**health**] restaurant, add, food, calorie, cup, cheese, fat, salt, minutes, pepper
0.71	[**sports**] game, team, play, season, miami, james, points, final, nba, player
0.69	[**science**] scientist, research, light, planet, star, particle, matter, space, earth, galaxy
0.69	[**technology**]apple, google, phone, iphone, device, app, microsoft, user, technology, company
0.67	[**family**] family, mother, children, father, son, daughter, parent, home, year, husband

Observe from Table 4, users have very different preferences for commenting and viewing (but not commenting) news articles. Among the top-10 topics attracted lots of comments, 9 of them are politics. For topics with higher user preference of viewing only, 3 are about sports, 3 are about science and technology, and 2 are about health. The results suggest that users are willing to express themselves through commenting on news articles about political issues (*e.g.,* government administration, tax and budget, immigration, and gay marriage). However, these political issues have less impact to most people's daily life, at least in short term. Different from sharing through social networks, commenting on news articles can be made anonymously and the comments are not pushed to the social network feeds. A user therefore has "more freedom" of expressing her opinion about a news article without the worry about offending some of her friends/followers who may hold different opinions about the political issues. On the other hand, when sharing a news article (*i.e.,* its URL) in her social network, a user usually adds a description or her comments to the article. Such descriptions/comments are push to her friends/followers.

We also observe that many comments are organized into conversations through replying to existing comments. A news article in this case serves as a starting thread of a temporal forum facilitating user discussions. Like in most forums, users participating the discussions are not strongly connected through social relationships.

To summarize the key observations made from Tables 3 and 4 based on topic modeling:

- Sports news often attracts large number of views. However, users are unlikely to share or to comment on news articles about sports compared to news articles of other topics.
- Health news has higher chance of being viewed and shared, but relatively does not attract large number of comments.
- Economy news is more likely to be shared and politics news is the most commented among all news articles users read.

3.2 Analysis by Named Entity

A news article often reports an event involving people, organization, location, and time. In this section, we conduct discriminant analysis based on the named entities recognized from the news articles, to find out the named entities that may attract large number of views, shares, or comments.

We utilized the Stanford NLP package[5] to extract names of people, organizations, and locations, from the news articles. Recall that we use V, S, and C to denote the sets of news articles that are most-viewed, most-shared, and most-commented. We now partition the news articles into 4 groups.

- $V - S$: This is the group of news articles that are among most-viewed articles but not in the most-shared articles. There are 1999 news articles in this group, and 17715 named entities are extracted.
- $S - V$: This is the group of news articles that are among most-shared articles but not in the most-viewed articles. There are 1561 news articles in this group, and 16866 named entities are extracted.
- $V - C$: This is the group of news articles that are among most-viewed articles but not in the most-commented articles. There are 1757 news articles in this group and 17617 named entities are extracted.
- $C - V$: This is the group of news articles that are among most-commented articles but not in the most-viewed articles. There are 1811 news articles in this group and 14700 named entities are extracted.

Based on the extracted named entities, each news article can be represented as a list of named entities contained in it. To find out which are the most discriminative named entities for identifying news articles in one group against another (*e.g.*, $V - S$ against $S - V$), many feature selection techniques can be applied directly [13]. We adopted *Odds Ratio* in our analysis for its effectiveness in many text classification tasks.

---

[5] http://www-nlp.stanford.edu/. Accessed 20 June 2013.

Table 5. The top-20 most discriminative named entities and topics for $S - V$ and $V - S$, respectively

Most discriminative NEs for $S - V$		Most discriminative NEs for $V - S$	
Named entity and [type]	Topic	Named entity and [type]	Topic
[O] S&P	economy	[P] Amanda Berry	crime
[O] FactSet	economy	[P] Ariel Castro	crime
[O] Fed	economy	[P] Gina DeJesus	crime
[O] Labor Department	politics	[P] Berry	unknown
[O] Federal Reserve	economy	[P] Michelle Knight	crime
[P] Ben Bernanke	economy	[P] DeJesus	crime
[O] Reuters Health	health	[L] Qusair	politics
[P] Tanya Lewis	science	[P] Knight	unknown
[O] Thomson Reuters	unknown	[P] Roger Federer	sports
[O] IBM	science	[P] Abigail Van Buren	columnist
[O] IMF	economy	[L] IL	unknown
[O] University of Pennsylvania	unknown	[P] Pauline Phillips	columnist
[L] Bangalore	unknown	[O] Mount Morris	unknown
[O] UBS	economy	[P] Jeanne Phillips	columnist
[P] Mike Smith	unknown	[P] Deval Patrick	crime
[O] Dow Jones	economy	[O] Foreign Ministry	politics
[L] German	unknown	[L] Golan Heights	unknown
[O] European Central Bank	economy	[L] South Korean	unknown
[O] National Academy of Sciences	science	[P] Jo-Wilfried Tsonga	sports
[O] Mayo Clinic	health	[P] Abby	unknown

Table 5 and Table 6 list the top-20 most discriminative named entities for the two groups $S - V$ and $V - S$, and the two groups $C - V$ and $V - C$, respectively. The type of each named entity determined by the Stanford NLP package (*e.g.,* [P]erson, [L]ocation, and [O]rganization) is indicated in the front of the name entity. Based on the news articles in which the named entity appear, we manually assign each named entity a topic. Nevertheless, it is hard to identify the topic of some named entities, particularly the named entities referring to country names or locations. Another reason for not being able to identify a topic is that, a name entity extracted is not a full name (*e.g.,* Berry).

Observe from Table 5, the top-20 most discriminative named entities are mostly organizations for $S - V$ while the most discriminative named entities for $V - S$ are mostly persons. The topics of named entities are quite consistent with that in Table 3, with economy being the dominate topic covering nearly half of the top-20 named entities. Many of these named entities are from the finance sector such as Federal Reserve, Ben Bernanke, Dow Jones, IMF, and European Central Bank. Again, we argue that news articles related to these named entities have higher chance of affecting many people in short time and are perceived to be useful to many users for sharing. Science and health cover a quarter. The sad stories about the kidnappings of Amanda Berry, Gina DeJesus, and Michelle Knight[6] gained large viewership but not many sharing.

---

[6] http://en.wikipedia.org/wiki/Kidnappings_of_Amanda_Berry,_Gina_DeJesus, _and_Michelle_Knight, Accessed 20 June 2013.

Table 6. The top-20 most discriminative named entities and topics for $C - V$ and $V - C$, respectively

Most discriminative NEs for $C - V$		Most discriminative NEs for $V - C$	
Named entity and [type]	Topic	Named entity and [type]	Topic
[P] Rubio	politics	[L] Space.com	science
[P] Lindsey Graham	politics	[P] Novak Djokovic	sports
[O] Republican Party	politics	[P] Woods	sports
[P] Harry Reid	politics	[O] Barcelona	sports
[P] John McCain	politics	[P] Iain Rogers	sports
[O] Tea Party	unknown	[P] Berry	unknown
[L] Palestinians	unknown	[P] Ariel Castro	crime
[P] Chuck Schumer	politics	[P] Mark Lamport-Stokes	sports
[O] Senate Judiciary Committee	politics	[P] Gina DeJesus	crime
[P] Netanyahu	politics	[P] Miriam Kramer	sports
[L] Americans	unknown	[P] Djokovic	sports
[O] Labor Department	politics	[P] Jo-Wilfried Tsonga	sports
[P] Schumer	politics	[O] Real Madrid	sports
[P] Mark Felsenthal	politics	[P] Michelle Knight	crime
[O] House Ways and Means Committee	politics	[P] Roger Federer	sports
[O] Pew Research Center	politics	[O] Bayern Munich	sports
[L] D-N.Y.	politics	[P] Mike Wall	science
[P] Roberta Rampton	politics	[O] Spurs	sports
[P] Rand Paul	politics	[P] DeJesus	crime
[P] Mahmoud Abbas	politics	[P] Knight	crime

Let us look at the named entities listed in Table 6. Almost all the named entities attracted large number of comments are from the politics topic. For named entities that attract large viewership but not commenting are mostly sportsman. The two observations are consistent with that from Table 4. Users are willing to comment on politics issues more freely (or even with anonymous ids) without sharing the comments with their friends/followers. On the other hand, news articles about sports gain a large readership but receive relatively fewer comments.

To summarize, the observations made from the analysis of named entities are consistent with the observations made from the analysis using topic modeling.

4   Related Work

User behavior understanding and analysis is a major research topic [5,7]. Particularly the studies on motivation of the use of social networks are related to our work to help to understand the possible reasons that a user would or would not share a news article after reading it. On the other hand, user behavior analysis on social platforms (*e.g.,* Twitter and Facebook) has attracted significant research interests [3,14]. However, social platform is much more complicated with many more factors (*e.g.,* number of friends, strength of the relationships, degree of activeness) affecting users' behavior. In our study, we are more focused on the textual content of the news articles.

The most related work to our study is the analysis of the relationship between different user actions (view, share, comment) reported in [1]. The authors found that the number of times people sharing a news article is related to the number of times people viewing this news article although the correlation is not very strong. This finding is consistent with our findings that users selectively share news articles depending on perceived usefulness of the topic of the news articles. The authors also reported that comparing to view action and share action, view action and comment action are even less correlated. We show in our study that politics topic receives large number of comments and sports topic receives large number of views but less commenting. In [1], the authors divided the news articles into different categories and found that the correlations between view action and other actions are diverse among categories. However, as the categories are predefined by news publishers, the number of categories is limited and may cover all news articles in fine granularity. In our study, we use topic modeling to infer the topics from the collection of news articles. Another major difference between our study is that, we use the most-viewed, most-shared, and most-commented news articles which are believed to be more representative for the view, share, and comment actions. The news articles used in [1] were randomly selected.

5   Conclusion

In this paper, we collected two months of most-viewed, most-shared, and most-commented news articles from a major news agency. Through topic modeling and named entity analysis we tried to answer the question: are most-viewed news articles most-shared or most-commented, and vice versa? Our analysis reveals that the sharing and commenting behavior from users is largely affected by the topic of news. Specifically, sports news articles receive large viewership but are less likely to be shared or commented; politics news articles are more likely to receive large number of comments; users like to share news articles about health and economy. We believe these findings are useful for news agencies in determining the best news promotion strategies to enlarge their readership. The findings are also helpful in the design of news personalization and recommendation systems. Although the lack of exact numbers of views, shares, and comments of the news articles in the data collection is considered as a limitation of this study, we believe the findings remain valid.

References

1. Agarwal, D., Chen, B.-C., Wang, X.: Multi-faceted ranking of news articles using post-read actions. In: Proceedings of the 21st ACM International Conference on Information and Knowledge Management (CIKM), pp. 694–703. ACM (2012)
2. Blei, D.M., Ng, A.Y., Jordan, M.I.: Latent dirichlet allocation. Journal of Machine Learning Research 3, 993–1022 (2003)

3. Cui, P., Wang, F., Liu, S., Ou, M., Yang, S., Sun, L.: Who should share what?: item-level social influence prediction for users and posts ranking. In: Proceedings of the 34th International ACM SIGIR Conference on Research and Development in Information Retrieval, pp. 185–194. ACM (2011)
4. De Francisci Morales, G., Gionis, A., Lucchese, C.: From chatter to headlines: harnessing the real-time web for personalized news recommendation. In: Proceedings of the Fifth ACM International Conference on Web Search and Data Mining (WSDM), pp. 153–162. ACM (2012)
5. Ellison, N., Steinfield, C., Lampe, C.: The benefits of facebook "friends:" social capital and college students' use of online social network sites. Journal of Computer-Mediated Communication 12(4), 1143–1168 (2007)
6. Hu, M., Sun, A., Lim, E.-P.: Comments-oriented document summarization: understanding documents with readers' feedback. In: Proceedings of ACM SIGIR Conference on Research and Development in Information Retrieval, pp. 291–298. ACM (2008)
7. Johnston, K., Tanner, M., Lalla, N., Kawalski, D.: Social capital: The benefit of facebook friends. Behaviour and Information Technology 32(1), 24–36 (2013)
8. Kwak, H., Chun, H., Moon, S.: Fragile online relationship: a first look at unfollow dynamics in twitter. In: Proceedings of the SIGCHI Conference on Human Factors in Computing Systems (CHI), pp. 1091–1100. ACM (2011)
9. Kwak, H., Lee, C., Park, H., Moon, S.: What is twitter, a social network or a news media? In: Proceedings of the 19th International Conference on World Wide Web (WWW), pp. 591–600. ACM (2010)
10. Lin, K.-Y., Lu, H.-P.: Why people use social networking sites: An empirical study integrating network externalities and motivation theory. Computers in Human Behavior 27(3), 1152–1161 (2011)
11. Liu, J., Dolan, P., Pedersen, E.R.: Personalized news recommendation based on click behavior. In: Proceedings of the 15th International Conference on Intelligent user Interfaces (IUI), pp. 31–40. ACM (2010)
12. O'Banion, S., Birnbaum, L., Hammond, K.: Social media-driven news personalization. In: Proceedings of the 4th ACM RecSys Workshop on Recommender Systems and the Social Web, pp. 45–52. ACM (2012)
13. Sebastiani, F.: Machine learning in automated text categorization. ACM Comput. Surv. 34(1), 1–47 (2002)
14. Xu, Z., Zhang, Y., Wu, Y., Yang, Q.: Modeling user posting behavior on social media. In: Proceedings of the 35th International ACM SIGIR Conference on Research and Development in Information Retrieval, pp. 545–554. ACM (2012)

What Users Do: The Eyes Have It

Paul Thomas[1], Falk Scholer[2], and Alistair Moffat[3]

[1] CSIRO and The Australian National University, Australia
[2] RMIT University, Australia
[3] The University of Melbourne, Australia

Abstract. Search engine result pages – the ten blue links – are a staple of document retrieval services. The usual presumption is that users read these one-by-one from the top, making judgments about the usefulness of documents based on the snippets presented, accessing the underlying document when a snippet seems attractive, and then moving on to the next snippet. In this paper we re-examine this assumption, and present the results of a user experiment in which gaze-tracking is combined with click analysis. We conclude that in very general terms, users do indeed read from the top, but that at a detailed level there are complex behaviors evident, suggesting that a more sophisticated model of user interaction might be appropriate. In particular, we argue that users retain a number of snippets in an "active band" that shifts down the result page, and that reading and clicking activity tends to takes place within the band in a manner that is not strictly sequential.

Keywords: Retrieval evaluation, user behavior, user model.

1 Introduction

Web and enterprise search systems process billions of queries per day, making them amongst the most highly-used computing services. A typical service provides a dialog box for query input, and in response generates a *search engine result page*, or SERP, which contains a ranked list of (often) ten query-biased summaries (or *snippets*), together with matching links to the underlying documents. Users are normally presumed to examine the SERP "from the top", reading the snippets in the order they are presented, making a decision about each in regard to the likely usefulness of the underlying document, and *clicking* to access those documents for which the snippet suggests relevance. If the bottom of the SERP is reached, users can access a second page of results for the same query; or reformulate the query to fetch a fresh page of (possibly overlapping) results; or switch to a different search system (again to get possibly overlapping results); or can exit their search entirely. Users might also undertake any of these actions even before reaching the bottom of the first SERP.

In this paper we take a fresh look at this presumed behavior, presenting the outcomes of a user experiment in which gaze tracking was coupled with an instrumented web browser in order to measure both the explicit actions users took while viewing a SERP (clicks and query reformulations), and also their implicit actions, as indicated by their gaze behavior.

R.E. Banchs et al. (Eds.): AIRS 2013, LNCS 8281, pp. 416–427, 2013.

2 Models and Metrics

Knowledge of user behavior allows better interfaces to be constructed, and hence allows more efficient searching. Another way we can exploit knowledge of user behavior is in understanding search effectiveness metrics. Given a query and a particular ranking of documents in a SERP in response to that query, it is natural to enquire whether or not the ranking is "good" compared to the SERP generated by some other system, or by some other configuration of the same system. To quantify search effectiveness, a range of metrics have been described, varying from simple ones such as Prec@k (the fraction of the first k documents in the SERP that are relevant) through to complex mechanisms such as normalized discounted cumulative gain (NDCG) [6].

Moffat and Zobel [11] drew a direct relationship between the user's behavior while reading the SERP and a metric for measuring retrieval effectiveness. They argued that search quality could be measured in units of "expected relevant documents identified per snippet examined", and that users could be modeled as starting at the top of the SERP, and proceeding from rank i to rank $i + 1$ with some probability p, with p adjusted according to the nature of the query and the persistence of the searcher. That is, they suggest that at rank i the user has probability p of next accessing rank $i + 1$, and probability $(1 - p)$ of exiting the search without examining any document snippets at ranks $i + 1$ or beyond. The resultant effectiveness metric, RBP, is formulated as a weighted sum over a vector of relevance-at-rank values,

$$\text{RBP} = \sum_{i=1}^{\infty} \left((1 - p)p^{i-1} \right) \cdot r_i,$$

where r_i is the relevance of the ith-ranked document as a fractional value between zero and one, with one meaning "completely relevant".

That is, the RBP metric can be thought of as being a direct consequence of a simple one-state, three-transition, *user model* in which the probability of exiting the reading state remains p throughout. Other possible models are then apparent: in Prec@k, the user model is that users read exactly k of the presented snippets; and in reciprocal rank, or RR, the user is modeled as reading until the first relevant document is encountered, and then exiting the reading state. Similarly, average precision, AP, defined as the average of the precision values at each depth at which a relevant document occurs, can also be regarded as being a *weighted-precision* metric:

$$\text{AP} = \sum_{i=1}^{\infty} \left(\frac{\text{Prec@}i}{R} \right) \cdot r_i$$

where $R = \sum_{i=1}^{\infty} r_i$ is the total relevance in the collection (for this query). That is, AP can also be regarded as being of the form $\sum_i w_i \cdot r_i$, where w_i is the *weight* assigned to the ith-ranked document. In the case of RR and AP the user model is *adaptive*, since the weights w_i are a function not only of i, but of r_i. Robertson [12] proposes a corresponding user model in which (for binary relevance values $r_i \in \{0, 1\}$) the user is assumed to proceed through the ranking examining snippets/documents until an identified relevant document is encountered, picked at random from amongst all of the R relevant documents for this query. Other *adaptive* metrics – ones in which the exit probability p is a function of relevance, $p_i = f(r_1..r_i)$ for some relationship $f()$, have also been described [17]. A "to depth k" truncated and scaled version of discounted cumulative gain (DCG) [6] is another example of a static weighted precision metric, in which w_i depends only on i. Note that DCG itself cannot be fitted to this weighted-precision structure, since the set of weights $1/(\log_2(i+1))$ used to discount the relevance scores r_i is a non-convergent series, and would give rise to a model in which the user is expected to read an arbitrarily large number of documents for each query that they pose.

Another metric has also been proposed recently – the *time-biased gain* (TBG) of Smucker and Clarke [13]. Rather than assessing user effort by counting the number of snippets viewed, Smucker and Clarke measure effort in terms of time spent on task. In this model of user behavior, inspection of snippets takes a certain length of time, and viewing of the underlying document adds a further variable time, depending on the length of the document, and whether it has been viewed previously. User willingness to continue reading down the ranking is assumed to erode as a function of time, rather than of snippets viewed, a further point of difference. Smucker and Clarke analyze the behavior of a set of 48 users, each spending up to ten minutes undertaking each of four search tasks. From this data they infer values for a number of critical parameters that drive their model, including probabilities that a document will be viewed, given that it is relevant (according to external relevance judgments), and the probability that it will be saved (regarded as being relevant by the subject), given that it has been viewed.

Common to many of these metrics is that the effectiveness value can be interpreted as being the rate at which relevance is accrued in terms of documents inspected (or, in the case of TBG, time spent) by a probabilistic user; and hence the only difference between these metrics is the estimate of how the user behaves. All of these models also share another feature – they are plausible only if users do indeed read "from the top"; or, at least, read SERPs in such a way that it can be logically equated in some way to a "from the top" reading order. A range of user studies have suggested that this is indeed the case, albeit with some variation [1,4,5,7]; and a key purpose of our study was to further explore that assumption.

3   User Experiment

To investigate user behavior, an instrumented web browser was used to access a commercial search service via its API. A total of $n = 34$ subjects were each asked to carry out six search tasks, after exploring the system via a training task. The six search tasks were of three different difficulty levels, following the categorization given by Wu et al. [16]. Table 1 lists half of the tasks, one of type *remember*, one of type *understand*, and one from the hardest category, *analyze*.

The browsing interface used in the experiments allowed users to click on documents and read them, but not open tabs or further windows. A pre-determined "starter query" was the first one run for each topic; thereafter, subjects were free to run other queries while they explored that topic, and to move to further pages in the results listing for any query. If a document was selected and opened for reading, it could only be closed by the user selecting one of two buttons, indicating whether the viewed document was "useful" or "not useful" for answering the information need. Only when that assessment had been lodged did the original SERP become accessible again. We took these

Table 1. Three of the test queries employed in the user study, together with the first query evaluated for each subject. The second and subsequent queries were at the discretion of the subjects.

Information specification	Starter query
(*remember*) You recently attended an outdoor music festival and heard a band called Wolf Parade. You really enjoyed the band and want to purchase their latest album. What is the name of their latest (full-length) album?	*wolf parade*
(*understand*) You recently became acquainted with one of the farmers at the local farmers' market. One day, over lunch, they were on a rant about how people are ruining the soil. They were clearly upset, so you're interested in finding out more. What are some human activities that degrade soil fertility?	*damage soil fertility*
(*analyze*) Your sister is turning 25 next month and wants to do something exciting for her birthday. She is considering some type of extreme sport. What are some different types of extreme sports in which amateurs can participate? What are the risks involved with each sport?	*extreme sport*

user-supplied judgments as being definitive of relevance for that user, and did not carry out any further judgments, working on the principle that the user's behavior is based on what they think at the time, rather than what an expert says via a post-hoc assessment. Users were asked to "collect a set of answer pages that in your opinion allow that information need to be appropriately met"; they were free to elect when they had reached that point, and move on to the next topic.

Search results were presented in SERPs that each contained ten links to documents, with seven of the links visible "above the fold" at the time the page was opened, and three more visible on scrolling. A set of "next page" links was provided at the bottom of each SERP, while a query box at the top of the SERP allowed fresh queries to be issued. The information need statement for the topic was displayed at the top of each answer page, as a reminder to the participant of what they were looking for. Figure 1 shows (part of) a typical SERP screen for one of the *analyze* tasks.

"Facelab" gaze-tracking equipment[1] monitored the user's gaze on the screen throughout each session. The stream of observations from the tracker was then reduced to *fixations* of at least 75 milliseconds duration within a 5-pixel radius; and sequences of fixations within the area of each displayed snippet were further amalgamated. That sequence was then integrated with the browser log data that noted user actions, including: queries and query reformulations; clicks and document opens; and document judgments made. The resulting processed data can be thought of as sequences of snippet numbers that follow the user's gaze, interspersed with notes about explicit actions undertaken, such as clicks, judgments, and query reformulations.

Topics were presented to participants in a structured manner so as to minimize any ordering effects. As an independent dimension of the exploration, we also systematically degraded the SERPs in half of the subject-topic combinations, using a technique described by Jones et al. [8]. In these *diluted* results, all of the odd-rank positions were replaced by documents that contained words matching the query, but were off-topic. In this paper we focus exclusively on the undiluted results; an analysis of the differences in user behavior arising from the dilution is part of a separate study [14]. Each of the

---

[1] http://www.seeingmachines.com/product/facelab/

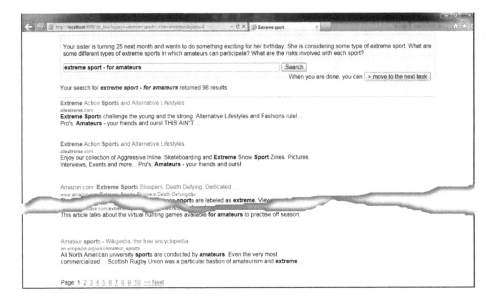

Fig. 1. A typical SERP as viewed by the study participants. The first seven links are visible when the page is opened, the other three, and the "next pages" buttons, are visible after scrolling.

34 users can thus be thought of as contributing three topics to the pool of data, with one topic drawn from each of the three categories shown in Figure 1.

The majority of the study participants were undergraduate or graduate students in STEM topic areas, all fluent in English (though many as a second language), majority male, and for the most part aged in their twenties. A total of 37 participants were identified initially, but technical issues meant that the data from three people was not used in the analysis. Ethics approval for the experimental design was granted by RMIT University's Ethics Advisory Board.

4   Results

We now examine some of the data we collected during our experimentation.

Click-Throughs. The relative frequency of click-throughs is shown in Figure 2, plotted as a function of snippet rank in the results page. The expected downward trend is present [7], and serves as a useful confirmation of two effects: the search service is more likely to place promising items near the top of the ranking; and users are more likely to view items near the top of the SERP. In combination, these two factors mean that click-throughs are more top-biased than document viewings.

Click information, and in particular whether clicked-on documents were subsequently marked as being useful, can be used to investigate whether participants were taking their search tasks seriously. For each pair of participants, the mean percentage agreement (calculated as the number of documents that were given the same relevance

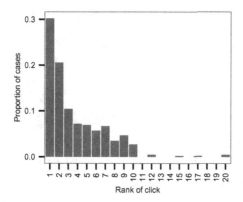

Fig. 2. Click-throughs averaged over topics and subjects, plotted by rank

rating by both participants, divided by the total number of documents that were viewed by both participants) was 79%. For the relevant-only class, the proportion of specific agreement is 85%. This is very high; for example, Voorhees [15] reports pairwise positive agreement of 42% to 49% between primary and secondary TREC assessors. However, it should be noted that the latter evaluation was carried out over a full set of TREC relevance pools, while our comparison is over the subset of documents that were clicked on by users, and hence likely to include a higher rate of relevant documents. In any case, the high level of agreement suggests that our user study participants were in fact attentive to their task.

Fixations. Figure 3 shows how the set of fixations was distributed over the rank positions in the SERP. In Figure 3(a), the distribution of first fixation points for the subject-topic-query combinations is plotted. The top snippet in the SERP dominates, and is the first one read 38% of the time. But ranks two and three also attract a significant fraction of the first fixations, and the participants were more likely to start with either the second or third snippet than they were to start with the first. Snippets that fall below the bottom of the screen (ranks eight and above) are also sometimes the first one viewed; indicating that in some rare cases the user's first action is to scroll the results window.

Across all fixations recorded during the experiments, shown in Figure 3(b), snippets that are closer to the top of the results page are more likely to be viewed than snippets lower down. But the relationship is not monotonic, and the first rank position is not the one that is most frequently viewed – positions 3 and then 2 enjoy that status. The role of the number of snippets in each SERP, and of the location of the "fold" – the point below which users needed to scroll down the page in order to reveal more snippets – is apparent in this second graph. (Where users requested a second page of results for the same query, the snippets were labeled as being at ranks 11–20, and so on.) The three snippets below the fold are rather less likely to be viewed; and snippets on the second results page are even less likely to be looked at.

Fixation Progressions. We define a *jump* as the difference between consecutive fixations for the same subject and topic. For example, if the t th snippet viewed in the

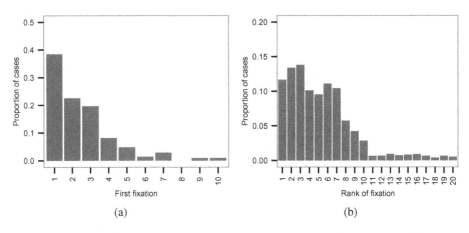

Fig. 3. Fixation distributions: (a) rank of first fixation for each submitted query; and (b) total fixations for each query. There were seven snippets presented "above the fold" on each SERP, and ten snippets in total on each SERP.

Table 2. Observed jump probabilities, expressed as fractions of a total of 2,633 overlapping two-fixation observations. A further 234 fixations occurred as singleton events, and were not included here. The median of this distribution is 1.0, the mean is 0.15.

$<$	-4	-3	-2	-1	$+1$	$+2$	$+3$	$+4$	$>$
0.047	0.033	0.049	0.069	0.230	0.347	0.104	0.046	0.032	0.043
		0.427			0.573				

SERP is at rank d_t, then the t th jump is given by $j_t = d_{t+1} - d_t$. An ideal "from-the-top" reader would have $d_t = t$ and hence generate a jump sequence of $j_t = +1$ values; while at the other extreme, a genuinely random reader would make a selection from $j_t \in \{-d_t + 1 \cdots +\infty\} \setminus \{0\}$ (assuming that the SERP is, in effect, infinite in length).

Table 2 gives an overview of the jump distribution observed in our experiments. Negative movements are nearly as likely as positive ones, with 57% of the jumps positive and 43% of the jumps negative. The median jump value is $+1$, as expected; however the mean jump value is only $+0.1$. At face value, these observations suggest that the document reading order is neither "from the top" nor random.

In fact, there is a certain amount of embedded structure in the jump sequence, but at a higher level than is revealed by Table 2. Table 3 lists observed occurrences of forwards and backwards jumps, first as overall totals matching the second row of Table 2, and then broken down by three conditioning categories: those jumps that are the difference between the first two fixations (that is, the first jump in each SERP displayed); those that took place immediately following a prior backwards jump; and those that took place immediately following a forwards jump. This is, each column of the table represents an estimate of the relative probability of backwards and forwards jumps (as shown by the parenthesized values), given one unit of knowledge of the gaze sequence. As has already been noted, the overall count of backwards jumps is only modestly smaller than

Table 3. Conditional probabilities of forward and backward jumps. Values in parentheses are observed proportional split between positive and negative jumps, in four different contexts. A positive jump is much more likely after a negative jump than it is in the other three contexts.

	overall	first	after $j_{t-1} < 0$	after $j_{t-1} > 0$
jump $j_t < 0$	1125 (0.427)	85 (0.392)	296 (0.295)	744 (0.527)
jump $j_t > 0$	1508 (0.573)	132 (0.608)	709 (0.705)	667 (0.473)

Table 4. Observed two-jump probabilities, expressed as fractions of a total of 2,416 overlapping three-fixation observations. The median of this distribution is 0.0, the mean is 0.33.

<	−4	−3	−2	−1	0	+1	+2	+3	+4	>
0.055	0.045	0.043	0.089	0.070	0.242	0.094	0.161	0.092	0.046	0.060
		0.303			0.242			0.454		

the overall count of forwards jumps. But when the estimates are conditioned by one prior event, a different picture emerges – after a backwards jump, it is very likely that the next transition will be forwards again; and after a forwards jump, there is heightened likelihood of a backwards jump.

Table 4 sums adjacent pairs of jumps to get a net change over sequences of three consecutive fixations. For example, the gaze sequence "1,3,2,3,4,3,5" would reduce to the 1-jump sequence "+2,−1,+1,+1,−1,+2" and then be further reduced to the 2-jump sequence "+1,0,+2,0,+1". As the table shows, when adjacent pairs of jumps are combined, the dominant outcome is "0" – around a quarter of the time the user will be looking at the same document again two steps from now. Table 5 provides further details. The most common 2-jump is "+1,+1"; with the "−1,+1" and "+1,−1" combinations also relatively common. The only double-negative combination in the top 12 is "−1,−1"; after that, the next double negative combinations are "−2,−1" at rank 16 (0.012), and then "−1,−2" and "−1,−3" at equal rank 22, with probabilities below 1%.

More importantly, the direction and magnitude of the first jump in each pair influences the second. Figure 4 explores this connection. Here, the horizontal axis gives the first jump, the vertical gives the second, and the level of shading gives the probability of the second jump conditioned on the first (so each column "adds up to 1"). Regardless of what jump has just happened, a jump of +1 (that is, reading down the results list) is very common, although this effect is weaker following a large positive (downward) jump since there are fewer results left. Other patterns are also evident. A jump in one direction (+ or −, down or up) is commonly followed by a jump in the other. In particular, jumps are commonly in the opposite direction and are of about the same magnitude, an effect that gives rise to the shaded band around the diagonal. This explains the tendency to an overall outcome of "0", in Table 4.

The relative abundance of these effects – jumps of +1, and jumps in one direction being followed by equal jumps in the other – might describe a user who is consciously or unconsciously looking at a result, often going back to some sort of "best so far" to compare it, then going forward a little and repeating the sequence.

Table 5. The most frequent two-jump combinations, expressed as a proportion of the 2,416 overlapping three-fixation observations

Comb.	prop.	Comb.	prop.	Comb.	prop.
$+1,+1$	0.128	$+1,+2$	0.037	$+1,-2$	0.024
$-1,+1$	0.098	$+2,-1$	0.033	$-2,+1$	0.023
$+1,-1$	0.096	$-1,+2$	0.029	$+1,-3$	0.017
$-1,-1$	0.044	$+2,+1$	0.027	$+3,+1$	0.014

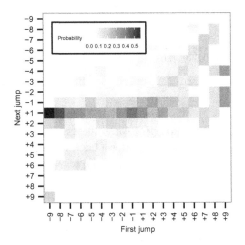

Fig. 4. Two-jump combinations. The horizontal axis gives the first jump in each pair; the vertical the second; and the shading gives the probability of this second jump conditioned on the first.

Taken together, these statistics suggest that there are a wide variety of reading behaviors, and the assumption that the average user reads a search results list from the top until they stop is somewhat simplistic, even if that is what click-through patterns might suggest. Instead, it appears that a modified sequential reading process takes place: searchers maintain a "zone of interest" that is a small number of snippets (two or three) wide, and read backwards and forwards freely within that zone, maintaining a localized set of potentially interesting snippets that are evaluated against each other before a click-through takes place. It is the zone that is likely to start near the top of the page, and then steadily progress downwards, rather than the fixations themselves.

It is also worth noting that some of the effect that has been observed may be due to the inherent imprecision of the gaze-tracking hardware and software (our tracker is generally accurate to within 10 pixels), and it might be that a sequence "$-1, +1$" reflects the user's eyes drifting slightly offline while reading a single snippet, and that only a single fixation was involved.

Exit From a SERP. Figure 5 shows the distribution of the lowest-ranked snippets that were viewed, for each query. Distinct peaks can be observed at ranks 7 and 10. These peaks are a consequence of the screen layout within the browser: 7 snippets showed

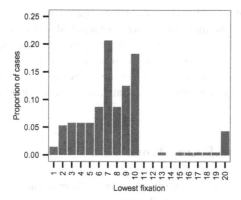

Fig. 5. Distribution of the ranks of the lowest snippet viewed for each query

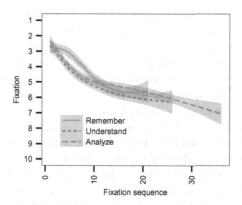

Fig. 6. Fixation rank as a function of fixation sequence. The three task types, in increasing order of complexity, were: *remember*, *understand* and *analyze*.

above the fold, and 10 were presented on each query page. The smaller peak at 20 similarly marks the end of the second page of results. Putting all modeling aside, there is clearly a strong influence on user behavior caused by presentation geometry. It seems questionable whether the default "ten results per page" is an optimal setting, since some users won't scroll at all. On the other hand, those that make the additional cognitive commitment to do so are rewarded with only three additional answers, before encountering an even more challenging hurdle in the form of a "next page" link. Investigating the influence of screen geometry, and the relative impact of the two barriers (needing to scroll, and needing to click on a link), is an interesting area for future work.

Impact of Task Type. Recall that participants in our user study carried out search tasks of three complexity levels: *remember*, *understand* and *analyze*. Figure 6 plots the mean fixation rank as a function of fixation sequence (fitted with a polynomial). For the simplest task category, *remember*, views were unlikely to move below the fold. On the other hand, for the more complex *understand* and *analyze* tasks, views were likely to continue to the bottom of the first results page. The different slopes also suggest that reading speed tended to be higher for more complex tasks. When users need to assemble a larger number of answer documents, they may be more inclined to scan the entire results list first, to get a feel for the range of answer documents that are available to them. For simpler tasks, a more common strategy seems to be to inspect the top rank positions more carefully, until one or two satisfactory items are found and the task is completed.

5 Conclusions and Future Work

Information retrieval systems provide searchers with multiple results in response to a query, typically formatted as a ranked list of document summaries. This paper investigated the long-standing assumption that users read through such a list from top to bottom, one item at a time.

Analysis of eye-tracking and click data from a study of 34 searchers showed that there are large variations in viewing behavior. While rank one was the most common single place to start looking, in over 60% of cases participants began their exploration of a results page from a different position; overall, the most frequently viewed positions were at ranks two and three. Examination of sequences of gaze movements showed that most users in fact shifted their attention freely within a zone of interest, typically consisting of two to three snippets. On average, this zone tended to start near the top of a results page, and shift slowly downwards. This detail is not apparent from click behavior alone, which suggests that click behavior is not a good proxy for viewing behavior and may not be a good proxy for users' decision processes or effort.

The majority of information retrieval evaluation metrics are based on either positional (static) or cascade (adaptive) models of user behavior, both of which assume linear, top-to-bottom reading patterns [3]. Given the findings above, it appears that these models are not capturing complexities that are present in searcher behavior. Investigating how such patterns can be incorporated into refined models, and how this might impact on evaluation metrics, is an interesting avenue for future work.

Our analysis also showed differences in gaze behavior for tasks of different complexity levels: for simple *remember* tasks, searchers tended to constrain their attention to the top half of the results list, with their zone of interest flattening out at around rank position five, presumably after they have found a sufficient number of relevant documents to satisfy their information need. For more complex tasks, users worked their way down the results list more quickly, and also to a greater depth, on average. This effect of task type on search behavior needs to be better understood. For example, different tasks might be approached with different expectations about the number of documents that need to be found; this might partially explain why users tended to read faster for the more complex tasks. We have investigated some of these relationships in other work based on the same user study [10]; and also explored the effect that answer quality has on user behavior [14].

A related issue is the potential impact that the instructions given to user study participants might have on their search behavior. Such effects have been observed when administering questionnaires, for example [9]. While prior work has demonstrated that framing artificial information needs in a task-based scenario can increase the fidelity of searcher behavior [2], the impact on gaze behavior when reading a search results screen is an open research question.

Acknowledgments. We thank Dingyun Zhu for his help running the experiments. This work was supported by the Australian Research Council.

References

1. Aula, A., Majaranta, P., Räihä, K.-J.: Eye-tracking reveals the personal styles for search result evaluation. In: Costabile, M.F., Paternó, F. (eds.) INTERACT 2005. LNCS, vol. 3585, pp. 1058–1061. Springer, Heidelberg (2005)
2. Borlund, P.: Experimental components for the evaluation of interactive information retrieval systems. J. Documentation 56(1), 71–90 (2000)
3. Chapelle, O., Zhang, Y.: A dynamic Bayesian network click model for web search ranking. In: Proc. WWW, Madrid, Spain, pp. 1–10 (2009)
4. Dumais, S., Buscher, G., Cutrell, E.: Individual differences in gaze patterns for web search. In: Proc. IIiX, London, England, pp. 185–194 (2010)
5. Granka, L.A., Joachims, T., Gay, G.: Eye-tracking analysis of user behavior in WWW search. In: Proc. SIGIR, Sheffield, England, pp. 478–479 (2004)
6. Järvelin, K., Kekäläinen, J.: Cumulated gain-based evaluation of IR techniques. ACM Trans. Information Systems 20(4), 422–446 (2002)
7. Joachims, T., Granka, L., Pan, B., Hembrooke, H., Gay, G.: Accurately interpreting click-through data as implicit feedback. In: Proc. SIGIR, Salvador, Brazil, pp. 154–161 (2005)
8. Jones, T., Hawking, D., Thomas, P., Sankaranarayana, R.: Relative effect of spam and irrelevant documents on user interaction with search engines. In: Proc. CIKM, Glasgow, Scotland, pp. 2113–2116 (2011)
9. Kelly, D., Harper, D.J., Landau, B.: Questionnaire mode effects in interactive information retrieval experiments. Information Processing & Management 44(1), 122–141 (2008)
10. Moffat, A., Thomas, P., Scholer, F.: Users versus models: What observation tells us about effectiveness metrics. In: Proc. CIKM, San Francisco, California (to appear, 2013)
11. Moffat, A., Zobel, J.: Rank-biased precision for measurement of retrieval effectiveness. ACM Trans. Information Systems 27(1), 2:1–2:27 (2008)
12. Robertson, S.: A new interpretation of average precision. In: Proc. SIGIR, Singapore, pp. 689–690 (2008)
13. Smucker, M.D., Clarke, C.L.A.: Time-based calibration of effectiveness measures. In: Proc. SIGIR, Portland, Oregon, pp. 95–104 (2012)
14. Thomas, P., Scholer, F., Moffat, A.: Fading away: Dilution and user behaviour. In: Proc. 3rd Europ. Wrkshp. HCI and IR, Dublin, Ireland, pp. 3–6 (2013)
15. Voorhees, E.M.: Variations in relevance judgements and the measurement of retrieval effectiveness. Information Processing & Management 36(5), 697–716 (2000)
16. Wu, W.C., Kelly, D., Edwards, A., Arguello, J.: Grannies, tanning beds, tattoos and NASCAR: Evaluation of search tasks with varying levels of cognitive complexity. In: Proc. IIiX, Nijmegen, The Netherlands, pp. 254–257 (2012)
17. Yilmaz, E., Shokouhi, M., Craswell, N., Robertson, S.: Expected browsing utility for web search evaluation. In: Proc. CIKM, Toronto, Canada, pp. 1561–1564 (2010)

Guess What You Will Cite: Personalized Citation Recommendation Based on Users' Preference

Ya'ning Liu, Rui Yan, and Hongfei Yan

School of Electronics Engineering and Computer Science,
Peking University, Beijing 100871, P.R. China
{liugoodness,rui.yan.peking,yhf1029}@gmail.com

Abstract. Automatic citation recommendation based on citation context is a highly valued research topic. When writing papers, researchers can save a lot of time with a system which can recommend a paper list for every citation placeholder. The past works all focus on the content based methods only. In this paper, we consider the citation recommendation as a content based analysis combined with personalization, using users' publication or citation history as users' profile and conduct to a personalized citation recommendation. After the combination of users' citing preference with content relevance measurement, we obtain an 27.65% improvement of the performance in terms of MAP and 31.67% improvement in recall@10 compared with state-of-art models for citation recommendation problem.

Keywords: Citation Recommendation, Personalization.

1 Introduction

Figure 1 is a fragment of one research paper, we call the fragment citation context. How much time do people have to spent in finding which two papers should be located in the placeholders of "[10, 6]". Looking for what papers to cite is often really time consuming. Paradoxically, the more paper an author knows, the harder it might be for them to figure out where the idea come from. There is a massive existing literature thesaurus in the world, and it is still expanding at an extremely impressive speed annually. Take the research field of Computer Science as an example, about 16000 research papers have been published within a single year, and will keep growing in the foreseeable years. For example, the number of publications in 2009 almost triples than that of 10 year before[16]. The information overload makes the citation recommendation problem more challenge and even more necessary: hence to find what you might be willing to cite is not just a piece of cake.

When people are writing their papers, it would be really energy saving that if there exist a system to recommend a candidate paper list for every citation placeholder in need of citation, so that the only concern for the author is to

R.E. Banchs et al. (Eds.): AIRS 2013, LNCS 8281, pp. 428–439, 2013.
© Springer-Verlag Berlin Heidelberg 2013

researchers [10, 6] proposed to use topic models to predict whether there should be a link (citation relation) between two documents.

Fig. 1. A Citation Context Demo

write and write while the system takes over citation stuffs. There are some researchers who are already aware of the necessity of citation recommendation and they have figured out some algorithms for computers to manage this. For example, in some previous works, citation recommendation is considered as an information retrieval problem, using the citation context as the query to issue, their systems search for papers to cite based on the "queries". The whole process is analogous to the standard procedure of search engines. Here, many methods could be employed to model the similarity between citation context and candidate papers, e.g., language model [8] and translation model [7]. Anchor text is actually another way of citation, like the method used in search engine, we can also compare the current citation context with other citation contexts whose reference is already known, then determine which paper should the citation context refers to. In a word, all these methods focus on the content based analysis. An obvious weakness for these methods is that they fail to take account of personalized user preference. In the real world, different users might have different reading scopes, different citing habits, and different tendencies to cite papers. To this end, citation recommendation should be personalized according to diverse users' preference. In this paper, we aim to recommend papers not only based on the content, but also the users' preference. The combined recommendation for literature citation shall be named as "personalized citation recommendation". Personalized citation recommendation is a new work. So there exist many challenges in the work: 1) How to get user information and build user profiles; 2) How to model user personalization; 3) How to combine user profile with content based algorithms.

In this paper, to the best of our knowledge, we are the first to consider citation recommendation in a personalized way. Our work can be incorporated into pervious research outputs and can further improve their performance. In our experiment, we incorporate the personalized component to language model and translation model for citation recommendation, while both of the models achieve a significant performance improvement.

2 Related Work

2.1 Literature Study

Citation recommendation is a paper recommendation task. There exist some achievements in paper recommendation researches. Blei et al. [1] analyze information on the web, get the reviewers' information, and recommend suitable papers to the reviewers. Chandrasekaran et al. [2] use the users' information in CiteSeer to recommend papers for them. They use the Hierarchical Tree structure to describe the users and papers' information, and edit distance is employed to measure the similarity between the user and the paper. B Shaparenko et al. [11] used language model and convex optimization to do the recommendation work, they use the cos similarity to recommend the top k related papers to the user. S. McNee et al. [9] use the already exist citation relationship between researchers, papers and other information to recommend paper to readers. Kazunari Sugiyamad et al. [13] recommend papers which may attract users based on users' recent research interests. They use users' paper information and users' citation information to form the personal profile. The similarity between user profile and paper information is used to get the rank list of recommend papers. D. Zhou et al. [17] combine multiple graph to one graph and use the graph information to recommend papers to users. Tang et al. [15] recommend papers according to users' interests and knowledge level in an e-learning system. After user finish one paper, they update the user's knowledge level according to the paper they read. Collaborative filtering[3,6,10] is also widely used in paper recommendation task. It works by recommending papers to the users based on papers which other similar users have preferred previously.

2.2 Citation Recommendation

Citation recommendation is a relatively new direction. In this direction not so many works have appeared. But recent years, some researchers realize the importance and meaningful of this work. And get some achievements in this filed. Trevor Strohman et al. [12] firstly consider the whole manuscript as the input of a retrieval system, and recommend a citation list for the whole manuscript. J. Tang et al. [14] apply Topic Model to the citation recommendation problem, they measure the similarity between the citation context and other papers according to the topic difference. Yang Lu et al. [7] use translation model to calculate the possibility of one citation context "translate" to one paper. Then recommend papers according to the possibilities. Qi He et al. [5] use the citation context in other papers as the description of the target paper, and recommend papers mainly on the basis of the description. Then, Qi He et al. expand their work in [5] and get the achievement in [4], they don't use the position information of citation context and predict the positions where a paper need citations.

3   Problem Formulation

In this paper, we need the following information as the system input:

Input: 1) The paper meta data information set P, which could contain most content information of the paper, including author, conference and citation information;2) a piece of citation context and the authors of the citation contexts.

Output: According to the input, the output of the algorithm is a ranking list of papers, ranked by the probability of being cited.

For convenience, we hence set some variables:

Citation Context (CC), indicates the context around the citation placeholder, and the paper fragment in Figure 1 is a citation context.

Content Relevance Degree (CRD), indicate the relevant measurement between a CC and a paper, which is based on the content of the citation context and paper content. This measurement can be a value getting from all previous works' model, such as language model or translation model.

User Tendency Degree (UTD). This value measures the tendency for a user to cite a paper.

Cite Possibility Degree (CPD). This measurement indicates the probability for a particular citation context to be associated with one particular paper.

In all, the citation recommendation is to provide such a system which outputs a paper list according to the calculated CPD given the specific citation context.

4   PCR Model

We call our model PCR (Personalized Citation Recommendation) model. This chapter will give a detailed introduction to PCR model.

Note that the whole process for a user u to cite a paper t. u got an opportunity to know paper t, got interests in it and read it; someday when u wrote a paper p and recalled t is relevant, the author u might write a description d about t and cited t at last. Before writing p, t already got a higher opportunity than other papers which u has not read.

The measurement between d and t is the CRD, and the measurement between u and t is the UTD. In previous works, CRD is used as the CPD, while UTD is ignored, which is quite insufficient. Actually, the author u will first get different UTD for different papers, then the individual citing behavior occurs. In other word, UTD is a prior of the CPD, it means the following formulas:

$$CPD = UTD \times CRD \qquad (1)$$

4.1   UTD (User Tendency Degree)

As mentioned previously, for every "paper-user" pair, we need to evaluate the UTD. Firstly, a user profile is needed at this step. It seems that there is no place where we can get existing information about the users. For junior researchers who have not published any paper yet, that might be correct. But for senior researchers, they have some publications, and their publications are actually the key factor to establish their preference profiles. For senior researchers we can get all we need from their publication history:

1). The paper set published by current user.

2). The author set who have collaborated with current user.

3). The author set who have been cited by current user.

Then, for junior researchers, we can recommend papers based on their mentor or other direction similar senior researchers' preferences. After getting one user's

Table 1. UTDs of Different Levels & Expand in Different ways

	Paper-self Expansion	Paper's Authors	Paper's Conference
User-self	UTD_{1_1}	UTD_{1_2}	UTD_{1_3}
User's Coauthors	UTD_{2_1}	UTD_{2_2}	UTD_{2_3}
User's Citation Authors	UTD_{3_1}	UTD_{3_2}	UTD_{3_3}

profile, given a paper, how can we measure the UTD between the current user and the target paper? In our work we consider the key points to the UTD is some "recommendations" and "expansions". "recommendations" from three levels of persons: user-self, user's coauthors and user's citation authors. They get different influence on user. "recommendations" get two types, one is written by the person, and the other is cited by the person, here we consider the two types as the same thing. After "recommended" by 3 types of persons. User can "expand" the "recommendation" in three ways: pay attention to the paper-self, pay attention to the paper's authors and pay attention to the paper's conference. According to these "recommendations" and "expansions", we can get 3 by 3 equals 9 probabilities which can be considered as the UTD prior (Table 1).

The following is a detailed description to every UTD, and list the formula of UTDs. In the formulas below, count(x, y) means the times which x cite y. count(x) means all the times x cite papers. count'(x) means all the times x cite authors. For example x only cite one paper and the paper has 3 authors, then count(x) is 1 and count'(x) is 3.

Variable u represent the current user, t represent the target paper. A represent target paper's author set, c represent the current paper's conference. A_{co} represent the author set who have collaborations with current user. A_{ci} represent the author set who have been cited by current user.

The first part is the "recommend" behavior of user-self. Obviously, compared with other papers, users are more familiar with papers which written or cited by themselves, this will lead to a relatively high UTD to these papers. High UTD not only influence the behavior to paper-self, it will also influence behaviors to paper's authors and conference. So we can get UTD_{1_1} to UTD_{1_3}.

1). UTD_{1_1}: The ratio of user-self's recommendation count to the target paper t, to user-self's recommendation count to all papers. The feature takes two users' behaviors into consideration: citing papers written by user-self, citing papers used to be cited by user-self. Firstly, every researcher have a relatively stable research interest; that means researchers' current research topic has a strong connection with past topics. So, papers written or cited by user-self have a relatively higher possibility of related with target paper t. At the other hand, users are usually more familiar with works published or cited by themselves. The two points may bring a higher tendency to target paper. So, given a target paper t, user-self's recommendation behavior is the first feature which should be considered. The formula of the feature like below:

$$UTD_{1\_1} = \frac{count(u, t)}{count(u)} \tag{2}$$

2). UTD_{1_2}: The ratio of user-self's recommendation count to the target paper t's author set A, to user-self's recommendation count to all authors. The feature takes one user's behavior into consideration: citing authors used to be cited by user-self. If the user cited one author multiple times, that means the author is highly understood, recognized and accepted by the user. After citing part of the author's papers, the user's focus may expand, he may get interests in all papers written by the author. Then, given one paper, except considering the paper-self, we can also consider the number of times that user cited the paper's authors. The measurement can be calculated in the following formula:

$$UTD_{1\_2} = \frac{\sum_{a \in A} count(u, a)}{count'(u)} \tag{3}$$

3). UTD_{1_3}: The ratio of user-self's recommendation count to the target paper t's conference, to user-self's recommendation count to all conferences. The feature takes one user's habit into consideration: read and cite papers from user's familiar conferences. If a user publishes in one conference multiple times or cites many papers from one conference, that means the user is familiar with the conference. And the user may read most of the papers published in the conference. So, papers from the conference may get a higher UTD compared with other papers. The feature expand in conference's way. Its formula like below:

$$UTD_{1\_3} = \frac{count(u, c)}{count(u)} \tag{4}$$

The past three features are all focus on user-self's behaviors, except user-self. User's coauthors also get the ability to "recommend" papers to users. So coauthors' papers or citations also give contributions in our model. The next 3 features all about user coauthors' "recommend" behavior.

4). UTD_{2_1}: The ratio of user's coauthor set A_{co}'s recommendation count to the target paper t, to A_{co}'s recommendation count to all papers. This feature focus on the user's behavior: know well about coauthor's work, read coauthor's papers. Users usually connect with their coauthors closely, this will lead to a high possibility for users to familiar with coauthors' works and read their papers. So papers "recommended" by coauthors give an influence on users, UTD_{2_1} is to measure the influence. The formula can be describe below.

$$UTD_{2\_1} = \frac{\sum_{a' \in A_{co}} count(a', t)}{\sum_{a' \in A_{co}} count(a')} \tag{5}$$

5). UTD_{2_2}: The ratio of user's coauthor set A_{co}'s recommendation count to the target paper t's author set A, to A_{co}'s recommendation count to all authors. This feature focus on the authors who write the user's coauthors' citations. The more times user's coauthors cite one author, the more possibility user can familiar with the author, and the familiarity will lead to future's citing behavior, the following is the formula which can calculate the feature's value:

$$UTD_{2\_2} = \frac{\sum_{a' \in A_{co}} \sum_{a \in A} count(a', a)}{\sum_{a' \in A_{co}} count'(a')} \tag{6}$$

6). UTD_{2_3}: The ratio of user's coauthor set A_{co}'s recommendation count to the target paper t's conference c, to A_{co}'s recommendation count to all conferences. Like UTD_{1_3}, when considering in coauthor's point of view, we can also expand in the conference way. The feature can be calculate by the formula below:

$$UTD_{2\_3} = \frac{\sum_{a' \in A_{co}} count(a', c)}{\sum_{a' \in A_{co}} count(a')} \tag{7}$$

Except user-self and coauthors, user's citation authors also get the ability to "recommend", if a paper, an author or a conference be "recommended" by user's citation authors many times, the user will also get a relatively high possibility to cite it. The following 3 UTDs expand in 3 ways(target paper-self, target paper's author, target paper's conference) to model user's citation authors' behavior. These features' calculations are similar with UTD_{2_1} to UTD_{2_3}.

7). UTD_{3_1}: The ratio of user's citation author set A_{ci}'s recommendation count to the target paper t, to A_{ci}'s recommendation count to all papers. Like UTD_{1_1} and UTD_{2_1}, this feature consider in paper-self way. Here is the calculation formula:

$$UTD_{3\_1} = \frac{\sum_{a' \in A_{ci}} count(a', t)}{\sum_{a' \in A_{ci}} count(a')} \tag{8}$$

8). UTD_{3_2}: The ratio of user's citation author set A_{ci}'s recommendation count to the target paper t's author set A, to A_{ci}'s recommendation count to all authors. This feature consider in target paper's authors way. Here is the formula to calculate the value:

$$UTD_{3\_2} = \frac{\sum_{a' \in A_{ci}} \sum_{a \in A} count(a', a)}{\sum_{a' \in A_{ci}} count'(a')} \tag{9}$$

9). UTD_{3_3}: The ratio of user's citation author set A_{ci}'s recommendation count to the target paper t's conference, to A_{ci}'s recommendation count to all conferences. Like UTD_{2_3}, the conference view is also taken into consideration, the feature's value can be calculated by the following formula:

$$UTD_{3\_3} = \frac{\sum_{a' \in A_{ci}} count(a', c)}{\sum_{a' \in A_{ci}} count(a')} \tag{10}$$

The 9 features are 9 priors to the CRD, then we can multiply one CRD value calculated by one previous model, then get 9 different CPDs. Combine the 9 CPDs, we can get the final score to rank the candidate papers for one citation context. The following chapter is detailed steps for the combination.

4.2   Combine UTDs with CRD

In this paper, we employ two models as the CRD measurement and consider them as our baselines. The first one is widely known language model[8], here we use one gram language model; the second is the new model from paper [7], named translation model with self-boosting on abstract. Then combine our UTD priors to the CRD. There also exist some problems in the process of combination, to solve these, we do the process in the following 2 steps:

Fill Up Value Gap. In the formula (1), we need to multiply UTD with CRD. But there exist a problem when do the multiplication. There may exist a value gap between UTD and CRD, the difference between different points for UTD and CRD doesn't in an order of magnitude. So, when multiply UTD with CRD, the effect for one of them may be very small. The situation due to the scale of data and the length of citation context. To deal with the situation, we add a shrink variable to the values we multiply, then the formula (1) becomes:

$$CPD = UTD^{\alpha} \times CRD^{(1-\alpha)} \tag{11}$$

Combine Scores. In our model, we have 9 different priors, after multiply with CRD, 9 different scores will appear. To get a final score for one author, we need to combine the 9 scores.

The citing problem is actually a classification problem. Given a CC and paper pair, it get two relationships: cite or not cite. We can get 9 scores to represent the pair. So the pair actually is a 9-D point. Some of the points are positive (the CC cite the paper), some of them are negative. This is a standard problem which SVM can solve. After doing classification, we can rank the papers according to the positive possibilities given by SVM.

But a new problem appears when we use SVM. One CC just cites one or a few papers, while all other papers are all negative points when combine with the CC. So negative points get the overwhelming majority. After tried, we solve the problem in the following way:

1). Add the positive points to the training set, randomly add equal quantity's negative point.
2). Train one SVM model.
3). Get a result according to the model in 2)
4). Repeat steps above n times, get n results, then calculate the average result as the final score. Here we fix n to 5, for it get a stable and good performance.

Then we can get one score for one author when considering a CC and paper pair. Many CC get more than one authors, average score from every authors perform best when compare with highest score or lowest score. So here we use the average score of CC authors as the final score.

Till now, we can get one score for every CC and paper pair. And then rank the papers according to the score for one CC. It's the output the citation recommendation problem want to get.

5 Experiment

5.1 Dataset

We get data mainly from three original: MAS (Microsoft Academic Search) API, MAS web site[1], Open access papers in the internet. The data was collected in the following steps:

---

[1] http://academic.research.microsoft.com/

Table 2. Performance for the PCR Model

Model	RDM	LM	LM_PCR	TM	TM_PCR
MAP	0.007	0.299	0.509	0.504	0.644
Recall@10	0.000	0.376	0.634	0.594	0.782

1. Pick up several seed literature venues such as ACL, CIKM, EMNLP, ICDE, ICDM, KDD, SIGIR, VLDB, WSDM, WWW, etc.

2. Get papers' meta data out of the selected seed venues ranged from 2000 to 2012 via MAS API, the meta data include: paper ID in MAS, paper title, paper published year, paper conference, paper authors, citing papers' ID, paper abstract, paper open access URL. At last we get 9492 papers' meta data.

3. Then we get the papers' meta data which cited by the 9492 papers. In the end we get 55823 papers' meta data.

4. According to the open access URL, we download 20171 pdf files and 22.49% of them are papers from the seed venues.

5. We get all citation links in our data set, and then we filter out the CC that we can get from the MAS web site, then 73236 cite relationships which send out by the papers from seed venues was fetched. Here a paper may cite another paper multiple times, because a paper may cite another paper in many places.

We pick up 1000 authors whose information is relatively complete in our data set, for every author, we put the last CC written by the author into the test data set. All the test data CCs' answer form the candidate data set. Then, we use the rest data as the training data.

5.2 Evaluation Metric

For every CC, every model can return a ranking list for papers. We consider the CC's citing papers as the answer. The following metrics can be used:

Recall: The fraction of citation contexts which can return the answers at top k result.

MAP (Mean Average Precision):

$$MAP(d_1, d_2, ..., d_n) = \frac{\sum_i \frac{R(d_i)}{i} \sum_{j<i} R(d_i)}{\sum_i R(d_i)} \quad (12)$$

$R(d_i)$ is a boolean function to indicate whether CC refer d_i.

5.3 Results

We use random result, one gram language model and translation model with self-boosting on abstract as the compared method. Our model, separately use language model and translation model as the CRD. Table 2 shows the experiment result, Figure 2 shows detailed information about recall.

In Table 2, RDM is the random result, LM means language model, LM_PCR means PCR use language model as CRD, TM means translation model, TM_PCR means PCR use translation model as CRD. From the results, we can see:

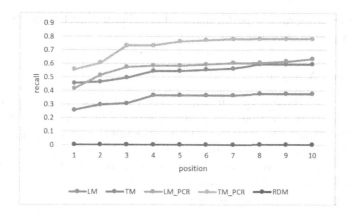

Fig. 2. Recall value of every position before 10

1. TM_PCR perform best and LM_PCR perform also better than not personalized language model.

2. No matter Language model or translation model, after employed in PCR model, all get an obvious improvement from 0.14 to 0.2 in MAP.

Because, the PCR model not only can use the content related information, but also can use authors' tendency information, it can maintain the results which CRD perform good, and promote the results which CRD perform pool, so the PCR model is effective and can improve the performance of the existing model.

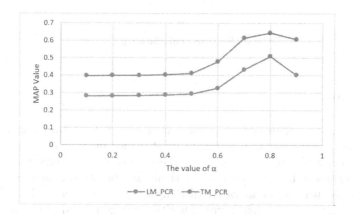

Fig. 3. Parameter tuning for the value of α

5.4 Parameter Tuning

In this chapter we tune the shrink parameter α as described in 4.2 In this paper, data set scale is described in 4.1, our citation context is fetched from MAS web site, after delete the stop words, the average citation contexts' length is 13.4

words. Figure 3 shows the performance of α value from 0.1 to 0.9, we can see set α to 0.8 performs best.

5.5 Feature Analysis

In our model, we chose 3 by 3 features, Figure 4 shows the performance after remove one of them. The item x_y means remove UTD_{x_y}. The last item "none" means remove none of the features which is the final result of our model. From the figure we can see the "recommendations" from user-self (written or cited by user-self) contribute more, and "expansions" in paper-self way give the most prompt to the model. The conclusion's reason is that, we get a relatively big effect decrease after removing one of them.

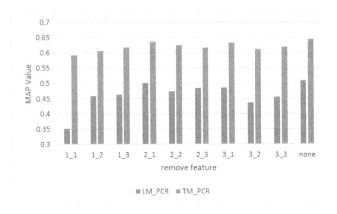

Fig. 4. Feature analysis for 9 UTDs

6   Conclusion

We propose recommend citation papers in a personalized way. Different users have different tendencies to papers, our PCR model quantize the tendencies and combine them with language model and the state-of-art translation model. Then get a performance prompt for both of them. In the future, we will try to use other models such as collaborative filtering or graph model as the UTD (user tendency degree). And other factors for citation recommendation will also take into consideration, for example papers' authority and popularity. We think the performance of personalized citation recommendation can be further enhanced.

Acknowledgments. This work is supported by FSSP 2012 Grant 2012115, NSFC Grant 61272340 and 61073082.

References

1. Blei, D.M., Ng, A.Y., Jordan, M.I.: Latent dirichlet allocation. The Journal of Machine Learning Research 3, 993–1022 (2003)
2. Chandrasekaran, K., Gauch, S., Lakkaraju, P., Luong, H.P.: Concept-based document recommendations for citeSeer authors. In: Nejdl, W., Kay, J., Pu, P., Herder, E. (eds.) AH 2008. LNCS, vol. 5149, pp. 83–92. Springer, Heidelberg (2008)
3. Goldberg, D., Nichols, D., Oki, B.M., Terry, D.: Using collaborative filtering to weave an information tapestry. Communications of the ACM 35(12), 61–70 (1992)
4. He, Q., Kifer, D., Pei, J., Mitra, P., Giles, C.L.: Citation recommendation without author supervision. In: WSDM, pp. 755–764. ACM (2011)
5. He, Q., Pei, J., Kifer, D., Mitra, P., Giles, L.: Context-aware citation recommendation. In: WWW, pp. 421–430. ACM (2010)
6. Konstan, J.A., Miller, B.N., Maltz, D., Herlocker, J.L., Gordon, L.R., Riedl, J.: Grouplens: applying collaborative filtering to usenet news. Communications of the ACM 40(3), 77–87 (1997)
7. Lu, Y., He, J., Shan, D., Yan, H.: Recommending citations with translation model. In: CIKM, pp. 2017–2020. ACM (2011)
8. Manning, C.D., Raghavan, P., Schütze, H.: Introduction to information retrieval, vol. 1. Cambridge University Press, Cambridge (2008)
9. McNee, S.M., Albert, I., Cosley, D., Gopalkrishnan, P., Lam, S.K., Rashid, A.M., Konstan, J.A., Riedl, J.: On the recommending of citations for research papers. In: CSCW, pp. 116–125. ACM (2002)
10. Resnick, P., Iacovou, N., Suchak, M., Bergstrom, P., Riedl, J.: Grouplens: An open architecture for collaborative filtering of netnews. In: CSCW, pp. 175–186. ACM (1994)
11. Shaparenko, B., Joachims, T.: Identifying the original contribution of a document via language modeling. In: Buntine, W., Grobelnik, M., Mladenić, D., Shawe-Taylor, J. (eds.) ECML PKDD 2009, Part II. LNCS, vol. 5782, pp. 350–365. Springer, Heidelberg (2009)
12. Strohman, T., Croft, W.B., Jensen, D.: Recommending citations for academic papers. In: SIGIR, pp. 705–706. ACM (2007)
13. Sugiyama, K., Kan, M.-Y.: Scholarly paper recommendation via user's recent research interests. In: Proceedings of the 10th Annual Joint Conference on Digital Libraries, pp. 29–38. ACM (2010)
14. Tang, J., Zhang, J.: A discriminative approach to topic-based citation recommendation. In: Theeramunkong, T., Kijsirikul, B., Cercone, N., Ho, T.-B. (eds.) PAKDD 2009. LNCS, vol. 5476, pp. 572–579. Springer, Heidelberg (2009)
15. Tang, T., McCalla, G.: Beyond learners' interest: Personalized paper recommendation based on their pedagogical features for an e-learning system. In: Zhang, C., Guesgen, H.W., Yeap, W.-K. (eds.) PRICAI 2004. LNCS (LNAI), vol. 3157, pp. 301–310. Springer, Heidelberg (2004)
16. Yan, R., Tang, J., Liu, X., Shan, D., Li, X.: Citation count prediction: Learning to estimate future citations for literature. In: CIKM, pp. 1247–1252. ACM (2011)
17. Zhou, D., Zhu, S., Yu, K., Song, X., Tseng, B.L., Zha, H., Giles, C.L.: Learning multiple graphs for document recommendations. In: WWW, pp. 141–150. ACM (2008)

Serendipitous Recommendation for Mobile Apps Using Item-Item Similarity Graph

Upasna Bhandari[1], Kazunari Sugiyama[1], Anindya Datta[1], and Rajni Jindal[2]

[1] School of Computing, National University of Singapore,
Computing 1, 13 Computing Drive, Singapore 117417
[2] Department of Computer Science, Delhi Technological University,
Shahbad Daulatpur, Main Bawana Road, Delhi-110042, India
{a0106246,sugiyama,datta}@comp.nus.edu.sg, rajnijindal@dce.ac.in

Abstract. Recommender systems can provide users with relevant items based on each user's preferences. However, in the domain of mobile applications (apps), existing recommender systems merely recommend apps that users have experienced (rated, commented, or downloaded) since this type of information indicates each user's preference for the apps. Unfortunately, this prunes the apps which are releavnt but are not featured in the recommendation lists since users have never experienced them. Motivated by this phenomenon, our work proposes a method for recommending serendipitous apps using graph-based techniques. Our approach can recommend apps even if users do not specify their preferences. In addition, our approach can discover apps that are highly diverse. Experimental results show that our approach can recommend highly novel apps and reduce over-personalization in a recommendation list.

1 Introduction

Concurrent with the phenomenal spread of smart-devices (*e.g.*, iPhone, iPad), the mobile application (app) market has experienced explosive growth. For instance, Apple's iOS App Store offers more than 550,000 unique apps to users in 123 countries, along with download counts exceeding 25 billion[1]. The enormous scale of the app market makes it difficult for users to discover apps that are relevant to their interests. In this context, it is tempting to apply recommender systems (RSs), which have been used successfully in a variety of domains like movies and books to alleviate the problem of information overload by suggesting items directly to users relevant to their interests.

In general, the effectiveness of RSs has been shown to be proportional to the data sparsity of the underlying application domain. In other words, the larger the fraction of the item corpus that has been experienced by users, the better the quality and coverage of recommendations from that corpus. Effectively, if an item has not been experienced at all, the RSs is not able to recommend items similar to it. This feature of RSs create a stiff hurdle for them to be applied in mobile app recommendations, as the rate of introduction of mobile apps is extraordinarily high, and the fraction of apps that have been experienced (downloaded) by users is extremely low.

---

[1] http://www.apple.com/pr/library/2012/03/
05Apples-App-Store-Downloads-Top-25-Billion.html

R.E. Banchs et al. (Eds.): AIRS 2013, LNCS 8281, pp. 440–451, 2013.
© Springer-Verlag Berlin Heidelberg 2013

The most popular approach in recommender systems is collaborative filtering (CF) [11,17,13] that works by recommending items to target users based on what other similar users have previously preferred. Another popular technique is content-based filtering (CBF) [7,6,21] that provides recommendations by comparing representations of content contained in an item with representations of content that the user is interested in. Both CF and CBF, however, are mostly aimed at generating accurate recommendations that is relevant to user's interests. The lack of "surprise" element in these recommendations owing to the fact that there are ratings available for only a small fraction of apps creates a major hurdle in overall user satisfaction of the user.

Recently, some researchers have focused on developing serendipitous recommendation systems [5], [12], [14], [16], [22], [1]. It is reasonable to say that a user would be happy with recommendation systems that offer less obvious choices. Suppose that we visit Amazon.com[2] to buy something online. To illustrate, after browsing a couple of items, Amazon.com provides us with lists such as *Recommended For You* or *Customer Who Bought This Item Also Bought*. Looking at them closely, users often observe that all of these items are already known. This may not be ideal for overall user satisfaction and experience with the system. For example, if a user browses a book written by *Dan Brown*, most of the recommendations for the user will be books by *Dan Brown*.

Serendipitous systems work on the basis of the assumption that the user may want to be surprised with something unexpected that he did not start out looking for. E-commerce Web sites, however, usually just offer a long list of search results. Therefore, users have little chance of finding out something different from their preferences. Another problem with existing recommendation systems is that they often recommend items which the users have rated or downloaded before. This limits the candidate apps to be recommended by pruning relevant but not yet rated or downloaded apps.

In order to provide serendipitous recommendations that solve the problems of existing recommendation systems, we first define serendipitous recommendation as the one that provides something diverse and novel, and then we propose a method for providing serendipitous recommendations by increasing item novelty and diversity. We leverage the user's preferences by tapping into the information about apps installed on mobile phones and recommend serendipitous apps using item-item similarity graph.

This paper is organized as follows: In Section 2, we review related work on serendipitous recommendation and state-of-the-art mobile app recommendation systems. In Section 3, we detail our graph-based approach to providing serendipitous recommendation for mobile apps. In Section 4, we present the experimental results for evaluating our proposed approaches and some user analysis. Finally, we conclude the paper with a summary and directions for future work in Section 5.

2 Related Work

In this paper, our goal is to construct a serendipitous recommendation system for mobile apps. Thus, we review related works on serendipitous and mobile apps recommendation systems in the following.

---

[2] http://www.amazon.com

2.1 Serendipitous Recommendation

Most of the recommendation approaches focus on recommending a list of items similar to the items previously seen and rated highly by the target user. However, much fewer works address serendipitous recommendations. Ziegler *et al.* [27] proposed a similarity metric using a taxonomy-based classification and uses it to compute an intra-list similarity to determine the overall diversity of the recommended list. They provide a heuristic algorithm to increase the diversity of the recommendation list. Zhang and Hurley [26] focused on intra-list diversity and optimized the tradeoffs between users' preferences and the diversity of the top-N results. They modeled the competing goals of maximizing the diversity of the searched list while maintaining adequate similarity to the user query as a binary optimization problem. Andre [5] proposed a method for performing serendipitous searches for Web information retrieval. They first defined the potential for serendipity as search results that are interesting but not highly relevant. In another publication, they discussed serendipity from human cognitive point of view [4]. They hypothesized that a reconsideration of serendipity from numerous angles may help refine new opportunities for designing systems to support, if not serendipity exactly, then the desired effects of serendipitous revelation. Lathia [14] found that temporal diversity is an important facet of recommender systems by showing how data of collaborative filtering changes over time. This work has explored temporal aspect of recommendation, but we focus on recommending serendipitous mobile apps to each user. Kawamae [12] emphasized the surprise of each user in the recommendation focusing on the estimated search time that the users would take to find the item by themselves. Their recommender system assumed that items recently purchased by an innovator, who has well-proven unpredictable trait, will surprise other users more than other items. Nakatsuji *et al.* [16] improved the drawback of Ziegler *et al.*'s approach described above. They proposed a method for identifying items that are highly novel for the user by defining item novelty as the smallest distance from the class the user accessed before to the class that includes a target item. Sugiyama and Kan [22] proposed a method for recommending serendipitous scholarly papers. They used the preferences gathered from other users (dissimilar users and co-authors) in the construction of the target researcher's user profile, used in matching candidate documents to achieve serendipitous recommendations. Recently, Adamopoulos and Tuzhilin [1] proposed an approach to providing unexpected recommendations by formalizing the Greek philosopher Heraclitus's concept, "If you do not expect it, you will not find the unexpected, for it is hard to find and difficult."

2.2 Recommendation for Mobile Apps

As a tremendous number of apps are readily available, users have difficulty in identifying apps that are relevant to their interests. Thus, recommender systems for apps have started to gain popularity. To understand how, where, and when apps are used compared to traditional Web services, Xu *et al.* [23] investigated the diverse usage behaviors of individual mobile apps using anonymized network measurements from a tier-1 cellular carrier in the United States. Yan and Chen [24] and Costa-Montenegro *et al.* [8] constructed recommendation system for apps by analyzing how the apps are actually used. Mobile devices are usually used in various contexts due to their ubiquitous nature. Davidsson and Moritz [10] developed a prototype system of app recommendation that achieves such context-awareness by exploiting GPS sensor information. Recommendation for apps needs to consider factors that invoke a user to replace an old app (if the user already has one) with a new app. Focusing on this point, Yin *et al.* [25] introduced the notions of actual value (satisfactory value of the app after the user used it) and tempting value (the estimated satisfactory value if the app seems to bring to the user) and regarded recommendation for mobile apps as a result of the contest between these two values. Based on the observations that app-related information in Twitter can precede formal user ratings in app stores, Lin *et al.* [15] developed a novel approach to recommending mobile apps in cold-start situations.

3 Proposed Method

The serendipitous recommendation works described in Section 2.1 have not addressed apps for smartphones yet. In addition, the recommendation systems for mobile apps described in Section 2.2 have not employed serendipitous recommendation. Thus, to the best of our knowledge, this is the first work on serendipitous recommendation for mobile apps. In this section, we explain our proposed approach.

3.1 Intuition of Our Proposed Method

The state-of-the-art recommendation systems have a key assumption, *"every item must be used at least once and every user must use at least one item."* According to this assumption, unfortunately, it is highly possible that recommender systems prune items that may be good but never get featured since nobody has used them yet. We mainly focus on increasing the aggregate diversity by discovering highly diverse and new apps to achieve serendipitous recommendations. In our approach, we define new apps as those which have never been downloaded or rated.

Graph-based techniques have been previously employed in recommender systems, but mainly focused on improving accuracy or maximizing diversity [3], [2]. These techniques are popular since they can avoid the problems of sparsity and limited coverage by evaluating the relationships between users or items that are not "directly connected" [18]. Thus, to generate serendipitous recommendations for mobile apps, graph-based methods are useful since they preserve some of the "local" relations in the data. In this section, we propose an approach to generating serendipitous recommendations based on apps installed on a target user's phone by using item-item similarity graph. We believe that, by using the list of apps already installed on a user's phone, we can capture a holistic view of user's preference and not relying on ratings given to a few apps so in turn what we are trying to do is focus on apps that the user has actually downloaded and used. Also, in many cases users download apps to test them out but never install them but we only take into account apps that are installed by the user. The main intuition is that, if there exists a path connecting two apps on a user's phone and the weights on each edge that constitutes this path are above a certain threshold of similarity, apps along this path which are not already downloaded by the user are candidates for serendipitous recommendations.

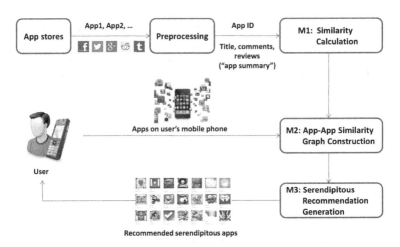

Fig. 1. System overview

3.2   Details of Our Proposed Method

Figure 1 shows an overview of our approach, consisting of the following three modules:

M1: Similarity calculation,
M2: App-app similarity graph construction, and
M3: Recommendation generation.

The main idea is that if two apps are connected by a path with highly weighted edges then these apps are also similar. Simply put, if there exists a path connecting two apps and the weights on each edge that constitutes this path are all sufficiently large, apps along this path which are not already downloaded by the user are good candidates for serendipitous recommendations to the user. The approach we have deployed is primarily for "casual discovery" of apps. We believe that, if a user specifically wants an app for a particular need, the user can download from the app store by searching for appropriate keywords. The only reason why a user would be interested in getting serendipitous recommendations is if the user is looking for interesting apps to try out. Thus, this approach is not aimed at finding apps that score high on the accuracy metric by being closer to user's interests but it scores high on the novelty and diversity from user's interest hence catering to serendipity. Apart from the modules mentioned above, we have preprocessing components for apps. These components are handled offline in order to reduce the computational cost of generating recommendations. At a high level, apps represent a set of apps from the app store. This subset of apps has been selected as apps that have been rated at least five times from our user database. Collecting actual usage data is the most ideal way to go about in generating recommendations. However, it is also difficult to collect real time usage data. Hence, we use comments or reviews as a substitute to narrow down on the subset of apps for this work (see "M1: Similarity Calculation" below for further details). Preprocessing, on the other hand, refers to a step that prepares data for similarity calculation. These can be truncations by removing punctuation, stop words, etc. The inputs from a target user are some apps that have already been installed on the user's mobile phone. The apps are used after M2 has completed constructing app-app similarity graphs to generate recommendations in M3 for the target user. In the following, we detail the three modules. Note that modules M1 and M2 aim at discovering apps while M3 aims at generating recommendations.

M1: Similarity Calculation

While item-based CF method computes similarities between item pairs by using rating patterns given to these two items by different users, our approach computes similarities between two apps by using meta-information about the apps as discussed earlier. Thus, input to this module is metadata such as app ID, title of the app and comments or reviews of apps obtained after preprocessing. While we use app ID as an index to keep track of the apps, we use app title, app description and comments (hereafter, "app summary") to construct feature vectors of apps. Then, we calculate similarity between apps.

For each app a, we transform a into a feature vector f^a as follows:

$$f^a = (w^a_{t_1}, w^a_{t_2}, \cdots, w^a_{t_m}), \tag{1}$$

where m is the number of distinct terms in app summary, and t_k $(k = 1, 2, \cdots, m)$ denotes each term. Using TF-IDF [19] scheme, we also define each element $w^a_{t_k}$ of f^a in Equation (1) as follows:

$$w^a_{t_k} = \frac{tf(t_k, a)}{\sum_{s=1}^{m} tf(t_s, a)} \cdot \log \frac{N_a}{df(t_k)},$$

where $tf(t_k, a)$ is the frequency of term t_k in the app summary, N_a is the total number of apps to recommend, and $df(t_k)$ is the number of app summary in which term t_k appears. Using feature vector for app defined by Equation (1), our approach computes similarity $sim(f^{a_i}, f^{a_j})$ between app a_i and a_j $(i \neq j)$ by Equation (2):

$$sim(f^{a_i}, f^{a_j}) = \frac{f^{a_i} \cdot f^{a_j}}{|f^{a_i}||f^{a_j}|}. \tag{2}$$

We consider all the apps in pair wise manner and generate similarity scores between them. The output is a list of similarity scores for each pair of apps ranging from 0 to 1. We employ cosine similarity since it is widely used and is effective in calculating similarity for short-text. For example, if we have 10 apps in our dataset, information about these 10 apps is first obtained from the app store, indexed and then cosine similarities are computed for $_{10}C_2$=45 app-pairs. These are then stored in a separate database to be used by the next module.

M2: App-App Similarity Graph Construction

The input to this module is a list of apps and the similarity scores between them computed by Equation (2) in M1. Let $G = (V, E)$ be an undirected and weighted graph, where V and E are a set of apps and a set of edges, respectively. Our approach creates an edge between two apps if the similarity between them defined by Equation (2) is greater than a predefined threshold. The similarity score is also used as a weight of the created edge. In order to control the size of the graph, we consider the top 30 most similar apps for every app. The output is app-app similarity graph that has vertices with the

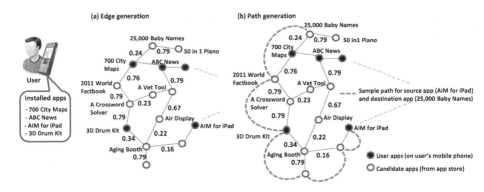

Fig. 2. Generation of (a) edge and (b) path from a given source (user's apps) to destination (candidate apps)

app IDs and edges with similarity scores between the vertices. Figure 2(a) shows the apps as vertices and edges (solid line) that connect the vertices marked with similarity between the apps.

M3: Serendipitous Recommendation Generation

At this stage, we have constructed app-app similarity graph that includes all the apps from our dataset. Now, we use the list of apps in a user's phone to start constructing paths from one app on the user's phone to another. In other words, we consider each app pair on a user's phone as source and destination for calculating paths between them. A path simply connects one app vertex to another which has similarity score above a threshold. We set the threshold to 0.4. Dotted line in Figure 2(b) illustrates the paths. By doing this, our approach can prevent each user's interests from too much drift, which commonly happens as the diversity of recommendations increases. It would not be useful to give highly diverse but less relevant apps to the user. Hence, to keep the interest of a user, we consider the apps installed on the user's phone to be the source and destination for the path construction. Adomavicius and Kwon [2] maximized the aggregate diversity of recommendations using max-flow algorithms in graph theory. Inspired by their approach, we find the application of the shortest-path finding algorithms to be extremely useful in the context of finding serendipitous items in the domain of mobile apps. The shortest-path algorithms aim to reduce the overall cost to traverse from a given source node to given destination node. In the app-app similarity graph, however, this cost is represented as the similarity between apps. Thus, during construction of the path, we take edges with low similarity to reach the destination, constructing the shortest path that connects the two apps. Paths are constructed for all the app-pairs on a user's phone. If an app-pair does not have a path connecting them, we eliminate such useless app-pair since it indicates lack of transitive relation between the two. The path construction step simply represents the app discovery problem and is useful for generating candidates for serendipitous recommendations. Thus, the output of this module is a list of serendipitous recommendations on the basis of apps installed on a target user's phone. This module thus generates recommendations by finding paths amongst the installed apps thus finding serendipitous apps to reduce over-specialization in recommendation lists.

4 Experiments

4.1 Experimental Data

Our dataset consists of 66,223 apps and 22,213 users in total, collected through a commercial project – Mobilewalla[3] [9]. Mobilewalla is a venture capital backed company that specializes in collecting, analyzing and presenting data related to mobile apps in four native stores, Apple iTunes[4], Google Android market[5], Blackberry native store[6] and Windows App store[7]. We implemented all modules with Java 1.7 and used MySQL v5.1 to store the similarity scores and recommendation paths. All modules and the database reside in the same computer (CPU: Intel CORE i5 2.27 GHz, Memory: 8 GBytes, OS: Windows 7).

4.2 Evaluation Measure

As described in Section 3.1, we define our serendipitous recommendation as the one that provides diverse and new apps. Thus, firstly, we evaluate our recommendations using normalized version of item novelty metric. Zhang and Hurley [26] introduced an item novelty measure in the course of their investigation on diversifying recommendation lists. Their approach, however, has a drawback; the measure can grow unbounded when the distance between two items becomes large. As such, we normalize the distance, $d(UMP_{apps}, R_{apps}^{srdp_j})$ between apps in user's mobile phone UMP_{apps} and serendipitous apps recommended to the user $R_{apps}^{srdp_j}$ against the maximum distance of $d(UMP_{apps}, R_{apps}^{srdp_j})$. This normalized item novelty measure, which we denote as $nITN_{R_{apps}^{srdp_j}}$, is thus defined as follows:

$$nITN_{R_{apps}^{srdp_j}} = \frac{1}{N} \sum_{j=1}^{N} \frac{d(UMP_{apps}, R_{apps}^{srdp_j})}{\max d(UMP_{apps}, R_{apps}^{srdp_j})}, \quad (3)$$

where N is the number of the recommended apps (in which we have set N=5, 10, and 20) and we refer to them as $nITN@5, nITN@10, nITN@20$, respectively. If the recommendation list contains apps similar (dissimilar) to user apps, this measure has a smaller (larger) value. Larger results indicate more surprise, resulting in serendipitous recommendations. We also employ another metric, diversity-in-top-N, which is defined as follows:

$$\text{diversity-in-top-}N = \frac{\left| \bigcup_{u \in U} L_N(u) \right|}{|U|}, \quad (4)$$

where u, U, and $L_N(u)$ denote a user, the set of all users, and the list of N items recommended for user u, respectively. This metric measures the aggregate diversity

[3] http://www.mobilewalla.com
[4] http://store.apple.com/us
[5] https://play.google.com/store?hl=en
[6] http://appworld.blackberry.com/
[7] http://www.windowsphone.com/en-us/store

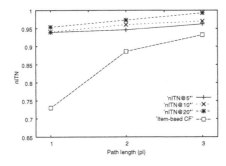 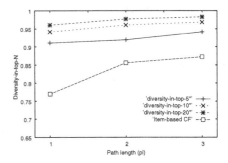

Fig. 3. Recommendation accuracy evaluated with $nITN@N$ (N=5, 10, 20) obtained by varying path length. ("*" denotes the difference between the results obtained by our approach and "item-based CF" is statistically significant for $p < 0.05$.)

Fig. 4. Recommendation accuracy evaluated with diversity-in-top-N (N=5, 10, 20) obtained by varying path length. ("*" denotes the difference between the results obtained by our approach and "item-based CF" is statistically significant for $p < 0.05$.)

using the total number of distinct items amongst the top-N items recommended across all users [2]. This measure also has the drawback in that it can grow unbound when the number of target users becomes large. As such, we normalize the total number of distinct recommended items for all users against the set of all users.

4.3   Experimental Results

We employ item-based collaborative filtering [20] as our baseline system. Item-based collaborative filtering works by calculating similarity between items. This approach regards two items as similar if users give similar ratings to items. We set threshold of similarity to 0.4, and then select all items (apps) that are less than the threshold as neighbors to predict ratings of apps. Our goal is to recommend serendipitous recommendation. That is why we select low similarity neighboring apps. Since only a handful of apps receive ratings by users, this method recommends a small pool of apps over and over again, contributing to the "rich gets richer" phenomenon. We employ binary ratings for the baseline system, namely, 1 and 0 for installed and uninstalled app, respectively. Figure 3 shows normalized item novelty ($nITN$) of recommended serendipitous apps. Higher $nITN$ score indicates larger serendipity. At path length, pl=3, our method outperforms the baseline (item-based collaborative filtering), and achieves the best with $nITN$ of 0.993 for the top 20 apps for all users. To measure the diversity, we evaluated recommended apps with diversity-in-top-N [2]. Figure 4 shows the top N diversity (N= 5, 10, and 20). Similarly, at pl=3, our method outperforms the baseline and achieves the best for the top 20 apps for all users.

As we mentioned in Section 3.2, we employed cosine similarity in module M1. On the other hand, Pearson correlation can be one of alternatives as similarity measure. However, we observe that Pearson correlation gives identical results with cosine similarity. Furthermore, both $nITN@5$ in Figure 3 and diversity-in-top-5 in Figure 4 outperform our baseline system, item-based CF. A two-tailed t-test at the all path length shows that the difference between the results obtained by our approach and "item-based CF" is statistically significant for $p < 0.05$.

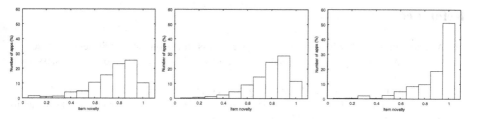

Fig. 5. Distribution of item novelty for User 1 (15 apps)

Fig. 6. Distribution of item novelty for User 2 (7 apps)

Fig. 7. Distribution of item novelty for User 3 (40 apps)

Having established the novelty and diversity of the recommended apps, we analyze the obtained results of recommendation qualitatively. A major challenge faced here was the lack of metrics to measure the new apps recommended. Since we do not have any prior data in terms of downloads or ratings for these apps, we cannot definitely say that which apps are relevant to each user, but by controlling the similarity threshold (we consider the top 30 most similar apps while graph construction), our approach can prevent user's interest from significant drift.

Figures 5, 6, and 7 show the distribution of item novelty for three sample users with various number of applications installed on their mobile phones when $nITN@20$ at $pl=3$. It ranges from 0.1 to 1.0, where 1.0 represents most diverse. Users 1 and 2 have installed 15 and 7 apps on each of their mobile phones, respectively. Our method can recommend about 30% and 25% diverse apps with $nITN > 0.9$ to User 1 and User 2, respectively. User 3 has 40 apps installed on his phone and 50% of the recommendations generated have $nITN > 0.9$. This indicates that, the higher the number of apps with the user, the greater the diversity of apps recommended, achieving a more desired novelty distribution. However, this does not mean that a smaller number of apps with the user would reduce the chances of being recommended diverse apps. Although Users 1 and 2 installed smaller number of apps compared with User 3, they can still obtain a notable novelty distribution score.

5 Conclusion

In this paper, we have developed a method for providing serendipitous recommendation for mobile apps by discovering highly diverse apps. Our approach captures user's preferences from apps already installed on the user's mobile phone and provides serendipitous recommendation by constructing app-app similarity graph. Our evaluation is still not complete as we need to develop additional metrics for verifying the accuracy of these serendipitous recommendations. This is a challenging task since any metrics for serendipitous recommendation have not been developed so far. While we focused on the domain of mobile apps, our approach can be applied to any domains with huge cardinality. In future work, we plan to justify the recommendations with newly developed metrics that can evaluate serendipitous recommendations.

References

1. Adamopoulos, P., Tuzhilin, A.: On Unexpectedness in Recommender Systems: Or How to Better Expect the Unexpected. Technical Report CBA-13-03, Stern School of Business, New York University (2013)
2. Adomavicius, G., Kwon, Y.: Maximizing Aggregate Recommendation Diversity: A Graph-Theoretic Approach. In: Proc. of the 1st International Workshop on Novelty and Diversity in Recommender Systems (DiveRS 2011), pp. 3–10 (2011)
3. Aggarwal, C.C., Wolf, J.L., Wu, K.-L., Yu, P.S.: Horting Hatches an Egg: A New Graph-Theoretic Approach to Collaborative Filtering. In: Proc. of the 5th ACM SIGKDD International Conference on Knowledge Discovery and Data Mining (KDD 1999), pp. 201–212 (1999)
4. Andre, P., Schraefel, M.C., Teevan, J., Dumais, S.T.: Discovery is Never by Chance: Designing for (Un)Serendipity. In: Proc. of the 7th SIGCHI Conference on Creativity and Cognition (C&C 2009), pp. 305–314 (2009)
5. Andre, P., Teevan, J., Dumais, S.T.: From X-Rays to Silly Putty via Uranus: Serendipity and its Role in Web Search. In: Proc. of the 27th International Conference on Human Factors in Computing Systems (CHI 2009), pp. 2033–2036 (2009)
6. Basu, C., Hirsh, H., Cohen, W.: Recommendation as Classification: Using Social and Content-Based Information in Recommendation. In: Proc. of the 15th National Conference on Artificial Intelligence (AAAI 1998), pp. 714–720 (1998)
7. Breese, J.S., Heckerman, D., Kadie, C.: Empirical Analysis of Predictive Algorithms for Collaborative Filtering. In: Proc. of the 14th Conference on Uncertainty in Artificial Intelligence (UAI 1998), pp. 43–52 (1998)
8. Costa-Montenegro, E., Barragáns-Martínez, A.B., Rey-López, M.: Which App? A Recommender System of Applications in Markets: Implementation of the Service for Monitoring Users' Interaction. Expert Systems with Applications: An International Journal 39(10), 9367–9375 (2012)
9. Datta, A., Dutta, K., Kajanan, S., Pervin, N.: Mobilewalla: A Mobile Application Search Engine. Mobile Computing, Applications, and Services 95(5), 172–187 (2012)
10. Davidsson, C., Moritz, S.: Utilizing Implicit Feedback and Context to Recommend Mobile Applications from First Use. In: Proc. of the 2011 Workshop on Context-awareness in Retrieval and Recommendation (CaRR 2011), pp. 19–22 (2011)
11. Goldberg, D., Nichols, D., Oki, B.M., Terry, D.B.: Using Collaborative Filtering to Weave an Information Tapestry. Communications of the ACM 35(12), 61–70 (1992)
12. Kawamae, N.: Serendipitous Recommendations via Innovators. In: Proc. of the 33rd Annual International ACM SIGIR Conference on Research and Development in Information Retrieval (SIGIR 2010), pp. 218–225 (2010)
13. Konstan, J.A., Miller, B.N., Maltz, D., Herlocker, J.L., Gordon, L.R., Riedl, J.: GroupLens: Applying Collaborative Filtering to Usenet News. Communications of the ACM 40(3), 77–87 (1997)
14. Lathia, N., Hailes, S., Capra, L., Amatriain, X.: Temporal Diversity in Recommender Systems. In: Proc. of the 33rd Annual International ACM SIGIR Conference on Research and Development in Information Retrieval (SIGIR 2010), pp. 210–217 (2010)
15. Lin, J., Sugiyama, K., Kan, M.-Y., Chua, T.-S.: Addressing Cold-Start in App Recommendation: Latent User Models Constructed from Twitter Followers. In: Proc. of the 36th Annual International ACM SIGIR Conference on Research and Development in Information Retrieval (SIGIR 2013), pp. 283–292 (2013)

16. Nakatsuji, M., Fujiwara, Y., Tanaka, A., Uchiyama, T., Fujimura, K., Ishida, T.: Classical Music for Rock Fans?: Novel Recommendations for Expanding User Interests. In: Proc. of the 19th International Conference on Information and Knowledge Management (CIKM 2010), pp. 949–958 (2010)

17. Resnick, P., Iacovou, N., Suchak, M., Bergstorm, J.R.P.: GroupLens: An Open Architecture for Collaborative Filtering of Netnews. In: Proc. of the ACM 1994 Conference on Computer Supported Cooperative Work (CSCW 1994), pp. 175–186 (1994)

18. Ricci, F., Shapira, L., Kantor, B.: Recommender Systems Handbook. Springer (2011)

19. Salton, G., McGill, M.J.: Introduction to Modern Information Retrieval. McGraw-Hill (1983)

20. Sarwar, B.M., Karypis, G., Konstan, J., Riedl, J.: Item-Based Collaborative Filtering Recommendation Algorithms. In: Proc. of the 10th International World Wide Web Conference (WWW10), pp. 285–295 (2001)

21. Sarwar, B.M., Karypis, G., Konstan, J.A.: Analysis of Recommendation Algorithms for E-commerce. In: Proc. of the 2nd ACM Conference on Electronic Commerce (EC 2000), pp. 158–167 (2000)

22. Sugiyama, K., Kan, M.-Y.: Serendipitous Recommendation for Scholarly Papers Considering Relations Among Researchers. In: Proc. of the 11th Annual International ACM/IEEE Joint Conference on Digital Libraries (JCDL 2011), pp. 307–310 (2011)

23. Xu, Q., Erman, J., Gerber, A., Mao, Z., Pang, J., Venkataraman, S.: Identifying Diverse Usage Behaviors of Smartphone Apps. In: Proc. of the 2011 ACM SIGCOMM Conference on Internet Measurement Conference (IMC 2011), pp. 329–344 (2011)

24. Yan, B., Chen, G.: AppJoy: Personalized Mobile Application Discovery. In: Proc. of the 9th International Conference on Mobile Systems, Applications and Services (MobiSys 2011), pp. 113–126 (2011)

25. Yin, P., Luo, P., Lee, W.-C., Wang, M.: App Recommendation: A Contest between Satisfaction and Temptation. In: Proc. of the 6th International Conference on Web Search and Data Mining (WSDM 2013), pp. 395–404 (2013)

26. Zhang, M., Hurley, N.: Avoiding Monotony: Improving the Diversity of Recommendations. In: Proc. of the 2008 ACM Conference on Recommender Systems (RecSys 2008), pp. 123–130.

27. Ziegler, C.-N., McNee, S.M., Konstan, J.A., Lausen, G.: Improving Recommendation Lists Through Topic Diversification. In: Proc. of the 14th International World Wide Web Conference (WWW 2005), pp. 22–32 (2005)

User-Aware Advertisability

Hai-Tao Yu[1] and Tetsuya Sakai[2]

[1] The University of Tokushima, Japan
yu-haitao@iss.tokushima-u.ac.jp
[2] Waseda University, Japan
tetsuyasakai@acm.org

Abstract. In sponsored search, many studies focus on finding the most relevant advertisements (ads) and their optimal ranking for a submitted query. Determining whether it is suitable to show ads has received less attention. In this paper, we introduce the concept of user-aware advertisability, which refers to the probability of ad-click on sponsored ads when a specific user submits a query. When computing the advertisability for a given query-user pair, we first classify the clicked web pages based on a pre-defined category hierarchy and use the aggregated topical categories of clicked web pages to represent user preference. Taking user preference into account, we then compute the ad-click probability for this query-user pair. Compared with existing methods, the experimental results show that user preference is of great value for generating user-specific advertisability. In particular, our approach that computes advertisability per query-user pair outperforms the two state-of-the-art methods that compute advertisability per query in terms of a variant of the normalized Discounted Cumulative Gain metric.

1 Introduction

Currently, the majority of major web search engines' revenue stems from sponsored search, which achieves a win-win-win situation for users, advertisers and search engine companies. For example, users can efficiently obtain their desired information or be navigated to specific websites. Advertisers get increased traffic and potential users. By satisfying users' needs and advertisers' desires, web search engines commonly get paid under a specific mechanism (e.g., cost-per-click [12]). Considering the huge profit margins, designing successful sponsored search technologies has attracted significant attention from search engine companies, as well as research communities. Increasing evidence points to the fact that showing ads should be avoided when users are not interested in ads and/or no ads match users' interests, otherwise, it may degrade user experience or drive them away [5, 20]. Therefore, deciding whether to display ads for a given query is a very important problem to tackle. To this end, Pandey et al. [18] have proposed the concept of advertisability for a given query, defined as the probability of ad-click on any of the displayed ads. A number of studies [1, 18, 21] have shown that each term that comprises a search query has its own inherent probability of receiving ad-clicks, and have attempted to quantify the advertisability of a query based on its query terms. The advantage of the query term based

R.E. Banchs et al. (Eds.): AIRS 2013, LNCS 8281, pp. 452–463, 2013.
© Springer-Verlag Berlin Heidelberg 2013

approach is that it can handle tail or even unseen queries. However, existing approaches do not consider whether a given query is likely to receive ad-clicks by a particular user. In this paper, we introduce the concept of user-aware advertisability, which incorporates user preference. Given a query with respect to a specific user (essentially a query-user pair), user-aware advertisability is defined as the probability that this user clicks on any ads displayed on the SERP (search engine result page). We define user preference as the user's tendency to click on a particular topical category, and represent it as a probability distribution over a set of pre-defined categories (detailed in Section 5.1). Compared with existing studies, our user-aware advertisability differs in the following aspects: (i) User-aware advertisability is computed per query-user pair rather than per query; (ii) We use the category information underlying each query-user pair to filter out the topically irrelevant queries when estimating a query term's probability of receiving ad-clicks. Table 1 illustrates the benefit of user-aware advertisability using toy examples. Suppose that the category information (Column 2) for each query (Column 1) can be automatically determined, and the two queries in Table 1 are the only ones that contain term *apple* in the set of past queries.

Table 1. Toy examples

Query	Category	Query frequency	Ad-click count
apple computer	Computers	10	5
apple crisp recipe	Shopping/Food	4	1

Existing methods don't consider the category information when computing the contribution of a query term to the query's advertisability. For example, the method proposed by Pandey et al. [18] computes a query term's probability of receiving ad-clicks as $\delta(w) = \frac{\sum_{\{q \in Q | w \in q\}} C^+(q)}{\sum_{\{q \in Q | w \in q\}} (C^+(q) + C^-(q))}$, where Q is the entire query set, $\{q \in Q | w \in q\}$ are queries that contain w, $C^+(q)$ is the count that query q received ad-clicks, $C^-(q)$ is the count that q received no ad-clicks. Suppose that two different users u_1 and u_2 enter the same new query, say, *apple*. Then $\delta(w)$ is computed as $\frac{6}{14} \approx 0.4286$, and the value is the same for both u_1 and u_2. In contrast, our approach first identifies the query's topical category with respect to a particular user, which may turn out to be *Computers* for u_1 just like *apple computer*, *Shopping/Food* for u_2 just like *apple crisp recipe* in Table 1. Then the advertisability for *apple* submitted by u_1 is computed as $\frac{5}{10}$, while that for *apple* submitted by u_2 is computed as $\frac{1}{4}$. Thus the statistics for the past queries that don't match the category underlying a query-user pair are filtered out.

In this study, we propose a method for computing user-aware advertisability and evaluate it using a commercial sponsored search data. Experimental results show that our approach can generate user-specific advertisability and outperforms the baseline methods that compute advertisability per query. The rest of the paper is organized as follows: Section 2 discusses related work. Section 3 formalizes user-aware advertisability, and Section 4 describes how the required probabilities were estimated. Section 5 presents experimental results and discussions. We conclude our work in section 6.

2   Related Work

To display highly relevant ads instead of driving users away, considerable work has been conducted from various aspects. Tyler et al. [22] formulated the problem of showing relevant ads as a context multi-armed bandit problem, where a user's query is used as the context. Wang et al. [23] proposed a mixture language model to find *good match* ads. To efficiently match ads against rare queries, Broder et al. [6] proposed a method for online rewriting of tail queries. A number of researchers [2, 11, 14, 15] studied how to use the sponsored search log to learn highly relevant ads using machine learning. For example, Hillard et al. [15] investigated the translation model to learn user click propensity. Ashkan et al. [2] proposed to model user's browsing and click behavior using contextual factors, such as the user's initial motivation and persistence of browsing the ad list.

Rather than finding relevant ads, Broder et al. [5] studied when to advertise in a supervised manner. They utilized ad relevance and result set cohesiveness as features. Pandey et al. [18] proposed the concept of advertisability to quantify the probability of seeing a click on any sponsored ads. They focused on tail queries and proposed a model that computes the advertisability of a query based on the individual query terms. Ashkan et al. [1] investigated the impact of query terms on the commercial intent of queries. They proposed a probabilistic model based on the assumption that the likelihood of receiving ad-clicks for a query is derived from the contributions of its composing terms. Cheng et al. [9] studied the user-specific features and demographic-based features to perform click prediction and showed that the accuracy can be improved through the personalized click model. Based on the user's motivation of entering a query, Dai et al. [13] classified queries into commercial and non-commercial. They used a supervised method to identify commercial queries. Cheng et al. [10] suggested to predict the user's search intent based on search behaviors. They argue that many information needs are actually triggered by what users have browsed.

None of the above mentioned studies considered the advertisability of a query for a particular user. We believe that our user-aware advertisability will be useful for effective presentation of ads on a SERP, e.g., deciding whether to display ads when a user submits a query.

3   User-Aware Advertisability

We define user-aware advertisability as the ad-click probability with respect to a query-user pair. More specifically, we formulate it as a conditional probability $p(x = 1|q, u)$, where x is a binary variable, $x = 1$ denotes the case that the user clicks on sponsored ads and $x = 0$ denotes the case of non-click. By assuming that each user's preference can be represented as his/her preference over a pre-defined set of topical categories, we decompose user-aware advertisability as:

$$p(x = 1|q, u) = \sum_{i=1}^{k} p(c_i|q, u) * p(x = 1|q, c_i) \tag{1}$$

where $p(c_i|q, u)$ represents the user preference of a topical category c_i given q, $p(x = 1|q, c_i)$ represents the probability of receiving an ad-click for query q given c_i. In the sponsored search log, some terms, such as *apple* and *camera*, have a high ad-click count. Others, such as *markov* and *equation*, rarely receive ad-clicks. Moreover, for the same term within different contexts of queries, the probability of receiving ad-clicks is different, e.g., *apple* in the context of queries *apple computer* and *apple crisp recipe* shown in Table 1 (Section 1). This observation leads us to hypothesize that: A specific term has its own probability of receiving ad-clicks, and this probability also depends on the underlying topic expressed by the query. Going further, we assume that the probability of receiving ad-clicks for a query with respect to a topical category can be derived from the contributions of its individual terms, which is expressed as:

$$p(x = 1|q, c_i) = \varphi(\{w \in q | p(x = 1|w, c_i)\}) \tag{2}$$

where $w \in q$ represents an individual term, $p(x = 1|w, c_i)$ indicates the probability of receiving ad-clicks for a query term with respect to a topical category, φ is a latent function that derives the query's probability of receiving ad-clicks with respect to a category from the contributions of its individual terms. In this study, we assume that the individual terms contribute towards a query's probability of receiving ad-clicks in a mutually-independent manner. Hence Equation 2 can be simplified as:

$$p(x = 1|q, c_i) = 1 - \prod_{w \in q}(1 - p(x = 1|w, c_i)) \tag{3}$$

Since the latter part of $\prod_{w \in q}(1 - p(x = 1|w, c_i))$ in Equation 3 is the product of probabilities that a term receives no ad-clicks, long queries tend to receive low values, and hence high advertisability values. To counter the bias towards long queries, we introduce the factor β as follows:

$$\begin{cases} p(x = 1|q, c_i) = (1 - \prod_{w \in q}(1 - p(x = 1|w, c_i))) * \beta \\ \beta = \frac{1}{\log_{avql}(\varepsilon + |q|)} \end{cases} \tag{4}$$

where $|q|$ denotes query length (the number of terms), $avql$ denotes the average query length for a training dataset. Given $avql$, β controls the extent that the individual terms can contribute towards a query's probability of receiving ad-clicks. This kind of length penalty is also discussed in previous studies [17, 19]. The small constant ε avoids division by zero when $|q| = 1$. Based on a pilot experiment with our training data (described in Section 5.1), we set $\varepsilon = 0.3$. By combining Equations 1 and 4, the user-aware advertisability is given as:

$$p(x = 1|q, u) = \sum_{i=1}^{k}\{p(c_i|q, u) * (1 - \prod_{w \in q}(1 - p(x = 1|w, c_i))) * \beta\} \tag{5}$$

To quantify user-aware advertisability with Equation 5, the category preference $p(c_i|q, u)$ and the term' probability of receiving ad-licks with respect to a topical category $p(x = 1|w, c_i)$ are required. In the next section, we detail how these probabilities are estimated based on a sponsored search log.

4   Probability Estimation

Here we first introduce some definitions and background that will be used throughout this study. When a user starts a search by submitting a query, the search engine returns a SERP. A SERP includes organic results (web pages), sponsored ads, related searches, etc. But this study focuses on the clicks on the organic results and sponsored ads. From the sponsored search log, we can obtain tuples of the following form: t: timestamp of viewing the SERP, u: user identifier that represents a user, q: query, d: a clicked web page, ad: an ad. From the data, we can construct an undirected 3-uniform hypergraph (or tripartite hypergraph) as $G = (V, E)$, where V is the set of nodes and E is the set of hyperedges. V consists of three subsets of nodes: $V^x = d$, $V^y = < q, u >$ and $V^z = ad$, where V^x, V^y and V^z denote the clicked web pages, query-user pairs and displayed ads respectively. A hyperedge $(d, < q, u >, ad)$ in E represents the resultant events when u submits q. Figure 1 illustrates an example, where circles, diamonds and rectangles represent clicked web pages, query-user pairs and ads respectively.

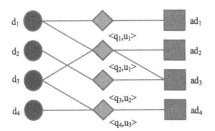

Fig. 1. A 3-uniform hypergraph

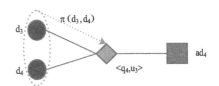

Fig. 2. Deducing user preference

Equation 5 (Section 3) requires the estimation of $p(c_i|q, u)$ and $p(x = 1|w, c_i)$. The former, the category preference for a given query-user pair, is estimated as:

$$p(c_i|q, u) = \frac{|c_i|}{\sum_{\{d_r \in D(q,u)|c_j \in \pi(d_r)\}} |c_j|} \tag{6}$$

where $D(q, u)$ denotes the set of clicked web pages when u submits q, π denotes a classifier that can effectively determine the categories of a web page, $\{d_r \in D(q, u)|c_j \in \pi(d_r)\}$ denotes the set of categories obtained by classifying the web pages in $D(q, u)$, $|c_i|$ denotes the count of c_i. As shown in Figure 2, for the query-user pair $< q_4, u_3 >$, the clicked web pages are d_3 and d_4. We deduce user preference as follows: Suppose $\pi(d_3) = \{c_1, c_2\}$, $\pi(d_4) = \{c_2, c_3\}$, we have $|c_1| = 1$, $|c_2| = 2$ and $|c_3| = 1$. With Equation 6, the category preference for c_1, c_2 and c_3 are computed as 0.25, 0.5 and 0.25 respectively. Then, the user preference underlying $< q_4, u_3 >$ is represented as $\{< c_2, 0.5 >, < c_1, 0.25 >, < c_3, 0.25 >\}$. For the web page classifier π, we utilize the method described by Bennett et al. [3, 4], using a pre-defined category hierarchy extracted from ODP (Open Directory Project)[1]. This method effectively overcomes the problems of error propagation and non-linear decision surfaces when classifying web pages into a

---

[1] http://www.dmoz.org/

pre-defined taxonomy. We refer the reader to the original papers [3, 4] for further details. We use this method as a black box for obtaining the topical categories of a web page. In Equation 5, the parameter k essentially denotes that the top-k categories are used to represent user preference (e.g, $k = 1$ means that only c_2 is used in the the above example). Based on a pilot experiment with the training data, we set $k = 3$.

Whereas, the click probability for a given term-category pair, which Equation 5 also requires, is estimated as:

$$p(x = 1|w, c_i) = \frac{\sum_{\{q \in Q|w \in q\}} C^+(q, c_i)}{\sum_{\{q \in Q|w \in q\}} (C^+(q, c_i) + C^-(q, c_i))} \qquad (7)$$

where $\{q \in Q|w \in q\}$ is the set of queries that contain term w, $C^+(q, c_i)$ is the count that query q with a topical category c_i received ad-clicks. $C^-(q, c_i)$ is the count that query q with c_i received no ad-clicks. The numerator is the total number of resultant ad-clicks when using term w to express information needs with respect to c_i. The denominator is the total number of times of using term w to express information needs with respect to c_i. Leveraging on the training data, we estimate $C^+(q, c_i)$ and $C^-(q, c_i)$ as follows: Suppose the categories of the clicked web pages corresponding to a past query-user pair are c_m and c_n, if this query-user pair resulted in ad-clicks, we generate two training triples as $(q, c_m, 1)$ and $(q, c_n, 1)$. If not, the training triples are $(q, c_m, 0)$ and $(q, c_n, 0)$ instead. At the same time, training pairs $(c_m, 1)$ and $(c_n, 1)$ or $(c_m, 0)$ and $(c_n, 0)$ are also generated, which are used to estimate the probability of receiving ad-clicks for an unseen query term w^*.

$$p(x = 1|w^*, c_i) = \frac{C^+(c_i)}{C^+(c_i) + C^-(c_i)} \qquad (8)$$

where $C^+(c_i)$ denotes the count of category c_i that received ad-clicks, $C^-(c_i)$ denotes the count of category c_i that received no ad-clicks.

When scaling up to the web-scale application, the training data for estimating the click probability for a given term-category pair can be learned in an off-line manner. For estimating the user preference, some collaborative filtering methods (e.g., Cao et al. [8]) can be used to deduce user preference instead of classifying each clicked web page as we have done in this paper.

5 Experiments

5.1 Data

We collected a 10-day click data from a major web search engine (April 1-10, 2013). The data from the first seven days were used for training and that from the remaining three days were used as the test data. Queries including characters outside a-zA-Z0-9 and the white space were removed. Our data set contains $10,590,386$ unique queries, $12,517,706$ unique users, $19,320,427$ query-user pairs, $10,905,297$ unique clicked web pages and a total of $1,718,906$ ad-clicks. The average query length ($avql$) for the training data is 3.1053. In this study, we manually extracted a part of the ODP categories that are suitable for commercial intents. There are totally 219 nodes with a maximum depth as 2. At the first category level, there are 15 nodes. At the second category level, there are 204 nodes. For example, the subcategories *Computers/Hardware* and *Computers/Software* are subsumed within the higher level category *Computers*. To perform a fine-grained differentiation of category preference by users, we use the two-level category hierarchy.

Query frequency is known to obey the power law. To investigate the feasibility of computing user-aware advertisability for both head and tail queries, we randomly extracted 200 queries with frequency counts at least 20 to form the HQS (head query subcollection), and another 200 queries with frequency counts lower than 20 to form the TQS (tail query subcollection). The corresponding users, clicked pages, ad-clicks were extracted accordingly. The basic statistics are summarized in Tables 2 and 3.

<table>
<tr><td colspan="2" align="center">Table 2. TQS</td></tr>
<tr><td>Item</td><td>Number</td></tr>
<tr><td>#distinct queries</td><td>200</td></tr>
<tr><td>#user</td><td>233</td></tr>
<tr><td>#query-user pairs</td><td>233</td></tr>
</table>

Table 2. TQS

Item	Number
#distinct queries	200
#user	233
#query-user pairs	233

Table 3. HQS

Item	Number
#distinct queries	200
#user	11803
#query-user pairs	11805

To demonstrate that queries and query terms cover diverse topical categories, we computed the *category span* of each query and query term. Here, category span means the number of categories that a given query or query term covers according to the categories of the clicked web pages as estimated by the method by Bennett et al. [3, 4]. Figures 3 and 4 plot the query count and query term count against category span.

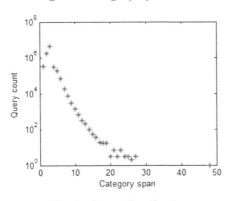

Fig. 3. Query distribution

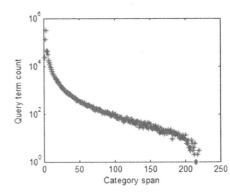

Fig. 4. Query term distribution

Not surprisingly, it can be observed that the query terms exhibit higher category spans than the entire queries. For example, the category span for the query *windows phone* is 11, while that for the term *windows* is 171. As the same term may be used in the context of diverse topical categories, this result suggests that it is important to take the category information into account when computing advertisability based on query terms. When estimating the ad-click probability of term *windows* in the *Computers* context, we don't want to use the statistics of term *windows* obtained in the *Housing* context.

5.2   Evaluation Metric

To evaluate the effectiveness of user-aware advertisability, we utilize the three-day test data portion of our data. Each test instance h in our test data H is a quadruple $(q, u, imp, cCnt)$, where q and u are the query-user pair, imp and $cCnt$ are the impression and ad-click count respectively. We rank all query-user pairs in the test data by user-aware advertisability and evaluate it using a measure similar to the nDCG (normalized Discounted Cumulative Gain) [7, 16]. nDCG measures how the system's ranked list deviates from the ideal ranked list L^*, i.e., the ranked list that we want to achieve. In our case, we require the ideal list to possess the following properties: (1) Query-user pairs with high clickthrough rates $(cCnt/imp)$ should be ranked higher; (2) Within the query-user pairs with the same clickthrough rate, those with larger $cCnt$ values should be ranked higher; (3) Within the query-user pairs with $cCnt$ of zero, those with larger imp values should be ranked lower. Thus, we want query-user pairs with high clickthrough rates and click counts, and we want to avoid queries that were shown many times but were never clicked. In accordance with the above three sort keys, we use the following function to define the gain for each h in H.

$$f(h, H) = \begin{cases} 10 * Round(\frac{cCnt}{imp}, 2) + \frac{cCnt}{10*max_H(cCnt)+1} & cCnt > 0 \\ \frac{1}{imp+10*max_H(cCnt)+1} & cCnt = 0 \end{cases} \quad (9)$$

where $max_H(cCnt)$ denotes the maximum count of ad-click in test collection H. To ensure a monotonically decreasing function, $Round(v, n)$ is introduced to return a number rounded to a specified number of digits, where v is the number to round, n is the number of digits to round the number to. By $Round(v, n)$, the ratio between ad-click and impression is divided into 100 intervals in our study, the different ratios within the same interval are viewed as the same. $f(h, H)$ is an ad hoc function that ensures that the three sort keys are applied exactly in that order. Table 4 illustrates some test instances sorted with $f(h, H)$, the user identifiers are partially omitted for privacy. Due to diverse users, *galaxy s4* appears in different test instances.

Table 4. The ideal order according to $f(h, H)$

Ideal order	Query	User identifier	Impression	Ad-click count
1	galaxy s4	***3868F4	9	3
2	galaxy s4	***A96C38	3	1
3	galaxy s4	***09676D	3	0
4	galaxy s4	***DA6E9C	52	0

The ideal list L^* ranks all instances in H by $f(h, H)$. On the other hand, we rank the same instances using our user-aware advertisability scores, computed using the ad-click statistics and category information from the training data.

This list is denoted by L. For an instance h at the r-th position in L, its gain value is defined as $g(r) = f(h, H)$. Then, the discounted cumulative gain is computed as $dcg(r) = \sum_{i=1}^{r} g(i)/log(i+1)$, and the $nDCG$ is computed as the ratio of the system's dcg and the ideal dcg. We compute $nDCG$ for various cutoff values.

5.3 Baseline Methods

We compare user-aware advertisability against two user-unaware baseline methods. Given a query, there are two hypotheses: $p(x = 1|q)$ that an ad-click occurs and $p(x = 0|q)$ that no ad-click occurs. The method of Log-likelihood-ratio proposed by Ashkan et al. [1] considers the ratio of the posterior probability of a query and is used for making a decision between these two hypotheses as:

$$log\frac{p(x = 1|q)}{p(x = 0|q)} = log[\frac{p(x = 1)}{p(x = 0)} \prod_{i=1}^{n} \frac{p(w_i|x = 1)}{p(w_i|x = 0)}] \tag{10}$$

Pandey et al. [18]' s advertisability for a given query is defined as:

$$\delta(q) = max_S(1 - \prod_{w \in S}(1 - \delta(w))) \tag{11}$$

where $\delta(w)$ denotes the probability of receiving ad-clicks for a query term, and for a parameter m, S is a subset of the set of all query terms from q, s.t. $|S| \leq m$.

5.4 Results and Discussions

The performances of our user-aware approach and the baseline methods are plotted in Figures 5 and 6, the x-axes represent the cutoff r, while y-axes represent $nDCG@r$. The circle indicates some example cutoff values that our user-aware approach outperforms the two baseline methods at the same time and exhibits a statistical significant difference (paired t-test, $p < 0.05$).

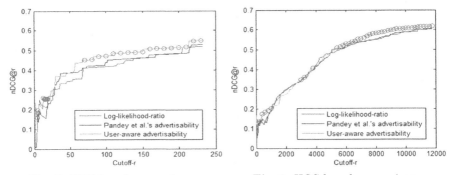

Fig. 5. TQS based comparison   **Fig. 6.** HQS based comparison

As shown in Figure 5, our user-aware advertisability slightly underperforms Log-likelihood-ratio for tail queries with $r \in [7, 12]$. Also, our approach slightly underperforms Pandey et al.'s advertisability with $r \in [37, 54]$. However, our approach significantly outperforms the baselines for many other cutoff values. In particular, for head queries (Figure 6), user-aware advertisability significantly outperforms the baseline methods for $r < 1055$ or $r > 5042$.

Due to diverse users, the frequent queries like *galaxy s4* in Table 4 (Section 5.2) constitute different sets of ties (i.e., query-user pairs with the same query). Because the baseline methods are user-unaware and compute advertisability per query, they assign the same advertisability score to a set of ties. Figures 5 and 6 show the results where the tied pairs were broken at random. Thus, we also considered the best-possible and worst-possible cases for the baseline methods: (1) For each set of ties, rank the tied pairs in the same order as the ideal list (UB: upperbound); (2) For each set of ties, rank the tied pairs in the reverse order of the ideal list (LB: lowerbound). Figures 7 and 8 show the performance of user-aware advertisability against the upperbound and lowerbound of the baseline methods, where the circle indicates some example cutoff values that user-aware advertisability outperforms the upperbound of two baseline methods at the same time and exhibits a statistical significant difference (paired t-test, $p < 0.05$).

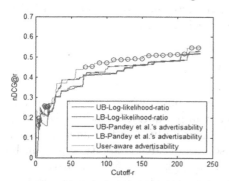

Fig. 7. TQS based comparison

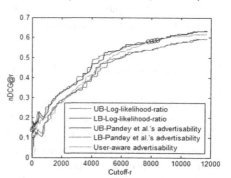

Fig. 8. HQS based comparison

As shown in Figures 7 and 8, while the upperbound and the lowerbound for the two baselines are indistinguishable for tail queries, there is a considerable gap between the bounds for the head queries. This reflects the fact that while most tail queries have a unique user, head queries have many users and therefore large groups of ties. From Figure 7, it can be observed that our user-aware advertisability steadily outperforms the baselines even the upperbounds for tail queries. From Figure 8, it can be observed that our approach is comparable to the two upperbounds for cutoffs $r < 1055$ or $r > 5042$.

So far, we have used the two-level categories from ODP. To explore the effect of the granularity of the categories on advertisability, we conducted an additional experiment using the top-level category only. For example, the category *Computers/Hardware* was reduced to *Computers*. Figures 9 and 10 show the results, where the circle indicates some example cutoff values that the top-level user-aware advertisability exhibits a statistical significant difference with the two-level user-aware advertisability (paired t-test, $p < 0.05$). As shown in Figures 9 and 10, the performance of the top-level user-aware advertisability and the two-level user-aware advertisability are significantly different. Intuitively,

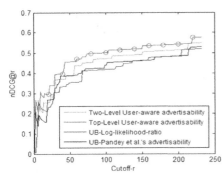

Fig. 9. TQS based comparison

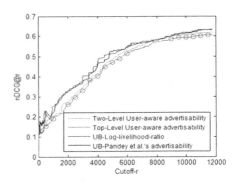

Fig. 10. HQS based comparison

two-level categories seem more effective than top-level ones, as they have more expressive power to reflect the user preference. However, the figures show that while it is true for head queries, the top-level user-aware advertisability actually do better for tail queries. This is probably because the category click statistics are sparse for tail queries and therefore relatively unreliable.

6   Conclusion and Future Work

We proposed the concept of user-aware advertisability, which computes the ad-click probability per query-user pair rather than per query. We believe that this will be useful for determining when and what to advertise for different users. Our experimental results showed that user-aware advertisability significantly outperforms two user-unaware baseline methods, especially for tail queries.

A limitation of our current study is that we have not taken into account factors besides ad-clicks, such as the user's entire ad-click history, query-ad relevance, the number and position of displayed ads, etc. Incorporating these features would be an interesting future research direction. We would also like to utilize user-aware advertisability in a real web search scenario.

Acknowledgements. We thank many researchers for their valuable helps, e.g., Dr. Bin Gao and his internships, Dr. Zhicheng Dou, Dr. Ke Zhou, etc.

References

[1] Ashkan, A., Clarke, C.L.A.: Term-based commercial intent analysis. In: Proceedings of the 32nd SIGIR, pp. 800–801 (2009)
[2] Ashkan, A., Clarke, C.L.A.: Modeling browsing behavior for click analysis in sponsored search. In: Proceedings of the 21st CIKM, pp. 2015–2019 (2012)
[3] Bennett, P.N., Nguyen, N.: Refined experts: improving classification in large taxonomies. In: Proceedings of the 32nd SIGIR, pp. 11–18 (2009)
[4] Bennett, P.N., Svore, K., Dumais, S.T.: Classification-enhanced ranking. In: Proceedings of the 19th WWW, pp. 111–120 (2010)

[5] Broder, A., Ciaramita, M., Fontoura, M., Gabrilovich, E., Josifovski, V., Metzler, D., Murdock, V., Plachouras, V.: To swing or not to swing: learning when (not) to advertise. In: Proceedings of the 17th CIKM, pp. 1003–1012 (2008)

[6] Broder, A., Ciccolo, P., Gabrilovich, E., Josifovski, V., Metzler, D., Riedel, L., Yuan, J.: Online expansion of rare queries for sponsored search. In: Proceedings of the 18th WWW, pp. 511–520 (2009)

[7] Burges, C., Shaked, T., Renshaw, E., Lazier, A., Deeds, M., Hamilton, N., Hullender, G.: Learning to rank using gradient descent. In: Proceedings of the 22nd ICML, pp. 89–96 (2005)

[8] Cao, B., Sun, J.T., Xiang, E.W., Hu, D.H., Yang, Q., Chen, Z.: PQC: personalized query classification. In: Proceedings of the 18th CIKM, pp. 1217–1226 (2009)

[9] Cheng, H., Cantú-Paz, E.: Personalized click prediction in sponsored search. In: Proceedings of the 3rd WSDM, pp. 351–360 (2010)

[10] Cheng, Z., Gao, B., Liu, T.Y.: Actively predicting diverse search intent from user browsing behaviors. In: Proceedings of the 19th WWW, pp. 221–230 (2010)

[11] Ciaramita, M., Murdock, V., Plachouras, V.: Online learning from click data for sponsored search. In: Proceedings of the 17th WWW, pp. 227–236 (2008)

[12] CNET: Another engine takes ads by the click (1996), http://news.com.com/Anotherenginetakesadsbytheclick/2100-1033_3-212736.html

[13] Dai, H.K., Zhao, L., Nie, Z., Wen, J.R., Wang, L., Li, Y.: Detecting online commercial intention (OCI). In: Proceedings of the 15th WWW, pp. 829–837 (2006)

[14] Graepel, T., Candela, J.Q., Borchert, T., Herbrich, R.: Web-scale Bayesian click-through rate prediction for sponsored search advertising in Microsoft's Bing search engine. In: Proceedings of the 27th ICML, pp. 13–20 (2010)

[15] Hillard, D., Schroedl, S., Manavoglu, E., Raghavan, H., Leggetter, C.: Improving ad relevance in sponsored search. In: Proceedings of the 3rd WSDM, pp. 361–370 (2010)

[16] Järvelin, K., Kekäläinen, J.: Cumulated gain-based evaluation of IR techniques. ACM Transactions on Information Systems 20(4), 422–446 (2002)

[17] Li, Y., Hsu, B.J.P., Zhai, C., Wang, K.: Unsupervised query segmentation using clickthrough for information retrieval. In: Proceedings of the 34th SIGIR, pp. 285–294 (2011)

[18] Pandey, S., Punera, K., Fontoura, M., Josifovski, V.: Estimating advertisability of tail queries for sponsored search. In: Proceedings of the 33rd SIGIR, pp. 563–570 (2010)

[19] Peng, F., Schuurmans, D.: Self-supervised chinese word segmentation. In: Hoffmann, F., Adams, N., Fisher, D., Guimarães, G., Hand, D.J. (eds.) IDA 2001. LNCS, vol. 2189, pp. 238–247. Springer, Heidelberg (2001)

[20] Raghavan, H., Iyer, R.: Probabilistic first pass retrieval for search advertising: from theory to practice. In: Proceedings of the 19th CIKM, pp. 1019–1028 (2010)

[21] Regelson, M., Fain, D.C.: Predicting click-through rate using keyword clusters. In: Electronic Commerce, EC (2006)

[22] Tyler, L., Dávid, P., Martin, P.: Showing relevant ads via lipschitz context multi-armed bandits. In: Proceedings of the 13th AIS (2010)

[23] Wang, L., Ye, M., Zou, Y.: A language model approach to capture commercial intent and information relevance for sponsored search. In: Proceedings of the 20th CIKM, pp. 599–604 (2011)

Assigning Library Classification Numbers to People on the Web

Harumi Murakami[1], Yoshinobu Ura[2], and Yusuke Kataoka[1]

[1] Graduate School for Creative Cities, Osaka City University,
3-3-138, Sugimoto, Sumiyoshi, Osaka 558-8585 Japan
harumi@media.osaka-cu.ac.jp
http://murakami.media.osaka-cu.ac.jp/
[2] Winspire,
9-310, Hachiban-cho, Wakayama 640-8157 Japan

Abstract. To help users select and understand people during searches for them, we present a method of assigning Nippon Decimal Classification (NDC), which is a system of library classification numbers, to people on the web. By assigning NDC numbers to people, we can assign not only labels to people but also build a NDC-based people-search directory. We use a relative index in NDC, which lists the related index terms attached to NDC. We developed a prototype based on this approach. We evaluated the usefulness of our proposed method and directory and found that extracting relative index terms from the titles of web pages outperformed comparative methods.

Keywords: NDC, library classification system, relative index, Web people search, people-search directory.

1 Introduction

The popularity of web people searches continues to rise as the number of people increases about whom the web can provide information. Most people search systems are based on keyword search. By keyword search, which is typically a search by a person name or a keyword, users distinguish different people from the search results. If the list is merely "person 1, person 2, and so on," users have difficulty determining which person they should select. Appropriate labels shown with people should help users select the person they want.

There is research that assigns labels to people. For example, Wan et al. separated web people search results and assigned titles to person clusters [1]. Ueda et al. assigned vocation-related information to person clusters [2]. Mori et al. extracted keywords contained in web pages [3].

In this paper, we present an approach of assigning labels to people to help users select and understand people. We use Nippon Decimal Classification (NDC), which is a library classification system in Japan, whose organization resembles the Dewey Decimal Classification (DDC). NDC is comprised of ten classes, each of which is divided into ten divisions, and each division has ten sections, and

R.E. Banchs et al. (Eds.): AIRS 2013, LNCS 8281, pp. 464–475, 2013.
© Springer-Verlag Berlin Heidelberg 2013

so on. The NDC number is constructed from three digits (with other optional digits after the decimal point.)

By assigning NDC numbers to people, we can assign labels to people and build a NDC-based people-search directory. For example, when we assign 312.8 (Politician) to a former Japanese prime minister *Naoto Kan*, users can browse 300 (Social sciences: class) to 310 (Political sciences: division) to 312 (Political history and conditions: section) and find him in the directory.

Although library classification systems were designed to classify library collections instead people, we exploit their advantages because many categorization schemes proposed for web resources lack the rigorous hierarchical structure and careful conceptual organization found in established schemes [4] such as library classification systems. In this paper, we use NDC, which resembles DDC both in its organization schemes and in having relative index terms. Moreover, NDC is the most popular library classification system in Japan. This research assigns NDC numbers to people on the web, and develops a NDC-based people-search directory.

Below, we explain our approach in Section 2 and examples of our implemented prototype in Section 3. Our experiments are described in Section 4. We discuss the significance of our research in Section 5.

2   Approach

2.1   Overview

Our approach uses a relative index in NDC. The relative index lists the related index terms attached to NDC numbers. For example, three index terms *talent, intellect, intelligence* are attached to 141.1 (Intelligence). There are 29,514 index terms and 8,551 NDC9 (version 9) numbers.

Our proposed algorithms are constructed from two processes: (1) extracting relative index terms from web pages, and (2) assigning NDC numbers to people (Figure 1).

2.2   Extracting Relative Index Terms

When HTML files of a person are given, after removing the HTML tags, we extract the relative index terms from the texts inside the title tags. When multiple index terms can be extracted, the longest-match method is used.

We deleted the following index terms that we consider unnecessary: (a) those that consist of one character, and (b) 100 manually selected terms that often appear on the web.

2.3   Assigning NDC Numbers

After the index terms are converted to NDC numbers, they are assigned based on the following scores:

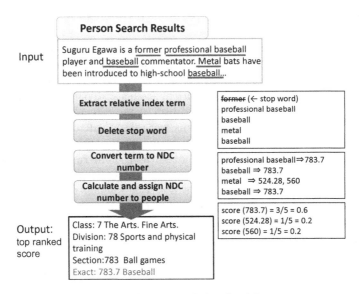

Fig. 1. Overview of the algorithm

$$score(ndc_i) = \frac{freq(ndc_i)}{\sum_{k=1}^{n} freq(ndc_k)} \qquad (1)$$

Where ndc is a NDC number and n is a distinct number of NDC numbers attached to a person.

2.4   Example

Consider the following sentence: "Suguru Egawa is a former professional baseball player and a baseball commentator. Metal bats have been introduced in high-school baseball..." *Former, professional baseball, baseball, metal,* and *baseball* are extracted as index terms. *Former* is removed because it consists of just one Japanese character. *Professional baseball* and *baseball* are converted to 783.7 (Baseball), and *metal* is converted to 524.28 (Metal. Alloy. Architectural hardware) and 560 (Metal engineering. Mine engineering).

The scores of 783.7 are 0.6 (3/5), 524.28 and 560 are 0.2 (1/5), respectively. These numbers can be attached to *Suguru Egawa*. For the top ranked score 783.7 (Baseball), its class is 700 (The arts. Fine arts), its division is 780 (Sports and physical training), and its section is 783 (Ball games).

3   Prototype

We implemented a prototype using our proposed method. This is an example of assigning the top five NDC numbers using the title documents in a dataset (see Section 4).

Figure 2 shows an initial screen of a NDC-based people-search directory. When a user selects 780 (Sports and physical training), Figure 3 is displayed. The upper side of the screen lists the list of the divisions of 780, and the lower side of screen shows the list of people assigned to 780. For example, *Suguru Egawa* (former baseball player) and *Ai Fukuhara* (table tennis player) are displayed, with five NDC numbers assigned to each. When a user selects a person, information about him or her (in this case, the search result pages of the designated person) is displayed.

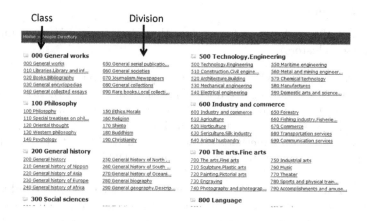

Fig. 2. Initial screen

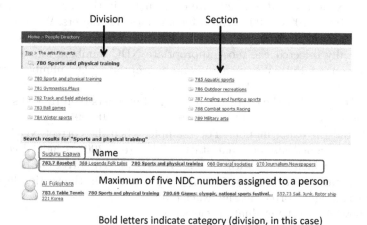

Fig. 3. Screen list of people

4   Experiment

4.1   Dataset

We describe a previously developed dataset [5]. The twenty person names used in related work [6] were selected as queries. 100 web pages (HTML files) were obtained for each twenty queries from web searches (i.e., $20 \times 100 = 2,000$ HTML files). We manually classified these web pages into different people. 152 people were found in all 2,000 web pages.

4.2   Experiment 1

We evaluated the usefulness of our algorithm that assigns NDC numbers to people (person clusters).

Method. We assigned NDC numbers to people (person clusters) with three methods using the following six documents (i.e., $3 \times 6 = 18$): (a) Tf-idf, (b) Cosine, and (c) Our method. The six documents were (1) Title, (2) Html, (3) Snippet, (4) Kwic50, (5) Kwic100, and (6) Kwic200.

The Tf-idf and Cosine methods do not use relative index terms. We treated a document of a person cluster as a query and a NDC label as a document. The numerator for calculating idf is the total amount of NDC numbers.

The Title is a document extracted from the title elements. The Html is entire document. The Snippet is a document given as a result of a Yahoo! search. In this paper, to examine co-occurrence information, we introduce concatenated text strings before and after person names. We call this "keyword in context (kwic)". Kwic50 is a concatenated document of 50 Japanese characters before a person's name and 50 Japanese characters after it (i.e., $50 + 50 = 100$ Japanese characters). Kwic 100 and Kwic200 are constructed in the same way except for using $100 + 100 = 200$ or $200 + 200 = 400$ Japanese characters. We removed the HTML tags from all documents. Figure 4 shows an example of the six documents.

We manually selected the most appropriate NDC numbers for each person (137 people out of 152). When there is no appropriate NDC number, we set it to "none." (i.e., 152 - 137 = 15 people.)

We checked whether the correct and assigned numbers (top ranked score) are the same in each class level (0-9), each division level (00-99), each section level (000-999), and the exact number. For example, when the correct NDC number is 783.7, the assigned number that starts with 7 (e.g. 700) is judged correct in the class level, which starts with 78 (e.g. 780) is judged correct in the division level, which starts with 783 (e.g. 783) is judged correct in the section level, and only 783.7 is judged correct at the exact level.

The following are the evaluation measures:

$$Precision = \frac{\text{correct answers by the method}}{\text{people to whom NDC was assigned by the method}} \qquad (2)$$

$$Recall = \frac{\text{correct answers by the method}}{\text{people to whom NDC was assigned manually}} \qquad (3)$$

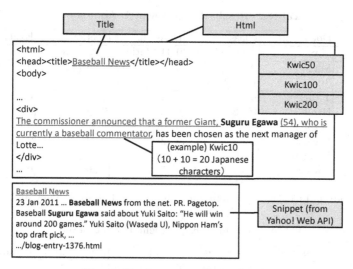

Fig. 4. Six documents for evaluation

$$F - measure = \frac{2 \times Precision \times Recall}{Precision + Recall} \tag{4}$$

$$Accuracy = \frac{correct\ answers}{people} \tag{5}$$

When calculating the Accuracy, *none* is judged correct when there is no correct NDC number for the people.

Results and Analysis. Table 1 shows the average Accuracy values in Experiment 1. Our method outperformed the comparative methods, suggesting its usefulness with relative index. For Accuracy, except for the class level, the Title was best among all the documents.

Table 2 shows the results for the exact numbers. Our methods were better than the comparative methods. In the six documents in our method, Title had good Precision and Accuracy, Snippet and Kwics had good Recall, and Kwic50 slightly outperformed the Title in the F-measure.

4.3   Experiment 2

Experiment 1 showed the overall effectiveness of our method using title documents. We evaluated the precision of our algorithm from another perspective using five-scale values.

Method. We evaluated whether the assigned NDC numbers (top ranked scores) were related to people by checking web pages by five values (5: very related; 4; slightly related 3: neutral; 2: not very related ; 1: unrelated).

Table 1. Result of Experiment 1: Accuracy

Method	Document	Class	Division	Section	Exact
Tf-idf	Max	0.44 (Title)	0.34 (Title)	0.23 (Title)	0.15 (Title)
Cosine	Max	0.43 (Title, Kwic200)	0.34 (Title)	0.25 (Title)	0.17 (Title)
Our method	Title	0.51	**0.45**	**0.36**	**0.25**
	Html	**0.52**	0.43	0.29	0.12
	Snippet	0.45	0.36	0.27	0.20
	Kwic50	**0.52**	0.42	0.29	0.23
	Kwic100	0.51	0.37	0.28	0.20
	Kwic200	0.47	0.37	0.26	0.16

Note: for Tf-idf and Cosine, the maximum values were described. They all used titles.

Table 2. Result of Experiment 1: Exact level

Method	Document	Precision	Recall	F-measure	Accuracy
Tf-idf	Max	0.08 (Title)	0.08 (Snippet)	0.07 (Snippet)	0.15 (Title)
Cosine	Max	0.12 (Kwic200)	0.10 (Html)	0.12 (Kwic200)	0.17 (Title)
Our method	Title	**0.18**	0.12	0.15	**0.25**
	Html	0.11	0.13	0.12	0.12
	Snippet	0.15	**0.14**	0.14	0.20
	Kwic50	0.16	**0.14**	**0.15**	0.23
	Kwic100	0.15	**0.14**	0.14	0.20
	Kwic200	0.13	**0.14**	0.14	0.16

Note: for Tf-idf and Cosine, the maximum values were described.

Table 3. Result of Experiment 2: Relatedness

Title	Html	Snippet	Kwic50	Kwic100	Kwic200
3.41	2.87	2.77	3.15	3.02	2.91

Results and Analysis. Table 3 shows the average values of relatedness. Title was best again (3.41).

From the above results of Experiments 1 and 2, we consider Title was best among six documents to extract relative index terms to assign NDC numbers to people.

4.4   Experiment 3

We investigated how many NDC numbers should be assigned to people using Title to develop a NDC-based people-search directory.

Method. We evaluated whether the top ten assigned NDC numbers were related to people by checking web pages by five values (5: very related; 4: slightly related; 3: neutral; 2: not very related; 1: unrelated).

Results and Analysis. Table 4 shows the cumulative relatedness for each rank in Experiment 3. For example, the average value of top ranked numbers was 3.43, and the top and second ranked numbers was 3.23. The average value of the top five ranked numbers exceeded 3.

We use NDC numbers not only to categorize people in a directory but also to display labels for them. The values of the top one or two are obviously better than the top three to five; however, if we only choose the top one or two, too little information is provided by the labels. We analyzed the top three to five ranked numbers and believe they are appropriate.

Table 4. Cumulative relatedness for each rank

1st	2nd	3rd	4th	5th	6th	7th	8th	9th	10th
3.43	3.23	3.17	3.12	3.04	3.00	2.98	2.94	2.91	2.89

In this paper, we extracted the top five ranked numbers to build a directory.

4.5   Experiment 4

We investigated how many people were found and the correct rates in each category (division) to evaluate the category's potential.

Method. We counted how many people were found in each 100 category (division): 000-990. We also counted the correct people in each 100 category to calculate the correct rate.

Results and Analysis. Figure 5 shows the Experiment 4 result. Html was the best for the number of people (5.47 people) and Title had the highest correct rate (39%).

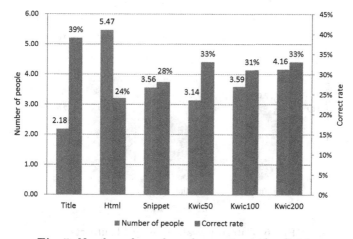

Fig. 5. Number of people and correct rate by division

4.6   Experiment 5

We investigated the usefulness of our developed prototype using 14 subjects.

Method. Our subjects were 14 undergraduate and postgraduate males whose average age was 22.8.

Since comparing six directories is complicated for the subjects, we chose three documents for our experiment: Title, Html, and Kwic50. We did not choose Snippet because it showed no advantage from previous experiments, and Kwic50 was chosen from Kwics, because it seemed the best.

We asked them three questions: Q1, Q2, and Q3.

(Q1) Is the NDC number attached to the person appropriate? (3: appropriate; 2: partially appropriate; 1: inappropriate).

The subjects evaluated pairs of NDC numbers and a person included in each ten category (division): 000 - 900 by checking HTML files. We used 110, 310, and 810 for 100, 300, and 800 because there was no people in categories 100, 300, and 800. We calculated the averages for each category.

(Q2) Is the list of people appropriate for each category? (3: appropriate: 2: partially appropriate; 1: inappropriate).

After question 1, the subjects evaluated the same ten lists in ten categories (000 - 900). We calculated the averages by each category.

(Q3) Rank the three people directory methods and explain why.

Finally, we asked the subjects for their overall comments.

Results and Analysis. Figure 6 shows the question results.

For the Title, the average values for Q1 were 2.01, 2.07 for Q2 and 1.50 for Q3. For all the questions, our prototype developed using Title was the best.

71% (10/14) of the subjects ranked Title best for Q3. The following are comments from two subjects who ranked Title best in Q3: "There is little useless information and its system is easy to understand." "The classification precision is good."

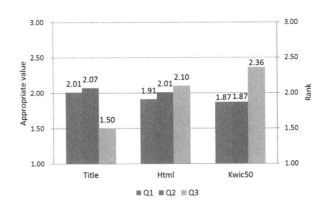

Fig. 6. Category evaluation by 14 subjects

5   Related Work and Discussion

5.1   Related Work

The initial idea of assigning library classification numbers to people was presented in a very short position paper [7]. In this new paper, we explain the algorithm and prototype in details and evaluate our algorithm and our developed prototype. In addition, we discuss the similarities and differences from various related work.

There is research that assigns labels to people. Wan et al. assigned titles (including vocations) [1], Ueda et al. assigned vocation-related information [2], Mori et al. assigned keywords to person clusters [3], and [5] extracts location information to people. WePS-2/3 conducted competitive evaluation on person attribute extraction on web pages [8]. No such research has assigned library classification numbers to person clusters.

Some research suggests NDC numbers or other terms in libraries. Kiyota et al. suggests LCSH subject headings and NDC numbers [9], and Ueda et al. suggests BSH subject headings and NDC numbers according to user input. They use web information sources as Wikipedia for matching without using relative index terms.

The automated subject classification of web documents is not new. Golub reviewed approaches to automated subject classification of textual web documents in different research communities (machine learning, information retrieval, and library science) and classified them into four categories: text categorization, document clustering, document classification, and mixed approach [10]. Our work belongs in the document classification category because we employed well-developed controlled vocabularies. Document classification is a library science approach.

Jenkins et al. organized web resources by DDC using simple classifiers [11]. They used a DDC thesaurus to match terms in documents. OCLC Scorpion is a well-known project that assigns DDC to web resources [12]. Our work resembles their approach because it compares the selected terms from documents to be classified with the terms in the vocabulary.

Frank et al. predicted Library of Congress Classifications (LCC) from LCSH subject headings and built an LCC browsing interface for a database of scholarly Internet resources [13]. They present a machine learning technique to assign LCC numbers to LCSH subject headings. This work is classified into the forth category, a mixed approach [10]. They did not evaluate their interface.

5.2   Discussion

Our experimental results show that, among six documents, Title had the best performance assigning NDC numbers to people on the web and developing a web people-search directory.

We believe that our work's main contribution is its successful assignment of library classification numbers to people on the web for displaying labels and building a people-search directory. To the best of our knowledge, this is the first research that assigns library classification numbers to people on the web.

Our paper also presents the titles of web pages as good sources to form virtual documents that represent people, which it does better than whole pages, kwic documents, or snippets. The kwic concept resembles window size. In expert searches, window sizes capture the proximity of terms and candidate mentions in documents [14]. Our finding is quite different from expert searches. This reflects the difference between the two tasks and provides new insights for web people searches and other types of people searches.

Although our research is limited to NDC and Japanese, our approach is easily applicable to other classification systems, such as DDC with similar organization and relative indexes or other terminology. People are one representative entity, and our approach can be applied to such entities as industries or place names.

6   Conclusions

To help users select and understand people, our method assigns Nippon Decimal Classification (NDC) to people on the web. We developed a prototype based on this approach and evaluated the usefulness of our proposed method and directory. Extracting relative index terms from the titles of web pages outperformed comparative methods.

Future work includes improving our algorithms for assigning NDC numbers to people. Second, we need to develop other kinds of datasets (e.g., more people, or famous/not famous people, etc.) to examine the effectiveness of the proposed method.

Acknowledgements. This work was supported by JSPS KAKENHI Grant Number 22500219, 25330385.

References

1. Wan, X., Gao, J., Li, M., Ding, B.: Person Resolution in Person Search Results: WebHawk. In: Proceedings of the Fourteenth ACM Conference on Information and Knowledge Management (CIKM 2005), pp. 163–170. ACM Press, New York (2005)
2. Ueda, H., Murakami, H., Tatsumi, S.: Assigning Vocation-Related Information to Person Clusters for Web People Search Results. In: Proceedings of the 2009 Global Congress on Intelligent Systems (GCIS 2009), vol. 4, pp. 248–253. IEEE Press, New York (2009)
3. Mori, J., Matsuo, Y., Ishizuka, M.: Personal Keyword Extraction from the Web. Journal of Japanese Society for Artificial Intelligence 20, 337–345 (2005)
4. Chan, L.M.: Exploiting LCSH, LCC, and DDC to Retrieve Networked Resources: Issues and Challenges. In: Proceedings of the Bicentennial Conference on Bibliographic Control for the New Millennium, pp. 159–178. Library of Congress, Washington DC (2001)
5. Murakami, H., Takamori, Y., Ueda, H., Tatsumi, S.: Assigning Location Information to Display Individuals on a Map for Web People Search Results. In: Lee, G.G., Song, D., Lin, C.-Y., Aizawa, A., Kuriyama, K., Yoshioka, M., Sakai, T. (eds.) AIRS 2009. LNCS, vol. 5839, pp. 26–37. Springer, Heidelberg (2009)

6. Sato, S., Kazama, K., Fukuda, K.: Distinguishing between People on the Web with the Same First and Last Name by Real-world Oriented Web Mining. IPSJ Transactions on Databases 46(8), 26–36 (2005)
7. Murakami, H., Ura, Y.: People Search using NDC Classification System. In: Proceedings of Fourth Workshop on Exploiting Semantic Annotations in Information Retrieval (ESAIR 2011), pp. 13–14. ACM Press, New York (2011)
8. Artiles, J., Borthwick, A., Gonzalo, J., Sekine, S., Amigo, E.: WePS-3 Evaluation Campaign: Overview of the Web People Search Clustering and Attribute Extraction Tasks. In: CLEF 2010 (2010)
9. Kiyota, Y., Nakagawa, H., Sakai, S., Mori, T., Masuda, H.: Exploitation of the Wikipedia Category System for Enhancing the Value of LCSH. In: Proceedings of the 9th ACM/IEEE-CS Joint Conference on Digital Libraries, p. 411. ACM Press, New York (2009)
10. Golub, K.: Automated Subject Classification of Textual Web Document. Journal of Documentation 62(3), 350–371 (2006)
11. Jenkins, C., Jackson, M., Burden, P., Wallis, J.: Automatic Classification of Web Resources using Java and Dewey Decimal Classification. Computer Networks and ISDN Systems 30(1-7), 646–648 (1998)
12. Automatic Classification Research at OCLC,
http://www.oclc.org/research/activities/auto_class.html
13. Frank, E., Paynter, G.W.: Predicting Library of Congress Classifications From Library of Congress Subject Headings. Journal of the American Society for Information Science and Technology 55(3), 214–227 (2004)
14. Balog, K., Fang, Y., de Rijke, M., Serdyukov, P., Si, L.: Expertise Retrieval. Foundations and Trends in Information Retrieval 6(2-3), 127–256 (2012)

Interactive Disaster Information Search System for Microblog by Minimal User Feedback

Sayaka Kitaguchi, Taiki Miyanishi, Kazuhiro Seki, and Kuniaki Uehara

Graduate School of System Informatics, Kobe University, Japan
kitaguchi@ai.cs.kobe-u.ac.jp

Abstract. During disastrous events, much information is posted on microblogging services. These postings sometimes contain important information concerning, for example, safety and support for afflicted people. However, due to the overwhelming volume of information on microblog, it is often difficult to find such useful information using the current microblogging search system. Given the background, this paper proposes two types of interfaces for effectively identifying useful information in the event of disasters. First, postings containing similar contents are grouped and displayed in the chronological order so that users could easily identify a group of messages directly relevant to their urgent needs. Second, a message chosen by the users is used to reformulate the initial search query to refine the search results. In order to show the effectiveness of the proposed interfaces, a user study is conducted on the Twitter Corpus collected during the event of the Great East Japan Earthquake in 2011.

Keywords: Twitter, Disastrous events, User Study, User Interface, Visualization, Interactive Search.

1 Introduction

In a disastrous event, much information is posted on microblogging services. For example, when the Great East Japan Earthquake occurred on March 11, 2011, numerous messages were posted on Twitter by the crowd of people. These postings, called *tweets*, naturally related to the event and sometimes contain critical information concerning safety and support for afflicted people. Due to the overwhelming volume of information, however, finding useful information for a specific region and/or a particular need is difficult for the current microblog search system.

Given the background, this paper proposes a disaster information search system on Twitter. The system searches for useful information for disaster victims and their supporters by focusing on the following aspects: (1) Our system uses Maximal Marginal Relevance (MMR) [3], a standard technique often used in multi-document summarization, to organize search results in terms of the contents of tweets, (2) our system displays the groups in the chronological order to organize search results in terms of when the tweets were posted, and (3) our system automatically extends the initial query by leveraging the tweet clicked by

R.E. Banchs et al. (Eds.): AIRS 2013, LNCS 8281, pp. 476–487, 2013.

the users in the initial search results to retrieve a new set of tweets supposedly more relevant to the users' particular information need. In order to investigate the effectiveness of the proposed interfaces, a user study is conducted on the Twitter Corpus collected during the event of the Great East Japan Earthquake.

The remainder of the paper is organized as follows: Section 2 details the framework and its components of our proposed disaster information search system. Section 3 describes the design of the user study. Section 4 reports on the results and discusses the implications. Section 5 summarizes the related work in comparison with the present study. Lastly, Section 6 concludes with a brief summary and possible future directions.

2 Interactive Disaster Information Search System

2.1 Interface

Figure 1 shows a screenshot of our proposed system. First, the users type a query that represents their information needs into the search box on the top of the screen (① in Figure 1). Then, the search results are grouped by sub-topics and is displayed in the left-most column (② in Figure 1). We set the number of tweets displayed in each group to $\log_3 N$, where N is the total number of tweets contained in the group. As the number of tweets presented in each group increases logarithmically with the total number of tweets in the group, the users can visually have a rough estimate of how actively the sub-topic is mentioned. When any tweet in a sub-topic group is clicked, the frame of the group is extended vertically and all tweets in the group are displayed.

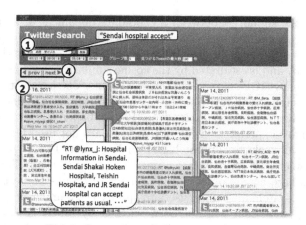

Fig. 1. Screenshot of the proposed system

Further, when any tweet is double-clicked, the system performs a search again but with a new, reformulated query by taking advantage of the contents of the clicked tweet, and displays new results in a new column (③ in Figure 1) on the right of the column containing the clicked tweet. Search results can be displayed up to three columns on a screen. When more columns are needed, the oldest, left-most column is pushed out to the left. Note that the old results are still kept by the system. When the users click the "prev" or "next" button at ④ in Figure 1, system slides all columns to the right or the left of the screen and shows hidden results.

2.2   Grouping Search Results

Due to the many active users, Twitter has a characteristic that when an exceptional event occurs, numerous tweets about the event are posted. Those tweets naturally contain topic-related terms, and thus it is possible to group them by sub-topics based on terms. By organizing search results into such groups, users would be able to find the relevant tweets more quickly by reading a few tweets in each group. This way, it is also possible to find minor sub-topics, which may be otherwise overlooked due to the small number of tweets despite its potential importance (e.g., information sent for/from isolated areas). In addition, the users could have a rough estimate of how actively each sub-topic is mentioned by looking at the size of the group as it reflects the total number of tweets in the group.

Our approach uses MMR for grouping related tweets. MMR is one of the extraction-based multi-documents summarization algorithms. It scores each document in terms of two aspects, that is, (a) relevance between a document and a query, and (b) dissimilarity between a document and already selected documents, and selects a document that has the highest score defined as:

$$\lambda Sim_1(d_i, q) - (1 - \lambda) \max_{d_j \in S} Sim_2(d_i, d_j), \tag{1}$$

where Sim_1 is the similarity between a candidate document d_i and a query q. In this study, a normalized search score returned by a search engine is used as Sim_1. S is a set of already selected documents (tweets). Sim_2 is the similarity between d_i and d_j and is estimated by the cosine similarity based on the inverted document frequency (IDF) of terms in the documents. The parameter λ ($0 \leq \lambda \leq 1$) controls the emphasis on relevance between the query and the document. High λ means little diversity among each group. In this paper, we set $\lambda = 0.8$ based on our preliminary experiment using developing data not used for evaluation.

MMR iteratively selects a tweet based on Equation (1) for specified times. The selected tweet is a representative message of each group. The number of selected tweets here corresponds to the number of groups to be generated by the system. Our system allows the users to specify the number of groups. Then, each remaining tweet that has not been selected by MMR is assigned to the most similar group based on Sim_2. Finally, the groups are sorted based on the average posting time of the tweets in each group in the chronological order. In order to reduce redundancy in the search results, our system displays only one tweet for multiple, duplicated tweets.

2.3   Query Reformulation by a Clicked Tweet

In disastrous events, there will be urgent needs for information related to, for example, damage or restoration in a specific region. However, users' queries tend to be short and ambiguous, resulting in a large amount of irrelevant information. For instance, when a user who would like to know the situation of damage in the Ishinomaki area may issue a query "Ishinomaki situation." Then, unrelated information such as a situation of medical supports or a situation of rations in Ishinomaki may be also presented. We propose the reformulation of a query to tackle this problem. In searching for relevant information, the users naturally select a tweet satisfying or related to their information needs. Then, our system takes it as a feedback and generates a new query using the selected tweet and searches for tweets similar to the selected tweet. Although the particulars of the query reformulation is different, this functionality is based on the report that search performance was significantly improved by taking advantage of a user-selected relevant tweet [8].

In reformulating a query, it is important to extract topical terms reflecting users' interest. A simple approach to identifying such on-topic vocabulary is to extract infrequent terms in a corpus based on IDF [2]. In addition, it is often the case that nouns are suited as topical terms. Based on these criteria, our system first performs morphological analysis with Kuromoji[3], an open-source Japanese morphological analyzer, to the selected tweet and extracts proper nouns, common nouns, and verbal nouns as query terms. Next, we eliminate stop words and morphemes composed of only two or less alphanumeric characters, and select the terms with M highest IDF values as a set of query terms Q_t. Let Q_o be a set of initial query terms given by the users at the beginning. Based on the two term sets, Q_t and Q_o, our system searches for tweets containing at least one query term from Q_t and one query term from Q_o. Using this functionality, the users can dig in potentially relevant information by simply clicking a tweet most pertinent to their interest without manually modifying the initial query.

3   Evaluation

3.1   Research Questions

In order to investigate the effectiveness of the proposed interfaces, we conducted a user study on the Twitter Corpus collected for the Great East Japan Earthquake occurred in 2011. Specifically, this study focused on the following questions:

- **The effect of grouping**: Can users find relevant tweets more efficiently by grouping search results compared to the one without grouping?
- **The effect of query reformulation**: Can users find more relevant tweets by query reformulation?
- **The effect of combination**: Is it effective to combine grouping and query reformulation?

---

[3] http://www.atilika.org/

3.2   Experimental Settings

Dataset. In this experiment, we used the Twitter Corpus provided by Twitter Japan Co., Ltd. for the Great East Japan Big Data Workshop[4]. This corpus consists of approximately 180 million tweets written in only Japanese for one week after the Great East Japan Earthquake occurred (i.e., from March 11 to 18, 2011). Figure 2 shows an example tweet in the corpus, which consists of four fields: (i) Tweet ID, (ii) User ID, (iii) Posting time, and (iv) Text (the English translation was inserted by the authors).

> (i) 46126534246932480(ii) 224956629 (iii) 2011-03-11 17:33:17
> (iv) w (Checked tweets
> that have been posted before the earthquake. I'm alive).

Fig. 2. Example tweets in the Twitter corpus

Microblog Search. We indexed the corpus with the Lucene[5] full-text search engine, where the language model with Bayesian smoothing using Dirichlet priors was employed. Here, we set the smoothing parameter μ to 2,500 based on our pilot experiment. Kuromoji was used for morphological analysis.

Baselines. The proposed system was compared with two interfaces, namely, Flat and Group, illustrated in Figure 3. The Flat (FL), which is similar to the official search interface of Twitter, displays a flat list of search results in the descending order of the relevance score. We used search scores returned by Lucene as the relevance score. The Group (GR) displays the search results grouped by sub-topics. Both FL and GR retrieve 100 tweets per page and present only one tweet for duplicated tweets having the same contents. More results can be retrieved by clicking a button labeled as "Read More" or "Search More." Our proposed system, illustrated in Figure 1, is hereafter referred to as "Group + Query Reformulation (GQR)." GQR displays grouped search results and provides a query reformulation leveraging the tweet selected by users. GQR also retrieves 100 tweets at once. We set M, the number of terms to be extracted from the selected tweet, to five based on our pilot experiment. The number of groups was experimentally fixed at five during throughout this experiment. The appropriateness of the number of groups is discussed based on a questionnaire. We evaluated the effect of grouping by comparing FL and GR, the effect of query reformulation by comparing GR and GQR, and the effect of combining grouping and query reformulation by comparing GR and GQR.

Tasks. We designed a task as a pair of an initial query and its information need. To evaluate the effectiveness of the proposed interfaces during disastrous events, it is important that the tasks reflect the real information needs. To this end, we focused on "inquiry tweets." We defined inquiry tweets as those asking

---

[4] www.biglobe.co.jp/pressroom/release/2011/04/27-1
[5] http://lucene.apache.org/core/

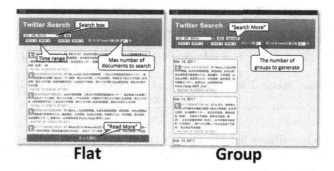

Flat   **Group**

Fig. 3. Screenshot of the baseline systems, Flat list (corresponding to the existing typical interfaces) and Group, used for our experiments

for certain information and thus contain the phrase, "please tell me" which is expressed in Japanese as " ", "", "", or ".." Inquiry tweets in the corpus can be seen as users' information needs and, especially in the time of disaster, they would reflect the most critical ones. There are of course many tweets containing the phrase but not related to the event of interest. To identify relevant questions, we took advantage of the "retweet" function of Twitter. A retweet is a tweet copying another tweet posted by others to disseminate the information. The fact that a tweet was retweeted many times means that many users found the tweet important and we used it as an indicator of the importance of a question. A total of 114,315 inquiry tweets were found in the corpus and were sorted in descending order of the retweet rate r_t of tweet t defined in Equation (2) each day.

$$r_t = \frac{\text{\# of times } t \text{ was retweeted on that day}}{\text{the total \# of times } t \text{ was retweeted}} \qquad (2)$$

Based on the ranking of tweets for each day, we selected inquiry tweets by manually examining them in the following steps.

1. Selected tweets related to the earthquake.
2. Removed redundant tweets, which ask the same questions as the already selected tweets.
3. Retained only tweets whose answers were found in the corpus.

A total of 36 inquiry tweets were selected. In this study, tweets containing RT at the beginning were simply regarded as retweets. This is partly because it is difficult to obtain tweet-retweet relations from only this corpus, and the precise relations are not very important to generate search topics. Then, search intentions were manually interpreted based on the selected inquiry tweets by the authors. The initial queries used for user study were also prepared from the intentions. Two examples of the constructed tasks are shown in Table 1.

Table 1. Examples of search tasks

Task#	Initial query	Search intention	Time-stamp
3	(Disneyland shelter)	I want to find shelters near Tokyo Disneyland.	2011/03/11 20:00
5	(Sendai hospital accept)	I want to find hospitals in Sendai which can accept patients.	2011/03/11 20:00

Time-stamp identifies when the inquiry tweet was retweeted most actively. We defined the time range for each task to be between the beginning of the corpus and 24 hours after its time-stamp. For example, in retrieving tweets for task#5 (cf. Table 1), the time range was specified from March 11 at 9:00 to March 12 at 20:00.

Procedure. We gathered 18 participants for the user study. Among them, 13 are male and five are female; 17 are students in computer science and one is an office worker; all in their 20's. Each participant performed a total of six tasks (two tasks for each system). The order of using the systems and performing the tasks were allocated equally based on Latin square. All pairs of a system and a task were carried out once. In each task session, the participant conducted a search using the initial query (see Table 1) and was asked to find five relevant tweets within five minutes. When they found five tweets, the session was closed. The following gives a precise procedure.

1. The participant received a general instruction of the study.
2. He performed the assigned tasks in the allocated order.
   (a) He received an instruction of the particular system to use, and went through a training task to become familiar with the interfaces and the tasks.
   (b) He performed the assigned two tasks. In each task, we automatically recorded the time taken to complete the task, the time taken to search by the system, and the tweets identified as relevant by the participant.
   (c) He filled in the questionnaire about the system used.
3. In the end, he filled in the questionnaire about the experiment.

4 Results and Discussion

4.1 Task Completion Time

Table 2 shows the average time taken to complete a task to evaluate the efficiency of the systems. Task completion time T is computed as $T_t - T_s$, where T_t is the time between the beginning and the end of a task by a participant; T_s is a processing time of a system to search the Twitter Corpus.

We observe that the task completion time for GR is shorter than those for FL and GQR, while there is little difference between FL and GQR. When looking

Table 2. Average task completion time with standard deviation, where the shortest time is shown in bold

System	Average time (s)	Standard deviation
FL	154.0	98.72
GR	**119.4**	74.27
GQR	160.0	80.49

Table 3. Average task completion time of GR and GQR for different orders of their use, where significant difference is indicated with †

System	GR→GQR	GQR→GR
GR	121.4	117.4†
GQR	143.3	176.7

at individual tasks, GR recorded the shortest task completion time for 64% of the tasks (not shown in Table 2). These results suggest that the grouping functionality implemented in GR has helped users gather relevant tweets more quickly. There's no time to lose in a critical situation, so that our system is helpful for volunteers to quickly find useful information and provide it to suffering people in the disaster area. We conducted a multiple comparison with Bonferroni corrected Wilcoxon signed-rank test where the significance level α was set to 0.05. However, we found no significant difference among the three systems and the advantage of grouping is inconclusive.

Comparing GR and GQR (the proposed system), the task completion time of GQR, was found longer than that of GR despite the fact that GQR is also equipped with grouping. A possible explanation is the difficulty of the interface to use. The interface for query reformulation implemented in GQR is not familiar to most users and is supposedly harder to learn than FL or GR. To investigate the interpretation, Table 3 shows the average task completion time of GR and GQR for different orders of system usage. The first row of Table 3 represents the order the two systems were used. For Example, GR→GQR means that the user first used GR and then GQR. A dagger (†) indicates a significant difference from GQR based on a Bonferroni corrected permutation test with 1000 times random sampling where the significance level α was set to 0.05.

We can see from Table 3 that the task completion time of GR is significantly shorter than GQR when the users used GR after GQR. In contrast, when users used GR before GQR, there was no significant difference. In other words, using GQR helped users to learn how to use GR but not the other way around. These results implicate that GQR is more difficult to learn than GR, which may explain the longer task completion time for GQR in Table 2. Moreover, in an additional questionnaire, some participants pointed out that the GQR interface is hard to use.

Table 4. Average P@5, sum of relevance scores, average P@5 without duplicates, and # of relevant tweets found only by each system with ±1 standard deviation

System	P@5	Relevance score	P@5 w/o duplicates	# relevant tweets found only by a respective system
FL	0.48 ±0.37	466 ±6.26	0.39 ±0.30	43
GR	0.54 ±0.40	534 ±5.81	0.39 ±0.30	54
GQR	0.53 ±0.34	502 ±5.81	0.40 ±0.26	61

4.2 Relevance of Search Results

Relevance Judgement. Through 108 task sessions (18 participants × 6 tasks from a total of 36 tasks), 462 tweets were marked as relevant by the participants. These results were assessed by two assessors per a pair of a task and a tweet. In total, three assessors participated in the assessment. They were students majoring in computer science. This section details the two types of relevance judgements we conducted.

First, we defined relevant tweets. Annotators assessed each tweet using a relevance grade ("relevant," "irrelevant", or "neither"). We regarded the tweets that were judged as "relevant" by two annotators as relevant and the others as irrelevant. As a result, 281 relevant tweets (61% of the all tweets found by the participants) were identified. Additionally, we defined an alternative relevance score of a tweet as the sum of the judgements by two annotators, where "relevant" was treated as two points and "neither" as one point.

Second, we identified relevant tweets similar to each other in order to evaluate the diversity of the information gathered by the participants. Annotators gave a particular label to a group of tweets with the same contents. As a result, 131 relevant tweets were labeled by 36 different labels, which correspond to 36 groups of tweets with the same contents for each.

Search Performance. We evaluated the effectiveness of the systems with precision at 5 (P@5) and the relevance score defined in Section 4.2. In this experiment, P@5 is defined in Equation (3). When the participants gathered less than five tweets during a task session, the remaining slots were treated as irrelevant tweets.

$$P@5 = \frac{\text{\# of relevant tweets gathered in a task session}}{5} \quad (3)$$

Table 4 shows the average P@5 and the sum of relevance scores by each system. The right two columns "P@5 without duplicates" and "# relevant tweets found only by a particular system" will be discussed later. It can be seen that the participants found more relevant tweets by GR and GQR than FL on average, which is presumably attributed to the fact that both GR and GQR group similar tweets. However, using Bonferroni corrected Wilcoxon signed-rank test ($\alpha = 0.05$), there was no significant difference among three systems.

We then evaluated search performance when duplicate tweets were removed. Intuitively, multiple tweets in the same group were regarded as one tweet in

Table 5. A list of questions asked in post-experiment questionnaire

	Question and Choices
Q1	Was the interface useful for finding relevant information? 5: Very useful 4: Useful 3: Neither 2: Useless 1: Very useless
Q2	How many irrelevant tweets did you have to read for finding relevant information? 5: Very few 4: few 3: Neither 2: Many 1: Very many
Q3	Do you want to use the interface to search microblog again? 5: Strongly agree 4: Agree 3: Neither 2: Disagree 1: Strongly disagree
Q4	Was the number of groups of tweets appropriate? 5: Too many 4: Many 3: Just right 2: Few 1: Too few
Q5	Did grouping make finding relevant information easier? 5: Very easy 4: Easy 3: Neither 2: Difficult 1: Very difficult
Q6	Did query reformulation make finding relevant information easier? 5: Very easy 4: Easy 3: Neither 2: Difficult 1: Very difficult

computing precision. We call this measure precision without duplicates. The result is found in Table 4. GQR scored slightly higher than the other systems but the difference is not significant.

For a more detailed analysis on individual systems, we then looked at the number of relevant tweets found only by a particular system, which indicates the novelty of search results. Comparing the results of three systems presented in Table 4, it is found that participants using GQR were able to find the largest number of tweets that were not found by FL or GR. For a concrete example, let us take the task #3 (see Table 1). While tweets (e.g., "Shelters near Tokyo Disneyland. Maihama Elementary School and Tokai University Urayasu High School are close") describing the places of shelters were found by all the systems, the participants using GQR found more detailed information, such as "Maihama Elementary School is small, so you should go to Horie Elementary School or Miakegawa Elementary / Junior High School." This result exemplifies the advantage of query reformulation using a clicked tweet for finding relevant tweets that are overlooked by the other systems.

4.3   User Satisfaction

Finally, we discuss the results of the questionnaire. Table 5 is a list of the questions asked upon the completion of the assigned tasks. The participants answered each question on a five-point scale.

Table 6 shows the results, where GR and GQR had higher scores than FL in Q1–Q3, which means that grouping and query reformulation were on average favorably accepted by the participants. In Q2 and Q3, there is a significant difference between FL and GR, but there is no significant difference between FL and GQR. The main reason would be the unfamiliarity of the query reformulation interface and the longer task completion time as discussed earlier. In Q4, we asked the appropriateness of the number of groups. As more than a half of the participants selected "just right", the number (five) used in this experiment seems appropriate. However, since the optimum number would depend on a type of task and the number of tweets to search, it would be ideal to dynamically set the number for a given query and the size of the data. Lastly, Q5 and Q6

Table 6. The questionnaire results, where the average and standard deviation (±SD) are reported. Significant improvement ($\alpha = 0.05$) with respect to FL is indicated by †.

System	Q1	Q2	Q3	Q4	Q5	Q6
FL	3.22 ±0.92	2.50 ±0.90	3.22 ±0.92	-	-	-
GR	4.00 ±0.58†	3.44 ±0.83†	3.89 ±0.57†	4.33 ±0.75	3.17 ±0.50	-
GQR	4.00 ±0.67†	3.17 ±0.90	3.72±0.73			3.89 ±0.81

indicate the satisfaction in grouping and query reformulation, respectively. Both questions had relatively positive responses, supporting their usefulness.

5   Related Work

Microblog has become popular since Twitter launched its service in 2007. Especially, in the last few years, the use of microblog in disastrous events has been drawing much attention. Vieweg et al. [13] analyzed messages posted on Twitter during disasters and reported the behavior of disaster information in microblog. Sakaki et al. [10] proposed earthquake detection by treating Twitter users as a sensor. In addition, an application for searching disaster information was also proposed. Abel et al. [1] presented Twitcident, a Web-based system for filtering and faceted searching for disaster information. The present study focused on the improvement of microblog search interfaces for disaster information.

With the popularization of microblog, microblog search has also been actively studied [12] , where traditional web search approaches were often adapted [6,7]. In addition, Efron et al. [4,5] proposed relevance feedback by using temporal properties of relevant tweets. Miyanishi et al. [8] proposed tweet selection-based relevance feedback, which uses a tweet selected by the users to refine search results and exploits temporal properties of refined search results. The purpose of this paper is not the improvement of search algorithm but the evaluation of the effectiveness of search interfaces including the grouping and the query reformulation particularly for disastrous events.

Microblog summarization is another research area related especially to grouping search results. O'Connor et al. [9] proposed the microblog search system by grouping search results similarly to our approach. Their approach identified groups of tweets by classifying search results based on the presence or absence of a high frequency phrase in a corpus, whereas our approach identified them based on textual contents of each tweet. Another summarization approach not using groups was proposed by Sharifi et al. [11].

6   Conclusion

In this study, we proposed and implemented the microblog search system, which provides two key features for efficiently find critical disaster information. One is to group search results and the other is query reformulation using a clicked tweet. In addition, we proposed a strategy to construct search topics reflecting real information needs during disastrous events by taking advantage of retweets. Through evaluation, our user study indicated that, on average, the users were able to find useful information more quickly by grouping, although the difference was not statistically significant. For query reformulation, there was no advantage as to the task completion time. Our analysis on the order of system use suggested that it was in part due to the unfamiliarity of the query reformulation interface. However, another analysis on the novelty of search results indicated that query reformulation was effective to find more detailed information than those found by the other systems.

For future work, we plan to improve the user interface for query reformulation and to perform a larger user study to validate the effectiveness of the proposed interfaces. Also, we would like to consider the credibility of information on Twitter since some information may be false whether deliberately or not. There is much existing work in this area and could be incorporated in our system.

References

1. Abel, F., Hauff, C., Houben, G.J., Stronkman, R., Tao, K.: Twitcident: fighting fire with information from social web streams. In: WWW, pp. 305–308 (2012)
2. Bendersky, M., Metzler, D., Bruce Croft, W.: Parameterized concept weighting in verbose queries. In: SIGIR, pp. 605–614 (2011)
3. Carbonell, J., Goldstein, J.: The use of MMR, diversity-based reranking for reordering documents and producing summaries. In: SIGIR, pp. 335–336 (1998)
4. Efron, M.: The University of Illinois' graduate school of library and information science at TREC 2011. In: TREC (2011)
5. Efron, M., Organisciak, P., Fenlon, K.: Improving retrieval of short texts through document expansion. In: SIGIR, pp. 911–920 (2012)
6. Metzler, D., Cai, C.: USC/ISI at TREC 2011: Microblog track. In: TREC (2011)
7. Miyanishi, T., Okamura, N., Liu, X., Seki, K., Uehara, K.: TREC 2011 microblog track experiments at Kobe University. In: TREC (2011)
8. Miyanishi, T., Seki, K., Uehara, K.: TREC 2012 microblog track experiments at Kobe University. In: TREC (2012)
9. O'Connor, B., Krieger, M., Ahn, D.: Tweetmotif: Exploratory search and topic summarization for twitter. In: ICWSM, pp. 2–3 (2010)
10. Sakaki, T., Okazaki, M., Matsuo, Y.: Earthquake shakes twitter users: real-time event detection by social sensors. In: WWW, pp. 851–860 (2010)
11. Sharifi, B., Hutton, M.A., Kalita, J.: Summarizing microblogs automatically. In: HLT-NAACL, pp. 685–688 (2010)
12. Soboroff, I., Ounis, I., Lin, J.: Overview of the TREC-2012 microblog track. In: TREC (2012)
13. Vieweg, S., Hughes, A.L., Starbird, K., Palen, L.: Microblogging during two natural hazards events: what twitter may contribute to situational awareness. In: CHI, pp. 1079–1088 (2010)

Building, Profiling, Analysing and Publishing an Arabic News Corpus Based on Google News RSS Feeds

Salha M. Alzahrani

College of Computers and Information Technology, Taif University, Taif, Saudi Arabia
s.zahrani@tu.edu.sa

Abstract. The aim of this paper is to give a detailed and explicit design, composition and documentation of a new Arabic News Corpus (ArNeCo). We used RSS feeds from Google news as a big container of article titles, and crawled the web to extract the text. About 11,000 documents with more than 6 million words were tagged as belonging to one of 6 domains: Business, Entertainment, Health, Science-Technology, Sports, and World. Metadata has been added to the corpus as a whole and to each domain independently. The developed corpus, called ArNeCo, has been analysed to ensure that it has a considerable quality and quantity, and published on the Internet for research purposes. This article aims to help potential users of ArNeCo to understand the nature of the corpus and to do information retrieval research in many ways such as in the formulation of queries, justification of decisions taken or interpretation of results gained. Besides the corpus, this article presents a method for developing corpora that can keep track of recent natural language texts posted on the Internet by using RSS feeds.

Keywords: Arabic corpus, RSS feeds, construction, profile, metadata, analysis, evaluation.

1   Introduction

A corpus is a collection of text documents in readable or audible formats which are digitized such that they can be processed on computers (Wynne 2005). A readable corpus is digitized in written formats whilst an audible corpus is implemented in different audio/sound formats. Both types exemplify patterns of a natural language that can be used for different studies and applications.

Arabic is the official language by the Middle East countries. There are thousands of Arabic books and millions of Arabic pages on the World Wide Web. The lack of freely available Arabic corpora is the motivation behind this work. Although it is extremely difficult to place limits on a natural language, neither on its number of vocabulary nor on its meaningful phrase structures, a new corpus for Arabic should attempt to be as representative as possible. Thus, we aim to support Arabic natural language processing (ANLP), language modelling, and information retrieval (IR) research by developing

R.E. Banchs et al. (Eds.): AIRS 2013, LNCS 8281, pp. 488–499, 2013.
© Springer-Verlag Berlin Heidelberg 2013

a method for collecting recent and ongoing documents from the Internet, and by building a text corpus for Arabic news. The major difference between ArNeCo and the previous Arabic corpora such as Arabic Gigaword (Graff 2007) and Arabic Newswire (Graff and Walker 2001) provided by Linguistics Data Consortium (LDC) is that our corpus is considered contemporary and freely accessed on the web.

2   Related Works

Current resources for Arabic corpora are few, outdated, very regional, and most of them are not available for free. Many researchers working on ANLP constructed their own datasets for their research purposes. For instance, Alzahrani and Salim (2009) constructed a dataset of 125 documents collected manually from Wikipedia for the purpose of gauging similarity and plagiarism detection in Arabic, Hmeidi et al. (1997) built a corpus of 242 abstracts collected from Saudi national conference proceedings for automatic indexing. However, such datasets are not considered a representative sample of the language due to the small amount of documents and language structures. On the other hand, Goweder and De Roeck (2001) constructed a corpus of 42591 news articles but it is very regional because it was collected from a single source.

Few other corpora which are not available for free to the public have been reviewed and listed by several researchers (Abdelali et al. 2005; Alansary al. 2007). The most popular of these include Arabic Gigaword (Graff 2007) and Arabic Newswire (Graff and Walker 2001) provided by Linguistics Data Consortium (LDC), Al-Hayat Arabic Corpus and An-Nahar Newspaper Text Corpus from European Language Resources Association (ELRA). Recently-built corpora include modern standard Arabic corpus (Abdelali et al. 2005), contemporary corpus of Arabic (Al-Sulaiti and Atwell 2006), and international corpus of Arabic (Alansary et al. 2007).

To enrich the resources, and overcome the limitations of current Arabic corpora, we present a new well-representative corpus for Arabic. In addition, we deploy a novel method of developing corpora that can keep track of recent natural language texts posted on the Internet by using RSS feeds.

3   Building ArNeCo: An Arabic News Corpus

3.1   Google News: A Rich Resource

To develop an Arabic news text collection from a rich resource, we used the Google News[1] in the Arabic world as a collector of news articles and stories from hundreds of sources. Google News service groups similar articles automatically and arranges them according to the last update. Thus, researchers using this corpus will have an inbuilt awareness of modern Arabic structure and vocabulary. A snapshot of Arabic Google news dynamic homepage is shown in Figure 1.

---

[1] https://news.google.com/?edchanged=1&ned=ar_me&authuser=0

Fig. 1. Arabic Google News Dynamic Homepage

As can be seen in the above figure, (1) refers to Arabic news service, (2) refers to the menu that displays the news' categories as follows: world, Arab world, business, science & technology, entertainment, sports and most popular, (3) indicates the article title, (4) refers to most similar titles, (5) gives links to the web pages that have the source of this article, (6) links to a list of all similar or related news articles. The last link forms a rich resource of similar language patterns, structures relations, and vocabulary connections stemmed from different writers in different locations. This is a great advantage for several applications such as detecting similar but not exactly the same patterns in a language.

In order to build a large and a representative reference corpus for Arabic, we defined well-selected criteria and adopted a structured method for corpus development. Section 3.2 discusses the criteria defined whereas section 3.3 explains the corpus builder method.

3.2   Criteria

Good selection of the corpus texts is coupled with good selection criteria. As Wynne (2005) stated: *"Criteria for determining the structure of a corpus should be small in number, clearly separate from each other, and efficient as a group in delineating a corpus that is representative of the language under examination"*.

There are six common criteria: text mode, type, domain, language or language varieties, location and finally date of the texts. Table 1 shows the criteria chosen to develop the ArNeCo corpus.

Google provides news articles not only from electronic newspapers but also from news channels that transcribe the news on their web pages. Table 2 lists some locations for many newspapers sources as Google collected from the web, and Table 3 shows the locations of some Arabic news channels.

Table 1. Criteria used for the development of ArNeCo

Criteria	Value
Mode	Electronic/digitized readable mode in UTF-8 encoding
Type	News articles
Domain	Popular news categorized in 6 domains: World, Sports, Science&Technology, Health, Entertainment and Business
Language	Modern Standard Arabic Language (without diacritics)
Location	Numerous Arabic news sources. See Table II and Table III.
Date	January-August, 2012

Table 2. Location of some Arabic newspapers sources

Location	Sources
Global Newspapers	Al-Arab, Al-Hayat, Al-Quds Al-Arabi, Asharq Alawsat, Al-Hayat, Asharq Alawsat, Algeria, Al-Chaab, Echourouk El Youmi , Al-Fadjr, Al-Khabar, Al-Massa
Saudi Arabia	Al-Jazirah, Al-Jeel,Al-Madinah, Naseej, Okaz, Al-Riyadh, Al-Watan, Al-Yaum, Arab News, Saudi Gazette
Syria	Al-Furat, Al-Jamahir, Al-Ouruba, Al-Thawra, Tishreen, Al-Wehda, Syria Times, Syria Today
Tunisia	Al-Chourouk, Al-Horria, as-Sabah
UAE	Akhbar Al-Arab, Al-Bayan, Al-Ittihad, Al-Khaleej, Emirates Today, Gulf News, Khaleej Times
Yemen	Al-Ayyam, Al-Gumhuriyah, Al-Mithaq, Al-Motamar, Naba Al-Haqiqa, Ray, Al-Sahwa, 26 September, Al-Shoura, Al-Thaqafiah, Al-Thawra, Al-Wahdawi, Al-Sahwa, Yemen Times, Yemen Observer
Morocco	Al-Alam, Attajdid, Al-Ayam, Bayane Al-Yaoume, as-Sabah
Oman	Al-Watan, Oman Observer, Times of Oman
Palestine	Al-Ayyam, Filasteen Al-Muslimah, Al-Hayat Al-Jadida, Al-Karmel, Al-Manar, Al-Massar, Al-Quds
Qatar	Al-Rayah, Al-Sharq, Al-Watan, Gulf Times, The Peninsula
Sudan	Al-Rayaam , Adaraweesh
Bahrain	Akhbar Alkhaleej, Alayam, Al-Wasat, Bahrain Tribune, Gulf Daily News
Egypt	Al-Ahram, Aqidati, Al-Gomhuria, Mayo, Al-Messa, Al-Osboa, Al-Siyassa Al-Dawliya, Al-Wafd, Watani, Egyptian Gazette, Egypt Today, Middle East Times, Al-Siyassa Al-Dawliya, Watani
Iraq	Azzaman, Alahali, Al-Jihad, Al-Mendhar, Nahrain, Al-Rafidayn, Al-Sabaah, Tareek Al Shaab
Jordan	Al-Arab Al-Yawm, Ad-Dustour , Al-Ghad, Al-Ra'i, As-Sabeel, Irbid News
Kuwait	Al-Qabas , Al-Rai-Al-Aam, Taleea, Al-Watan
Lebanon	Al-Aman, Al-Anwar, Al-Balad, Al-Intiqad, Al-Kalima, Al-Kifah Al-Arabi, Al-Liwaa, Al-Nahar , Al-Massira, Al-Mustaqbal, Al-Ousbou' Al-Arabi, Al-Safir, Al-Sharq, Al-Waie, Al-Watan Al- Arabi
Libya	Al-Fajr Al-Jadid, Al-Jamahiriyah, Al-Shams, Al-Zahf Al-Akhdar

Table 3. Arabic news channels and their locations

Base	Channel
Qatar	Al-Jazeera
Dubai	Al-Arabiya
United States	Al-Hurra, MBC
Lebanon	CNN (AR), Al-Manar, Future TV, LBC
Iraq	Al-Iraqiya
Saudi Arabia	Al Ekhbaria
UK	BBC (Ar)

3.3   Google News RSS Feeds: An Overview

According to Wikipedia, RSS is a family of web feeds formats which can be used to publish continuous updated work such as news and blog entries. Any RSS document contains some metadata such as the source URL, title, publisher, date, full text or summary, etc. that are usually specified in XML format to facilitate the use of data as elements with start-tag and end-tag. Thus, using RSS feeds is potentially valuable for parsing the XML elements into valuable news items. A sample of RSS source document taken from Arabic Google news webpage is shown in Figure 2.

```
- <rss version="2.0">
  - <channel>
      <generator>NFE/1.0</generator>
      <title>أخبار - أعمل Google 15</title>
      <link>http://news.google.com.sa?ned=ar_me&hl=ar</link>
      <language>ar</language>
      <webMaster>news-feedback@google.com</webMaster>
      <copyright>&copy;2009 Google</copyright>
      <pubDate>Thu, 25 Jun 2009 10:15:15 GMT</pubDate>
      <lastBuildDate>Thu, 25 Jun 2009 10:15:15 GMT</lastBuildDate>
```

Fig. 2. Google RSS feeds source file

The most valuable XML element found in the Google news RSS feeds is <item> which is shown in Figure 3. The <item> element describes each news article by giving some sub-elements such as <title>, <link>, <category>, <pubDate>, and <description>, where they can be extracted and used to build our corpus collection and its metadata.

3.4   ArNeCo Builder: A Detailed Method

After investigating the RSS files, we developed a method for collecting Arabic news documents using systematic and sequential steps shown in Figure 4.

In the first step called RSS feeds aggregator, we collected the RSS feeds from Arabic Google news web page. Two methods were used in this stage, latest-news and searched-news. In the latest-news method, the corpus builder was run to navigate to the

```
- <item>
  <title>مجموعة دبي المصرفية تنهي نزاعا وتحصل على حصة 48% في شعاع - الاقتصادية</title>
  <link>http://news.google.com/news/url?
    fd=R&sa=T&url=http://www.aleqt.com/2009/06/25/article_
  <guid isPermaLink="false">tag:news.google.com,2005:cluster=http
  <category>أصل</category>
  <pubDate>Thu, 25 Jun 2009 06:16:28 GMT</pubDate>
  <description><table border="0" cellpadding="2" cellspacing="7"
    style="font-size:85%;font-family:arial,sans-serif"></font><
    serif"><br /><div style="padding-top:0.8em;"><img alt="" h
    href="http://news.google.com/news/url?
    fd=R&amp;sa=T&amp;url=http://www.aleqt.com/2009/06/2
    48% في شعاع</b></a><br /><font
    دبي المصرفية تنهي نزاعا وتحصل على حصة 48.4% في شعاع. وقال بنك شعاع أن الصفقة التي تأتي عقب<b>"
    المتفق عليها في الاتفاق الأصلي. وأضاف البنك أن الاتفاق الجديد يمثل سعر تحويل قدره 2.91 درهم )
    0.793 درهم 1.28 على سعر إغلاق السهم أمس وهو 127% للسهم بعلاوة نسبتها )دولار.</f
    class="p" href="http://news.google.com.sa/news?ned=ar_m
     &raquo;</b></nobr></a></font></div></font></t
</item>
```

Fig. 3. News items in the RSS feeds

URLs of all related articles from Google News for every article appears in the main page (see number 4 and 6 in Figure 1). Each Google News page has an RSS feeds file which could be downloaded and saved as xml file under a specific domain as specified by our criteria (see Table 1). On the other hand, in the searched-news method we aimed to search different keywords under each domain. For example, the Arabic keyword "انفلونزا الخنازير" which means "H1N1 Flow" was searched in Google News and the results page that contains the RSS feeds for retrieved documents were downloaded and categorized under the health domain.

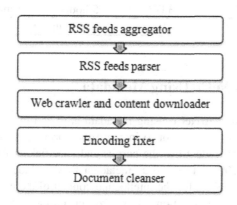

Fig. 4. ArNeCo Builder Algorithm

RSS feeds parser in the second step was used to read collected RSS files and parse the XML elements. The most valuable element is <item> which is shown previously in Figure 3. For this purpose, the parser was developed to extract an array of <item>s from each RSS file and parse the <item>'s tags such as <title>, <link> and <description>. Then in the third step, the value of the <link> tag was passed to a web crawler built in PHP[2]. The crawler visits the URL and extracts the content of the webpage but keeps the encoding as it is. The crawler was run for each domain for several hours, and the collected news articles were downloaded and stored under each domain separately. To unify the encoding of the collected webpages, another method namely *encoding fixer* in our ArNeCo corpus builder was used (i) to detect the document encoding and (ii) to convert the Windows-1562 and other encodings to UTF-8 encoding. The last step was utilised to cleanse the collected documents and strip HTML tags, diacritics, symbols, and English/Latin words and characters. For this purpose, a document cleanser method was employed to refine documents and obtain just-Arabic texts. The number of RSS feeds files and collected articles along with the construction time for each domain are shown in Table 4.

Table 4. RSS files and articles numbers, and the construction time of the corpus

Domain	No of RSS.xml	No of Articles	Crawling Time	Encoding& Cleansing Time
World	152	3621	6 hours	5 min
Business	33	280	1 ½ hour	30 sec
Entertainment	35	865	2 hours	1 min
Health	80	2379	4 hours	2 min
Sci-Tech	29	543	44 min	1 min
Sports	167	3377	5 hours	3 min
Total	496	11065	≈20 hours	≈ 12 min

4   Profiling ArNeCo Using Metadata

The purpose of profiling ArNeCo using metadata is to add more value to the corpus collection and at the same time not to increase the corpus size. In this regard, some descriptive metadata that identifies the corpus and specifies its functionalities should be defined (Wynne 2005). The corpus metadata may include the name of corpus, producer, agency responsible for the intellectual content of the corpus, contact details, date of creation, date of publication, place, size, encoding, version, last updated and others. ArNeCo metadata sample file is shown in Figure 5. On the other hand, one metadata file was created for each category/domain including ID, name, size and last updated date and time. Sub-metadata was added for each article to give its identifier, title, link and publication date in the category as presented in Figure 6.

---

[2] PHP: Hypertext Preprocessor, see php.net

```
<?xml version="1.0"?>
<corpus>
    <titleStmt>
        <title> Arabic News Corpus: ArNeCo </title>
    </titleStmt>
    <publicationStmt>
        <agency>Taif University</agency>
        <agency> University of Technology Malaysia </agency>
        <developer>Salha M. Alzahrani</developer>
        <supervisor>Naomie Salim</supervisor>
        <supervisor>Robert M. Colomb</supervisor>
        <publisher>Salha M. Alzahrani</publisher>
        <distributor>Salha M. Alzahrani</distributor>
        <dateOfCreation>May-Dec,2009</dateOfCreation>
        <dateOfPublication>Jan,2010</dateOfPublication>
    </publicationStmt>
    <corpusStmt>...
    <categoryStmt>...
</corpus>
```

Fig. 5. ArNeCo Corpus Metadata

```
<?xml version="1.0" encoding="utf-8"?>
<category ID="A" name="Business">
    <document>
        <docID>A1</docID>
        <title>رؤوس المال الاقتصاد - الجزيرة</title>
        <link>http://www.google.com/hostednews/afp/...</link>
        <pubDate>Thu, 25 Jun 2009 05:22:28 GMT</pubDate>
    </document>
```

Fig. 6. Business Category Metadata

5   Analyzing and Evaluating ArNeCo Corpus

The aim of constructing ArNeCo is to provide a freestanding representative corpus of the modern Arabic language. The corpus consists of news texts collected by crawling the web from hundreds of sources and locations addressed by Google news RSS feeds. Accordingly, the developed corpus may constitute well-representative resource for Arabic language engineering. To justify this claim, firstly, ArNeCo has thousands of articles distributed over six different domains: Business, Entertainment, Health, Science &Technology, Sports and World. Secondly, there are, in each domain, similar news articles about the same subject written by different authors/news agencies. Such similar documents enrich the vocabulary usage besides the language structures, varieties and dialects. Thirdly, ArNeCo has a considerable size, digitized format, and unified encoding which allows us to investigate how well is representative. Table 5 gives a statistical summary of the corpus for being analysed and assessed.

To ensure that the collected articles have considerable amount of unique words, we studied the contribution of the document in each category to the corpus. We used the documents from two different domains: 'Business' as it has the smallest number of documents versus 'World' as it has the largest.

As can be seen in Table 6, the number of statements (Stmt#), words (W#) and distinct words (#DW) is increased as more articles being added to the dataset. Figure 7 visualizes the contribution of the document to the corpus in both domains. It can be seen that when the number of documents increased, new distinct words and vocabulary appears.

Table 5. Statistical summary of the corpus

Domain	No of Articles	Size in MB	No. Of Stmts	No. Of Words	No. Of Distinct Words
Business	280	2.34	22735	172888	20025
Entertainment	865	10.5	103524	907997	56962
Health	2379	21.9	187495	1702451	77570
Sci-Tech	543	6.77	54388	544410	38798
Sports	3377	34.4	308570	2810031	1066145
World	3621	32.3	22735	172888	97976
Total	11065	108.21	699447	6310665	1357476

Table 6. Contribution of 'Business' and 'World' datasets to the corpus

	'Business' category				'World' category		
Article#	Stmt #	W#	DW #	Article#	Stmt #	W#	DW #
10	901	6049	2155	10	551	3866	1769
20	1499	11129	3321	20	1306	8216	2632
40	3118	20711	5617	40	3748	45493	11551
80	7302	53501	10741	100	8787	80975	16804
...							
100	8517	66285	12246	500	42412	386927	49192
...							
200	16412	126784	17418	1000	81723	755784	69505
...							
280	22735	172888	20025	3000	98143	1535754	97976

To assess the ArNeCo corpus, Zipf's law was investigated (Goweder and De Roeck 2001; Sarkar, De Roeck et al. 2004; Abdelali et al. 2005; Alotaiby et al. 2009). Zipf's law means that "given some corpus of natural language utterances, the frequency of any word is inversely proportional to its rank in the frequency table". Therefore, it is a useful indicator for gauging the data sparseness and providing the evidence of any imbalance in the corpus.

According to Zipf's law, the relationship between the frequency of the words in the corpus, i.e. the number of occurrences of the word, and the rank of the word, i.e. its position in the list, is a constant k. The relationship appears as straight line with slope -1 in the ideal state. For this purpose, we developed a MATLAB function that reads the words from plain text documents in the corpus and displays the frequency of the words against their rank. To reduce the list of words, this function displays only the words which were used at least twice. We investigated the Zipf's distribution on each domain as a separate dataset, then on the whole corpus. The results were displayed in descending order so that the most frequent word has rank number one, second most frequent word has rank number two and so on. Figure 8 plots the ranks versus frequencies on logarithmic scale for 'Business' category. The slope is not near to the ideal state because this domain has the smallest number of documents but with relatively big number of redundant words appeared more than twice.

However, as the number of documents in the corpus increased, the Zipf's distribution becomes better. Figure 9 shows ranks versus frequencies for the list of Arabic words in the whole corpus shown in logarithmic scale for both axes. The curve is near to the ideal situation (straight line with slope -1). This indicator shows that the ArNeCo is representative and imbalanced.

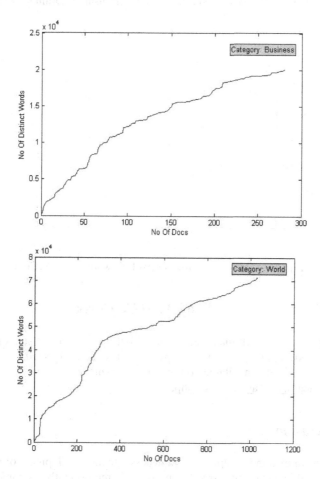

Fig. 7. Contribution of the document to the corpus in case of 'Business' and 'World'

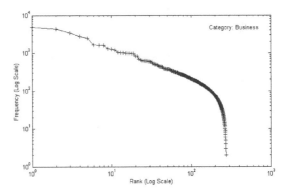

Fig. 8. Zipf's law, the rank versus frequency of the word using logarithmic scale on x and y axis for 'Business' category

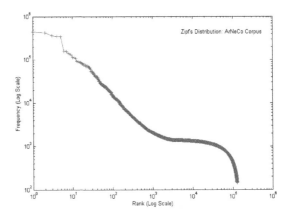

Fig. 9. Zipf's law, rank versus frequency of the words in 'ArNeCo' corpus

6   Publishing and Archiving ArNeCo Corpus

ArNeCo corpus is not an ultimate goal by itself but it is a step that supports the future research on ANLP. Therefore, the corpus is currently published to the research community and freely available online for download on the following link: http://www.c2learn.com/anlp/corpus.php.

7   Conclusion

The limitations of existing Arabic corpora necessitate the development of a new corpus for modern Arabic language. ArNeCo presents a representative sample for Arabic wherein thousands of news articles have been tagged under six categories to cover more language varieties and vocabulary. The corpus consists of more than 11,000 documents with more than 6 million words which has been already published and archived online. More importantly, the use of RSS feeds in our corpus builder provides a different method for constructing corpora which keeps track of recent natural language texts posted on the Internet. That is, the present corpus may be enlarged, modified, and updated easily. The method for corpus builder can be further used to construct corpora for other languages using Google RSS feeds. However, publishing the current ArNeCo with such representative size is not an end. The use of RSS feeds from dynamic web content, such as news and blogs, facilitates increasing the number of documents and allows automatic derivation and generation of the corpus metadata.

References

Abdelali, A., Cowie, J., et al.: Building A Modern Standard Arabic Corpus. In: Workshop on Computational Modeling of Lexical Acquisition, Croatia (2005)

Al-Sulaiti, L., Atwell, E.S.: The design of a corpus of Contemporary Arabic. International Journal of Corpus Linguistics 11(2), 135–171 (2006)

Alansary, S., Nagi, M., et al.: Building an International Corpus of Arabic (ICA): Progress of Compilation Stage. In: 7th International Conference on Language Engineering, Cairo, Egypt (2007)

Alotaiby, F., Alkharashi, I., et al.: Processing Large Arabic Text Corpora: Preliminary Analysis and Results. In: Second International Conference on Arabic Language Resources and Tools, Cairo, Egypt (2009)

Alzahrani, S.M., Salim, N.: On the Use of Fuzzy Information Retrieval for Gauging Similarity of Arabic Documents. In: Second International Conference on the Applications of Digital Information and Web Technologies (ICADIWT 2009), London Metropolitan University, UK (2009)

Goweder, A., De Roeck, A.: Assessment of a significant Arabic corpus. In: Arabic NLP Workshop at ACL/EACL 2001, Toulouse, France (2001)

Graff, D.: Arabic Gigaword, 3rd edn. Linguistic Data Consortium, Philadelphia (2007)

Graff, D., Walker, K.: Arabic Newswire. Linguistic Data Consortium, Philadelphia (2001)

Hmeidi, I., Kanaan, G., et al.: Design and implementation of automatic indexing for information retrieval with Arabic documents. Journal of the American Society for Information Science 48(10), 867–881 (1997)

Sarkar, A., De Roeck, A., et al.: Easy measures for evaluating non-English corpora for language engineering: Some lessons from Arabic and Bengali. Technical Report Number 2004/05 Department of Computing (2004)

Wynne, M.: Developing Linguistic Corpora: a Guide to Good Practice. Oxbow Books, Oxford (2005)

RSOL: A Trust-Based Recommender System with an Opinion Leadership Measurement for Cold Start Users

Jiun-Yuan Wang and Hung-Yu Kao[*]

Institute of Computer Science and Information Engineering,
National Cheng Kung University, Tainan, Taiwan, R.O.C.
hykao@mail.ncku.edu.tw

Abstract. The cold start problem is a potential issue in computer-based information systems that involve a degree of automated data modeling. Specifically, the system cannot infer a rating for users or items that are new to the recommender system when no sufficient information has been gathered. Currently, more websites are providing the relationships between users, e.g., the trust relationships, to help us alleviate the cold start problem. In this paper, we proposed a trust-based recommender model (*RSOL*) that is able to recognize the user's recommendation quality for different items. A user's recommendation quality contains two parts: "*Rating Confidence*"- an indicator of the user's reliability when rating an item, and "*Proximity Prestige*"- an indicator of the user's influence on a trust network. In our experimental results, the proposed method outperforms the *Collaborative Filtering* and trust-based methods on the Epinions dataset.

Keywords: Recommendation System, Trust Network, Cold Start Problem.

1 Introduction

1.1 Background

The recommender system is an important technology to help users find relevant and useful information in the information explosion era. For example, there are recommenders for movies, music [4], etc., such as MovieLens and Netflix. Recommender system analyze many factors, including the user's explicit preferences (rating history and user/item latent features), implicit preferences (the trust network), and other users' profiles, and recommend the items (movie, music, etc.) to users.

With the development of the internet, more and more websites, such as Epinions.com have provided the trust relationships between users, so trust-based recommendation methods have been highly developed. The trust-based methods use the information from the given user's neighbors in a trust network for recommendations.

In this paper, we expect to predict the ratings of users who have fewer rating profiles to be observed. To consider enough ratings for reliable users, we proposed a *Recommender System with Opinion Leadership* model (*RSOL*) that combines two indicators: *Rating Confidence* and *Proximity Prestige*. The name also represents a solution of a recommender system; that is why we named our model *RSOL*.

---

[*] Corresponding author.

R.E. Banchs et al. (Eds.): AIRS 2013, LNCS 8281, pp. 500–512, 2013.

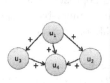

Rating Matrix				
	i_1	i_2	i_3	i_4
u_1	3		2	
u_2	1	3	5	4
u_3		2		1
u_4		1	3	

Trust Network				
	u_1	u_2	u_3	u_4
u_1	X	1	1	1
u_2	X	X	X	1
u_3	X	X	X	1
u_4	X	X	X	X

Example 1: Suppose we have four users: u_1, u_2, u_3, and u_4. u_1 trusts u_2, u_3 and u_4. u_2 trusts u_4. u_3 trusts u_4. u_4 does not trust anyone. Additionally, we have the rating profiles of the four users. We want to know the rating of item i_3 rated by user u_1. We compare two methods, *Collaborative Filtering* and the Trust-based method, with our method-*RSOL*. We illustrated the three different methods with the figures below:

Collaborative Filtering

Rating Matrix				
	i_1	i_2	i_3	i_4
u_1	3		2	
u_2	1	3	5	4
u_3		2		1
u_4		1	3	

User Simialrity Matrix				
	u_1	u_2	u_3	u_4
u_1	X	-0.422	-0.87	0.157
u_2		X	0.05	0.69
u_3			X	-0.246
u_4				X

Rating Matrix				
	i_1	i_2	i_3	i_4
u_1	3		2	
u_2	1	3	5	4
u_3		2		1
u_4		1	3	

Item Simialrity Matrix				
	i_1	i_2	i_3	i_4
i_1	X	0.006433	-0.111443	-0.073782
i_2		X	-0.024985	0.093384
i_3			X	0.045423
i_4				X

RSOL

RC Matrix				
	i_1	i_2	i_3	i_4
u_1	0.362877059	0.036878964	0.069810914	8.68E-16
u_2	0.055500449	5.79E-16	0.034825143	0.150458111
u_3	1.93E-16	0.288260094	0.241635502	0.876603364
u_4	0	0.203888517	0.19119152	0.048372841

PP Matrix	
	PP
u_1	0
u_2	0.25
u_3	0.25
u_4	1

RC+PP Matrix				
	i_1	i_2	i_3	i_4
u_1	0.362877	0.036879	0.069811	8.68E-16
u_2	0.15275	0.125	0.142413	0.200229
u_3	0.125	0.26913	0.245818	0.563302
u_4	0.5	0.601944	0.595596	0.524186

$$R_{u_1,i_1} = \frac{0.1424 \times \frac{13}{4} + 0.2458 \times \frac{3}{2} + 0.5955 \times \frac{4}{2}}{0.1424 + 0.2458 + 0.5955} = 2.1702$$

The predict ratings are *User-based CF*: 1.5931, *Item-based CF*: 3, Trust-based method: 2.9375, and *RSOL*: 2.1702. The example shows us that the performance of our *RSOL* model is the best among the three methods. Significantly, $u1$ is a cold start user who has fewer ratings; our *RSOL* model can address the cold start user problem. However, *Collaborative Filtering* and trust-based methods fail on the cold start user problem.

2   Related Work

How to infer an indirect trust is a key issue of the trust-based recommendation system. Two different approaches have been proposed for inferring the trust: model-based

[2, 5-8] and memory-based [1, 3, 10]. In model-based approaches, a model should be learned; the model stores the model parameters. In memory-based approaches, no model will be learned first; it learns by exploring neighbors from dataset.

TidalTrust [1] is a trust-based method; it is a modified breadth-first search algorithm in a trust network. It predicts that people who users trust highly at the shortest distance are the most important users. The *TidalTrust* algorithm explores all the users at the shortest distance from the source user, and then it averages their ratings, weighted by the trust value between the source user and the users being explored. To compute the indirect trust value between user u and v, it aggregates the trust value between u's direct neighbors, weighted by the direct trust values of u and its direct neighbors. *TidalTrust* uses ratings that are dependent on the users at shortest distance, but it does not consider that whether we should trust these users about the target item. Additionally, *TidalTrust* only considers the users who are at the shortest distance; it ignores the trustworthy users who are slightly farther from the source user in the trust network.

MoleTrust [10] is also a trust-based method. The idea of *MoleTrust* is similar to *TidalTrust*. *MoleTrust* also weights the ratings of trusted users with a trust score, but it considers all users up to a maximum depth. However, the larger the maximum depth is, the higher the cost of *MoleTrust*, so previous works consider the users up to a maximum depth of 6. Because *MoleTrust* considers the users who are close to the source user, within a maximum depth of 6, it does not consider different set of users who are also appropriate to target item. It loses many users who are trustworthy or have rated the target item but are far from the source user.

TrustWalker [3] has been introduced as a random walk method that combines a trust-based and item-based recommendation to predict the rating of single items. *TrustWalker* performs random walks on the trust network to find ratings for the target items or similar items. The prediction from *TrustWalker* is based on the ratings from these trusted users up to a certain depth (which is 6) and the similar items rated by them. However, when finding the trusted users who can appropriately predict an rating for a target item, *TrustWalker* is not dependent on the target item but only on the users on the trust network. It may lose the users who are trustworthy about the target item because of the sparsity of trust network.

3   Method

Our model consists of two indicators: the *Rating Confidence* for each user on different items and the *Proximity Prestige* of user on the trust network. First of all, we do the item clustering, and then calculate the distance between users' preferences and characteristic of target item and *Proximity Prestige* on different sub-network. We then return the ratings of each user with high recommendation quality. In the following subsections, we will discuss the details of our *RSOL* model.

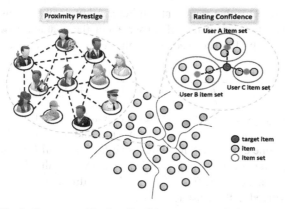

Fig. 1. Concepts of Rating Confidence and Proximity Prestige

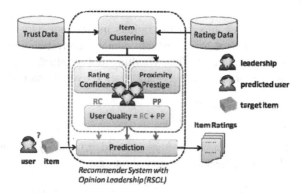

Fig. 2. Recommender system with opinion leadership model

3.1   Rating Confidence

When we want to predict the rating for a cold start user on an unrated target item, we need to know users who should I trust toward the target item. For the reason, we cluster all items. Due to the items in same cluster have similar characteristic on ratings for each other; they will be helpful to the target item rating prediction. We employ *K-Means* clustering method to find similar characteristic of items on a sparse data. Employing latent feature vectors to cluster sparse data has been used successfully in the previous study, such as [13].

$$RC(u, c_k) = \log_{10} \left(\frac{Max\ D}{d_{u,c_k}} \right) \tag{1}$$

where $D = \{d_{u,c_k} | d_{u,c_k} = |\hat{h}_u - v_{c_k}|\}$, for each user $\hat{h}_u = \dfrac{\sum_{i \in I_{u,c_k}} r_{u,i} \times h_i}{\sum_{i \in I_{u,c_k}} r_{u,i}}$

Here, c_k denotes the center of the kth cluster, which the target item belongs to. U_{c_k} denotes a set of users who have rated at least one of the items in cluster c_k. v_{c_k} is the vector of c_k. h is a vector that represents an item. Additoinally, we use the Euclidian distance to compute the confidence of a user about the characteristics of the target item. j_u denotes the preference vector of the user u and i is the target item's characteristic vector.

$$d(i, j_u) = \sqrt{(i_1 - j_{u1})^2 + (i_2 - j_{u2})^2 + \cdots + (i_d - j_{ud})^2} \tag{2}$$

We have two types of *Rating Confidence*, Global and Local. Global *Rating Confidence* calculates the distance between the user and the centroids of the clusters. Every item in the same cluster will have the same *Rating Confidence* for a user who is involved in the cluster. Local *Rating Confidence* calculates the distance between the users and the items in a cluster. Every item will have different *Rating Confidence* for different users involved in the cluster.

Item Representation

Matrix Factorization [6] decomposes the ratings matrix into two lower dimension matrices $P \in R^{|U| \times d}$ and $Q \in R^{|I| \times d}$ which contain corresponding vectors with length k for every user and item. The resulting dot product, $q_i^T p_u$, captures the interaction between user u and item i – the user's overall interest in the item's characteristics.

$$\hat{r}_{ui} = q_i^T p_u \tag{3}$$

To determine the latent feature vectors (p_u and q_i), the system minimizes the regularized squared error on the set of observed ratings:

$$\min_{P^*, Q^*} \sum_{(u,i) \in R_o} \left(r_{ui} - P_u Q_i^T \right)^2 + \lambda(\|P_u\|^2 + \|Q_i\|^2) \tag{4}$$

Here, R_o is the set of the (u,i) pairs for which r_{ui} is observed.

Thus, *Matrix Factorization* characterizes every user and item by assigning them a latent feature vector. We use the item feature vector q_i to represent each item.

Example 2: Fig. 3 is an example of *Rating Confidence*. Suppose we have three users: Alan, Bobby, and Claire. None of them have watched movie 1; Alan has watched movie 2 and 3. Bobby has watched movie 4 and 5. Claire has watched movies 6 and 7. Training the *Matrix Factorization* model with $k = 2$ yields two matrices P and Q consisting of user and item factor vectors:

$$R = \begin{bmatrix} 0 & 5 & 4 & 0 & 0 & 0 & 0 \\ 0 & 0 & 0 & 3 & 1 & 0 & 0 \\ 0 & 0 & 0 & 0 & 0 & 4 & 2 \end{bmatrix}, \quad Q = \begin{bmatrix} 0.75 & 0.83 \\ 1.1 & 0.2 \\ 0.1 & 1.2 \\ 0.2 & 1.2 \\ 0.9 & 1.0 \\ 1.3 & 0.3 \\ 0.9 & 1.1 \end{bmatrix} \xrightarrow{\text{yields}} P_{u,m1} = \begin{bmatrix} 0.65 & 0.64 \\ 0.375 & 1.15 \\ 1.16 & 0.56 \end{bmatrix}$$

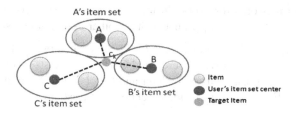

Fig. 3. An example of using *Rating Confidence* to find trustworthy users

Here, matrix R is the user item rating matrix and matrix Q is the item latent features learned by the *Matrix Factorization* model. $P_{u,m1}$ denotes the centroids representing the three users preferences. The distance is between the centroid of the user's item set and the target item's feature vector $(Dist(Alan, m1) = 0.214,\ Dist(Bobby, m1) = 0.492,\ Dist(Claire, m1) = 0.490)$. The shorter the distance between user and target item is, the higher the *Rating Confidence* of the users $(RC(Alan, m1) = log \frac{0.492}{0.214} = 0.3615$, $RC(Bobby, m1) = log \frac{0.492}{0.492} = 0$, $RC(Claire, m1) = log \frac{0.492}{0.490} = 0.0017$). In this example, Alan has the highest *Rating Confidence* toward the target item among these three users.

3.2   Proximity Prestige

Prestige as a measure of the prominence, applies only to directed graphs, taking into account the differences between sending and receiving relationships. *Proximity Prestige* is the average distance between users i and another user j that is in user $i's$ influence domain:

$$Proximity = \frac{\sum_j dist(n_j, n_i)}{I_i} \qquad Proximity\ Prestige = \frac{I_i/(|U| - 1)}{Proximity} \qquad (5)$$

Here, I_i is the influence domain, and $dist(n_j, n_i)$ is the distance from user i to user j.

This indicator is the ratio between the number of users in the influence domain and the average distance of these users to user i. If user i is unreachable, PP = 0; if all users are directly tied to user i, PP = 1. If the numerator is large, the value of PP will be large. The meaning of the numerator is the number of users that user i will influence. Additionally, if the denominator is small, the value of PP will be large. The meaning of the denominator is the distance between the user i and the users in his influence domain. If the user i is closed to these users, it is more probable that other users will trust this user i.

We have two types of *Proximity Prestige*, Global and Local. Global *Proximity Prestige* considers a user prestige in the original trust network. We consider every user's influence domain and the average shortest path between the users in the influence domain. Local *Proximity Prestige* considers a user's prestige in the sub-network. The networks are divided according to the users included to a cluster. There are different trust networks for every cluster, and we consider every user's influence domain and the average shortest path between the other users in these sub-networks.

Example 3: Fig. 4 is an example of *Proximity Prestige*. Suppose we have seven users: Alan, Bobby, Claire, David, Eric, Federer, and Gerel. Alan trusts Claire. Bobby trusts Alan, David, and Gerel. Claire trusts Federer and Gerel. David trusts Alan and Claire. Eric trusts Bobby. Federer trusts David. Gerel does not trust anyone.

$$
\text{Dist} = \begin{bmatrix} 0 & 1 & 3 & 1 & 2 & 2 & 0 \\ 0 & 0 & 0 & 0 & 1 & 0 & 0 \\ 1 & 2 & 0 & 1 & 3 & 2 & 0 \\ 3 & 1 & 2 & 0 & 2 & 1 & 0 \\ 0 & 0 & 0 & 0 & 0 & 0 & 0 \\ 2 & 3 & 1 & 2 & 4 & 0 & 0 \\ 2 & 1 & 1 & 2 & 2 & 3 & 0 \end{bmatrix}
\qquad
M_{PP} = \begin{bmatrix} A & 0.53 \\ B & 0.16 \\ C & 0.55 \\ D & 0.55 \\ E & 0 \\ F & 0.416 \\ G & 0.654 \end{bmatrix}
$$

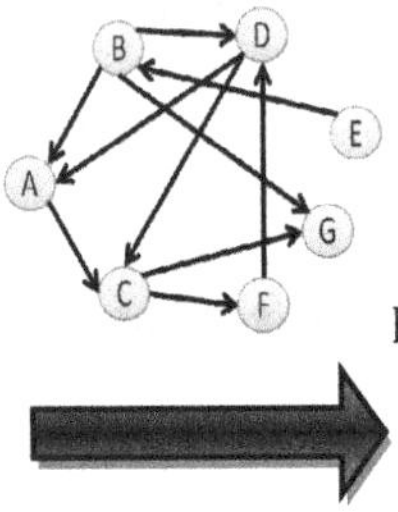

$$
PP_A = \frac{5/6}{9/5} = 0.46, \ PP_B = \frac{1/6}{1/1} = 0.16, \ PP_C = \frac{5/6}{9/5} = 0.46, \ PP_D = \frac{5/6}{9/5} = 0.46
$$

$$
PP_E = \frac{0/6}{0/0} = 0, \ PP_F = \frac{5/6}{12/5} = 0.0027, \ PP_G = \frac{6/6}{11/6} = 0.54
$$

Fig. 4. An example of using *Proximity Prestige* to find trustworthy users

Here, *Dist* stores the distance between the all users and M_{PP} store the *Proximity Prestige* of all users. We also show the operation of *Proximity Prestige* for all users above. A: 0.53, B: 0.16, C: 0.55, D: 0.55, E: 0, F: 0.416, G: 0.654. As User G has the most people in his influence domain (A: 5, B: 1, C: 5, D: 5, E: 0, F: 5, G: 6) and the average distance between user G and other users is short (A: 1.8, B: 1, C: 1.8, D: 1.8, E: 0, F: 2.4, G: 1.83), user G has the highest value for *Proximity Prestige* of the seven users. Thus, user G has the highest prestige in the trust network.

3.3   Rating Prediction and Explaining Recommendation

The values of the RC and PP metrics are used in conjunction with the *RSOL* model to present item-dependent trust-based recommendations. When we want to know the rating that a user would give a target item, the recommended rating is computed by the ratings of a set of users who are trustworthy. The selection process considers a user's RC toward the target item and the PP that a user has on trust network:

$$
r_{u_g,i} = \frac{\sum_{\{u \mid r_{u,i} \neq 0 \ and \ i \in I_{c_k}\}} [(RC_{u,i} + PP_u)/2] \times \bar{r}_{c_k}(u)}{\sum_{\{u \mid r_{u,i} \neq 0 \ and \ i \in I_{c_k}\}} (RC_{u,i} + PP_u)/2}
\qquad
\bar{r}_{c_k}(u) = \sum_{\{j \mid j \in I_{c_k} \ and \ r_{u,j} \neq 0\}} \frac{r_{u,j}}{|I_{c_k}|} \qquad (6)
$$

Here, u_g denotes the given user, i denotes the target item, I_{c_k} denotes a set of items in a cluster k, and $\bar{r}_{c_k}(u)$ denotes the average rating of user u in cluster c_k. $RC_{u,i}$ denotes the RC of user u for target item i, and PP_u denotes PP of user u in trust network. $r_{u_g,i}$ -denotes the predicted rating of given user u_g for target item i.

4   Experiments

4.1   Dataset Description and Experiment Design

The Epinions dataset [9] is very sparse (99.99% and 99.97%). It contains 49k users with at least one rating, of which 16k users (34.3%) are cold start users who have less than 5 ratings (similar to previous works [3, 10]). It is important to consider the performance of the recommendation system for cold start users. The statistics for the Epinions rating data are summarized in Table 1.

Table 1. Statistics for the Epinions dataset

Rating Data	Epinions
#-of-User	49,288
#-of-Item	139,783
#-of-Rating	664,824
Min Rating	1
Max Rating	5
Avg. Rating	3.99
Rating Sparsity	99.98%

Trust Data	Epinions
Nodes	49,288
Edges	487,183
Avg. Node Degree	19.77
Avg. Shortest Path	4
Diameter	14
Avg. Trustor	2,070
Avg. Trustee	3,338
Trust Network Sparsity	99.96%

Table 2. The number of ratings, users, and items in four types of cold start users. CS-1 denotes cold start user who has one rating, and so on

	Density	#Rating	#User	#Item
CS-1	0.000192	7,739	7,739	5,201
CS-2	0.000362	7,874	3,937	5,518
CS-3	0.000485	8,751	2,917	6,188
CS-4	0.000619	9,268	2,317	6,461

Table 2 shows the number of the cold start users, ratings they have, and items included, and the density of the user item matrix.

4.2   Comparison Methods and Evaluation Metrics

In our experiments, we compare the results with two baselines and three state-of-the-art methods. The following is the description of the labels we use to denote the methods:

User-based CF: We implemented the user-based Collaborative Filtering method [12], with the *Pearson Correlation* as the similarity measure. *Item-based CF*: We implemented the item-based *Collaborative Filtering* method [11] with the *Pearson Correlation* as similarity measure. *TidalTrust* is the trust-based approach from a previous study [1], proposed by Golbeck. *MoleTrust*: This is the approach in a paper [10], which is similar to *TidalTrust*. We use max_depth=6 for *MoleTrust* as well. *TrustWalker* is the approach in a paper [3], which combine the trust-based and item-based recommendations. $RSOL_{RC(Global)}$ and $RSOL_{RC(Local)}$: This method is one version of our *RSOL* model in which we only consider the RC metric for all <user, item> pairs. $RSOL_{PP(Global)}$ and $RSOL_{PP(Local)}$: This method is another version of our *RSOL* model in which we only consider the PP metric for all users on a trust network in different item clusters. $RSOL_{All}$: This is the full version of the *RSOL* model. We combine the two user metrics to help us choose the trustworthy users.

We perform leave-one-out cross validation in our experiment which is the same as the previous works [1, 10, 11]. In the leave-one-out cross validation, we try to predict a target item rating by using the remain ratings and the trust relationships between users in trust network. In our experiment, the evaluation metric we use to measure the error is the Root Mean Squared Error (*RMSE*) which is defined as follows:

$$\text{RMSE} = \sqrt{\frac{\sum_{<u,i>\in R_{train}}(r_{ui} - \hat{r}_{ui})^2}{|R_{train}|}} \tag{7}$$

As the paper [3] discussed, the purpose of using trust is primarily enhancing the *Coverage* without sacrificing the *Precision*. We use the *Coverage, Precision, F-Measure* metric that is mentioned in the paper.

$$\text{Precision} = 1 - \frac{\text{RMSE}}{4} \tag{8}$$

$$\text{F} - \text{Measure} = \frac{2 \times \text{Precision} \times \text{Coverage}}{\text{Precision} + \text{Coverage}} \tag{9}$$

4.3   Evaluation Results

Fig. 5 is the results of *RMSE* for different values of the parameter k, which is one of the versions of the *RSOL* model. We use a different threshold for *RC* to select the reference users to conduct our experiments. The result of the $RSOL_{RC(Local)}$ is better than the $RSOL_{RC(Global)}$, because $RSOL_{RC(Local)}$ considers the *RC* of every user for different items. We can select different set of the trustworthy users according to the target items in a cluster that we want to predict. In contrast, $RSOL_{RC(Global)}$ just selects the same set of the trustworthy reference users for different target items in a cluster.

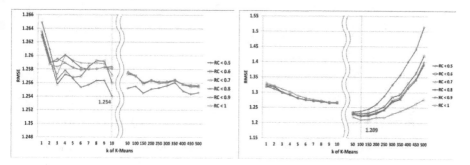

Fig. 5. RMSE of $RSOL_{RC(Global)}$ and $RSOL_{RC(Local)}$ for different values of k

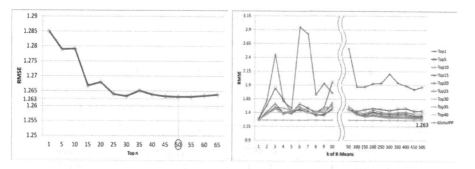

Fig. 6. RMSE of $RSOL_{PP(Global)}$ and $RSOL_{PP(Local)}$ for different values of k

Fig. 6 is the *RMSE* for different values of the parameter k in two versions of the *RSOL* model. We use Top-n users with highest *PP* to select the reference users to perform our experiments. Fig. 10 shows us that the result of Global *PP* is better than Local *PP*. Now we have two metrics, Local *RC* and Global *PP*, that have smaller square errors. We combine these two metrics to help us find trustworthy users.

Fig. 7 shows us that the combination of Global *PP* and Local *PP* is the best of the four previously mentioned versions of our *RSOL* model. By using two metrics, we can find the trustworthy users who are have the highest recommendation confidence for the target items and prestige in the trust network. The two metrics help us decide which benefits the predictions.

As shown in Table 3, also shows the *F-Measure* together with *Precision* and *Coverage* for all methods. When comparing the *RMSE* of "Local" and "Global" shows that considering the effect of items in different cluster reduces the square error. It shows that all four versions of *RSOL* model outperform all other methods according to the combination of precision and coverage. Notably, *RSOL*'s coverage is 29.83% more than that of *TrustWalker*, which makes *RSOL* model is best in terms of *F-Measure*.

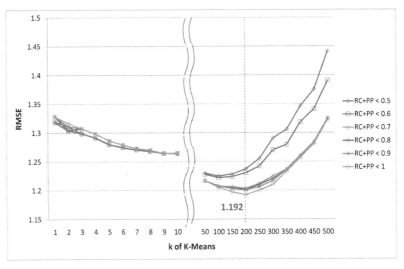

Fig. 7. RMSE of the *RSOL* model for different values of k

Table 3. Summary of all comparison methods in terms of *Precision*, *Coverage*, and *F-measure*

Method	Cold Start User		
	RMSE	**Coverage (%)**	**F-Measure**
User-based CF	1.464	16.34	0.259
Item-based CF	1.295	21.26	0.316
TidalTrust	1.244	60.92	0.626
MoleTrust	1.532	57.75	0.594
TrustWalker	1.192	74.22	0.701
RSOL$_{RC(Global)}$	1.254	100	0.814
RSOL$_{PP(Global)}$	1.263	100	0.811
RSOL$_{RC(Local)}$	1.209	100	0.821
RSOL$_{PP(Local)}$	1.250	100	0.817
RSOL$_{All}$	1.192	100	0.825

In Fig. 8, each node represents a user and each edge is a trust relationship between two users. On the right, the color of the nodes corresponds to their coreness value. The node degree scale is also displayed on the left, showing the maximum degree of the network. We show the Top 100 users selected by one version of our *RSOL* model – *Proximity Prestige*. We found that these users located on the center of the image (these nodes are large and red), so we can explain that our network has the characteristic of a core/periphery structure. The core is a complete subgraph and the periphery is a collection of nodes that do not interact with each other. The core nodes have short path distances between a pair of nodes. Because the core nodes control the flows between peripheral nodes, selecting users is helpful for the predictions.

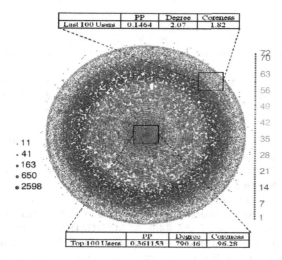

	PP	Degree	Coreness
Last 100 Users	0.1464	2.07	1.82

	PP	Degree	Coreness
Top 100 Users	0.361153	790.46	96.28

Fig. 8. The visualization of the nodes degree and coreness in a trust network

5   Conclusions

Recommender systems are important technology for helping users find relevant and useful information in the information explosion era. The *Sparsity* of the user item ratings data not only fails to compute the similarity between two users but also forces the trust-based methods to consider the ratings of indirect neighbors who may not be trustworthy, which may decrease the performance of the recommender system. To address this problem, we proposed the *Recommender System with Opinion Leadership* (*RSOL*) model to consider the user's recommendation quality, which includes the user's RC for different items and the user's influence on the trust network. *RSOL* is an item-dependent model that can consider a set of appropriate user for each different item. We performed an evaluation on the Epinions dataset; the results of experiments show that *RSOL* outperforms both *Collaborative Filtering* methods and trust-based methods, especially in terms of *Coverage*.

This study suggests two interesting directions for future work. First, we want to evaluate the *RSOL* model on other available datasets. Second, in addition to the cold start user problem, the cold start item problem is also a more and more important task for recommender systems. We plan to investigate the extension of the *RSOL* model for this task. In addition, the trust concept we considered in this paper does not integrate text information, such as the user's reviews of items. However, people may trust or distrust people on certain item because of the reviews they have written. User reviews may be a good indicator of the intensity of the underlying text effect. Combining the review and trust information models for recommendations is also a direction for future work.

References

[1] Golbeck, J.A.: Computing and applying trust in web-based social networks, University of Maryland at College Park. p. 199 (2005)

[2] Jamali, M., Ester, M.: A matrix factorization technique with trust propagation for recommendation in social networks. In: Proceedings of the Fourth ACM Conference on Recommender Systems, pp. 135–142. ACM, Barcelona (2010)

[3] Jamali, M., Ester, M.: TrustWalker: a random walk model for combining trust-based and item-based recommendation. In: Proceedings of the 15th ACM SIGKDD International Conference on Knowledge Discovery and Data Mining, pp. 397–406. ACM, Paris (2009)

[4] Koenigstein, N., Dror, G., Koren, Y.: Yahoo! music recommendations: modeling music ratings with temporal dynamics and item taxonomy. In: Proceedings of the Fifth ACM Conference on Recommender Systems, pp. 165–172. ACM, Chicago (2011)

[5] Koren, Y.: Factorization meets the neighborhood: a multifaceted collaborative filtering model. In: Proceedings of the 14th ACM SIGKDD International Conference on Knowledge Discovery and Data Mining, pp. 426–434. ACM, Las Vegas (2008)

[6] Koren, Y., Bell, R., Volinsky, C.: Matrix Factorization Techniques for Recommender Systems. Computer 42(8), 30–37 (2009)

[7] Ma, H., Yang, H., Lyu, M.R., King, I.: SoRec: social recommendation using probabilistic matrix factorization. In: Proceedings of the 17th ACM Conference on Information and Knowledge Management, pp. 931–940. ACM, Napa Valley (2008)

[8] Ma, H., Zhou, D., Liu, C., Lyu, M.R., King, I.: Recommender systems with social regularization. In: Proceedings of the Fourth ACM International Conference on Web Search and Data Mining, pp. 287–296. ACM, Hong Kong (2011)

[9] Massa, P., Avesani, P.: Trust-aware bootstrapping of recommender systems. In: ECAI Workshop on Recommender Systems. Citeseer (2006)

[10] Massa, P., Avesani, P.: Trust-aware recommender systems. In: Proceedings of the 2007 ACM Conference on Recommender Systems, pp. 17–24. ACM, Minneapolis (2007)

[11] Sarwar, B., Karypis, G., Konstan, J., Riedl, J.: Item-based collaborative filtering recommendation algorithms. In: Proceedings of the 10th International Conference on World Wide Web, pp. 285–295. ACM, Hong Kong (2001)

[12] Wang, J., de Vries, A.P., Reinders, M.J.T.: Unifying user-based and item-based collaborative filtering approaches by similarity fusion. In: Proceedings of the 29th Annual International ACM SIGIR Conference on Research and Development in Information Retrieval, pp. 501–508. ACM, Seattle (2006)

[13] Xu, W., Liu, X., Gong, Y.: Document clustering based on non-negative matrix factorization. In: Proceedings of the 26th Annual International ACM SIGIR Conference on Research and Development in Informaion Retrieval, pp. 267–273. ACM, Toronto (2003)

A Tamil Lyrics Search and Visualization System

Karthika Ranganathan, B. Barani, and T.V. Geetha

Anna Univesity, India
{karthika.cyr,baraniskb}@gmail.com,
tv_g@hotmail.com

Abstract. The availability of Tamil lyrics available on the web is growing rapidly. It has been difficult for the user to search for lyric characteristics, such as emotion, genre, rhyming features, pleasantness and rhetorical style, from a large data set. In order to increase the interestingness of Tamil lyrics to the user, we have developed lyric visualization using statistical modeling. A collection of 10000 lyrics from various Tamil lyrics books and web sites is used in order to explore the internal and external features of the individual lyric. These data have been incorporated into a multi-search engine, in which, the user will have the facility to use keywords search based on a well-known "weighting" factor called term frequency–inverse document frequency (TF-IDF), a semantic search based on the Universal Networking Language (UNL) and a lyricist search based on features style model. However, it is a challenging task to visualize each lyric with different characteristics. So, we have designed a flower like structure, which has been created using a graphics2D tool, to visualize each lyric characteristic and increase the interest of the user in the lyric search. Moreover, different statistical approaches have also been handled to identify the lyric characteristics. The proposed visualization has been evaluated using various parameters to distinguish the comfort and inclination of the user. The relevance of the document displayed in the search, and the accuracy of the genre and emotion have been characterized, using a precision and recall mechanism.

Keywords: Information retrieval, search interface, information extraction, multi-search, lyrics, usability testing, text input, user interface design, information visualization, visual design and evaluation methods.

1   Introduction

In Computer Science, research and development depend upon the human understanding of computer knowledge. Nevertheless, NLP (Natural Language Processing) is the process developed to make computers understand human languages. NLP is a branch of artificial intelligence, which is mainly concerned with linguistics and improves the interaction between computer and human languages. Texts based on both theories and technologies are analyzed using the NLP [1]. This increases the interest of computer scientists with a view to develop different languages, and make it convenient for native speakers. In NLP, speech recognition, machine translation, information extraction, text generation and text mining are the

R.E. Banchs et al. (Eds.): AIRS 2013, LNCS 8281, pp. 513–527, 2013.
© Springer-Verlag Berlin Heidelberg 2013

current trends. This paper focuses mainly on text mining in NLP. Applications such as pattern detection and constructing unstructured texts are highly attractive in NLP [2]. The former is concerned with the recognition of patterns in natural language texts using data mining, and the latter is largely involved in constructing the keywords into useful information using text mining. The main aim is to extract the data from the corpus and visualize the results in a 2d format [3]. In text mining, text categorization, text clustering, concept/entity extraction, sentiment analysis, document summarization, information extraction, machine learning and entity relation modeling are highly dependent on the language components. While most text mining tools focus on processing English documents, mining from documents in other languages offers a new host of opportunities. In this article, Tamil text documents were used to perform the text mining tasks.

Lyric mining is also known as text mining or knowledge discovery, from the lyric databases. Computational creativity is particularly very challenging, as it requires understanding and modeling knowledge, which cannot be fully formalized [4]. It requires standard NLP tools for analyzing the song lyrics. The processing of a lyric varies from normal text processing. For instance, song lyrics exhibit specific properties different from traditional text documents; the lyrics may use 'slang' language or differ greatly in the length and complexity of the language used, and also song lyrics exhibit a certain structure as to how they are organized as blocks. Tamil is one of the longest surviving classical languages in the world. The growth of the internet has made it possible for users to access a large amount of music data, like lyrics, music sound signals etc. In Tamil lyrics, the use of the LaLaLaa Framework has been proposed to analyze lyrics for various purposes, and to generate lyrics in Tamil, given the music and theme [4].

2   Related Work

Simile, metaphor, rhyme, pleasantness, repetition, onomatopoeia, epanalepsis and polyptoton are the different features of lyrics [5]. The pleasantness scoring studied by the previous work [6] describes the pleasantness of Tamil words, by language dependent methods based on meaning, phoneme and grammar, and by language independent methods based on voice and articulation. The statistics in the lyrics were used to find the regularly used alphabets [7], words, and meaningless words for a thorough analysis of the lyrics. Metaphor is an implicit simile [8], which does not involve explicit words such as 'like' or 'as' for comparing two terms. The other features in the lyric, such as rhyme, bag-of-words, part-of-speech and simple text statistic, were extracted for genre classification, and it was claimed that various genres will have different feature sets [9]. Bag-of-word is another common approach in text retrieval to index documents using the tf-idf calculation. This method has been used to describe the importance of the terms and discriminate between the documents. It is assumed that different genres of music will exhibit different styles of lyrics; the rhyming patterns are defined to extract the rhyme features from the lyrics. Tagging of words was also performed using a Part-of-speech approach, in which words were tagged according to their definition, and the textual context they appeared in. In addition, some statistical measures were also performed, based on the word or character frequencies. Based on the features discussed above the genre of the lyric can be classified. The similarity of the songs is defined with respect to the differences in distributions across clusters, in order to identify interesting genres.

Visualization is done for a lot of data such as texts, company profiles, stories, poems, lyrics, and so on, for easy retrieval of information, rather than to analyze the whole document. There are a lot of visualization techniques such as graphs, hierarchy, treemaps, pie charts, fractals, lyricon, and so on. Taxonamising visualization techniques using the data state model, help to reuse the visualization techniques and use them broadly [10]. The hierarchical aggregation of the visualization techniques, makes them visually scalable and less cluttered [11]. Fractals can also be used to visualize lyrics, but they can take only one feature as input [12]. Lyricon, is the technique that creates multiple icons, based on both tunes and lyric keywords. It uses multiple icons, since it is complex to visualize the lyric in a single icon. It enables the users to understand both the sound and the content of the lyric [13].

Text and music information are retrieved, through the integration of the audio and text features. It is done using visualization, namely, the self-organizing map (SOM) [14]. The music slide showed a technique to create a slideshow, according to the story of the lyric. The slideshow is created using personal photos, based on the contents of the lyric [15]. The text visualization of song lyrics visualizes lyrics using musical sparklines, taking into consideration three components, namely, musical, linguistic, and contextual features [16]. Visualization techniques that take multiple variables are classified into four types, namely, geometric projection (eg: scatter plots), pixel-oriented techniques (eg: bar graphs and pie charts), hierarchical techniques (eg: treemaps), and iconographic techniques (eg: Chernoff faces, glyphs) [17].

The visualization of information through the above discussed methods does not cover all the information in one diagram; it requires graphics, which gives us the freedom to create a visual of our choice. The features can then be passed to the visual as parameters, to show the variations in the output. Thus, visualization helps to get the information quickly from a data, rather than analyzing it word by word, which takes a lot of time.

3   Description

3.1   Lyrics Gathering

Lyrics gathering is considered to be an important step in the present work. Initially, a large set of lyrics has been collected along with other information, such as lyricist's name, title of the movie and the year of release. This process involves two steps, i) gathering lyric information, and ii) representation of the lyrics.

(i) Gathering lyric information

Tamil websites and various Tamil lyric books were used to collect large sets of lyrics. For instance, "Thenkinnam", a Tamil website was used to download the lyrics. This page contains most of the lyrics along with their information. The information which is available on the web is as follows: Movie's name, Lyricist's name, Singer's name,

Composer's name, Year of the lyric, tune of the lyric and rhythm of the lyric. Other resources such as books and journals have also been used to collect the lyrics.

(ii) Lyric representation

The gathered lyrics and the information available on the lyrics are represented in an XML() format. XML was used as a database to store a large set of data. This format is also helpful in retrieving data, and it is easy to add or remove tags from the format. The XML format for the lyric is represented as:

```
<Xml-document>
<Title> title of the lyric </Title>
<Movie> name of the movie </Movie>
<Music> composer name for the lyric </Music>
<Lyricist> lyricist name for the lyric </Lyricist>
<Singer> singer name for the lyric </Singer>
<Tune> tune name of the lyric </Tune>
<Rhythm> rhythm name of the lyric </Rhythm>
<Year> year of the lyric </Year>
<Lyric>
<Chorus> opening or first unit of the lyric </Chorus>
<Anti-chorus> second unit of the lyric </Anti-chorus>
<Charanam> third unit in the form of stanzas </Charanam>
</Lyric>
</Xml-document>
```

3.2   Multi-search Engine

Figure 1 shows the schematic representation of a multi-search engine; this provides three different searching facilities for a user, viz, keyword search, semantic search and lyricist search. For a given query term, the keyword search will provide the relevant documents based on the weighting factor of TF-IDF, whereas the concept search will give the relevant lyric documents based on the semantic representation, UNL. However, when the user gives the lyricist's name as a search query, then the lyricist search gives all the relevant documents based on the style of the lyricist.

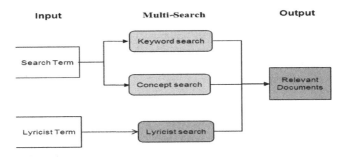

Fig. 1. Multi-Search Engine

Keyword Based Search

Most of the search engines available on the web are based on keyword search. In this system, the weighting factor, tf-idf has been used to determine the relevant documents, based on the query term. In order to determine the weight, it is much more necessary to perform a two-step process, such as stop words removal, and identifying the root word, using a morphological analyzer for the document set. When both the processes are done, then derives the term count (TF) and inverse document frequency (IDF) based on the given formula 1:

$$TF\text{-}IDF(t,d,N) = TF(t,d)*\log(1+N/d(t)) \qquad (1)$$

where, TF (t,d) is the number of times a given t (term) appears in that d (document), N is the total number of documents and d(t) is the number of documents containing the term. Once the weighting calculation has been processed, the relevant documents were retrieved for further processing. The obtained relevant documents were then ranked, according to the higher value of the document, which has been determined by summing all the tf-idf terms in the document. Semantic based Search
In semantic based search, when the user gives the concept as a query term in the offline process, the list of concept words related to the query term is identified based on the universal word, a semantic representation of UNL (universal networking language). The documents are initially retrieved, based on the concept of the tf-idf weighting factor. The relevant documents are subsequently ranked, based on the higher value of the document, which is calculated by summing all the tf-idfs of the concept term. To determine the weight, the concept term frequency (t_cf) from the document is calculated, based on the formula 2:

$$t_cf(t) = \sum_{i=1,...n} [tf+cf_i(t)] \qquad (2)$$

where, n represents the number of concept terms, tf is the number of times the term t occurs in the document, and $cf_i(t)$ is the number of times the concept term occurs in the document.

The inverse document frequency (idf) is usually obtained, by dividing the total number of documents (N) by the number of documents containing the term (d(t)), and then taking the logarithm of that quotient, equation 3.

$$idf(t,N) = \log(1+N/d(t)) \qquad (3)$$

Then, the tf-idf for the term is calculated, using equation 4

$$tf\text{-}idf(t) = t_cf(t) * idf(t,N) \qquad (4)$$

Lyricist Search

When the user gives the query as to the lyricist's name, the lyricist search provides the relevant documents, depending upon the author's name. Here, only a limited number of lyricists such as Kannadasan, Vaali and Vairamuthu were used. For searching the relevant documents and for ranking, the lyricist's style is considered to be an important feature. Each lyricist has followed a different style, based on the internal and external features of the rhyme, words corresponding to pleasantness, and also words which are freshly used in the lyric. However, the pleasantness of the lyric is identified by using five models. Of these, three are language dependent, based on the meaning of the word and the phonetic and grammatical elements of Tamil, and the remaining two models are language independent based on the place and manner of articulation [5].

3.3   Rhyming Score

The Tamil language has three different rhyme schemes, Edhugai, Monai and Iyaibu. This scheme is based on internal and external rhymes, specified in Tamil grammar, yappilakkanam. According to Tamil grammar, if the first two letters are identical for two words in a rhyme, it is called monai (Example 1a). Likewise, if the second and the last two letters of the two words in a rhyme, they are called edhugai (Example 1b) and iyaibu (Example 1c), respectively.

Examples 1:

a) *paRavai* and *pachchai* rhyme in monai as they start with the same letter.
b) *aruvi* and *viruppu* rhyme in edhugai as they share the same second letter.
c) *yaakkai* and *vaazhkkai* rhyme in iyaibu as they share the same last letter.

Moreover, one may find that two words can rhyme in more than one pattern also, see example 2a and 2b.

Examples 2:

a) *aruvi* and *kuruvi* rhyme in edhugai and iyaibu.
b) *kavidhaikaL* and *kavignarkaL* rhyme in all the three schemes.

Monai between different words within a line also has different names. The one existing between the first and second words within a line is *inai monai*. Ex : annaiyin anpil ellOrum thiLaikka
Monai between the first and third word is *polippu monai*. Ex : akamenum iniya akaththinil mEvum
Oruu monai is the one which exists between the first and fourth word. Ex : asaivilaa nanneRi viLangum aRivaal
The *kulai monai* is the one between the first, second and third words. Ex : avaniyum arutkaN amaindhu malara
Monai between the first, second and fourth words is *kilkkatuvay monai*.
Ex : arundhamizh azhakum pozhindhadhu adhandhalai
A *merkatuvay monai* is that which occurs between the first, third and fourth words.
Ex : arumpum inimaiyum adhanvazhi aNikoLum
If all the four words within a line match, then it is a *murru monai*. Ex : aRaneRi angE arasena aaki
   The positional categorization discussed above, applies to edhugai and iyaibu also, by considering the second and last letter of the words in each line accordingly. Here,

we also refer to this kind of categorization as internal rhyme.
The rhyme can be further sub-categorized, based on the nature of the letters. If the monai is only due to the consonants, not the vowels, then it is a *varukka monai*.
Ex : **pu**laakkaLam seydha kalaaath thaanaiyan
     piRangunilai maatath thuRandhai yOnE
The monai between long vowels is called as *nedil monai*.
Ex : **vaa**lipaththil manmadhan
     leelaikaLil mannavan
The monai based on the three classes of consonants, is called an *ina monai*. Since there are the hard class (vall-inam), the soft class (mell- inam) and the middle class (idai-inam), there exist the *vallina monai* (Example 3a), *Mellina monai* (Example 3b), and *idai-ina monai* (Example 3c).

Example 3 :

a) **the**yvam thozhaaaL kozhunaR RozhudhezhuvaaL
    pevyenap peyyum mazhai
b) **mO**ppak kuzhaiyum anichcham mukamdhirindhu
    nOkkak kuzhaiyum virundhu
c) **vaa**mmeyyaak kaNtavatruL illai enai
    vaaimaiyin nalla piRa

The nature of the letter sub-categorization discussed above, applies to edhugai and iyaibu also, by considering the second and last letter of words in each line accordingly. Depending upon the above classifications, the scoring is determined by assigning the initial values of 1 for murru, 0.75 value for kuzhai, kizhkadhuvaai, meRkadhuvaai and 0.5 value for inai, pozhippu and oru categories.

Based on the nature of the letter classification, varukka is assigned an initial value of 1, and 0.75 values for the nedil and 0.5 for ina categories. The rhyming score is calculated by summing all the values in the lyric, based on this classification; equation 5.

$$\text{rhyme\_score} = \text{abs} \left(\sum \text{all above values} / \text{number of senetences in the lyric} \right) \quad (5)$$

3.4   Freshness Score

The algorithm involved in identifying the freshness of a word is given below:
- Construct a timeline (5 year gap) in the lyric dataset and group the lyrics under each timeline.
- Identify the unique words in each timeline.
- Give the freshness score for each word as given below
- Compare each word in the current era (timeline) with all the previous eras.
- If any match is found then, the Freshness score - > 1
- Else, Calculate: Cumulative document frequency using equation 6; Number of eras the word has occurred.

$$\text{Cumulative document frequency (CDF)} = (\{d : t \in d\} / D) \quad (6)$$

where, D is the total number of lyrics in the previous era and {d: t € d} is the number of lyrics where the word w appears in th previous era

$$freshness\_score = CDF * Inverse (Number of eras the word occurred) \qquad (7)$$

Depending upon the above pleasantness, rhyming and freshness scoring models, the relevant documents are ranked by using the equations 8 & 9:

$$style\_scoring (L) = \sum_{d=1...n} p_d + r_d + f_d \qquad (8)$$

where, n represents the total number of lyricist documents, p_d is the pleasantness score, r_d is the rhyme score and f_d is the freshness scoring

$$ranking\_score = P (d/D) * style\_scoring \qquad (9)$$

where P (d/D) is the probability of the number of lyricist's documents occuring in the total number of lyric documents lot of time.

4   Proposed Visualization

For a given query term, depending upon the user's requirements, the process of the search retrieves the relevant documents either by the keyword based or by the semantics based or the lyricist based methods. The obtained relevant lyric documents have different lyric characteristics, which are difficult for the user to identify. In order to improve the intention of the user in the lyric search engine, and also to know the lyric characteristic information, we propose a "flower like structure" model. This can be drawn by using the Java code in graphics2D for the center (ellipse), stem (rectangle), petals (ellipse), leaves (polygon), thorns (polygon), and colors for the petals and leaves, so that a flower is drawn. After generating the flower, the characteristics of each lyric are extracted, and given as parameters to be represented in the visual. The parts of the flower indicate each characteristic, which is given in a range, so that the parts size and color vary according to the parameters. The different lyric characteristics associated with the lyric are as follows:

4.1   Statistical Count

The words in each sentence pass through the morphological analyser, to identify the root word and its grammatical properties.
- The average word count is calculated by dividing the total number of words by the total number of lines in the lyric. In the visualization, this count determines the number of petals composed for the flower like structure.
- The average number of characters in a lyric is calculated from the total number of characters in each word divided by the total number of words. These determine the length of the petal in the proposed structure.

Here, both the numbers and the length of the petal increase or decrease, depending upon the counts.

4.2   Rhetorical Style

Simile

The lyric input has searched for words, like pondRa, pola, nikarththa, aNai, aNaiya, maadhiri, pol which are used in a simile using their Unicode. If the words are identified, then the simile count is incremented. Here, the flower structure represented in the central part of the flower depicts the simile (blue=no simile, green=medium similes and red=high similes).

Repetition

The reuse of words in a sentence in the lyric is identified by checking their positions. If the words are identified, a flag is set. The existing Agaraadhi API, will be used to find the meaning of the words in the lyric. If the words have the same meaning, then the repetition count is incremented.

Onomatopoeia

The reuse of words in a sentence in the lyric is found by checking the positions. If found, a flag is set. The Agaraadhi API is used to check whether the word has a meaning or not. If there is no meaning, then the onomatopoeia count is incremented.

Polyptoton

In a polyptoton, the lines in the lyric are tokenized, and each line token is sent to the analyzer to find if there are any root words and their derived words. If found, the polyptoton count is incremented. Eg: idi idithu mazhai pozhinthathu.

Epanalepsis

The word or words in the beginning and end of each line in a lyric are checked. If they are found to be the same, the epanalepsis count is incremented. Eg: kankal irandal un kankal irandal.

Metaphor

Metaphoric words are investigated, by taking the words before and after the simile words, such as pondRa, pola, nikarththa, aNai, aNaiya, maadhiri, pol. The words taken are stored in a file. A count is maintained to know the number of metaphoric words used in a lyric, from the file. Eg:maanvizhi, thenmozhi.

Except for the simile, all the remaining counts of each rhetorical style show the number of thorns in the proposed visualization structure.

4.3   Genre Classification

For Genre identification, six different types of genres such as occasion, event, relationship, character description, philosophy and nature are considered. If none of the genres is identified, then the lyric is considered as a "miscellaneous" genre. The genre classification was performed using the following algorithm:

- The stop words and pronouns are removed, and the root words are found, using the morphological analyzer.
- The seed data in each genre consists of five songs.
- A list is maintained for each genre containing the word pair exclusive for each genre, with its frequency. The word pairs are then checked with the corpus to classify the genre for the rest of the data.
- The word pair score is incremented if found in the lyric, and any exclusive word pairs are appended to the list.
- The genre's word pair with the highest score is set as the genre for the new lyric.
- If a lyric is not matched with any word pair then it is kept in a separate genre, namely, "miscellaneous".
- The miscellaneous genre is again iterated with the newly appended word pairs to get classified.
- If not classified, then it is kept as a separate genre.
    This identification represents the color of the petal in the flower structure.

4.4   Emotion Detection

For emotion detection, six different types of emotions such as happiness, sadness, anger, love, fear, and surprise were considered. Initially, the set of keywords for each emotion is identified, and the percentage for each emotion of a lyric is calculated by counting the words that are matched with the keyword specified. Associate a lyric to an emotion, which gets a higher percentage. This represents the color of the inner petal in the flower structure.

4.5   Morpholgical Endings

Extract the possible case endings from the root word using the morphological analyzer. Count the number of occurrences of each case ending. The percentages of the case endings used in a lyric are examined, by dividing the number of case endings used by the total number of words in that lyric. This represents the length of the stem in the proposed flower structure.

4.6   Different Scores (Freshness, Rhyme and Pleasantness)

The freshness score is described above, and the value of the score is represented in the central part of the flower structure as a spot. If the freshness count is equal to 0, then it represents the black spots; else the central part of the flower represents the yellow spots. However, the rhyme score is calculated based on the above explanation, and it is used in the proposed structure to determine the number of leaves in the flower. The pleasantness score calculation is shown in the above description, and it determines the color of the leaves in the structure. If the pleasantness count is equal to 0, then it shows a dark green color; else it represents light green as the leaf color.

5   User Interface

The user interface which has been developed, consists of multi-search interfaces, such as keyword search, concept search and lyricist search. Figure 2, shows the implementation of the main search engine visualization window. Here, when the user gives the word as the input, depending upon the requirements, the user can select any of the search technique, and retrieve the relevant documents.

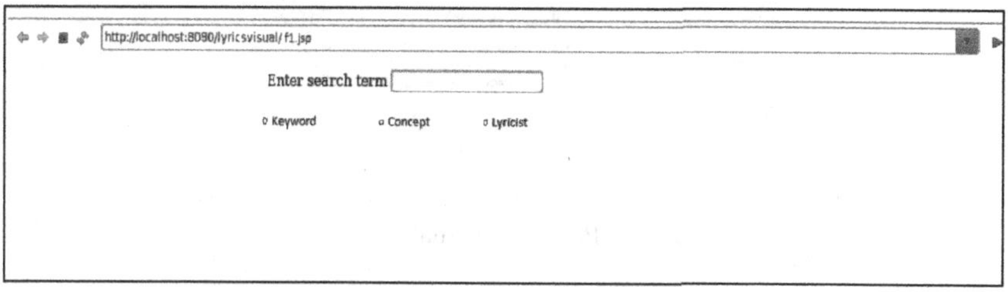

Fig. 2. Main Search Engine interface, snapshot

In the main visualization window, when the user enters a search term and the desired search technique, the output for the search term will be displayed. Here, the user gets the relevant documents according to the searching technique, that the user clicks. The output of the search term provides the relevant documents along with the information of the song's title, the TF-IDF count for the lyric, movie's name, singers of the lyric, composer, year of the lyric, and also the proposed visualization button. Figure 3 shows the output where the user enters the search term, and clicks the keyword search, then the relevant documents along with the lyric information are displayed.

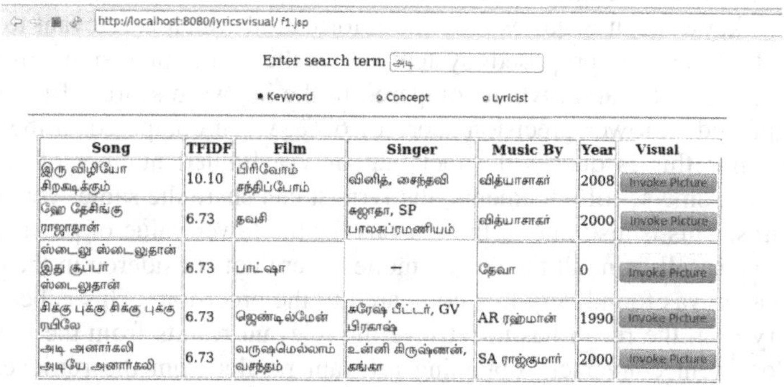

Song	TFIDF	Film	Singer	Music By	Year	Visual
இரு விழியோ சிறகடிக்கும்	10.10	பிரிவோம் சந்திப்போம்	விளிந், சைந்தவி	வித்யாசாகர்	2008	Invoke Picture
ஜே தேசிங்கு ராஜாதான்	6.73	தவசி	சுஜாதா, SP பாலசுப்ரமணியம்	வித்யாசாகர்	2000	Invoke Picture
ஸ்டைலு ஸ்டைலுதான் இது குப்பர் ஸ்டைலுதான்	6.73	பாட்சா	–	தேவா	0	Invoke Picture
சிக்கு புக்கு சிக்கு புக்கு ரயிலே	6.73	ஜென்டில்மேன்	கே.ஜே. யேசுதாஸ், GV பிரகாஷ்	AR ரஹ்மான்	1990	Invoke Picture
அடி அனார்கலி அடியே அனார்கலி	6.73	வருஷமெல்லாம் வசந்தம்	உன்னி கிருஷ்ணன், கங்கா	SA ராஜ்குமார்	2000	Invoke Picture

Fig. 3. User interface keyword search, snapshot

When the user clicks the button of the "Invoke picture" for the particular lyric, then the proposed visualization of the flower like structure will be displayed , which is shown in figure 4. This structure provides all the characteristics of the lyric for the relevant document.

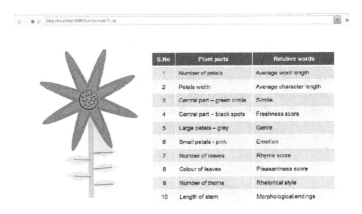

Fig. 4. Proposed Visualization

6   Evaluation

We evaluated our system in the lyric domain, and tested it with a set of 10000 documents. The test set is consist of two types of queries such as term and concept. A random sample of 50 queries for each type query was chosen. This queries were selected from the linguistics which are based on lyric features. To evaluate the effectiveness of the two types of queries, precision and recall mechanism were used. From figure 5A, it is evident that the obtained results using precision and recall for the search, suggested the importance and relevance of the documents. In the keyword search, the precision shows 78%, which is due to the retrieval of all the documents relevant to the user search term. The main disadvantage of using keyword search is the ignorance of the document, when the search engine failed to retrieve the concept of the given keyword; it acquires only the information which is relevant to the given keyword. However , the proposed system shows the higher precision value of about 86% for the concept search, when compared to the keyword search. But, the lyricist search displayed a lower precision score of 67%, when compared to the other two search systems; this is due to the fact that only a limited number of lyricists are available. For some set of documents, the lyricist can share the same score for all the style features. This is also one of the reasons for the lower value of precision scores. Note that, the recall from all the search models were not considered in the evaluation since the value was found very low compared to the precision . This is because, for a given query term the recall has to retrieve the relevant results from the total number of lyric document conversely obtaining relevant results from the retrieved data. In order to improve the recall value, higher level of semantic features will be considered to extract the meaning of the context for a given query term.

Figure 5B represents the precision and recall score for each genre. For identifying the accuracy of the genre, a 10000 lyric document set was considered. The result shows that 27% of the lyrics are miscellaneous, and to improve the precision score of the genre, we consider the three factors:
- Changing the set of songs kept in the seed data of each genre.
- Finding the noun pairs from two or more lines, instead of finding them from just one line.
- Using the compound analyser to get more word pairs.

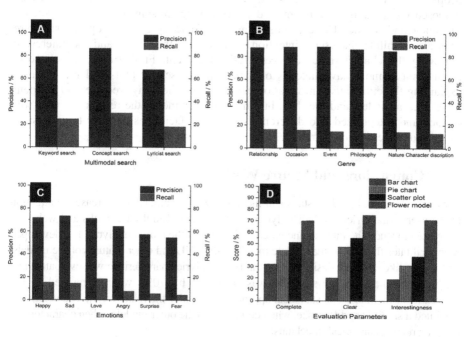

Fig. 5. Precision and Recall score for (A) multimodal search, (B) genre, (C) emotions and (D) Evaluation parameters

Figure 5C represents the precision and recall score of emotion detection. Here, the values are too low, due to the fact that the emotion database does not contain the largest amount of data. This improves the accuracy only by increasing the number of 'emotion' words in the emotion DB.

Figure 5D shows the user evaluation for the proposed visualization. The proposed visualization system is compared with three visualization techniques such as the bar chart, pie chart and the scatter plot. Here, we have focused on evaluating how well the user gets the information about the lyric's characteristics and checked whether the user will able to get the requirements completely. For this, we have selected persons in the age group 20 – 40 to perform the evaluation. About 40 students (20 males & 20 females) from Anna University and 40 random people were involved in this study. In order to obtain critical reviews, the evaluation was also performed by 4 linguistics in tacola lab, Anna University, India. The evaluation can be made, by using the parameters shown below:

Question 1: Complete (the user can get all the characteristics of the lyrics)
Question 2: Clear (the user can understand the characteristics clearly)
Question 3: Interestingness (the user can feel interested in this structure)

The users were asked to give a score from 1 to 5, where the score 5 denotes the highest value. The results from students showed lots of interest over the visualization model and the statistics showed 89% interest from students and 87% from random people. However, the linguistics showed only 73% interest, due to the fact that the proposed visualization requires more data acquisition for some critical words such as Metaphor and Simile. These results show the efficiency of our proposed structure. This also exhibits the user's intention in searching the lyrics, and the interest in retrieving the characteristics of every lyric document. Furthermore, the proposed mechanism is more advantageous over bar graphs, scatter plots and pie charts in explaining the cumulative information clearly. The other ways require user to spend more time to understand the data, but in the flower model the results are very well defined and categorized into different aspects, this facilitates the user to understand easily and makes it more attractive.

7   Conclusions and Future Work

Lyric visualization, based on statistical modeling was developed, to increase the attention of the user in the lyric search. The lyrics gathered from Tamil lyric books and web sites were used to study the internal and external features of the individual lyric. The developed lyric facilitates the user to manipulate the TF-IDF, UNL and other features of the models. The flower like structure designed to visualize each lyric characteristic was evaluated, and the interestingness of the structure was increased by 70%, when compared to the conventional methods. The statistical approach to identify the relative lyric characteristics exhibited a significant difference, when compared to the other models, when characterized using a precision and recall mechanism.

In future, an animated illustration of the flower model will be developed, to fascinate the users. In addition to exploring the design space for visualizing the lyrics of the individual song, it will be more interesting to explore visualizations, by comparing and contrasting multiple songs. It is also interesting to investigate the user's desire for a rich language, for querying lyrics; for example, in addition to searching with basic search terms, the user can directly search for lyrics that have a particular kind of feature.

References

1. Kao, A., Poteet, S.: Text Mining and Natural Language Processing – Introduction for the Special Issue. Journal of ACM, 1–4 (1994)
2. Mahedero, J.P.G., Martınez, A., Cano, P.: Natural Language Processing of Lyrics. In: Proceedings of the 13th Annual ACM International Conference on Multimedia, NewYork, USA (2005)

3. Oh, J.: Text Visualization of Song Lyrics, Center for Computer Research in Music and Acoustics, Stanford University (2010)
4. Dharmalingam, S., Karky, M.: LaaLaLaa – A Tamil Lyric Analysis and Generation Framework. In: World Classical Tamil Conference (June 2010)
5. DiYanni, R.: Glossary of Poetic Terms, http://highered.mcgrawhill.com/ sites/0072405228/.../poetic_glossary.html
6. Giruba Beulah, S.E., Ranganthan, K., Suriyah, M., Madhan Karky, V.: Pleasantness Scoring Models for Tamil Lyrics. In: IICAI Conference, Tumkur, India, pp. 1561–1571 (2011)
7. Ranganathan, K., Elanchezhiyan, K., Geetha, T.V., Parthasarathy, R., Karky, M.: Frequency Analysis of Tamil Alphabets. In: National Seminar on Tamil Linguistics, Annamalai University, India (2011)
8. Glucksberg, S., Keysar, B.: Understanding Metaphorical Comparisons: Beyond Similarity. Princeton University Press (1990)
9. Mayer, R., Neumayer, R., Rauber, A.: Rhyme and Style Features for Musical Genre classification by Song Lyrics. In Master's thesis, Vienna University of Technology, Austria (2008)
10. Chi, E.H.: A Taxonomy of Visualization Techniques using the Data State Reference Model, Xerox Palo Alto Research Centre (2010)
11. Elmqvist, N., Fekete, J.-D.: Hierarchical Aggregation for Information Visualization: Overview, Techniques and Design Guidelines. IEEE (2010)
12. Hearn, D., Pauline Baker, M.: Three-Dimensional Object Representations in Computer Graphics, 2nd edn., pp. 362–404. Pearson Edu. (1997)
13. Machida, W., Itoh, T.: Lyricon: A Visual Music Selection Interface Featuring Multiple Icons, Ochanomizu University, Tokyo, Japan (2009)
14. Neumayer, R., Rauber, A.: Multi-Modal Music Information Retrieval -Visualisation and Evaluation of Clusterings by Both Audio and Lyrics. In: 8th International Conference on Computer-Assisted Information Retrieval (2007)
15. Xu, Jin, T., Lau, F.C.M.: Automatic Generation of Music Slide Show Using Personal Photos. In: 10th IEEE International Symposium on Multimedia, pp. 214–219 (2008)
16. Chan, W.W.-Y.: A Survey on Multivariate Data Visualization, Department of Computer Science and Engineering, Hong Kong University of Science and Technology, Clear Water Bay, Kowloon, Hong Kong (June 2006)
17. Cava, Winckler, M., Pimenta, M.S., Nedel, L.P.: On Evaluating Information Visualization Techniques. In: Advanced Visual Interfaces, Trento, Italy (May 2002)

Improving Speech Recognizer Using Neuro-genetic Weights Connection Strategy for Spoken Query Information Retrieval

Noraini Seman, Zainab Abu Bakar, and Nursuriati Jamil

Computer Science Department, Faculty of Computer & Mathematical Sciences
MARA University of Technology (UiTM)
40450 Shah Alam, Selangor, Malaysia
{aini,zainab,liza}@tmsk.uitm.edu.my

Abstract. This paper describes the integration of speech recognizer into information retrieval (IR) system to retrieve text documents relevant to the given spoken queries. Our aim is to improve the speech recognizer since it has been proven as crucial for the front end of a Spoken Query IR system. When speech is used as the source material for indexing and retrieval, the effect of transcriber error on retrieval performance effectiveness must be considered. Thus, we proposed a dynamic weights connection strategy of artificial intelligence (AI) learning algorithms that combined genetic algorithms (GA) and neural network (NN) methods to improve the speech recognizer. Both algorithms are separate modules and were used to find the optimum weights for the hidden and output layers of a feed-forward artificial neural network (ANN) model. A mutated GA technique was proposed and compared with the standard GA technique. One hundred experiments using 50 selected words from spontaneous speeches were conducted. For evaluating speech recognition performance, we used the standard word error rate (WER) and for evaluating retrieval performance, we utilized precision and recall with respect to manual transcriptions. The proposed method yielded 95.39% recognition performance of spoken query input reducing the error rate to 4.61%. As for retrieval performance, our mutated GA+ANN model achieved a commendable 91% precision rate and 83% recall rate. It is interesting to note that the degradation in precision-recall is the same as the degradation in recognition performance of speech recognition engine. Owing to this fact, GA combined with ANN proved to attain certain advantages with sufficient accuracy.

Keywords: Spoken Query Information Retrieval, Speech Recognizer, Artificial Neural Network, Genetic Algorithm, Feed-forward Network.

1   Introduction

Speech-driven text retrieval or also known as spoken query information retrieval aims to search information in a textual document collection using a spoken query. Interests in providing speech access to web contents have increased steadily as the web has become an important source of information. Speech is natural for most people, and

R.E. Banchs et al. (Eds.): AIRS 2013, LNCS 8281, pp. 528–539, 2013.
© Springer-Verlag Berlin Heidelberg 2013

thus it can provide a more usable and favorable interaction. Different approaches have been proposed to allow access to web contents using speech. Spoken dialogue system is a traditional option; however the textual information lacks the required structure. The limitations of the speech channel are also a problem, because it is not possible to send much information over it. One solution is to extend an existing web browser using speech [1]. Other approaches are based on the automatic generation of dialogue systems for specific web content [2]. Finally, spoken queries information retrieval (IR) systems that use speech as input to an IR engine provided a natural solution to overcome the major limitations of the speech channel. Speech recognition which decodes human voice to generate transcriptions has of late become a practical technology. It is feasible that speech recognition is used in real world computer-based applications, specifically, those associated with human language.

A related area of research is spoken document retrieval (SDR), whose aim is inverse: to index and retrieve relevant items from a collection of spoken audio recordings in response to a text query. A lot of effort has been invested in SDR and good results have been obtained [3]. However, spoken query information retrieval is a more difficult task, because spoken queries contain less redundancy to overcome speech recognition errors. Initiated partially by the TREC-6 spoken document retrieval (SDR) track [4], various methods have been proposed for spoken document retrieval. Barnett et al. [5] performed comparative experiments related to spoken query text retrieval, where an existing speech recognition system was used as an input interface for the INQUERY text retrieval system. They used as test inputs 35 queries collected from the TREC 101-135 topics, dictated by a single male speaker. Crestani [6] also used the above 35 queries and showed that conventional relevance feedback techniques marginally improved the accuracy for spoken query text retrieval.

The abovementioned cases focused solely on improving text retrieval methods and did not address problems of improving speech recognition accuracy. In fact, an existing speech recognizer was used with no enhancement. In other words, speech recognition and text retrieval modules were fundamentally independent and were simply connected by way of an input/output protocol. However, since most speech recognizers are trained based on specific domains, the accuracy of speech recognition across domains is not satisfactory. Thus, as can easily be predicted, in cases of Barnett et al. [5] and Crestani [6], a relatively high speech recognition error rate were detected thus considerably decreased the retrieval accuracy. Additionally, speech recognition with a high accuracy is essential for interactive retrieval.

Motivated by these problems, we proposed a method to integrate speech recognition and retrieval methods where our aim is to improve speech recognizer and then allow the IR engine to retrieve text documents relevant to the given spoken queries. Since spoken queries language is dependent on the target collections, we adapt statistical language models used for speech recognition based on the target collection, so as to improve both the recognition and retrieval accuracy. The direction of this work is composed into several sections. Section 2 provides an overview of the speech recognizer. The details of the methods and implementation are described in Section 3. Section 4 describes the experimental and performance evaluation of the speech recognizer and retrieval. In Section 5, the experimental results are reported and discussed. Finally, the conclusion is drawn in Section 6.

2   Speech Recognition System Overview

In recent years, there has been an increasing interest in classification approaches to improve the recognition of speech sounds. Various approaches have been experimented to develop the speech recognizer or classifier and over the years, three speech recognition approaches are established. Dynamic time warping (DTW) is the oldest approach and is an algorithm for measuring similarity between two speech sequences which may vary in time or speed [7][8]. However, this technology has been replaced by the more accurate Hidden Markov Model (HMM) that has become the primary tool for speech recognition since 1970s. Hidden Markov Model (HMM) is a statistical model in which the system being modeled is assumed to be a Markov process with unknown parameters. This algorithm is often used due to its simplicity and feasibility of use.

However in late 1980s, artificial intelligent (AI) based approaches were considered for training the system to recognize speech using artificial neural network (ANN) algorithms. This technology is capable of solving much more complicated recognition tasks, and can handle low quality, noisy data, and speaker independence. Researchers have started to consider ANN as an alternative to HMM approach in speech recognition due to two broad reasons: 1) speech recognition can basically be viewed as a pattern classification problem, and 2) ANN can perform complex classification tasks [9]. Given sufficient input-output data, ANN is able to approximate any continuous function to arbitrary accuracy. However, the main obstacle faced by NN model is a longer learning time when the data set becomes larger. NN learning is highly important and is still undergoing intense research in both biological and artificial networks. A learning algorithm is the heart of the NN based system. Error Back-Propagation (EBP) [10] is the most cited learning algorithm and a powerful method to train ANN model [11]. However, there are several drawbacks in the EBP learning algorithms; where the main basic defect is the convergence of EBP algorithms which are generally slow since it is based on *gradient descent* minimization method. Gradient search techniques tend to get trapped at local minima.

Recently, many researchers tried to overcome this problem by using stochastic algorithm, such as Genetic Algorithms (GA) [12], since they are less sensitive to local minima. Genetic Algorithm (GA) based learning provides an alternative way of learning for the ANN, which involves controlling the learning complexity by adjusting the number of weights of the ANN. However, GA is generally slow compared to the fastest version of gradient-based algorithms due to its nature of finding a global solution in the search space. Thus, to have better convergence time, we proposed the fusion of global search GA method with matrix solution second order gradient based learning algorithm known as Conjugate Gradient (CG) in a two-layer Feed-Forward NN architecture. Our proposed neuro-genetic weights connection strategy method combined GA in the first layer and CG in the second layer to achieve optimum weights for the feed-forward network. Our algorithm aims to combine the capacity of GA and CG in avoiding local minima and the fast execution of the NN learning algorithm.

3   Methods and Implementation

The general idea towards this work is to generate a speech recognizer capable of producing accurate text transcription of isolated spoken Malay utterances for textual documents retrieval. Malay language is a branch of the Austronesian (Malayo-Polynesian) language family, spoken as a native language by more than 33,000,000 persons distributed over the Malay Peninsula, Sumatra, Borneo, and numerous smaller islands of the area and widely used in Malaysia and Indonesia as a second language [13]. The improved speech recognizer is done by implementing genetic algorithm (GA) with Artificial Neural Network (ANN) to determine the suitable network architecture and to improve the recognition performance in an offline mode. The overall process of this model is described as a block diagram as shown in Fig. 1.

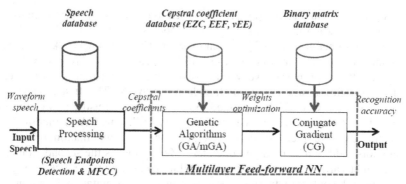

Fig. 1. Block diagram of the isolated spoken Malay speech recognition system

All the waveform speech input went through the first block of speech processing techniques that involved spectral analysis, speech boundary or endpoint detection methods, time axis normalization and feature extraction to form cepstral coefficients of vector input signals. The pre-processing block designed in speech recognition aims towards reducing the data complexity before the next stage start to work with the data.

Classification is the next step to identify input speeches based on the feature parameters: Energy Zero-Crossing Feature (EZF), Energy-Entropy Feature (EEF) and variance Energy-Entropy (vEE) [14][15]. These different feature parameters data were generated from three different dataset collections that contain accurate start and endpoint words segment detection [14][15]. A two-layer feed-forward neural network with one hidden layer and one output layer was used in this work. Only one hidden layer was utilized as it has been proven that an ANN with one hidden layer was sufficient in performing process mapping arbitrarily [16]. Our approach combined genetic algorithm (GA) with matrix solution methods to achieve optimum weights for hidden and output layers. The proposed method is to apply genetic algorithm (GA) in the first layer and conjugate gradient (CG) method in the second layer of the FF ANN architecture as depicted in Fig. 2. These two methods are combined together using proposed dynamic connection strategy, where a feedback mechanism exists for both algorithms.

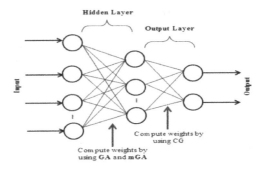

Fig. 2. The two-layer ANN architecture for the proposed weights connection strategy of Neuro-Genetic learning algorithms

In this study, trial and error approach was used to determine the optimum topology of the network. It was found that the optimum topology of the network could be best estimated using a network with 20 hidden neurons. Using this network topology, the training and validation errors were 1.9143×10^{-5} and 1.6126×10^{-4} respectively.

In this work, we proposed two variations of genetic algorithm (GA) that can be applied for weights searching in the first layer of ANN. The first strategy is the primitive or straight GA which is applied to ANN phenotype using a direct encoding scheme and we followed exactly the work done by [17]. This GA methodology used the standard two point crossover or interpolation as recombination operator and Gaussian noise addition as mutation operator. Meanwhile, as the second strategy, we proposed slight variations of the standard GA known as **mutation Genetic Algorithm (mGA)**, where the only genetic operator to be considered is mutation. The mutation is applied using a variance operator. The stepwise operation for **mGA** can be described as follows:

Step 1: Uniform distribution technique will be used to initialize all the hidden layer weights of a closed interval range of [-1, +1]. A sample genotype for the lower half gene from the population pool for input (n), hidden units (h), output (m) and number of patterns (p) can be written as in Equation (1).

$$\begin{vmatrix} x_{11}\mu_{11}x_{12}\mu_{12}...x_{1n}\mu_{1n}x_{21}\mu_{21}x_{22}\mu_{22}... \\ x_{2n}\mu_{2n}...x_{h1}\mu_{h1}x_{h2}\mu_{h2}...x_{hn}\mu_{hn} \end{vmatrix} \qquad (1)$$

where, range (x) initially is set between the closed interval [-1, +1]. Each values of variance vectors (μ) is initialized by a Gaussian distribution of mean (0) and standard deviation (1).

Step 2: The fitness for the population is calculated based on the phenotype and the target for the ANN.

$$netOutput = f(hid * weight) \qquad (2)$$

where, hid is the output matrix from the hidden layer neurons, $weight$ is the weight matrix output neurons and f is the sigmoid function is computed as in Equation (3) and (4).

$$RMSError = \sqrt{\frac{\sum_{i=1}^{n}(netOutput - net)^2}{n * p}}$$

(3)

$$popRMSError_i = norm(RMSError_i)$$

(4)

Step 3: Each individual population vector ($\mathbf{w}_i$, $\mathbf{\eta}_i$), $i = 1, 2,..., \mu$ creates a single offspring vector ($\mathbf{w}'_i$, $\mathbf{\eta}'_i$) for $j = 1,2,...,n$ as in Equation (5) and (6).

$$\eta'_i(j) = \eta_i(j)\exp(\tau'N(0,1) + \tau Nj(0,1))$$

(5)

$$w'_i(j) = w_i(j) + \eta'_i(j)Nj(0,1)$$

(6)

Step 4: Repeat **step 2**, if the convergence for the mGA is not satisfied.

Meanwhile, the weights for the output layer is computed using the conjugate gradient (CG) method where the output of the hidden layer is computed as sigmoid function [f(.)] for the weighted sum of its input. The CG algorithm is a numerical optimization technique designed to speed up the convergence of the back-propagation algorithm. It is in essence a line search technique along any set of conjugate directions, instead of along the negative gradient direction as is done in the steepest descent approach. The power of the CG algorithm comes from the fact that it avoids the calculation of the Hessian matrix or second order derivatives, yet it still converges to the exact minimum of a quadratic function with n parameters in at most n steps [11]. The conjugate gradient algorithm starts by selecting the initial search direction as the negative of the gradient as in Equation (7) and (8).

$$\underline{p}_0 = -\underline{g}_0$$

(7)

$$\underline{g}_i = \nabla \underline{F}(\underline{x})|_{x=x_k}$$

(8)

where $\underline{x}$ is the vector containing the weights and biases and $\underline{F}(\underline{x})$ is the performance function, that is the mean square error (MSE). The search directions ($\underline{p}_i$) are called *conjugate* with respect to a positive definite Hessian matrix if,

$$\underline{p}_i^T \underline{A}_{pi} = 0 \quad \text{for } i \ne j$$

(9)

where $\underline{A}$ represents the Hessian matrix [$\nabla^2 \underline{F}(\underline{x})$].

The above condition can be modified to avoid the calculation of the Hessian matrix for practical purposes and is given as in Equation (10).

$$\nabla \underline{g}_i^T \underline{p}_i = 0 \text{ for } i \ne j$$

(10)

The new weights and biases are computed by taking a step with respect to the learning rate (α_i) along the search direction that minimizes the error as in Equation (11).

$$\underline{x}_{i+1} = \underline{x}_i + \alpha_i \, \underline{p}_i \tag{11}$$

where, the learning rate (α_i) for the current step is given by Equation (12).

$$\underline{p}_{i+1} = -\underline{g}_{i+1} + \beta_{i+1} \, \underline{p}_i \tag{12}$$

where the scalar (β_i) which can be viewed as a momentum added to the algorithm [16] is given by one of three common choices where we adopted *Fletcher and Reeves* formula for the current implementation.

$$\beta_i = \frac{\underline{g}^T_{i+1} \underline{g}_{i+1}}{\underline{g}^T_i \underline{g}_i} \tag{13}$$

The algorithm iterates along successive conjugate directions until it converges to the minimum, or a predefined error criterion is achieved. As is obvious from the above steps, the conjugate gradient algorithm requires batch mode training, where weight and bias updates are applied after the whole training set is passed through the network, since the gradient is computed as an average over the whole training set [11]. In this work, since the network architecture is a two-layer feed-forward ANN, the input nodes in the first layer started with the range compression for the applied input (based on pre-specified range limits) so that it is in the open interval (0,1) and transmitted the result to all the nodes in the second layer, which is the hidden layer. The hidden nodes performed a weighted sum on its input and then passed through the sigmoidal activation function before sending the result to the next layer, which is the output layer. The output layers also performed the same weighted sum operation on its input and passed through the sigmoidal activation function to produce the final result. The vital and challenging task is to find suitable rules of joining two different techniques for the given ANN architecture. The combination of the GA and the CG method provides much possibilities of joining the two different methods [17].

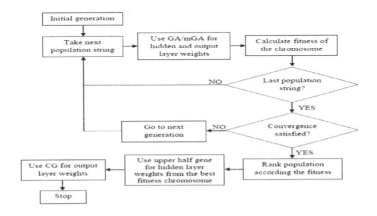

Fig. 3. The proposed dynamic weights connection strategy process diagram

The above flowchart (Fig. 3) illustrates our proposed method: dynamic connection strategy for combining these two methods, where the CG method is called after one generation run for GA/mGA method. The best fitness population is halved and the upper half is saved as the weights for output layers. Then, the GA/mGA ran for the remaining generation.

4   Experiments and System Evaluation

We conducted 100 experiments to evaluate the performance of the spoken query information retrieval. First, we described the experimental set-up and the results of our proposed method compared to the standard ANN error back-propagation (EBP) baseline system. We also compared the standard GA+ANN model against our proposed mGA+ANN model. For evaluating speech recognition performance we used the standard word error rate (WER) as our metric. On the other hand, we used precision and recall (Eq. 14-17) with respect to manual transcription to evaluate the retrieval performance. Let Correct (q) be the number of times the query q is found correctly, Answer (q) be the number of answers to the query q, and Reference (q) be the number of times q is found in the reference.

$$\text{Precision } (q) = \frac{Correct(q)}{Answer(q)} \tag{14}$$

$$\text{Recall } (q) = \frac{Correct(q)}{Re\,ference(q)} \tag{15}$$

We computed precision and recall rates for each query and reported the average over all queries. The measurement was not weighted by frequency, for example, each query $q \in Q$ is presented to the system only once, independent of number of occurrences of q in the transcriptions.

$$\text{Precision} = \frac{1}{|Q|} \sum_{q \in Q} \Pr\,ecision(q) \tag{16}$$

$$\text{Recall} = \frac{1}{|Q|} \sum_{q \in Q} Re\,call(q) \tag{17}$$

All experiments were conducted on the *hansard* documents of Malaysian House of Parliament. The *hansard* documents consists of Dewan Rakyat (DR) Parliamentary debates session for the year 2008. It contains spontaneous and formal speeches and it is the daily records of words spoken by 222 elected members of DR. The *hansard* documents comprises of 51 live videos and audio recording files (.avi form) of daily parliamentary session and 42 text files (.pdf form). Each part of parliamentary session contains six to eight hours spoken speeches surrounded with medium noise condition or environment ($\geq$ 30 dB), speakers interruption (Malay, Chinese and Indian races) and different speaking styles (low, medium and high intonation or shouting). The reason of choosing this kind of data is due to its naturalness and spontaneous speaking styles during each session.

For the purpose of this study, eight hours of one day Parliament session document was selected as our experimental data. The document collection consists of 12 topics, 120 speakers and a total of 148,411 spoken words. After thorough data analysis, the most frequently words were determined from eight hours of one day Parliament session document. The quantitative information shows that only 50 words were most commonly used by the speakers with more than 25 repetitions. The selection of 50 words are the root words formed by joining one or two syllables structures (CV/VC – consonant or vowel structure) that can be pronounced exactly as it is written and can control the distribution of the Malay language vocalic segments. However, the vocabulary used in this study consisted of seven words as presented in Table 1 for the purpose of spoken queries input. Each word was selected according to their groups of syllable structure with maximum 25 repetitions and spoken by 20 speakers. Thus, the speech data set consists of 3500 utterances of isolated Malay spoken words. For the experiments, all the audio files were re-sampled at a sampling rate of 16 kHz with frame size of 256 kbps. All signal data were converted into a form that is suitable for further computer processing and analysis.

Table 1. Selected Malay words as speech target sounds

Words	Structures	Occurrences
ADA (*have*)	V + CV	3037
BOLEH (*can*)	CV + CVC	5684
DENGAN (*with*)	CV + CCVC	7433
IALAH (*is*)	VV + CVC	4652
SAYA (*i*)	CV + CV	6763
UNTUK (*for*)	CV + CVC	4101
YANG (*that*)	CVCC	4718

5   Results and Discussion

A total of 3500 data collection were used as inputs for modeling purposes. The data were equally divided into training and testing set. The network was obtained after undergoing a series of training using two different algorithms. In order to improve network generalization ability, early stopping techniques was applied to CG training. In this technique, validation error was monitored during the training process. When the validation error increased over a specified number of iterations, the training was stopped to prevent over fitting. For weights evolved using GA, the number of generation was used to stop the iteration.

The word recognition results obtained based on 95% confidence interval for the training and testing sets of all the methods used in the study is depicted in Fig. 4. Fifty experiments were done to choose perfect Hidden Neurons Number (HNN) for the ANN model. We identified the network configuration with the best HNN is (50-20) of multilayer feed-forward (FF) network structure.

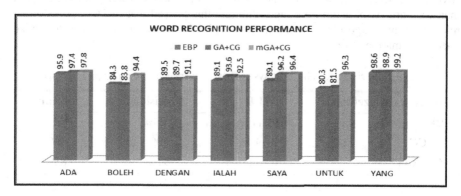

Fig. 4. Word recognition performance based on 95% confidence interval for training and testing sets with three different methods

The maximum number of epochs for network training was set to 1,000 after observing that convergence was reached within the range. As can be seen from Fig. 4, the proposed algorithm using mutation Genetic Algorithm (mGA) and Conjugate Gradient (CG) yielded 95.39% of overall classification rate. The proposed method outperformed the other two training networks where 91.57% was obtained from the fusion of standard GA and CG. Meanwhile, standard ANN using EBP algorithm yielded 89.54% that is the lowest among the other two algorithms. Although the difference in overall classification performances between standard GA and CG (GA+CG) and the mGA with CG (mGA+CG) may deemed insignificant, the difference between the two algorithms becomes more significant when the individual confusions matrices and 95% confidence interval plots are examined.

The degradation in recognition is very noticeable on all the vocabulary words except for the word "ADA" and "YANG". The spreads in confidence intervals of the words "BOLEH" and "UNTUK" obtained with the GA+CG algorithm are 16.25% and 18.55% respectively. Whereas the spreads for the same words obtained with the mGA+CG method are 5.6% and 3.7% respectively. Therefore, the mGA+CG lead to more accurate and reliable learning algorithm for training of FF network than the standard GA+CG algorithm. Since the calculation started with random initial weights, each run produced different results even though the network architecture was maintained. Thus, in order to obtain an optimal solution, repeated runs were practiced and only the best result was recorded.

As mentioned earlier, precision and recall methods were used to evaluate retrieval performances. Prior to evaluation, the spoken query was transcribed by the speech recognizer and the best hypothesis was processed by the IR engine to obtain the list of documents relevant to that query. Each of the speech recognizer's performance is measured and the result is given in Table 2. As expected, we obtained very good performance on the proposed method of mutation GA and CG (mGA+CG) fusion. It is interesting to note that as precision and recall rates increase indicating a better retrieval performance, the WER reduces indicating improved word recognition accuracy. Owing to this fact, GA combined with CG is proven to possess probable advantages. Moreover, the performances in the validation sets were considered better than standard ANN using EBP algorithm and this proved that mGA+CG fusion is a reliable learning algorithm and has high potential for further improvement for spoken query information retrieval.

Table 2. Precision-Recall for IR system based on speech recognizer performance

Speech recognizer model	WER	Precision	Recall
EBP	10.47%	56%	42%
GA+CG	8.44%	80%	63%
mGA+CG	4.62%	91%	83%

6   Conclusions

This paper reports on an experimental study of improving speech recognition engine for a better retrieval of text document retrieval based on spoken queries. Despite the limitations of the experimentation presented here, the results showed that the use of speech recognizers at the front end of spoken query information retrieval is quite robust with low error rate of 4.62%. Based on the results obtained in this study, ANN is an efficient and effective empirical modeling tool for estimating the speech process variable by using other easily available process measurements. The use of multilayer feed-forward network with delay values in model input variables is sufficient to give estimation to any arbitrary accuracy. Even though the conventional EBP method is widely used, GA is preferable as the optimal solution searching is population based using gradient information. As presented in this study, integrating mutated GA with CG as second order gradient based learning method can also improve mean square error (MSE) to reduced WER of the speech recognizer and increased the recognition rate up to more than 95%. Despite the success of the proposed neuro-genetic weight connection strategy, the speech recognition model has room for improvement. Much effort is needed to improve GA method for speeding up the learning process in ANN model for the purpose of spoken query IR systems.

Acknowledgements. This research was supported by Research Management Instiitute (RMI), UiTM under research grant: 600-RMI/DANA 5/3/RIF (403/2013).

References

[1] Vesnicer, B., Zibert, J., Dobrisek, S., Pavesic, N., Mihelic, F.: A Voice-driven Web Browser for Blind People. In: Eurospeech (2003)
[2] González-Ferreras, C., Cadeñoso Payo, V.: Development and Evaluation of a Spoken Dialog System to Access a Newspaper Web Site. In: Eurospeech (2005)

[3] Garofolo, J.S., Auzanne, C.G.P., Voorhees, E.M.: The TREC Spoken Document Retrieval Track: A Success Story. TREC-8 (1999)

[4] Garofolo, J.S., Voorhees, E.M., Stanford, V.M., Jones, K.S.: TREC-6 1997 spoken document retrieval track overview and results. In: Proceedings of the 6th Text REtrieval Conference (1997)

[5] Barnett, J., Anderson, S., Broglio, J., Singh, M., Hudson, R., Kuo, S.W.: Experiments in spoken queries for document retrieval. In: Proceedings of Eurospeech (1997)

[6] Crestani, F.: Word recognition errors and relevance feedback in spoken query processing. In: Proceedings of the Fourth International Conference on Flexible Query Answering Systems (2000)

[7] Itakura, F.: Minimum prediction residual principle applied to speech recognition. IEEE Transactions on Acoustic, Speech and Signal Processing 1975 23(1), 67–72 (1975)

[8] Sakoe, H., Chiba, S.: Dynamic programming algorithm optimization for spoken word recognition. IEEE Transactions on Acoustic, Speech and Signal Processing 26(1), 43–49 (1978)

[9] Panayiota, P., Costa, N., Costantinos, S.P.: Classification capacity of a modular neural network implementing neurally inspired architecture and training rules. IEEE Transactions on Neural Networks 15(3), 597–612 (2004)

[10] Rumelhart, D.E., Hinton, G.E., Williams, R.J.: Learning internal representation by error propagation. In: Parallel Distributed Processing, Exploring the Macro Structure of Cognition. MIT Press, Cambridge (1986)

[11] Duda, R.O., Hart, P.E., Stork, D.G.: Pattern Classification, 2nd edn. Wiley-Interscience, New York (2001)

[12] Goldberg, D.E.: Genetic Algorithm in Search, Optimization and Machine Learning. Addison-Wesley, Reading (1989)

[13] Britannica, Encyclopedia Britannica Online (2007),
http://www.britannica.com/eb/article-9050292

[14] Seman, N., Abu Bakar, Z., Abu Bakar, N.: An Evaluation of Endpoint Detection Measures for Malay Speech Recognition of an Isolated Words. In: Proceedings of the 4th International Symposium on Information Technology (ITSim 2010), pp. 1628–1635 (2010)

[15] Seman, N.: Coalition of Genetic Algorithms and Artificial Neural Network for Isolated Spoken Malay, PhD. Thesis, Universiti Teknologi MARA (UiTM) (2012)

[16] Hornik, K.J., Stinchcombe, D., White, H.: Multilayer Feedforward Networks are Universal Approximators. Neural Networks 2(5), 359–366 (1989)

[17] Ghosh, R., Yearwood, J., Ghosh, M., Bagirov, A.: Hybridization of neural learning algorithms using evolutionary and discrete gradient approaches. Computer Science Journal 1(3), 387–394 (2005)

Author Index